Bodies and Artefacts
VOLUME 1

Historical Materialism Book Series

The Historical Materialism Book Series is a major publishing initiative of the radical left. The capitalist crisis of the twenty-first century has been met by a resurgence of interest in critical Marxist theory. At the same time, the publishing institutions committed to Marxism have contracted markedly since the high point of the 1970s. The Historical Materialism Book Series is dedicated to addressing this situation by making available important works of Marxist theory. The aim of the series is to publish important theoretical contributions as the basis for vigorous intellectual debate and exchange on the left.

The peer-reviewed series publishes original monographs, translated texts, and reprints of classics across the bounds of academic disciplinary agendas and across the divisions of the left. The series is particularly concerned to encourage the internationalization of Marxist debate and aims to translate significant studies from beyond the English-speaking world.

For a full list of titles in the Historical Materialism Book Series available in paperback from Haymarket Books, visit: www.haymarketbooks.org/series_collections/1-historical-materialism.

Bodies and Artefacts

Historical Materialism as Corporeal Semiotics

VOLUME 1

Joseph Fracchia

Haymarket Books
Chicago, IL

First published in 2021 by Brill Academic Publishers, The Netherlands
© 2021 Koninklijke Brill NV, Leiden, The Netherlands

Published in paperback in 2023 by
Haymarket Books
P.O. Box 180165
Chicago, IL 60618
773-583-7884
www.haymarketbooks.org

ISBN: 978-1-64259-821-6

Distributed to the trade in the US through Consortium Book Sales and Distribution (www.cbsd.com) and internationally through Ingram Publisher Services International (www.ingramcontent.com).

This book was published with the generous support of Lannan Foundation and Wallace Action Fund.

Special discounts are available for bulk purchases by organizations and institutions. Please call 773-583-7884 or email info@haymarketbooks.org for more information.

Cover art and design by David Mabb. Cover art is a detail of *A pattern of life 4, plan of Letchworth Garden City on Morris & Co. design*, limited edition of 19 linocut prints on fabric (2019).

Printed in the United States.

10 9 8 7 6 5 4 3 2 1

Library of Congress Cataloging-in-Publication data is available.

To my parents: George Fracchia and Vera Rose Zarzana Fracchia
To my Teachers and Friends: Eugene Lunn and Kosmas Psychopedis

'Small History', drawing by Erik Dahl, 1995. With kind permission by Erik Dahl.

Contents

VOLUME 1

Acknowledgements XIII
Notes on Notes IX

Introduction: Exposing the Corporeal Roots of Historical Materialism and Moving toward a Corporeal Semiotics 1

PART 1
Reconstructing Historical Materialism 'Up from the Body': The Corporeal Foundations of a Materialist Conception of History and the Guiding Threads of a Historical-Materialist Wissenschaft

Introduction to Part 1 43

1   An *Aufhebung* of Philosophy and the Genesis of a Materialist Conception of History: Objectification and Marx's Corporeal Turn 49

2   From the First Corporeal Fact of Human Being to the Moments of History: Corporeality, Modes of Objectification, and Ways of Worldmaking 93

3   The Dimensions and Methodological *Leitfaden* of a Historical-Materialist *Wissenschaft* 146

PART 2
Toward a Historical-Materialist Cartography of Human Corporeal Organisation (in Outline): On the Corporeal Constitution of Human Experience, Behaviour, and Realities

Introduction to Part 2 213

4   The Body Is Not a Tabula Rasa: Clearing a Path toward a 'Hidden Bodily Problematic' 216

5 Toward a Corporeal Cartography: Methodological Preliminaries   268

6 A Historical-Materialist Cartography of Human Corporeal Organisation (in Outline): On the Corporeal Constitution of Patterns of Human Experience, Behaviour, and Realities   292

7 On the Corporeal Constitution of Cognition and Subjecthood   502

   Conclusion to Part 2: What It Is Like To Be a Human: Corporeally-Constituted Patterns of Human Experience and Subjecthood   547

Bibliography   555
Index   596

Acknowledgements

The history of this project goes back thirty years, and also has a longer prehistory that made it quite literally conceivable. This book is obliquely autobiographical in the sense that so many people from so many parts of my life contributed to its making in many and varied, yet all essential ways. Given space enough and time, I would gladly paint detailed portraits of those wonderful people and explain the diverse ways they made it possible. As one of them would say in such a circumstance: Alas ... But I will try to express my inexpressible gratitude to those whose teaching – whether in classrooms, dining rooms, or pubs – made my life into one of learning and enabled me to fabricate this written artefact.

This project began around 1990 when I was preoccupied with still nebulous thoughts about bodies and history that derived from issues, raised in my dissertation, about the epistemological consequences of the separation of mental and manual labour for the relation between theory and practice. While musing about these matters, and rather frustrated by the tendency in the ever-growing 'cultural-turn' literature to disappear the 'natural body' by treating it only as the bearer of the cultural meanings inscribed on it, I came across two books – *The Roots of Thinking* by Maxine Sheets-Johnstone and *The Body in Pain* by Elaine Scarry – that inspired this entire project. Against the background of their work, I happened to read yet again Karl Marx's manuscript *The German Ideology*; and a seemingly offhand statement of what should be the obvious, a comment that I had read past many times, finally caught my eye, namely: 'the first fact for the study of human history is that of human corporeal organisation'. Reading that statement through the prism of Sheets-Johnstone's exposure of the bodily roots of thought, and Scarry's excavations revealing the body as the interior structure of artefacts, suggested a way to focus my still diffuse thoughts about bodies and history into the corporeal problematic addressed in this book. I would never have been able even to conceive of this project without the inspiration of Sheets-Johnstone's and Scarry's work. And I cannot thank them enough not only for their insights, critiques, and suggestions, but also for their interest and encouragement, and their willingness to visit the first course that I gave on this project to discuss their ideas with my students.

As I mulled over the idea of a kind of synthesis of Sheets-Johnstone, Scarry, and Marx, I became convinced that it could be done – but was not at all certain whether I would be able to do it. And I would never have been able either to formulate it or to pull it off, more or less to my own satisfaction at least, were it not for the project's prehistory. That prehistory dates to January 1971, and is a tale of three professors, teachers, and friends who changed and enriched my life.

In late December 1970, I had just returned from a four-month trip around Western and Southern Europe in a VW bus. Back in school at the University of California, Davis, for the Winter trimester, I wanted to take a course on European history. The only one that fit my schedule was something called Modern European Intellectual History. Without at that time having any idea what the title meant, let alone what the course contents would be, I stumbled into that class taught by Eugene Lunn. When the lecture ended fifty minutes later, I stumbled out with, as we said in those days, my mind blown. I really had no idea what he had been talking about. But I did know that after three years of just passing time at the university, I finally found what I really wanted to study – and have been studying ever since. It is no exaggeration to say that Gene changed my life in fifty minutes. Although I have no idea whatsoever where I would be now if I had not attended that lecture, I do know that I would never have written this book. But, I did attend that lecture, which led to my eventual enrolment in the Ph.D. programme at Davis, with Gene as my dissertation director, and ultimately to this book project. Among the many things I learned from Gene about theory and practice, thinking, teaching, and living was how to ask big questions, how to think and formulate questions in what Leo Lowenthal referred to as a supradisciplinary manner. Without his teaching I would never have been able even to ask the questions that this book attempts to answer.

Between my undergraduate and Ph.D. years at UC Davis, I entered the M.A. programme at the University of California, Santa Barbara. Although I had become passionate about studying history, I felt painfully out of place in graduate school and seriously considered quitting. In that ambivalent state of mind, I took courses from Professor John Talbott who, probably without knowing it, but through his example as a teacher truly concerned about his students, not only persuaded me to stay in graduate school, but also taught me a great deal about teaching, and profoundly inspired my own.

Having chosen to focus on modern German Intellectual History, I needed to learn the language. Studying in Göttingen in 1973–74, I took courses from social and political theorist Kosmas Psychopedis, who later served on my dissertation committee. I returned to Göttingen and worked with Kosmas during the 1978–9 academic year. In 1980, Kosmas returned home to Greece and taught at Panteion University in Athens. When I mentioned in a letter that I wasn't progressing well on my dissertation because of having to spend too much time working to finance my education, he responded with an invitation to come to Athens, where I spent a year living with him and his wife Olympia Frangou-Psychopedis and working on my dissertation. I learned an immense amount from Kosmas about so many things, most pertinent here: how to perform the kind of meticulous immanent critique that is a necessary aspect of answering supradisciplinary questions. And from both Kosmas and Oly I learned an immense amount about hospitality, generosity, and the practice of 'material values' addressed in the Conclusion to this book.

I very much wish that Gene and Kosmas were here to see what I've done with what they taught me. Sadly, Gene died rather young in 1990, just as I was beginning this project. I did have the opportunity to discuss it with Kosmas during several trips to Greece before his also premature death in 2004. I like to think they would be pleased with the finished work, but I imagine they would in any case have a good laugh.

My gratitude also to the following for their varied and indispensable contributions to the pre-history of this project:

An meine lieben FreundInnen in Göttingen, Hannover, Bremen, und Berlin, die mich in ihr Leben einbezogen haben und die mir die wunderbare deutsche Sprache in ihrer komplexen Deutlichkeit beibrachten, für die unvergesslichen Erinnerungen, die wir seit der Studentenzeit in den früh 70ern gemeinsam erschaffen haben – u.a. die bis tief in die Nacht andauernden 'mit-mit' Diskussionen (mit Marx-mit Bier – oder umgekehrt), und hier vor allem an Esther Böhlcke, Mac Hottmann, Susanne Dräger, Norbert Voß, Karl Möhlmann, Ulrike Ganter, Andreas Poltermann, Olga Drossou, Emil Sander, Rudi Brenneke, Reinhard Schroeder, Achim Heerde, Helmut Reichelt, Christian Erzberger; auch an den umgepflanzten Oregondeutschen und Germanisten Alexander Mathäs, und an die ehemals nach Oregon umgepflanzte, in die Heimat zurückgekehrte, jetzt Berlin bewohnende Germanistin Elke Liebs. Ich bedanke mich herzlich für die vielen Gespräche, Einsichten, Vorschläge, Unterstützung, Ermutigung, Kritiken, und Kneipensymposien. Einen weiteren Dank an Helmut Reichelt für die Einladung nach Bremen 1999, die zu einem Forschungsstipendium vom Deutschen Akademischen Austauschdienst führte, und auch zu vielen Gesprächen im Laufe der Jahre, die zum geistigen Inhalt der vorliegenden Arbeit wesentlich beigetragen haben – und dessen köstliche Käsespätzle mich körperlich genauso wesentlich geprägt haben.

To Patricia Penn Hilden for all that I learned from our very many discussions during the years we spent sharing an office in graduate school, and for all she taught me about writing. In response to my asking why she had gasped the first time she read one of my papers, she explained in shocked surprise: 'there's neither a literary reference nor a single metaphor in the whole thing!' Should she read this book, she will encounter several lines of poetry, most of which I learned from her recitation of them during our conversations. And she may well gasp again, this time at the abundance of what I hope are not overly forced metaphors. Alas ...

To Dennis DaVia, Daniel Doyle, David Travis, and Nahum Dimitri Chandler for friendships formed in Davis, California, for half a century of learning and laughing together, and for contributing in so many ways to making me into the person who wrote this book.

As noted above, the history proper of this book began with my encounter with the works of Sheets-Johnstone and Scary that prompted me to formulate the *Fragestellung* and pointed me in the direction I wanted to take. And my gratitude to the many people whose significant contributions enabled me to complete this long see-saw ride.

To then (1991/92) four-year-old Jessye Schwartz Brick who played a crucial role in the moulding of this Scarry/Sheets-Johnstone inspired problematic into the project it became. On several occasions, I accompanied Jessye and her father, my friend and colleague Howard Brick, to a nearby park on sunny afternoons. While she and the other children were swinging, sliding, and generally enjoying themselves, I spun out my ideas while Howard listened, posed questions, and offered insightful critiques and suggestions. Through these playground dialogues I began to fashion my amorphous ideas into a more or less workable form. Throughout the entire project Howard remained a willing, sympathetic and gentle, but appropriately relentless critic. His editorial work on several chapters was invaluable; his enthusiasm, encouragement, and friendship even more so.

To historians Daniel Pope and Jeffrey Ostler, friends and colleagues who spent countless hours over the last thirty years listening to me talk about this project, contributing expertise in several areas, critiquing drafts of various chapters, and offering perspicacious and much-appreciated suggestions, but most of all for their friendship and encouragement – and of course their most excellent senses of humour.

To William Hagen, an invaluable advisor since my graduate student years, my gratitude for his willingness to respond to all my questions about early modern European history, for his *rücksichtslose Kritik*, and for his reminder not to let the theoretical tail wag the historical dog.

To Richard Lewontin who through an odd sequence of coincidences offered me a desk in his lab in Harvard's Museum of Comparative Zoology where I spent four months working on this book in 1995. One afternoon a few days after I arrived, Dick wanted to talk about my project. Some hours later I walked out of the building into a stunning early-autumn New-England sunset, with a headache – a headache caused by having to think so hard about Dick's very many insightful and challenging questions, comments, and suggestions. I did initially feel rather pleased, musing that I had more or less held my own in the conversation. But that feeling lasted only a few seconds – until I remembered that this was my history project, while he is a geneticist, and also that I had been thinking about this project for a good five years, while he for about five minutes. That was the first of many such headaches I got from conversing with him. And from his interactions with all those in his lab – undergraduates, graduate students, post-docs, and invited guests like me – it is obvious that Dick's heart is as big as his mind. At least as valuable as the intellectual contributions he made to all who have had the opportunity to work with him are the fact and example of his generosity and support. I know I am not the only one who would say that his interest in, and his enthusiasm and encouragement for, what I was trying to do gave me the hope that I could do it, and the confidence to do it.

To Timothy Reiss for his many insights and great patience as I pestered him with queries about Descartes, Foucault, the French language, and many other matters; also, for encouraging me some years ago to write an article on Foucault and Marx from which I derived much of the material for Chapter 11 and the narrative logic of Chapter 12.

To John Foster for years of discussions, suggestions, critical, insightful, and extremely helpful readings of various parts of the manuscript, and for his friendship, support, enthusiasm, and encouragement.

To Carlo DaVia for his always amusing (and constructive) comments on several chapters, for his pathological punctuation policing, for the lively, fruitful, and enjoyable disputes prompted by his resolute rejection of most everything I had to say about the history of 'Western' philosophy – and especially for his expert guidance that kept me from stubbing my toes while venturing out onto the linguistic field of classical Greek.

The breadth of this project has sent me across many disciplinary boundaries into areas about which I knew nothing and still know little. Although I feared I might be viewed as a dilettantish interloper, I was fortunate to find people in various disciplines who were as welcoming as they were helpful. These include: paleoanthropologist John Lukacs, cognitive psychologist Dare Baldwin, astrophysicist James Schombert, and English historian Randall McGowen. A special thanks to philosophers Mark Johnson and Beata Stawarska, and to linguist Spike Gildea who welcomed me into their disciplines, who always responded patiently and graciously as I bombarded them with questions, who lent me their expertise both in a good many discussions and also in their critiques of various chapters, who gently nudged me back on the proper path whenever I strayed too far as I traversed their fields, and whose enthusiasm and encouragement provided a reassuring boost by allaying my fears of disciplinary trespass.

All of the above-named, who spent hours responding helpfully and patiently to my endless questions and proofreading requests, surely deserve an apology for all of their time that I took up. But because their generous donation of their time and expertise produced valuable insights, critiques, and suggestions crucial to making this book into that which it has become, it would be disingenuous of me to apologise. All I can offer, gladly and sincerely, is my deepest gratitude.

To all the students who took my courses over my many years of teaching, and from whom I learned so much about teaching. A special thanks to the students in the seven courses I gave on aspects on this project. I am so grateful for having had the opportunity to present this material to such wonderful students whose interest and enthusiasm were inspirational, and whose questions and comments helped me so much in formulating these ideas. I benefitted not only from the exchange of ideas with them in the classroom, but also from several of their research papers that made substantive contributions to this book, and whose authors are cited in the notes. And the comments of several students, that my courses on *Bodies and Artefacts* had changed the way in which the see the world, that they can no longer walk down the street without looking at 'artefacts' and seeing the body in their 'interior structure', provided welcome affirmation of the project and equally welcome encouragement during its extended production process.

A special thanks to five former students. To Max Novick, who took the first course I gave on this project in 1994, for the many insightful (and highly amusing) discussions during and since his undergraduate years, and for his critical reading of, and valuable suggestions on, issues raised especially, but not only, in Part 1. To Erik Dahl, wherever he may be, who also took that first course in 1994. When viewing the drawings he had done for his senior-thesis project, I found one entitled 'Small History', and knew immediately that I wanted it for the cover or frontispiece of this book, should it ever be finished. When I asked during his thesis defence whether my course had anything to do with the drawing, he softly replied, in very deliberate Erik fashion, with a definitive 'Maybe'. When I asked if I could photograph the drawing for use in the book, he kindly replied by giving it to me; and it now hangs on the wall of one of the two most corporeally-important rooms of any house: the dining room. To Eric Merchant and Ian Maurer for their generous, patient, and humorous help with all things mathematical. To Leslie Johnson who was one of the several student research assistants who helped me over the years. I thank them all. But a special thanks to Leslie who worked the longest and whose thorough and conscientious work on a variety of topics saved me an immense amount of time. Were it not for her, I would still have at least another couple years of work to do. On the other hand, because she was so good at uncovering matters I hadn't considered, and then had to address, she did cause me a good bit of extra work ...

ACKNOWLEDGEMENTS

As is evident from the vast number of citations throughout this book, I was thoroughly dependent on, and benefitted immeasurably from, what Marx called 'the most solid form of social wealth': the accumulated knowledge produced by others. To all those whom I know only by name, and whose works I have used, my gratitude – and my hope that I have neither misused nor abused them. And to anyone who might read this book I would like to acknowledge that I am painfully and embarrassedly aware that, despite its excessive length, there are too many gaping holes in the analysis – too many crucial issues begging for sustained discussion, some of which are briefly addressed, some intimated, some not mentioned at all, and doubtless many of which I'm not even cognisant. I can only hope that, despite its shortcomings, this book might make a small contribution to that 'most solid form of social wealth' and perhaps suggest lines of inquiry leading to further deposits that might fill in some of the many blank spaces in the text.

A common theme in the above tributes is the encouragement that I received from so many. Inertia is of course a force. But it was never the only thing that kept me going over the thirty years that I worked on this project. Despite all too many moments of frustration at my ignorance, and of doubt about whether I would ever complete it, the enthusiasm and encouragement of friends, colleagues, students, and even some to me hitherto unknown people who came across my work and contacted me not only sustained me through the whole, drawn-out process, but also made it into what Gene Lunn ever so rightly referred to as 'serious fun'. I am so grateful to all of you for that.

Finally, a few readers of parts of this manuscript have purported to find a 'humane' quality to it. I could not imagine a higher compliment, and I certainly hope that it is true. If there actually are any traces of humaneness, they derive not only from all of those mentioned above, but first and foremost from my family. My unending gratitude to my parents, George and Vera Fracchia, for the security, generosity, and love that gave me the opportunity to do so many things that they, whose lives were filled with making a living and caring for their family, were never able to do – including getting the education that produced this book, and the opportunity to travel, including several stays with our many relatives in the Sicilian town of Piana degli Albanesi from where my mother's family emigrated. From the moment I arrived, unannounced and a complete stranger, on Zio Franco's doorstep in 1970, I was welcomed into the extended family and have experienced a kindness, generosity, and wisdom to which I can only aspire – and which are not insignificant to the pursuit of a better world.

In 1939, with Nazism ensconced in Germany, fascism elsewhere, Stalin in the USSR, world war on the horizon, and himself in exile, Bertolt Brecht, writing *To Posterity*, asked:

> What times are these when a conversation about flowers is almost a crime
> Because it includes a silence about so many evil deeds?

Crucial here is that in those very dark times (frighteningly similar to our own present) Brecht made a point of insisting, quietly but poignantly, that such a conversation is *almost* a crime. In the closing lines of the same verse, he regrets that

> We who wanted to pave the path for friendship
> Could not ourselves be friendly.

As countless philosophers and theoreticians have indefatigably reiterated, there are many things that the common sense of everyday wisdom cannot explain. For that we need and have theory. But Brecht's poem makes clear that amid the increasingly deafening noise of world-history, we must retain that everyday wisdom – precisely because it points to everyday values whose cultivation is an essential building-block of a world beyond exploitation and oppression. Conversations about flowers and acts of friendship will not alone change the world. But if we are unable to converse about flowers or be friendly, it is doubtful that we will be able to construct a humane one.

The lives of my parents and of my many now-departed cousins in Piana were, as are the lives of the still-living generations there, humane lives filled with what William Wordsworth called those 'little, nameless, unremembered acts of kindness and love' that make up 'that best portion of a good [person's] life'. Such 'little, nameless acts of kindness and love', however, must not remain unremembered. For, they might be called, to paraphrase Walter Benjamin, 'chips of a messianic praxis' in everyday life: a quotidian practice of humane values, despite the limits that an unjust world imposes on the possible. Theodor Adorno's dictum to the contrary notwithstanding, those acts of kindness and love show that there is a right way to live in a false world. I cannot thank them enough for that invaluable insight.

My thanks also to the editors of the following journals and book for permission to use parts or all of the following essays that first appeared in their publications:

History and Theory:
'Marx's *Aufhebung* of Philosophy and the Foundations of Historical-Materialist Science', 1991.

'Dialectical Itineraries', 1999.

Historical Materialism:

'On Transhistorical Abstractions and the Intersection of Historical Theory and Social Critique', 2004.

'Beyond the Human Nature Debate: Human Corporeal Organization as the "First Fact" of Historical Theory', 2005.

'The Capitalist Labour Process and the Body in Pain: The Corporeal Depths of Marx's Concept of Immiseration', 2008.

'The Philosophical Leninism and Eastern "Western Marxism" of Georg Lukács', 2013.

Intellectual History Newsletter:

'Foucault, Marx, and the Historical-Materialist Horizon', 1998.

Social Autonomy and the Critique of Capitalism eds. W. Bonefeld and K. Psychopedis 'The Untimely Timeliness of Rosa Luxemburg', 2005.

Finally, my thanks to Danny Hayward, Simon Mussell, Jennifer Obdam and Noortje Maranus for their editorial work, and especially for the patience and endurance it must have required, not only to edit this whole thing, but also to respond to my incessant questions.

Notes on Notes

Sequences of page numbers separated by a comma (e.g. p. 3, p. 4.) indicate different passages cited *within* one of my sentences. Sequences of page numbers separated by a semi-colon – e.g. p. 3; p. 4; p. 7; pp. 35–6 – indicate passages I cite in *different* sentences in the same paragraph; these are generally preceded with the notation: 'Following citations in this paragraph, p. x; p. y; p. z'. If within such a sequence there is a sentence in which I cite two different passages, those two will be separated by a comma as in the bolded part of this example: Following citations in this paragraph, p. 5; p. 11; **p. 35, p. 47**; p. 62; p. 110.

On several occasions I cite the same work several times in the same or sequential paragraphs. In order to reduce somewhat the already rather large number of footnotes, I note, in a given footnote, 'all citations in this paragraph', or 'all citations in this and the following paragraph' – and then cite the work and the page numbers.

Translations of passages cited from German texts, and for which only the German source is given in the notes, are mine.

Introduction: Exposing the Corporeal Roots of Historical Materialism and Moving toward a Corporeal Semiotics

> Einen Denker verstehen,
> gerade auf rechtzeitige Weise,
> heißt,
> über ihn hinausgehen.
>
> (To understand a thinker,
> precisely in a timely manner,
> means
> to go beyond him.)
> ERNST BLOCH[1]

∴

0.1   Introductory

Sketching 'the real prerequisites' of a materialist conception of history, Karl Marx began by noting the tautologically obvious point that 'the first premise of all human history is naturally the existence of living human individuals'.[2] But

---

[1]   Ernst Bloch 1975, p. 73.
[2]   This and following citation, Marx 1845 in Tucker 1978, p. 149, my italics. Translation altered. Marx's term, *körperliche Organisation*, literally means 'corporeal organisation', which I prefer to Tucker's more generic rendering as '*physical* organisation' that smacks more of mechanical physics than organic biology. Also worth mentioning is the reasoning behind my translations of Marx's terms for that of which 'corporeal organisation' is the 'first fact'. Throughout *The German Ideology* and elsewhere, Marx uses *Betrachtung der Geschichte* or *Geschichtsbetrachtung* (literally, the 'observation') of history; and he refers also to the *Betrachtungsweise* (mode or manner of observing history). Although '*Betrachtung*' generally means to observe, to render that in English as 'the observation of history' sounds a bit awkward. Other possibilities would be 'historical reflection' or 'historical study'. But I choose instead to translate *Geschichtsbetrachtung* as 'historical theory' because Marx's reflections in *The German Ideology* on the content of history, the logic of historical change, and the methodology of historical analysis certainly qualify as studies in historical theory – a translation that also seems etymologically appropriate because the term 'theory' derives from the classical Greek θεωρεῖν meaning to

he immediately rendered this seemingly superficial point profound by drawing the also obvious, but far-reaching consequence of this premise for the study of human history, namely: if the first premise is 'the existence of *living* human individuals', then 'the first fact to be established is the *corporeal organisation* of these individuals and *their consequent relation to the rest of nature*'.

Unfortunately, neither in the unfinished work in which this corporeal comment appears, *The German Ideology* co-authored with Friedrich Engels in 1845, nor in any of his later works did Marx ever systematically elaborate this somewhat casual, but nevertheless very striking comment, at once both profane and profound. He did, however, later refer to the reflections in *The German Ideology* as his and Engels's 'settling of accounts with our erstwhile philosophical conscience', and as the site where they achieved 'self-clarification'.[3] I take that comment quite seriously and contend that in *The German Ideology* Marx, together with Engels, took the decisive step in confronting the challenge that he set for himself in the last of the *Economic-Philosophical Manuscripts of 1844* – where he undertook (as later editors appropriately entitled that manuscript) a 'Critique of the Hegelian Dialectic and of Philosophy in General'.

I would argue, however, and do so in Chapter 1, that while Marx did successfully confront Hegel's idealist dialectic in the *Economic-Philosophical Manuscripts of 1844*, he had not yet succeeded in escaping that 'erstwhile philosophical conscience', nor in breaking with 'philosophy in general'. For, what he proposed in the *Manuscripts* as an alternative to Hegel's idealist philosophy of history was a materialist philosophy of history – antithetical to Hegel's, but still a *philosophy* of history. Although he had embarked on a materialist voyage and was listing toward corporeality, he still steered a philosophical course. Only in *The German Ideology* did he achieve the 'self-clarification' that directed him to a rather different materialist course leading away from philosophy, heading instead in a historical direction. While navigating this new course, he began to figure out how 'to give a materialist basis to the writing of history'.[4] In so doing, he supplanted his earlier materialist *philosophy* of history with a materialist *conception* of history: a conception of history, grounded in the 'first fact' of 'human corporeal organisation', from which he derived a set of fundamental

---

look at, to view, to behold. Thus, 'human corporeal organisation' is 'the first fact' to be established for 'historical theory' – and thus also, as I argue in Chapter 3, for historical study and analysis.

3   Marx 1859 in Tucker 1978, pp. 5–6. On the status of *The German Ideology* as 'text', see Appendix 1.1.

4   Marx 1845 in Tucker 1978, p. 156. In this comment Marx credited the English and French as the first to attempt (in his view unsuccessfully) to give a materialist basis to the writing of history. He clearly thought he had succeeded where they had failed.

assumptions or premises [*Voraussetzungen*] about how human beings make their own history, but not as they please – premises intended to serve, not as a 'recipe or schema' to be imposed on history, but as the *Ausgangspunkt* and the *Leitfaden*, the starting point and the guiding threads, of historical-materialist analysis.⁵

This radically new, corporeally-based conception of the content of history required, accordingly and no less importantly, an entirely new approach to the production of historical knowledge – a consequence too often overlooked by critics both amicable and averse. In short: in *The German Ideology* Marx not only closed the ledger on his 'philosophical conscience', but also embarked on the new project that would occupy him for the rest of his life: the development of a historical-materialist *Wissenschaft* on the foundation of his newly-, but still only partially-articulated 'materialist conception of history' – on the basis of which he could and would then undertake a 'radical' critique of political economy in order to grasp its object of analysis, the capitalist mode of production, by its corporeal roots.⁶

Having achieved 'self-clarification', Marx and Engels left the unpublished manuscript (figuratively at least, perhaps also literally) to the 'gnawing criticism of mice'. Although the *German Ideology* finally appeared in published form in 1932, it never attracted the attention drawn to the *1844 Manuscripts* first released in 1927 – just as the insightful comment from the *German Ideology* about human corporeal organisation was overshadowed by the section on alienation (*Entfremdung*) in the *1844 Manuscripts*. Accordingly, Marx's *Aufhebung* of philosophy is often either disdainfully dismissed as 'so-called', as much ado about nothing, or viewed regretfully as marking his abandonment of 'human-

---

5 Marx 1845 in Tucker 1978, p. 155.
6 I prefer, and will use throughout, the German *Wissenschaft* rather than the English 'science'. The reason is that the latter is too closely identified with natural science and the use of natural scientific methods. The key issue here is that although generalities in the natural sciences might have the force of law, this is not the case in the 'human sciences', the humanities and social sciences. Consequently, those 'human sciences' require different methodologies and especially a more flexible attitude toward generalities that do not have the immediate explanatory force of natural scientific laws. Because the term *Wissenschaft* refers more generally to the systematic study of, and body of knowledge about, a given content, it appropriately leaves more leeway for each *Wissenschaft* to articulate a methodology appropriate to its own contents. And for a *Wissenschaft* that seeks to grasp what Ranajit Guha calls the 'historicality' of things (see Chapter 8, note 14), Oskar Negt's reference to historical materialism as a 'research direction' is most appropriate. See Negt in Nelson and Grossberg 1988, pp. 211–34, esp. p. 230. See also Callinicos (1982, p. 163) who refers to a historical-materialist *Wissenschaft* as a 'research programme'.

ist' philosophy for an economically-determinist theory of history.[7] Therewith his comment establishing human corporeal organisation as 'the first historical fact' is either overlooked or quickly forgotten.

In my view, however, this seemingly parenthetical positing of human corporeality as history's first fact is arguably the single most insightful and single most radical statement that Marx ever made (radical in the sense of 'grasping the thing by its roots' or, in the case here at hand: by its flesh and bones) – and certainly the one with the most far-reaching implications.[8] Though Freud excluded it from his list of mind-shatteringly decentring and humbling Copernican revolutions in Western intellectual history (his list was limited to Copernicus, Darwin and, somewhat immodestly, himself), I contend that this single sentence designating human corporeal organisation as the first fact of human history amounts to such a Copernican upheaval. For, this corporeal-centric claim situates *Homo sapiens* as one among all of the other faunal forms on planet Earth – all belonging, by virtue of their organic, animate corporeality, to the same taxonomical kingdom, yet all differentiated by the unique, species-specific corporeal organisation of each. And by taking corporeal organisation as his starting point for the study of human being-in-the-world, Marx not only

---

7 Here I want to offer a rather unorthodox response to the question concerning Marx and 'humanism'. Regardless of which Marx is favoured, and regardless of whether the shift is dated to the period after the 1848 Revolutions, as had been the dominant interpretation after the publication of the *1844 Manuscripts* and *The German Ideology* in the 1930s, or pushed forward to *The German Ideology* 1845 as Louis Althusser claimed, there has been general unanimity that Marx's early philosophical works (through 1848) were suffused with a 'humanism' that he later supplanted with the scientific study of economics. My heterodox claim upends the prevailing view of the 'early humanist' vs. the 'late economist' Marx. I argue contrariwise that the 'late' Marx whose emergence is marked by the designation (in 1845) of human corporeal organisation as the first fact of history is in at least one very important sense significantly *more* 'humanist' than his earlier self. By this, I do not mean to attribute to Marx the traditional Western notion of humanism deriving from classical and Renaissance Europe that makes 'man' into 'the measure of all things'. I mean rather a very material humanism: by understanding 'human corporeal organisation' as the first fact of human history, and by attempting to reconstruct everything (see Terry Eagleton's comment in next section) 'up from the body', Marx took the very radical step of beginning with the corporeal foundation of *Homo sapiens* and with the corporeal roots of human existence and history. His historical-materialist 'humanism' is grounded in, and based upon, the species-specific corporeal organisation of human beings. I do not again address directly the question of a 'corporeal humanism' in the 'late' Marx. But this entire book supports the claim that a consistent 'humanism' must begin with the 'first [biological] fact' of 'human corporeal organisation'. And I do argue specifically (in Parts 1 and 4) that Marx's 'late works', especially the *Grundrisse* and *Capital*, are saturated with categories derived from this 'corporeal humanism'.
8 Marx, Introduction to *Contribution to the Critique of Hegel's 'Philosophy of Right'* in Tucker 1978, p. 60.

effected his *Aufhebung* of traditional Western philosophy, but also laid the foundation of a truly materialist conception of history.[9]

Although it is unlikely that Engels (or, for that matter, Marx himself) fully realised the far-reaching breadth and depth of the implications of that declaration of human corporeal organisation as the first historical fact, he was nevertheless certainly correct in his graveside speech that eulogised Marx for having done for human history what Darwin accomplished for natural history.[10] I take Engels's encomium not only as appropriately high praise for both Marx and Darwin as thinkers of equal and exalted stature in their respective disciplines, but also as an acknowledgement of the complementarity of Marx's materialist conception of human history and Darwin's materialist conception of the histories of all organisms – both of which are grounded in the fundamental premise of, and both take as the starting-point of their research programs, the species-specific corporeality of the particular organisms (whether finches, tortoises, mockingbirds, or human primates) whose histories they sought to reconstruct. Although some might dismiss this estimation of the relation between Marx and Darwin as a rather fancifully imagined affinity, I endeavour here in this introduction to evoke what Coleridge called a willing suspension of any disbelief

---

[9] This is the first of many occasions throughout this work when I shamelessly appropriate Heideggerian, or concoct Heideggerian-like, categories for their somewhat clumsy, but effective descriptiveness, and fill them with historical-materialist content.

[10] See Engels, Speech at Marx's Graveside in Tucker 1978, p. 681. Engels's comment may be, and has been, (in my view mis-)taken to mean that Marx completed Darwin by applying Darwinian evolutionary laws to human history. But Marx's comment that Darwin had provided 'the natural-historical basis' for historical materialism by no means requires conflating natural history and history by reducing the later to the human form of the later. Marx himself opposes such a conflation in several comments in the *Economic-Philosophic Manuscripts of 1844*, *The German Ideology* of 1845, and in *Capital* where he expressly distinguishes human beings and human history from other animal species and their 'natural histories'. And in referring to those passages, Engels categorically concluded that 'it is impossible to transpose without further ado the life laws of animal societies onto human ones'. Therefore, the more likely intent of Engels's comment resides in its literal meaning: that in his own discipline Marx was a thinker of equal standing with Darwin in his – a reading supported by Engels equation of the value relative to their disciplines of Darwin's theory of natural selection and Marx's of surplus value. Understood in this way, the parallel formulation of Marx and Darwin as revolutionary thinkers in their respective disciplines is consistent with my claim below that bridging the gap between the evolutionary history of hominids and the history of *Homo sapiens* needs two supports. It is in this context also worth noting, as John Foster has pointed out in several works, most recently in his majesterial *The Return of Nature*, that Engels's understanding of evolutionary processes was rather more sophisticated and nuanced than the rather crude and reductionist Herbert-Spencerian brand of social Darwinism imputed to him by a good number of his interpreters. (See Foster 2020, Part Two, pp. 171–298).

that this claim might provoke; and I invoke the argument developed in the following pages as a case for its plausibility.

To begin to grasp the significance and implications of this fundamental axiom of a materialist conception of history (which go far beyond Marx himself), it is necessary to view it in two dimensions: in relation to the past, to the history of Western philosophy from its canonically recognised birth in classical Athens through Hegel; and in relation to a future as a new conception of history whose breadth, depth, and implications have not at all been fully recognised – not even by Marx himself. To do so, I begin with an exploration of what Marx meant by an *Aufhebung* of philosophy, specifically: with an elaboration of that *Aufhebung* as a fundamental corporeal break with the Western philosophical tradition since Socrates. I shall argue that Marx's new materialist conception of history is not a speculative philosophy of history of the Hegelian kind claiming to encompass and explain the course of human history from beginning to end, but an outline of a few fundamental corporeal premises that frame and guide an open-ended research strategy. Then, to explain the Copernican importance of this new corporeally-grounded conception of history and the fields of study that it opens, I endeavour to map the boundaries and sketch the contours of a historical-materialist horizon broad enough to encompass both Marx and Darwin.

0.2   Marx's *Aufhebung* of Philosophy

The first question to be asked: what did Marx mean in viewing his own work as a historical-materialist *Aufhebung* of philosophy? In approaching this question, it is necessary to remember that Marx's most important precursor and the greatest influence on him, Hegel, had claimed, not without a certain, albeit geo-culturally parochial logic, that his own work represented the culmination and conclusion of philosophical inquiry. Thus, to understand Marx's meaning in claiming that his *Aufhebung* of Hegel's philosophy was at once an *Aufhebung* of 'philosophy in general', it is first necessary to understand the particular sense in which Hegel could somewhat legitimately contend that his work was the culmination of philosophy – that is, and more accurately: the culmination of the 'Western' philosophical tradition since Socrates.[11]

---

11   My reason for not addressing in any detail the recently much-discussed question of Spinozan themes in Marx is presented in Appendix 0.A.

Although they differed in their evaluations, both Hegel and Marx felt that the unity of the 'Western' philosophical tradition lay in its consistent definition of the mind-body relationship. Corporeally speaking, traditional 'Western' philosophy has (with a few literally eccentric exceptions) been top-heavy. The foundational moment in its birth in classical Athens was a denigration of the body as the merely animal side of human being, the elevation of the mind to the status of the truly human, and therewith thought, reasoning, mental labour, as the properly human form of labour. Since Socrates, 'Western' philosophy has differentiated human beings from animals on the basis of the human mind and its capacity for Reason. In *Phaedo* Socrates did not mince words when expressing his conviction that the body was the cause of all error, misery, unhappiness, violence, etc., and his contention that the mind could not discover truth until death had liberated it from its corporeal incarceration. Echoing Socrates when telling his tale of the cave, Plato allegorically denounced the body as enslaver of the mind, and pronounced manual labour a life-sentence of servitude and ignorance.[12]

Insisting that 'the first principle of all action is leisure', Aristotle at least admitted that the leisure necessary for philosophising was dependent on the satisfaction of material needs; and he attributed the early development of mathematics in Egypt to the fact that the priestly caste that spawned mathematicians had very early become a leisure class.[13] He was, accordingly, not at

---

12 In *Phaedo* Socrates launched a rather vehement attack on the body, which he saw as an 'imperfection' contaminating the soul, the source of 'innumerable distractions' from the search for truth and of diseases, it 'fills us with loves and desires and fears and all sorts of fancies and a great deal of nonsense', and 'wars and revolutions and battles are due simply and solely to the body and its desires'. Consequently, 'we are in fact convinced that if we are ever to have pure knowledge of anything, we must get rid of the body and contemplate things by themselves with the soul by itself' (Plato, *Phaedo*, in Plato 1961, pp. 49, p. 95. See also the *Allegory of the Cave* in ibid., pp. 747 ff.).

13 Aristotle, *Politics* in Aristotle, 1941, p. 1307; Aristotle, *Metaphysics* in Aristotle 1941, p. 691. Following Citation, ibid. VIII.2,1337b8–15, in Aristotle 1941, p. 1306. Because βάναυσος has been translated as both 'mechanical' (by Jonathan Barnes) and 'vulgar' (by Richard McKeon), and because both, especially together, seem most appropriate for this passage, I have included both. Also in *Politics*, Aristotle wrote: 'Not that a life of action must necessarily have relation to others, as some persons think, nor are those ideas only to be regarded as practical which are pursued for the sake of practical results, but much more the thoughts and contemplations which are independent and complete in themselves; since acting well, and therefore a certain kind of action, is an end, and even in the case of external actions the directing mind is most truly said to act' (ibid. 1325b21 ff., in Aristotle 1941, p. 1282). My thanks to Carlo DaVia for making me aware of these passages and explaining the fine points obscured in translation.

The consistency of this philosophical attitude is indicated by Hegel's approving cita-

all enamoured of manual labour of any kind; nor, unsurprisingly, did he think much of those who laboured with their bodies: 'And any occupation, art, or science, which makes the body or soul or mind of the freeman less fit for the practice or exercise of virtue, is mechanical and vulgar [βάναυσος]; wherefore we call those arts mechanical and vulgar which tend to deform the body, and likewise all paid employments, for they absorb and degrade the mind'. This distaste for manual labour carried with it, unsurprisingly, a disdain for manual workers and artisans (expressed in the appellation βάναυσοι, from βάνοσ signifying furnace or forge). Aristotle seemed as unconcerned as Plato that this definition relegated the ignorant many, whose manual labour was the necessary precondition of the philosophising of the few, to a less than fully human status. And it is worth noting parenthetically, with the help of Robert Garland, how this distaste of manual labour among the classical Athenian philosophers ironically exemplifies a slightly revised version of Voltaire's, perhaps apocraphyl, but certainly acerbic aphorism about historical analysis: that 'history is a pack of misconceptions we play on the dead'. For, this disdain for those who worked with their hands was directed not only at blacksmiths, metalworkers, house painters, cobblers, and carpenters, but also at those engaged in plastic arts, such as potters, vase painters, jewellers – including the sculptors who chiselled blocks of marble into those much-admired figures taken by Hellenophiles as mute witnesses testifying to the 'Golden Age' of Greek culture.[14]

The legacy of the first 'Western' philosophers, then, was a particularistic definition of truly human being as knowing being, as the work of appropriating the objects of the world by transforming them into objects of knowledge – a definition of human being that, of course, privileged philosophy as the definit-

---

tion of Aristotle's comments on the underlying but immediately forgotten social prerequisite of mental labour. And in the *Philosophy of Right* Hegel goes to great lengths to justify this forgetfulness by exposing the irrelevance of material needs and labour to a philosophical definition of freedom: see the transition from 'bourgeois society' (*die bürgerliche Gesellschaft*) to 'the state' (*der Staat*).

14 This information on crafts and arts from Garland 2009, p. 87. This oft-quoted, but never cited statement about history, or more accurately, about historians, is attributed to Voltaire, but no one with whom I have consulted seems to know its source – although Timothy Reiss found a similar quote attributed to Napoleon (personal correspondence). But regardless of when and by whom it was coined, the phrase is for my purposes quite useful. The phrase is rendered variously in English as a 'pack of lies' and as a 'pack of tricks' played on the dead. Although somewhat different in meaning, both seem apprpropriate. But because of personal preference, I will use 'pack of tricks' when the phrase occasionally reappears in the following.

ively human form of work.¹⁵ Nature and the body were considered pertinent to philosophy only insofar as they could be known (although the same cannot be said of the desires of these very corporeal philosophers for, to put it anachronistically, knowledge of bodies 'in the biblical sense').¹⁶ Any other attributes and activities rooted in the body, such as physical needs and the practice of satisfying those needs, were mired in the realm of necessity – at best subordinate elements of the analysis and ultimately philosophically irrelevant.¹⁷

For this reason, moreover, those first 'Western' philosophers also concluded that the material dimension of life was ultimately irrelevant politically. Because of its innate dependence on the satisfaction of material needs and its mortality, the body could have only a subordinate place in the philosophical analysis of society and no place in a philosophical definition of freedom and morality. Although freedom (as Aristotle hinted in his comment about the leisure of Egyptian philosophers) may have a material prerequisite, the notion of material or economic freedom was a contradiction in terms. Corporeality is animality, subjected to material needs. Only the immaterial mind, *Geist*, can be free and can make moral choices – hence Socrates's conclusion that the ability to know the truth that will set one free is possible only after death frees the mind

---

15 See Chapter 4 for a critique of Hannah Arendt's (in my view specious) differentiation of the 'work' of the mind (philosophy and the arts) that produces durable products from the 'labour' of the body whose products (in German called *Lebensmittel*, the means of life) are consumed and seem (to her mind's eye) to have disappeared. But Arendt completely dismisses what she apparently considers the rather banal corporeal fact that the consumption of *Lebensmittel* is crucial to the metabolic process that renders life itself durable.

16 For some musings on the relevance of the rather sensual depictions of the social sites and conversational contexts of philosophical discourse in the Platonic *Dialogues*, see Appendix 0.2.

17 We should not be deceived by Foucault's contrast of the apparently more liberated 'pagan' Greek sexuality with the later Victorian 'sexual regime' (Foucault 1990b). While it is not at all difficult to admit that Greek sexuality was more emancipated than its Victorian successor, it is far too much to conclude (and a careful reading of Foucault shows that he doesn't either) that the Greeks gave the body its due and that Greek philosophy respected the body. Socrates's tirade against the body as the source of all that is evil and false in the world (see note 12 above), does include a recognition that unsatisfied bodily desires (not least sexual desire) could overwhelm the mind's rational capacities – which is why he concluded that the mind could only reach the truth after the death of the body. And although Foucault depicts the classical Greek view of sexuality as much more sensual and sensible when contrasted with Victorian values, it is also evident that whatever their corporeal and emotional experience of sex may have been, the philosophers, when philosophising about sex, prescribed the pleasurable uses of the body not, so they claimed, for the sake of sensual pleasure itself, but for the sake of philosophy: satisfy potential bodily distractions in order afterward better to think.

from its confinement in its corporeal prison. With the body and material needs deprived of any essential place in the definition of freedom, so, too, was the question of socio-economic justice. The locus of freedom was effectively displaced onto, and limited solely to, the political sphere in which the individual could appear, not as kin to animals trapped in the realm of material necessity, but as a free, self-determining citizen and distant cousin of the deities. Thus, along with the idealist definition of the relation between human being and the world as one of knowledge, a commensurate definition of freedom as primarily a matter of mind became the other main pillar of the Greek legacy to the Western philosophical tradition.

This dual legacy remained consistent for more than two millennia, at least through (and, I would argue, well beyond) Hegel. Among philosophers, few, if any, of Linnaeus's predecessors and successors, would have appreciated the irony with which he named the human species *Homo sapiens* – which he apparently intended as an insult to his conspecifics, affixing to them the same epithet that he attached to the ape species *Simia sapiens*.[18] It is, in any case, the consistency of this idealist philosophical anthropology that lends tautological profundity to Hegel's insistence that 'all philosophy is idealism', and credence to Alfred North Whitehead's observation that 'the European philosophical tradition ... consists of a series of footnotes to Plato'.[19]

Hegel doubted not his lineage as a direct descendant of the Greek philosophers. He also understood his good fortune to be alive in the historical era in which, so he thought, the social world was on the verge of becoming rational and thus knowable. The problem with Greek society, he argued, was a social reality that limited freedom to a certain class of people – a social order that

---

18 Further discussion of Linnaeus's naming of the taxon *Homo sapiens* in Appendix 0.3., 'Linnaeus and *Homo sapiens*'.

19 Whitehead 1979, p. 39. Descartes' inquiry into the subject/object relation is generally considered the beginning of the qualitatively new problematic that differentiates 'modern' (Western) philosophy from 'classical' philosophy. Although it would, of course, be anachronistic to attribute a subject/object relation to Greek philosophy, the more important issue is that both the 'classical' conception of the mind/body relation and the 'modern' conception of the subject/object relation are rooted in a mind-body dualism that privileges the former and posits knowing as the truly human relationship to the world. In confronting his *genius malignus*, Descartes purified the mind of bodily influences just as thoroughly as did Socrates before him with his denunciation of the body and his insistence that the mind could know truth only after death freed it from bodily interference – and, after him, Hegel whose recounting of the phenomenological odyssey of *Geist* chronicled the painstaking and protracted, but ultimately victorious epistemological purge that cleansed the mind of all intrusive corporeal traces and culminated in absolute knowledge of the corporeally unadulterated absolute idea.

imposed particularity on, and thus contradicted, the very concept of freedom which is, by definition, universal. In his own time, however, with the spread of the French Revolutionary ideas of universal freedom, the elimination of arbitrary privilege, and the universal applicability of the law, Hegel believed he was witnessing the dawning of an age of enlightenment and rationality in which the social order and political institutions would finally come to correspond to their concepts, that is: would finally fulfil the criteria of philosophy.[20] And since the real had become rational (or was about to become so; for the idealist Hegel, when the idea is present, reality will follow), philosophy could become absolute. The knowledge and freedom sought by the Greeks, which Socrates had relegated to a life after death when the mind would be emancipated from the body and its inevitable interruptions, were both, in Hegel's view, about to be realised in this world. This is why he felt justified in depicting his work as leading, finally, to absolute knowledge. And because his age was the one in which history had reached its goal of freedom, he could look back from his vantage point when history had revealed its meaning and comprehend the logic driving the entire process. This is the modest meaning of his statement about Minerva's philosophical owl beginning its flight at dusk.[21]

Although he drew rather different conclusions, Marx clearly agreed with Hegel's insistence that 'all philosophy is idealism' and, thus, with Hegel's claim that his magnificent philosophical edifice succeeded in solving the philosophical problems bequeathed to Western intellectual history by the Greeks. Nevertheless, he found unappealing the 'grotesque craggy melody' of Hegel's philosophical composition.[22] Appalled by the discrepancy between Hegel's exalted philosophical claim that history had reached the realm of freedom and the rather drearier state of the real, material world, Marx would doubtless have endorsed Kierkegaard's acerbic observation that '[t]he philosopher constructs

---

20   Psychopedis 1982, p. 72. See also below, Chapters 3, 10, and the Conclusion for further comment on the intimate relation between the philosophically idealist insistence that the mind is truly human, while the body only animal, and a liberal conception of freedom (e.g. that animating the French Declaration of the Rights of Man and Citizen and the US Declaration of Independence) as a political and legal 'procedural' matter. My argument is not that such freedoms are unimportant. On the contrary, they must be a part of any meaningful notion of freedom. My point is rather that without guarantee of the material wherewithal necessary for people not just to have, but also to realise, the rights to life, liberty and the pursuit of happiness, those procedural rights alone are inadequate.

21   Hegel 1975, *Rechtsphilosophie* in *Werke* VII, p. 28. This is a variation on a recurring theme, previously expressed in Isaac Newton's perhaps apocryphal acknowledgement that 'If I have seen further, it is by standing on the shoulders of giants'.

22   Marx, Letter to his father, 10 November 1837, in Tucker 1978, p. 7.

a palace of ideas and lives in a hovel'.[23] Pondering that gap, Marx found himself caught 'in the embarrassment of having to speak of material interests'; and to relieve this embarrassment, he began, as editor of the *Rheinische Zeitung* (1842–43), to concern himself with 'economic questions'.[24] This concern, however, eventually led him into a deeper and more radical analysis, until, in writing the *German Ideology* in 1845, he traced the roots of economic questions in particular and material matters in general to 'human corporeal organisation'. And it was this understanding of the materiality of human existence, this recognition of human corporeal organisation as the prerequisite and framework of human history, that provoked his call for the *Aufhebung* or transcendence of philosophy.

Against traditional philosophy's idealist conception of the properly human mind as an effectively disembodied mind free from, and unconcerned with, bodily needs and distractions, of proper *human* being as essentially *thinking* being, and against its elevation of the history of philosophy as the proper history of humanity, Marx started with what he considered the material premises of human existence and therewith of human history and its study. Conceiving of human beings as much more than just thinking beings, Marx announced in the *Theses on Feuerbach* the foundation of his materialist conception of history by redefining the subject-object relation as that between the sensually-acting (*sinnlich-tätige*) subject(s) and the object(s) of their action.[25]

By sensuous activity, Marx meant all forms of interactions between human beings and the world. From this perspective, even thinking is a sensual activity, an interaction of mind and world through which are produced the diverse forms of knowledge that constitute culturally specific world-views that in turn *in-form* human behaviours.[26] Through sensuous activity, then, the human species (any species for that matter, albeit in varying degrees) alters the physical world of the nature outside itself. In so doing, human beings produce species-specific, socio-culturally diverse worlds through the labour of fabricating material objects, the establishment of social relations and development of modes of communication, and through the perception and apprehension of the world that are the foundational for ways of looking at (*Weltanschauungen*) and modes of knowing it. In what is arguably the single most important concept in historical-materialist vocabulary, Marx conceptualised the sensu-

---

23   Søren Kierkegaard cited in Hyppolite 1969, p. 100.
24   Marx 1859 in Tucker 1978, p. 3.
25   See the first of Marx's 'Theses on Feuerbach' 1845 in Tucker 1978, p. 143.
26   As Konrad Lorenz (1972, pp. 22–3) reminds, the term 'information' itself primarily means 'giving form'. This use of 'in-form' will recur often throughout this work.

ous activity through which human beings build their worlds by fashioning the objects, the artefacts, that those worlds contain and out of which they are made, as *Vergegenständlichung* or 'objectification'.[27] I undertake a thorough elaboration of this crucial concept in Chapter 2. The important matter here, however, is that a sensuously-active, objectifying subject is obviously and necessarily a very corporeal subject. Marx's historical-materialist redefinition of the subject-object relation thus points directly to the fundamental historical-materialist axiom that human corporeal organisation is the first fact of history and historical theory.

A definition of the subject as a sensually-acting, objectifying being forces consideration not just of the mind, but also of the entire array of corporeal attributes that both require and enable humans to act – in short, the body, more specifically for *Homo sapiens*, the 'mindful body'.[28] This redefinition of human being set the mind squarely in the body as only one, even if perhaps the single most important, attribute – but also as one that was not independent of the body as traditional philosophy had since Socrates maintained. Engels summarised Marx's break with Hegel with his appropriately corporeal witticism that Marx turned the upside-down Hegel right-side up and put him back on his feet so that he could apprehend the world, not as mediated through the idealist

---

[27] 'Objectification' is a very literal translation *Vergegenständlichung* into English. The problem is that the literal English translation, 'objectification', has come to carry rather different connotations than does *Vergegenständlichung* in German. Here I will just note that what is now generally meant by 'objectification' in English would in German be *Verdinglichung* or 'reification'. Further comment on these terms, and their translations and connotations, follows the Introduction to Chapter 1. A detailed elaboration of *Vergegenständlichung* follows in Chapters 1 and 2.

[28] On 'mindful bodies' see Sheets-Johnstone 2011 and 2011a. Michael Steinberg's elaboration of what he terms 'thinking bodies' is remarkably similar to Sheets-Johnstone's: 'We are not thinking beings at all but bodies that think and without the body thinking wanders into irrelevance'; '[l]ike all other animals, we are thinking bodies. Just because an organism cannot tell us what it knows doesn't mean that it knows nothing' (see Steinberg 2005, p. 23; p. 41). For reasons to be elaborated in greater detail in Chapter 7 on 'Corporeality and Cognition', although Steinberg and Sheets-Johnstone fill the categories, respectively, the 'thinking body' and the 'mindful body' with similar contents, I prefer Sheets-Johnstone's 'mindful body' that better captures what both she and Steinberg describe, namely: a mind that is situated in a brain, and a brain that is situated in a species-specific body. And while thinking might be the jewel in the cognitive crown, the realm of cognition is broader and deeper and additionally includes, as Steinberg alludes, not only conscious thought processes, but all forms of awareness including perception and what Michael Polanyi calls 'tacit knowledge'. I should add that this notion of the mindful body is not to be confused with either yoga practices that aim to still the body in order to liberate the mind or with the now ubiquitous trivialisation of 'mindfulness' in popular culture.

lens of the philosopher, but as mediated through human corporeal organisation, through the human mindful body.[29] This shorthand formulation refers on the one hand to his critique and *Aufhebung* not only of Hegel's philosophy, but also of 'philosophy *überhaupt*'; and it refers on the other to his corporeal redefinition of the essential relation between human being and the world, the allegedly truly human form of which traditional philosophy had conceptualised as a relation of knowing.[30]

As Hegel understood that his own ability to write the 'culmination of philosophy' lay in having the good fortune to live in a time when the philosophical dream of freedom seemed about to be realised, so too did Marx understand that he was living in an age in which the dynamism and sheer power of capital had demystified social relations and exposed the world-transforming and world-making capacities of labour. Nevertheless, although Marx's materialist conception of history is unthinkable without the problematic that he inherited, and although his materialist conception of history is in a sense only one step beyond Hegel's, it was actually a two-step process, the first of which was a step into a qualitatively new 'paradigm', fully incommensurate with that which had dominated Western thought for over two millennia. But that was only the first step. For, Marx's materialist conception of *history* was more than just a philosophical-materialist inversion of Hegel's idealist philosophy. It also presented fundamental challenges to the production of knowledge, to epistemology.

In the preface to his *1844 Manuscripts*, Marx wrote that his encounter with 'Feuerbach's discoveries about the essence of philosophy made necessary a critical confrontation with the philosophical dialectic'.[31] Feuerbach's inquiry was concerned with a critique of the *contents* of philosophy. As is, however, evident from Marx's very Feuerbachian materialist philosophy in the *1844 Manuscripts*, a redefinition of the contents of knowledge does not alone constitute an *Aufhebung* of philosophy. A thorough *Aufhebung* of philosophy would also require a confrontation, not just with the contents of knowledge, but also with the nature of knowledge production. And this is what Marx began to undertake in *The German Ideology*.

With his positing of human corporeal organisation as the 'first fact' of historical theory, and his consequent corporeal redefinition of the subject-object

---

29   Engels 1886, *Ludwig Feuerbach und der Ausgang der klassischen deutschen Philosophie* in *Marx-Engels Werke* (hereafter MEW), Vol. 21, p. 293.
30   These far-reaching claims can only be sketched here in the most general and therefore inadequate form. They will be addressed in detail in three chapters of Part 1.
31   Marx, *1844 Manuscripts* in MEW, EB I, p. 470.

relation as one of sensuously-acting, objectifying subjects interacting with nature and each other, Marx radically reconstituted the content, the *what*, of historical knowledge. But this was only the first step, only half of the problematic. For, his corporeal redefinition of the subject/object relation effectively decentred the knowing subject, deprived that subject of its privileged position as overseer and thus knower of all. And this decentring presented a fundamental challenge to knowledge production. In order to take his corporeal *Aufhebung* of philosophy seriously and pursue it systematically, Marx not only had to initiate a massive project of reconsidering, from this new corporeal perspective, the contents of *Wissenschaft*. He also had to respond to the epistemological challenges presented by taking corporeal organisation as the 'first fact', that is: he would have to fashion the means of knowledge production 'up from the body'. In responding to these epistemological challenges, he articulated a historical-materialist set of guiding threads pertaining to *how* we know. Marx's *Aufhebung* of philosophy, then, was a two-step process, consisting, first, of redefining in historical-materialist terms, the *contents*, the *what*, of historical knowledge and, second, of establishing the epistemological guidelines, the *how*, the methodology, of knowledge production in order to elucidate how corporeally-decentred subjects can produce meaningful knowledge about themselves and their history.[32] To complete his *Aufhebung* of history, in short, Marx would have to make an 'epistemological break' with the philosophical tradition whose descendant he was.[33]

---

32   In *History and Class Consciousness*, Georg Lukács insisted that 'orthodoxy' in Marxism 'does not imply the uncritical acceptance of the results of Marx's investigations. It is not the "belief" in this or that thesis, nor the exegesis of a "sacred" book', but rather 'refers exclusively to method' (1971, p. 1). While I fully agree that the question of method is a crucial one, I am rather uneasy about the tyrannical strains inherent in any notion of 'orthodoxy'. A 'belief' in the orthodoxy of a given 'method' can just as easily lead to narrow-minded dogmatism as can 'belief' in a 'sacred' book. And while I argue throughout Part 1 of this book that Marx laid the foundation for distinctive historical-materialist methodology, my understanding of that methodology is, as I elaborate in some detail in Chapter 11, rather different from, and certainly rather more open than, Lukács's.

33   While I borrow Althusser's term, and agree with him on the timing of, Marx's 'epistemological break', I see that break rather differently than Althusser. My view of Marx's 'epistemological break' is developed throughout Part 1, but especially in Chapter 3 and Appendix 1.3. it should also be noted that when speaking of an '*Aufhebung* of philosophy', Marx did not mean that further philosophical inquiry is worthless. He was reacting against the specifically idealist Western philosophical tradition from Socrates through Hegel that privileged mind over body, and that therefore treated human history, human worldmaking, as the work of a mind allegedly freed from material influences. Once the subject-object relation is defined such that the human mind is put back into the human body, and the philosopher is put back into society, traditional philosophy, that had conceived itself as '*an independ-*

0.3   Marx's Wager on Reconstructing History 'Up from the Body'

Marx was, as Étienne Balibar observed, a thinker 'of eternal new beginnings, leaving behind him *many* uncompleted drafts and projects'.[34] And that uncompleted project of fully elaborating a theory of history grounded in corporeal organisation as its first and fundamental fact was doubtless the biggest gamble of all. The magnitude of Marx's corporeal challenge to historical theory is best conveyed by Terry Eagleton's formulation of the question animating Marx's project: 'What if an idea of reason could be generated up from the body itself, rather than the body incorporated into a reason which is always already in place? What if it were possible, in a breathtaking wager, to retrace one's steps and reconstruct everything – ethics, history, politics, rationality – from a bodily foundation?'[35] At first glance, 'breathtaking' seems a polite understatement for this wager; 'audacious', 'foolhardy', or perhaps 'impertinent' would seem more appropriate. For, in addition to the breathtaking immensity of the project, the attempt to rethink 'everything' from a 'bodily foundation' is, as Eagleton recognised, necessarily 'fraught with perils': 'how could it safeguard itself from naturalism, biologism, sensuous empiricism, from a mechanical materialism or false transcendentalism of the body every bit as disabling as the ideologies it seeks to oppose? How can the human body, itself in part a product of history, be taken as history's source? Does not the body in such an enterprise become simply another privileged anteriority, ... spuriously self-grounding'.[36]

Marx, of course, did not win his wager. But his failure to win was not, in my view, a result of having succumbed to any of the perils that Eagleton noted. On the contrary, and as I shall argue throughout this work, he successfully navigated between the traps of a false universalism and an arbitrary eclecticism. His failure to win resulted rather from the presumptuousness of his wager; for, he obviously did not, nor could he, succeed in reconstructing 'everything'. Indeed, he barely scratched the surface, or better: he barely laid the foundations for his reconstruction project. For, it was, and remains, a wager that neither Marx

---

ent branch of knowledge', 'loses its medium of existence' (Marx [1845] in Tucker 1978, p. 155; my italics).

34   Balibar 2017, p. 6. In this passage Balibar calls Marx a 'philosopher'. I write 'thinker' instead to correspond with my argument concerning Marx's *Aufhebung* of philosophy – and because the term thinker encompasses Marx's various activities as theoretician, critic of social forms, and historian.

35   Eagleton 1990, p. 197. Eagleton also notes that Nietzsche and Freud also made the same wager. But the transhistorical logic of their respective theories of 'the will to power' and instinctual drives result in rather narrow, one-dimensional views of history.

36   Eagleton 1990, p. 197.

nor anyone else could possibly win. One individual's lifetime pitted against the lifespan of a more than 2000-year-old philosophical tradition does not make for great odds.

But before dismissing Marx's wager, it would be worth taking a closer look and determine exactly what it was on which he placed his bet. Perhaps he was not so foolish as to bet on such an impossible wager – or at least not so foolish as to bet on his own efforts alone. Perhaps he was completely aware of the odds against him, and therefore changed the terms of the wager. Perhaps his work was not at all intended to be complete in itself, that is: perhaps (contrary to so much interpretive literature) he was not at all trying to write a Hegelian-like speculative philosophy of history that would encompass everything essential about history from the beginnings of humanity through the present and into an 'inevitable' communist future. Perhaps he understood that the only way to win the wager would be to contribute to the construction of a materialist conception of history, of a historical-materialist 'paradigm' with a set of 'guiding threads' outlining the 'research strategy' of a historical-materialist *Wissenschaft* whose ongoing project would be to 'reconstruct everything from a bodily foundation'.[37]

This, of course, is what I think Marx was betting on – and also why I think that there is still much to be won by backing him. My backing of that wager, however, does not take the form of a simple defence of Marx grounded in the simplistic assumption that a 'proper' interpretation of his theories would suffice to win. For at the very least, it is necessary to show that a materialist conception of history based on human corporeal organisation is compatible with the great strides in fields ranging from evolutionary biology and paleoanthropology to the social sciences and humanities in the nearly century-and-a-half since his death. But those great strides should not themselves be simplistically taken as *a priori* proof that the materialist conception of history, which Marx presented only in the barest outline, is itself outdated. This book, therefore, intends to back Marx in his corporeal wager by substantiating and elaborating both the paradigm of a materialist conception of history and the research strategy of a

---

37   There is a large debate, involving Thomas Kuhn himself, over what exactly is meant by a scientific 'paradigm'. Here I shall sidestep that debate and explain only how I use it in this work. By 'paradigm' I mean a set of assumptions about the contents of a science of *Wissenschaft*, the logic that governs that content, and the methods used to analyse that content; in consequence of which I use 'normal science' as the deployment of those methods in the analysis of that content. The term 'guiding threads', which Marx used in *The German Ideology* to designate his foundational assumptions about history and his methodological guidelines for its analysis is addressed briefly in note 38 below and elaborated in detail in Chapter 3.

historical-materialist *Wissenschaft* along the lines of Marx's insights, but well beyond anything that he himself did or even could address. In one sentence, the (perhaps presumptuous) purpose of this book is to pursue and elaborate the profound and far-reaching implications of Marx's claim that 'human corporeal organisation' is the foundation of historical theory and the starting point for historical inquiry. In terms of Marx's own writings this undertaking might be seen as an attempt to elaborate his meditations on the corporeal roots of history presented especially in the first section of *The German Ideology*, and to extrapolate their implications beyond, yet in keeping with the historical-materialist logic of, his own reflections.

Like Marx's undertaking, mine too must confront the perils that Eagleton enumerated. To recognise the theoretical dangers is, of course, not enough to disarm them. That disarming can in any case only be accomplished, if at all, through the actual development of the argument itself. But here it is worth specifying the terms on which I am backing Marx in his wager. I take Marx's materialist conception of history to be a paradigm: a set of assumptions or, as Marx himself put it, of 'guiding threads' (*Leitfaden*) that in turn establish the foundations for the systematic study of history, a research strategy for a historical *Wissenschaft*. Such a modest understanding of what Marx was claiming with his general statements about history not only helps us better to understand what he wagered, but also provides a good reason to continue backing him. For he has not lost the bet as long as his guiding threads and research strategy continue to produce knowledge. And my goal will be to articulate those 'guiding threads' derived from human corporeal organisation – those *Leitfaden des Leibes* ('guiding threads of the body', to appropriate and give a historical-materialist twist to Nietzsche's very appropriate term[38]) – and to show that those corporeal-based guiding threads are capable of opening new horizons of knowledge production.

In addition to these monumental risks of being swamped by the immensity of the project, and of succumbing to either the false universalism of traditional Western philosophy or the arbitrary eclecticism so prevalent in poststructur-

---

38 Nietzsche 2019, pp. 347–8. In a fortuitous, but perhaps telling, coincidence, Nietzsche's choice of terms that introduce this passage, *Am Leitfaden des Leibes*, has an affinity with Marx's terminology – and for that reason will be cited at some length as an introduction to Chapter 1. In the Preface to the *Critique of Political Economy* Marx strategically used the term *Leitfaden* or guiding threads as a methodological preface to his general outline of a material conception of history (Marx 1859 in Tucker 1978, p. 4). With this usage Marx reiterated a methodological discussion in *The German Ideology* cautioning that the general outline of a materialist conception of history is not a grid to be forced onto history, but a path of inquiry, an analytical itinerary (Marx 1845 in Tucker 1978, p. 155).

alist/postmodernist 'interventions', there are at least two more profane risks, namely banality and boredom. This project could be charged with banality for belabouring the obvious; 'everyone knows' that the 'the first prerequisite for human history is the existence of living human beings', and that 'we can't live without our bodies'. But here it is worth recalling Stephen Jay Gould's comment that '[n]o biases are more insidious than those leading to the neglect of things everyone knows about in principle'.[39] Although 'insidious' may seem too strong a word in this context, Gould's reference to familiarity breeding neglect is certainly *apropos*. It is, as I shall argue throughout, no caricature to say that there have been in fact rather few serious attempts in the Western philosophies of history to 'give the body its due' – and by 'serious' I mean attempts that treat the body as more than an unruly bearer of the mind or a passive site of inscription or discipline.[40] For though the body has been and continues to be the object of a great deal of attention, that attention has been of the kind that briefly calls its object to centre stage only in order quickly to domesticate and dismiss it. What Marx said of the political economists' treatment of 'use-value' is overwhelmingly true of treatments of corporeality in traditional Western philosophy and also among its poststructuralist and postmodernist antagonists: despite their hostility to one another, one significant point of convergence between traditional 'logocentric' philosophy and its poststructuralist/postmodernist critics is that both (freely in different ways, but nevertheless) reduce human corporeal organisation, the 'natural body', to a 'simple prerequisite' – and then summarily neglect it.[41]

The risk of boredom results from the possibility that this project might be viewed as yet another attempt to reconstruct Marx, to explain 'what Marx really meant' – a topic that, according to Étienne Balibar, has long since lost its 'charm' in scholarly circles.[42] I do not, however, consider 'charm' the sole, or even a necessary criterion for evaluating the use-value of the products of intellectual labour. And although I do indeed devote Part 1 to reconstructing what I think Marx 'really meant' (not least in order to show that he did *not* mean many of the things that numerous and varied interpretations have purported to find in his texts), that is only the starting point. The bulk of the book (with the partial

---

39   Gould 1977, p. 289.
40   This phrase is from Sheets-Johnstone 1992.
41   This phrase is Marx's which he uses to describe how the Political Economists defined and dismissed 'use-value' as 'a simple prerequisite' – which will be treated in detail in Part 1. The phrase itself will appear often in a variety of contexts, all of which have in common, as Gould put it, 'the neglect of things everyone knows about in principle'.
42   The phrasing is from Étienne Balibar (1992, p. 38) who referred to the question of the relation between Marx and Foucault as one that by the 1990s had lost its charm.

exception of Part 4) aims to elaborate and develop Marx's insights by tapping into fields ranging from evolutionary biology to cultural studies – fields whose contributions to the production of knowledge (that is: to that which Marx himself designated 'the most solid form of social wealth') he could have at most only dimly imagined.[43] Moreover, I make no claim to have determined what Marx 'really *would* have said' were he still alive to witness the great developments in knowledge of the world. Rather, I adopt what I take to be his principles and insights, and I attempt to complement and supplement them with, where necessary adjust them to, research advances in fields relevant to grasping history by its corporeal roots.

That Marx's materialist conception of history and his historical-materialist research strategy can be complemented, supplemented, and enriched in so many ways by research advances since his lifetime is a tribute to his intellectual endeavours. For if, in paraphrase of Ernst Bloch (see headnote), 'to understand [a great theory], precisely in a timely fashion, means to go beyond [it]', then that is because its 'rational core' does not come undone with the historical explanation of its genesis and historical context.[44] Rather, that which remains 'scientifically [*wissenschaftlich*] animated' and 'progressive' in a theory is neither confined to nor exhausted in the historical time of its origin.[45] Because the 'core ideas' of great theories are, Bloch insists, never erstwhile, 'whoever turns toward them is not looking backward'. Rather, 'we reach back to great thinkers according to the measure of the not-yet-past [*Nicht-Vergangenen*] in them because they themselves reach forward toward us and are co-workers in that space which is not the space of the past'. Great theories are those that are necessarily incomplete; they are not definitive, closed books, the last work on a subject, but instead an introduction to it; they open analytical horizons and offer guiding methodological threads that reach far beyond the lives of their creators. In the present case, if we grasp what Marx considered the corporeal core of historical materialism, we can then see the many ways in which his theory points beyond itself and reaches forward well into our own time.

One of the tasks of this book, accordingly, is to suggest how the results of 'Darwinian' paleoanthropological studies supplement and enrich, widen and

---

43   Marx 1973 [1857–58], p. 540. Because of its rich and varied implications, esp. its intimations about Marx's vision of a society of emancipated individuals, this definition of knowledge (*Wissenschaft*) as 'the most solid form of social wealth' will appear frequently in the following.
44   Ernst Bloch 1975, p. 73.
45   Ernst Bloch 1975, p. 7. Following two citations, ibid., p. 8. For a brief discussion of recent works that would bury Marx in the nineteenth century, see note 74 below.

deepen the theoretical foundation of Marx's materialist conception of history and indicate its theoretical expanse (a theoretical expanse that is quite possibly much more extensive than he himself realised). And I might add, as an addendum to Bloch's comment, that going beyond a thinker, here Marx, and understanding how his theories can be supplemented by later research enables us to return to him with a greater understanding of the corporeal depths of his materialist conception of history and of the breadth of the research horizons opened by that conception. I intend therefore, as Richard Halpern aptly described his own undertaking, 'to "return to Marx" in an unabashed and somewhat systematic way in order to lay the basis of my own argument'.[46] My concern in any case is not with Marx himself but with the logic and the consequences of, and the possibilities opened by, a materialist conception of history. Thus, while it is of course necessary to begin with Marx's own works, this book is not a gamble on Marx alone. I place my bet, not on Marx, but rather *with* him: I back his historical-materialist wager on the possibility of writing the history of 'everything' up from 'a bodily foundation'. To do so, I undertake a systematic reconstruction of a materialist conception of history up from its corporeal foundations – a reconstruction that begins with Marx, and then attempts to go through and beyond, but nevertheless with him, along paths he delineated and with itineraries he proposed.

This interpretation of bodies and history cuts obliquely across the grain of the two rather antagonistic approaches toward the body, both of which, curiously, emerged in roughly the post-war era, came to prominence in the 1960s and 1970s, and both of which remain foundational paradigms for inquiry in their respective fields, namely: Darwinistic sociobiological approaches that treat bodies essentially as bearers of genes, and view history as developing according to a selectionist logic; and poststructualist approaches insisting that the only historically relevant matter pertaining to bodies are the ways in which they are constructed and inscribed by cultures. Sociobiological proponents find no commonality between Marx and Darwin other than perhaps a distantly related materialism, and generally dismiss Marx's theory as teleological or ideological, in contrast to Darwin the scientist. Poststructuralists, on the other hand, treat both Marx's and Darwin's writings as textual targets of deconstructive analysis, and find in both false essentialist assumptions about human beings that result in particularist conclusions parading as universal principles. In my view, however, these polar opposite positions mirror each other. Whereas sociobiology views the body through the prism of genes, poststructuralists

---

46   Halpern 1991, p. 62.

view the body through the prism of culture. But both approaches see only one dimension of corporeality and treat the body only as an object, whether of genetic or cultural construction.

I have a rather different take on the matter. For, if we accept 'human corporeal organisation' as the foundation of a materialist conception of history, it becomes evident that Marx's wager is not so different from that of his contemporary, Darwin, who sought to explain the logic governing the evolution of the corporeal organisation and the ethology of all species, *Homo sapiens* included. And given their common focus on corporeal organisation, it is worth pausing a moment to consider the affinities between the two – and in contrast to sociobiological and cultural constructionist approaches.

0.4   Historical-Materialist Horizons: Darwin and Marx

However much we are surprised, shocked, stunned, delighted, amused and/or bemused by the corporeal resemblances between the 'higher' primates and humans (and despite Darwin's disgusting doubts about the humanity of 'savages' and the detestable yet recurring racist use of simian epithets), no visitor to a zoo would mistake any of the great apes for a human being – and not just because the humans are not encaged. Rather, it is obviously because of an unmistakably human corporeal form: a 'universal', that is to say a species-specific corporeal form that – regardless of age, sex, or race, regardless of the particular cultural meanings with which it has been inscribed, the disciplinary practices to which it has been subjected, and the culturally specific thoughts that it carries around in its head – is immediately recognisable as human. As noted above, the mainstream of the Western philosophical tradition subjected this obvious fact of a human corporeal organisation to what Gould called the 'insidious bias' of familiarity breeding neglect, even contempt. And as I shall indicate shortly, despite all the effort it has recently put into deconstructing traditional philosophy's denigration of the body, much poststructuralist/postmodernist writing shows a similar contempt for and neglect of what it dismisses as the merely 'natural' or 'physical' body.[47] In consequence, there were in 1988 when evolutionary biologist Ernst Mayr expressed his disappointment over the fact, and there are still 'many philosophers [and many other practitioners of *les sciences humaines*] who write as if Darwin had never existed', and

---

47   This will be touched on in the next section of this introduction and elaborated more thoroughly in Chapter 4, 'The Body is not a Tabula Rasa'.

who have not heeded Mayr's insistence that the human sciences cannot neglect natural scientific insights.[48]

With philosophers and other practitioners of the 'human sciences' treating the body as a simple prerequisite of history (whether as the vessel bearing the mind that allegedly defines *Homo sapiens*, or as the blank slate awaiting cultural inscription, or the locus of amorphous drives awaiting discipline), the study of the body and/in history has been more or less abandoned to the natural scientists – who, along with a growing number of social scientists, are justifiably appalled at this relegation of human biology to the status of a 'simple prerequisite' of 'truly human' being. Such sociobiologically-oriented thinkers insist that through the application of selectionist models, natural science can take over, and better accomplish, what had been the task of the human scientists, namely: the explanation of culture and history. Nevertheless, however accurate Mayr's statement about the neglect of Darwin in the human sciences may be, there is certainly more than one way of agreeing with it.

The most visible form of agreement in the US is from the many researchers who have responded to E.O. Wilson's (now half-century old) call to develop and advance a science of human sociobiology. Wilson and like-minded researchers in the natural and social sciences – those whom Niles Eldredge calls 'ultra-Darwinians'[49] – insist on the principle of scientific reductionism and, accordingly, that 'cultural evolution' must be explained in terms of, or by analogy with, the 'laws' of natural selection and adaptation. Sociobiologists and their social-scientific following insist that the human body has the same basic drives and is thus subjected to competitive struggle and the same selectionist laws that allegedly animate the animal kingdom. In formulations as short-sighted as they are succinct, Richard Dawkins maintains that a body is merely 'the genes' way of preserving the genes unaltered' and Melvin Konner that '[a]n organism is, in essence, a gene's way of making another gene'.[50]

No longer a vessel for the mind as in traditional philosophy, the body – or, more broadly, human corporeal organisation – is now consigned to the equally passive role as the vessel in which genes replicate themselves; and the bodily attributes of the individual organism are considered only in a quantitative comparison of relative fitness vis-à-vis those of conspecific individuals.[51] For

---

48   Mayr 1982, p. 71.
49   Eldredge 1995, pp. 35 ff.
50   Dawkins 1989, p. 23. See also Konner 1991 in Sheehan and Sosna 1991, p. 109.
51   The brevity with which I have for introductory purposes summarised the fundamental premises, assumptions, and conclusions of these three intellectual traditions (mainstream Western philosophy, sociobiology, poststructuralism/postmodernism) necessarily over-

sociobiologists, the uniqueness of humans vis-à-vis other species lies in their culture-producing genes which gives humans a qualitatively different history, but one still subject to the principle of scientific reductionism and thus ruled by the same transhistorical logic of selection. Thus, although rooted in the body, sociobiology also fails to give the body its due. It is a kind of shortcut that all too easily subjects the complexities of human histories to a monocausally selectionist version of Darwin's evolutionary insights.

While sociobiology claims that culture is a product of genes and evolution and thus can only be fully explained by selectionist models derived from evolutionary biology, those whom I shall call (in paraphrase of Eldredge) cultural 'ultra-constructionists' reject any and all (except their own) universalist claims about culture and history, and insist instead that all meaning (scientific meaning included) is wholly constituted by, as an effect of, some kind of structured semiotic system, e.g. a system of linguistic or cultural signs.[52] To understand the meanings of things therefore, it is not necessary to look outside the semiotic system through which meanings are constructed. The ultra-constructionist position on corporeality is most succinctly summarised in Anthony Synnott's (rather universalist) claims that 'the body and the senses are socially constructed', that '[t]he body is *not* a "given", but a social category with different meanings imposed and developed by every age, and by different sectors of the population', and that 'the body social negates the body physical'.[53] It is easy enough to agree that all human bodies are inscribed with

---

simplifies them. But here I am concerned only with a kind of general mapping, an overview that will situate my undertaking in relation to these others. For a discussion of sociobiological attempts to apply Darwinistic principles to the study of human history, see Fracchia and Lewontin 1999.

52 Kimberlé Crenshaw has a stronger term for claims of this ilk, namely: 'the vulgarized social construction thesis' (Crenshaw 1991, p. 1296). Crenshaw does not, nor do I, deny the power of essentialising processes of categorisation that hierarchically divide and evaluate people according to essentialised categories based on such constructions as race, ethnicity, gender, or sexual orientation; nor, accordingly, does either of us deny the value of anti-essentialist deconstructionist critiques of such categorisation processes. But as necessary as such deconstructions are, she does not, nor do I, find them sufficient. As she puts it: 'Vulgar constructionism ... distorts the possibilities for meaningful identity politics by conflating at least two separate but closely linked manifestations of power. One is the power exercised simply through the process of categorization; the other, the power to cause that categorization to have social and material consequences. While the former power facilitates the latter, the political implications of challenging one over the other matter greatly' (ibid., p. 1297). To this I would add only, but significantly, that it is necessary to grasp the social and material sources of the power that can cause categorisations to have social and material consequences.

53 Synnott 1993, pp. 1; 2–4; 5 my italics. Because of their prevalence in the contemporary stud-

socio-culturally specific meanings; and it is equally easy to appreciate the great contribution of ultra-constructionist analyses in exposing and deconstructing culturally-specific meanings inscribed on bodies. But it is certainly possible to deconstruct cultural constructions of the body without having to 'negate' the body physical – and thus without having also to deny the rather fundamental factors that *Homo sapiens* is, by virtue of its corporeal organisation, a culture-creating animal, and that human corporeal organisation is therefore a constitutive factor in the construction and content of cultural forms. And it is one of the purposes of my project to explain that possibility: to show that and how a historical-materialist deconstruction can, by exposing the corporeal foundation of human histories, see deeper into the life of made-things, cultural constructions included.

It should be obvious, moreover, that the human 'body physical' is always already a 'body social': human sociability is a necessary consequence of the corporeal framing of human modes of reproduction and child-rearing, and of the specifically human modes of production required for the satisfaction of material needs, the diverse forms of which, despite much variance in the particulars, are all distinctly and uniquely human – and that is because human corporeal organisation is the 'form-determinant' [*Formbestimmung*] of their range, of the extent and limits of their variation.[54] And the 'body cultural' (a more appropriate term than 'body social' for what Synnott describes) is the human body conceived as constituted by the culturally-specific meanings inscribed on it. The diverse meanings imposed on bodies, however, are not at all wholly arbitrary, but are, I shall argue, rather easily revealed as socio-culturally specific refractions of the 'body physical'.

Between these two extremes there are those who understand that the gap is more than an epistemological illusion, who recognise the need to bridge it, and whose suggestions are more measured and modest. Stephen Jay Gould, for example, suggests the need to view cultural achievements against the background of 'biological potentiality', the bodily capacities that made them possible: the larger human brain and voice box enabling conceptual thought and

---

ies of social and cultural constructions of the body in the humanities and social sciences, I shall in the course of this book elaborate in some detail the critique of cultural ultra-constructionism to which I allude in the rest of this paragraph. See Chapters 4, 8, and 9.

54 As Marx uses the term especially but not exclusively in the *Grundrisse*, *Formbestimmung* or 'form-determinant' is determinant only in the sense that a given sense establishes or 'determines' a range of possibilities, but which of those possibilities becomes realised is a historical contingency, albeit an understandable and explicable, that is to say, non-arbitrary contingency. I address 'form-determinant' again in Chapter 1, Chapter 3, and Appendix 1.2; and the term recurs frequently throughout this entire work.

language, the opposable thumb enabling humans to fashion tools, paintings, etc.⁵⁵ By calling attention to the culture-constructing capacities of human corporeal form, Gould points to the materiality of the body as the central category in both the evolutionary natural sciences and the human sciences, and thus as the site where the bridge between biology and culture, human natural history and human history, might be built. And this in turn brings us back to Marx and Darwin, whose common concern with corporeal organisation might point towards bridging the gap between the natural and human sciences.

In a crossed-out comment in the manuscript of *The German Ideology* that can retrospectively be taken as a kind of anticipation of Darwin, Marx presciently noted that 'We recognize only one single *Wissenschaft*, the *Wissenschaft* of history. History can be observed from two sides; it can be divided into the history of nature and the history of human beings. Both sides are however inseparable; as long as human beings exist, the history of nature and the history of human beings mutually condition [*bedingen*] each other'.⁵⁶ Having thus established a unity in difference of the natural and social/historical sciences, it is not surprising that Marx celebrated (albeit somewhat chauvinistically) the publication of Darwin's *Origin of Species* fourteen years later. As he commented in a letter to Engels after having read the *Origin*: 'Although developed in a crude English manner, this is the book that contains the natural historical basis for our view'.⁵⁷ In addition to their stylistic objections, Marx and Engels later expressed some reservations and criticisms of certain of Darwin's specific theses. They particularly objected to his Malthusianism which they thought led to his monocausal reliance on the 'struggle for survival' to explain natural selection – a criticism shared by many prominent Darwinists.⁵⁸ The emphasis on struggle could all too easily become 'nothing but a phrase'⁵⁹ that just as easily raises the spectre of a nature (in Alfred, Lord Tennyson's formulation) 'red in tooth and claw'. Such a view neglected, as Engels pointed out, that 'the mutual interaction of natural bodies includes harmony as well as collision, struggle as well as cooperation'.⁶⁰ And Marx was amused that Darwin 'recognizes, among

---

55   Gould 1981, p. 328.
56   Marx, *Die Deutsche Ideologie* in *Marx-Engels Werke*, Vol. 3, p. 18. In his manuscript Marx crossed out this passage, but it is certainly consistent with and accurately represents his historical-materialist viewpoint.
57   Karl Marx, letter to Friedrich Engels, 19 December 1860, in *Marx-Engels Werke* (MEW) Vol. 30, p. 131.
58   E.g. Richard Lewontin, Richard Levins, Stephen Jay Gould, Niles Eldredge.
59   Marx, letter to Ludwig Kugelmann, 27 June 1870, in Marx and Engels 1975, p. 225.
60   Engels, letter to Pjotr Lawrowitsch Lawrow, 12–17 November 1875, in MEW, Vol. 34, pp. 169–72; Engels, letter to Karl Kautsky, 10 February 1883, in MEW, Vol. 35, pp. 431–3. Marx and

the beasts and plants, his own English society with its division of labour, competition, opening of new markets, "inventions", and Malthusian "struggle for survival"'.[61] Nevertheless, both he and Engels seem always to have held Darwin in the highest regard, viewing him as a benchmark of scientific progress; and they immediately recognised both the materialist underpinnings and the revolutionary implications of Darwin's work. Despite his 'crude style', Darwin had, they believed, delivered the 'death-blow' to teleology in the natural sciences, thereby initiating what Freud would later call a Copernican revolution in the study of *Homo sapiens*.[62] Darwin had made it possible to bridge the gap between the natural sciences and a materialist conception of history and to develop a single *Wissenschaft* with two distinct, but corporeally-related dimensions.

Certain that Darwin had provided an evolutionary-materialist underpinning to their materialist conception of history, though without having elaborated in any systematic detail why this was so, Marx and Engels confidently continued their attempts to decipher the contemporary capitalist economy and only peripherally pursued their historical-materialist inquiries into the evolution of human corporeal organisation. But even if the affinities between Darwin and Marx are obvious, conviction without elaboration and explanation tells us little about the exact relation between them or, more precisely in terms of the question to be discussed here, about the relation between an evolutionary conception of human prehistory and a materialist conception of human history.[63] Though Marx was convinced that Darwin had provided the prehistorical

---

Engels also had a brief skirmish over Darwin in an exchange of letters between August and October 1866 (*MEW*, Vol. 31, pp. 247–9, 256–61). Marx maintained that Darwin's work had been overtaken by P. Tremaux's *Origine et Transformations de l'Homme et des autres Etres*, while Engels replied that there is 'nothing' to Tremaux's work because neither did he understand geology nor was he capable of the most ordinary literary-historical critique. As late as 1866 Marx wrote to Ludwig Kugelmann recommending Tremaux's work as 'an advance over Darwin'. But afterward, references to Tremaux in Marx's writings and letters disappear, while Darwin continues to be referred to as the dean of natural history.

61   Karl Marx, letter to Friedrich Engels, 18 June 1862, in *MEW*, Vol. 30, p. 249.
62   Marx to Lasalle, 16 January 1861, in *MEW*, Vol. 30, p. 578. See also Engels *MEW*, Vol. 19, p. 205: '*Darwin hat der metaphysischen Naturauffassung den gewaltigsten Stoss versetzt*'.
63   A note on terminology. The more common usage of human 'prehistory' is in reference to 'preliterate' societies. That is not my usage, for in my view, all human societies are historical (and I would even argue that all life forms are as well). Here I will use human 'history' to refer to the history of *Homo sapiens*. And I use 'human natural history' and 'human prehistory' interchangeably to refer to the evolutionary process (through the *Australopithecines* and the earlier *Homo species*) that preceded *Homo sapiens* and from which the species emerged.

foundation for a materialist conception of history, the missing elaboration of the relation between his own work and Darwin's remains to be articulated.[64]

Darwin for his part was fully aware that his too was (to borrow Eagleton's phrase) a 'breathtaking wager' with revolutionary implications. Though he had developed his notions of evolution and natural selection long before 1859, he was very cautious and hesitant about publishing them. As Gould suggests, the main reason for 'Darwin's Delay' in publishing his theory of evolution may well have been 'that he espoused but feared to expose something he perceived as far more heretical than evolution itself, namely: philosophical materialism'; for '[n]o notion could be more upsetting to the deepest traditions of Western thought than the statement that mind – however complex and powerful – is simply a product of brain'.[65] Though apparently more hesitant to publicise his views than Marx, Darwin was certainly a materialist fellow traveller and no less iconoclastic.

In terms of content, the affinities between Darwin's materialist conception of human prehistory and Marx's materialist conception of history lie in their unabashedly materialist focus on corporeal organisation. They both unapologetically focus not only on the fact that the human mind is always an embodied mind, but also on the more important fact with more far-reaching implications that *Homo sapiens* is a mindful body. Human corporeal organisation can thus be conceived as mid-point and link between the disciplines. It points 'backward' toward paleoanthropology and the evolution of that corporeal organisation, and also forward to the worlds that humans have built for themselves with this corporeal organisation. Though students of human evolution disagree,

---

64 For further discussion of how Marx and Engels saw their work in relation to Darwin's, see Appendix 0.4, 'Marx, Engels and Darwin'. For comment on paradigms and research programmes in Marx's and Darwin's undertakings, see Appendix 0.5.

65 Gould 1977, pp. 21–7. Perhaps because of his personal caution or modesty, Darwin's iconoclasm has fared far better than Marx's. This is actually a bit curious, for both theories have been brutally misused. Marx's work was obviously abused by Stalinism and its avatars – and there are countless interpretations holding Marx responsible for the brutalities committed in his name. Darwin, however, has remained untainted by the bloody history of certain forms of social Darwinism, especially the social Darwinist justifications of the subjection of and murderous brutality toward the victims of European and US American imperialism since the late nineteenth century, and of course in the social-darwinistically justified genocidal policies of the Nazis among others. Unlike Marx, however, Darwin is seldom called to account (nor should he be; nor, for the same reason, should Marx) for what has been done in his name. And the political history of Marxism has only compounded the theoretical problems resulting from a century-and-a-half of Marx-interpretation that preferred to see economics, rather than human corporeal organisation as the foundation of his materialist conception of history.

often vehemently, in their causal explanations of the emergence of human beings – whether the key element in human evolution was bipedality, the opposable thumb and toolmaking, the sharing of food and sociability, the larger brain and language and culture, etc. – they all nevertheless recognise the evolved human body as the source of *Homo sapiens*' unique social and cultural capacities, that is to say: they all analyse human evolution in terms of the emergence of human corporeal organisation. And this last fact of paleo-anthropology, the emergence of the corporeal organisation of *Homo sapiens*, is of course for Marx the 'first fact' of historical materialism, of an approach that would seek to analyse human socio-cultural history up from the body.[66]

The affinities between Marx and Darwin extend beyond content to methodology as well. Darwin's theory of evolution was built on a combination of careful observation and highly-educated (and very good) guesswork. Nevertheless, it was still only a hypothesis that suggested the foundations and outlines of a radically new way of looking at the world. Darwin too made a kind of breathtaking wager in providing the premises and general outlines of a research programme that no single person could ever exhaust. He obviously did not live long enough to substantiate all his insights, and to do so required discoveries far beyond anything he could have concretely imagined. The first problem that had to be solved, one of which Darwin himself was aware, was the lack of an explanation of the means of transmission of traits from one generation to the next. The genetic studies of Darwin's younger contemporary, Gregor Mendel, offered a means of solving the transmission problem. But it still took until the mid-twentieth century before Ernst Mayr, G. Ledyard Stebbins and Theodosius Dobzhansky, among others, constructed the 'modern evolutionary synthesis' that applied Mendelian-based genetics, complemented by population genetics, as the means of explaining the transmission of traits. It was this synthesis, finally achieved nearly a century after his treatise *On the Origin of Species* appeared (in 1859; eight years before the publication of the first volume of *Das Kapital*), that won Darwin his wager by turning his hunches and hypotheses into a solid foundation for the science of evolutionary biology.

---

66 Though I disagree somewhat with her specification of how to give content to the study of the 'natural' dimension of human history, Kate Soper (1981, p. 76) captures in formal terms what is implied by Marx's adoption of an evolutionary dimension on which he developed a materialist conception of history as that which traces how human beings make their own history and, in the process, themselves. She writes: 'if Marx can be said to transcend rather than reproduce, albeit in inverted form, the discourse of an opposition between natural and social, it is because he refuses once and for all to offer a "philosophic" solution to the question of the relations between natural and social determinations and therefore opens up this question to scientific investigation'.

Countless deterministic interpretations notwithstanding, my contention is that, like Darwin, Marx too explicitly understood his various general theoretical statements about the assumptions of historical analysis, about the content of history and the causes of historical change, not, as noted above, as a grid or schema to be imposed on history, but as *Leitfaden*, guiding threads, and therefore as in themselves and 'apart from empirical content' only empty and 'worthless abstractions' in need of critical development.[67] Consequently, the project of elaborating Marx's initial insights into a materialist conception of history and of developing a historical-materialist *Wissenschaft* is an ongoing one that is in many respects still in its early phases – however well-developed certain aspects (e.g. the critique of capitalism) may be.

Thus, although both Marx and Darwin made general statements, although both were fully aware of the abstract and inadequate character of those statements and insisted on the need for further critical elaboration, posterity has treated them very differently as thinkers. Allen Megill, for example, contrasted Darwin, whom he considered the scientist who transcended his time, to a Marx whom he considered imprisoned in the philosophical rationalism of his own time.[68] What I am suggesting here is to give Marx the same treatment that Darwin received, and for the same reasons. And if we adopt such a perspective, then we can approach Marx's and Darwin's projects as complementary – as the two sides of a single historical-materialist *Wissenschaft*. In so doing, we might also begin to construct a lasting bridge across C.P. Snow's well-known abyss between the 'two cultures'.

Precisely because of their common interests in human corporeal organisation, a Darwinian materialist conception of pre-history and a Marxian materialist conception of history may be said to be reaching across Snow's abyss at its narrowest point. And this is why the theories of Marx and Darwin, the *Leitfaden* proposed, and the research programs initiated, by each, are more promising sites than most for the building of the bridge. This is because, to borrow again Gould's succinct formulation, cultural production must be viewed against the background of 'biological potentiality'.[69] If, as Norman Geras has quipped, no fish can be Mozart,[70] this is not just because of its minute brain. Ignoring for the sake of argument the fact that the capacities of the human brain are intimately

---

67   Marx 1845 in Tucker 1978, p. 155.
68   See Fracchia 2003. For further comment on the similarities between Darwin's and Marx's projects and why they should be accorded similar respect, see Appendix 0.4, 'Marx and Darwin: Paradigms and Research Programs'.
69   Gould 1981, p. 328.
70   Geras 1983, p. 109.

related to the corporeal form in which they evolved, even if a fish had a brain equipped with human-like capacities, it is the lack of corporeal instruments and dexterities capable of writing music and playing musical instruments that would still prevent it from composing concertos. That is the sense of Antonio Gramsci's response to his son's inquiry about what human life would be like if our brains were as big as those of elephants. Appealing, in effect, to the first corporeal fact of a materialist conception of history, he asked his son in turn to consider what good a larger brain would be without hands.[71]

Though inseparable, 'biological potentiality' and the actual production of culture(s) are not the same. The bridge must therefore be suspended from two supports. For however essential evolutionary biology is to the study of human history, it can alone cast only a pale illumination on that history – sociobiological claims to the contrary notwithstanding. If we acknowledge both the difference between the natural and human sciences, yet also the need to bridge the gap between them and to write history 'as though Darwin existed', then we can also acknowledge the profundity of Marx's insistence, noted above, on a single *Wissenschaft* consisting of the two 'inseparable' dimensions of human natural, evolutionary prehistory and the human history of *Homo sapiens*.

0.5 Corporeal Semiotics: A First Encounter

The determination of human corporeal organisation as the foundation of a materialist conception of history is of course only the first step in reconstructing human histories 'up from the body'. The next step is to learn how to decipher the worlds that human beings make, the societies and cultures humans construct in order to detect in them the signs of corporeality – that is, to articulate what I call a 'corporeal semiotics'. The categorial starting point for this corporeal semiotics is Marx's notion of 'objectification' (*Vergegenständlichung*). Objectification refers to the process of making, the very corporeal activity of sensuously-acting subjects building their worlds by fashioning the objects, the artefacts, that those worlds contain and out of which they are built. As Elaine Scarry notes in reflecting on Marx's corporeal-rooted notion of objectification, the common tendency to see him only as a critic of capitalism neglects his broader contribution as 'our major philosopher on the nature of material objects'.[72] And recognising the centrality of corporeality in that philosophy, she explains that Marx 'soberly, often movingly' portrays the made-object 'as

---

71 Gramsci 1973, p. 271.
72 Scarry 1985, p. 179. Following citations in this paragraph, ibid., p. 247; p. 281; pp. 242–3; p. 278.

a projection of the human body': 'he breaks open the sensuous object (now a table, now a wall of bricks, now a bolt of lace) and finds located in the interior structure of each our bodies'. Succinctly and precisely put, the body is for Marx 'the interior structure of the artefact'. And continuing along Scarry's line of thinking: if the body is the interior structure of the artefact, then the artefact will necessarily bear signs of corporeality, signs of the corporeally-grounded purpose – the needs, wants and desires – behind its making, signs of the corporeal capacities and dexterities that enabled it to be made, signs of the process by which it is made, and signs of its social life after it has been made. To decipher the different layers of meaning embedded in these signs is the task of a historical-materialist corporeal semiotics.

Having established objectification as the fundamental historical-materialist category conceptualising the relations between human beings and their world(s), the next step involves determining the modes of objectification and the kinds of artefacts commensurate with each that collectively and cumulatively make-up human worlds. Based on Marx's own discussion of the 'moments' of history, I argue that human worlds are made through the three modes of material, social, and semiotic objectification and are made up of material artefacts, social and semiotic artefacts. There are two elements of clumsiness in this categorisation that will be addressed in detail in the following chapters, but that require brief clarification here at the outset.

At first hearing the reference to 'social' and 'semiotic' artefacts no doubt seems strange; and there is admittedly a certain categorial fuzziness here, for in my view all made-objects (be it a table or the concept 'table') are at once 'material', 'social', and 'semiotic', These claims will be elaborated in detail below. But for introductory purposes let us take the example of language, the most ethereal of semiotic artefacts which are in turn the least solid of these three forms that I designate as artefactual: linguistic artefacts, those 'mouthy little noises we call words' (Susanne Langer), consist materially of 'agitated layers of air' (Marx) shaped and emitted by our supralaryngeal tract in the production of verbal signs through which are expressed socially determined meanings. And if we remember that each kind of artefact also bears the attributes of the other two, then we can, while acknowledging their shared dimensions, readily enough differentiate between material artefacts such as a table, social artefacts such as an institution or established patterns of social behaviour, and semiotic artefacts such as linguistic signs.

A second terminological clumsiness needing clarification is the seeming redundancy of proposing a corporeal-semiotic analysis of 'semiotic artefacts'. Since the publication of the Saussurean *Course in General Linguistics* in 1916, the dominant form of semiotic analyses of linguistic signs and cultural symbols has been structuralist and synchronic, that is: a given set of linguistic or cultural signs is designated the object of analysis; and the analytical aim is to explain how the internal logic of the sign system structures the meaning of individual signs of which the set consists (see Chapters 8 and 9). But the object of analysis is taken as a given, as existing – and no inquiry is made into the diachronic element of its making. And this points to the reason behind my somewhat clumsy terminology. Since the components of languages and cultural forms are signs and symbols, it is certainly justifiable to deem them 'semiotic'. And because I do not take sets of linguistic signs or cultural symbols as *given*, but rather approach them as *made*-objects, it seems justified to refer to them as artefacts. A historical-materialist study of signs and symbols as artefacts therefore inquires into the process and purpose(s) of their making as factors pertaining their meanings. As with all artefacts, the making of linguistic signs and cultural symbols is a corporeal process: human corporeal organisation is intimately involved in, and in-forms, language production (Chapter 6); and the meanings embedded in linguistic signs and cultural symbols are refracted encounters among human corporeal beings and between those beings and the world (Chapters 8–10). In short, a historical-materialistically grounded 'corporeal semiotics' rests on a set of assumptions that is rather different from the Saussurean-based synchronic approach, and that therefore requires a rather different methodology that approaches linguistic signs and cultural symbols as made-objects, as semiotic artefacts. Thus, although the notion of a corporeal-semiotic analysis of semiotic artefacts is somewhat clumsy because of the repetition of terms, it is neither redundant nor inaccurate.

With those clarifications, the twofold task of a corporeal semiotics grounded in the historical-materialist notion of objectification can be presented. A corporeal semiotics must uncover the traces of human corporeal organisation inescapably present in the interior structure of all artefacts – whether small or vast, whether material objects, social forms and practices, or linguistic and cultural signs; and by thus giving corporeal breadth and depth to the analysis of past and present socio-cultural forms, it provides a corporeal foundation for the substantive critique of social forms – which also entails the articulation of a corporeally-grounded vision of human freedom.

0.6   Overview

This book consists of four parts. Part 1 comprises three chapters that together seek to reconstruct Marx's materialist conception of history starting from the 'first fact' of human corporeal organisation and draw the consequences for a historical-materialist *Wissenschaft*. The first chapter is concerned with the genesis of Marx's materialist conception of history; the second with the contents of this new 'historical materialism';[73] and the third with the *Leitfaden* or guiding threads of a historical-materialist research strategy or *Wissenschaft*. In these chapters I am concerned primarily with reconstructing 'what Marx really meant', by which I mean: with understanding the categorial apparatus and the logic of the materialist conception of history that Marx began to articulate, and the methodology of the historical-materialist *Wissenschaft* that he began to outline.

There have of course been so many attempts to reconstruct the logic of Marx's materialist conception of history that the question, as noted above, seems to have long since lost its charm. But there are at least two good reasons to undertake yet another attempt. One is that analytical short-sightedness continues to attribute to Marx all too many things that in my view he obviously did *not* mean; and the net effect of short-sighted interpretations, combined with the relegation of Marx to the nineteenth century, is to foreclose further inquiry into a view of history and a research strategy that not only has much to offer in itself, but also opens analytical horizons that have only been glimpsed.[74] As

---

[73] A note on terminology: While I will often use the term 'historical materialism' in the course of this work, it is necessary to establish exactly how I shall use it by commenting on Marx's usages. Marx always referred to his theory as a *materialistische Geschichtsauffassung* or materialist conception of history. And although he did use the adjective and adverb, *geschichtsmaterialistisch* (historical-materialist), he did not use 'historical materialism' as a noun. The problem with 'historical materialism' as a noun is its connotations, seemingly implying an 'ism', an established and rather fixed body of thought or ideology – which of course is not what I take Marx's theory to be. Thus, although I will often use 'historical materialism' as a noun to avoid repetition, I intend it to refer to a 'conception' of history and a set of *Leitfaden* or guiding threads of a research strategy (see also note 38 above).

[74] This relegation of Marx to the nineteenth century is effected in different ways: by economists who claim that Marx mistook the birth pangs of capitalism for its death throes; by poststructuralist/postmodernists who view Marx's work as perhaps interesting but passé modernist; by intellectual historians such as Allan Megill and Jonathan Sperber who both concluded that, as Sperber put it, Marx was 'more a figure of the past than a prophet of the present'; and by some erstwhile Marxists like Gareth Stedman Jones who wants 'to put Marx back in his nineteenth-century surroundings'. Sperber's and Stedman Jones's comments are cited in Louis Menand, 'He's Back: Karl Marx, Yesterday and Today', in *The New Yorker* (10 October 2016), p. 90. The books from which the citations come are: Sperber, *Karl Marx: A Nineteenth-Century Life* (NY: Liveright, 2013); Gareth Stedman Jones, *Karl Marx: Greatness and Illusion* (UK: Penguin Books, 2016). I wholeheartedly agree with Menand's response to Sperber and Jones that 'you can put Marx back into the nineteenth century, but you can't keep him there. [Marx] wasted a ridiculous amount of time feuding with rivals and putting out sectarian brush fires, and he did not even come close to completing

Samir Amin put it so clearly, it is necessary 'to continue the work that Marx merely began', albeit 'with unequaled power'; we must 'not ... stop at Marx, but ... start from him. For Marx is not a prophet whose conclusions, drawn from a critique of both reality and how it has been read, are all necessarily "correct" or "final." His opus is not a closed theory. Marx is *boundless*, because the radical critique that he initiated is itself boundless, always incomplete, and must always be the object of its own critique ..., must unceasingly enrich itself through radical critique, treating whatever novelties the real system produces as *newly opened fields of knowledge*'.[75]

Amin's reference to the 'boundless, always incomplete' nature of Marx's own work points to the second reason for my reconstructionist undertaking in Part 1: of the many previous efforts, none has, to my knowledge at least, begun with what Marx posited as the 'first fact' of history nor systematically attempted to rethink the histories of society and cultures 'up from the body'. And that is exactly my intent in Part 1: to show *that* and *how* Marx did indeed take human corporeal organisation as the starting point of a materialist conception of history and as the foundation of his critique of capitalism.

I noted above that Marx's *Aufhebung* of philosophy was a two-step process of first elaborating a materialist conception of history, and then following through and drawing the epistemological consequences of taking human corporeal organisation as the foundation of human history. The goal of Part 1, therefore, is to follow Marx through that two-step process: to show *that* and *how* he took human corporeal organisation as the starting point of a materialist conception of history and of a historical-materialist *Wissenschaft*. The first two chapters of Part 1 are concerned with elaborating a materialist conception of history 'up from the body'. Chapter 1 chronicles Marx's development from the philosophical materialism of the *1844 Manuscripts* to the materialist conception of history in *The German Ideology*. Chapter 2 focuses on the crucial historical-materialist category *Vergegenständlichung*, 'objectification' and elaborates its contents in terms that Marx indicated but never articulated. A corporeal revision of the contents of historical theory did not alone constitute an *Aufhebung* of philosophy. As noted above, a corporeally-grounded materialist conception of history necessarily decentres the knowing mind. Thus, a second step addressing the epistemological consequences of this decentring of the mind for the production of knowledge would be required. And Chapter 3 follows Marx

---

the work he intended as his magnum opus, "Capital". But, for better or worse, it just is not the case that his thought is obsolete' (ibid., p. 90).

75   Amin 2010, pp. 9–10; '*boundless*' Amin's italics, '*newly opened fields of knowledge*', mine.

through this second step that constituted an 'epistemological break' and completed his *Aufhebung* of philosophy.

Part 2 consists of four chapters devoted to the cartographic project of mapping human corporeal organisation. The first two of these chapters are, albeit in different ways, prefatory to the third chapter in which I sketch a historical-materialist map of human corporeal organisation. Chapter 4 situates my project in relation to, and sets it in relief from three kinds of discourses about the body: cultural ultra-constructionist approaches that purport to have taken a 'corporeal turn', but that view the body only as a passive site of cultural inscription: some Marxist approaches that have taken the turn toward a bodily problematic, but have not, in my view, turned far enough nor delved deeply enough; and the existentialist approaches of Martin Heidegger and Hannah Arendt who both glimpsed, before turning away from, what Heidegger called the 'hidden problematic' of the body. Chapter 5 addresses methodological matters concerning the cartographic project. These include: building the conceptual apparatus to be used; formulating the principles guiding the selection of topics and issues addressed; formulating the principles guiding the presentation of the material and the organisation of the narrative; and determining the methodological place-value of the sketch, the extent and limits of its value. Chapter 6 presents a somewhat detailed, but necessarily incomplete cartographic sketch of human corporeal organisation; this sketch highlights the capacities and limits that together establish the range of history-making possibilities embedded in human corporeal form. Chapter 7 concludes Part 2 with a set of reflections, derived from that cartographic portrait, on corporeality and cognition – a relation of fundamental import in the constitution of both the general forms of consciousness and cultural variations of those forms.

Part 3 consists of three chapters aimed at elaborating the contents and methodology of a corporeal semiotics that renders visible that, and articulates the ways in which, human corporeal organisation forms the interior structure of artefacts, made-objects. Chapters 8 and 9 present, respectively: a critique of the semiotically-driven 'linguistic turn' deriving largely, though by no means exclusively, from the 'Saussurean' *Course in General Linguistics*; and a critique of the ensuing 'cultural turn' characterised by the adoption and application of the semiotic principles elaborated in the *Course* to the study of culture.[76] The

---

76   For reasons I shall explain in the Introduction to Chapter 8, my concern is not with the author Ferdinand de Saussure many of whose reflections on language were less certain and more flexible than some of the rigid, almost dogmatic formulations in the *Course in General Linguistics* that was put together by two of Saussure's former students. My concern instead is with the text published posthumously in Saussure's name and with its

two-fold purpose of these critiques is not to deny the validity and value of semiotic analyses of language and culture, but rather: to establish the limits of such approaches that essentially treat language and culture as synchronic structures, sealed off from worldly influences, yet whose allegedly arbitrarily constructed meanings impose themselves on the world; and to raise crucial questions and illuminate crucial issues pertaining to what we might call (in a Heideggerian vocabulary) the 'Being-of-Language-(and Culture-)in-the-World', but that lie outside the range of synchronic semiotic vision. The critique presented in these two chapters is aimed at determining what I can adopt, what I must adapt or alter, and what I must reject from the Saussurean-based semiotic tradition on the basis of which I shall develop my alternative. While I agree with the claim of the Saussurean *Course* that a pan-chronic synthesis is not viable, I do not find the synchronic analysis of the structure of language and culture sufficient to understand either. I therefore attempt to construct a pan-chronic *standpoint* from which to survey both the synchronic structure and the diachronic life of language and culture in the world.

Having presented this critique of purely synchronic approaches to the semiotics of language and culture, I then turn in Chapter 10 to the central task and centrepiece of this undertaking: the outline of a historical-materialistically grounded 'corporeal semiotics'. This undertaking is more than a little eccentric and consists of a methodological fusion of Marx, Elaine Scarry, and Walter Benjamin. It is based on the assumption, frequently exemplified by Marx and explicitly formulated by Scarry, that 'the body', human corporeal organisation, is the 'interior structure' of artefacts. I trace in some detail Scarry's elaboration of the corporeal interior of both individual artefacts (whether material, social, or semiotic) and of what she calls 'vast artefacts', by which she refers explicitly to modes of production and implicitly to cultural forms. Then, guided by Benjamin's historical-materialist monadology, I approach artefacts, both small (e.g. individual objects) and vast (e.g. modes of production), as monads, each reflecting the entire course of human history, each from its own particular perspective. I follow Benjamin in excavating (or, in his words, 'exploding') artefactual monads to reveal the layers of meaning embedded in them – meanings that derive from the particular form of human corporeality that frames human interaction with the world and each other, and that are mediated through specific modes of production and commensurate socio-culture forms. And borrowing Scarry's understanding of artefacts as 'ordinarily' beneficial to human

---

adventures in the linguistic and cultural turns of the twentieth and into the twenty-first centuries. I shall therefore refer to the *Course* itself or use 'Saussurean' to refer to the *Course* and the semiotic tradition to which it gave rise.

beings, I establish a limited set of corporeally-grounded norms that can serve as both a means of social critique and a partial but indispensable measure of human freedom.

Part 4, consisting of four chapters, puts the theory developed in the previous three parts into practice in an analysis and critique of capital's culture of quantity; it reconsiders Marx's analysis of the capitalist mode of production 'up from the body' and shows how an understanding of the corporeal roots of Marx's materialist conception of history adds broader and deeper dimensions to his critique of capitalism and its quantitative culture. Chapter 11 addresses methodological issues pertaining to a corporeally-grounded historical-materialist analysis and critique of culture forms. And it does so by enlisting the aid of Michel Foucault. Contrary to the partisans of each who see Marx and Foucault as incommensurable, I argue that both wrote from within a historical-materialist horizon; and I explain how a fusion of the two helps us to understand both the genealogy and the archaeology of capital's culture of quantity. Chapter 12 traces the genealogy of capital's culture of quantity. Because I obviously cannot, in one chapter, provide a thorough genealogy of the diverse paths and forms of the emerging capitalist mode of production in Europe and the new 'quantificational thinking', I borrow from Fernand Braudel the notion of the *longue durée* and from Norbert Elias the notion of a developmental curve in order to trace the general trajectory of the emergence of capital's quantitative culture.[77] Chapters 13 and 14 are both archaeological in nature. Chapter 13 derives capitalist social geography and its culture of quantity from the fully-developed commodity form as it exists where capitalist relations of production predominate. And Chapter 14 plumbs the corporeal depths of Marx's concept of immiseration, exposing how a labour-process based on a quantitative notion of value is a systematic attack, launched in and sustained beyond the workplace, on the bodies and minds of workers.

If I were to attempt a concise summary of what differentiates my approach from much of the work done on the body in recent decades, it would be this: Rather than treat the body as an *object* fully constituted by language, discourse, representation, performative action, discipline, repressive and/or ideological state apparatuses, I approach human corporeal organisation as the site of (decentred) human subjecthood and therefore as the foundation on the basis of which human beings make their own histories – but not as they please. Such an approach will necessarily have consequences for a vision of human freedom.

---

77 Braudel's notion of the *longue durée*, Elias's of the developmental curve, and Crosby's of 'quantificational thinking' are addressed in the Introduction to Chapter 12.

I therefore conclude the book with a set of reflections on how an understanding of human corporeal organisation as the 'first fact' of human history not only gives corporeal breadth and depth to the critique of socio-cultural forms, but also provides crucial corporeal content to visions of human freedom and dignity – to the dream of an emancipated society ordered according to the principle, 'From each according to ability, to each according to need'.

PART 1

Reconstructing Historical Materialism 'Up from the Body': The Corporeal Foundations of a Materialist Conception of History and the Guiding Threads of a Historical-Materialist Wissenschaft

∶∶

Introduction to Part 1

> *Am Leitfaden des Leibes.* – The human body, in which the most distant and most recent past of all organic development again becomes living and corporeal, through which and over and beyond which a tremendous inaudible stream seems to flow: the body is a more astonishing idea than the old 'soul'. In all ages, there has been more faith in the body, as our most personal possession, our most certain being, in short our ego, than in the spirit (or the 'soul', or the subject, as school language is now wont to say instead). It has never occurred to anyone to regard his stomach as a strange or, perhaps, a divine stomach: but to conceive his ideas as 'inspired', his evaluations as 'implanted by a God', his instincts as activity in a half-light – for this propensity and taste in men there are witnesses from all ages of mankind.
>
> FRIEDRICH NIETZSCHE, *The Will to Power*[1]

∴

Part 1, as noted above, consists of three chapters in which I undertake an exegetical reconstruction of Marx's materialist conception of history and a historical-materialist *Wissenschaft* up from the 'first fact' of human corporeal organisation. Chapter 1 is entitled and addresses 'Marx's *Aufhebung* of Philosophy and the Genesis of a Materialist Conception of History'. The notion of a Marxian *Aufhebung* of philosophy has often been oversimplified by a misrepresentation of a comment by Engels (so common that it has made its way into *Wikipedia*) that Marx stood Hegel's dialectic on its head, and then dismissed it as much ado about nothing. But as Engels quickly corrected himself after having expressed that notion, Marx 'more accurately' turned the Hegelian dialectic 'from its head on which it had stood and placed it on its feet'.[2] And as I shall argue in this chapter, Marx's *Aufhebung* of philosophy consisted not simply of turning Hegel right-side up through an inversion of an idealist into a materi-

---

1 Nietzsche 1968, pp. 347–8, translation slightly altered. German: Nietzsche 2019, § 436.
2 Engels 1975, pp. 259–307, p. 293.

alist philosophy, but also of replacing philosophical inquiry with a historical *Wissenschaft*.

This *Aufhebung* of philosophy was a two-step process, the analyses of which will occupy the two parts of Chapter 1. The first step was taken, with the help of Ludwig Feuerbach, in the *Economic-Philosophical Manuscripts of 1844*, and consisted of a redefinition of the subject-object relation. In contrast to traditional Western philosophy that treated that relation as one of knowing, a relation between a knowing subject and the object of knowledge, Feuerbach redefined it as a relation of objectification (*Vergegenständlichung*) between sensuously-active (*sinnlich-tätige*), embodied subjects and the objects produced through their activity. Despite his move in the direction of embodied, sensuously-acting subjects, Feuerbach's materialism was still rather idealist, conceiving of that activity in terms of religion and philosophy and asking only that it recognise its sensuous source. While Marx adopted Feuerbach's notion of objectification and the subject-object relation it entailed, he deepened it by extending it beyond the realm of thought and conscience to labour and the making of human worlds. Although this emphasis on labour and the making of human worlds put him on the verge of history, it is fair to say that in the *1844 Manuscripts* Marx did not go beyond this inversion of Hegel – which is clear from his rather abstract philosophical reflections about the course of history. And in his historical reflections, developed through his critique of Feuerbach in *The German Ideology*, Marx established human corporeal organisation as the 'first fact' of history; in so doing, he took the second step beyond philosophical materialism, put both feet firmly on historical ground, and completed his *Aufhebung* of philosophy. This step consisted of a partial return to Hegel whose albeit idealist approach nevertheless treated history as the product of the dialectical relation between subjects and objects, as something that human beings make, although not always as they please.

As is clear from its title, Chapter 2 proceeds 'From the First Corporeal Fact of Human Being to the Moments of History: Corporeality, Modes of Objectification, and Ways of Worldmaking'. Having in the first chapter made a case for the corporeal activity of objectification as the fundamental category of a materialist conception of history, the next step in this reconstruction of a materialist conception of history 'up from the body' is to elaborate what I call the various 'modes' of objectification. This step, undertaken in Chapter 2, is all the more important since objectification is all too often (including by sympathetic and usually insightful critics like Theodor Adorno and Max Horkheimer, Agnes Heller, Jean-François Lyotard, and Jean Baudrillard, to name a few) rather unimaginatively limited exclusively to labour and economic production. Such a one-dimensional understanding of objectification reduces Marx's theory to one concerned only with material needs, which easily leads to the mistaken conclusion that Marx advocated an environmentally destructive 'Promethean' productivism and to a reductionist view of culture.

Marx himself may appear to have contributed to this narrow interpretation of objectification. Against those who take the history of religion, politics, art, and/or literature as the real history of humanity, he insisted that 'the history of industry ... is the open book of essential human powers'.[3] Borrowing from Elaine Scarry, Eagleton interpreted this passage to mean that the history of industry is 'the materialized text of the human body'.[4] I agree that the history of industry is to be viewed as *a* 'materialized text of the human body', but would immediately add that Marx's own statement is too narrow as a definition of the contents of a materialist conception of history and the tasks of a historical-materialist *Wissenschaft*. First of all, this passage must be taken in context – as a counter to those who ignore the history of industry as not of the properly human realm. But more importantly, and as he clearly states in those powerful passages, also in the *1844 Manuscripts*, that treat the apprehension of the world through sense perception as a mode of objectification, Marx did not limit objectification to the production of material goods. Productive labour does have a dynamic and transformative capacity that affects in definitive ways the content of those other, also fundamentally human modes of objectification – social and semiotic: labour played an essential role in the evolution of the human body itself, of human corporeal organisation and the bodily instruments and corporeal dexterities in the human bodily toolkit; and through labour humans transform the natural world and construct human worlds. With the transformations of humans' relation to nature, their modes of interacting with each other (society) and their modes of thinking about, and representing, their world (intellectual labour or culture) are also transformed. With this rather schematic formulation, I intend simply to point out that for a materialist conception of history, the making of histories consists of at least three specific, yet interrelated 'moments'; and corresponding to each of these three moments is a mode of objectification that produces three different yet interrelated kinds of artefacts. These modes of material, social, and semiotic objectification are both made possible and also limited by the corporeal organisation that 'in-forms', that gives form to, the material, social and semiotic objects produced. Taken together, these three modes of objectification are, to borrow a term from Nelson Goodman, the three 'ways of worldmaking'; and together

---

3 Marx 1844 in Tucker 1978, p. 89.
4 Eagleton 1990, p. 198.

these three ways of worldmaking make human worlds – worlds made in the image of human corporeal organisation, and consisting of material, social and semiotic artefacts whose interior structure is human corporeal organisation.

Chapter 3 outlines 'The Guiding Threads and Research Strategy of a Historical-materialist *Wissenschaft*'. The two previous chapters elaborating human corporeal organisation as the fundamental precondition and form-determinant (*Formbestimmung*) of human modes of objectification will have presented a two-part argument backing Marx's wager on human corporeal organisation as the first fact of a materialist conception of history and his attempt to rethink everything *up from the body*. But the attempt to rethink *everything* up from corporeality necessarily has consequences for thinking itself and poses fundamental challenges to intellectual labour and knowledge production. The task of Chapter 3, therefore, is to articulate those consequences and confront those challenges by developing what Marx referred to as the *Leitfaden* (guiding threads) of a historical-materialist *Wissenschaft*.

Marx's most succinct expression of this challenge is in his discussion of the 'moments of history', among which he lists that which traditional philosophy held to be the *only* truly human moment of history, namely: the moment of consciousness in its various forms. Further specifying his *Aufhebung* of philosophy, he wrote: 'Morality, religion, metaphysics, all the rest of ideology and their corresponding forms of consciousness thus no longer retain the semblance of independence. They have no history, no development in themselves; but [people], developing their material production and their material intercourse, alter, along with this their real existence, their thinking and the products of their thinking'.[5] Here Marx established an inextricable, though non-reductionist link between ideas and the material world. Consequently, he had to redefine the social locus of the knowing subject and of intellectual labour. In contrast to philosophy, for which the knowing subject is situated both in the centre and above the world it observes, Marx had, to borrow a poststructuralist term, 'decentred' that subject.[6] By positing corporeal organisation as the first fact of history, Marx initiated a corporeal turn that amounts

---

5 Marx 1845 in Tucker 1978, pp. 154–5.
6 It is perhaps worth noting parenthetically that one who is considered an icon of postmodernism, Michel Foucault, yet who himself claimed not to be 'up to date' on the question of postmodernism, identified Nietzsche, Freud, and Marx as having 'founded anew the possibility of interpretation', as having recognised 'the incompleteness of interpretation, the fact that it is always fragmented'; and he pointed to Nietzsche and Marx as engaged in operations devoted to decentring the sovereign subject. See Foucault (1964, pp. 61, 63) on 'Nietzsche, Freud, Marx'; and Foucault 1972, pp. 12–13. Foucault expressed his perplexity over postmodernism in an interview with Gerard Raulet in Spring 1983, reprinted in Foucault 1990a, p. 33.

to a radical decentring of the sovereign knowing subject of traditional Western philosophy. And he did so by defining the locus of intellectual labour as one branch *among*, rather than *above*, the other branches of the social division of labour. Marx's *Aufhebung* of philosophy, his version of a critique of Western 'logocentrism', then, consisted of exposing the relation between mental and manual labour, the precise nature of which his philosophical predecessors had overlooked by privileging their own activity. This redefinition of the social locus of intellectual labour forced Marx to reject the conceptual absolutism inherent in the philosophical positing of the primacy of mind over body. As a result of this reduction of the power of thought, he confronted a difficult epistemological dilemma that he tried to solve by carrying out a radical reappraisal and recrafting of the tools of the intellectual trade.

The third and final chapter of Part 1 addresses this many-sided epistemological dilemma that, ironically, arises *although*, and also *because*, the starting point of this science is the concrete material life-process of the real, historically existing, sensually active individuals. I shall argue that Marx's *Aufhebung* of philosophy and its truth claims required the abandonment of a speculative philosophy of history recounting a transhistorical story from the first emergence of a 'human nature' conceived as *Homo sapiens* through to its culmination in the victory of rational thought; it required him to lay the barest foundations of a research strategy, of an open-ended historical-materialist *Wissenschaft*; and it required him to fashion methodological solutions to the various dimensions of this epistemological dilemma and to maintain what I call an 'epistemological tension' between the abstractions of theory and the details of empirical analysis – to recognise that both are necessary to knowledge production yet each is necessarily insufficient.[7]

As noted above, Part 1 focuses on Marx's own writings in order to reconstruct his outline of a materialist conception of history up from its roots in human corporeal organisation and to raise the kinds of corporeal matters that have barely been addressed and the kinds of corporeal questions that have rarely been posed. In this way an exegesis of Marx's writings points well beyond Marx himself. And in order to be successful, my undertaking must at the very least respond to two major challenges. The first of these challenges, to be addressed in Part 2, is to integrate into historical materialism the great strides taken in the 'Darwinian' disciplines of evolutionary biology and paleoanthropology in the many years since Marx's death in order to grasp the biological potential for cultural production that resides in human corporeal organisation, and to

---

7 See Fracchia 1991.

understand how human corporeal organisation in-forms sociocultural forms. The second challenge, to be addressed theoretically in Part 3 and exemplified historically in Part 4, is to explain the most disparate sociocultural forms as all having the same human corporeal organisation as their interior structure – and in so doing to avoid the false extremes of a suffocating universalism and an eclectic cultural relativism. A successful response to these challenges would show not only how these developments enrich a materialist-conception of history, but also how in having gone beyond Marx, we can return to him and better understand the corporeal depths and richness of his theoretical endeavours.

CHAPTER 1

An *Aufhebung* of Philosophy and the Genesis of a Materialist Conception of History: Objectification and Marx's Corporeal Turn

1.1 Introduction and a Note on Terminology

The concept of *Vergegenständlichung* or 'objectification' is in my view the most fundamental concept of a materialist conception of history – and also the concept with the most far-reaching implications. A thorough elaboration of objectification in all of its dimensions and forms is thus crucial to backing Marx's 'breathtaking wager'. There is a great deal of debate over what Marx meant by the term *Vergegenständlichung* – a debate that can briefly but effectively be exemplified with Agnes Heller's notion of the 'two Marxes': a young Marx whose 'paradigm of work' encompassed diverse forms of 'objectification' ranging from economic labour to intellectual and aesthetic work; and an older, 'mature' Marx who had discarded the variegated category of objectification, narrowed its range to economic labour, and subsumed it under an 'paradigm of [economic] production'.[1] My position, however, is that Marx

---

1 Agnes Heller (1976, p. 40) states that 'Later on, Marx makes a basic distinction between objectivation [*Objektivation*] and objectification [*Vergegenständlichung*]'; and she later (1981) follows up on this with the claim that although 'Objektivation' and 'Objektivierung' were common coin in Marx's early writings, he later abandoned them for what she sees as the narrower, work-based model of *Vergegenständlichung*. I am not sure exactly what to make of this statement. First of all, 'Objectivation' is rarely to be found in Marx's writings. The only usage I could find is in *Zur Kritik der Hegelschen Rechtsphilosophie* (MEW, Vol. I, 224) where Marx uses the term in criticising Hegel's inversion of the subject's predication: instead of viewing, like Hegel, the real subject as result, Marx insists, on the contrary, that it is necessary 'to begin with the real subject and observe its objectivation'. Marx does use a similar term, *Objektivierung*, in a few scattered references in the *Grundrisse*; but there he uses the term in apposition and as synonymous with *Vergegenständlichung* (Marx 1973 [1857–58], p. 356). The more important point, however, is that after having insisted that Marx differentiated the two terms, Heller then suggests a retrieval of the concept of Objectivation in such a way as to exclude work, but to include 'three components' in what she dubs a 'sphere of objectivation-in-itself', namely 'the *use* of man-made objects, observing the culturally defined ensemble of customs, and the use of ordinary language' (Heller 1981, p. 79, my italics). The rather large gap in this formulation is that it addresses only the *use*, but precludes consideration of the *making*, of the objects, customs, and ordinary language that are being used. In contrast to Heller's insistence that Marx limited *Vergegenständlichung* to a work-based, that is, a production-based model, I am con-

never abandoned the broad notion of objectification elaborated in the *1844 Manuscripts*, even if he did, in his later writings, narrow his analytical focus in order to decipher the exploitative logic of work under capitalist conditions of production. And my purpose in this chapter and the next is: first, to show that objectification is the fundamental concept of a materialist conception of history; then to present the diverse modes of objectification that Marx specifically addressed, and to elaborate those to which he only alluded. Before that task can be taken up, however, there is an extra and dual difficulty to be addressed concerning the translation of the noun *Vergegenständlichung* and the adjective and adverb *gegenständlich* into English.

The first part of this dual difficulty concerns normal lexicon translations and dictionary definitions. As both adjective (needing declension) and adverb, '*gegenständlich*' is rendered into English as 'objective' and 'objectively' respectively. But as Raymond Meyer comments on his own attempt to translate *gegenständlich* into English: '[s]ince "objective" carries too strongly the meaning "expressing or dealing with facts or conditions as perceived without distortion by personal feelings, prejudices, or interpretations"', he chooses to translate it instead as 'objectual'. Explaining his choice, he continues: '"Objectual" means "having to do with, relating to an object or objects", as, for example, in the phrase "objectual activity"; it can also mean "relating to or being an object for a subject, for consciousness"'.[2] The adverbial counterpart to this very sensible translation would be 'objectually'. Meyer's use is unfortunately idiosyncratic. And if I do not adopt his usage, it is only because all the standard English translations of Marx's writings use instead 'objective' and 'objectively' rather than 'objectual' and 'objectually'. It is therefore all the more crucial to remember, when encountering the terms 'objective' and 'objectively' in English translations of Marx, that they should not be understood in terms of traditional English-language notions of 'objective', and that their meanings are more accurately, if somewhat awkwardly, captured by Meyer's neologisms.

The second cause of confusion over *Vergegenständlichung* arises from a common usage that has developed in the last decades in some poststructuralist and feminist works that focus on 'the gaze'.[3] There is in these works, and in English

---

vinced, and will argue in detail in Chapter 2, that he used it in a much broader sense relating to making in general – which includes the making or 'production', not only of objects, but also of customs, languages and other semiotic systems. Suffice it to say here *contra* Heller that in the *1844 Manuscripts*, Marx even refers to sense-perception as a form of *Vergegenständlichung*.

2 See Raymond Meyer in Honneth and Joas 1988, p. xi. Here Meyer cites *Webster's Ninth Collegiate Dictionary*.

3 This is particularly true in the literature on vision and the gaze which criticises 'ocular-

usage more generally, a common and misleadingly easy elision of the terms 'object' and 'thing'. For example, the 'male gaze' is said to 'objectify' women. In German, however, there is a rather significant difference between *Gegenstand* (object) and *Ding* (thing) – a difference embedded deeply in the history of German-language philosophy. And to render in German that which is intended by the English phrase that the male gaze produces the 'objectification' of women, one would have to say it produces the *Verdinglichung* or 'reification', the thing-a-fication, of women. For Marx and historical-materialist vocabulary more generally, there is a fundamental difference between *Vergegenständlichung* or objectification and *Verdinglichung* or reification: the former is a perfectly normal, and actually unavoidable human activity consisting of the making of objects, while the latter refers to its alienated form. And it is also crucial to keep this distinction in mind through the following elaboration of why objectification, *Vergegenständlichung*, is the fundamental concept of a materialist conception of history.

1.2   A Materialist Redefinition of the Subject-Object Relation:
       Vergegenständlichung as Sensuous Activity and Historical Process

Marx began his university studies in Bonn at the age of seventeen. A year later, he transferred to Berlin at a time when Hegelian idealist philosophy dominated the intellectual scene. Marx admitted to being thoroughly imbued on his arrival in Berlin with an 'idealist' outlook, which he tried to express in his somewhat sappy poetic efforts. But he quickly found unappealing the 'grotesque craggy melody' of Hegel's idealism; as expressed in a letter to his father shortly after arriving in Berlin, he had 'arrived at the point of seeking the idea in reality itself'; and referring to the profane origins of theology and its somewhat secular counterpart, idealist philosophy, he concluded that '[i]f previously the gods had dwelt above the earth, now they had become its center'.[4] In his doctoral dissertation written in 1841, Marx pursued his budding materialist interests into the philosophies of Democritus and Epicurus. But his materialism took a more concrete turn with his experience as editor of the *Rheinische Zeitung* from 1842–44. During this period he was forced to deal with very immediate

---

centrism' by conflating the objectifying vision that enables us visually to delineate objects with the reifying gaze (see Chapter 6). For an example of this conflation, see Lewen 1993. For a thorough discussion and critical evaluation of the attack on 'ocularcentrism' in twentieth-century French thought, see Jay 1993.

4   Marx, Letter to his Father, 10 November 1837, in Tucker 1978, p. 7.

material matters such as land distribution, laws prohibiting wood theft, conditions of the regional peasantry, free trade and tariffs; and 'for the first time' he found himself, as he retrospectively put it, 'in the embarrassing position of having to speak about so-called material interests'.[5] Also during this period Marx encountered the materialist philosophy of Ludwig Feuerbach, whose major work was *The Essence of Christianity*, and became an enthusiastic but 'momentary' Feuerbachian.[6] And it was this dual concern with materialist philosophy and the material matters of everyday economic life that would push Marx from the materialist philosophy that he proposed and already partially criticised in the *Economic-Philosophical Manuscripts of 1844* to the materialist conception of history that he began to articulate in *The German Ideology* of the following year.

This first chapter is devoted to tracing the genesis of Marx's concept of objectification from its origins in Feuerbach's materialist philosophy through Marx's appropriation and redirection of the term that led him to a materialist conception of history. The first part of this chapter focuses on what Marx punningly referred to as the 'Feuer-bach', literally the 'fiery-brook', and hailed as 'the purgatory of the present' that he had to pass through on his way forward to 'truth and freedom'.[7] The second part focuses on Marx's deployment of objectification in the *Economic-Philosophical Manuscripts of 1844* where, though still in a very Feuerbachian framework, he took a rather un-Feuerbachian turn toward the analysis of labour as a mode of objectification. In so doing, he provided a (very abstract) materialist alternative to the idealist anthropology on which the mainstream of Western philosophy since Plato had been based. Against the idealist determination of human being as a thinking being and therefore of thought as the highest and uniquely human activity, Marx began to understand human being as an embodied 'natural being', i.e. as part of nature, but with unique, nature-transforming capabilities. Though Marx focused on the objectifying activity of labour in the *Manuscripts*, they contain also several comments, often brilliantly insightful in their brevity, that allude to other kinds of objectifying activity or what I shall call 'modes' of objectification. In the concluding third part of this chapter, I shall trace the development of Marx's thought as he struggled to develop his materialist conception of history. That conception itself will be the focus of the next chapter. In concluding this chapter, my concern is to show how Marx's un-Feuerbachian analysis of labour as objecti-

---

5 Marx 1859 in Tucker 1978, p. 3.
6 This was Engels's later description of Marx, himself, and the 'young' or 'left' Hegelians in general. See Engels 1886, in *MEW*, Vol. 21, p. 272.
7 Marx, in *MEW*, Vol. 1, pp. 26–7.

fication not only disrupted the Feuerbachian method that he had used when he began writing the *Manuscripts*, but also led him to a partial reconsideration of Hegel. Marx's approach to labour as an activity, as making, pointed beyond Feuerbach's rather static concern with the finished products of objectification. This led him to reconsider Hegel's notion of the production of human worlds, i.e. of history, as a process. But having gone through the 'Feuer-bach', Marx's reconsideration of Hegel's approach to history was a very materialist one, the result of which would be the materialist conception of history first outlined in *The German Ideology* of 1845.

On his way to 'self-clarification' Marx flirted with various categories, drawn from his intellectual predecessors, that pertained to the transformative relations between human beings and the worlds they inhabit. In his earlier works he generally used Hegel's notion of *Entäusserung*, before subjecting it to a biting critique in the last of the *Economic-Philosophical Manuscripts* of 1844. While it is unclear whether Marx ever read Schopenhauer, he did on rare occasion use the very Schopenhauerian terms *Objectivation* and *Verobjektivierung*.[8] But none of these terms expressed adequately the material interrelations between humans and their worlds that Marx would attach to category of *Vergegenständlichung* or 'objectification' nor, consequently, did they assume a similar methodological significance as the central category of his thinking about history. 'Objectification' appeared rather suddenly in Marx's 'Excerpts from James Mill's *Eleméns d'économie politique*' and, more prominently, in the *Economic-Philosphical Manuscripts*, both written in 1844, that is: during the period in which he and Engels were 'momentary Feuerbachians'.[9] It seems that Ludwig Feuerbach did indeed coin the category *Vergegenständlichung* as one of conceptual foundations of his sensualist philosophy; and it would quickly become the foundational category in Marx's thinking about history.[10]

Feuerbach developed his notion of objectification as the quintessentially human sensuous activity in opposition to Hegel's idealist definitions of subject

---

8   Arthur Schopenhauer in *Die Welt als Wille und Vorstellung* (1818) (in *Ausgewählte Schriften*, Sigbert Mohn Verlag [no place or date given]) uses the term 'Objektivation' to signify the visible manifestations of will or, as Patrick Gardiner puts it, 'the will as it appears under conditions of external perception' (Gardiner 1972, Vol. 7, p. 328). Though couched in terms of a rather static metaphysic of the dynamic principle of will (i.e. the will's 'objectivation' is a visible manifestation rather than a product), the elements of Schopenhauer's category could conceivably lend themselves to a materialist redefinition in terms of work. Such sparse and rather different usage of these terms does not suggest that Marx was significantly influenced by Schopenhauer, or even that he had read him. See note 1 above.

9   Engels 1886, in *MEW*, Vol. 21, p. 272.

10 On Feuerbach and Marx, see Alfred Schmidt 1973.

and object. Hegel, like his philosophical predecessors since at least Socrates, defined the relation between human beings and the world in a thoroughgoing idealist manner. What differentiated 'man' from other animals was the human mind: unlike other animals, human beings are knowing beings; and the essence of human being is to know the world, to make the things of the world into objects of knowledge, into concepts and ideas. For Hegel, accordingly, the essentially human form of labour that goes into the making of uniquely human worlds is intellectual labour; and the real work of making history is thus that of the philosophers. Historical eras can therefore be differentiated by their *Zeitgeist* defined in terms of each era's great philosophical systems. Since knowledge production is cumulative (though dialectical) and since a philosophical work is concerned with the history of knowledge rather than with the various individual philosophers who contributed to its making, Hegel sublated the various *Zeitgeister* into one *Weltgeist*. The *Weltgeist* is *not* a metaphysical entity, but a methodological fiction, that is: a very consciously posited *construction* of a transhistorical knowing subject that, in the philosophical presentation of history as the history of thought, could serve as *the* knowing human subject who progressively accumulates the knowledge produced in each philosophical epoch. *Geist* is posited as the 'general intellect' of the species.

Hegel's conceptualises the labour of *Geist*, i.e. intellectual labour, as *Entäusserung* (externalising) and *Setzen* (positing). In order to extend its reign over the natural as well as the human world, in order to make the world philosophical, Hegel's *Geist* externalises itself. Posited as the quintessential philosopher, *Geist* must come to know the world; and its temporary externalisation in the dirty businesses of work, politics, history, etc. serves the philosophical purpose of conceptualising those spheres, of writing the philosophy of work, politics, history, etc. The goal of Hegel's long argument in both the *Phenomenology* and the *Encyclopedia* is systematically to purify objects of their materiality, and human being of the taint of corporeality. *Geist*'s laborious odyssey in these works consists of a progressive cleansing of itself from bodily influences and the progressive extension of its 'knowledge-power' over objects.[11] *Geist* subjugates the world by conceputalising it as an object of knowledge which relegates the world's sensuousness to the status of the contingent and as such philosophically uninteresting. In his well-known but often misunderstood 'Master-Slave' chapter of the *Phenomenology*, for example, Hegel finds the work of the

---

11   The term 'knowledge-power', made commonplace if not coined by Michel Foucault, and echoing Marx's notion of *Wissenskraft* (see Chapter 14 note 106) is most apt here.

slave philosophically significant only insofar as it provides *Geist* with food for thought on its long phenomenological journey toward absolute knowledge, the actual material product being relevant only insofar as it plays a role in the knowledge process: since *Geist* in the form of the slave recognises the product as its own, it comprehends itself as the maker and shaper of the world – the product of labour is reduced to a mere medium of self-knowledge, and the slave remains a slave. For Hegel, the most thoroughgoing idealist among philosophers, the albeit necessary positing of the self in external objects, in the material world, is an act of alienation that must be recouped by subjecting the external object to the rule of thought; the object's alien materiality is dissolved through its elevation to the status of an object of knowledge. Externalisation in the idealist framework is necessary, but it is necessarily a negation and thus alienation which must itself be negated if the world is to come under the reign of philosophy.

In his attempt to give philosophy a sensuous, materialist foundation, Feuerbach criticised the idealist inversion that resulted in the elevation of an abstract entity, the concept (that Hegel called *das Werkzeug des Geistes*, 'the tool of mind'), to the status of the essential. In Feuerbach's view, Hegel's positing of the idea as the essential was pure mystification and a denigration of the sensuous being both of humans and objects. He chastised Hegel and his predecessors for reducing human beings to merely thinking beings and objects to mere objects of thought. Anticipating what Nietzsche would later and much more emphatically call nihilistic, Feuerbach argued that philosophy and religion were themselves alienated in their negation of the inescapable sensuousness of the world and human being and in their insistence that pure contemplation or an unworldly afterlife was the essence of humanity. In his most well-known work, *Das Wesen des Christentums* (1841), Feuerbach described the alienated character of religion as the result of the fact that 'Human beings first displace their essence *outside of themselves* before they find it in themselves. ... Human beings have objectified [*vergegenständlicht*] themselves, but have not recognized that object as their own essence'.[12] That is, it is in the nature of human beings to fashion a world in their own image. But in those cases where people end up fetishising their own creations, where they attribute their own powers, the powers that enable them to create, to their creations themselves, there is a case of alienated objectification. In contrast to Hegel, then, Feuerbach conceived of externalisation or objectification as not in itself an alienated activity; rather alienation occurs in those specific manifestations in which human

---

12   Feuerbach 1841b, *Das Wesen des Christentums*, in Feuerbach 1976, Vol. V, p. 31.

beings project their own attributes onto a product of their own creation, by whose measure humans are invariably inadequate.

This characteristic usage of *Vergegenstandlichung* also provides a perfect example of Feuerbach's critical method: the first step is to recognise when the human world is characterised by 'doubling' [*Verdoppelung*], that is when humans cannot find themselves in their own objectifications; the next step is to recognize the displacement of the human essence onto some entity, whether God or *Geist*, as alienation; then the final step is to overcome alienation by retrieving as human attributes those which have been projected onto transcendental forms. The notion of 'objectification' thus underlays the critique of alienation: humans are alienated from the worlds they themselves have made *precisely because* they themselves have, through their objectifying activity, made these worlds in their own image, but cannot find themselves in them. Humans are not at home in the 'palaces of ideas' that they have themselves built.[13]

For Feuerbach the means to overcome the doubling inherent in idealist abstraction was the philosophical rehabilitation of the sensuous attributes of being (*Sein*), including the corporeal sensuousness of human being,[14] as well as objects (*Gegenstände*). Against the idealism of traditional philosophy Feuerbach wanted to render the world and its human inhabitants sensuous (*sinnlich*). Rather than flee empiricism as a taint on pure thought, Feuerbach embraced it as the essence of human beings and therefore the starting point of philosophy. He undertook to redefine philosophy and render it concrete by insisting that philosophy must recognise that '*empirical activity* is also a philosophical activity, [must] recognize that seeing is thinking, and also that the *sense apparatuses* [*Sinneswerkzeuge*, literally: "sense tools"] are *organs of philosophy*'. He concluded accordingly that '[o]ne must philosophize under the direction of the senses'.[15] To do so, one must also rethink the nature of human beings from a sensuous rather than an idealist perspective.

The 'old philosophy', Feuerbach charged in his *Grundsätze der Philosophie der Zukunft* (1843), had as its starting point the idealist anthropological insistence: 'I am an abstract, an only thinking being; the body does not belong to my essence'. Feuerbach's 'new philosophy', on the contrary, would begin with

---

13 The reference is to Kierkegaard's quip that philosophers built palaces of ideas, but in hovels. See above, Introduction, note 19.
14 See Löwith 1984, p. 310.
15 Feuerbach 1841a, 'Einige Bemerkungen über den "Anfang der Philosophie" von Dr. J.F. Reiff', in Feuerbach 1975, Vol. III, p. 132.

the materialist anthropological claim: 'I am a real, a sensuous being: The body belongs to my essence; indeed, the body in its totality is my self [*mein Ich*], my essence itself'.[16] Feuerbach found the traditional philosophical differentiation of human beings and other animals on the basis of thinking to be too narrow and too simplistic. He maintained that not only humans' capacity for thinking, but more so their 'entire essence' is their 'difference from animals'. In terms that Marx would echo (and occasionally plagiarise) in his discussion in the *1844 Manuscripts* of both human species-being and of the un-alienated sensuous apprehension of the world, Feuerbach explained:

> The human being is not a particularistic being like the animal, but a universal one, and therefore not a limited and unfree, but an unlimited, free being; for universality, limitlessness, freedom are inseparable. And this freedom does not exist merely in a particular capacity, in *the power of thinking*, in reason – this freedom, this universality reaches through the entire human being. The animal senses are surely sharper than the human, but only in relation to certain things that stand in a necessary relation to the animal's needs, and they are sharper precisely because of this determination, this exclusive limitation to particular things. The human does not have the sense of smell of a hunting dog or a vulture; but only because the human sense of smell is one that is more comprehensive of all kinds of smell, therefore one that is freer ... Where a sense raises itself above the limitation of particularity and its bondage to needs, there it raises itself to an *independent*, to a *theoretical* significance and worth. Universal sense is *understanding* [*der Verstand*], *universal* sensuousness [is] *rationality* [*Geistigkeit*]. Even the lower senses of human beings, smell and taste, are raised to rational [*geistigen*], to scientific [*wissenschaftlichen*] acts. The smell and taste of things are objects of the natural sciences.[17]

Following a brief explanation of the 'universality' of the human stomach that is not confined to limited sorts of nourishment, and having observed that a human with the stomach of a lion or horse would cease to be human, Feuerbach draws the general conclusion that the 'new philosophy makes the *human being* in *connection with nature*, the basis of human being, into the-

---

16   Feuerbach 1843, 'Grundsätze einer Philosophie der Zukunft', in Feuerbach 1975, Vol. III, p. 302.
17   Ibid, p. 318.

single, universal, and *highest object* of philosophy – that is, will make *anthropology* in *connection with physiology* into a *universal science*'.[18]

Feuerbach's philosophy was of crucial importance for Marx. Feuerbach's rehabilitation of the essentially sensuous nature of being and beings, humans as well as natural objects, his rehabilitation of the body, his depiction of the universality of the human bodily sense organs, and his use of the concept of objectification (not to mention the penchant for using italics) all contributed to Marx's own move toward materialism. Marx momentarily but rather laboriously wielded Feuerbach's categories and method in his *Critique of Hegel's Philosophy of Right*, then again in his critique of Hegel's idealist positing of the idea as the essence in *Die heilige Familie*.[19] His most well-known Feuerbachian writing, which is my concern here, was of course the still very philosophical critique of capitalism in the *Economic-Philosophical Manuscripts* of 1844. The methodology and categorial apparatus of Marx's exposé of alienated labour, his contrast between alienated labour under conditions of private property and labour as free, sensuous, self-fulfilling objectification in communism, and his critique of the power of money in bourgeois society were all thoroughly indebted to Feuerbach.

The content of Marx's critique of 'Alienated Labour' came, however, not from Feuerbach, whose notion of the sensuous activity of objectification Marx was already beginning to find too 'passive'. It most likely came rather from Arnold Ruge, a 'left-Hegelian' with whom Marx collaborated from about 1842 until breaking with him in July 1844.[20] According to Karl Löwith, it was Ruge who treated work as a 'liberating activity' with 'universal significance', beyond the production of mere value and money, and as a 'means toward the production of man and his own in the natural world'.[21] Ruge also insisted, echoing a theme raised and then dropped in Hegel's analysis of lordship and bondage, that in class societies it is the working classes whose activity results in the construction of human society and culture.[22] It is thus not surprising that the first of Marx's works in which the 'proletariat' assumes a place of importance is the Introduction to his *Critique of Hegel's Philosophy of Right* – written at the end of 1843 and early 1844, during which time Marx and Ruge were co-editors of the *Deutsch-Französischen Jahrbücher*.

---

18 Ibid, p. 319.
19 See *Die heilige Familie*, in MEW, Vol. 2, pp. 60–1.
20 Marx's polemic, 'Kritische Randglossen zu dem Artikel eines Preussen' (1844), was aimed at Ruge. See MEW, Vol. 1, pp. 392–409.
21 Löwith 1984, p. 273.
22 Ibid.

Once Marx embarked on the study of labour in the *Economic-Philosophical Manuscripts of 1844*, it then became his primary concern for the rest of his life. The *Manuscripts*, however, are very deceptive both for internal reasons and because of the conditions of their reception. As has often been noted, the lack of organisation of these unedited manuscripts and their tortured philosophical prose make them extremely difficult to read. But it is doubtful that even a good editor could have had much success, for there are deeper reasons for their obscurity. One is that the opacity of Marx's language results from his own in-between position – between Hegel's philosophical idealism, Feuerbach's philosophical sensualism, and his own later historical materialism toward which he had begun moving with his newfound emphasis on labour. And this makes them not only difficult to read, but even harder to understand, and still more challenging to comprehend. Suspended between Feuerbach and Hegel, influenced by, yet critical of both, Marx pursued in the *Manuscripts* two related, but distinct endeavours that he was not yet able to reconcile or to supersede. What we have in the *Manuscripts* (and, as we shall see in the next chapter, in *The German Ideology*) is not a finished product, but records of a thought process *in statu nascendi*. It is in these works that we can read Marx thinking – and because of both the complexity of the issues involved and Marx's still-developing views on them, it is a rather convoluted thought process.

The difficulty in understanding and evaluating the *Manuscripts* was only enhanced by the conditions of their discovery and publication. Published after the transformation of Marxist theory into economic reductionism and during the transformation of 'really-existing socialism' into a system of Taylorism with terror, the striking and, in general, relatively comprehensible, but perhaps too well-known chapter on 'Alienated Labour' seemed to offer the hope of a rejuvenation of Marx and an alternative 'Western Marxism'. This chapter is almost invariably the focus of attention – and is generally considered the quintessential expression, of the 'early Marx'. While I would agree that this chapter is the quintessential expression and the culmination of Marx's early development, it is my contention that the almost exclusive attention paid to the discussion of alienated labour is misplaced and has had rather serious consequences for the understanding not only of Marx's concept of objectification and its role in his intellectual development, but also of the construction and character of his materialist conception of history.

The section on 'Alienated Labour' is deceptive. The deception results from the understandable fact that in his Feuerbachian critique of alienated labour, Marx discusses objectification only in terms of labour. But the excessive focus on this section creates the illusion that Marx re-interpreted Feuerbach's notion of sensuous activity, of objectification, exclusively in terms of labour and thus reduced objectification to, by conflating it with, labour. This very one-dimensional interpretation of a very rich and multi-faceted category has allowed interpreters to reduce a materialist conception of history to an exclusive preoccupation with labour and thus to claim that Marx was a Promethean productivist or, as Adorno once allegedly sputtered in an ill-humoured but oft-quoted quip, that Marx wanted to turn the world into 'a giant workhouse'.[23] But throughout the other manuscripts Marx provides a very rich discussion of sense perception as objectification and he alludes, among other activities, to theory production, language and sociability as forms of objectification.

For now, however, it is necessary to emphasise that Marx integrated labour into his thought as one mode of objectification – certainly as the most important mode for the understanding of alienation and, soon, for the delineation of social form and exploitation, but nevertheless as one of several modes of human objectification. Telling in this regard is that Marx does not discuss objectification as work, but work as objectification, that is: he does not equate objectification with labour, but treats labour as a mode of objectification. Objectification is the name for this genus of activity, of which work/labour is one species. When objectification is collapsed and reduced to labour, when the two are treated as synonymous, it is virtually impossible to see what Marx was up to in both the *Manuscripts* and *The German Ideology*. And in order to understand where labour fits into Marx's overall scheme, and therewith to understand also the convoluted dynamic of the *Manuscripts*, it is worth struggling through the tortured philosophical prose of the last manuscript on Hegel where Marx discusses various modes of objectification, including labour.

In contrast to Hegel's notion of *Entäußerung*, in which the thinking subject temporarily 'externalises' itself into the alienated objectivity of the world before withdrawing into contemplation of the absolute idea, the concept of *Vergegenständlichung* redefines that 'externalisation' as normal, not alienated – and in so doing calls for a reconsideration of the subject-object relation. Feuerbach redefined the subject as the 'sensuously-acting' (*sinnlich-tätig*) subject and the object as the sensuous (*sinnliches*) object of that activity. Because only an embodied subject can be a 'sensuously-acting' subject, this redefinition rehabilitates the body, corporeality, from the mere animalistic prison to which it had been consigned by the Western philosophical tradition. But as Marx was to complain in his *Theses on Feuerbach*, Feuerbach's sensuously-

---

23 For a convincing case that Marx's materialist conception of history is profoundly ecological, see Foster 2000. For Foster's rebuttal to those accusing Marx of Promethean productivism, see esp. pp. 134 ff. Adorno's comment is reported by Jay 1973, p. 57.

acting subject was rather 'passive'[24] – that is, although Feuerbach countered philosophy's 'logocentric' definition of human nature by rehabilitating aesthetics, the senses and sense perception, as the properly human activity, he neglected those forms of sensuous activity like labour which actually transform the world. Marx's notion of objectification was, in short, much broader and deeper than Feuerbach's. Marx by no means excluded sense perception (nor intellectual labour) from his notion of objectification; and he insisted that all forms of objectification are active and transformative.

However, the addition of labour as a mode of objectification had two far-reaching consequences that would ultimately push Marx toward his *Aufhebung* of philosophy: the concern with labour obliged him to take seriously, not just the sense organs of the sensuously-active subject, but also the whole range of 'bodily instruments' embedded in 'human corporeal organisation' that make possible human objectification in the mode of labour; it enabled him, as Elaine Scarry put it, to discover human corporeality in the 'interior structure' artefacts. And 'artefacts', as I shall argue below, refers to all artefacts that make up human worlds, which consist not just of 'material' artefacts, but also of (also material) social and semiotic ones as well. The rest of this chapter, accordingly, will be devoted to analysing Marx's redefinition of the subject-object relation and his consequent re-working of the concept of objectification, and to introducing the 'world-making' that it entails and that is essential to the understanding of historical materialism as 'corporeal semiotics'.[25]

Marx's rethinking of the subject-object relation within the framework of his expanded notion of objectification has two dimensions which I shall address in inverse order of their appearance in the *Manuscripts*. In his critique of Hegel and 'philosophy in general' in the last manuscript, Marx offers, against traditional philosophical definitions of human beings as thinkers, a materialist redefinition of human being that is the first crucial step toward his *Aufhebung* of philosophy. And in his critique of 'Alienated Labour' he situates the human animal as both a part of nature and as a unique part. These (abstract) determinations, though still carried out within the Feuerbachian framework of a philosophical-materialist anthropology, would be crucial to the development of a historical-materialist anthropology or what Marx calls 'the assumptions' underlying the materialist conception of history that he developed in *The German Ideology*.

---

24 Marx 1845, First Thesis on Feuerbach, in Tucker 1978, p. 143.
25 I have borrowed 'worldmaking' from Goodman 1978. In the next section on 'Modes of Objectification' I shall address the 'ways of worldmaking' be found in Marx's historical-materialist perspective.

Hegel's dialectic is based on the assumption that the uniquely and truly human form of labour is mental or intellectual labour; and the dialectic itself progressively transforms, by disembodying, the subject into a knowing subject who confronting the world and its contents as objects of potential knowledge. Marx, by contrast, proposes and elaborates a fully corporeal dialectical relation between 'real, material human beings' and nature. Like Feuerbach, he is incensed that Hegel defines the 'subject' as 'self-consciousness', which in its Hegelian mental purity is an 'abstraction from the human being' that leads directly to the equation of 'externalisation' with 'alienation'.[26] In contrast to Hegel's idealist definition of the subject-object relation and his consequent identification of externalisation as alienation, Marx finds it 'wholly natural' that the 'self-externalisation' of 'a living, natural being equipped and endowed with objective, i.e. material essential powers', 'a real, corporeal human being who stands on the solid, well-rounded earth', should establish 'a *real* objective world, a world in the form of externality, that is a world not belonging to its essential being'. Such 'an objective being acts objectively, and it would not act objectively if the objective (*das Gegenständliche*) did not reside in the very nature of its being'. This objective being 'creates, establishes, only objects because it is established by objects, because it is at bottom *nature*. In the act of establishing it thus does not fall out of its 'pure activity' into a *creation* of the *object*; rather its *objective* product only confirms its *objective* activity, that is, its activity as the activity of an objective, natural being'.[27] With this verbiage Marx reminded idealist philosophers that the human being is more than just mind, is also and essentially a natural corporeal being dependent on nature, and for whom the production of objects, 'externalisation', is not only a necessary, but an essential life-activity. The human being *should* not be lost in 'externalisation', in the objects it produces, because it is its nature to produce, create. Alienation is therefore not an existential state, but a social consequence. Elaborating, Marx writes:

> The *human being* is immediately a *natural being*. As a natural being and as a living natural being, the human being is on the one hand equipped with *natural powers*, with *life powers* – an *active* natural being. These powers exist in it as dispositions and capacities, as *drives*; on the other hand, as a natural, embodied, sensuous, objective being, the human being is a sentient,[28] conditioned and limited being as are animals and plants.

---

26 Marx 1844 in Tucker 1978, pp. 114–15.
27 Ibid.
28 The German term is *leidendes*, which can be translated as both passionate and suffering.

That is: the *objects* of its drives exist outside of it as independent *objects*; but these objects are objects of its *need*, as *objects* that are indispensable and essential for the activation and confirmation of its essential powers. That the human being is a *corporeal*, living, real sensuous, objective being full of natural powers means that it has *real, sensuous objects* as the object of its being, of its life-expression or that it can only *express* its life in/on/through real, sensuous objects.[29]

This is a rather complex way of stating what should be the mundane point that minds do not labour (not even mentally) without bodies; and it is precisely the essential 'objectivity', the materiality and corporeality, of human being that makes the human being 'immediately a natural being'. To sustain and maintain itself, this objective natural being is dependent on objects outside of it for the satisfaction not only of its needs, but also its wants and desires. Hegel's disembodied *Geist*, 'without eyes, without teeth, without ears, without everything [corporeal]',[30] is 'a being that does not have its nature outside of itself is not a *natural* being, does not participate in the system of nature. A being that has no object outside of itself is not an objective being. A being that is itself not an object for a third being has no being as its *object*, that is, does not have objective relations; objectively its being is not objective'. To ground a theory of history in *Geist* is to base it on a contradiction in terms, for 'an unobjective being is a *non-being*'. To forget or neglect, while acknowledging in principle, this primary fact of human corporeality and its consequent needs, and to reduce history to the activity of mind (whether that activity be defined as philosophical as in Hegel, or cultural/signifying as in poststructuralism), can only result in an inflated and false idealist conception of human being and human activity – one that reduces human activity to only thinking and neglects the manifold ways in which, in addition and also through thinking, human beings objectify themselves in building their own worlds.

Whereas philosophy strictly demarcates human beings from other animals on the basis of *Geist*, Marx insists that human beings, as corporeal creatures, are, like all other corporeal creatures, also 'natural beings'. He does not at all deny that the human species is (like every other species) unique; but he roots his differentiation of human beings not apart from, but *within* the natural

---

Because Marx's meaning seems to be something between the two, I find it best rendered as 'sentient' or 'animate' as used by Maxine Sheets-Johnstone and Elaine Scarry (see Chapter 7).

29 Marx 1844 in Tucker 1978, p. 115.
30 Marx 1844 in Tucker 1978, p. 124. Following two citations, ibid., p. 116.

world: 'The human being is not only a natural being, but it is a human natural being'.[31] Characteristic of this human natural being is that the process through which it satisfies its needs is a transformative process; it transforms those needs, the being whose needs they are, and the world which it makes over in its own image. Consequently, Marx concludes, 'History is the true natural history of humanity'.[32] Thus his anticipated insistence a few paragraphs earlier that 'consistent naturalism or humanism distinguishes itself both from idealism and materialism, constitutes at the same time the unifying truth of both, and is alone capable of comprehending the act of world history'.[33] But before turning to the question of history and the problems with this still philosophical formulation of what history is, it is necessary to pursue further Marx's depiction of the uniqueness of the human animal and its objectifying activity which he attempts to elaborate, in confusing philosophical terminology, in the manuscript on 'Alienated Labour', specifically in his discussion the alienation of human beings from their 'species being'.

1.3   Objectification, Objectifying Labour, and Human Species-Being

Because of the common conflation of labour and objectification in Marx-interpretation, it is worth prefacing this discussion by reiterating that Marx inherited the concept of objectification from Feuerbach who applied it to philosophies and theologies, that is: exclusively to products of mental labour. Having adopted objectification from Feuerbach, Marx then adapted it and applied it to labour as well, which in the *1844 Manuscripts* constituted his great advance over Feuerbach. After 1844, what became his life-long attempt to decipher the social hieroglyphics of capital resulted in his usage of 'objectification' almost exclusively in discussions of labour. Throughout the *Manuscripts*, however, Marx deployed the term more broadly, often with brilliantly insightful brevity, to a variety of other human activities including sense perception, speech and language, knowledge production (*Wissenschaft*), and social relations, both public institutional and more personal social relations such as love and friendship. The detailed articulation of what I shall call 'modes of objectification' will be taken up in the next chapter. Here, however, my purpose is two-fold: to explain Marx's use of one of those modes, labour, the production of

---

31   'Der Mensch ist nicht nur Naturwesen, sondern er ist menschliches Naturwesen' (MEW, EB I, p. 579).
32   'Die Geschichte ist die wahre Naturgeschichte des Menschen' (MEW, EB I, p. 579).
33   Marx 1844 in Tucker 1978, p. 115.

material objects, as that which differentiates the human species from all other animal species; and to show that the attributes of labour are not definitive for all modes of objectification, that, as noted above, Marx does not treat objectification as synonymous with, or as a mode of labour.

Like all other animals, human beings are 'species-beings' [*Gattungswesen*[34]] – which simply means that all human beings share the definitive attributes of their species. Like the life of other animal species, human 'species-life' [*Gattungsleben*] consists physically in the fact that the human being (like the animal) lives from 'inorganic nature'. Having established the comparison, Marx then proceeds to differentiate human species-being from that of all other species. He explains that 'as the human being is all the more universal than the animal, all the more universal is the range of inorganic nature from which it lives'.[35] Non-human species are 'one-sided' in the limited extent of the range of their productive capacities and therefore of their environmental niches. Marx acknowledges that animal species also 'produce' – they 'build nests, houses, like the bee, beaver, ants' – but their production is limited: 'they only produce what they immediately need for themselves or their offspring'; they produce 'one-sidedly', 'only under the dominion of immediate physical need' and in a manner that only reproduces its own physical being. 'An animal's product belongs immediately to its physical body, whilst man freely confronts his product'.[36] An

---

34   One of the conceptual pillars of the Feuerbachian framework of the *Manuscripts*, *Gattungswesen* can be translated into English as either 'species-being', which is the usual translation of Marx's usage, or as 'species-essence' – and which I shall use here. 'Species-being' is useful insofar as it indicates that in defining the human species Marx is concerned with, to borrow Heidegger's term, human 'being-in-the-world' which he defined as a natural being, dependent on nature, but equipped with the bodily instruments to engage in the transformative activity of objectification. But it should be noted that this translation can also be somewhat misleading, since 'Wesen' can be translated as 'essence' as in a constant, *a priori* human essence. The term has as such a long history in the German idealist tradition against which Marx was struggling as he attempted to attain 'self-clarification'. Used in the framework of the doubling of the world in which the human essence appears in alienated form, *Gattungswesen* as 'species-essence' entails a closed speculative philosophy of history whose telos will be reached with the negation of this negative state of alienation – of which the *1844 Manuscripts* smack more than a little. It is this static element of the concept 'Wesen' that Marx rejects in the sixth thesis on Feuerbach – a rejection that also led to heated debates on whether or not Marx had a concept of human nature (which I address in the Chapter 2). In my view, in short: 'species-*being*' indicates where Marx was heading, while 'species-*essence*' indicates where he came from and what he was struggling to get beyond; and both should be kept in mind in interpreting this term.

35   Marx 1844 in Tucker 1978, p. 75. See below, note 41, for comment on the notion of 'inorganic nature'.

36   Hannah Arendt turned this distinction between the immediate consumption of a product

animal 'forms things in accordance with the standard and need of the species to which it belongs'. Human beings, by contrast, produce 'universally' in that they 'make all nature into their *inorganic* [sic; see below] body, both insofar as it [nature] is an immediate means of life, and insofar as it is the material, the object, and the tool of his life activity'.[37] Human beings, furthermore, 'produce in freedom' and reproduce 'the whole of nature' because they 'know how to produce in accordance with the standard of every species, and know how to apply everywhere the inherent standard to the object. For that reason, human beings also produce according to the laws of beauty'.[38] The consideration of animal production is useful for elaborating key aspects of objectification that Marx did not (adequately) address, and I shall return to it shortly. Here it is necessary to focus on what these comments are trying to express about the human species.

The profundity of these seemingly superficial and certainly convoluted statements lies not in their reiteration of what should be the obvious facts that the human species, like all other species, is first of all a natural species with an inevitable dependency on nature, and that however much humans may modify their means of obtaining their life from nature, they cannot eliminate their dependency on the nature of which they are necessarily a part. Their profundity lies rather in Marx's *use* of these simple facts: he does not treat them as 'a simple prerequisite', but rather posits them as the foundation of what will soon emerge as his materialist conception of history. These simple facts embedded in human corporeality are rendered profound against the background of a Western philosophical tradition that denigrated and excluded the body and

---

and its continued 'free-standing' existence into an ontological one between labour which 'only' produces products for immediate consumption and 'work' whose 'works' are long lasting. By following the Western philosophical tradition and denigrating 'labour' as the merely animal side of human life, while elevating 'work' as properly human, Arendt reduces corporeality to, at best, a simple prerequisite and apparently finds trivial and properly neglected the familiar fact that the consumption of the transitory and thus despised product of 'labour' results in the continued existence of the body that consumes it. Viewed from the perspective developed here, the fact that the products of what Arendt calls 'labour' are consumed means that their meaning is the perpetuation of human life itself – a not unimportant, even if obvious fact recalling the tautological profundity of Marx's comment that the first prerequisite for human history is the existence of living human beings.

37 Marx 1844 in Tucker 1978, p. 75.
38 Marx 1844 in Tucker 1978, pp. 75–6. Marx always used 'der Mensch' to speak of human beings generically, which despite its masculine article, is gender neutral in content. I will accordingly not follow the standard rendering of 'der Mensch' as 'man' but will instead, always and without further comment, translate 'der Mensch' as 'human beings' or 'humanity'.

human dependence on nature as the mere animal dimension of human life; traditional philosophy found the body relevant only as an object of knowledge, but not as a crucial means of knowledge production. Since these simple facts are so fundamental that they can serve as the basis of a conception of history, and since too many interpretations of Marx have read much more into these statements than they say, it is necessary to understand exactly how these facts fit into Marx's argument.

First of all, it is necessary to clear up some conceptual confusion. In the passage cited above, Marx referred to nature with the misleading misnomer 'inorganic body'. This term seems to posit a qualitative distinction between humans who are presumably 'organic' and the rest of nature which he seems to designate as 'inorganic'. But humans, of course, live, as do all other species, from organic as well as inorganic nature. Thus, what he means by 'inorganic body' is more accurately rendered in the next sentence (see above) where he simply states that nature is 'the body' of human and all other organic beings.[39] Or as he formulates it more accurately elsewhere in the *Manuscripts*, in the *Grundrisse* and *Capital*, nature is the 'extended body' of human beings.[40] These terms more appropriately capture the intimate and inseparable link of dependence that binds human beings to nature. As our 'extended body', nature is much more than a mere instrumental and therefore disposable means to an end, something that can be used up and destroyed. Nature is not just the indispensable means of life; more fundamentally, it is the precondition of life. And this understanding of nature as our 'extended body' is not only the strongest refutation of the misplaced accusation that Marx advocated a 'Promethean productivism', but it is also the starting point for a historical-materialist ecology; for it makes immediately and graphically obvious that the wholesale or 'universal' exploitation, and therewith destruction of nature, of our own extended body, would be tantamount to suicide.[41] Like all creatures, human beings live on the nature of

---

39 Marx 1844 in Tucker 1978, p. 75.
40 Marx used the term 'extended body' [*verlängertes Leib*] explicitly in the *Grundrisse* (1973 [1857–58], p. 493). In *Capital* he explained that since production is necessarily a metabolic process between human beings and nature, nature itself thus 'becomes one of the organs of [human] activity which [human beings] annex to [their] own bodily organs' (Marx 1990 [1967], p. 285).
41 Engels makes this point emphatically in his much-maligned essay 'On the Role of Labour in the Transition from Ape to Human' in the *Dialectics of Nature*. There he establishes a link between environmental destruction and the decline of civilizations. See also Foster 2000. Nevertheless, Marx's description of nature as the 'inorganic body' of human beings has led many to pounce on this pronouncement as proof of his 'Promethean productivism'. In their review and refutation of such claims, however, John Foster and Paul Burkett

which they are a part. As Judith Butler put it so succinctly: 'The body is in the natural world not as an ontologically separate entity, but a relation process between terms that can become separated or unified. The body is in and of nature to the degree that this ongoing process, if disrupted or destroyed, can expose the body to precarity, and is an ongoing interchange that requires renewal – and the conditions for renewal'.[42] 'What matters' therefore, as Yrjö Haila and Richard Levins conclude, 'is not whether we modify nature or not, but how, and for what purpose, we do so'.[43]

As becomes clear in his further elaboration of the 'relative universality' of humans vis-à-vis other species, Marx's point is to contrast the astonishing range of what we would today call 'ecological niches' in which human beings can make themselves at home with the rather narrow range of other animal species. In contemporary terms, what Marx was saying is that non-human animal species are governed by fairly rigid instinctual programs that evolved through their accommodation to (and forming of) their specific niches; those species are for that reason confined to their own relatively local habitat, condemned to a narrow niche. The technological one-dimensionality of other animal species results in the geographical one-dimensionality of their range.[44] The history

---

have convincingly argued that such a conclusion derives from a misunderstanding of Marx's use of the terms 'organic' and 'inorganic'. Based on a careful etymological study of the terms, they show that Marx 'referred to nature (other than the human body) as the inorganic body of humanity in conformity with the scientific vocabulary of his day, wherein organic referred to bodily organs, whereas inorganic meant unrelated to bodily organs' (Foster and Burkett 2000, p. 412). Thus, although Marx intended his references to nature as the 'inorganic' and the 'extended' body of human beings as synonymous, to avoid confusion on this point in the following I shall use only the latter term which, to mix sensory metaphors, is more palatable to our ears. And it must be emphasised of course that because *all* organisms live from the nature outside of their own bodies, that external nature is for them as well their 'extended body' which, as Lewontin and Levins argue, they also alter in order to suit themselves in building a niche. In this regard, the difference between human beings and other species in their respective relations to external nature lies in the vast quantitative difference in the degree to which human beings alter that external nature – a quantitative difference so great that it constitutes a qualitative difference of the kind that is essentially what is implied in the epithet 'anthropocene' that designates the span of human history as on par with geologic epochs.

42 Butler 2019, p. 15.
43 Haila and Levins, cited in Foster 2000, p. 254.
44 Marx 1844 in Tucker 1978, p. 76. In *Capital* Marx noted the rudimentary capacity of certain species to fabricate and use tools (which was virtually unrecognised until Jane Goodall made public her observations on tool-use among chimpanzees in 1960), and obviously correctly noted that this is a very rare exception and is not an essential characteristic of the life-activity of any other but the human species. In discussing the means of labour, Marx considered tools and technology. Anticipating Jane Goodall's observations on 'tool-use'

of all animal species except the human animal, *Homo sapiens*, is the history of their biological evolution; and their only possible responses to qualitative environmental changes are either speciation, the adaptive process that transforms an older species into a new one, or extinction.

In contrast to the one-dimensional, genetically determined, environmentally specific manner in which all non-human species build their own worlds, humans are not so limited, or more accurately: human limits are more elastic. Human beings can effect qualitative changes in almost any environment to make it hospitable to themselves. Marx's comments that human beings produce 'consciously', 'freely', 'according to the measure of every species',[45] and for reasons beyond their immediate physical needs – all this is simply a philosophically convoluted way of saying that because human beings can produce 'universally', they are not relegated to a particular environmental niche. The uniqueness of the human species lies in the fact that its productive capacities, informed by the imagination, are multi-dimensional. Humans can produce as artefacts, as made-objects, that which 'immediately belongs to the physical body' of other species, and can mimic and improve on the bodily instruments of, and the artefacts instinctually produced by, those species: the means of preserving water like the humps of camels or the dams of beavers, warm clothes modelled to make up for the lack of fur, nets like those of spiders for trapping, sonar machines to hear like bats, airplanes to fly like birds, submarines to swim like fish, etc.

---

by chimpanzees that occasioned so much surprise (van Latwick-Goodall 1971, pp. 35–7, pp. 227–9, pp. 240–1, pp. 277–80), Marx recognised that 'the use and creation of means of labour is in germ characteristic of various animal species' (Marx 1990 [1867], p. 296). But he also recognised (along with many contemporary students of human evolution) that the systematic use and creation of tools is unique to the human species. In this respect, he therefore cited approvingly Benjamin Franklin's definition of humans as 'toolmaking animal(s)' (ibid., p. 296). But his point was not to valorise tool-making *per se* and, therewith, tool-using *cum* productivism as an end in itself. Rather as the context shows, Marx adduced Franklin's definition, not as a definition of human being in general, but to characterise one of the 'simple moments' of the uniquely human labour-process, the uniquely human ability to produce tools or means of their labour that are separate from their own corporeal organisation. According to the logic of Marx's overall materialist conception, human being is more appropriately described as objectifying being. And it is unique to humans, not to be limited by their own bodily instruments, but to produce the 'means of objectification' – tools for labour, words and languages for semiotic production, and institutions for social objectification.

45 Similar notions of the universality of human being in contrast to the narrowness of the life-activity of other species are found in Herder, *Sprachphilosphie*, cited in Liebrucks 1964, p. 59.

This 'universality' of human productive capacities establishes the 'universality' of the geographic range of *Homo sapiens*. The range of human worlds, of the ecological niches that humans can build for themselves, though not strictly speaking 'universal' (body limits such as the need for oxygen, for example, place altitudinal limits on human habitation), is certainly unique in its breadth. In a comment updating Marx's language, but substantiating much of what he was trying to convey about human 'universality', biological-anthropologist John Relethford has noted that much of human biology reflects the fact that our ancestors were tropical animals.[46] Translated into Marx's terms, this means that human evolution can be seen as the development of the corporeal organisation, the bodily instruments and capacities, to produce 'universally', to transform the natural world so that humans could move out beyond their natural tropical habitat. That is: proto-human species were able to break the bounds of the narrow, 'local' ecological niche of its origins and spread from the forested edges of the African savannah, that most paleoanthropologists locate as the niche inhabited by the earliest hominids, to the ends of the earth and come to inhabit virtually all (terrestrial) regions of the planet from deserts to polar caps and almost everywhere in-between – in short, to inhabit more different kinds of geographical and climatic zones than perhaps any other species except those bacteria that live on and off of humans and follow them wherever they may go.[47] Because of its ability to transform even hostile environments into comfortable homes, and to be able to produce in those environments fully adequate means of subsistence, it is not too much to say that, in contrast to other species, the geographic range of *Homo sapiens* is certainly planetary if not truly 'universal'.[48]

---

46 Relethford 1994, p. 248.
47 As Niles Eldredge explains: 'Culture enabled our ancestor *Homo erectus* to travel north from the tropics in the very teeth of a major glaciation event one million years ago. Fire, clothing, and spears were all that it took to create the greatest expansion of an ecological niche recorded in the entire history of life: species are rarely seen moving into entirely different climatic regimes – let alone moving from the topics into the frozen steppes of higher latitudes. And it was culture, learned behavior in the form of agricultural revolution, that ten thousand years ago took us out and away from the very local ecosystem is in which our ancestors and all other species, like spotted hyenas and wild dogs, have always lived'. This is, as Eldredge says, 'worth pausing over', for 'absolutely every other kind of organism, from bacteria to sexually reproducing species of plants and animals, lives in groups inside of local ecosystems. But now, all of a sudden, humans have started to do something very different; with the invention of agriculture in a number of different places starting about ten thousand years ago, humans abruptly began to live *outside* local ecosystems' (Eldredge 2004, pp. 116–17).
48 Obviously, we cannot take 'universal' too literally, for humans cannot (yet) live above cer-

This ability to produce 'universally' makes it possible for human beings not only to *be*, but also to *feel* everywhere at home. In contrast to Novalis's definition of philosophy as 'homesickness, the wish to be everywhere at home', Marx's materialist conception of history exposes that homesickness as a case of philosophical alienation: 'It is precisely in the re-working (*Bearbeitung*) of the objective world' that *Homo sapiens* 'preserves itself as a species-being. This production is his active species life. Through and because of this production, nature appears as *his* work and his reality. The object of labour is, therefore, the *objectification of man's species life*; for he duplicates himself not only in consciousness, intellectually, but also actively, in reality, and therefore he contemplates himself in a world that he has created'.[49] Human beings can, in this formulation, *be* everywhere at home because they can everywhere *build* themselves homes.

In this convoluted half-materialist, still half-idealist vocabulary Marx was trying to convey what are essentially Darwinian notions. When he speaks of conscious life-activity that transforms nature and builds human worlds, he is simply making the same point that students of human evolution make in defining *Homo sapiens* as an animal with the biological potential to produce culture. In more contemporary terms, he is simply defining human species-being in terms of the human ability to produce beyond any kind of instinctual programming and beyond immediate physical needs, to supplement 'nature' with, and transform it through, 'culture'. As the non-genetic transmission of information through learning, culture enables humans to produce imaginatively rather than only instinctually, thus consciously shaping the worlds they inhabit. And precisely because this comment about the 'universality' of human production is one of several of Marx's comments often mistaken as a promotion of Promethean productivism, it is worth emphasising that he uses the term as a descriptive delineation of the qualitative range of human capacities, but *not* as a prescriptive advocacy of their unregulated and quantitatively unlimited use.[50]

---

tain altitudes with too little air, too low temperatures, where nothing can grow. But it is clear from the context that Marx uses 'universal' to contrast the much vaster range of human habitats with the 'one-dimensional' ranges of other species.

49 Marx 1844 in Tucker 1978, p. 76.

50 Marx's above-mentioned view of nature as the 'extended body' of humans (and all other species), which entails recognition that the destruction of out natural 'extended body' would be suicide, is a rather explicit refutation of 'Promethean productivism'. Further refutations of the Promethean-productivist charge against Marx will be adduced throughout this book. See particularly, Chapters 10 and 14. Two more recent refutations of the

Though Marx's comment on the unconscious character of animal production is intended as further differentiation of humans vs. other species, this explicit acknowledgement that animals produce raises two key matters pertaining to objectification, whose clarification is crucial to the development of my argument. These are: whether self-conscious intentionality is a necessary attribute of objectification; and the relation between corporeal form and the form of the objective world of artefacts that a species produces.

The paradigm of self-consciously intentional objectification is of course labour. But the question here, however, is whether labour is the definitive model for all modes of objectification. An answer to that question can be gleaned from Marx's discussion of intentionality in the human labour-process. When outlining its general form in *Capital*, Marx further distinguishes the human labour-process from that of other species by differentiating between the 'worst architect' and 'the best bee'. One English translation of *Capital* has loosely but accurately rendered Marx's specific comparison of how bees and architects build their domiciles in a more general form: 'the architect raises the structure in the imagination, before erecting it in reality'.[51] Though this rendering tends to minimise the importance of human corporeal organisation in the labour-process, it nevertheless captures the sense of Marx's specific example and his definition of the *human labour-process* not just as intentional, but as self-consciously intentional – as a process at whose end 'a result emerges that was already in the mind of the worker in the beginning, i.e. that already existed ideally. The worker not only effects a transformation of the natural [object of labour], but also realizes his/her purpose'.[52] And John McMurtry is justified in citing this translation and in referring to this ability to 'raise a structure in the imagination' and then to 'erect it in reality' as the 'projective consciousness'.[53] Despite common references to certain jobs in the capitalist productive process as mindless, McMurtry is certainly correct in his insistence that the 'projective consciousness' is a 'special property' of human labour.[54] Although there is no doubt that this projective consciousness is a key attribute of *Homo sapiens* and

---

charge of 'Promethean Productivism' from a 'Marxist ecology perspective' are Foster 2000 and Burkett 2014.
51 Cited in McMurtry, 1978, p. 22. McMurtry cites the English translation of *Capital* by Samuel Moore and Edward Aveling; the generalisation in this sentence is in keeping with the examples that Marx provided, though he does not himself provide a general summary of these examples.
52 Marx 1990 [1867], p. 284.
53 McMurtry 1978, p. 22.
54 McMurtry does call attention to Marx's insistence on the corporeal dimensions of human labour, on 'bodily instruments' (1978, p. 34), but he categorises these bodily instruments

the one that enables humans to produce 'universally', this does not necessarily answer the question of whether the human labour-process is the definitive model for all modes of objectification. The answer to this question depends, in turn, on the answer to the question of whether this 'projective consciousness' or self-conscious intentionality is a necessary attribute of objectification or, to put it another way, whether self-consciousness is a necessary attribute of intentionality.

If the projective consciousness is definitive of objectification, then self-conscious intentionality must be an attribute of all objectification. The intentional projective consciousness is certainly engaged in all forms of labour, whether manual, intellectual, or aesthetic, as well as in speech and other performative acts, and numerous other kinds of objectifying activities. But in Marx's usage, at least, not all objectifications can be considered self-consciously intentional.[55] In the *1844 Manuscripts*, for example, he embarks on a brief but profound discussion of sense perception as a mode of objectification (see Chapter 2); and in both the *Manuscripts* and *Capital* he speaks of animal production which, as such, is a mode of objectification. But neither of these can be considered acts of a 'projective consciousness'. And the same is true of such collective products as languages and cultural forms. Like beaver dams and spider webs, languages and cultural forms are not simply given, but are rather made, produced. And they are produced with purpose, even if not with the self-conscious intentionality of the projective consciousness with which people make tables or formulate sentences. They are, in short, objectifications that, however, cannot be grasped as such if the conscious intentionality of human labour is taken as the model of objectification. It would therefore be more accurate to define objectification as those activities through which an organism effects a purposeful and meaningful transformation of some aspect(s) of the world – regardless of whether it is motivated by conscious intention, habit, or even instinct. The purpose, for example, of a spider's instinctual programme that enables it to build a web is to procure sustenance. In this manner, an activity may be said to be 'intentional', better: purposive, even if the organism's labour is not activated by a 'projective consciousness'. In this case the inten-

---

and corporeal capacities as 'other' and focuses on the 'special property' of the 'projective consciousness'.

55 The temptation to attribute self-conscious intentionality to all forms of objectification is perhaps enhanced by the fact, noted by Terry Eagleton, that Marx generally used the individualistic production of artists and artisans as his model of material production or objectification (Eagleton 1990, p. 204). But the question with which I am here concerned is whether self-conscious intentionality is a necessary attribute of objectification.

tionality and purpose are embedded in the organism's 'tacit knowledge' (see Chapter 7) that enables it to know instinctually what it needs to do and can do.

Understanding objectifying labour as a purposive, even if not a consciously intentional transformation of environment, and thus as an attribute of all species, provides a comparative perspective that puts into relief the relation between an organism's corporeal organisation and the world or niche it creates for itself; and this is the second matter indicated by Marx's discussion of animal production. We are so used to looking at 'nature' or the 'environment' as everything that is not human, that we tend to overlook the productive processes that go on in 'nature'. But Marx's comment on non-human species as the unconscious producers of their (albeit 'one-dimensional') worlds implies that they too engage in their own species-specific objectifying activity through which they transform 'nature' or their 'environment' by building themselves worlds or, ecologically expressed, niches in their own bodily image. As Richard Levins and Richard Lewontin have argued in grounding a 'dialectical biology', all species are the subjects and objects of their own evolution. That is: in contrast to the un-nuanced notion that (non-human) species simply plop themselves down pre-established 'niches' in 'the environment', Levins and Lewontin insist that each species creates its own niche by modifying, according to its bodily capacities and in accordance with its needs, the world outside itself, what we call 'nature'. The degree of modification certainly varies, but the greater the modification, that is, the more pronounced the artefactual, the more we can see in those artefacts the bodily needs and capacities of their makers. For embodied in all artefacts is the embodiedness of their producers – their species attributes, the capacities and needs embedded in the species phenotype.

As subject and object of its own evolution, each organism produces a world made in the image of its own mindful body, a world whose boundaries are established by the dialectic of needs and capacities residing in its corporeality. If all species can be said to be capable of objectification, then the key to understanding the different ways in which various species objectify themselves must necessarily lie in the particular corporeal organisation of each species: the nature of its bodily toolkit, its bodily instruments, its corporeal capacities and dexterities, needs, and constraints which establish the range, the possibility and limits, of a species' possible objectifications.[56] As mentioned above,

---

56 The insistence that the projective consciousness is the definitive attribute of objectification and is thus the unique activity of human beings tends, as evidenced by McMurtry's own analysis, to focus only on the mental side of human labour, the projective consciousness, and thereby to reduce the corporeal capacities and bodily instruments required for erecting the idea in reality to the neglected status of 'simple prerequisites'. This is not only

Marx noted that in its life-activity lies the entire character of a species. He could have added that in the objective world produced by that life-activity lies its corporeal organisation. Or elaborating Elaine Scarry's rendering of Marx's insight that 'the body is the interior structure of the artefact', we might say that the corporeal organisation of a species is the interior structure of the objective world it builds. Articulating the relation between corporeal organisation and artefactual worlds and learning to read human worlds as products of the various modes of human objectification, itself a function of human corporeal organisation, is exactly what is entailed by historical materialism as 'corporeal semiotics' – and that will be the focus of Parts Two to Four. Here, however, it is necessary to consider Marx's reconsideration of Hegel and his turn toward history.

1.4 Between Hegel and Feuerbach: A Philosophical-Materialist Conception of History

The excessive attention paid to the manuscript on alienated labour not only leads to a mistaken reductionist conflation of objectification with labour, but also makes it difficult to follow the trajectory of Marx's intellectual development as it runs through the *Manuscripts*. For in the last of the manuscripts, the 'Critique of the Hegelian Dialectic and Philosophy in General', there are unmistakable hints that Marx had already begun to move beyond the Feuerbachian position presented in the section on 'Alienated Labour'. As noted above, Marx's striking Feuerbachian critique of alienated labour must be seen as exactly that: another Feuerbachian foray, prompted perhaps by Ruge, but one that could be added to Feuerbach's critiques of religious and philosophical alienation and Marx's own earlier critique of political alienation in Hegel's *Philosophy of Right*. From a Feuerbachian standpoint, Marx's critique of alienated labour was thoroughly successful. Feuerbach was crucial for Marx's intellectual development – the *1844 Manuscripts* are simply unthinkable without him; and Marx acknowledged his obligation to Feuerbach as 'the only one who maintained a serious, a critical relation to the Hegelian dialectic' and truly went beyond 'the old philosophy'.[57] Yet however enthusiastic Marx's momentary Feuerbachianism was, it

---

a problem in itself, but it also occludes the intimate relations between corporeal organisation and the particular worlds that each species builds in its own image. McMurtry has a place for corporeal capacities and bodily instruments in his chart of 'human nature', but after listing them, he never addresses them again.

57   Marx 1844 in Tucker 1978, p. 107.

was certainly momentary; for his newfound concern with labour quickly disrupted the Feuerbachian framework and pushed him in the direction of history.

Having cast more than a glance at labour, Marx grew dissatisfied, not only with Feuerbach's neglect of it, but also with any approach that acknowledges labour as an activity definitive of human species-being, but views it narrowly as a means to self-knowledge, while neglecting its remaking the world and therewith too human life – which in different ways was the case both in Hegel's well-known Master-Slave narrative and in Marx's own discussion of 'alienated labour'. The very materiality and dynamism of labour – its transformative character that alters the face of nature, brings new objects into the world, and produces human worlds – could not be contained by a Feuerbachian framework; nor could the very important question concerning the origins of alienation be answered within that framework. For although Feuerbach posited objectification as a process, he did so very abstractly and as a *fait accompli*, without concern for the specific content of the process. It is therefore more accurate to say that Feuerbach's focus was not on the *process* of objectification, the production of social objectivity, but on the *product* of objectification, the existing alienated state of the world. This is true too of Marx's critique in the manuscript on 'Alienated Labour' in which he, like Feuerbach, begins with the 'actual fact' of alienation.

There is, however, already in the last few paragraphs of the manuscript on 'Alienated Labour' an indication of the problems with Feuerbach's rather static approach.[58] With tortured and totally unsatisfying logic, Marx attempted to provide an explanation of how it comes about that human beings alienate themselves from their labour. It is first worth noting that although Marx introduced this discussion with the Feuerbachian category of 'alienation' (*Entfremdung*), he used in the discussion itself the Hegelian category of 'externalisation' (*Entäußerung*). More telling, however, is the convoluted circularity of his

---

58 Axel Honneth and Hans Joas argue that in so doing, in incorporating Feuerbach's ideas into, as simply an element of, his larger project, Marx neutralised them and robbed them of their 'emancipatory power'; they also argue that as Marx moved to social critique in his later works, the 'anthropological' concern 'retreat[ed] more and more into the background' (Honneth and Joas 1988, p. 23). As I shall argue below on the exegetical point, the two are not mutually exclusive, and the focus on one or the other is the result of a choice – as Honneth and Joas put it earlier in the book: the result of a fully conscious methodological choice. The larger and more germane point to a materialist conception of history is whether it is possible to maintain the Feuerbachian dimensions while developing a critique of specific social forms such as the capitalist mode of production. In the following two chapters I shall show why *Capital* could not have been written on the basis of the methodology and conceptual apparatus of the *1844 Manuscripts*.

pseudo-explanation that explains private property as both the cause and the consequence of externalised (*entäußerten*) labour. Though he provided a rich and insightful portrait of alienated labour and could generally trace it to the private ownership of property, he was unable to develop a clear explanation of how alienated forms came to be constructed in the first place.[59] His lack of success here resulted from having brought a philosophical interpretation to a problem that, Marx began to realise, needed historical explanation.

And it is at this point that Marx's increasing suspicions of the passivity of Feuerbach's still philosophical materialism and his increasing impatience with Feuerbach's ahistorical methodology provoked a reconsideration of Hegel. Hegel's anthropogenetic understanding of (the albeit idealist form of intellectual) labour as the process of human self-production[60] offered a way to get beyond the static materialism he had adopted from Feuerbach. Marx reconsidered Hegel's positive side in the midst of his section which later editors entitled 'Critique of the Hegelian Dialectic and Philosophy in General'. This title injects an often overlooked degree of instability into the *Manuscripts* as a whole; for, its uncompromising directness seems to imply that Marx bid a categorical and final farewell to Hegel and philosophy, to which he now steadfastly opposed a Feuerbachian materialism, but the content of this manuscript is much less certain and much more complex.

Perhaps the best way to see and explain the very real instability in this last manuscript, and thus in the *Manuscripts* as a whole is to read the first of Marx's *Theses on Feuerbach*, (1845) as a kind of retrospective recognition that the *1844 Manuscripts* contained two unreconciled critiques. The *Manuscripts* begin with a Feuerbachian critique of idealist philosophy that Marx expan-

---

59 Saito (2017, pp. 32–44) attempts to refute the charge of circularity that has also been levied by other commentators (e.g. Ignace Feuerlicht, Michael Quante). As much as I admire Saito's thorough analysis of the ecological dimensions of Marx's materialist conception of history, I do not find this argument convincing; for it seems to me that Saito here reproduces in even greater detail the circularity in which Marx was caught. Be that as it may, the more important issue (of which this circularity is only a symptom) is that in the *1844 Manuscripts* Marx was still trapped, as Saito puts it, in 'philosophy' from which he 'decisively distanced himself' in the *Theses on Feuerbach* and *The German Ideology*. But Saito does not consider 'Marx's rejection of philosophical questioning' an 'epistemological break'. My argument, however, (developed throughout Part 1, especially Chapter 3, and also in Appendix 1.3.) is that Marx broke not only with philosophical questioning, but also with philosophical modes of answering those questions, that his *Aufhebung* of philosophy consisted not only of a redefinition of the contents of knowledge, but also the nature of knowledge production – which together constitute an 'epistemological break'.

60 Marx 1844 in Tucker 1978, p. 112.

ded greatly by introducing the sensuous activity of labour into the Feuerbachian framework. And while doing so, he began to realise that Feuerbach's materialism was not only not materialist enough, but also too 'passive'; and he developed a renewed appreciation for Hegel who, despite his idealism, had displayed greater insight into history as a process than did Feuerbach. And the Theses on Feuerbach prefacing *The German Ideology* can be read as Marx's dawning recognition that the *Manuscripts* contained unreconciled elements: Feuerbach's important but limited philosophical-materialist critique of idealism; and Hegel's also important, albeit idealist understanding of the logic of historical processes. *The German Ideology* itself can thus be understand as an attempt to reconcile the strengths, and go beyond the weaknesses, of both Hegel and Feuerbach.

Marx's first thesis begins with an expression of impatience with the static character of Feuerbach's sensualist philosophy, which, Marx came to realise, viewed 'reality, sensuousness, only in the form of an object or of observation [*Anschauung*]'.[61] Though Feuerbach shifted the locus of knowledge from abstract thought to sensuous apperception, apprehension, and appreciation of sensuous objects, he remained a philosopher in defining thought as the highest human activity. He therefore remained passive before objects, accepting them as given. Feuerbach wanted to know human sensuous activity and the sensuousness of objects (*Gegenstände*), without grasping 'human activity itself as objectifying (*gegenständliche*) activity'.[62] Echoing his comments in the last manuscript on Hegel's positive side, Marx then praised idealist philosophy for having grasped history as a process and for developing the 'active side' of human life, albeit in abstract form and without acknowledging the sensuous nature of that activity. This active dimension of Hegel's thought would in turn serve as the basis for a criticism of what he saw as the passivity of Feuerbach's thought, a criticism that was only reinforced by Marx's inclusion of labour as a key form of objectification. Unlike his earlier *Critique of Hegel's Philosophy of Right* that treated Hegel's political philosophy as mere alienation, he now found within that alienated philosophy a dynamic, historical element that helped him to put his own materialist premises in historical motion. Though *The German Ideology*, as Marx later noted, was his work of self-clarification, this first thesis on Feuerbach points retrospectively to his reconsidered critique of Hegelian dialectics in the final section of the *Manuscripts* as very much a part of that process of self-clarification.

---

61 Marx 1844 in Tucker 1978, p. 143, translation slightly altered.
62 Marx 1844 in Tucker 1978, p. 143.

In this critique Marx accepted Hegel's evaluation of his own philosophy as the solution and therewith the culmination of Western philosophical history.[63] But, he insisted, Hegel's thought contains 'a double mistake': as was discussed above, half of that double mistake was Hegel's conflation of *Entäusserung* or externalisation (that which Marx was in the process of conceptualising as the quintessential human activity of *Vergegenständichung*) with *Entfremdung* or alienation.[64] And this led to the other half of Hegel's 'double mistake', his purely idealist or philosophical concept of labour. Because he proceeded from traditional philosophy's anthropological assumption that the mind is quintessentially human, and its activity the truly human activity, 'the only labour that Hegel knows and recognizes is abstract, mental [labour]'.[65] Once this idealist determination of the nature of human beings and their 'proper' activity, was effected, human history could (and had to be) conceived as the history of human thought as exemplified in the work of its best practitioners, that is, in the history of philosophy.

In turning the tables on Hegel and arguing that alienation lay not in objectification, but in the philosophical illusion that thought alone makes the world go around and forth, Marx was more or less simply reiterating Feuerbach's critique. Yet while dragging Hegel too through the 'Feuer-bach', Marx mined elements in Hegel's thought that both pointed beyond its narrow idealist boundaries and increased his discontent with Feuerbach's rather static materialism. In Hegel's idealist philosophy Marx found the insights and the methodology that, given the proper materialist content, could overcome the passivity of Feuerbach's materialism and address the question that he raised but failed to answer in concluding the manuscript on 'Alienated Labour', the question of how alienated forms came to be constructed in the first place. Rather than delivering, as did Feuerbach, a solely negative critique of Hegel's philosophy as alienation, Marx recognised in Hegel's work what he would later call a 'rational core' (although it must immediately and emphatically be added that there would be much more to Marx's project that simply extracting the rational core from its alienated shell – see Chapters 2 and 3). Though he objected to Hegel's

---

63   See Marx 1844 in Tucker 1978, p. 112. This seemingly immodest evaluation is actually much more modest than it seems, somewhat along the lines of Newton's alleged comment that he saw further only because he stood on the shoulders of giants.
64   Against this idealist reduction of objectification to externalisation and against the conflation of externalisation and alienation, Marx insisted, as Helmut Reichelt has argued, 'on a sharp differentiation between *Vergegenständlichung* and *Entäusserung*' (Reichelt 1983, p. 17).
65   Marx 1844 in Tucker 1978, p. 112. The German original: 'Die Arbeit, welche Hegel allein kennt und anerkennt, ist die *abstrakt geistige*' (*MEW*, EB I, p. 574).

idealist definition of essentially human labour as mental labour, Marx found 'the greatness of Hegel's *Phenomenology*' in the fact that it 'grasped the self-production of human beings as a process', that it 'grasped the essence of labour and comprehended the objective [*gegenständlichen*] human beings, [the] true, because real human beings, as the result of their own labour'.[66] It was from Hegel that Marx gained a more sophisticated understanding of the transformative nature of labour conceived as the dialectical process involving subject and object which produces human worlds and history. And he came to agree (formally) with Hegel that this production process, once reconceputualised in materialist terms, must be the concern of what he would elaborate as a historical-materialist *Wissenschaft*.

Thus, in the short time (April–August) that he spent writing the *Economic-Philosophical Manuscripts of 1844*, Marx took a long intellectual journey and accomplished much. Following Feuerbach, he undertook a materialist redefinition of the subject-object relation as the 'sensuously acting' subject and the object of that activity. He extended the range of that sensuous activity by considering labour which, in turn, prompted the beginnings of more serious thought about the process of objectification, its various peculiarly human modes, and about its corporeal prerequisites. While 'reducing' human being to that which it is, namely, like all other species a form of natural being, he delineated the uniqueness of human natural being that enables it to transform nature and to produce and live 'universally'. While human labour is but one form of objectification, it is the one form whose transformative power is unique among the objectifying practices of all species, and by means of which human beings transform the natural world on such a scale as to remake it in the image of their own corporeal organisation. And the very dynamism of labour pushed Marx beyond Feuerbach's static framework and toward a critical reconsideration of the processual, historical, and anthropogenetic character of Hegel's dialectics. Yet, although that focus on labour pushed the other forms of objectification into the background of his own work, it does not mean, as I shall elaborate in the next chapter, that Marx eliminated them from a materialist conception of history.

For all that, however, if we view the *1844 Manuscripts* from the perspective of the materialist conception of history that he developed in the following year, Marx in a certain sense stood still. Taking as his analytical object 'human being' as a 'species-being' and defining its history as anthropogenetic, as the process in which this species-being produces its own nature, Marx had not yet overcome

---

66 Marx 1844 in Tucker 1978, p. 112.

the temptation to produce another speculative philosophy of history – materialist rather than idealist, but one that like Hegel's, was universal in its claims and transhistorical in its contents. Such an unqualified notion of anthropogenesis, common in speculative philosophies of history, all too easily slips into a kind of Whiggishness, that is: a view of history as the progressive unfolding of human species-being, as an ascending arrow from 'primitive' to 'true', civilised and cultivated human being. And several of Marx's comments in the *1844 Manuscripts* certainly seem to imply that he directly or indirectly treated history as the progressive humanising of both nature and human being in both quantitative and qualitative terms. Of the ascent of human being in general, for example, Marx wrote: 'Neither objectively nor subjectively is nature immediately given in a form adequate to the *human* being. And as everything natural must come to be, so the human being also has its act of becoming. History is the true natural history of human being'. And what is true of human being in general is also true of each of its attributes. Commenting on the sense organs he writes that 'The forming of the five senses is a labour of the entire history of the world down to the present. The sense caught up in crude practical need has only a restricted sense'.[67]

Such statements have two very serious consequences. First of all, it is, to say the least, exceedingly derogatory to call the finely tuned sense organs of gathering and hunting peoples 'only narrow' and 'subject to raw practical need'. And it is not at all sensical to imagine that the fine-tuning of the senses has reached its historical best in today's 'modern' world, in which the overwhelming sensory bombardment numbs the perceptual capacities of the senses. Moreover, the only kind of history that can be written on this basis is simply a situating of the object of analysis in its proper place the line of progress. Such an approach to history allows us only to measure what we have gained, but not to treasure what we have lost.[68] It is not necessary to reject the notion of anthropogenesis in the first passage, nor the beauty of the sentiment and vision in the second,

---

67 Marx 1844 in Tucker 1978, p. 89.
68 For example, what enabled Hegel to develop a unitary philosophy of history as one of ascent is that he systematically eliminated as 'contingent' everything that does not fall into his notion of history as rational and progressive. Hence his brutal comments about (mostly non-Western) peoples not included in his progressive historical panorama as not having a history and the not so subtle implications that if people without history are human, they remain somehow not fully human – primitive, uncivilised. It should also be noted that the flip-side of Whiggish speculative philosophies of history as the story of 'man' progressively making 'man' is the Romantic view of history as equally linearly, but on a trajectory of decline rather than ascent – a view that also tends toward romanticising the 'noble savage'.

in order to recognize that if taken too literally, they can impose a unilinear trajectory of progress and thus create serious problems for a historical study. And there has been far too much evidence over the last few centuries of historical writing based on a unilinear notion of anthropogenesis that has explicitly or implicitly treated the 'West' as the bearer, often also the founder, of civilisation and progress – and have thus explicitly supported or implicitly lent credence to the 'white man's burden' of conquering, dominating, and 'developing' peoples designated as 'uncivilised'.

The truth of anthropogensis lies in the fact that humans, like all other species, make their own worlds; but unlike all other species, humans build worlds that fundamentally transform and, for better or worse, 'humanise' nature. Although all species to some degree remake the world in their own image in the process of building their niches, each species' niche and the degree to which each species remakes the world is of course rather limited – in obvious contrast to the human species which has transformed virtually all parts of the world in building its own niches. As Marx put it in the *Manuscripts*, through human labour, nature is 'humanised', i.e. human worlds – whether on the scale of a gathering and hunting society or that of industrial capitalism – are constructed, and humans develop and define themselves by producing the worlds in which they live. But as our era of growing ecological crises unmistakably shows, the quantitative degree to which humans remake the world should not be simply be assumed to be qualitatively positive. Thus, before 'anthropogenesis' could become a useful category for historical theory, it would have to be divested of the unilinear progressivism generally attached to it, and deposed from its position as the directional grid superimposed on the course of history.[69] If thus divested and deposed, as Marx began to do in *The German Ideology*, the notion of anthropogenesis may be considered a guiding thread, a starting point for the study of how various groups of people make their histories and their own worlds – just as an 'arachnogenetic' approach would be the starting point for a study of how spiders make their own worlds.

In the *1844 Manuscripts*, however, and despite all of his new insights about the subject-object relation, human history, categories and methodology, Marx remained within the confines of a philosophical problematic. And though he was but a step away from a materialist conception of history, it was a rather large step. Perhaps the best measure of the *Manuscripts* is to realise that he himself did what he had considered impossible, namely: to go further than

---

69 See Chapter 4 for a discussion of some Marxist interpretations that have inadvertently come too close to this Whiggishness by treating human nature as in the process of progressively becoming.

Feuerbach in the direction of materialism, but still remain within the confines of philosophy. Criticising Feuerbach's limited materialism, Marx wrote that 'insofar as Feuerbach is a materialist, he does not consider history, and insofar as he considers history, he is not a materialist. With him, history and materialism diverge completely'.[70] This evaluation of Feuerbach, however, applies perhaps more so to Marx himself; for, in the *Manuscripts* he was both more materialist than Feuerbach in his definition of the subject-object relation, and he was becoming more historical in his Hegelian influenced commitment to anthropogenesis. But not yet able to take the next big step to history, Marx had gone further than Feuerbach 'without ceasing to be a philosopher'.[71] Nevertheless, the result of Marx's dual critical consideration was to push him beyond philosophy altogether, beyond 'the early Marx', toward what he referred to as his *Aufhebung* of philosophy and toward his materialist conception of history. Precisely because he did not rest content with the accomplishments of the *Manuscripts*, because he was dissatisfied with the point that he had reached, he, in collaboration with Engels, subjected himself to a process of 'self-clarification' that would result in the outlines of a materialist conception of history and the guidelines of a materialist *Wissenschaft* of history.

1.5   *The German Ideology* and the Foundations of a Materialist Conception of History[72]

If Marx began work on the *Manuscripts* with both feet rooted in philosophy, by the time he finished them, he had taken a crucial step toward both materialism and history. This step consisted of his redefinition of the subject-object relation from which followed a definition of objectification as bodily activity, a conceptualisation of labour as a form of objectification, and an understanding of human histories as anthropogenetic processes. Marx's focus on objectifying work as the means through which human beings transform nature and construct human worlds quickly led to the realisation that the conceptual framework of the *Manuscripts* was inadequate. He realised that the content of his materialist redefinition of subject and object as a relation of human beings interacting with nature and each other in order to satisfy their material needs

---

70   Marx 1845 in Tucker 1978, pp. 171–2.
71   Marx, 1845 in Tucker 1978, p. 166.
72   Going even further than Tucker and Megill who dismiss its importance, Terrell Carver (2013) makes the claim in the title of his article that 'The German Ideology Never Took Place'. For my response, see Appendix 1.1. 'Was there a *German Ideology*?'.

and their desires could not be contained by either a Feuerbachian materialist or Hegelian idealist framework. He began to rethink the way he had conceived the relations between objectifying subjects and the objects of their objectifying activity, to reconsider 'up from the body' the implications of his new definition of the subject-object relations, and to revise his notion of labour, no longer as a matter and measure of alienation, but as the means by which the 'real living individuals' satisfy their needs and sustain their lives. In short, he began to reconsider history not from a speculative philosophical viewpoint but from the viewpoint of real living individuals always already imbricated in a specific set of social relations, themselves framed by a 'mode of production' (a new concept introduced in *The German Ideology*). And he needed to develop a new, commensurately historical conceptual apparatus to express these ideas. This meant that any *a priori* anthropological determination of human being or a human essence, though necessary for purposes of historical orientation, could only be an abstract determination of human possibilities; it could not, however, serve as the teleological foundation of a speculative philosophy of history.

If by the end of the *Manuscripts* Marx still had one foot bogged down in philosophy, he was in motion, and his momentum would free that other foot as well. This work of planting both feet unquestionably on historical ground is what Marx together with Engels carried out in *The German Ideology* where they achieved what Marx later referred to as 'self-clarification'.[73] And though his footing was still wobbly on this new terrain, he had taken the definitive step and passed the point of no return.

For this reason, I disagree with all variations on Robert Tucker's designation of Marx's Preface to the *Critique of Political Economy* as 'the *locus classicus* of the materialist conception of history'. In keeping with this determination, Tucker initiates his anthology of Marx's with the Preface; and he reduces *The German Ideology* to simply 'a restatement, minus much of the German philosophical terminology, of the theory of history adumbrated in the manuscripts of 1844'.[74] Analytical Marxists (e.g. Gerald Cohen, William Shaw, Jon Elster) also treat the Preface as the essence of Marx's theory in the form of a collection of apodictic explanatory principles that *are* the materialist conception of history. In a different path to the same place, Allan Megill recognises *The German Ideology* as 'the most important', but also the 'lengthiest' presentation of the materialist conception of history. He therefore chooses 'to simplify matters' without, he claims, 'doing any great violence to the overall view' by focusing on the Preface

---

73   Marx, 1845 in Tucker 1978, pp. 5–6.
74   Tucker's commentary to the Preface and *The German Ideology* in Tucker 1978, p. 3, p. 146.

whose 'greater compression' makes it 'a more apt candidate for explication' and 'brings to light fissures in the historical materialist view that are not so readily visible in other, more leisurely accounts'.[75]

My contention, however, is that, regardless of the reason, when the Preface is lifted out of the context of Marx's own intellectual development and designated as the *locus classicus* of historical materialism, it is invested with an explanatory value far beyond what Marx explicitly stated – and that inevitably distorts his meaning both in the Preface and, through myopic hindsight, in *The German Ideology*. Tucker's approach lends itself to a static and reductionist reading of Marx's general comments and turns them into *the* fundamental tenets and explanatory principles of Marx's materialist conception of history thereby *creating* 'fissures' that were not there in Marx's formulation.[76] I therefore take very seriously Marx's own retrospective comments, in the Preface itself, that refer to *The German Ideology* as the work in which Engels and he 'settle[d] [their] accounts with their erstwhile philosophical conscience' and achieved the 'self-clarification' that enabled them to set out on their new path and that led to their willing abandonment of the unpublished manuscript to the 'gnawing criticism of mice'.[77] *The German Ideology* is Marx's first attempt to formulate a materialist conception of history on the basis of his materialist redefinition of the subject-object relation. The unpublished text is in dire need of editing; it is filled with false starts, repetitions, second beginnings, and with unclear, somewhat muddled, but nevertheless insightful comments, sometimes infuriatingly provocative for want of elaboration. But the positive side of that lack of editing is that we can see Marx (in the Feuerbachian section at least, most of which he wrote) realising, and struggling with, the scope of the 'breathtaking wager' he had made. It is in this text, in short, that we can read Marx thinking.[78]

---

75 Megill 2002, p. 185.
76 Viewing the writing of the 1859 Preface in historical context, which included Marx's justifiable fear of the Prussian censors who could have prevented the book's publication and distribution, Arthur Prinz has argued that Marx consciously did 'violence' to his own theory by specifically avoiding any mention of class and class struggle, and therefore that the purged discussion in the Preface cannot be considered an adequate summary of Marx's materialist conception of history. See Prinz 1969.
77 Marx 1845, Preface to the *Critique of Political Economy*, in Tucker 1978, pp. 5–6. See also Marx's letter to Karl Leske in which he wrote: 'It seemed to me very important that a work polemicizing against German philosophy and current German socialism should precede my positive construction [of an economic analysis of capitalism]' (*MEW*, Vol. 27, p. 448).
78 My thanks to Thomas Kemple for the title of his book from which I borrowed and adapted the phrase *Reading Marx Writing* (Kemple 1995).

It is therefore worth struggling with all the difficulties of an unfinished manuscript in order to get a kind of first-hand view of the complexity and profundity of Marx's materialist conception of history that is not at all conveyed by the brief prefatory summary he scribbled out in 1859. This is why I argue that the neglect of *The German Ideology* does indeed, Megill's claim notwithstanding, do 'great violence to the overall view'. This is also why I shall argue that if there is a *locus classicus* of the materialist conception of history (which is not at all to say that Marx, as he himself clearly realised, solved all of the problems that he explicitly noted and specifically addressed), then it is the Feuerbach Section of *The German Ideology*. And only against the background of the more fully developed positions in *The German Ideology* is it possible to understand how to read and evaluate the summary presentation in the Preface itself.

The conceptual indicator of Marx's qualitative break with his philosophical past is the fate of the Feuerbachian conceptual and methodological framework of the *Manuscripts*. As discussed above, the *1844 Manuscripts* were framed between the categorial binary of species-being and alienation; and Marx's task there was to expose a 'doubled' world in which the human essence or species-being was deformed in an alienated existence. The methodological consequence of that framework only required him to proceed from alienation as 'an actual fact' and to catalogue the ways in which that alienation separated people from the human 'species-essence'. After the *Manuscripts*, however, these categories lost their place of primacy in Marx's work.

The concept of species-being, so crucial to the Manuscript on Alienated Labour, disappears altogether. In the sixth of the *Theses on Feuerbach* which serve as the preface to *The German Ideology*, Marx rejected the concept of a species-being or essence. In criticising Feuerbach's abstraction from the historical process, he wrote: 'Feuerbach resolves the religious essence into the human essence. But the human essence is no abstraction inherent in each single individual. In its reality it is the ensemble of the social relations'.[79] Here Marx clearly and categorically rejected the ahistorical notion of a fixed and *a priori* human essence,[80] and he replaced it with a notion of 'real living indi-

---

79 Marx 1845, '6th Thesis on Feuerbach', in Tucker 1978, p. 145. See above, note 35, for comments on Marx's use of *Gattungswesen* in *Manuscripts* and 'menschliches Wesen' in *The German Ideology*.

80 If 'species-being' can be said to resurface in Marx's later writings, having metamorphosed into 'human nature in general', it is clear from the context that the category, though necessary, is, within the framework of a materialist conception of history, no longer sufficient to bear the theoretical weight that it did in the *1844 Manuscripts* where it served as the foundation of the entire theoretical edifice, that is: as the foundation of a materialist philosophy of history.

viduals'[81] whose lives are conditioned by the world in which they live and which they themselves produce and reproduce.[82] With this historicised perspective on human being(s), Marx had cleared the way to begin an analysis of real human beings in their concrete historical activity. This historicised perspective on human beings also forced him to rethink the causes of, and to redefine, the unhappy state in which he found them which he begins to conceptualise as 'exploitation'.[83] Accordingly, 'alienation' [Entfremdung], the other categorial pole of the *Manuscripts*, is mentioned in *The German Ideology* only in passing, and then sarcastically as a means of 'remaining comprehensible to the philosophers'.[84] Marx certainly continued to use the Feuerbachian notion of an inverted world and the category of 'alienation' in his later writings (in *Capital*, for example, in his exposure of the inverted, alienated world of capitalism in the chapter on commodity fetishism and in his critique of the debilitating and dehumanising character of the capitalist labour-process). But the category of alienation no longer held the conceptual place of honour, nor did it any longer have to bear the methodological weight that was required of it in the *Manuscripts*.

Marx's supplanting of the 'alienation' of human 'species-being' with the 'exploitation' of the 'real living individuals' was no merely nominal shift. 'Ex-

---

81 Marx 1845, in Tucker 1978, p. 155.
82 Two points need to be made about Marx's replacement of the concept of 'species-essence' with the 'ensemble of social relations'. First, the ensemble of social relations is meant in neither a deterministic nor an economically reductionist sense. The single most important element in this ensemble is, for Marx, class. But it is not the only factor nor, necessarily, the determining causal factor in a given historical event. In contrast to a Hegelian-like approach, individuals are not defined simply as manifestations of their 'class essence'. Rather, the ensemble of social relations which shape personality, consciousness, and behaviour encompasses not only the relations of production, but all social relations: education, socialisation, culture etc. (See Negt 1988, pp. 221; 227–30). The 'ensemble of social relations', then, defines the specific world in which individuals live and which structures their choices, but does not determine how they will choose. The second point is that since social relations change, so too does the character or 'nature' of human beings. This does not mean that there are no constants in human life. As Perry Anderson has argued, Marx's conception of those constants 'clearly has a biological origin, in the sense that the human physiognomic structure is that of a specific animal species [which] endows us with certain potentials, physical powers, and certain dispositions as well' (Anderson 1988, p. 334). It simply means that the specific character of human beings in a given era cannot be determined a priori, but only in reference to the ensemble of social relations.
83 I think Megill (2002, p. xx) is absolutely correct when he says that the late Marx's primary concern was exploitation. But in contrast to Megill, and as I explain in the following chapters, I consider that an expansion rather than a contraction of his field of vision.
84 Marx 1845 in Tucker 1978, p. 161.

ploitation' is not just 'alienation' by another name. The philosophical-materialist concept of alienation depicts an existing perversion of the human essence and presents the overcoming of alienation in the form of a moral 'ought' and an act of conscience: people ought to realise that they themselves are the source of the values they project onto gods and *Geister*; and the act of recognition is the act of revolution. The historical-materialist concept of exploitation, however, depicts an unequal relation among human beings through which some benefit unfairly from the labour of others, and whose overcoming requires practical political action and a revolutionary transformation of social relations. Rooted not vaguely in a generic 'history' as is alienation, but more deeply and concretely in specific socio-historical forms, the category of 'exploitation' demanded a new methodology. If the Feuerbachian methodology required Marx only to expose and describe the various dimensions of alienation, the materialist conception of history developed in *The German Ideology* required him to *explain* those dimensions and the other debilitating consequences of the capitalist labour-process as embedded in and produced by the normal functioning of that process – itself a fundamentally exploitative process.

In a way that registering the 'actual fact' of 'alienation' never did, Marx's newfound focus on 'exploitation' forced him to explain its origins in the 'mode of production' and especially the 'social relations of production' – categories quite absent from the *Manuscripts*, but derived from his materialist conception of history, and indispensable to the writing of *Capital*. The *Capital* that Marx wrote is quite literally *unthinkable* – that is: it could not have been thought – from the standpoint and with the categorial apparatus of the *Manuscripts*. Had he attempted a critique of his contemporary world with the categories of the *1844 Manuscripts*, the result would have been a much different and rather tedious book – a kind of economic version of his *Critique of Hegel's Philosophy of Right* that would tirelessly (and tiresomely for the reader) chronicle the 'actual fact' of labour alienated from human species-being under conditions of 'private property'.

Instead, as Neil Davidson put it so pointedly, what was new in *The German Ideology* was the conviction that 'the course of human development' could only be adequately explained 'on the basis of a more fundamental underlying social process – *production*'.[85] It is here, Davidson continues, that Marx introduced the category of the 'forces of production', a category with two aspects: 'One is the means of production which include nature itself, the capacity to labour, the skills brought to the process, the tools used, and the techniques with

---

85   Davidson 2012, p. 127. Following two citations in this paragraph, ibid., p. 129.

which these tools are set to work. The other is the labour process, the way in which the different means of production are combined in the act of production itself'. Although *The German Ideology* introduces production as the foundation of his materialist conception of history, it was still plagued by categorial confusion. But as Davidson argues, 'the final elaboration' of the concepts introduced there was accomplished a year later in *The Poverty of Philosophy*. Here Marx replaced the shaky category, the 'form of intercourse', with that of 'social relations', a specific form of which, namely the 'social relations of production', combines with the forces to constitute a 'mode of production'. The *Capital* that Marx wrote was made possible because he had by 1845 put both feet on historical ground and followed through in his theorising about the epistemological, methodological, and categorial consequences of that step. And the product of that theorising was the materialist conception of history whose fundamental assumptions, methodological guiding threads, categorial apparatus were first (and still incompletely) presented in *The German Ideology*.

Crucial here is that the introduction of the concept of the 'mode of production', consisting of the forces and means of production, was the categorial development that made *Capital* possible. It is moreover imperative to grasp the contours of this newly-introduced concept. For the 'mode of production' is not just a matter of the 'economy', but more akin to the Greek notion of οἰκονομία. Following his first mention of the term, he explains crucially: the 'mode of production must not be considered simply as being the reproduction of the physical existence of the individuals. Rather it is a definite form of activity of these individuals, a definite form of expressing their life, a definite *mode of life* on their part'.[86] Thus elaborated, the 'mode of production' is the 'form-determinant' (*Formbestimmung* – to import a term that Marx did not systematically deploy until the *Grundrisse*, 1857) that in-forms, gives form to, and frames not only the particular practice of labour but also, and more broadly, the 'mode of life' in a given society.[87]

Because the term 'form-determinant' is so essential, both to his materialist conception of history and to the present work, and because of the long history of reductionist and determinist misinterpretations of that conception of history, it is also imperative to determine immediately and exactly what is entailed, and what is not, by the notion of 'form-determinant'. In explaining Marx's break, his move from a teleological delineation of the stages of history grounded in 'metaphysical remnants' to a genealogical mode of analysis,

---

86 Marx 1845 in Tucker 1978, p. 150.
87 For further elaboration of the crucial (and in this book recurring) concept, *Formbestimmung* or 'form-determinant', see Appendix 1.2.

Richard Halpern perfectly captures Marx's notion of determination; writes he: 'The determinism for which [a materialist conception of history] can legitimately argue is more modest; it agrees with the etymological sense of the word as a limit on the field of the possible rather than an irresistible compulsion in any one direction'.[88] It is therefore absolutely essential, at this point and throughout this entire work, *not* to conflate this notion of *determination* understood as a framing, as a delineation of the range of possibilities and limits, with a notion of *determinism* understood as a logically necessary relation in which a given antecedent results in a given consequent, a proposition of the form 'if x, then y'. Not only would such a conflation thoroughly misrepresent Marx's notion of *Bestimmung* or determination, but it is also wholly antithetical to Marx's dialectical approach and to the logic of a materialist conception of history.

Precisely because *The German Ideology* establishes the variable modes of production as the form-determinants of modes of social life and the key to a historical-materialist understanding of social forms and their histories, it represents Marx's fundamental break with his philosophical past and the (not yet completed) foundation for his later critique of capitalism; and it can rightly be considered the work in which Marx not only attained 'self-clarification', but also accomplished his *Aufhebung* of philosophy. In keeping with their notion that *The German Ideology* is just a restatement of the *Manuscripts*, Tucker and Megill, among many others, reject the notion of a qualitative break between the *Manuscripts* and *The German Ideology*. Tucker's comment that *The German Ideology* is simply a 'restatement' of the *1844 Manuscripts* 'minus much of the German philosophical terminology' was cited above. Echoing Tucker, Megill claims that 'Marx's fabled historical materialism' was already 'sketchily present' in the *Manuscripts* and only 'articulated in detail in the *German Ideology*'. He insists further that the *Manuscripts* 'laid the basis for the entirety of Marx's sub-

---

88   Halpern 1991, p. 11. The bracketed [a materialist conception of history] is my replacement of Halpern's reference to 'Marxism', some strands of which were only too willing to deploy a much stronger, reductionist notion of determination.

Marx most often used 'form-determinant' in the *Grundrisse* and *Capital*, when discussing the relations between the general character of products of labour as 'use-values', and in their particular capitalist form as commodities bearing exchange-value. In such cases, he defined the exchange-value as 'form-determinant', as that which determines the particular socio-historical form assumed by products of labour or use-values within the capitalist mode of production and exchange. But if throughout this work I use 'form-determinant' somewhat more broadly than Marx typically did, my uses are, I think, in keeping with his meaning as that which gives form by setting the range and limits of the possible in a particular context (see also Chapter 3).

sequent intellectual career', and that Marx 'never abandoned his conclusions of that year'. These claims all too cavalierly neglect Marx's own statement that he attained 'self-clarification' with the *Aufhebung* of philosophy that he effected in *The German Ideology* – a claim that Megill dismisses as needing 'no extended discussion'. Convinced that there is no qualitative shift between 1844 and 1845, Megill with the same ease waves off Althusser's notion of an epistemological break by simply asserting that Althusser's claim is 'widely recognized' to be 'vastly overstated'.[89]

I would argue, however, that although there is a wager in the *Manuscripts*, it is not the 'breathtaking' one that Eagleton described. It is rather the one that is intimated in the last manuscript where Marx developed a renewed appreciation for Hegel's historical sense – one that concerns only the content and would consist in giving materialist content to Hegel's philosophy. Such a wager, however, would have been a philosophical-materialist one based on a simple materialist inversion of Hegel, on turning Hegel right-side up and standing him on his feet. This is in essence the wager attributed to Marx by all those interpretations which insist that Marx's was a speculative philosophy of history that traced the Whiggish evolution of freedom. Though as monumental as Hegel's, such a philosophical wager would be nowhere near as breathtaking as the historical-materialist bet that Marx made in *The German Ideology* and which Eagleton described so well. For Marx's materialist conception of history has radical epistemological consequences for a historical *Wissenschaft* and for the human sciences in general, most of which are raised and some of which are solved in *The German Ideology*, but others remained the source of over two decades of puzzlement before Marx could solve them and publish *Capital*.

Therefore, and though I rather fundamentally disagree with his depiction of its contents, I fully agree with Althusser that *The German Ideology* represents a qualitative break in Marx's thought, and one so fundamental that it is rightly called it an 'epistemological break'. The difference is that whereas Althusser sees this break in terms of a rejection of humanist philosophy for materialist philosophy, I see it as a rejection of philosophy *'überhaupt'* for a materialist conception of history and a historical-materialist *Wissenschaft*. The detailed

---

89   Megill 2002, p. 39, p. 134, p. 67, p. 159. I agree with Althusser who insisted that there was an 'epistemological break' in Marx's development and also with his designation of *The German Ideology* as the site of the break. But I have a very different take on the nature and implications of that break. I elaborate my view of the break throughout Part 1, but especially in Part 3. For further discussion of Althusser's position and of two more recent reflections on questions of continuity and change in Marx's intellectual development, see Appendix 1.3.

elaboration of the 'epistemological break' consisting of a new materialist conception of *history* and new guidelines for a materialist *Wissenschaft* of history are the concerns of the following two chapters.

CHAPTER 2

From the First Corporeal Fact of Human Being to the Moments of History: Corporeality, Modes of Objectification, and Ways of Worldmaking

2.1 Marx's Corporeal Turn and the Genesis of a Materialist Conception of History

In the first pages of *The German Ideology* Marx states his historical premises that, he insists, 'are not arbitrary ones, not dogmas, but real premises' which can be 'established empirically' and from which one 'can only abstract in the imagination'.[1] Separating his own position from the narrowly mental view of *Homo sapiens* characteristic of the 'German ideologues', Marx explains that 'the premises from which we begin ... are the real individuals, their activity and the material conditions under which they live, both those which they find already existing and those produced by their own activity'. Emphasising in effect that we must not neglect what everyone knows in principle, he repeats that 'the first premise of all human history is naturally the existence of living human individuals'. In order to take seriously the 'existence of *living* human individuals', it is necessary pursue all the implications of the 'first fact' of human history, to understand, 'the corporeal organisation of these individuals and their consequent relation to the rest of nature'.[2]

Though Marx had insightfully, if unsystematically, discussed dimensions of corporeality in the *Manuscripts*, this positing of 'human corporeal organisation' as the 'first fact' for historical theory and writing marks a radical corporeal turn. As he put it in the following paragraph: 'One can differentiate human beings from [other] animals through consciousness, through religion, through whatever else one wants [Marx's own undertaking in the *Manuscripts*]. [Human beings] themselves begin to differentiate themselves from animals as soon as they begin to produce their means of life, a step that is conditioned [*bedingt*] through their bodily organisation'.[3]

---

1 All citations in this and next paragraph, Marx 1845 in Tucker 1978, pp. 149–50. Here I have combined two of Marx sentences into one and altered slightly their sequence.
2 The English translation of '*körperliche*' as 'physical' rather than 'corporeal' is misleadingly vague. See Marx 1845 in Tucker 1978, p. 149.
3 Marx 1845 in Tucker 1978, p. 150. I added '[other]' to this sentence because it more accurately

It is first worth noting a grammatical and a terminological shift that occur here. Whereas in the *Manuscripts* Marx's differentiation of humans from other animal species takes place in the passive voice as it were, as a description of 'an actual biological fact', he now formulated this differentiation in the active voice. Though we should perhaps not make too much of this grammatical shift, it is nevertheless appropriate that in place of the analytical distinction between humans and other species and in place of the *a priori* discussion of a species-being or essence found in the *Manuscripts*, the emphasis here is on observing the historical process by which the human species comes to distinguish itself from other species. And though we also should not make too much of another terminological shift, it is appropriate that whereas in the *Manuscripts* he always used the singular *'der Mensch'* which fit his notion of species-being, he now uses the plural, *'die Menschen'* when speaking of the 'real, living individuals' who make their own history.

More importantly, by grasping the corporeal roots of human history, Marx raised the question not just of the difference between human beings and other animal species, but also of the genesis of that difference, i.e. the evolutionary perspective on how humans, a part of nature, separate themselves from other natural species through the unique character of their activity. In so doing, he situated history, materialistically conceived, in the greater scheme of human 'natural history', that is the evolutionary history of *Homo sapiens*. This designation of 'human corporeal organisation' as the starting point of his materialist conception of history completed Marx's rethinking of the subject-object relation and of the contents of history that was the crucial first step in his *Aufhebung* of the philosophy. In contrast to the philosophical tradition he inherited, a tradition that treated human history as the work of the human mind, and therefore as a history completely discontinuous with, and of a completely different order from, 'natural history', Marx's establishment of the corporeal premises of history gave *avant la lettre* a decidedly Darwinian form to his determinations of human being. As noted above in the Introduction, the point at which Darwin's and Marx's theories converge is precisely 'human corporeal organisation' which is not only the 'first fact' for human history, but the 'last fact' as it were of human evolutionary history, that is in paleoanthropological terms, the emergence of 'anatomically modern' *Homo sapiens*. 'Human corporeal organisation' is thus the node from which one can look 'backward'

---

captures the basic premise of a corporeally-grounded materialist conception of history. For, by having posited human 'corporeal organisation' as the 'first fact' of human history, Marx situated the human animal as one among other animal species that are differentiated from one another on the basis of their corporeal organisation.

to the evolutionary process that produced it, and 'forward' toward the histories whose production it made possible.

No sooner had Marx established human corporeal organisation as the 'first fact' of history and indicated some of its aspects than did he immediately state that he 'naturally' could not expand on these matters here. The missing elaboration of this fact could easily lead to the conclusion that he used it as only a rhetorical ploy intended to score polemical points against 'German ideology'. Such a conclusion is seemingly validated by Marx's next sentence in which he seems to back away from this 'first fact': 'Of course, we cannot here go either into the actual physical make-up of human beings, or into the natural conditions in which man finds himself – geological orohydrographical, climatic and so on'.[4] It would, however, be too hasty to conclude that he did not intend it seriously. For in the next, and final, line of this paragraph, Marx reiterated the foundational importance of this 'first fact' and its consequences for a historical *Wissenschaft*: '*The writing of history* must always set out from these natural bases and their modification in the course of history through the action of human beings' (my emphasis).[5] To broaden somewhat Fredric Jameson's apt description, 'Marx's materialism is less a philosophical position than a commitment to ... living and [objectifying] bod[ies]'.[6] And his historical-materialist *Wissenschaft* is an open-ended commitment to writing the histories of, and up from, those living and objectifying bodies in their existentially necessary relation to the natural worlds they inhabit.

Nevertheless, Marx's failure to follow up on the 'physical make-up' of human beings and the 'natural conditions' in which they find themselves rendered his theory vulnerable to two kinds of charges and the bias of neglect. One charge is that levied by Jürgen Habermas who felt that Marx was on the right track with his claim that human history was an extension of human evolutionary history, but takes him to task for not having shown *how* the two are related, or, to borrow again Mayr's formulation, for not having shown how to write history after Darwin. The other charge results from the fact that Marx's unelaborated comments about the body, followed immediately by a lengthy discussion of labour for the satisfaction of bodily needs, seem to imply that he treated the body far too narrowly as only a needy and labouring body. Finally, Marx's seeming

---

4 Marx 1845 in Tucker 1978, pp. 149–50.
5 Marx 1845 in Tucker 1978, p. 150.
6 Jameson 2014, p. 111. Jameson writes: 'Marx's materialism is less a philosophical position that a commitment to the living and working body'. For reasons explained in this and the following chapter, I argue that Marx's broad notion of 'objectification' includes, but is not limited to work or productive labour. Hence my alteration of Jameson's statement.

neglect of human corporeal organisation influenced even sympathetic writers such as Norman Geras and John McMurtry who, in seeking to elaborate Marx's notion of 'human nature', only acknowledged its corporeal dimension with a passing nod; and neither elaborated this dimension beyond its being the locus of bodily needs (McMurtry explicitly justified his own 'reticence' with an appeal to Marx's).[7] In this way the corporeal foundation of a materialist conception of history became relegated to the status of a 'simple prerequisite'. Neglected thereby too were Marx's quiet incorporation of this 'first fact' of 'human corporeal organisation' into the crucial categories that appear on the first page and in the first chapter of *Capital* (e.g. use-value and concrete labour), as well as his use of corporeal norms to measure the depth of capitalist immiseration (see Part 4). To counter these charges, it is necessary here to look more closely at the reasons why Marx did not feel it necessary in *The German Ideology* to consider these natural foundations of human history.

Marx's two immediate concerns in *The German Ideology* render his practical decision not to follow through with a comprehensive delineation of a materialist science of history understandable, if regrettable. After the initial Feuerbach chapter with its profound reflections on a materialist conception of history and its consequences, Marx's purpose in *The German Ideology* was to 'settle accounts' with his philosophical contemporaries (Max Stirner and Bruno Bauer among others) which produced a long, often tedious tirade, though not completely devoid of insight. Accordingly, and unfortunately, he only delved deeply enough into his corporeally-rooted materialist conception of history as was necessary to provide an alternative way of looking at history. And his other increasingly pressing concern was, as he put it in the well-known eleventh thesis on Feuerbach, not just to interpret the world, as had the philosophers, but to change it. In *The German Ideology*, this meant the sketching of a theoretical basis that would ultimately enable him to decipher and explain the exploitative character of the capitalist mode of production. In order to grasp the structural and functional logic of the capitalist valorisation process, he needed economic categories rooted in, and incorporating, human corporeal organisation and the necessary relation between human beings and nature.

In addition to these purely practical reasons, there is a still practical, but, more importantly, theoretically legitimate reason not to have gone into great detail in discussing the corporeal and natural circumstances. As Marx noted, it is 'the writing of history' that must take these factors into account. That is, the concrete historical analysis of a specific society in a specific place and at a

---

[7] See Geras 1983 and McMurtry 1978. See Chapter 4 below for further discussion of their positions.

specific point in socio-historical time is obliged to address the geographically specific natural conditions (geology, climate, etc.); and these factors as well as the relevant aspects of human corporeal organisation would also make themselves felt in the analysis of each historically specific mode of production, in the particular labour-processes, the particular system of needs and the particular contents of the productive process of each geographically situated society. Marx could assume, in short, that the historically relevant data from the natural sciences – data about climate, geology, bodily needs, geo-culturally specific wants, etc. – would automatically insert themselves into a concrete historical-materialist study of each geo-historically specific socio-economic form. For these reasons he was justified in not going into concrete detail on corporeal form and natural preconditions. Nevertheless, he could have elaborated more fully, even on this abstract level, the various dimensions of corporeal organisation and natural preconditions to which he alluded; and he could have specified precisely why he 'naturally' did not feel obliged to address them at that point. Had he done so, it could have prevented a great deal of misunderstanding of his project. It might also have forced him to explain the necessity of both, and the relation between, the abstraction of theory and historical writing which, as I shall show in the following, is certainly integral to the position propounded in *The German Ideology*. Finally, it also might have forced him to make explicit the implications of these factors for the specificity of cultural forms which are certainly not free-floating and arbitrary, but intimately related to geographical space, historical time, and social practice.

2.2   The Moments of History

Having established 'human corporeal organisation' as the first premise of history and the first fact for historical theory, and labour as the crucial factor in the production of human worlds and history, Marx then jumped the gun, as it were, and made a logical, but nevertheless false start. He immediately proceeded to take stock of history thus conceived, to differentiate the various historical forms of property and of the division of labour. He then concluded this section by reiterating his critique of philosophy's 'nihilism' in the course of which he provided a brief yet compact outline of his own methodological assumptions. There are several categorial problems with this sketch. But my concern here is that though it is a perfectly logical next step following the presentation of the basic premises of a conception of history, the problem is that Marx had not yet finished establishing his premises, which he then takes up again following the methodological discussion. The result is not only sequential disorder, but also (and not unlike the two-step in the Biblical creation narrative) a somewhat confusing historical-materialist version of a dual genesis. Here I shall neglect the sketch of the forms of property and division of labour (which Marx himself, in the chapter on 'Pre-Capitalist Economic Forms' in the *Grundrisse*, fundamentally reworked – and in so doing dispensed with the atavistic Whiggishness of his discussion of property forms in *The German Ideology*; see below); and I shall address instead Marx's self-interrupted discussion of the corporeal premises of history.

Linking his renewed elaboration of the premises of history to his initial concern, Marx repeated that, in contrast to the German philosophers who are 'devoid of premises', he began his historical reflection with the 'real premises' of 'all human existence'. He then proceeded to delineate what he called the 'moments' of human existence or human life-activity, the discussion of which requires two preliminary comments.[8] First of all, it is crucial that these 'moments' *not* be understood chronologically as successive moments in a linear sequence. When understood chronologically, as is too often the case, the result is a mirror theory of consciousness, a 'mechanistic deformation of the base-superstructure relation',[9] and an economically reductionist, linear stage-theory of history. Rather, as Marx explicitly stated, these 'moments' are 'not to be understood as [...] different stages' but as different 'sides' of human life-activity, as constitutive elements of human being-in-the-world. Graphically helpful in this regard is Walter Benjamin's notion of a 'constellation', varying in concrete form, but always and necessarily consisting of these same 'moments'. The second preliminary comment is that I intend to rewrite Marx's discussion which, though somewhat confusing in enumeration, treats five such moments of history. In discussing these five moments, I shall explain why I am reducing their number to three which correspond to the three modes of objectification that follow from them.

'The first premise of human existence and therefore of all history', Marx wrote, is 'that people must be in a position to live in order to be able "make history". But life involves before everything else eating and drinking, a habitation, clothing, and many other things'.[10] To satisfy this premise is to satisfy the material needs determined by human 'corporeal organisation'. Having already observed that humans distinguish themselves from other animals once they begin to produce their own lives, he consequently drew the conclusion that

---

8   Marx 1845 in Tucker 1978, p. 155, p. 157.
9   Brüggemann 1973, p. 82.
10 All citations in this and the following paragraphs discussing the 'moments' of human life-activity from Marx 1845 in Tucker 1978, pp. 156–8.

'the production of the means to satisfy these needs' is 'the first historical act'. Accordingly, 'the first step of any conception of history' must be 'to observe this fundamental fact in all its significance and all its implications and to accord it its due importance'.

Giving full due to this seemingly trivial, but ever so true proposition that the satisfaction of bodily needs is necessary for survival, without which there would be no history, has not proven easy. Examples of familiarity breeding what Stephen Jay Gould called 'the insidious bias of neglect' are legion precisely when it comes to the body which 'everyone knows about in principle', and which for that reason is generally treated as a simple prerequisite for the 'real' work of analysing cultural constructions and/or culturally specific ways of disciplining of the body. There have, for example, been countless theoretical variations on the theme that 'man' does not live by bread alone – which have served as the justification for neglecting the obvious fact (and its far-reaching consequences) that humans certainly do not live without bread. The different cultural meanings derived from the fact that some eat rye bread, some wheat, and others white bread, some with seeds, some without, some leavened, some not, or that some live in houses of stone, others in houses of wood, ice, grass, or glass, are very interesting and very important questions. But they are not the only interesting, nor, *if* one were forced to choose, are they collectively the single most important question. For the bottom line is that everybody must eat something sometime, keep their body temperature normal, etc. – and it must be added, the questions of how they obtain what they eat, how they shelter and clothe themselves are not at all immaterial to the forms and content of cultural sign systems.

This premise thus acquires biological depth and methodological import when we inquire into what it entails. When Marx refered to these needs as eating, drinking, abode, clothes, and 'many other things', these are shorthand forms of saying that the body needs a certain number of calories to reproduce its cells, a certain amount of liquid to prevent dehydration, a certain amount of shelter to maintain its temperature within a fairly narrow range. Under 'still much else' we might include the equally obvious bodily needs for a certain amount of oxygen, rest and sleep, no doubt too for a certain amount of exercise. As I shall argue in Parts 3 and 4, a historical-materialist historiography not only requires that questions concerning the socio-cultural specificity of needs and their satisfaction be addressed, but also provides the means with which to address them. Here, however, we remain on a higher, species-level of abstraction and it is not yet necessary to address that level of concreteness.

Marx's next step, which I consider out of place, is to consider the dynamic of needs and the production of means to satisfy them as the dynamic force of historical change. He explained that 'the satisfaction of the first need (the action of satisfying, and the instrument of satisfaction which has been acquired) leads to new needs'. He then designated this 'production of new needs' as 'the first historical act'. Aside from the confusion that arises from this second designation of 'the first historical act', there is another source of confusion that arises from the placement of this statement. While this statement does follow (albeit not necessarily – human needs had remained relatively static over millennia) from the first historical premise about the existence of really-living human beings, it pertains rather to the nature and logic of historical *change* – and therefore does not belong in a discussion of those foundational premises or 'moments' of human *existence*. This dynamic dialectic of needs and technology is not a premise of history or a necessary 'moment' of human life-activity, but a consequence of it – and its misplaced presence here, in a formulation with intimations of inevitability, lends credence to economic-determinist interpretations of historical materialism.[11] But its status as an essential 'moment' of history is refuted not least by the fact that gathering and hunting peoples not subject to conquest by other peoples possessing superior technology and weaponry had been able to maintain their way of life (basic needs and rudimentary technology) for millennia, some into the present. I shall therefore exclude this dialectic of needs and technology from the 'moments of history' and consider it below after having completed discussion of the other 'moments' which is, in my view, a more appropriate place for discussing this question.

The third relation that Marx addressed is a double relation that he counts as two moments. That is, that 'human beings, who daily remake their own life, begin to make other people, to propagate their own kind: the relation between man and woman, parents and children, the family'.[12] The family, however, is not just a biological entity. It is 'in the beginning the only social relationship'[13] –

---

[11] This point appears to lend credence to those who want to view Marx as a technological determinist. Marx's purpose, however, was not to establish a law of necessary technological development and social evolution; rather he was simply delivering a materialist explanation of the impetus for technological development and, consequently, social evolution. As will be shown in Chapter 3, this comment is only a general (and abstract) statement for purposes of orientation, not as an iron law of historical change. This notion of a(n irregular) dialectic of needs, production, new needs, etc. can very easily be read as the basis of a technologically determinist theory of history as did, for example, Gerald Cohen in *Karl Marx's Theory of History: A Defense* (Cohen 1978). Since one purpose of this entire book is to show that this is not the case, I will simply note my disagreement and let my reasons appear in the course of the argument, most notably in the discussion in Chapter 3 of the well-known chapter in the *Grundrisse* on pre-capitalist economic forms.

[12] Marx 1845 in Tucker 1978, p. 156.

[13] Ibid.

whence it follows that 'the production of life, both of one's own in labour and of fresh life in procreation, now appears as a double relationship: on the one hand as a natural, on the other as a social relationship'.[14] With this analysis of the socio-economic function of the family and of human beings as necessarily social beings linked through both material production and biological reproduction, Marx broke decisively with classical liberalism's 'Robinsoniad' view of human beings as atomised, isolated individuals in a state of nature who then form society. Human beings are always already social beings and the natural, biological act of reproduction is also always already a social act that reproduces the society by perpetuating its population. And because politics, whether institutionalised or not, is essentially the ordering of social relations among a population, I would include it in this moment as well.[15] For these reasons, and though Marx counted this double relation as two moments, I prefer to restructure this moment of human existence using the generic category of social relations whose various dimensions include the social relations of material production, the social relations of biological reproduction, and the social relations of power.[16]

Before embarking on his discussion of the last moment, that of consciousness and language, Marx summarised his comments about social and biological reproduction by pointing out what he feels is immediately obvious, namely that 'a materialist connection [*Zusammenhang*] exists among people which is structured or conditioned [*bedingt*] by their needs and by the mode of production and is as old as people themselves – a connection that ever assumes new forms and thus presents a "history" *even without* the existence of some political or religious nonsense that additionally holds people together'.[17] In order to avoid misinterpreting this statement as a reductionist relation between the material base and political/cultural superstructure, it is necessary to recognise its counterfactual nature. Here Marx simply insisted that the modes in which the human animal satisfies its needs and reproduces itself are social, that the material basis of human life, rooted in human corporeal organisa-

---

14 Marx 1845 in Tucker 1978, p. 157.
15 Hegel notwithstanding, though there are peoples without states, it is doubtful that there are any without politics, without the *nomos* or ordering of πόλις or social relations See Clastres 1989.
16 After he finished his discussion of what he initially called the 'third circumstance', Marx paused before addressing the question of consciousness that he will address, as he notes, only after he had 'already considered four moments, four sides of the primary historical relations' (Marx 1845 in Tucker 1978, pp. 157–8) – which indicates that he has counted this double relationship as two moments, thus making 'consciousness' the fifth moment.
17 Marx 1845 in Tucker 1978, p. 157; translation altered.

tion, has a material basis that would mandate human social relations, even if there *were* no language and cultural forms, even without what he calls (human) consciousness – as was the case, according to paleoanthropologists, with the pre-linguistic yet very socially producing *Homo habilis* and *Homo erectus*. Having made that necessary point, Marx then proceeded to analyse the moment of consciousness – but by no means as an afterthought.

The particular wording of Marx's introduction of the moment of consciousness seems to treat it as a chronological moment: 'only now', as he introduces his statement, 'after having considered four moments, four sides of the primary historical relationships, do we find that [people] also have "consciousness"'. The temporal designation, 'only now', is however a comment *only* on the order of discovery. It is by no means a statement about causal primacy that would deny consciousness its status as a constitutive moment and reduce it to epiphenomenal status. Marx's point here was simply to establish, against traditional philosophy, that human consciousness is not disembodied and free-floating, rather: 'from the start, mind, (*Geist*) is afflicted with the curse of being "burdened" with matter, which here makes its appearance in the form of agitated layers of air, tones, in short, as language'.[18] The allusion here to the materiality of language and the bodily instruments required to agitate those layers of air to form words, in short, to language as a mode of objectification, will be addressed in detail in the next section. Here I want to focus specifically on what he had to say about consciousness and forms of thought.

Not only is language dependent on a corporeal organisation capable of making meaningful agitations in layers of air, but the contents of language that, for Marx, make up the forms of consciousness, derive from social interaction: 'Language is as old as consciousness – language *is* practical real consciousness that exists for other human beings and therefore also for me. And language, like consciousness, originates in the need, the necessity, for interaction with other human beings. ... Consciousness is thus from the very beginning a social product and remains so as long as human beings exist'.[19] Just as mind is not pure and free-floating, but firmly rooted in corporeal organisation, so

---

18   This and following citation, Marx 1845 in Tucker 1978, p. 158; translation altered.
19   Marx 1845 in Tucker 1978, p. 158. Following citation ibid., 154. I have altered the translation in the *Marx-Engels Reader*. There *das bewußte Sein* is translated 'conscious existence' which, while not wrong, severs the link between 'conscious being' and 'consciousness' that is explicit in the German wording that describes '*Das Bewußtsein*' as '*das bewußte Sein*'. The entire sentence in the original is: '*Das Bewußtsein kann nie etwas Andres sein als das bewußte Sein, und das Sein der Menschen ist ihr wirklicher Lebensprozess*'. In a similar formulation referring to '*the discreteness yet inclusiveness of the individual and the social*', Henri Lefebvre writes: 'This unity is the foundation of all society: a society is made up of

too are the forms of consciousness rooted in the historically specific experience of individuals. And as he put it a few pages earlier while describing the contents of consciousness: 'Consciousness can never be anything else than conscious existence'. The German wording makes even more explicit the link between consciousness (*das Bewußtsein*) and conscious being [*das bewußte Sein*] as consciousness of one's being. And that 'being', as Marx continued, is one's 'actual life-process'. The 'life-process' of individuals means the totality of their life-activity whose moments are the aforementioned. The primary (but by no means the exclusive) factor structuring social form and therewith a given individual's life-activity and therewith, in turn, his/her consciousness of, outlook on, the world is that individual's place in social geography, in the social division of labour. But 'life-activity' refers to all the moments, the totality of experience, of all that pertains to and is included in the 'moments of history'. Whereas idealist philosophy insists that 'consciousness determines life' and accordingly takes consciousness as itself 'the living individual', Marx, having insisted that life determines the forms of consciousness, began with 'the real living individuals and treat[ed] consciousness as *their* consciousness'.[20]

The rather profound epistemological consequences of this historical-materialist perspective on the forms and contents of consciousness for intellectual labour or *Wissenschaft* will be addressed in the next chapter. Here, however, only two summary points need be made about the forms of consciousness and their linguistic expressions. First, as indicated by the reference to language as 'agitated layers of air' and by the implication that experience derives from a dialectic of corporeally-based, socially mediated needs and the corporeally-based, socially mediated capacities to satisfy those needs, Marx saw consciousness and language as inescapably burdened with 'body matters' (though in a sense rather different from Judith Butler's use of the phrase; see Chapter 4). Secondly, the forms and contents of consciousness are the conscious expressions of socially-constituted individual experience, itself structured fundamentally by modes of production and social reproduction within which those individuals satisfy their corporeally-based needs and desires, and which are fundamentally rooted in site-specific interactions with the natural world. This 'conscious-being' or 'life-process' consisting of the dual interaction of individuals among themselves and with nature provides the contents of, in-forms, consciousness. Thus, consciousness and language as its 'practical expression' are not at all epiphenomenal afterthoughts, but rather essential moments of history that, like

---

individuals, and the individual is a social being, in and by the content of his life and the form of his consciousness' (Lefebvre 2009, p. 72).

20   Marx 1845 in Tucker 1978, p. 155.

the other two moments, are both constituted through and constitutive of 'the real life-process', the 'mode of life', of human beings as social beings.

In this brief discussion of the moments of history, Marx began to elaborate history 'up from human corporeal organisation' and managed to sketch only the broadest outlines of a materialist conception of history. As mentioned above, he (and we) would have been much better served had he sustained this reflection on history throughout the entire *German Ideology*. As also mentioned above, though objectification is in my view the fundamental category of a materialist conception of history, it hardly makes an appearance in *The German Ideology* where Marx laid the foundation of his materialist conception of history. This is something he might well have addressed there had he not gotten involved in long-winded verbal battles with his contemporaries. Thus, what I intend to do here might been seen as developing Marx's reflections on the corporeal roots of history in the Feuerbach section of *The German Ideology*; and I will do so by establishing and elaborating the links between the moments of history and what I will call 'modes of objectification'.

2.3   Modes of Objectification and the Artefactual Contents of Human Worlds

2.3.1   *Introductory Considerations*

In the previous section I attempted to bring a bit of order to Marx's presentation of the moments of human being and history by subjecting it to a historical-materialist measure of consistency. The consequence was to reduce what Marx presented as five moments to three, namely: the 'economic' production of material goods; the 'social' production of relations among people, both of a given generation as well as over succeeding generations; and the 'cultural' production of the semiotic forms and contents that make up the 'materiality' of consciousness. My larger purpose in bringing consistency to this discussion of the moments of history, however, is to use it as a framework to bring categorial order to Marx's many, often scattered but always insightful comments about the most varied activities which he subsumed under the category of objectification. In the previous chapter I mentioned briefly the categorial order that can be gleaned from a consideration of Marx's unsystematic comments about various kinds of objectification, namely that they could be subsumed under three 'modes of objectification:' material production, semiotic production, and social production. And these three 'modes of objectification' correspond to what Marx delineated as the three moments of human being and human activity: the production of material artefacts, the production of semiotic artefacts (the production of language, symbolic forms, knowledge, and of sensual apprehensions); and the production of social artefacts, ranging from the public (politics as the institutionalisation and 'normativising' of social relations) to the personal (love, friendship). The elaboration of these modes of objectification as the activities required by the moments of history, and through which human beings build their own worlds and make their own histories, is the task of this section.[21] But first, a few comments on terminology, specifically on my usage of 'artefact' and then on the terms 'material', 'social', and 'semiotic' that I use to designate the three distinct modes of objectification and the kind of artefacts produced by each mode.

Etymologically, 'artefact' derives from the Latin combination of *ars*, comparable to the Greek τέχνη, meaning art or skill, and *factus*, the past participle of *facere* meaning 'to make'. An artefact is thus something made by human art and skill. In contemporary everyday speech, however, 'artefact' is seldom used or understood to signify 'made-objects' in general. The most commonly understood meaning of 'artefact' is rather archaeological, more specifically: paleoarchaeological. The term conjures up images of relics and ruins, shards and shattered remnants of a 'dead' way of life. When we encounter artefacts in museums, most of us will marvel at them, at their beauty, at the craft that overcame the rudimentary technological conditions – and perhaps even find them almost sublime as traces of worlds that, though themselves all too human, are all too foreign to us. Unless our ears have been attuned to their speech and our mind can comprehend their very corporeal language, artefacts are mute. And

---

21 This parallelism between what I have called the three moments of history and the three modes of objectification helps to explain a noticeable absence that seemingly calls into question my claim that 'objectification' is the fundamental category of a materialist conception of history. For if it is such a fundamental category, one must wonder why it appears in *The German Ideology* which, I have claimed, lays the most complete (though still sketchy) foundation of a materialist conception of history scarcely more often than 'species-being' and 'alienation'. The reason is that in elaborating historical theory, Marx only had to ascertain the moments of history. It certainly would have been most helpful, as a means of forestalling economically reductionist interpretations of his materialist conception of history, had he also elaborated the modes of activity, the modes of objectification, required by those moments. His failure to do so led to strange critiques by Heller, Markus, etc. who set up an opposition between a paradigm based in production and one based in work and objectification. In this respect his allusion, after discussing the first moment of satisfying needs, to the making of tools to satisfy those needs and thus produce new needs as what he in my view mistakenly refers to as a second moment is confusing, because here he goes beyond the moment of satisfaction of needs to at least hint at the objectifying activity required by that moment – something he did not do with the other moments and which lends itself to an economic-determinist dialectic of needs and technology as in the analytical Marxists Jon Elster, William H. Shaw and G.A. Cohen.

the hushed tones in museums might well be as much a result of ignorance as of reverence. The brief descriptions provided by the museum offer an inkling of understanding of the displayed artefacts, thus giving us a modicum of comfort. Those descriptive tags placed in their proximity tell us in effect that the artefacts are signs of life that once was and have entire life-stories to tell, autobiographies to narrate.

What I propose is to expand the notion of what constitutes an artefact, to 'liberate' the term 'artefact' from museums and restore to it its broader meaning as a 'made-object'. For, from a historical-materialist viewpoint, *all* made-objects are artefacts; like those in museums, all made-objects are signs of life and have entire have entire life-stories to tell, autobiographies to narrate, biographies to be written. A historical-materialist approach to artefacts, then, would do well to emulate archaeologists who know how to unlock the open secrets of artefacts and reconstruct the lives that they signify, who know how to 'make silent stones speak' and tell their stories.[22] To develop a means of unlocking the histories of those artefacts and reading their open secrets, that is, to develop the guiding threads of what I call a 'corporeal semiotics', will be the specific task of Chapter 10. But crucial to that corporeal semiotics is the understanding of the modes of objectification presented in the following.

As made-objects, artefacts presuppose the very corporeal activity of making, of producing something that, as Ferruccio Rossi-Landi put it, 'does not exist "in nature", and that for its existence requires (or has required) intervention by [human beings]'.[23] This process is of course what Marx meant by objectification. I suggested above that Marx's notion of objectification is broad enough to encompass all modes of making from material making, to social making, to semiotic making. This suggestion must be elaborated in detail, and that is the purpose of this section. And just as I shall extend the concept of objectification to cover material, social and semiotic making, I shall extend the concept of the 'artefact' to cover the products of those modes of making, to include not only material, but also social and semiotic artefacts.

This set of categories is certainly not without problems or fuzziness. One question that immediately arises is whether semiotic objects and social, especially personal relations, can meaningfully be called artefacts and products of

---

22   The phrase is borrowed from Schick and Toth (1993) who make 'silent stones speak' (the title of their book) in order to trace 'Human Evolution and the Dawn of Technology' (their subtitle). But the idea of making the relic speak aptly describes the archaeological undertaking regardless of the kind of artefact.

23   Rossi-Landi 1983, p. 120. Following citation in this paragraph, ibid., p. 127.

'objectification'. This question is best addressed in the appropriate sections below – although I should note, here, however, that what Rossi-Landi says of recognising the homology between language and labour holds too for referring to linguistic signs and social relations as artefacts: the oddness has 'a methodological and demystifying power'. The more immediate problem of fuzziness to be addressed here can best be formulated in terms of the questions that my categorisation raises: is the categorial distinction between 'material', 'social', and 'semiotic', modes of objectification and kinds of artefacts a valid one? Are not material objects also bearers of meaning? And are not semiotic objects also material? Is not, as Marx clearly understood, and as postmodern theorists have constantly and correctly insisted, materiality also an attribute of the sign? Are not material and semiotic artefacts also social artefacts? And are not social artefacts also material and semiotic?

The first thing to note here, however, is that affirmative answers to those questions are not fatal to this categorisation. Of course, material objects bear meaning – for the mind and, we must not forget, for the body as well. As Terry Eagleton correctly states, because the human labour that produces material objects 'works nature up into human meaning'; labour is 'a signifying activity'.[24] And materiality is of course an attribute of semiotic objects. Yet, one need not deny the materiality of signs in order to maintain a distinction between material and semiotic objects. Granted, cultural proscriptions can and often do carry such material force that a starving person might reject nourishment from the tabooed object. Yet it is nevertheless true that a starving person, for example, differentiates immediately between the materiality of food and the materiality of the signifier 'food'. The materiality of the food that goes into the mouth and nourishes the body is of a rather different kind from the materiality of the agitated layers of air that come out of the mouth in the form of those little noises we call words. And as long as the different modes of materiality between, say, the signifier 'food' and actual food that is edible and nourishing are kept in mind, then the validity of this categorial differentiation between 'material' and 'semiotic' objects can, I think, be sustained.

'To sum up', with Rossi-Landi, 'let us say that both linguistic artefacts and what we call here "material" artefacts are completely material'.[25] Insisting on the validity of these albeit somewhat fuzzy categories, Rossi-Landi continues: 'If, bearing these warnings in mind, we draw a distinction between (simply)

---

24   Eagleton 2011, p. 232.
25   Rossi-Landi 1983, p. 123. Following citations in this paragraph, ibid. For my purposes, of course, linguistic artefacts are one form of semiotic artefacts, and I contend that Rossi-Landi's comments hold as well for all semiotic artefacts.

linguistic artefacts and (simply) material artefacts, it is because "material" is a term that intuitively and unitarily brings to mind goods that are usually described as "material", the goods which are *more commonly* spoken of as products or artefacts'. And most pertinent to my tripartite categorisation, is Rossi-Landi's insistence in this context that both 'linguistic' and 'material' artefacts are 'also constitutively social' – to which I would only add that social artefacts are both material and sign-bearing semiotic artefacts. As I shall elaborate in the following, each of these forms of objectification and artefact bears the attributes of the other two, yet each is also unique enough to be meaningfully differentiated from the other two.

A final matter of introductory clarification concerns Marx's comments on modes of objectification that are unsystematic, scattered, and provocative but unelaborated, generally leaving many gaping holes. The following discussion will thus consist of much interpolation, much borrowing from theories that are isomorphic with Marx's general outlook on objectification, and also, where useful in elaborating the modes of objectification, of critical confrontations with other theories. And that precisely is the goal of this discussion: to elaborate the three modes of objectification, the production of material, semiotic, and social objects that together make up the production of human worlds – all of which, despite the infinite but not unlimited diversity in their specific contents, consist of made-objects: of material, semiotic and social artefacts. To adopt and adapt a term from Nelson Goodman, these three modes of objectification may be considered 'ways of worldmaking'. For the fundamental attribute of objectification is that it is transformative and creates a human object, an artefact; and the three transformative or objectifying activities together produce human worlds that consist of material, semiotic, and social artefacts.[26] Although the three modes of objectification can, as I shall do here, be temporarily separated for analytical purposes, it is crucial that they be considered the three dimensions of a constellation, of a 'mode of life', another crucial term that Marx introduced in *The German Ideology* but unfortunately never systematically elaborated, and to which I shall return in concluding this chapter.

2.3.2 *Material Objectification and the Making of Material Artefacts*

The mode of material objectification was discussed in the previous chapter in differentiating between human production and that of other animal species. There the two essential and unique attributes of human labour as a mode of objectification were addressed, namely: the 'projective consciousness' that dif-

---

26 See Goodman 1978.

ferentiates self-consciously intentional human labour from the instinctual yet purposeful production of other animals; and the relation between the corporeal organisation of a given species and the world(s) it produces in the image of the bodily instruments and corporeal capacities belonging to that species. Here, accordingly, it will only be necessary to provide a brief discussion of the moments of the labour-process, and then conclude by drawing the conclusions for human history of the powerfully transformative character of those two unique attributes of the peculiarly human form of labour.

Early in volume one of *Capital*, and in order to put in relief the unique attributes of the capitalist labour-process, Marx first provided a sketch of the 'labour process in general', the common attributes of all labour 'independent of every specific social form'.[27] He began this necessary, but necessarily abstract discussion with a definition of labour that acknowledges its inevitable corporeality. Labour, he wrote, is 'first of all a process between human beings and nature, a process by which man, through his own actions, mediates, regulates and controls the metabolism with nature'. In labour humans 'set in motion the natural powers that belong to their corporeality, arms and legs, head and hands, in order to appropriate the natural material in a form that is useful for their own lives'. The labour-process, then, presupposes the labouring subject which itself obviously presupposes 'human corporeal organisation' whose needs and desires provide the telos of production and whose corporeal instruments and capacities provide the means of production; and it presupposes the natural world that provides the materials of production.

Having defined the elements of the labour-process, Marx next delineated its 'three simple moments'. These are: 'purposeful [*zweckmässige*] activity or labour itself, its object, and its means'.[28] The labour-process itself consists of the activation of the objectifying subject 'be-labouring' [*verarbeiten*] an object with some particular means of labour [*Arbeitsmittel*] which may only be 'the dexterities embedded in the human hand' that effects a transformation of the raw materials into an artefact, a made-object.[29] In summarising labour as a mode of objectification, he explained:

> In the labour process ... human activity, via the instruments of labour, effects an alteration in the object of labour which was intended from the

---

27 This and following citations, Marx 1990 [1867], pp. 283–4. For comment on Agnes Heller's argument that there are two unreconciled paradigms in Marx's theory, one of work and one of production, see Appendix 2.1.
28 Marx 1990 [1867], p. 284.
29 Marx 1973 [1857–58], p. 85.

outset. The process is effaced [*erlischt*] in the product. The product of the process is a use value, a piece of natural material adapted to human needs by means of a change in form. Labour has become combined with its object. Labour is objectified [*vergegenständlicht*], and the object belaboured [*verarbeitet*]. What on the side of the worker appeared in the form of unrest now appears, on the side of the product, in the form of being, as a fixed, stable characteristic.[30]

Portrayed 'in its simple and abstract moments', the labour-process is 'purposeful activity for the production of use-values [or use-objects[31]], appropriation of nature for the satisfaction of human needs'; regardless whether these needs 'spring from the stomach or the imagination',[32] this process is 'the universal condition of the metabolism [*Stoffwechsel*] between human beings and nature, the eternal nature-imposed condition of human life, and therefore independent of every form of this life, and therefore equally common to all social forms'.[33] To put it most succinctly the moments of objectifying labour are the labouring subject who purposefully and consciously 'belabours' an object in order to produce a product. These are the fundamental moments of all modes of objectification, though it should be recalled, especially for the following discussion of semiotic objectification, that 'purposeful' does not require conscious intentionality (see Chapter 1). But precisely because the human labour-process is based on conscious intentionality, we can say with McMurtry that objectifying labour employs the projective consciousness. And because the projective consciousness itself presupposes learning and language, which facilitates learning and expands the productive imagination, it gives human labour a transformative power that no other species has – that power to produce 'universally', to enable humans to make themselves everywhere at home by transforming nature and building human worlds.[34]

---

30   Marx 1990 [1867], p. 287.
31   Marx used *Gebrauchswert* (use-value) and *Gebrauchsgegenstand* (use object) interchangeably. Where and why he does so will be discussed in detail in Chapter 13.
32   Marx 1990 [1867], p. 125.
33   Marx 1990 [1867], p. 290.
34   Marx's referred to this process as the 'humanising' of nature (Marx 1844 in Tucker 1978, pp. 84, p. 111). This notion of 'humanising' nature can be taken in a strong teleological sense that the goal of human history is to subordinate nature to human purposes – a sense that is often alluded to especially in the *1844 Manuscripts*. Or it can be taken in the weaker sense alluded to in the discussion (Chapter 1) of Lewontin's notion of the organism as subject and object of its own history, the consequence of which for this discussion here is that niches are not found but produced by the interaction of the organism as subject trans-

2.3.3 *Social Objectification and the Making of Social Artefacts*

Former British Prime Minister Margaret Thatcher is notorious for her mistakenly apodictic quip that 'There's no such thing as society. There are individual men and women and there are families'. This statement, of course, was anything but original. The tradition of atomistic individualism goes back at least to Hobbes, and it has been the mainstay of mainstream economics for which society is a population of individuals who are rational economic actors engaged in a competitive struggle for accumulation; and it has also been a mainstay of various forms of social Darwinism from Herbert Spencer to contemporary cultural evolutionists whose application of natural selection as a transhistorical explanation of 'cultural evolution' has as its starting point a population of individuals locked in a competitive struggle for cultural survival.[35]

But these positions seem to me to be rather naïve. Although there have been real-life cases of Robinson Crusoes, of individuals surviving decades alone in the wilderness, these examples of isolation are exactly that: isolated. And they are certainly inadequate as a model of human being. For aside from those very few isolated examples, human beings are of necessity social beings; their sociality is a necessary consequence of human corporeal organisation for the reproduction of both individuals and of the species (Marx's 'third moment' of human being). The question therefore is not whether individual human beings will or will not have relations with others. That is as unavoidable for humans as it is for other social species. And in this regard Maurice Godelier's simultaneous situating of the human species among, and differentiating it from, other social species points us in a fruitful direction: 'Human beings, in contrast to other social animals, do not just live in society, they *produce society in order to live*'.[36] The questions thus become: what kind of social relations do human beings produce and what forms do objectified social relations, or social artefacts, assume?

Before proceeding, I should note that I am fully aware of the degree of terminological awkwardness involved in defining social relations in terms of objectification and as social artefacts. Because social relations, public and private, involve people, the association of social relations and objectification,

---

forming the 'external world' into a niche in which it can live. In this perspective, every organism reworks nature and builds a world, however great or small, in the image of its own corporeal organisation. This latter sense is in my view more consistent with the logic of a materialist conception of history, and it is the sense in which I shall allude to human beings constructing 'human worlds'.

35 See Fracchia and Lewontin 1999.
36 Godelier 1988, p. 1.

especially when considering such intimate relations as friendship and love, must at first glance be somewhat off-putting – especially in today's cultural world and for speakers of English. Part of the oddness for speakers of English in referring to social relations as objectifications stems from differences in theoretical vocabulary. In the previous chapter I addressed the very crucial difference between *Vergegenständlichung* ('objectification') and *Verdinglichung* ('reification'), and that discussion should be recalled here. But to specify further why it makes sense to speak of social relations as objectifications, it is worth looking at Marx's *Umfunktionierung* or redefining of a vocabulary he adopted from Hegel.

In Hegel's great philosophical *Bildungsroman* chronicling the odyssey of mind, social institutions make up what he calls '*objektiver Geist*' or 'objective mind'. Hegel, of course, defined these social institutions purely politically, that is, in terms of the state. He differentiated 'prehistoric' from 'historic' peoples along the dividing line of the existence of a state. Societies without a state are in his view prehistorical and essentially pre-human. This is because, for Hegel, the state is the institutionalisation or the objectification of reason – that is, the state is reason made objective, reason existing materially in the world. Although Hegel posited the state as the rational means of ordering social relations, it had not always existed in rational form; only at the 'end of history' would the state acquire a form commensurate with its concept. It required, in short, a long historical process of 'rationalisation', from the imperial to the monarchical to the bourgeois to the constitutional monarchical state until in this last manifestation the state acquired a form commensurate with the dictates of reason.

Be that as it may, our concern here is that although Marx was influenced by and adopted Hegel's notion of 'objective *Geist*', he also had to adapt the idealist category to fit it into his materialist conception of history. This required a broader and deeper redefinition of the social that included, but was not limited to, the solely political. And it required dispensing with the idealist fetish, *Geist*. So instead referring to them as *objektiver Geist*, Marx spoke of the institutionalisation or materiality of social relations as '*die gesellschaftliche Objektivität*' or 'social objectivity'. And here, in order to differentiate further Marx's vocabulary from the common English-language conflation of 'objectification' and 'reification' it should be emphasised that Marx's use of 'social objectivity' refers not to people themselves, but to the established (whether in institutions or through performative reiteration), tangible, and efficacious relations among them – all of which are objectified, some of which may also be reified.[37] And as I shall

---

37   For a study of the reified social relations characteristic of the capitalist labour-process, see Chapter 14 below.

argue in the following, the term 'social objectification' effectively encompasses both 'public' and 'private' social relations.[38]

The seeming oddness of referring to social relations as objectifications, finally, might contribute to their much-needed denaturalisation. As is well-known, the most effective ideological defence of any status quo is to convince people that it is 'natural' and thus always has been and always will be – perhaps best exemplified by the political economists' universalising projection of the isolated individual as 'rational economic actor' into the distant evolutionary ancestry of *Homo sapiens* and into all possible human societies. To think of social relations as artefacts, products or objectifications of human social interaction is to denaturalise and to demystify them – and to open up the possibility that what has been made can be remade. Rossi-Landi, who, as we have seen, extends the notion of the artefact to language, notes that it would require a 'further extension' to apply it to 'social and legal institutions'.[39] Though he does not elaborate this extension, he nevertheless insists that such institutions are artefacts. The missing elaboration of the artefactual character of social relations is the task of this part.

---

38   It is certainly not unheard of to use the term 'object' in the depiction of personal relations. The most frequent usage of 'object' to signify a subject involved in a personal relation is to be found in depth psychology and psychoanalysis. Freud, for example, stated quite bluntly that 'love strives after objects' – 'objects' here clearly referring to other people (Freud 1962, p. 64). And post-World War II, post-Freudian depth psychology perpetuated at least this aspect of Freud. W. Ronald D. Fairbairn developed 'An Object-Relations Theory of Personality' and by 'object relations' he meant not relations with things, but with other people; and later Heinz Kohut developed a notion of 'self-objects' whose loss entailed also 'the loss of the object's [that is, the loss of the other person's] love'. See Fairbairn 1964 and Kohut 1974. While these examples have a point to make about the relation between a given ego and its others, the problem with them, the reason they cannot serve as the foundation of historical-materialist theory of intersubjective relations, is that they are one-dimensional and unidirectional. Though these approaches all focus on intersubjective relations, they all take the individual, isolated ego as the starting point. Given this their starting point, the relation between an ego and other egos is reduced, by methodological default if not categorial design, to a relation between a given ego and its others, which in turn reduces intersubjectivity to a relation between an ego and its object. While a reference to another person as the 'object of one's affections' is as harmless as it is common in everyday parlance, and though such an approach may have well positive psychoanalytic results for the treatment of an individual patient, the treatment of that other subject only as an object that gives or withholds that which the subject being treated (the object of psychoanalysis) desires is wholly inadequate for a historical-materialist theory of intersubjective relations.

39   Rossi-Landi 1983, p. 123.

2.3.3.1 Public Social Relations

Since Marx agreed with none of Margaret Thatcher's theoretical precursors, it is safe to assume that he would have disagreed with her atomistic individualism as well. The reason for this, as expressed in what I renamed his second moment of history, is that in his view human beings are inescapably social beings. In the discussion of method in the Introduction to the *Grundrisse*, Marx presented his critique of the demography of political economy based on atomistic individualism. The hallmark of political economy and the source of its shortcomings, Marx argued, was that it took as its starting point the population without having determined the components of the populations, its 'subgroups' or classes, nor the logic of their internal relations. Though the 'population [...] is the foundation and the subject of the entire social act of production', to take it as the analytical point of departure is to begin with 'a chaotic notion of the whole' that is blind to 'the classes of which it is composed' and the 'elements on which they rest'. For this reason, the further determinations of this chaotically conceived population would 'move analytically towards ever more simple concepts, from the imagined concrete towards ever thinner abstractions' rather than produce 'a rich totality of many determinations and relations'.[40] Or as he later summarised it more succinctly: '[s]ociety does not consist of individuals, but expresses the sum of interrelations, the relations within which these individuals stand'. Whereas a census would, from Thatcher's perspective, suffice to understand society, Marx insists on mapping social objectivity (*die gesellschaftliche Objektivität*) and charting social geography – which required him to track down the 'inner bonds' that hold society together and govern the relations and distribution of people in social space (see Chapter 3).

Social objectivity is, for Marx, well: objective, an efficacious reality. In all societies, public social relations are objectified, made objective. In modern capitalist societies, social relations are objectified in the form of established law, in constitutions enforced by the power of a state. In non-capitalist social forms, social relations may be objectified through the medium of politics, religion, or other media; in non-capitalist social forms what Althusser called the 'structure in dominance' might be, for example, the Greek πόλις or the Medieval Catholic Church. Despite claims by Hegel and the many other Western thinkers, who made the existence of an institutionalised state the criterion of 'real' societies with a 'history', it is a great fallacy to assume that objectified social relations only exist where power is objectified in durable institutions. According to Pierre Clastres, it is precisely this fetishism of the state and its

---

40 Marx 1973 [1857–58], p. 100. Following citation, ibid., p. 265.

institutionalisation of power that has blinded Western political science and anthropology to the social and political logic of the South American peoples or any peoples who are, as he put it, 'enemies of the state'.[41] Clastres exposed the fallacy and futility of trying to impose categories taken from the analysis of states (hierarchy, command-obedience relations, powers of taxation, etc.) on societies whose social relations precluded an institutionalised state with all the attributes normally associated with it.

In his study of four such stateless societies, Clastres found no concrete institutions on the state-model, but he did find that these societies do very much have an objective political logic – albeit one that is 180 degrees opposite that of Western states. Social and political relations in these societies are objectified, not in concrete institutions, but in roles, practices, and mutual obligations that are concretised in memory, objectified performatively, and confirmed and reinforced in and through their efficacy. Power is not formalised and institutionalised in a monarch or some kind of putatively representative body, nor is it a command-obedience relation enforced by the weapons of police and/or military. Power is rather enacted performatively through persuasion and compromise. Because the purpose of the 'economy' in these societies is not accumulation, but the satisfaction of the needs of the group's members, the leader's economic role is not to tax 'subjects', but to distribute his own surplus to those members of the group who might temporarily be without. And because the leading figure or chief has no power to command obedience, a leader who failed to provide for the well-being of the group would be deposed simply by being ignored. These societies, Clastres shows, are societies structured such that sovereign power resides not with the leader, but with the group – and such that the political structure itself discourages the emergence of a top-heavy political hierarchy.

A different, religious example of the objectification of social relations is provided by the history of Christianity which itself can be seen as a sequence of increasingly concrete objectifications of God as pure spirit: first in Jesus who is both God and man; then in the Holy Spirit residing in each of the believers as both the spirit of God and the spiritual bond that holds together the believers as members of a Christian community; and finally in the institutions of the Christian Church (in both its Catholic, and later in its several Protestant forms).

Whether the bond established to govern and cement social relations is a spiritual one or, as will be discussed next, one of love, or a set of non-institutional but ritually institutionalised performances, or a constitution and legal system

---

41   Clastres 1989.

that defines its citizens as 'isolated individuals', to name just a few possibilities, the objectification of social relations constitutes social objectivity as 'artefactual', as a made social form that is efficacious in framing the behaviour patterns of its members – in establishing the social limits whose transgression invites ostracism. Again, however awkward it may sound to speak of established social relations as 'artefactual', it still has the indispensable advantage of stating explicitly that social forms and relations are not natural, they are not the inevitable products of an unchangeable nature consisting of isolated individuals in competition for scarce resources – as has been maintained by those ranging from Hobbes, Smith and Malthus to sociobiologically-based cultural evolutionists, and to Margaret Thatcher, all of whom, with varying degrees of subtlety (ranging from treating it as merely epiphenomenal of the fundamentally individual struggle for survival to the simple statement of absolute disbelief), have denied the existence of 'society'. But whatever their particular form, it is the facticity, the organisation (whether performative or institutional), the very objectivity of social relations that allows them to be recognised as objects of analysis for the social sciences.

2.3.3.2   Private Social Relations

To speak of private social relations as artefacts of social objectification is not only an awkward mouthful, but also seems at first glance to be doubly troubling. First of all, the term 'private social relations' appears to be a contradiction in terms. But the point here is simply that while all relations among people are social, and although the designations 'private' and 'public' are themselves social designations, it nevertheless makes perfect sense to designate some as 'private' or 'personal' in order to differentiate them from relations in public spheres. Whereas, for example, the family is designated as 'private' in bourgeois societies, it is also quite public in feudal society in which birth into a 'private' noble family confers immediate and public social and political power.

The second, and more troubling aspect of this term has to do with the designation of personal relations as artefacts of social objectification – a discordant note that already arises when considering public social relations as objectified artefacts, but that is even more accentuated with personal relations. It is, however, easy enough to acknowledge the prescribed procedures in all societies for the public recognition and legitimation of private relationships as forms of objectification – forms that often employ an object as a sign of the objectified relationship: a licence as a sign conferring official public sanction on the private relation of marriage; the wedding ring as the object signifying the institutionalised objectification of love. Yet although the English-language reference to one's beloved as 'the object of one's affections' is commonly taken for granted without reflection on the literal meaning of the words, it still sounds a bit strange to refer explicitly to personal relations themselves, be they of love, friendship, or of enmity and hatred, as objectifications. This requires a bit more explanation.

In referring to such personal relations as themselves objectifications, Marx drew on a usage in Hegel's philosophy that was reformulated by Feuerbach (and that is not unlike similar formulations in existentialist philosophy and interactionist social psychology[42]). Hegel's well-known chapter in the *Phenomenology* on the struggle for recognition has two selves standing in an antagonistic relation because their desires, as Hegel presents them, are mutually exclusive. Each subject encounters the other as an object, but both want to be recognised as a subject. This gives rise to a struggle to the death, which is broken off when the weaker chooses to recognise the other as subject rather than be killed. In his sensualist critique of Hegel, Feuerbach found in Hegel's antagonistic rendition of the process of mutual recognition a rather alienated form of human interaction that began with the false assumption of atomised and antagonistic individuals. Feuerbach insisted, and Marx was clearly influence by this, that human beings are inevitably social beings and that the recognition of the other as inevitably linked to the self is simply a recognition of our shared humanness. As Feuerbach put it succinctly, 'the most important, most essential sensual object for a human being is a human being'; and he refers to a human being outside of the self with the 'concept of the thou', the other as 'an objectified I'.[43]

Marx's clearest expressions of personal relations as objectification are found in the *1844 Manuscripts* – in the section on 'the power of money in bourgeois society' where he commented on sensibilities, passions, desires, and pleasures in both their alienated and their emancipated form.[44] There he maintained that these bodily attributes, which the Western philosophical mainstream since Socrates treated primarily as disturbances, obstacles to thought and the attainment of truth, are essential components of human being; and he

---

42   Existential and depth psychology commonly use the term 'object relations' to refer to people. See Csikzenthmihalyi and Eugene Rochberg-Halton 1981.
43   Ludwig Feuerbach, *Grundsätze der Philosophie der Zukunft*, para. 41: '*das wichtigste, wesentlichste Sinnesobjekt des Menschen [ist] der Mensch selbst*'; and para. 32: der *Begriff des Du, des gegenständlichen Ich*. Cited in Honneth and Joas 1980, p. 22.
44   It is interesting that Marx addresses personal relations such as love or friendship within a larger discussion of the sensual apprehension of the world. He can do so because he does not limit the senses to the five sense organs, nor sensual activity to sense perception. Among the senses he also includes what would generally be called emotions such as willing and loving – also sensibilities and passions that are only truly affirmed insofar as their object is for them 'sensual', that is: tangible, real. See Marx 1844 in Tucker 1978, pp. 101–5.

maintained further that these sensibilities and passions are only truly affirmed insofar as 'their object [*Gegenstand*] is for them sensual [i.e. tangible, real]'.[45] From these he drew several conclusions, the one of relevance here is: 'insofar as the human beings are human, that is that their sensibilities, etc. are also human, the affirmation of their object by another is his/her own pleasure as well'. He then proceeded to explain how money perverts these sensibilities and passions, insofar as their realisation depends on whether or not the individual has the money to buy the objects of desire. In the inverted and perverted world in which money rules, the personal qualities of an individual reside not in their persons, but in their *porte-monnaie*.

Drawing on Shakespeare's *Timon of Athens*, Marx, somewhat incorrectly, called money the 'universal whore' that, dubbed more accurately as the 'universal pimp', turns all persons and objects into whores in the form of commodities. Echoing his earlier discussion of the capitalist reduction of the manifold diversity of human sense organs to the one-dimensional sense of having, Marx described a process in which what in a free unalienated situation would be objects of passion, desire, and sensual joy are reified into things that can be had for the right price. Capitalism and money thus do in practice what Hegel (and much depth psychology) does in theory, namely: conceive of the 'natural' social relationship as an antagonistic one in which the self is inevitably at odds with the other even if the other is the object of the self's desire – in which case the desiring self wants 'to have' the other as object. From this perspective, not even love can be conceptualised outside the sense of having.

What Marx meant in speaking of people as objects [Gegenstände] and of personal relations as objectification is, however, something quite different from the reification of love through the sense of having. His concern was not simply an individual ego that has another person for its object. His concern was, rather, with two egos that have each other for their mutual and not at all obscure objects of desire. And his analysis is of the product of social objectification, the social artefact. This social artefact is not one of the subjects turned into an object, but of the relation itself objectified, made real (be it one of love, friendship, or hatred). Rather than reify subjects, an attempt to view social relations as objectifications leads us to focus specifically on the relations established or made, the tangible and efficacious bonds between people.

He exemplified this in a discussion of what love would be like in a world not dominated by the 'sense of having'. Where there is 'a human relationship' among people, 'you can only exchange love for love, trust for trust, etc. [...] Each

---

45   All citations in this paragraph from Marx 1845 in Tucker 1978, pp. 101–2.

of your relations to other people – and to nature – must be a specific expression of your actual individual life that corresponds to the object of your will'.[46] For Marx, then, to speak of personal relations as objectification is to speak of a concrete intersubjective relation between real people – what is meant by the everyday euphemism that the beloved is 'the object of one's affections'. This is quite different from the intellectual tradition following Socrates, that defined 'true' love philosophically as the love of truth or wisdom, and also from literary tendencies that portray the beloved as an unattainable object of desire (e.g. courtly love poems, Dante's poems to Beatrice, Petrarca's to Laura). The sublimation of unfulfilled erotic feelings may be expressed, objectified in monumental works of art that elevate the unattainable beloved onto an unreachable pedestal. But the transformation of the unreachable beloved into a Muse or an *objet d'art*, into the sublimated sensuality of love poetics in written or painted form, is something much different from the sensual poetics of love in which, not poetic images however sublime, but the really living, sensuously active lovers themselves are *objets* of each other's affections. In the vocabulary used here, both are objectifications, but the former is semiotic, the latter social.

Marx, then, simply reiterated the obvious fact that actual love and desire between embodied human beings have as their object not ideas, but real, sensual, embodied human beings. And his point was that the realisation of love and desire should depend only on the mutual attraction of people who have each other as the objects of their love; and the realisation of love is an objective relation to which both have committed themselves, an objectification of their subjective desires: the establishment of an objective, i.e. really-existing, love relationship, regardless of whether 'institutionalised' by church, state, or mutual assent is an objectification of love. This can be graphically depicted by glancing, as does Marx, at the opposite case, namely: 'if you love without evoking love in return – that is, if your loving as loving does not produce reciprocal love; if through a *living expression* of yourself as a loving person you do not make yourself a *loved person*, then your love is impotent – a misfortune'.[47] Unrequited love has no object, and is thus not objectified love.

---

46 Marx 1845 in Tucker 1978, p. 105.
47 Ibid.

2.3.4　Semiotic Objectification and the Making of Semiotic Artefacts[48]

Bedeutung ist immer schon Vergegenständlichung

[Meaning is always already objectification]
BRUNO LIEBRUCKS[49]

∴

If the 'projective consciousness' is at work in defining the consciously intentional purposefulness of labour, this is, as noted above, not necessarily the case with all forms of objectification. Nowhere is this more evident than among the different modes of production of meaning through semiotic objectification. The modes of production of meaning can be formally divided between those that involve the projective consciousness and those that do not. Intellectual and artistic labour and speech acts are structurally identical with labour, and certainly involve the projective consciousness. But others – like sense perception and the production of sensory impressions or speaking and the production of language – do not. Sense-perception, for example, is no longer considered a passive process, but one in which the sensory organs play a constitutive role in constructing percepts. Although it is certainly purposeful, it cannot be said to be consciously intentional as is the projective consciousness that mentally preforms its objects. Similarly with the production of languages or symbolic forms: while the individual speech act, the individual deployment of a culturally specific symbol, intellectual and artistic labour can all be said to be intentional acts of a projective consciousness, this does not hold for the production of language or cultural and symbolic forms. Languages, cultures, and their specific symbolic forms are obviously not 'natural', but are human artefacts, products of human objectification. The neglect of the made character of semiotic artefacts and

---

48　Other writers have sought to create names for objects produced by the mind. Alfred Kroeber, for example, coined what Julian Huxley (1960) called that 'delightful word "mentifact"'. And Richard Dawkins (1976) coined the notion of 'memes'. Both of these are perfectly legitimate terms for signifying mental objectifications. But I prefer to use 'semiotic artefacts' because it directly refers to the products of semiotic objectification and because it highlights more effectively the madeness of signs.

49　Liebrucks 1964, p. 197.

of the objectifying activity that made them, all too easily allows one to focus on the mere facticity of languages or symbolic systems whose great diversity then easily enables one to conclude that they are 'arbitrary'. 'Vast' semiotic artefacts like languages, symbolic forms, etc. are, however, socially, collectively produced, certainly with purpose, but not with the conscious intentionality of the projective consciousness in making a table, formulating a sentence, or writing a poem.[50] Their production is such an elongated and an ongoing process that it is impossible to point to the act of their making. Yet they are nevertheless made-objects, artefacts in an ongoing process of being made, produced, by human beings and invested with meaning by human beings – even if the intentionality of the making was not self-conscious, and even though the maker was a collective subject or, better, a collection of subjects, rather than an individual projective consciousness. The following discussion of the production of semiotic objects will begin with sense-perception as objectification, then move to language production and speech acts as forms of semiotic objectification, and conclude with a few comments about the 'higher' forms of linguistic objectification: intellectual and aesthetic labour in/and the production of cultural forms

2.3.4.1   Sense Perception as Objectification

Though the manuscript of some fourteen pages that later editors entitled 'Private Property and Communism' seems to announce a discussion of economic forms, Marx, unexpectedly at first glance, devoted almost half of the discussion to the question of the senses and sensuousness – and in so doing he penned some of his most striking and visionary prose. A second glance, however, makes this discussion of the senses in this context more understandable. For throughout the *Manuscripts*, Marx was never concerned with the kind of socio-economic 'details' he would address in *Capital*; his focus was rather on portraying the attributes of human alienation in contemporary capitalist society and anticipating the attributes of an emancipated humanity under communism. Though he only cursorily mentioned Feuerbach in this section, it is here that he developed some of his most Feuerbachian, and also most profound and emancipatory insights about the senses and sensibility. Though the designation of sense perception as a mode of objectification might also seem unexpected and strange, here Marx, following Feuerbach's lead, effected a materialist transformation of the central tenet of German idealist philosophy,

---

50   I adopted the notion of 'vast artefact' from Elaine Scarry who explains that Marx treats the mode of production as a 'vast artifact'. This notion from Scarry's *The Body in Pain*, and her general argument there that the body is 'the interior structure' of artefacts, will be discussed in detail in Chapter 10 as the foundation of a 'corporeal semiotics'.

namely that the subject constructs and determines (i.e. establishes the determinations of) the object as an object of a knowing subject, and thereby produces it as a known object, an object of knowledge. But Marx countered that tradition's treatment of the senses of passive media, conduits of raw material, sense data, that is then worked into knowledge by the mind. Instead, he insisted, in a sensual-materialist manner, that sense perception itself is a corporeal process of knowledge production.

No doubt influenced by Friedrich von Schiller, though concerned not just with an aesthetic education, but with aesthetic, that is: sensual, life-activity, Marx contrasted the one-dimensional pseudo-sensuality effected by private property with the free cultivation of a multi-dimensional sensual life-activity that he anticipated in a communist society. In his earlier commentary on James Mill, Marx had described the basic purpose of private property as producing in order 'to have', more specifically, to have as one's own to the exclusion of others. Expanding on this theme in the *Manuscripts*, he argued that private property causes the atrophy of the bodily sense organs as they are subsumed by the cancerous growth of the sense of having. Under the conditions of capitalist private property, the objects in the world have meaning for us only 'in the sense of immediate, one-sided enjoyment, ... in the sense of possession, in the sense of having. ... Private property has made us so stupid and one-sided that an object is only *ours* when we have it – when it exists for us as capital, or when it is directly possessed, eaten, drunk, worn, inhabited, etc., in short *used* by us. ... In place of *all* these physical and mental senses there has therefore come the sheer estrangement of *all* these senses – the sense of having'.[51] Under private property, the potential wealth of the senses is reduced to the sense of having – or having not: 'The sense that is entangled in raw practical need is a one-dimensional sense. For the starving [person] it is not the human form that exists, but only its abstract being as food; it could just as well be there in its crudest form, and it would be impossible to say wherein this feeding activity differs from that of animals. The care-burdened, needy person has no sense for the most beautiful drama; the dealer in minerals sees only their mercantile value, but not the beauty and the unique nature of the minerals; he has no mineralogical sense'.[52]

---

51 Marx 1844 in Tucker 1978, p. 87. Marx pointed to Moses Hess as the one who explicated the alienated sense of 'having' as opposed to emancipated 'being'.

52 Marx 1844 in Tucker 1978, pp. 88–9. The estranged identification of 'having' with 'being' has always been ubiquitous in advertising which essentially tells us that if we 'have' this or that commodity, we will 'be' attractive, glamourous, sexy, healthy, happy, wealthy, and wise, etc. A more recent theme exemplifies the reification of social relations, in which commodity

Marx contrasted this with a future following the abolition of private property in which a new person will emerge, a new subject with a new relation to the world its natural objects and its human products, and able fully to realise the manifold potential for the different modes of objectification residing in human corporeality. In a world beyond private property, need and pleasure will have lost their 'egoistical nature' and nature will have lost its 'mere utility', 'use' will have become 'human use' and an 'all-sided' sensual apprehension of the world will replace the one-dimensional perception of all objects only as possible possessions: 'each human relation to the world – seeing, hearing, smelling, tasting, feeling, thinking, being-aware, willing, acting, loving – in short all organs of human individuality as well as the organs that in their form are immediately social organs, are in their objective [*gegenständlichen*] orientation, or in their orientation to the object, the appropriation of that object, the appropriation of the human world'.[53] The emancipation from a social form ruled by private property 'is thus the complete emancipation of the human senses and attributes'. When no longer yoked to the proprietary appropriation of objects, the truly human senses will become attuned, each according to its sensory instruments and capacities, to the various attributes of the 'object' being apprehended, or 'appropriated'. Emancipated senses 'relate themselves to the matter for the sake of the matter itself'; and in so doing emancipated sense become organs of aesthetic cognition, of non-conceptual knowledge. As Marx noted in a comment rich in epistemological implications: 'The senses will have become, in their immediate practice, theoreticians'. And that theoretical praxis of the senses will consist of 'relating to a thing for its own sake, to the thing itself' whereby 'need and pleasure will have lost their *egoistic* nature and nature will have lost its mere utility insofar as use [of nature] will have become *human* use'.[54]

---

possession is peddled as the familial bond that ties its owners – as exemplified in, among others, Subaru and Chevrolet commercials: have (i.e. buy) a Subaru or Chevy and be part of that car's family.

53   All citations in this paragraph from Marx 1844 in Tucker 1978, p. 87. Against the insistence common among later critics (e.g. Martin Heidegger, Theodor Adorno, Jürgen Habermas, Jean Baudrillard, environmentalist and some feminist critiques) that Marx treated nature as simply an object of 'use' in the sense of 'using-up', of destructive consumption, this passage emphatically shows that Marx's notion of human 'use' is quite opposite that of capitalist utilitarianism.

54   See Gibson 1966, and Part 2 below. What Marx said in his Hegelian-Feuerbachian language is similar to what J.J. Gibson called 'perceptual systems'. And albeit in a different vocabulary and with a different purpose, Marx's comments on perception have a certain affinity with those of later phenomenologists who likewise argue that perception is not simply a passive intake of that which is impressed upon the senses, but rather an act of the perceiving subject who 'evidences', who 'brings forth the presence' and 'truth' of things. See Sokolowski 2000, pp. 160–1.

In a world emancipated from the crude sense of having, 'objective reality [the world of objects] becomes ... the world of human essential powers' and 'all *objects* become for human beings the *objectification* of their own selves', become, that is, 'objects which confirm and realize their individuality'.⁵⁵ Each emancipated sense turns its particular theoretical powers toward the objects of the world and apprehends them aesthetically, that is: sensually. With the development of the theoretical powers of each and every sense comes both the cultivation of a multiplicity of ways of sensually apprehending an object as well – a kind of synaesthesia; for through this multiplicity of sensual apprehension we gain an aesthetic sense of the multi-dimensionality of the object itself: 'An object becomes to the eye other than to the ear, and the object of the eye is another object than that of the ear. The uniqueness of every essential power is precisely its unique essence, that is the unique mode of its objectification, of its objectively real living being. Not only in thought, but with all senses, human being is affirmed in the objective world'.

The manifold exercise of the various senses opens new worlds to perceptual apprehension and thereby transforms the perceiver as well: 'Only through the objectively unfolded richness of man's essential being is the richness of subjective human sensibility (a musical ear, an eye for beauty of form – in short, senses capable of human gratifications, senses confirming themselves as essential powers of man) either cultivated or brought into being. For not only the five senses but also the so-called mental senses, the practical senses (will, love, etc.), in a word the human sense, the humanness of the senses, comes to be only through its object, through humanized nature'.⁵⁶ We need not accept the rather problematic Whiggish overtones in this formulation that entails an underestimation of the sensual acuity of those in pre-capitalist societies not ruled by private property and the sense of having in order to appreciate Marx's visionary comment that combines a notion of the historicity of the senses with the potential of an emancipated sensuality: 'the cultivation [*Bildung*] of the five senses is a labour of the entire history of the world down to the present' – a cultivation that, he notes in concluding, 'is required to make man's *sense human*, as well as to create the *human sense* corresponding to the entire wealth of human and natural substance'.

---

55   All citations in this paragraph from Marx 1844 in Tucker 1978, p. 88.
56   Marx 1844 in Tucker 1978, p. 89. Following citation, ibid. The translation in the *Marx-Engels Reader* renders *Bildung* as 'formation'. While that is not incorrect, I prefer to translate it with the equally correct term 'cultivation' because of its stronger connotations of an ongoing historical process of developing, growing.

Marx's early critique of capitalism – and an aspect that remained constant throughout his entire life, even if never again addressed so directly and emphatically – is then that it subordinates the body's senses to the socially constructed, alienating medium that is the sense of having. The result is the hypertrophy of the sense of having and commensurate atrophy of the body's perceptual systems and, accordingly, a one-dimensional, alienated apprehension of the world in order to have its objects for one's own exclusive use. And his vision is of a world beyond capital in which the senses and sense perception have come into their own, a world to which the subject is attuned because all senses are emancipated and primed to perceive the object in its various modes of being for the human eyes, for the human ears, etc. Under unfree social conditions, sense perception is not properly an objectifying activity, but a reifying and purely instrumental one that turns all objects into things to be possessed and used up. In an emancipated world, on the contrary, human senses will be properly aesthetic, producing percepts derived from the being, rather than the having, of their objects.

2.3.4.2 Linguistic Objectification

Given the hegemony in the contemporary discursive regime dominated by structuralist, poststructuralist, and postmodernist variants grounded in what are all too often taken to be axioms established by the 'official Saussure' of the *Course in General Linguistics*, any talk of 'linguistic objectification' will no doubt provoke dismay.[57] This is because the process of 'linguistic objectification' as I use it here rehabilitates a set of elements essential to speech and language but dismissed as irrelevant by the exclusively synchronic approach of the *Course*. Concerned only with the synchronic structure of language and the formal logic of linguistic signification, the *Course* and its devotees dismiss the entire diachronic realm in which language is used, its *raison d'être* performatively exemplified, and its purpose realised. An exclusively synchronic approach to language thus excludes: the corporeal prerequisites of speech, the social prerequisites of language, dialogically-engaged speaking and listening subjects, and the referents of signs of the signs they use and therewith the world about which they speak. In short, a synchronic approach dismisses everything relevant to an understanding of that with which this section is concerned,

---

57 The reference to the author of the *Course in General Linguistics* as the 'official Saussure' was coined by Ferruccio Rossi-Landi to differentiate the much more nuanced work Ferdinand de Saussure whose ideas about language were formulated more as hypotheses than as the kind of dicta that fill the *Course*. This too will be addressed in greater detail in Chapter 8.

namely: linguistic objectification. As preparatory to my elaboration of a corporeal semiotics in Chapter 10, I present a rather lengthy critique of the *Course in General Linguistics* and its consequences for the understanding of language and culture solely as formal or synchronic semiotic systems (Chapters 8 and 9). Here, however, I focus exclusively on sketching the guidelines of a historical-materialist approach to language in terms of linguistic objectification.

First, however, a word on terminology is in order. The English term 'language' carries heterogeneous meanings that, because easily conflated, can be confusing. The conceptual apparatus of the *Course* is in this regard much clearer and has become, moreover, the *lingua franca* of semiotic studies of language and culture. From here on through the rest of this book, whenever the use of the English 'language' might be ambiguous, I will add the French terms for clarification purposes. The key terms are the following:

Langage is the superordinate concept that designates the general faculty of speech and all that pertains to speech. *Langage* is as such 'many-sided and heterogeneous' and 'straddl[es] several areas simultaneously – physical, physiological, and psychological'.[58] It encompasses two major subdivisions sub-divisions: *langue* and *parole*. This very heterogeneity, the *Course* insists, prevents *langage* from being the analytical object of a science of linguistics.

Langue in its everyday meaning designates (with corporeal appropriateness) a 'tongue', e.g. English, Chinese, etc. In the linguistic tradition emanating from the *Course*, however, *langue* has a more specialised, and yet more abstract meaning, designating 'a system of signs in which the only essential thing is the union of meanings and sound images'. In this context, then, *langue* is the purely formal structure of the system of signs that functions according to the particular semiotic logic of signs which underlies each and every particular tongue. *Langue* designates the particular systems of linguistic signs that given social groups use as their means of speech production.

Parole designates 'speaking', the 'executive side of speech', speech acts that entail speakers and listeners, a language/*langue* that serves as a means of both expression and communication, and the referents about which something is expressed. This is the diachronic dimen-

---

58 Saussure 1959, p. 9. Following citations: the discussion of *langue*, ibid., p. 15; discussion of *parole*, ibid., p. 13.

sion of speech which is excluded from the synchronic 'science of linguistics' delineated in the *Course*.

From a historical-materialist viewpoint, *langage*, the general faculty of speech, can be viewed as analogous to Marx's notion of the 'labour-process in general'. As in the labour-process, the objectifying activation of the corporeal capacities and the bodily instruments of speech effects a transformation of raw materials into artefacts. In the linguistic mode of objectification, historical-materialistically conceived, the purposeful activity is both signification and communication. As in the labour-process, the means of labour (*Arbeitsmittel*) or tools are both internal or corporeal and external or artefactual. The corporeal means of labour are the body's own instruments: the vocal, auditory, and the respiratory organs, and the raw material is air. Respiration provides the raw material for language by drawing air through the surpralaryngeal tract. This linguistic labour produces 'agitated layers of air' (Marx) and transforms them into made linguistic objects, into those 'mouthy little noises we call words' (Susanne Langer).[59] As Rossi-Landi puts it, '[i]t is enough for a sound to bear the mark of man for us to consider it in some way produced, rather than simply emitted, *and therefore to recognize in it the characteristics of the artefact*'.[60] 'All the sound material that makes up language', he continues, 'is the fruit of human work; it does not exist in nature *in that way*, with those modifications that adapt it to the purpose for which it is formed'.

In elaborating the artefactual character of relatively small-scale linguistic products, 'words, sentences, discourses and the like', Rossi-Landi writes that these 'are also human products, artefacts; they do not exist in nature without human intervention, and their presence immediately and unequivocally reveals the presence of [human beings]'.[61] This is equally true of the vaster arte-

---

59   Marx 1845 in Tucker 1978, p. 158; Langer 1979, p. 61. A rather literal adaptation of Marx's depiction of the general labour-process (Marx 1990 [1867], p. 287) to the general faculty of speech could be rendered as follows: 'In the speech process, human activity, via the instruments of speech [the body's vocal tract], effects an alteration, intended from the outset, in the object of speech (i.e., air). The process of speech production is effaced [*erlischt*] in the spoken product, the utterance. The product of the process is a use value, a piece of natural material [air] adapted to human needs [communication through signification] by means of a change in form [words, verbal signs]. Speech is objectified [*vergegenständlicht*], and the object [air] be-laboured [*verarbeitet*]. What on the side of the speaker appeared in the form of unrest now appears, on the side of the product [the utterance] in the form of being, as a fixed, stable characteristic'.
60   Rossi-Landi 1983, p. 122, my italics. Following citation, ibid.
61   Ibid. Maurice Godelier makes the point that should be obvious, but has been subjected to the insidious bias of neglect, namely: that mental and material practice are inseparable,

facts that are the various languages/*langues*. Because of the ease with which a language is normally deployed in everyday speech acts, language usage appears to be 'natural' or 'instinctual'. The combination of those 'mouthy little noises' into meaningful utterances may well be governed by what Noam Chomsky calls a 'language-acquisition device' embedded in the brain, or by what Steven Pinker calls a 'language instinct'. That, of course, cannot be determined here. But assuming, for the sake of argument, that Chomsky and Pinker are correct, that 'device' with an inherent capability to use language belongs to the set of corporeal instruments for speech production. Languages themselves, the specific sets of syntactical and semantic rules that govern and give content to the 'production of the expression of meaning' (this awkward phrase is, for reasons discussed below, most apt) may be more appropriately viewed as external tools: artefacts purposely (if unintentionally) produced in order to function as the tools, the means of the linguistic production of meaning.

Although speech may well be as 'natural' to humans as flying to birds or swimming to fish, it does not follow that even what we call 'natural languages' are 'natural'. 'Natural' languages are so-named to differentiate them from languages that are consciously constructed in a premeditated fashion (e.g. Esperanto, sign-language for the deaf, computer-programming or mathematical languages). But the name itself is a misnomer. For, although 'natural languages' do 'arise in an unpremeditated fashion',[62] they clearly do not 'exist in nature without human intervention', and they are no less artefactual than artificial languages. Although not produced by intentional human design, the speech acts that go into the production of 'natural languages' are purposeful. *Langue* is produced through the practice of *parole*.

Such a claim that understanding the genesis of language might help us to understand its systemic logic is categorically rejected by those of a structuralist or poststructuralist inclination. But the rejection of this claim by Émile Benveniste, one of the earlier proponents of a synchronic and structuralist analysis of language, provides a perfect example of the methodologically-induced myopia mentioned above. Benveniste is of course correct in stating that 'we can never get back to man separated from language and we shall never see him inventing it'. It is instead only 'a speaking man whom we find in the world, a man

---

which is another way of saying that human manipulation of objects always and necessarily engages both mind and body or, better, the thinking body – that labour (human objectification) and language are inseparable moments of social practice. See Godelier 1988.

62 as the Wikipedia definition of 'natural language' succinctly condenses the views of many on this matter. http://en.wikipedia.org/wiki/Natural_language.

speaking to another man'. And he properly rejects as 'pure fiction' the 'naïve concept of a primordial period in which a complete man discovered another equally complete, and between the two of them language was worked out little by little' (although it seems rather a 'pure fiction' of his own making than a 'naive concept' that anyone actually espouses). But all he has to offer, it seems, is a syllogistic shortcut, based on a non-sequitur, that produces an even greater (and not very useful) fiction, namely: because we can never get back to man without language to witness its invention, we can find only 'a speaking man [...] in the world, a man speaking to another man'. From this point, he leaps to the (by no means necessary) conclusion that therefore 'language provides [*enseigne*] the very definition of man' (should we not also ask whether 'man' provides the very existence and definition of language???).

The fictional character of this vision of two linguistically-abled 'men' speaking to one another, apparently having emerged fully fluent from the mind of language, is only magnified by his insistence that unlike 'the pick, the arrow, and the wheel [that] are not in nature' but are rather 'fabrications', 'language is in the nature of man, and he did not fabricate it'.[63] The endless, often vehement arguments among the many and varied specialists over the question certainly lends itself to the view that a conclusive genealogical reconstruction of the evolution of language might well be impossible. Nevertheless, despite the heated debate over the particulars, there is general agreement among students of human evolution that the stages of speech and language can be correlated to the general stages in the evolution of *human* being – from *Homo habilis* who had only the rudiments of language, to *Homo erectus* who had a primitive 'proto-language' to fully loquacious *Homo sapiens* (see Chapter 6). And even assuming that knowledge gap will never be filled, it is still quite a leap of faith to jump from that ignorance of the details to the secular-creationist conclusion that language did not evolve, was not 'fabricated', but rather just *is* the 'very definition of man'. And as Roland Fletcher succinctly formulated the obvious: '[T]here is no evidence that our current form of language is much more than

---

63   In an interesting bit of evolutionary inversion, Benveniste (1971, pp. 223–4) insists that language is not a fabricated 'instrument'; and to speak of language as fabrication is 'to put man and nature in opposition'. However, if there is one thing on which students of evolution agree, it would be that the fabrication of 'instruments' in the form of tools long preceded the advent of language (although there is much disagreement over how long). And as Jane Goodall among others have shown, tool-use is not exclusive to humans. Although one could argue that the earliest tools were 'natural' and that it is only with language that sophisticated tools were 'fabricated', such an argument would be no less specious than Benveniste's that language is 'natural' but 'tool-making' is not. It seems to me that either both are 'natural', or neither.

50,000 years old. We were becoming human long before that, and our humanness is founded in our distant past, not uniquely created by our most recent forms of behavior'.[64]

The problem with Benveniste's argument (that I am tempted to call his 'fabrication') is that he obviously thinks of 'fabrication' as involving what John McMurtry called the 'projective consciousness' in the premeditated making of an object, linguistically speaking, in the invention of an artificial language. But as I argued above *contra* McMurtry, 'objectification' (essentially synonymous with 'fabrication') can be purposeful without being intentional or premeditated (see Chapter 1). As Rossi-Landi puts it: 'If languages [*langues*] were not products and language in general [*langage*] were not work, they would be something purely natural, that is, hypo-historical, like digestion or respiration, or else they would be something purely non-natural, that is, meta-historical'.[65] Recalling Marx's and Engels's insistence that 'language, like consciousness, only arises from the need, the necessity, of intercourse with other human beings', Rossi-Landi provides a more realistic and analytically more useful alternative to Benveniste's fully-formed *Homo loquens*.[66] And he does so by reminding us that neither human beings nor language emerged fully formed in the world, that each must be viewed 'dialectically', with an eye to the *formation* of its meaning:

> When we speak of a *man's* need for relations with other *men*, we do not by this mean that all these men are already formed. Instead, they form themselves precisely in the process of instituting these relationships. When we say that *man has* among other needs, that of expressing himself and communicating, we are describing a given fact related to the present situation, in which men already exist in that measure of completion that evolution has permitted. ... Once the phase of early animal and instinctive forms of immediate appropriation of objects existing in nature is overcome, only human work can satisfy a human need; and only such a complex work as linguistic work can satisfy the complex human need for expression and communication. The complexity of this labour is determined by the complexity of the need and, in turn, determines it – exactly as occurs with manipulative or transformative work.[67]

---

64   Fletcher 1993, p. 18.
65   Rossi-Landi 1983, p. 37.
66   Marx 1845 in Tucker 1978, p. 158.
67   Rossi-Landi 1983, pp. 37–8. Following citations in this paragraph, ibid., p. 38; p. 42. It should go without saying that just as the universal production of such basic products as food,

'Language too', Rossi-Landi therefore concludes, is also 'human work and languages are its necessary objectification'. Like all human work, linguistic work is social, and it is 'the social nature of language itself ... that presides over the formation and repeated use of the materials that make up languages'. Thus, what seems to Benveniste the 'naturality of speech' is actually 'a sociality[,] ... the product of long practice on the part of the individual and of a long tradition of social living. It is a *social pseudo-naturality*'.

In contrast to the *Course* that views *langue* as the social side of *langage*, but relegates speakers and *parole* to the 'individual private side', Rossi-Landi argues that *parole*, the individual speech acts, are fundamentally social as well.[68] He takes his cue from Marx's comment in the *Grundrisse* that individuals are 'related to a language as [*their*] own only as the natural member[s] of a human community. Language as the product of an individual is a non-thing [*ein Unding*]. ... Language itself is just as much product of a community, as in another aspect it is the existence of a community – it is, as it were, the communal being speaking for itself'.[69] Wielding this insight against the argument of the Saussurean *Course*, Rossi-Landi insists:

> Linguistic work lies rather on the side of *langage* in so far as, being collective rather than individual, it stands in opposition to *parole* and, being work rather than product, to *langue*. By making *langage* a simple combination of *langue* and *parole*, we preclude the study of the collective and communitarian techniques of language. The bi-partition between language and speech must be replaced by a tri-partition: linguistic work

---

shelter, etc. is always mediated by socio-culturally specific models and techniques, so too is speech production governed by the grammatical (syntactical and semantic) blueprints of a socio-culturally specific language. It is also worth noting that even if the 'language instinct' (Pinker) is natural and resides in a 'language acquisition device' (Chomsky) situated in our brains, it does seem rather indisputable, as several unfortunate cases of children cut off from human contact have shown, that without the social dimension, i.e. without speech and interlocutors, the 'language acquisition device' will not be activated, will fail to function.

68 Because linguistic objectification in the form of individual speech acts is the work of the projective consciousness, it is more homologous to the labour-process. Rossi-Landi insists that the dismissal of *parole* by Saussure and his structuralist and poststructuralist successors betrays their refusal to acknowledge language as the product of language production or linguistic objectification. This refusal, he concludes, 'has a marked ideological imprint, the nucleus of which is constituted by a refusal to recognize the founding power of work and thus also the explicative and revolutionary power of the notion of work' (Rossi-Landi 1983, p. 152).

69 Marx 1973 [1857–58], p. 490.

(collective) produces the language (collective) on and with which individual speech is exercised. The products of this speech flow back into the same collective reservoir from which its materials and instruments have been drawn.[70]

It is therefore necessary, he concludes, to 'replace individual speech [*parole*] with a *collective* speech and examine the relationships between a language [*langue*] and a speech [*parole*] which are both collective'. This redefinition of *parole* as collective speech enables Rossi-Landi to articulate the relation between an individual speech act, which is always already collective speech, and *langue*: 'Each of us, when we speak, puts back into operation not only a collective language, but also a collective and therefore communicative speech. It is precisely for this reason that we understand one another. If the modalities of our [linguistic] work, that is, the work processes as embodied in actual operations on the one hand, and the materials and instruments ... were not *already* collective, we would never succeed in understanding one another'.

Langue can and should be temporarily quarantined, methodologically etherised and, like T.S. Eliot's evening against the sky, laid out upon a table and probed in order to gain an understanding of its anatomy and physiology, its internal structure and immanent logic. Once the desired insights have been attained, however, the anaesthesia must be allowed to wear off. If, however, the methodological fiction that excised *langue* from *langage* and *parole* is allowed to persist, and if, following Saussure, *langue* is taken as the 'unique and true object of linguistics ... studied in and for itself',[71] then the patient remains laid out on the table, a kind of living corpse – yet one whose post-mortem effects burden the brain of the living insofar as *langue* is (mis)taken as the producer of meaning and thus the essential and formative factor in human consciousness and cognition. However, a historical-materialist (or any) approach that focuses on the entire process and practice of *langage* will seek to awaken the anaesthetised *langue*, bring it back into the world of the living, re-join it with *parole* as one of the two essential moments of the process of linguistic objectification. Once *langue* is reintegrated into the world of the living, it loses the illusion, born of its isolation, of being mistaken as the sole producer of meaning and thought (and subjecthood, see Chapter 7). Instead, it can be understood as the key instrument and material of linguistic objectification, the means through which speakers produce and communicate the expression of meaning.

---

70   Rossi-Landi 1983, pp. 39–40. Following citations in this paragraph, ibid., p. 148; p. 151.
71   Saussure 1959, p. 232.

As Bruno Liebrucks insists, in my view accurately: because 'real language [*Sprache*[72]] is only there where it is spoken', language itself is 'intentional doing'. This 'intentional doing', moreover, is a tripartite relation: a 'subject-subject-object relation',[73] and it is (as I shall, for the moment, paraphrase his formulation) a matter of an individual communicating some meaning about something, through language, to another individual.[74] The speaking individual is never isolated and individual, but rather involved in an obviously social subject-subject-object relation whose purpose is the *production* and communication of meaning that is *expressed* in a language (*langue*) that is itself a collective product. This formulation, however, raises at least three issues that, for purposes of both elaboration and substantiation, must be addressed here briefly (and more specifically in Part 3).

First of all, there is a good deal of often vehement debate over what seems to me the false binary opposition of language as signification vs. communication.[75] The general trend in this debate is that those concerned with animal

---

72   Liebrucks 1964, p. 58. '*Sprache ist – auch – absichtliches Tun. Denn wirklich Sprache ist nur, wo gesprochen wird*'. It is worth noting that unlike the fine differentiations in French between *langage* and *langue*, the German *Sprache* can signify either or both *langage* and *langue*. On the one hand, this may have made it more difficult for a German speaker to isolate *langue* as a system of signs as a necessary step in deciphering the logic of linguistic signs. On the other hand, it may have made it easier to avoid the reification of *langue* that begins in the *Course* and was furthered by its followers and thus to remember, as did Liebrucks that language is both language and the linguistic act of speaking/communicating.

73   Liebrucks 1964, p. 3. Liebrucks's argument is aimed at philosophers who, while recognizing the linguistic character of knowledge (*Erkenntnis* which, he says is *sprachlich* or 'linguistic'), have neglected the essential communicative dimension of language; having focused only on the relation between the knowing subject and the object and knowledge, they have seen only one 'a moment of the entire knowledge-process'. The same can be said of those whose only interest in the analysis of *langue* and the relation between signifier and signified. From a phenomenological perspective, Robert Sokolowski has a similarly critical take on the approaches that attribute agency to structures: 'Formal structures are not ends in themselves, but instruments in the disclosure of things. ... The mind that constitutes meaning and its formal structures does so ultimately to evidence the truth of things' (Sokolowski 2000, pp. 173–4).

74   Liebrucks 1964, p. 3. I have purposefully paraphrased Liebrucks's comment about 'subjects' – '*ein Subjekt dem anderen Subjekt in der Sprache etwas über die Dinge mitteilt*' (p. 3) – and used 'individuals' because I do not here want to address the more complicated matter of 'subjects'. The problem of the subject will be addressed specifically in Chapter 7 and periodically throughout Part 3. Here I want to focus on the fact that *parole*, speech acts, the activation of *langue*, is also social because it requires an interlocutor. And *apropos* talking to oneself, Liebrucks also notes that 'in communicating something about things to another person, I communicate it to myself. In giving, I receive' (ibid., p. 3).

75   See Chapter 8 below.

behaviour tend to focus on the question of communication and subsume both the signalling of other species and the language of the human species under the category communication. The semiotically inclined are appalled by this seeming conflation of signals and linguistic sign systems; but instead of just differentiating the semiotics of language from the semiotics of signals, they reduce communication to signalling, whereby the opposition between language and signals becomes one of signification vs. communication – an opposition made more rigid by the methodologically fictional isolation of *langue* from considerations of why languages exist, that is, from the purpose of the human faculty of speech (*langage*), and from the actual use of languages in speaking (*parole*). Yet, in the world of our early human(oid) ancestors, it is hard to imagine language evolving except socially, i.e. through communication. Without interlocutors seeking to communicate some meaning(s), there would be no need for a language in which to express that meaning, thus no need to invent it.[76] We need not deny that *langue* has always been by its very nature a semiotic system, and has developed into an extraordinarily complex system. Nevertheless, in the land of the living (and again: notwithstanding the need temporarily to isolate it for analytical purposes), *langue* must be viewed as also and necessarily a system of communication, an integral *means* in the subject-subject-object relation that is linguistic work or linguistic objectification.

This understanding of the faculty of speech or *langage* as necessarily involving both signification and communication follows from the historical-materialist focus on the entire process of linguistic objectification through which meaning is *produced*. This is in contrast to those who, following the *Course* and focusing exclusively on the semiotic system, conclude that the system of signs is itself and alone the producer of meaning. It is, however, worth noting that even the *Course* makes the much more modest claim that *langue* 'is a system of signs *expressing* ideas' (my emphasis).[77] Although at first glance the two might

---

76 Although language not only facilitates thinking, but also makes possible abstract thinking (with all its advantages and disadvantages), it is, contrary to exaggerated claims, not necessary for cognition. In encountering a threatening dog, for example, one can certainly think and react appropriately without representing, signifying, or conceptualising it to oneself that 'this is a mad dog and I must away'. And although our conscious articulated thoughts are impossible without language, they are deeper, richer than language embedded in what Michael Polanyi calls 'tacit knowledge' which he views as foundational to all conscious knowledge (see Chapter 7). It seems safe to say that language developed through attempts to communicate thoughts and also stimulated thinking in turn.

77 Saussure 1959, p. 16. The translation reads: 'Language is a system of signs that express ideas'. The original is '*La langue est un système de signes exprimant des idées*' (Saussure 1983, p. 33). I have altered the translation accordingly.

appear synonymous, the difference between 'expressing' and 'producing' ideas is perhaps subtle, but certainly significant; it is what I tried to capture above with the awkward phrase 'the production of the expression of meaning' whose appropriateness I promised to elaborate. This is most effectively done by giving historical-materialist content to the terminology in the *Course* that delineates the branches of linguistics – which also entails rethinking the relations among them.

The *Course* divides *langage*, the general faculty of speech, into the synchronic logic of the linguistic system, *langue*, and the diachronic linguistics of the contingent, *parole*; and the elevation of *langue* to the norm 'of all other manifestations of *langage*', to the 'unique and true object of linguistics' as a science, reduces the interest in *langage* and/or *parole* to a merely antiquarian or dilettantish pastime. A historical-materialist twist of this terminology, however, not only redefines its contents, but also realigns the relations among the branches of linguistics. *Langage* is reconsidered as linguistic objectification or the mode of linguistic production. The *means* of linguistic production are the corporeal tools of speech and its reception, that is, the vocal apparatus of the speaker and the acoustic apparatus of the interlocutor through which speech is *produced* and consumed. The *materials* of production are of two kinds: the layers of air agitated and formed into mouthy yet meaningful little noises; and *langue*, the system of signs in and through which speakers *express* their meanings. *Parole* is the *production-process* itself, the work of speaking, the linguistic intercourse of interlocuting individuals. And the *product* of linguistic production is of course their dialog.

These redefinitions and this realignment do not at all deny the value of the synchronic analysis of *langue*, but rather situate it in the much larger process of which it is an integral part. And it should also reawaken interest in an element discarded by a synchronic semiotics, yet essential to a consideration of language as linguistic objectification, namely: the referent, that to which the sign is supposed to refer, but which in synchronic semiotics is called onto the stage only in order to be immediately banished. My argument for the rehabilitation of the referent will be made in detail in Chapter 8, but here a comment will suffice to establish its place within a historical-materialist approach to linguistic objectification.

In a formulation that alludes to the referent (while also concurring with the *Course* on the expressive nature of language), Liebrucks writes that language is 'the expression of an impression'.[78] If construed narrowly, this phrase

---

78 'Sprache ist der Ausdruck eines Eindrucks', Liebrucks 1964, p. 173. Here *Sprache* refers to both speaking (*parole*) and that with which one speaks (*langue*).

could be taken to mean a one-to-one nomenclatorial relation between thing and word. I choose to focus on the motivated indeterminateness of the term 'impression', that is: impressions are formed through encounters with objects in the world (whether material or 'immaterial' – even figments of the imagination are objectified, materialised when put into words); but they of course vary among individuals and cultures. Nevertheless, those impressions that are expressed in speech acts and through language/*langue* are spoken with the intention of communicating to another (or even to oneself) some meaning about some thing(s) in the world, a referent. Without something to talk about, a referent, language has no purpose. Although perhaps incidental to understanding how meaning is expressed in *langue* taken as a semiotic system, the referent of linguistic signs, that which provokes the impression expressed in language, is nevertheless essential to understanding the meanings produced through linguistic objectification. This is captured succinctly, beautifully, and perfectly in Walt Whitman's apostrophe to

> You objects that call forth from diffusion my meanings
> And give them shape[79]

2.3.4.3 Note on Intellectual and Aesthetic Objectification

Following these lengthy discussions of sense perception and language production, this treatment of intellectual labour and artistic production as also forms of semiotic objectification will be perhaps surprisingly brief. This is in part because it does not require any great stretch of the imagination to consider intellectual and aesthetic labour as forms of objectification. The production of ideas and of art is the form of semiotic objectification most homologous to material objectification: both are 'purposeful activities' of subjects using the tools and materials of their trade, concepts and ideas, and transforming 'raw' thoughts or images into intellectual or aesthetic artefacts. As with material objectification, the purposefulness of these two forms of semiotic objectification derives from the projective consciousness, that ability to raise a structure in the imagination and then erect it in reality.

Despite this isomorphism of intellectual and aesthetic with material objectification, there are limits to the comparison. This mistake is evident in claims that those who occupy that branch of the social division of labour devoted to the production of ideas, i.e. academics and intellectuals, are 'proletarians

---

79 Whitman, 'Song of the Open Road' in Whitman 1958, p. 137.

of the mind'.⁸⁰ And Fredric Jameson's comment on the problems with this notion is applicable to the notion of 'aesthetic proletarians' as well. Jameson warned, 'One cannot without intellectual dishonesty assimilate the "production" of texts ... to the production of goods by factory workers: writing and thinking are not alienated labour in that sense, and it is surely fatuous for intellectuals to seek to glamorize their tasks ... by assimilating them to real work on the assembly line ...'.⁸¹ On the other hand, this should not be taken to imply that only academics and intellectuals work with their minds, or that only those who make a living as artists are aesthetic. As Antonio Gramsci clearly and correctly stated, all people are intellectuals, though not all have the social function of being an intellectual;⁸² and analogously, all people have an aesthetic sensibility, though not all have the social function of being an artist. Thus, just as the analysis of material objectification or manual labour in a given social form must focus on its specific social constitution, so too must the analysis of intellectual and aesthetic labour also address their specific social constitution. The question of the social constitution of intellectual labour, and Marx's attempt to find methodological solutions to the epistemological problems resulting from it, will be addressed in some detail in the following chapter.

2.4   Concluding Considerations: Objectification, Artefacts, and History

In the previous chapter I argued that by taking 'human corporeal organisation' as the 'first fact' of historical theory, Marx effected a corporeal reconstitution of the subject-object dialectic grounded in the concept of objectification. In this chapter I began with Marx's enumeration of the moments of history and, by systematising his many scattered comments on the topic, derived from them three corresponding modes of objectification enabled and required by human corporeal organisation. And because each of these three modes of human objectification is inherently social, what Liebrucks said of language (or what I have termed more broadly semiotic objectification) is applicable to the other two modes as well, namely that they are subject(s)-subject(s)-object(s) dialectics. These three modes of objectification are all transformative, producing artefacts that do not exist 'in nature'; as such they are 'ways of worldmaking' that, taken together, produce the totality of human worlds of material, semi-

---

80   This is common in the recent debate, especially among the Italian 'Postworkerists' such as Antonio Negri.
81   Jameson 1981, p. 45.
82   Gramsci 1971, p. 9.

otic, and social artefacts. By way of concluding this chapter I would like to make two comments of explanation and qualification, both pertaining to artefacts and history: the first concerns the relation between the history of artefacts and their meaning(s) – and therewith the significance of this lengthy elaboration of objectification; the second concerns the relation among the three modes of objectification in transforming nature and making history.

First, I would like to address a question that will doubtless be asked of this extended discussion of the three moments of history and the three modes of objectification: the 'so what?' question: Even if you are right in whittling down the moments of history and in elaborating three corresponding modes of objectification, so what? Why is it so important? What work does it do? The most important work performed by this elaboration of objectification is that it forces us to approach what I have called material, semiotic, and social objects not merely as things existing in their brute facticity, but as artefacts. The difference is that the term 'artefact' should force us to remember that all artefacts are made-objects that, as such, have a history – and one that does not consist solely of what happens to the object *after* it has been made.

Despite the various forms it has assumed, the age-old battle over how to determine the meaning of a thing can be described as one between the same essential antagonists manifested in a variety of ways, i.e. whether the meaning of a thing is determined by: its past or its present; diachrony or synchrony; history or structure; *Genesis* or *Geltung*. In the long and broad wake of *Course* of 'the official Saussure', synchrony has been privileged over diachrony; and where structuralist analysis has dominated, history has been increasingly banished from the determination of an object's meaning. Nowhere is this more evident than in structuralist and poststructuralist literary and cultural studies. And nowhere is it more succinctly formulated than in Roland Barthes's notion of 'the death of the author' and the birth of the 'text'.

Various formalist approaches from the New Criticism to Deconstruction have provided a much-needed corrective to the practice of over-historicising literary texts to the point of disappearing their aesthetics; and the value of such analyses that exclude everything outside the text and focus exclusively on its internal logic is not at all in question here. However, as Marx said of dialectics (and Derrida intimated in referring to his own work as 'limited'), every methodology must 'know its own limits'.[83] And while certain purposes can be served by the temporary methodological exclusion of such factors as the author's life,

---

83   Derrida, 1981, p. 63. See Chapter 3, note 54 for source of, and comment on, Marx's recognition of the limits of the dialectic.

authorial intent, the historical context in which the author lived and the social conditions of literary production within which the author worked, the permanent exclusion of these factors crucial to its production, its making, is to reify the text, to turn it into a thing and deprive it of its madeness, its artefactuality.

Similarly in cultural studies after the 'cultural turn' – as, for example, in a volume edited by Arjun Appadurai, entitled *The Social Life of Things* and devoted, as its subtitle states, to the analysis of 'Commodities in Cultural Perspective'.[84] Telling about these essays is that things are treated as givens and their existence taken for granted (as is the hypostasis of the commodity form which I will only note here). As is revealed by a quick glance at the table of contents, the essays are grouped around aspects of the post-production afterlife of 'commodities', on their 'exchange, consumption, and display', 'prestige, commemoration, and value', and on 'transformations in commodity codes'.

All of these are of course interesting and important topics, and there are obviously many very good reasons to read a work of literature or philosophy or history as a text. Such readings that refuse to look at a work of art or any artefact as simply a mirror of the author's intent, the historical context, etc. have certainly proven their value in deciphering the internal, systemic logic of a text, cultural form, etc. Certainly true, too, is that over time artefacts of any kind come to assume meanings quite different from that which was the purpose of their production. On the other hand, however, a study of artefacts, made-objects, that completely excludes the history of their making renders them vulnerable to being filled with meanings that are projections of the critic's imagination; and it is difficult to find a structuralist-based study that, while claiming to focus exclusively on the text to the exclusion of authorial intent, does not at some point attribute an intent, derived solely from the reader's textual analysis, to the text's author. But even if such questionable attribution can be avoided, the more fundamental issue is that such a purely 'textual' approach to artefacts (again, whether material, semiotic, or social) addresses only their post-production half-life, and completely ignores the not irrelevant questions of why and how it came into being, why human beings made it, what the purpose and process of its production were, thus depriving them of their own lives and meaning. Severed from its history and rendered lifeless, the artefact becomes, in another rephrasing of Voltaire's witticism, a means of using the dead to play a pack of tricks on history.

---

84 Appadurai 1986. Cultural studies after the 'cultural turn' (one aspect of which, as evident in Appadurai's title and subtitle, is the tendency to conflate the 'social' and the 'cultural') are addressed in greater detail below (Chapter 9).

We do not have to reduce the meaning of an artefact to authorial intent in order to realize that the artefact may have a much different history and meaning from that which is constructed through a denial of its history – especially if followed, as often happens, by a projection of our own meanings onto it. I would therefore counter the structuralists' one-dimensional either/or, either history or structure, with the historical-materialist both/and, both structure and history, both synchrony and diachrony.[85] From a historical-materialist viewpoint, the production of an artefact (its producers and their purpose in producing, the means, materials, and relations of its production, etc.) is no less (and no more) crucial as what happens to it after it has been produced. And the most important reason for this lengthy elaboration of why material, semiotic and social things should be considered artefacts, products of material, semiotic, or social objectification, is precisely that it forces us to focus on the madeness of artefacts, and therewith too on their makers and of the purpose and meaning with which they are invested at the time, and in the act, of their making. By viewing artefacts as products of an objectifying process, however, it becomes clear that their history long precedes their existence, and can be traced all the way back through the actual production process to the needs and desires (regardless, as Marx put it, of 'whether they spring from the stomach or the imagination') that defined their purposes and prompted their production – the history, that is, that is not irrelevant to the lives and meaning of artefacts nor to the human worlds comprised by them (See Chapter 10).

My second comment concerns the relation between the three modes of objectification and the making of history, specifically, the kinds of transformation effected by the three modes of objectification. Through the bodily activity of objectifying interaction with nature, human beings (always in social groups) create worlds of artefacts, human worlds. In so doing humans not only transform the 'naturally' given world and their relations to it, but also their modes of interacting with each other (social objectification, society) and their modes of thinking about, and representing, their world (semiotic objectification); in short, they transform themselves. Here it must be emphasised that I am not talking in terms of transhistorical laws that entail a specific direction for history – simply about the facts that humans' relations both to nature and to each other in the process of satisfying their social and material needs ($οἰκονομία$), and that the way they understand and give meaning to those relations (culture), are inextricably imbricated in each other. It must therefore also be emphasised

---

85   This will be elaborated in detail in the following chapter on a 'historical-materialist *Wissenschaft*'.

that this categorisation of modes of objectification is not intended as a rigid grid to be imposed on the material of history, on human activity. As was noted above, language could be categorised as an artefact produced by social objectification almost as easily as it can be classified a semiotic one. And intellectual labour could easily be classified as a branch of the social division of labour. But crucial to my set of categories is the nature of the artefacts produced by a particular form of objectification – and given this criterion, it is perfectly reasonable at this stage of the analysis to categorise language and intellectual labour as semiotic rather than social or material objectification. But it is imperative that the categories remain flexible or, better, that we remain flexible enough in our thinking to recognise overlaps and nuances. If so, then this categorisation can be used heuristically and effectively, not only as the basis of elaborating a historical-materialist theory of worldmaking, but also as a basis from which to point out, against false binaries (e.g. Habermas's separation of the economic sphere from the 'life-world'), that making, speaking, and inter-subjective relations all have their roots in human corporeal organisation and though identifiably distinct, they are the inextricably intertwined moments of human being and history.

Finally, although this will be discussed in greater detail in the next chapter, a brief comment is in order here on why a historical-materialist *Wissenschaft* 'privileges', as the starting point of its analyses, labour and the production of material artefacts. As Maurice Godelier succinctly formulates the fundamental historical-materialist hypothesis, '*human beings have a history because they transform nature*'.[86] And all three modes of objectification discussed above are certainly transformative. The historical-materialist reason for positing material objectification as the 'first among equals' is the difference in kind between the transformations effected by material objectification and those effected by semiotic and social objectifications. While social objectifications establish the relations among human beings within a given relation to the natural world and while semiotic objectifications determine how human beings give meaning to their relations to each other and the natural world, both leave the natural world in a certain, key way 'untouched'.

I hesitate to use the word 'untouched', but perhaps an example will help qualify what I mean here: the railroad trains invented in the early Industrial Revolution could be signified as 'trains', 'iron horses', 'speed demons', etc. – different signs carrying different meanings which create different relations to the referent. But this new object of diverse significations was a product of material

---

86   Godelier 1984, p. 1.

objectification; and trains and all that pertains to them, from tracks to stations to seating arrangements, had a transformative effect on all the 'moments' of history. The velocity at which trains could travel, Wolfgang Schivelbusch has argued, transformed the very perceptions of speed and distance. Though the seating in trains may have been socially segregated, the cosmopolitan character of the clientele in railway stations restructured the composition of the 'crowd'. The train tracks that cut across the Great Plains, through the Rockies, and to the Pacific forcibly redefined the relation between people and nature and intensified the confrontation between Euro- and Native Americans. What was left of the diminishing Native American lands, already subject to systematic expropriation in the name of private ownership of nature, was now being severed by iron rails and iron horses that disrupted their relation to nature and destroyed their way of life. Material objectification, whether in producing handtools or weapons, cultivating a field, or building the greatest of material artifices, cities, immediately touches and transforms the natural world; in so doing it transforms the relations between human beings and the natural world and produces new kinds of objects that become the objects of semiotic objectification.

Thus, *if* forced to choose (and I very purposefully emphasise the counterfactual), a materialist conception of history would choose 'material objectification', the mode of production, as the single most transformative form of objectification. But precisely because the foundational premise of historical materialism and dialectical thinking is that the three 'moments of history' and the three 'modes of objectification' are the inextricably intertwined moments of a constellation, one must from a historical-materialist standpoint refuse to respond to a question demanding a single and exclusive answer – or even to a question demanding a definitive answer about what is essential and what is epiphenomenal; a historical-materialist *Wissenschaft* must rather reconstruct the 'totality' of human worlds which necessarily consist of the artefacts produced by all the modes of objectification enabled by the capacities inherent in human corporeal organisation.[87] Consequently, though the labour of material objectification within a given mode of production may be the starting point of a historical-materialist analysis, it is certainly not the end point. For, as Marx adds immediately upon introducing the concept of a 'mode of production' in *The German Ideology*: 'The mode of production must not be considered simply as being the reproduction of the physical existence of the individuals. *Rather, it is a definite form of activity of these individuals, a definite form of expressing*

---

87 For a discussion of Marx's views on labour and work and a critique of Hannah Arendt's ontology of the same, see Appendix 2.2.

their life, a definite mode of life on their part.⁸⁸ In this regard, a given mode of production is the form-determinant (*Formbestimmung*) that frames (but does not determine with the iron necessity) the range, the possibilities and limits, of a given 'mode of life' or, as he alternatively puts it, of the 'real life process' of 'really living individuals'.⁸⁹

The 'mode of life' or 'real life-process' of a given social group consists not only of material, but also of social and semiotic objectification. And although the differentiation of these three modes of human objectification is valid for analytical purposes, the fact that all three modes are inherently social establishes a synaesthesia among them: human labour is social and literally and figuratively unthinkable without semiotic objectification – as are social objectifications in the form of institutions and durable relations of any human form. And the labour of semiotic objectification is unthinkable without human sociability which itself is mediated through the labour required to reproduce the lives of individuals and succeeding generations. Those objects that become referents of human sign systems (whether linguistic or cultural/symbolic) are those whose attributes catch the eyes and ears, nose, stomach, and feeling, in short, the senses of human beings, those objects whose 'affordances' (J.J. Gibson) become imbricated in human material practices, those objects that, as part of human life-experience, become part of the 'conscious being', the consciousness of human beings.⁹⁰ Even if the mode of material objectification is the form-determinant that frames a mode of life of a given social group, the 'real life-process' of the members of that group is formed by the synaesthesia of these three modes of objectification – by their interaction with nature and with each other while producing and living within semiotically produced webs of meaning. Historical-materialist *Wissenschaft*, accordingly, must consider all three modes and establish the constellation of relations among them that together give shape to a socio-cultural form. How to do this will be taken up in the next chapter – but first, my final qualification concerning the question of what is, and is not meant, by objectification.

---

88 Marx 1845 in Tucker 1978, p. 150; Marx italicised only *mode of life*; but because all that is expressed in this statement is, for my purposes, of the utmost importance, I italicised the whole sentence. Following citation, ibid.
89 On *Formbestimmung* or 'form-determinant', see Appendix 1.2.
90 In my view, J.J. Gibson's notion of 'affordances' is a crucial conceptual means of understanding the subject-object relation in a non-essentialist manner, of acknowledging that and how different subjects can perceive and apprehend the same object in a variety of ways – all meaningful. This term will reappear throughout this work, and is particularly important in Chapters 8 and 9. Further discussion of 'affordances' in Appendix 2.3.

In a passage that I could imagine Nietzsche greeting as akin to his notion of a 'will to power',[91] Marx wrote: 'The wealthy human being is ... the human being *in need of* a totality of human life-activities – the human being in whom self-realization exists as inner necessity, as need'.[92] As we saw above in the discussion of 'human nature', the evolved human being is for Marx a creature with species-specific bodily instruments and powers, capacities, and limitations, and with a need, inhibited only by an unjust social order, to utilise those instruments and capacities and realise the vast potential residing in them. This notion (like Nietzsche's will to power and striving for the *Übermensch* as self-realisation) can be and not infrequently has been interpreted in a rather heroic manner. By this I mean neither the Stalinist nor the Nazi caricatures of the heroic, but the more subdued heroism of those literary archetypes Prometheus or Faust – a vision of humans as makers, doers, defiers, etc. which some feminist critics have criticised as a male vision of the world. Those critics are tautologically correct in arguing that a materialist conception of history is all about making and using. The problem, however, is that the notion of making that such critics attribute to Marx is a rather one-dimensionally monumental notion of making – a notion that adequately describes distorted productivist (e.g. Soviet) interpretations of Marx's materialist conception of history, but not Marx's historical-materialist conception itself.

Marx's notion of objectification is rather different. From his viewpoint, all human beings, whether male or female, are, by corporeal definition, inevitably objectifying beings, 'makers' who inescapably practice all three modes of objectification. 'A human and natural subject with eyes, ears, etc., living in the world and in nature' will inevitably be engaged in the production of material objects whether building dams or making a meal, in the production of semiotic objects in perceiving and speaking, and in the production of social objects in the intersubjective relationships that everyone builds. Making may of course be as monumental as Faust's land-reclamation project. But it may also be as profoundly simple as attuning oneself to the other, whether object or person. Above we encountered Whitman's hailing of the objects 'that call forth from diffusion [his] meanings and give them shape'. And he also attuned himself to other individuals/subjects whom he encountered on the open road:

---

91 Feuerbach is one of the few modern thinkers about whom Nietzsche had something good to say and Nietzsche's 'will to power' in many ways resembles Feuerbach's notion of an unalienated human being. It is unfortunate that Nietzsche never had the opportunity to read Marx's *Economic-Philosophical Manuscripts of 1844*.

92 Marx 1844 in Tucker 1978, p. 91. Translation slightly altered.

> Listening to others, considering well what they say,
> Pausing, searching, receiving, contemplating,

Or making may be as selflessly heroic as what Wordsworth called 'those little nameless unremembered acts of kindness and love' that make up 'the best portion of a good [person's] life'. Or as aesthetic as Wordsworth's objectification of those sentiments into words. True, Marx's theory is all about making and use, but so too, his theory argues, is human life. Human beings cannot not make; we cannot not use the objects of the world. The crucial question thus becomes not whether we make and use, but what we make and how we use.

Finally, Marx's comment about the inner necessity of self-realisation aims at the ultimate project of making. That comment not only resonates with, and exponentially expands the scope of, Nietzsche's notion of the human 'will to power', but it resonates too with a crucial term that emerged in the Black and other Power Movements of the 1960s and in the feminist movement, and that has now become an integral (and too often unfortunately trivialised) part of everyday speech and action, namely: 'empowerment'. The goal of Marx's own theory-making was a society 'in which the free development of each is the precondition for the free development of all' – one which allows us to engage in the ultimate project of making, that is to be makers of ourselves, i.e. to be free.[93]

---

93   Marx and Engels 1848 in Tucker 1978, p. 491.

CHAPTER 3

The Dimensions and Methodological *Leitfaden* of a Historical-Materialist *Wissenschaft*

3.1 Introductory

In the previous two chapters I presented my take on the terms of Marx's wager to reconstruct human history up from human corporeal organisation. Chapter 1 traced his attempts to establish the foundations of a corporeally-grounded materialist conception of history on the basis of which he sought to win the wager; and Chapter 2 elaborated what he considered the fundamental and transhistorical 'moments' of human existence – those moments that I designated material, social, and semiotic objectification, the modes and range of which are delineated by the capacities and limits embedded in human corporeal organisation, and the specific form or constellation of which by socio-cultural and geographical factors. As moments of human existence, these are *ipso facto* moments of all human histories – and therefore also crucial issues of analysis for a historical-materialist *Wissenschaft* seeking to comprehend those histories.

But precisely as transhistorical constants, these moments are necessarily lacking the specificity and particularity of their concrete and diverse historical manifestations; they are empty of historical content, pure forms that can only be abstractly conceived. Although they provide the indispensable foundation of a materialist-conception of history, these moments cannot in themselves reveal concrete knowledge of particular human beings inhabiting a particular social form in a particular geographical space, and at a particular point in historical time. They can serve only as the (albeit necessary) starting point of a historical-materialist *Wissenschaft*. There remains, accordingly, a long way to go from that necessarily abstract historical-materialist *conception* of history to writing the concrete history of the 'really-existing, active people' in a given society.[1]

---

1 Marx 1845, in Tucker 1978, p. 171. Marx used such terms as 'really existing individuals' or 'living human individuals' (ibid., p. 149) in *The German Ideology* to differentiate his material-corporeal take on human being from the idealist focus only on the mind. For similar reasons elaborated throughout this chapter (see esp. concluding paragraph to section 3.3.3 below, and note 51), these very important terms will recur rather often in this and the following chapters.

That journey is made all the more difficult by the obstacles to knowledge production inherent in a materialist conception of history itself. For, if human corporeal organisation is taken as the 'first fact' of human history, and the mind is, accordingly, firmly situated in the body, then the historical-materialist attempt to produce knowledge 'up from the body' will inevitably confront epistemological challenges. The two most formidable of these are: that the knowing subject is deprived of its traditional, philosophically-privileged position as the locus of 'pure reason' standing above the world about which it speaks; and that the conceptual tool of intellectual labour is deprived of the potency that traditional philosophy had invested in it. To phrase the epistemological challenge in historical-materialist terms: historical-materialist knowledge production, or *Wissenschaft*, must first determine what kinds of work can and cannot be done with the traditional conceptual tools of intellectual labour; and once, that range and its limits are determined, it is necessary to figure out how to overcome the 'natural' limitations of the means of knowledge production. The purpose of this chapter is, accordingly, two-fold: to specify the epistemological dilemmas resulting from a corporeally-based materialist conception of history; and to follow Marx carefully as he devised methodological solutions to resolve them.

These epistemological obstacles presented by his newly-developed historical-materialist theory forced Marx to recognise that although theoretical labour can and must lay the foundation for historical-materialist knowledge production, it cannot alone finish the job. And in responding to the epistemological challenges posed by his materialist conception of history, Marx elaborated the methodology and ongoing tasks of an open-ended historical-materialist *Wissenschaft*, best understood as comprising three inextricably linked dimensions, each of which is necessary, and each necessarily insufficient. The first dimension is that of historical theory, specifically: the materialist conception of history as elaborated in the previous two chapters. And the other two dimensions, that will be addressed in this chapter, are: social theory or the critique of social form (e.g. *Capital*); and historiography (which I take in its general and etymologically literal meaning of writing history, and which, in historical-materialist terms means the analysis and presentation of concrete, corporeally-grounded materialist histories of really-existing individuals inhabiting really-existing societies, each of which has been grasped in its particularity through the critique of social form).[2]

---

2 Here I take the term 'historiography' in a very general, etymologically literal manner to designate the writing of histories of any analytical object that is considered to have been, or to

The following elaboration of this three-dimensional, historical-materialist *Wissenschaft* will follow Marx as far as he went, most notably in key passages on methodology in *The German Ideology*, the *Grundrisse* and *Capital*, and also as exemplified in his own intellectual labours. But it will also require both interpolation to fill the empty spaces left by silences in his own works and extrapolation to follow his methodological *Leitfaden* (guiding threads) beyond that which he himself explicitly addressed. Only after having discussed these methodological matters will it be possible to understand the full meaning and significance of Marx's *Aufhebung* of philosophy, of his epistemological break with his erstwhile philosophical past, and of the praxis of historical-materialist *Wissenschaft*.

There has been, of course, a long line of thinkers, going back at least to Plato with his philosophical monarch, who insist that politics must be guided by knowledge – and *a fortiori* by knowledge-producers. And up to a point, Marx has a place in this line. For, although his eleventh thesis on Feuerbach castigates philosophers who only interpret the world, Marx obviously was not suggesting that knowledge production be halted or suspended in favour of the politics of changing it. As is evident from his own lifetime preoccupation, he obviously saw the work of knowing the world as integral to changing it. Nevertheless, suffering from (in his own words) 'the embarrassment of having to talk of material matters', of attempting to write history 'up from the body', he was, as I shall argue throughout this chapter, much more circumspect about the nature of knowledge production and consequently held, as I suggest in concluding, a more modest and nuanced, and therefore potentially more efficacious notion of the relation between knowledge and politics, between theory and praxis, than that of his philosophical predecessors – and that of some of his followers as well.

---

be, really existing – whether people, events, things, ideas, belief systems, societies, nations, institutions, or any of the myriad topics about which historians have written. This etymologically literal usage of historiography is rather more general than disciplinary uses of the term. Among academic historians, 'historiography' typically denotes one of two somewhat overlapping, but rather different undertakings: either a survey of historical literature in particular fields or on particular topics, and that accounts for variant analyses and arguments advanced by different authors or perhaps different schools of thought; or a set of reflections on the logic of history, on questions such as how historical objects are constituted and conceptualised, which people, events, etc. are considered worthy of historical analysis, how causality is determined, how to interpret meaning, and, since the publication of Hayden White's *Metahistory* (1973) and the importation of French semiotic-based theories of textuality in the 1970s, the concern with forms of narrativity and the textual character of historical documents. These issues addressed in this second form of 'historiography' are matters, often subsumed under the rubric of philosophy of history, but are perhaps more properly denoted by what Peter Novick called a 'once respectable word', namely: 'historiology' (Novick 1988, p. 8).

3.2 On the Epistemological Challenges of a Materialist Conception of History and Marx's Methodological Solutions

As depicted in Plato's fictional account of the birth of philosophy, human beings were originally enchained in a subterranean cave (inspired by Athenian-controlled mines at Laurion on the Attica peninsula where slaves mined the metal used for weapons and currency, for power and wealth). With their bodies bound in darkness and able to catch sight only of shadowy appearances that filled their merely perceiving minds with deceptive notions delivered through the body's unreliable senses, these cave-dwellers were incapable of comprehending the essence of things. Some, however, were somehow (how, we are never told) released from their bonds. Escaping the darkness and emerging into the sunlit ether of pure thought, these emancipated ones could now peer with their liberated mind's eye into the essence of things and see them as they truly are; they could, in short, philosophise. Having thus become able to see truth, these newly freed and enlightened spokespersons of sovereign philosophy had also acquired the wisdom to rule – to be philosopher-monarchs.[3]

Perhaps because overwhelmed by their understandable joy in their newfound freedom that allowed them to gaze on truth, and/or because bedazzled by the bright sunlight, the newly emancipated never thought to inquire into how and why they (few among a great many) were emancipated, nor to consider that there may have been epistemological strings attached to the liberation of their conceiving mind's eye from their perceiving and deceiving bodily senses. But the hidden cost of ignoring these rather crucial questions surrounding their emancipation from the cavern of corporeal deceit was to succumb to another kind of illusion: a misconceived notion of the philosophical self as unfettered and unadulterated mind, accompanied by a misplaced faith in

---

3 The suggestion that Plato's cave was modelled on the mines of Laurion is from George Thomson's *The First Philosophers* (1949, p. 214, pp. 241–3). To avoid misunderstanding: my intent here is neither to indulge in a diatribe against the Western philosophical tradition, nor to deny its contributions to the formulation of civil or 'procedural' political and legal freedoms that constitute and preserve free citizen-subjects, that grant them the right freely to cultivate their conscience, to speak their minds, to be protected by laws guaranteeing those rights, and to participate as citizens in governance. It is however not necessary to deny the importance of such freedoms in order to point out their limitations – limitations resulting from the fact that such procedural freedoms, while not empty, guarantee only the *right* to life, liberty, and the pursuit of happiness, but not the things themselves. And for those deprived of the material wherewithal, of the 'substantive' freedoms that enable people to realise those rights and pursue their happiness, such civil freedoms are rather hollow. This is addressed further in the Conclusion that sketches 'A Corporeally-Grounded Vision of Human Freedom and Dignity'.

the omnipotence of pure thought. Basking in, yet blinded by, the bright light outside the cave, they remained as oblivious as did Plato to the obvious particularity of their own newly acquired standpoint, and of the knowledge they would produce from it.

It is in this regard worth noting the rub, the loose thread, hidden in plain sight but unseen by its philosophical author, that unravels the neat explanatory logic of the narrative. As is evident to a historical-materialist glance, something is missing in this creation story – a story that has been variously identified as 'allegory', 'analogy', 'metaphor', and 'parable'. But in one respect, at least, it verges on a fairy tale – and reveals itself as such. Significant in this regard is that while positing freedom from the corporeal cavern as the precondition of pure thought, both the emancipated ones in Plato's narrative and Plato himself were rather unconcerned with their past, with their own history that, in their view apparently, only began outside the cave. Celebrating the fact of their emancipation, they evince no curiosity about the process of emancipation, no interest in the rather pertinent questions of who was freed, how, and why – and at what costs, both epistemological and social.

But Plato's narrative is unwillingly telling in what it does not tell. Couched in the passive voice, his passing comment on the moment of emancipation ('Consider, then, what *being released* from their bonds … would naturally be like, if something like this *should happen to* them') renders it rather fabulous. For, this passive voice, that avoids posing those not unimportant questions of who was freed, how and why, lends a certain sorcerous tinge to the liberation.[4] Without having considered these questions, the first philosophers remained in the dark about their uniquely privileged and, according to the narrative, rather *fortunate* (in both senses of this signifier's non-synonymous signifieds: 'favourable' and 'lucky') standpoint, that is: about the particular social ground on which the foundations of philosophy were laid, and therefore too about the particularity of the knowledge produced from that standpoint.

Although Aristotle at least acknowledged that freedom from manual labour was the prerequisite for true philosophising, he took that prerequisite simply as a given; and he did not bother to draw the epistemological consequences of that

---

4 In addressing the emancipation from the cave, Plato writes: 'Consider, then, what being released [λύσις, the freeing, releasing] from their bonds and cured of their foolishness would naturally be like, if something like this should happen to them. When one was freed [passive of λύω, to free] and suddenly compelled [passive of ἀναγκάζω, to compel] to stand up, turn his neck around, walk, and look up toward the light'. Cited from Plato's *Republic*, translated by C.D.C. Reeve (Indianapolis: Hackett Publishing, 515c, p. 209); my italics. My thanks to Carlo DaVia for the annotations on translation.

emancipation of the mind from the labour of the body. But it is precisely the socially-constructed separation of material and mental labour that constitutes knowledge production as a privileged branch of the social division of labour, allocated to, and as the preserve of, those intellectual labourers socially constituted and sanctioned as thinkers and knowers. And this separation not only lays the foundation of intellectual presumption, but also sets the epistemological traps in which intellectual labour all too easily finds itself caught. As Marx put it: from 'that moment when a separation of material and mental [*geistige*] labour appears, consciousness can really imagine itself as something other than consciousness of existing life-activity, can really imagine something without imagining something real – from this moment on, consciousness is able to emancipate itself from the world and to begin the construction of "pure" theory, theology, philosophy, morality, etc.'[5]

From his historical-materialist perspective that exempts neither mental labourers nor the products of their mental labours from having been afflicted with the 'curse' of materiality, Marx viewed this presumption as philosophical self-delusion. And reversing a tradition dating back to Socrates, he turned the tables by insisting that intellectual labourers were themselves in the dark concerning the socially-constituted nature of their own mental labour, of their own putatively pure thought. Countering philosophy's illusion of self-emancipation, he insisted instead that '[t]he phantoms formed in the human brain are also, necessarily, sublimates of their material life-process, which is empirically verifiable and bound to material premises'. Therefore, '[m]orality, religion, metaphysics, all the rest of ideology and their corresponding forms of consciousness no longer retain the semblance of independence. They have no history, no development; but people, developing their material production and their material intercourse, alter, along with this their real existence, their thinking and the products of their thinking'.[6] Marx's insistence that ideas have no independent history in an imaginary realm of pure thought, but are instead rooted in the world and thus have a social history, neither trivialises them nor reduces them simply to 'ideology' or 'false consciousness'. His point, rather, is the not so astonishing one that as the world changes, so too do ideas – the flip-side of which is that ideas become ideological if and when their producers mistake the socio-historically particular knowledge that they produce for universal and eternal truth. In this way Marx traced the roots of mind-body dualism, the definitive characteristic of traditional Western philosophy, back

---

5 Marx 1845 in Tucker 1978, p. 159.
6 Marx 1845 in Tucker 1978, pp. 154–5.

to its origins in the social separation of material and mental labour; he revealed philosophical mind-body dualism as itself simply a mirror-image of that social division of labour seen from the particular viewpoint of mental labour.

Gramsci noted that although all people are intellectuals, they do not all have the social function of being intellectuals and granted the socially-privileged position of knowledge-producers. In what could be considered a succinct summary of Marx's position on the social constitution of intellectual privilege, Michel de Certeau writes that 'a group misconstrues the society in which it is inserted when it fails to recognize itself as a particular social category in the relations of production and in power relations'.[7] He might have added that such a group not only fails to recognise itself, but misconstrues too the particularity of the knowledge it produces. The establishment of a specific group of socially-constituted intellectual labourers as *the* knowing subjects not only allows them to think themselves free of material interests, but also hypostatises the means or tools of intellectual labour, concepts and ideas, to the status of both the 'true' and the 'real'. This, as Marx pointed out in *The German Ideology*, allows socially-constituted knowers to put their faith in their own disciplinarily-specific language as the vehicle for expressing truth, yet prevents them from recognising the deceptively abstract character of the language they use:

> For philosophers, one of the most difficult tasks is to descend from the world of thought to the actual world. *Language* is the immediate actuality of thought. Just as philosophers have given thought an independent existence, so they had to make language into an independent realm. This is the secret of philosophical language in which the form of words has their own content. The problem of descending from the world of thoughts to the actual world is turned into the problem of descending from language to life. ... Philosophers would only have to dissolve their language into ordinary language, from which it is abstracted, to recognize it as the distorted language of the actual world, and to realize that neither thoughts nor language in themselves form a realm of their own, that they are only *expressions* of actual life.[8]

By remaining blind to the particularity of their socially-constituted standpoint, intellectual labourers can easily claim not only a privileged access to truth, but a socially-privileged role as truth-sayers. Rephrased along the lines of Gram-

---

7 de Certeau 1997, p. 129.
8 Marx 1845 in *Marx-Engels Werke*, Vol. 3, pp. 432–3.

sci's comment about intellectuals: although all people use language, the social division of mental and manual labour designates a specific social group as the masters of thought who have privileged access to transcendent entities, whether spiritual or temporal, whether deities, essences, or the future, and who speak for and to the unenlightened masses while claiming to lead them to the promised land.

The mismeasure of its own place in the social division of labour has been commonplace in the Western intellectual tradition. The first consequence of a materialist conception of history, however, is to decentre all subject positions – not excluding that of the masters of intellectual production.[9] As Michel Foucault recognised, Marx had been engaged, well before the structuralist turn, in the project of decentring and deconstructing what would later be dubbed philosophical logocentrism; and he did so by situating the locus of intellectual labour as one branch among, rather than above, the other branches of the social division of labour. By exposing the relation between mental and manual labour, the nature of which his philosophical predecessors had myopically overlooked while privileging their own activity as above all special interests, free-floating, and interested in nothing but truth, Marx revealed that traditional philosophy had been standing, not on solid epistemological ground, but instead on an epistemologically unstable rug – that he unceremoniously pulled out from underneath its feet.

In so doing, however, Marx put himself in the rather ironic position of having to confront the dilemma that he had himself posed: he had to figure out how to produce efficacious knowledge from a shaky standpoint that was, he insisted, neither as lofty in elevation nor as magisterial in breadth as its occupants imagined. A historical-materialist decentring of intellectual labour and of the knowing subjects who perform it immediately problematises the production of knowledge, contests truth claims, and requires rejection of the conceptual absolutism inherent in the philosophical positing of the primacy of (the philosopher's) mind over body. By turning intellectual labour right-side up and planting the thinker's feet on *terra firma*, a materialist conception of history recognises those feet as belonging to a subject socially constituted as a knowing subject, and trying to grasp, as the object of its knowledge, the world on which it stands, in which it inheres, and of which it is a part.

---

9 Marx's critique of philosophy and his redefinition of the social locus of the knowing subject, the intellectual labourer, is a direct and fundamental corporeal critique of what Derrida would call the 'logocentric' tradition. And, as Foucault recognised, it is a critique devoted to decentring the sovereign subject. See Foucault 1964 in Ormiston 1990, pp. 61, 63; and Foucault 1972, pp. 12–13.

In exposing the social particularity of the standpoint of intellectuals, this 'uprighting' also poses a number of serious challenges to the entire enterprise of knowledge production – challenges that Marx recognised early on in *The German Ideology* of 1845, but which took him a good deal of time and effort to solve. By reining in the belief in the pure freedom and pure power of thought, he burdened intellectual labour, his own included, with a many-sided and most challenging epistemological dilemma: a historical-materialist *Wissenschaft* understands itself as one moment of the social division of labour, but wants to raise itself above its own limited perspective in order to gain knowledge about the whole; a historical-materialist *Wissenschaft* aims both to recognise the limits on the power of thought, and to avoid relativism and scepticism, while striving to present historical reality in its concrete totality; a historical materialist *Wissenschaft* must necessarily utilise the conceptual tools of thought in order to portray reality, while knowing simultaneously that those tools necessarily abstract from its concrete diversity. In short, precisely because its claims concerning the *a priori* power of intellectual labour are much more modest than those of traditional philosophy, a historical-materialist *Wissenschaft* must confront a much more challenging task in its attempt to reconstruct reality in thought. As noted above, this is a problem that arises although, and also because, the starting point of this *Wissenschaft* is the concrete, material life-process of the real, historically existing and acting individuals. Thus, we might say that by putting mental labour in its social place, Marx himself concocted the epistemological obstacles that he had to overcome in order to win his 'breathtaking wager' on reconstituting intellectual labour 'up from the body' And he tried to solve these dilemmas through a radical reappraisal and recrafting of the tools of the intellectual trade.

Marx's response to these epistemological challenges was cautious, perhaps impatient, but certainly lengthy and complex; and it resulted in the development of the epistemological principles and the methodological *Leitfaden* (guiding threads) of a materialist *Wissenschaft* of history. The first step was the easier since it was only negative. This was to acknowledge the dilemma and, through a critique of the philosophical tradition in which he was raised, to delineate the limits on thought. This is what Marx undertook with Engels in *The German Ideology*. As we will see, however, throughout the *Grundrisse* and into *Capital* he remained concerned with defining these limits and trying to determine how to overcome them in order to produce knowledge of concrete reality while using necessarily abstract tools. The more difficult second step following from the first was the positive building of a historical *Wissenschaft* on a very modest epistemological foundation. Together, these two concerns entailed methodological reflections on the both the necessity and the inadequacy of historical theory, on the relation between historical theory and the critique of social form, and on the place of specific historical analyses and historical writing.

Nothing, perhaps, has been more common in Marx-misinterpretation than to assume that the content of the form is given with the form itself, which then all too quickly and easily leads to the reductionist and determinist conclusion that nothing more need be done than filling in the blanks of a pre-established grid in order to produce a historical-materialist analysis (e.g. the mistaken assumption that the conceptual presentation in *Capital* suffices to write the histories of really-existing capitalist societies – see below). But content is more slippery than formalists would have it. Rather than determining the specific contents, form determines the range, delineates the limits, of possible contents. And what makes such misinterpretations even more curious is that Marx provided, right in the midst of his presentation of the content of a materialist conception of history, a compact and absolutely crucial methodological discussion of the relation between *the abstract form of historical theory* and *the concrete content of historical analysis*. Along with the methodological discussion in the Introduction to the *Grundrisse*, this seldom-acknowledged discussion in the *German Ideology* is in my view the most significant and telling elaboration of historical-materialist methodology that Marx ever put in writing. In this brief two-paragraph discussion, we see Marx not only thinking through to their logical conclusion the epistemological dilemmas following from the historical-materialist attempt to write history 'up from the body', but also indicating how to develop methodological solutions to those dilemmas.

Marx began by stating that the study of real material human beings in their interaction with nature and with each other is the only adequate approach to the depiction of reality; and he concluded that once the focus is on 'the active life-process' of the 'real living individuals', history ceases to be 'a collection of dead facts as it is with the empiricists or the imagined action of imagined subjects as it is with the idealists'.[10] In announcing its obsolescence, he in effect pronounced his *Aufhebung* of philosophy which 'as an independent branch of knowledge loses its medium of existence' when confronted with this new materialist conception of history. With the end of such 'speculation', the way had been cleared for 'real, positive science [*Wissenschaft*], ... the representation of the practical activity, of the practical process of development of human beings'.[11] The most that remained to satisfy the philosophical propensity for

---

10   Marx 1845 in Tucker 1978, p. 155.
11   Ibid. A comment on Marx's use of the notion of 'positive science' is necessary here to avoid confusion. As these passages should make clear, Marx's use of this term is not to be confused with the positivism deriving from Comte which insists on inexorable laws of social

universal statements is 'a summing-up of the most general results that can be abstracted from the observation of the historical development of human beings'.[12] He immediately added, however, that 'viewed apart from the study of real history', such general statements are only 'abstractions which have in themselves *no value whatsoever*'. Their only remaining function is 'to facilitate the arrangement of historical material, to indicate the sequence of its separate strata. But they by no means afford a recipe or schema, as does philosophy, for neatly trimming the epochs of history'. In contrast to the philosophers who take universality as truth's touchstone, Marx saw in universal statements only abstractions incapable of descrying the concrete particularities of history.

Marx, however, did not dispense with such statements altogether, but maintained instead that, if consciously acknowledged as abstractions, they do have a necessary, albeit limited, role to play. Such transhistorical abstractions in the form of both premises of history (e.g. human corporeal organisation, the satisfaction of material needs) and categories (e.g. mode of production) can, as he noted, 'serve to facilitate the arrangement of historical material, to indicate the sequence of its separate strata'. As I show in the next section, 'arranging the historical material' and differentiating history's 'separate strata', although preliminary, are nevertheless essential steps toward the analysis of the various societies that comprise each particular stratum.

Given the not uncommon tendency to hypostatise the well-known sketch of the dynamics of historical change in the Preface to *A Contribution to the Critique of Political Economy* (1859) into an alleged materialist philosophy of history, it is worth noting that Marx preceded that sketch with the rather unambiguous insistence that it consists only of 'guiding threads' (*Leitfaden*) to his concrete historical studies. And establishing the guiding threads was all that he was concerned to do in reflections on history in *The German Ideology*: the general overview of the premises and content of history, along with the considerations of the nature of historical change, are intended to be only a first sketch, not a finished portrait. The generally overlooked consequence of this modest definition of the role of transhistorical statements is that all of Marx's utterances that appear to be apodictic universals are actually very self-conscious abstractions. As guides for historical-materialist knowledge-producers, they are useful

---

evolution. Rather, it must be viewed in the context of his critique of his philosophical predecessors and contemporaries whose works Marx viewed as hopelessly abstract; and it refers, of course, to the need to study empirically human beings within the 'ensemble of social relations' and in the concrete process of producing the means to satisfy their material needs.

12   Marx 1845 in Tucker 1978, p. 155. Following citations, ibid, my italics.

abstractions. But prior to being given content and corrected by the results of concrete historical-empirical analysis, they are simply abstractions – invaluable abstractions, but certainly not statements of universal truth. As Samir Amin expressed it so well when commenting on Marx's approach in relation to that of Pierre Dardot and Christian Laval 'whose analyses concerning the articulation between anthropology and sociology [Amin] share[s]': 'when examining the "practical activity of individuals" ..., I attempt never to separate the transhistorical (but not transcendent!) anthropological foundation from the sociohistorical framework in which that activity takes place'.[13] Or as Marx himself perspicaciously noted (in the midst of a scathing attack on Mr Jeremy Bentham whom he would call, had he 'the courage of [his] friend Heinrich Heine, a genius in the way of bourgeois stupidity'): to develop a principle aimed at understanding human affairs, one must deal 'first with human nature in general [that is: in the abstract], and then with human nature as historically modified in each epoch'.[14]

The German Ideology, then, presents Marx's redefinition (in abstract terms) of the content of history to match his materialist definition of the subject and object. He not only set Hegel on his feet, but also did the 'much more' that was made necessary by that inversion: he performed a thorough critique of the philosophical mode of knowledge production and, in so doing, illuminated the dilemmas that a historical-materialist *Wissenschaft* would have to confront and that established the necessary but limited, because still abstract, value of the tenets of historical-materialist theory (elaborated above in Chapters 1 and 2). The next step would be to go beyond critique and define the positive content of that historical-materialist *Wissenschaft* – a step that entailed the delineation of the relation between historical theory and the critique of social form and then between social critique and historical writing.

In his concluding comments to these paragraphs, Marx pointed to the directions that a historical-materialist *Wissenschaft* would take by pointing out the challenges it must address: 'our difficulties begin only when we set about the observation and arrangement – the real depiction – of our historical material, whether of a past epoch or of the present. The removal of these difficulties is governed by premises which it is quite impossible to state here, but which only the study of the *actual life-process* of the individuals of each epoch will make evident'.[15] Although it does not explicitly name the difficulties, this passage does indicate the two tasks involved in this second step: first, conducting

---

13 Amin 2014, p. 31. Amin's reference is to Dardot and Laval 2012.
14 Marx 1990 [1867], pp. 758–9, n. 51.
15 Marx 1845 in Tucker 1978, p. 155; my italics.

empirical research and analysing each era on its own terms; and second, solving the epistemological problems resulting from the historical-materialist restrictions on the power of thought. Only upon having performed these two tasks could Marx complete *Capital*. And his writings of the next two decades were devoted to accomplishing this dual purpose. Consequently, the first studies for *Capital*, the *Grundrisse* and the *Critique of Political Economy*, even *Capital* itself, might be viewed not only as excavations of the capitalist economy, but also as experiments in historical-materialist methodology aimed at resolving the epistemological dilemmas that erect formidable obstacles to writing history 'up from the body'. In the remainder of this chapter I trace the methodological path along which Marx sought to surmount these epistemological obstacles; and I argue that he did so by establishing a three-dimensional historical-materialist *Wissenschaft* that moves from historical-materialist theory, to the critique of social form, to historical-materialist historiography.

3.3 Beyond Historical-Materialist Theory to the Deciphering of Social Forms

3.3.1 *Delineating Social Form(s) as Analytical Object(s)*

If with *The German Ideology* Marx had set both feet clearly on historical ground, his footing was nevertheless a bit wobbly. This still uncertain footing derived from the fact that he had only just begun to think through the problem of the diverse and discrete logics of historically specific modes of production towards which his reflections on the content of history were leading. This is most clearly manifested in two competing formulations in *The German Ideology* that both pertain, albeit in very different ways, to the problem of how to define the object of analysis. With the first formulation Marx made a transhistorical, teleological, and ultimately reductionist claim, while the second statement anticipates his own 'mature' and consistently historical-materialist position. This is but one of several examples in the *German Ideology* of contradictory positions existing side-by-side in an unreconciled tension – which is, of course, confusing. If, however, we acknowledge the contradictory positions and then trace Marx's thinking about them in his later works, noting which he chose to adopt and explaining why and how he did so, then we are in a better position to understand his thought-process *in statu nascendi*. And this issue is all the more important because it is the point at which Marx made a choice between a transhistorical philosophy of history and a historical-materialist *Wissenschaft*.

The particular issue that prompted these two formulations was Marx's attempt in *The German Ideology* to delineate the capitalist mode of production as an object of analysis. Since commodity production and exchange were not limited to the modern capitalist era, the demarcation of the capitalist mode of production was not a straightforward task. And Marx's first inclination was to look back over his shoulder at Hegel and formulate an all-too Hegelian-like statement of a philosophy of history:

> This conception of history depends on our ability to expound the real process of production, starting out from the material production of life itself, and to comprehend the form of intercourse connected with this and created by this mode of production (i.e. bourgeois society [*die bürgerliche Gesellschaft*] in its various stages), *as the basis of all history*; and to show it in its action as state, to explain all the different theoretical products and forms of consciousness, religion, philosophy, ethics, etc., etc., and trace their origins and growth from that basis; by which means, of course, the whole thing can be depicted in its totality (and therewith too the reciprocal action of these various sides on one another) can be depicted in its totality.[16]

The concept of 'totality' has of late given rise to much suspicion – somewhat understandably when, as with Hegel and Lukács, the totality is totalising.[17] And Marx's positing of bourgeois society as 'the basis of all history' clearly entails a Hegelian-like transhistorical teleology and also a mechanistic and reductionist understanding of the base-superstructure relation – both of which can serve as the basis for a totalising because unitary, transhistorical logic. In addressing these matters, it will be necessary not only to consider the counter-positions that Marx presented in *The German Ideology*, but also to reach beyond, toward his later works – especially the *Grundrisse* whose chapter on 'Pre-Capitalist

---

16   Marx 1845 in Tucker 1978, p. 164, my italics.
17   In depicting Marx's thought as much more than a simple inversion of Hegel's, Althusser characterises the latter's dialectic as based on the category of a totality whose moments are mere manifestations of its essence, and with an expressivist notion of causation; for Marx's dialectic he proposes the category of a 'social whole' consisting of several 'relatively autonomous' layers, 'determined in the last instance' by the mode of production. I think, however, that Althusser underestimated the historical dimension, and exaggerated the synchronic and 'philosophical' character, of Marx's 'mature' work (Althusser 1986, p. 21). While he insisted that each relatively autonomous layer has its own time and history, his category of 'overdetermination' already lends itself to an expressivist notion of causation. And when the specific histories of each relatively autonomous layer are not written, and each is simply treated as a moment of overdetermination, what is left of structural causality hovers uncomfortably close to expressivist causality. See Althusser 1987, pp. 186–8.

Economic Forms' is crucial to understanding the direction in which Marx was heading on both of these issues, namely: toward the realisation that the logic of a materialist conception of history is antithetical to such a totalising totality.

Marx's claim that bourgeois society should be understood as the 'basis of all history', posits the bourgeois-capitalist present as the telos of the entire course of world history. Had he pursued this excessively teleological line of inquiry, he would not have gone beyond a speculative, albeit materialist, philosophy of history, and would have produced only a materialist inversion of Hegel. In this case he would already have abandoned the historical-materialist undertaking that he had barely initiated and effectively given up on his wager to reconstruct everything 'up from the body'. However, *The German Ideology* also contains a comment on the rather arbitrary nature of technological development for most of human history that not only undermined the possibility of a universal and unitary philosophy of history, but also, after Marx worked out its consequences in the *Grundrisse*, became the basis of his presentation in *Capital*.

In discussing the evolution of technology Marx wrote that 'it depends purely on the extension of commerce whether the productive forces achieved in a locality, especially inventions, are lost for later development or not. As long as there exists no commerce transcending the immediate neighbourhood, every invention must be made separately in each locality, and mere chances such as irruptions of barbaric peoples, even ordinary wars, are sufficient to cause a country with advanced productive forces and needs to have to start right over again from the beginning'.[18] Because, then, of both the contingent character of technological development and the constant threat of the loss of technology for most of human history, Marx realised that it would be wholly inaccurate to posit bourgeois society as the telos of the entire course of world history – and therefore impossible to write a philosophy of history that would be both universal and consistently historical-materialist. It is, on the contrary, only relatively recently that technological development has acquired its own immanent logic: 'Only when commerce has become world commerce and has as its basis large-scale industry, when all nations are drawn into the competitive struggle, is the permanence of the acquired productive forces assured'.[19] Here Marx clearly argued that only the capitalist mode of production has an immanent devel-

---

18   Marx 1845 in Tucker 1978, p. 180.
19   Ibid. This insistence on the contingency of technological development, by the way, lends credence to my argument in the previous chapter that the notion of necessarily progressive dialectic of needs and technology insinuated by Marx's abbreviated formulation of such a dialectic as 'the second moment' and 'first historical act' be eliminated from the 'moments of history'.

opmental logic that provides the material prerequisites for the preservation of technology and the material incentive for its development – and consequently that there was no transhistorical logic inexorably driving history toward modern bourgeois society.

In *The German Ideology*, these two views of history existed side-by-side, and in an unacknowledged and unreconciled tension. Eventually Marx opted for the latter, which is in keeping with the new conception of history he was still in the process of developing. Perhaps the key category that led to his preference for the latter, more differentiated understanding of the historical specificity of social forms was that of the 'mode of production' itself. This category first noticeably appears in Marx's writings in *The German Ideology*. But as can be seen from the confused results of his attempt to differentiate historical epochs according to their 'division of labour' and 'forms of property', the 'mode of production' was splashing around amid other categories and had yet to assume the fundamental importance that it eventually would in the *Grundrisse* and *Capital*.[20] In these later works, he would elaborate the category fully and use it to differentiate among discrete and incommensurable social forms. This in turn would eliminate all vestiges of a universal and teleological philosophy of history and prompt Marx to a more nuanced approach to history.

A crucial indication of the historical nuance provoked by Marx's turn toward the analysis of discrete modes of production appears in the Introduction to the *Grundrisse* where his insistence on the historical specificity of categories is at once a rejection of their transhistorical application. While seeking to delineate the capitalist mode of production as an object of analysis, he qualitatively differentiated it from preceding modes of production; and he strictly limited the range of applicability of categories drawn from the latter. Although his statement that 'human anatomy contains a key to the anatomy of the ape' seems on first hearing to echo the formula that posited bourgeois society as the 'basis of all history', his elaboration shows that he now rejected the transhistorical teleology inherent in the earlier formulation.[21] In a *de facto* critique of that earlier teleological position, he now carefully emphasises that while the later society does provide a key to the character of its predecessors, categories from the later society cannot be directly and immediately applied to the former. He clarified this with the example of the 'modern concept of labour' which 'shows strikingly how even the most abstract categories, despite their validity – precisely because of their abstractness – for all epochs, are nevertheless, in the

---

20   Marx 1845 in Tucker 1978, pp. 150–4.
21   Marx 1973 [1857–58], p. 105. Following citations in this paragraph, ibid, p. 105; p. 106, my italics; p. 106.

specific character of this abstraction, themselves likewise a product of historic relations, and possess their full validity only for and within these relations'. In conclusion he stated: 'Although it is true ... that the categories of bourgeois economics possess a truth for all other forms of society, this is to be taken only with a grain of salt. They can contain them in a developed, or stunted, or caricature form etc., but always with an *essential difference*'. Any analysis which does not recognise this difference is bound falsely to posit the present era as telos: 'The so-called historical presentation of development is founded, as a rule, on the fact that the latest form regards the previous ones as steps leading up to itself, and, since it is only rarely and only under quite specific conditions able to criticize itself[,] ... it always considers them one-sidedly'. Here Marx presented a critique, not only of bourgeois universalising of economic categories that subsumed the past by treating it only as a path to the present, but also of his own earlier tendency, in the *1844 Manuscripts* and still lingering in *The German Ideology*, to do the same.

Although the identifiable set of historical-materialist 'moments' (the modes of material, social, and semiotic objectification discussed in the previous chapter) is common to all social forms, a glance at the course of history reveals that the particular constellations of these moments vary 'with an essential difference'. And although the sequence of those constellations can be explained *ex post facto*, that sequence cannot be subsumed under a unitary, transhistorical teleology that would treat history's 'separate strata' as simply a logical and necessary progression of steps on a unitary path to the present. In order to avoid a narrowly one-sided, teleological treatment of a given society as but a steppingstone to the capitalist here-and-now, Marx insisted that each society be considered on its own terms, specifically: in terms of the particular way in which people in each society reproduce their lives, that is: in terms of their mode of production. Thus, the first step in moving from the transhistorical abstractions of historical theory to the more concrete, but still abstract analysis and critique of a given social form is to differentiate and delineate the particular mode of production that 'in the last instance' gives form to each social constellation and that in-forms the discrete mode of life in each society.

In the Introduction to the *Grundrisse* Marx provided a succinct explanation of the value and limits of the transhistorical abstractions that make up a materialist conception of history, and thus also of the epistemological obligation to move beyond those transhistorical abstractions to the analysis of discrete socio-economic forms:

> *Production in general* is an abstraction, but an understandable [*verständige*] abstraction in so far as it really brings out and fixes the common

element and thus saves us repetition. Still, this *general* category, this common element, sifted out by comparison, is itself segmented many times over and splits into different determinations. Some determinations belong to all epochs, others only to a few. [Some] determinations will be shared by the most modern epoch and the most ancient. No production will be thinkable without them. ... [N]evertheless, just those things which determine their development, i.e. the elements which are not general and common, must be separated out from the determinations valid for production as such, so that in their unity – which arises already from the identity of the subject, humanity, and of the object, nature – their essential difference is not forgotten.[22]

Summarising, he concluded: 'There are characteristics which all stages of production have in common, and which are established as the general ones by the mind; but the so-called *general preconditions* of all production are *nothing more than these abstract moments with which no real historical stage of production can be grasped*'.

In order to grasp a given 'historical stage of production', it is first necessary to determine the historical boundaries or 'historicity' of a given socio-economic form – which Marx did for the capitalist mode of production (in deed, if not explicitly in word) with two of the most striking discussions in *Capital*. Marx's presentation of the structure and logic of the capitalist mode of production in *Capital* might be seen as framed by these two discussions: by his exposé in the concluding section of the initial chapter devoted to deciphering 'the sensual, supersensual thing' that is the commodity and the fetishism that inheres in it; and by his disclosure, in the book's penultimate chapter on 'the so-called originary accumulation', of the painful history of displacement that established the preconditions and prerequisites of the capitalist mode of production.[23] Most

---

22   Marx 1973, p. 85, translation slightly altered. Following citation, ibid., p. 88, my italics.
23   Two notes on translation and terminology. First, Rubin (1981, p. 21) notes that many critics have found in Marx's reference to the commodity as a *sinnlich übersinnliches Ding* (Marx 1990, p. 85) 'something incomprehensible and even mystical'. This unfortunate tendency is not helped by Fowkes's translation (1990, p. 163) that renders *sinnlich übersinnliches Ding*, I think inadequately, as 'a thing which transcends sensuousness'. Marx's formulation implies that both qualities of sensuousness and beyond sensuousness are combined in the commodity, but not that the commodity is a thing which transcends sensuousness altogether, as this translation implies.
     Second, in this passage, and throughout this work, I follow Rosalind Morris who, based on her critique of mistranslations and misunderstandings Marx term, *die ursprüngliche Akkumulation*, has rendered it as 'originary accumulation'. And for the sake of consistency

obviously striking about these chapters are their contents, insights, and powerful presentation. Less obvious, though equally striking once one notices it, is that there is a certain sense in which these very memorable chapters do not belong in *Capital*. These discussions are more historical in content and as such are not integral to the dialectical unfolding of the categories that Marx uses to build a kind of model of the structure and logic of the capitalist mode of production. Although neither is necessary to the categorial presentation, their placement, standing as portals into and out of the abstract conceptual presentation, is not without significance. For, both serve to delineate and contextualise the capitalist mode of production – yet in different ways.

The fetishism section includes a brief comparative history of socio-economic forms, in which Marx 'took flight' to other modes of production in order to contextualise and historicise capitalism, to differentiate it from all other modes of production – and to reveal that atomistic and possessive individualism (what Adam Smith called the 'certain propensity in human nature to truck, barter and exchange') is not an essential attribute of human beings, but a particular kind of behaviour required by a particular mode of production, by the competitive market economy. And in the analysis of originary accumulation he presented a brief history of capital's always exploitative, often violent ascendance to socio-economic dominance made possible by expropriation and the creation of a class of people completely cut off from the means of production and thus a potential source of wage-labour. For analytical purposes in the early stages of *Capital*, Marx, like the capitalist, took this supply of potential wage-labourers for granted. But, that supply, he was careful to note, 'does not come from nature'; and in so doing he pointed to his historical explanation of its origins in the discussion of originary accumulation at the end of the first volume of *Capital*.[24] Together, these two discussions exemplify the necessary complementary historical tasks that must be taken up in order to move from theoretical abstrac-

---

throughout this work, not only not only do I use 'originary accumulation' when writing in my own voice, but I have taken the liberty of changing every usage of 'primitive accumulation' in passages cited from English translations of Marx's writing to '[originary] accumulation' and also in passages cited from other authors (except where 'primitive accumulation' appears in the title of their work). I address the meaning of Marx's use of *ursprüngliche Akkumulation* and questions of translation in greater detail in Appendices 3.1 and 12.8.

24 Marx 1990 [1867], p. 273. I return to this issue in Chapter 14. Marx and Weber both knew full well that the trading economies of the great Middle Eastern and Asian empires were much more advanced than that of the urban islands in Europe's late Middle Ages; and both sought to explain the uniqueness and unparalleled growth of Western capitalism. But in contrast to Weber who explained it in terms of a particular kind of formal or instru-

tions to a portrait of the concrete totality of a really-existing society, namely: the delineation of the historical specificity, the 'historicity', of a given society that is addressed in the remainder of this section; and the writing of its history, or historical-materialist historiography that, however, can only be properly addressed below (see 3.4) following discussion of two further methodological matters pertaining to the critique of social form.

Although Marx did not provide in *Capital* itself an explicit explanation of his inclusion of these somewhat excursive historical discussions, he did so elsewhere in passages crucial to understanding his undertaking. In his notes on theories of surplus value he briefly but precisely differentiated his own method from that of 'classical economy'; and although he alluded neither to commodity fetishism nor to originary accumulation, this note seems to offer a succinct explanation of why he included those discussions in *Capital*. Classical economy, he explained, 'is not interested in elaborating how the various [socioeconomic] forms come into being. Because it starts from those forms as given premises, it seeks instead to reduce them to their unity by means of analysis'.[25] More discerning minds, however, would use analysis to differentiate among, to delineate the genealogy and explicate the particular logic of, the various 'social strata': 'analysis', Marx insisted, 'is the necessary prerequisite of genetical [*genetisch*] presentation, and of the understanding of the real, formative process in its different phases'. And in a pregnant phrase pointing toward both the chapter in *Capital* that denaturalises the fetishised forms of classical economy and the chapter on 'originary accumulation' explaining the emergence of a 'free' labour-force as the genealogical prerequisite of capitalist production, he concluded: 'classical economy fails, is lacking, in that it does not conceive the *basic form of capital*, i.e., production designed to appropriate other people's labour, as a *historical* form, but instead as a *natural form* of social production'. Thus, although *Capital* is primarily an abstract conceptual presentation of the structure and essential logic of the capitalist mode of production and valorisation-*cum*-exploitation process, it does contain, in strategically-placed discussions, rather explicit hints illuminating the boundaries, the historical specificity, of the capitalist mode of production – its preconditions, its peculiar production process and unique developmental logic.

---

      mental rationality born of an ascetic Protestant mentality, Marx explained it in terms of a fundamental transformation of the social relations of production through process of separation of individuals from the means of production who, with no other means of making a living, were a potential source of wage-labour.

25   Marx 1971, pp. 500–1 (translation slightly altered; cf. *Marx-Engels Werke*, Bd. 26.3, p. 491). Next citation ibid.

Despite those historical hints, however, the analysis presented in *Capital* does not alone suffice to tell the concrete and diverse histories of various capitalist societies. To do that, a historical-materialist *Wissenschaft* must engage in historical-materialist histography. Pointing to this next necessary step in a similar passage in the *Grundrisse*, Marx wrote that 'our method indicates *the point where historical investigation must enter in*, or where bourgeois economy as a merely historical form of the production process points beyond itself to earlier historical modes of production'.[26] And in a sentence that both anticipates *Capital*, and establishes its necessary, but limited methodological place-value, he adds: 'in order to develop the laws of bourgeois economy, therefore, it is not necessary to write the *real history of the relations of production*. But the correct observation and deduction of these laws, as having themselves become in history, always leads to primary equations – like the empirical numbers e.g. in natural science – which point towards a past lying behind this system'. These 'indications [*Andeutungen*], together with a correct grasp of the present', so he concluded with a comment most relevant here, 'also offer the key to the understanding of the past – a work in its own right which, it is to be hoped, we shall be able to undertake as well'.[27] Before that 'real history' could be undertaken, however, several methodological matters still needed resolution, most importantly: determining the relation between the mode of inquiry and the mode of presentation.

3.3.2   *The Mode of Inquiry: 'Flushing Out the Inner Bond'*

As with any science, the necessary first step in what Marx designated the 'mode of inquiry' (*Forschungsweise*) is to identify the object of analysis. For a historical-materialist inquiry, this entails the differentiation of history's separate social strata according to their modes of production and the delineation of their historical boundaries. Although an indispensable first step, this dual process of identification and delineation is quite literally a 'superficial' process that classifies societies on the basis of their socio-economic appearance –

---

26   This and following citations in this paragraph, Marx 1973 [1857–58], pp. 460–1, my italics.

27   Nicolaus appends the following very relevant note to Marx's statement of hope about a future historical project: 'On 22 February 1858, Marx wrote to Lassalle that he was planning three works: (1) a critique of the economic categories or the system of bourgeois critically presented, (2) a critique and history of political economy and socialist, and (3) a short historical sketch of the development of economic relation of categories (*Marx-Engels Selected Correspondence*, Moscow n.d., p. 125). Marx referred here to the third work, which he never produced in completed form'. Nicolaus notes in conclusion that the section on 'original accumulation in the "Chapter on Capital"' would 'no doubt have formed part of it' (Marx 1973 [1857–58], p. 461, n. 56).

but that tells us little about their 'essence', the logic of their inner workings. Thus, once the society under analysis has been identified and differentiated, the next step is to proceed to the empirical study and analysis of that society on its own terms, to dig deeper in order to flush out the 'inner bond' that is the *form*-determinant of the mode of life in a given society, the framework within which individuals make their own history – and that is the key to deciphering its particular systemic logic.

Marx commented on his 'mode of inquiry' in the Afterword to the second edition of *Capital* in response to a Russian reviewer of the first Russian edition. Here he approvingly cited the reviewer for having 'so accurately portrayed' his (Marx's) rejection of the claim 'that the general laws of economic life are one and the same, regardless of whether one applies them to the present or the past', and also for having recognised that 'each historical period possesses its own laws'.[28] Because each social form possesses its own qualitatively distinct logic, it is impossible to impose, without appropriate modification, the categories and logic derived from the capitalist mode of production onto pre-capitalist forms – and thus impossible to write a universal and unitary philosophy of history. While acknowledging the praise, however, Marx faulted the wording of the review for leaning too much toward presenting his analysis as an '*a priori* construction' – which he attributed to the reviewer's failure to distinguish between his (Marx's) 'mode of inquiry' and 'mode of presentation' (*Darstellungsweise*).

The purpose of inquiry and research, he explains, is 'to appropriate the material in detail, to analyse the different forms of development' and to prepare the material for written presentation.[29] This research and preparation, however, is not free of premises. Marx's general premise was that the data which appear to the observer, the phenomena, are not isolated and independent facts which have meaning in and of themselves. In contrast to a purely empirical approach, the task of historical-materialist inquiry is to penetrate beyond surface appearances and to find the essential structure of a society, i.e. the structure within which phenomena gain their meaning and can correctly be interpreted. The goal of the inquiry, then, is not only to 'appropriate the material in detail, to analyse its different forms of development', but also 'to flush out their inner bond [*innres Band*]'. The 'presentation' question will

---

28   Marx 1990, p. 101.
29   This and following citation, Marx 1990, p. 102. 'Inner connection' is Ben Fowkes's translation of *das innere Band* (see Marx, Afterword to the Second German Edition of *Capital* Vol. I., in *Marx-Engels Werke*, Vol. 23, p. 27). Because it connotes greater cohesiveness than does 'connection', I translate *das innere Band* as 'inner bond'.

be addressed in the next section. First, however, it is necessary to look more closely at this notion of 'inner bond'.

It is often inferred, from its inaccurately-alleged primacy of the 'economic', that a materialist conception of history takes the mode of production as the locus of the 'inner bond' in all social forms. As is evident from the discussion of 'Pre-Capitalist Property and Production' in the *Grundrisse*, however, this inference is incorrect. The *Grundrisse* as a whole can be meaningfully understood as a record of Marx's mode of inquiry while struggling 'to appropriate the material in detail, to analyse its forms of development'. And the chapter on 'Pre-Capitalist Property and Production' can be seen as a theoretical interlude summarising the results of his empirical labours. Here he once again tried to solve a problem that he had already taken up, albeit unsuccessfully, in *The German Ideology* with the categories of the division of labour and forms of property, that is: to delineate the objects of social analysis by differentiating among discrete and incommensurate social forms. In the *Grundrisse*, Marx made a qualitative distinction between capitalist and pre-capitalist modes of production that defies all attempts to discover or construct a unitary transhistorical logic; and in so doing he explained the complexity of the relation between economy and society, between economic 'base' and social 'superstructure', in non-reductionistic, non-deterministic terms.

Although he occasionally used the terms 'bond' and 'real bond' in the *Grundrisse*, he did not, until *Capital*, specify either what he meant by 'inner bond', or how he deployed it. Nevertheless, his inquiry into 'Pre-Capitalist Property and Production' is properly described as a search for the 'inner bond', as an attempt to locate that 'inner bond' in pre-capitalist and capitalist social forms. The 'inner bond' is that which mediates the social relations among, and the socialisation of, individuals within a given socio-economic form – that which establishes the logic or 'laws' of a given social form. It is necessary, in short, to grasp the inner bond before one can even decide which analytical categories are to be used in analysing 'people' in 'society'.

During his 'flight' to pre-capitalist modes of production to decipher commodity fetishism, Marx made two interrelated discoveries of methodological import for flushing out the inner social bond.[30] In this conceptually challenging and somewhat convoluted chapter Marx determined that in pre-bourgeois modes of production the pursuit of wealth is never a purpose unto itself. Because economic activity in non-capitalist societies is embedded in society and ordered according to extra-economic, social ends, there is nothing 'out

---

30   Marx 1990 [1867], p. 169.

there' that can be designated as an 'economy' with its own *raison d'être* and its own set of needs whose satisfaction is necessary for its survival. In such societies, therefore, the notion of an austerity programme of the kind periodically launched in capitalist societies, and which essentially asks people to tighten their belts and go without so that the economy can satisfy its need for nourishing profit, would appear as illogical and irrational as it actually is. Economy and society are moreover so inextricably intertwined that it is analytically misleading to attempt to isolate an economic 'base', and impossible to understand the 'essence' of such societies, by focusing solely on the mode of production. It is, on the contrary, the unique double characteristic of the capitalist mode of production that the pursuit of wealth is a purpose unto itself and functions according to the regularities of commodity exchange. Or to put it in the clearer terms with which Karl Polanyi, almost a century later, made exactly the same point in speaking of a 'great transformation' from pre-capitalist societies to capitalist societies: in the former the 'the economy is embedded in social relations' and 'run on non-economic motives', while in capitalist societies 'social relations are embedded in the economic system'.[31]

For capitalism, the inner bond is, of course, the commodity situated in, as the cornerstone of, the mode of production. Because, however, of the qualitatively different relation between economy and society in pre-capitalist social forms, it cannot simply be assumed that the mode of production is always the locus of the inner bond. Marx explained this intimate, but not reductionistic relation between the mode of production and the inner bond in a note in the first chapter of *Capital* where he responded to a critic who reviewed his *Critique of Political Economy* in 'a German-American publication'. Referring to Marx's comment in the Preface that the mode and relations of production condition the legal, political, and cultural superstructure, the critic explained that while it may be true of the contemporary world, it certainly was not true of feudal Europe where Catholicism was dominant, nor of Athens or Rome where politics dominated. 'One thing is clear', Marx replied, namely that 'the Middle Ages could not live from Catholicism nor could the ancient world live from politics'. On the contrary, it is 'the manner in which they gained their livelihood that

---

31   See Karl Polanyi 1957, p. 57. Godelier (1988, p. 50) also explains that 'social relations [e.g. kinship] become dominant when they serve as framework and direct social support for the process of appropriation of nature – in short, when, whatever their other functions, they function as relations of production'. Godelier notes that while 'inspired by Marx', this 'hypothesis ... is not to be found in his work in this form'. My argument, on the contrary, is that this is exactly the point that Marx made in the chapter in the *Grundrisse* on 'precapitalist economic forms'. For further comment on the imbrication of economy in society in non-capitalist societies, see Appendix 3.2.

explains why there politics, and here Catholicism, played the main role'.[32] It is, in short, precisely because the economy in non-capitalist modes of production is 'embedded in social relations' and 'run on non-economic motives' that the πόλις or the Catholic Church could assume the role of the inner bond. But in the Athenian πόλις, the Roman republic and empire, and in feudal Europe, it was the mode of landholding that determined who would exercise power in and through the πόλις or the Church. Thus, although the inner bond always stands in a direct relation to the mode, and specifically to the social relations, of production, its locus in non-capitalist societies is situated outside of (though not unrelated to) the mode of production; and in those societies, such non-economic elements as kinship, the πόλις or the Church might serve as the inner bond (or what Althusser called the structure-in-dominance) that gives each society its specific form of cohesiveness and its particular contents.[33]

When Marx maintained that the materialist conception of history nevertheless remains a valid mode of inquiry into non-capitalist societies, this is not because the mode of production is the *exclusive* form-determinant of social relations; it is rather because the way in which any society reproduces itself materially, i.e. its mode of production, is the primary form-determinant that establishes the limits on the possible range of social relations and that frames the life-activity of really-existing individuals. Where the economy is embedded in society, the inner bond, as Marx and Polanyi both explain, will be forged socially, rather than economically. What makes capitalist societies historically unique, as Marx and Polanyi also agree, is that capitalist society, in contradistinction to all hitherto existing societies, *is*, as Polanyi put it, embedded in, and fundamentally formed by, the economy: not only does the capitalist mode of production frame the general form of capitalist societies, but its 'cell-form', the commodity, also serves as the cohesive inner bond of societies in which commodity production and exchange prevail.

Much misinterpretation follows from the mistaken assumption that Marx defined human beings as *Homo oeconomicus* – differing from Adam Smith only by his focus on the productive, labouring human rather than on the 'trucking, bartering and exchanging' one. This is possibly why Polanyi's analysis has often

---

32   Marx 1990 [1867], pp. 175–6, n. 35.
33   I introduced Marx's notion of 'form-determinant' [*Formbestimmung*] in Chapter 1 as that which establishes the range, and establishes the limits on, a set of possibilities. Below (Chapter 3.D.) I will explain the relation between the mode of production and the inner bond as that between different levels of 'form-determination'. On 'structure in dominance', see Althusser and Balibar 1987, p. 108. See also ibid., p. 319 for Ben Brewster's definition of the terms in the glossary that he provides with his translation.

been welcomed as an apparent antidote to Marx. But if one considers carefully Polanyi's own formulation of pre-capitalist relations between economy and society, it actually reaffirms Marx's differentiation of pre-capitalist from capitalist social forms. Marx's discovery of the inner bond of capitalist societies (and only of capitalist societies) in the mode of production itself, in the commodity situated in the economic structure, expresses exactly the same point that Polanyi makes with his assertion that the society in capitalist societies (and only in capitalist societies) is embedded in the economy, rather than the inverse. And Marx and Polanyi fully agreed on one great irony: that if there is any society in which the socio-cultural superstructure may be meaningfully viewed as determined by the economic base, it is certainly capitalism in which the economy, freed from social control, becomes the determinant and arbiter of social relations and cultural forms (the hegemony of capital's 'culture of quantity' will be elaborated in Part 4).

This differentiation of the capitalist from other modes of production in terms of the relation between economy and society clearly suggests a correspondingly differentiated, non-reductionist understanding of the relation between their economic 'base' and socio-cultural 'superstructure'. This rejection of any reductionist notion of the relation between 'base' and 'superstructure' enabled Marx to view societies as discrete constellations. And while the economic 'base' should be given a certain priority, it is also necessary to determine exactly what that 'certain priority' entails. And to do so, it is worth taking a closer look at Engels's curbing of the causal efficacy of the first 'moment' of a materialist conception of history.

Against determinist interpretations of his and Marx's work, Engels insisted that 'the history of the production and reproduction of life' is '*in the last instance* the determining moment'; and he dismissed the claim that the economic is the *only* determining moment as 'a meaningless, abstract, absurd phrase'.[34] This notion of 'last-instance' determination is to be understood neither as a linear or mechanistic causal explanation in the form of 'if x, then y', nor as what Althusser called Hegel's expressivist causality that treats all aspects of the appearances as mirroring manifestations of a 'base' understood as essence.[35] The mode of production is not some kind of *a priori* from which can be derived, purely conceptually (i.e. without concrete historical analysis), an understand-

---

34   Engels, letter to Joseph Bloch, 21 September 1890, in Tucker 1978, pp. 760–5. The German is: '*das in letzter Instanz bestimmende Moment*'. If *bestimmen* may be rendered in English as 'determine', it is in the less reductionist sense of 'determination' meaning 'to fix the boundaries of', 'to limit in extent and scope'.
35   See Althusser and Balibar 1987, pp. 184, pp. 186–7.

ing of the particular social behaviour, political institutions, cultural contents, and the history of a given society; nor does it determine *the* course of history.

As Raymond Williams explained, on the contrary, a historical-materialist notion of 'determination' refers rather to the 'setting of limits' (to which should also be added the counterpart of limits, namely: possibilities).[36] Thus, to refer to the mode of production as the 'base' or the 'last instance' simply recognises its fundamental role as the *form*-determinant of a given social form, as that which establishes the boundaries of a given social world and frames the context within which people make their own history, but does not determine the contents of the histories that people actually make within that context. And the analytical task of a historical-materialist *Wissenschaft* is therefore to reconstruct how people make their own history within determinate, yet open-ended social forms. The first step in the analysis of a discrete social form is to chart social geography, to map the topography and the distribution of people in social space. Such a mapping that illuminates the categories to be used in analysing 'people' in 'society' provides a necessary framework for the analysis of the society in its historical specificity – but a still very abstract one.

With this qualitative differentiation between discrete and incommensurate social forms Marx solved the problem of the contradictory formulations raised, but not resolved, in *The German Ideology*. In contrast to both Hegel's philosophy of history, which teleologically subsumed the entire course of history to its 'result' and approached the past only as the prehistory of the present, and his own earlier, similarly teleological formulation of the bourgeois-capitalist present as the 'basis of all history', Marx's new method is quite different: rather than equate the prehistory of bourgeois society with the history of pre-bourgeois societies in their own historical specificity, he now sought to establish the guiding threads for the critique of social forms and for writing the concrete history of a discrete social forms. That same differentiation of capitalist from pre-capitalist social forms, the recognition that the latter which were *not* dominated by, and regulated according to, the logic of commodity production and exchange, required Marx to use the terms 'base' and 'superstructure' only as heuristic abstractions whose concrete content and relations can only be determined through the analysis of individual social forms. With these reflections on how to differentiate discrete social forms, Marx established a relation between historical theory and social theory that avoided both the diachronic determinism of a transhistorical teleology and the synchronic determinism of a reductionist base-superstructure relation.

---

36 Williams 1977, p. 85.

3.3.3 The Mode of Conceptual Presentation and Its Methodological Place-Value

After the work of inquiry has discerned the inner bond of a given social form, the next step is to develop a theoretical model of its structural and functional logic. Despite his extensive research into other social forms, Marx was of course primarily concerned with capitalism; and that was the only social form that he ever elaborated in any detail. Strictly speaking, a discussion of Marx's presentation of the capitalist mode of production does not belong here, where my concern is with the general outlines of a historical-materialist *Wissenschaft*. Yet because this is the only case in which Marx systematically applied the *Leitfaden* of his materialist conception of history to the critique of a specific social form, it is worth discussing precisely because it sheds so much light on his methodology, his use of abstractions, the range of his concepts, and especially the methodological place-value of *Capital* in a historical-materialist *Wissenschaft*. In short, it exemplifies his methodological solutions to the above-mentioned epistemological dilemmas.

While it is easy enough to detect the commodity as the inner bond of societies where commodity exchange *prevails*, this discovery does not alone suffice to delineate the boundaries of capitalist society as an analytical object. The difficulty in doing so is evident in the classical political economy of Adam Smith and his acolytes who mistook the obvious point that commodity production and, particularly, commodity exchange are not exclusive to the modern capitalist era as evidence that the human 'propensity to truck, barter, and exchange' is an innate and universal behaviour grounded in human nature – from which they concluded that capitalist commodity exchange is the epitomic realisation of a very natural and universal mode of human being. Marx, however, took claims of the universality of commodity exchange with but a grain of conceptual salt. Undeceived by the seeming ubiquity of commodity exchange, he carefully drew the historical boundaries of 'modern' commodity exchange. In contrast to the subsidiary role played by its historical antecedents, 'modern' commodity exchange was, in consequence of the development of commodity *production*, rapidly becoming the form-determinant of economic and social life. This focus on commodity *production* enabled him not only to delineate the boundaries of capitalism as a historically-specific socio-economic form, but also to expose the historical specificity of the allegedly 'natural' human 'propensity to truck, barter, and exchange'.

In so doing, he was able to explain rather clearly, not only why the economy is the locus of the inner social bond in those societies in which commodity production prevails, but also why, in capitalism, the economy is itself the social form-determinant that had attained a historically anomalous degree of autonomy from extra-economic control. As Marx recognised, this real separation of the economy from society was also the prerequisite for a science of economics. In pre-capitalist societies, in which economic activity is always subordinated to extra-economic ends, the economy did not exist in this isolated form; hence his comment that 'we never find among the ancients a study of what form of landed property, etc. is the most productive, creates the greatest wealth. Wealth never appears as the purpose of production. ... The study is always of what kind of property creates the best citizens'.[37]

In capitalist economies, however, the systematic pursuit of ever-increased profit through commodity production and exchange is a goal unto itself. And because a mature capitalist economy is neither embedded in, nor dominated by, social controls (even if its anarchic tendencies may perhaps be somewhat regulated), but runs according to its own economic logic, it presents itself clearly and distinctly as a potential object of scientific analysis. Under capitalist conditions of production, the economy truly is the 'base' of capitalist social forms: that in which society is embedded. Marx's purpose here, however, was not to establish a deterministic relation between base and superstructure. Rather, this characterisation enabled him to both to delineate the capitalist mode of production as an object of analysis and, in contrast to the political economists and their successors, to delineate its historical specificity.

Because Marx established a qualitative break between capitalist and pre-capitalist economic forms, he could not simply and immediately project onto the latter the economic categories derived from the former. He did not seek commodity production and exchange, clothed perhaps in some disguise, as the secret of all social forms. Nor did he project *Homo oeconomicus*, that fictional 'rational economic actor' imagined by economists, backward onto all hitherto existing societies. His goal in *Capital* would be the more modest one of writing a genealogy and an archaeology of the capitalist mode of production and an abstract biography of its life-cycle. This life-cycle began not with the proto-capitalist exchange of the ancient world nor even with the well-developed Asian markets, both of which remained subject to strict extra-economic social controls. It began rather, as sketched in the *Communist Manifesto*, with the rudimentary form of commodity production that emerged on the urban islands amid the Medieval European manorial economy and with an inherent dynamic that eventually reclaimed the countryside (see Chapter 12).

Having, through his mode of inquiry, 'flushed out' the inner bond of capitalist society and delineated its historical boundaries, Marx could take the next

---

37 Marx 1973 [1857–58], p. 487.

step beyond the mode of inquiry. That would involve (as he impatiently lectured the Russian reviewer mentioned above) addressing issues involved in the mode of presentation – a presentation that, in the case of the capitalist mode of production, consists of a conceptual reconstruction beginning with the commodity as the inner social bond and proceeding toward the visible surface of society. In this respect, there are structural parallels between Hegel's conceptual presentation in his *Logic* and Marx's in *Capital*. But it would be a mistake to assume that the two are identical in purpose, or that they play the same role in each thinker's overall project.

Hegel's *Logic* not only establishes the form of his inquiry, but also provides the criteria for winnowing its contents. At each step along Hegel's phenomenological path – as he moves through the philosophy of nature to the philosophy of *Geist*, and then through the various dimensions of *Geist* from anthropology, to psychology, the political-ethical sphere, history, and finally to absolute *Geist* in the form of religion, art and philosophy – both the dialectical form of argument and presentation, and also the specific, narrowly idealist content, are predetermined by the rigid pattern established in the *Logic* and imposed on each particular inquiry. And any content falling outside that pattern is dismissed as contingent and irrelevant. At the end of this 'circle of circles', as Hegel called his philosophy, the encyclopaedia of knowledge is complete and nothing essential remains to be said.

It is often assumed, among both his friends and foes, that Marx's *Capital*, like Hegel's *Logic*, is to be understood as the *concrete* presentation of the essential, as a closed book within whose covers is included all that needs to be known about its subject matter. This comparison, however, is far too hasty. In order both to understand why it is rash and to grasp the methodological place-value of *Capital*, its efficacy and its limits, it is necessary to go back to the *Grundrisse* and consider Marx's abstrusely formulated, but epistemologically rich musings on the value of the concept and the nature of the mode of presentation.

In formal agreement with Hegel, Marx defined the logic, the 'scientifically [*wissenschaftlich*] correct method', of presentation as the 'unfolding' of the categories, the ascent from the simplest category to the most concrete.[38] Having arrived at the inner bond as a result of the inquiry, the next step is to turn around and retrace the steps. The inner bond, which is the end point or goal of the inquiry, is thus the starting point of the presentation, and the course of the presentation consists of developing the increasingly concrete categories out of the simplest. And if this 'unfolding' is successfully performed, Marx

---

38   Marx 1973 [1857–58], pp. 100–1.

elaborated in the Afterword to the second edition of *Capital*, 'if the life of the subject-matter is ideally reflected as in a mirror, then it may appear as if we had before us a mere *a priori* construction'.[39]

The counterfactual formulation of this statement points to the deceptive appearance of the conceptual presentation, thus indicating that the interpretative problem does not end here. For, the formal logic of presentation explains only the sequence according to which the concepts are to be analysed and 'unfolded'. It does not, however, automatically define the epistemological value nor, accordingly, the methodological place-value of the conceptual presentation, i.e. its relation to historical reality. Thus, the *formal* identity of Hegel's and Marx's definition of the logic of presentation should not lead us to conclude that Hegel and Marx placed the same epistemological value on their respective works. Such a conclusion creates the illusion that Marx's *Capital* is identical to Hegel's *Logic* not only in structure but also in purpose, that *Capital* is Marx's presentation of the concrete totality of capitalist society. Because of their radically different evaluations of the content of the concept, however, Hegel and Marx also differed radically in their epistemological evaluations of the conceptual presentation.

Since Hegel had posited the *a priori* essentiality of the concept, he could contentedly conclude that the conceptual presentation *is* the concrete presentation of reality. And because in the Hegelian framework reality had come to correspond to philosophy, its presentation is literally a closed book; and there remains little for a historical *Wissenschaft* to do except perhaps the illustrative activity of filling in the details by subsuming the empirical data to their concepts. Any phenomena, however, that cannot be defined as manifestations of a conceptual essence are for that reason considered contingent and arbitrary. And insofar as philosophical logic is based on necessity, any contingent and arbitrary elements, while perhaps interesting as historical curiosities, are philosophically unsatisfying and thus irrelevant.

As was shown above, however, Marx's materialist analysis of the mode of intellectual production limited the range of the concept by depriving it of its essentiality. As will be shown below, this limitation forced Marx to reconsider the criteria of scientific knowledge in general and the role of the 'contingent' in particular. In the meantime, however, it is necessary to consider his critique of Hegel's evaluation of the conceptual presentation; for it is on the basis of this critique that he redefined those criteria.

---

39   Marx 1873, Afterword to the Second German Edition of *Capital* in *Marx-Engels Werke*, Vol. 23, p. 27.

Marx discussed the necessarily abstract character of a purely conceptual presentation in several places. In the section on 'Method' in the *Grundrisse*, after having revealed Hegel's 'illusion of conceiving the real as the product of thought concentrating itself, probing its own depths, and unfolding itself out of itself, by itself', he then rejected the generative power that Hegel attributed to the concept: 'the method of rising from the abstract to the concrete is only the way in which thought appropriates the concrete, reproduces it as the concrete in the mind. But this is by no means the process by which the concrete itself comes into being'.[40] And throughout *Capital* Marx injected regularly reminders that, in this general analysis of the capitalist mode of production, he posited a 'normal' or pure, that is to say: a conceptually ideal situation, rather than a historically real one. He made this point most explicitly and unmistakably in the third volume where, when comparing the effect on profit rates of different compositions of capital in different branches of production, he added the qualification: 'In a general analysis of the present kind, *it is assumed throughout that actual conditions correspond to their concept* or, and this amounts to the same thing, that actual conditions are depicted only in so far as they express their own general type'.[41] Recognising the crucial importance of this passage, Helmut Reichelt maintains that it *'must be the starting point of every serious study of Marx's work and that future interpretations will have to be judged according to the degree to which they follow and develop its implications'*.

Marx's goal, then, was not to subsume reality to the concept, but to produce knowledge about reality by means of concepts. However, those same historical-materialist tenets which allowed him to see through the philosophical fetishism of concepts also forced him to renounce the philosophical luxury of positing the primacy of the concept. He was thus confronted with the above-mentioned epistemological and methodological dilemma: obliged to use the concept as the indispensable tool of intellectual labour, as the necessary means to carry out the reconstruction of reality in thought, yet while knowing that this tool and its product are necessarily abstract. To solve this dilemma, Marx could not follow Hegel and proclaim that the conceptual presentation *is* the presentation of historical development in its concrete totality. Rather, he had to reduce the claims attached to the conceptual presentation and then figure out how to approach the concrete totality by means of abstract concepts. And he solved this problem by means of an epistemological break with the philosophical tradition.

---

40   Marx 1973 [1857–58], p. 102.
41   Marx 1981 [1894], p. 242, my italics. Following citation, Reichelt 1973, pp. 76–7, my italics.

The recognition of the epistemological limitations of concepts does not mean that the conceptual presentation is worthless, simply that it is limited. Although the conceptual presentation is reduced to a more modest role than that allotted it by philosophy, it is nevertheless a role which is essential to historical-materialist knowledge production. Rather than posit the conceptual presentation as that of the real, Marx defined its epistemological value in the limited terms of what Kosmas Psychopedis called an 'abstract presentation of the essential'.[42] The purely conceptual presentation temporarily abstracts from real existing, but 'contingent', elements that do not correspond to the concept of capital in order to construct a model of the capitalist mode of production. In so doing it presents the essential in its pure, and therefore historically abstract, form. Marx, in short, developed methodological solutions to epistemological problems – solutions that, precisely because of their modesty, enable a greater understanding of analytical objects.

This evaluation of the abstract character of the conceptual presentation represents, according to Psychopedis, Marx's 'methodological breakthrough'.[43] From the viewpoint of Marx's philosophical predecessors, for whom the essential is, by definition, the real substance, the notion of an 'abstract presentation of the essential' is a contradiction in terms. Whereas Hegel could maintain that the ascent from the simplest to the most complex attains the essence and encompasses all that is relevant to the philosophical conception of the concrete totality, and could eliminate anything that did not fit into the conceptual presentation as merely contingent and thus philosophically uninteresting, Marx could make no such assumptions.[44] The conceptual ascent is the dialectical means of presenting the essential moments of the mode of production and, in so doing, of exposing the exploitative logic inherent in the relations of production yet hidden by the illusion of the free market and the formal equality of capitalist and worker entering into the labour contract. But while culminating in the presentation of capitalism's immanent logic, that conceptual ascent never leaves the realm of the abstract. As Psychopedis summarises:

---

[42] Psychopedis 1984, p. 219.
[43] Ibid.
[44] As Hegel unambiguously stated in his *Philosophy of Nature* (Hegel, *Werke*, Vol. 9, p. 35), since nature consists of chance, arbitrariness, and disorder, 'it is the greatest impropriety [das *Ungehörigste*] to demand of the concept that it should comprehend such contingencies [*Zufälligkeiten*]'. For Hegel this was true not only of nature, but also of such natural 'contingencies' in the social world as who owns how much. (Hegel, *Werke*, Vol. 7, 1975, p. 112).

Marx's methodology formally differentiates itself from Hegel's approach in terms of the specific place-value [*Stellenwert*] that the concept of the social essence assumes within the totality of political-economic categories. Marx's theory suggests the possibility of an abstract thematizing of the essential moments of the 'whole' *before* the derivation of its parts. ... This means that Marx's mode of presentation assumes that the essential moments of results at which theory arrives at the end of the research process can be abstractly presented, indeed, *must* be abstractly presented in order to get at the character of the 'essence' of the production process that is veiled by its mediating moments. ... Only *after* the presentation of the essence as an abstraction can, according to Marx's approach, the mediating moments be presented that lead in turn to a presentation of the society in its concrete totality, that is as a unity of essential moments and of phenomenal moments and forms of social intercourse.[45]

Crucial in this passage are not only the differentiation between Hegel's and Marx's determinations of the relation between essence and appearance, but also what that differentiation means for determining what Psychopedis calls the 'place-value' of Hegel's conceptual presentation in the *Logic* and Marx's in *Capital*. Because this term 'place-value' is so crucial not only to the issue here at hand, but also throughout the following chapters, it requires further comment.

With the introduction of this notion of the 'place-value' or, as he calls it elsewhere with greater descriptive precision, the 'methodological place-value' of a given work, Psychopedis does more than call attention to the fairly obvious point that no text should be taken at face-value. He insists that it is necessary to grasp, not only what the text itself says (the exclusive interest of structuralist and poststructuralist approaches), but also its methodological place-value. To ascertain a text's 'methodological place-value' it is necessary to determine its *value*, that is: its range of efficacy, the work that it can and cannot do. And that determination depends not only on the 'inside' of the text, but also on its 'outside', that is: on the *place* that it occupies and the role that it plays within a given system of thought. And because the *place-value* of a given text is methodologically established on the basis of the fundamental assumptions of a given system of thought, it also requires situating that given text within the broader system of thought that produces it. And I would argue that if these issues pertaining to the methodological place-value of a text are not addressed, it will likely not be possible to determine what that text says – or at least what it means.

---

45   Psychopedis 1984, p. 173. Following reference in this paragraph to 'methodological place-value' (ibid., p. 158).

In the case at hand: because Hegel determined the concept to be not only an accurate representation of the concrete, but also as itself the 'real', the methodological place-value of his conceptual presentation is, accordingly, as the concrete presentation of the essential. Marx, however, while making use of concepts as the necessary means of presenting the essential structure and logic of the real, also recognised their abstract character and limited value. This recognition, in turn, required him to deflate the methodological place value of the conceptual presentation, to understand it as an *abstract* presentation of the essential – and thus as a necessary step toward, but by no means a complete presentation of, the concrete totality itself. The determination of methodological place-value will, as noted, play a crucial role in the following chapters, both in terms of establishing the limits of cultural ultra-constructionism and in constructing my alternative notion of a corporeal semiotics. Here, however, it is necessary to consider further Marx's modest determination of the methodological place-value of the conceptual presentation and its consequences.

Because for Marx the albeit necessary conceptual presentation is also necessarily abstract, its long ascent reaches only a plateau, the first stage of a much longer climb toward the concrete totality.[46] The historical elements that Hegel's philosophy excluded as 'contingent' are, from a historical-materialist viewpoint, essential elements of the concrete totality. Since Marx conceived of the conceptual presentation as an abstract presentation, he could not simply ignore that which does not fit into it. In order to reach the concrete totality, he was methodologically required descend again into the empirical world in order to reintegrate the temporarily 'contingent' elements excluded from the

---

46 That Marx understood *Capital* as an abstract presentation of the essential structure and functioning of the capitalist mode of production is clearly indicated in a number of places. In the Preface to the First Edition, Marx stated that although the natural scientist can use microscopes or experiments, the historical-materialist scientist obviously cannot and is, thus, forced to rely on the powers of abstraction (Marx 1990 [1867], p. 90). And it is this conscious use of abstraction to which Marx pointed on the numerous occasions throughout *Capital* when he posited a normal or pure, that is, an historically abstract, situation in order more sharply to focus on the essential structure of the capitalist mode of production. Finally, and most clearly, in the third volume of *Capital*, after mentioning the existence of local variations of the profit rate, he temporarily dismissed them because: 'In a general analysis of the present kind, it is assumed throughout that actual conditions correspond to their concept or, and this amounts to the same thing, actual conditions are depicted only in so far as they express their own general type' (Marx 1981, [1894], p. 242). And the crux of Reichelt's comment noting that Marx regularly acknowledged that his portrait is of capital 'insofar as it corresponds to its concept' is to point out that Marx understood *Capital* is an abstract presentation of the essential.

abstract conceptual analysis, that is: to reintegrate the historical actors who are necessary factors in the project of moving from the abstract conceptual to the concrete historical presentation of a given society.

In order, then, to solve the epistemological dilemmas resulting from a materialist conception of history and its relativising of the power of thought, Marx recognised and worked through the unavoidability of having to reconstruct concrete reality in inescapably abstract categories. He showed the necessity of theoretical or conceptual analysis, but without reducing reality to concepts. Instead, his 'positive science' insisted on the need to include that which does not correspond to the purely conceptual and, therefore, on the need for ever-renewed empirical analysis as theory's self-critique. In short, he redefined the notion of the 'essential' vis-a-vis traditional philosophy. That which for Hegel was merely contingent and could thus be conveniently ignored, was for Marx essential to an understanding of the history of a given society in its concrete and contradictory totality.

For Marx, the purpose of the dialectical presentation is not to trace the entire course of human history, but to explain conceptually the logic of a particular social form and, in so doing, to map its social topography. And like Hegel's *Logic*, Marx's *Capital* is also a depopulated undertaking: its primary concern is with the structures within which people make their own histories, but that prevent them from making those histories as they please. As Fredric Jameson put it succinctly yet precisely: *Capital* 'is not a book about people but rather about a system'.[47] And for this reason Marx offers, in the preface to the first edition of *Capital*, 'a word to avoid possible misunderstandings', and explains: 'I do not depict the forms in a rosy light. But *here* individuals are treated *only insofar as they are personifications of economic categories*. My standpoint, from which the evolution of the economic formation of society is viewed as a process of natural history, can less than any other make the individual responsible for relations whose creature he socially remains, however much he may subjectively raise himself above them'.[48]

---

47 Jameson 2014, p. 53.
48 Marx 1990 [1867], p. 92, my emphasis. In a peculiar 'post-*Marxist*' reading of this prefatory comment, Paul Smith (1988) completely fails to see that this is a very self-conscious *methodological* statement, and instead reads it as an ontological reduction of individuals to bearers of economic categories. (See Smith 1988, p. 40). Smith also has a most peculiar way of citing this paragraph: he neglects the first sentence, begins with the third, then cites a passage from one of Marx's earliest works, his *Critique of Hegel's Philosophy of Right* written in 1843, and then returns to cite the second sentence – and a few pages later justifies this interjectional citation which neglects the immense literature on the 'young' and 'mature' Marx with the rather wobbly claim, 'I think it can be argued that there is a certain

Now, aside from the fact, noted by both Polanyi and Marx, that it is, of all societies, those where capitalist relations of production prevail that most effectively reduce people to the status of bearers of *economic* categories, it is crucial to recognise – and this cannot be emphasised enough – that Marx's decision in *Capital* to treat people only as personified economic categories was *both a methodological decision, and a temporary one*. He made the *methodological* decision, at this particular stage of knowledge production, to treat really-living individuals as economic categories in order, in this work, to develop a historically abstract model of the structural and functional logic of the capitalist mode of production and to create a map of capitalist social topography, in short: to depict capital 'insofar as it corresponds to its concept'. Despite all the uproar over Marx's temporary treatment of people as bearers of categories, it describes nothing more or less than what all social scientists do when building models: sociologists, anthropologists, and political scientists forego a consideration of really living people, which is to say: they too depopulate society and treat individuals as inhabitants of social roles or bearers of categories of class, kinship, etc., or as numerical units, in order to do the same thing that Marx attempts in *Capital*, namely: to build a model of a social form.

The difference, however, is that this self-conscious methodological reduction of people to economic categories is for Marx only *temporary*. The model provides the general logic and a general topographical outline of a given social form. But it does not, cannot, nor even wants or attempts to provide a concrete portrait of the 'real life-process' of the 'really living individuals' who occupy the various social spaces. This part of the portrait can only be filled in through concrete historical analysis – without which the outline of social topography would only be, as Marx said on several occasions, empty 'abstractions' that 'in themselves have no value whatsoever'.[49] This is where, according to the logic of Marx's theory at least, if not to that of standard social science, the necessary, but necessarily abstract historical-materialist theory or model of a given society must be given concrete content, must be repopulated, through historical writing. I return to that issue below. First, however, and because 'really-living

---

consistency' in Marx's early and later works (ibid, p. 11). Smith's undertaking in this book, his attempt to come up with a theory of subjectivity that does not reduce individuals to mirrors of social objectivity, is of the utmost importance. But his equal and opposite reaction to a misreading of Marx's methodological statements combined with an illegitimate conflation of comments from 1843 and 1867 leads him off into the realm of abstract theory and misses the key role that historical analysis of experience must play in the analysis of subjectivity. A similar misreading of what Marx clearly intended as a methodological statement is found in Paul du Gay 1997, pp. 289–94.

49 Marx 1845 in Tucker 1978, p. 154.

individuals' were not the only temporary exclusion Marx made in order to construct his critique of capitalist socio-economic form, it is necessary to complete the list of excluded elements that must be re-integrated in order to give concrete historical content to the abstract model of social form.

In the abstract presentation of capitalism Marx excluded everything except that which was essential to the structure and functioning of the capitalist mode of production. Among the elements consciously left out of his presentation are: first, all classes except those two, the capitalist and wage-labouring classes, that are immediately involved in the production and expropriation of surplus value; this very self-conscious reduction of differential class relations to the binary of capital and labour requires the reintegration and situating of other classes as the analysis moves from abstract theory to historical specificity; second, and to repeat, 'the real, living individuals' who are in *Capital* methodologically but temporarily reduced to personifications of economic categories; third, national variations in capitalist evolution, what Ernst Bloch called 'dissynchronicities' (*Ungleichzeitigkeiten*) both among capitalist societies (different rates of development) and within each capitalist society (the persistence and/or emergence of pockets of economic activity not part of the capitalist valorisation process proper, but whose new social position and politics are structured by that process, and the persistence of cultural forms);[50] fourth, so-called 'superstructural' elements (e.g. the peculiarities of political power or cultural values) that might affect the workings of pure capitalist production and exchange; and fifth, the forms of consciousness of really-existing individuals. None of these factors is necessary to decipher the exploitative logic of the capitalist mode of production and its valorisation process, but *all* are essential to grasping particular capitalist societies, each in its historical specificity. Consequently, the further course of a historical-materialist *Wissenschaft* seeking to overcome its own socially-constructed epistemological limitations and to move toward the understanding of its analytical objects in their historical specificity is the project of giving concrete content to the abstract conceptual presentation.

---

50   This includes the determination of the position, limits, and possibilities of 'dyssynchronous' pockets within the social whole. For example: the persistence of pockets of individual artisan-like production within industrial capitalist society (the situation of the *Mittelstand* in Weimar Germany's industrial capitalist economy); or the persistence of churches in an overwhelmingly secular and 'rationalised' society. On the unwieldy category of the 'dissynchronous', see Ernst Bloch's use of '*Ungleichzeitigkeiten*' in Bloch 1973, pp. 104–26. For Althusser's terminological variation on this notion, his insistence that each social sphere (e.g. economics, politics, aesthetics, philosophy, science) has its 'peculiar time and history', see *Reading Capital*, Chapter 4, esp. pp. 98–100.

This redefinition of what is essential to historical understanding thus contains an accompanying demand for a return to empirical analysis, now informed by an understanding of the social geography that frames the lives of 'really-existing individuals', in order not to exclude or subsume, but to reintegrate the 'contingent'. The proper understanding of the inner bond of a society (e.g. the capitalist mode of production) can only be gained through theoretical abstraction. But the complete understanding of the history of societies (e.g. the various bourgeois societies) demands empirical analysis of the 'contingent' which does not correspond to the conceptual model. This approach to knowledge production recognises the existence of an inescapable epistemological tension between conceptual and empirical analysis. The role of theory is to reach the inner bond behind the empirical data, and that of empirical analysis to give content to and, where necessary, to correct theoretical abstraction. Each is necessary, and each alone is necessarily insufficient. This dialectical movement which accepts the tension, yet tries to reduce the gap, between theory and empiricism, is movement in the direction of the concrete totality. But the presentation of the concrete totality cannot be contained in a closed book at the end of which the reader has attained 'absolute knowledge'. From a historical-materialist standpoint, *Wissenschaft* is an open-ended research project whose process of inquiry is not, nor ever can be, complete – an 'experimental science' based on certain 'guiding threads' about the content of history and historical change. The history of the capitalist era has been delineated, and its fundamental socio-economic logic articulated, in *Capital*. But to take *Capital* as a complete presentation of the concrete histories of the 'life processes' of 'really-living individuals' is to mistake its methodological place-value – and to commit to what Alfred North Whitehead called 'the fallacy of misplaced concreteness'.[51] *Capital* must instead be read as an albeit crucial introductory, but nevertheless as only the *first*, chapter of an open book on the histories of those societies in which the capitalist mode of production predominates.

---

51 Whitehead 1967, pp. 50–1. By this point the reader will have often encountered citation of Marx's oft-used terms, the 'real life-process' of 'really-living individuals' or of 'really-existing individuals' – terms that will also appear often in the following pages. Here I might append a plea for patience regarding the frequent recurrence of these terms. Although my usage of these seemingly simple, almost redundant, but ever so important, corporeally-materialist terms might well seem excessive, perhaps even obsessive, I do so with a crucial purpose in mind, namely: to avoid 'the fallacy of misplaced concreteness' by calling constant attention to, in order to maintain, the necessary epistemological tension between, the conceptual presentations of theory and empirically-grounded historiography – a tension that, properly maintain, will prove to be a very positive one for historical-materialist knowledge production.

3.4 From Social Theory to Historiography: The Ongoing and Obligatory Tasks of an Open-Ended Historical-Materialist *Wissenschaft*

The preceding analysis, from Chapter 1 through the previous section of this chapter, has been concerned with historical and social theory that comprise the first two dimensions of a historical-materialist *Wissenschaft*. One means of summarising that discussion of theoretical issues, of providing a transition to the following discussion of the third historiographical dimension of that *Wissenschaft*, and of illuminating the relations between those three dimensions, is through Marx's notion of 'form-determinant'. I introduced 'form-determinant' above (Chapter 1) as that which frames, by establishing the range of and limits on, a given field of possibilities. And what I have addressed throughout these first three chapters are the various levels of form-determination that establish the range, the possibilities and limits, of the life-activity of really-existing human beings inhabiting specific social forms.

The primary, in the sense of the broadest level of form-determination is the 'first fact' of a materialist conception of history: the species-specific corporeal organisation that establishes the possibilities and sets the limits on the range of possible histories of any given species; and the purpose of Chapters 1 and 2 was to reconstruct historical-materialist theory up from this corporeal form-determinant.[52] After having spent those two chapters articulating Marx's corporeally-grounded historical-materialist theory, I began this chapter by enumerating the epistemological challenges confronting a *Wissenschaft* that would take human corporeal organisation as its 'first fact'. I then proceeded to address the methodological means (a historical-materialist delineation of analytical objects; establishing the modes and means of inquiry and presentation) by which Marx sought to respond to those challenges. In so doing, I elaborated what could be called the secondary and tertiary historical form-determinants, both of which belong to the dimension of social theory, to the analysis and critique of social form(s). The secondary level of form-determination would be the mode of production that frames the way in which the inhabitants of a given society reproduce their very corporeal being; and the tertiary form-determinant, always related, if in varying ways, to the mode of production, is the particular inner bond of a given society that gives it its particular form (e.g. kinship relations, the πόλις, the Church, the commodity). My analysis up

---

52   While the materialist conception of history theoretically establishes corporeal organisation as the first historical fact, it does not elaborate specifically *how* corporeal organisation 'in-forms' human history. I suggest how that question might be answered in the four chapters that make up Part 2 of this book.

to this point might therefore be summarised as having drawn a series of narrowing concentric circles of form-determination, each of which places narrower limits on the possibilities of making histories, and that together prevent human beings from making history as they please. And determining the geometry of both the transhistorically corporeal and the historically-specific socio-economic circles is the work of the first two dimensions of a historical-materialist *Wissenschaft*: historical theory and social theory.

However: those narrowing circles of *form*-determination do not determine the *contents*. While form-determinants circumscribe the possibilities of how people can make their own history, they do not prescribe the histories that people actually make. And it is therefore necessary to proceed to the next dimension of a historical-materialist *Wissenschaft* and engage in historical-materialist historiography in order to grasp and write the histories of the real life-activity of really existing individuals. Put in the context of Marx's own work: if his materialist conception of history as outlined in *The German Ideology* is not a universal philosophy of history but an abstract presentation of history's essential moments, and if *Capital* is an abstract presentation of the capitalist mode of production insofar as it corresponds to its concept, then it is clear, both that the abstractions of historical and social theory are necessary elements and steps of a historical-materialist *Wissenschaft*, and that they insufficient to paint a complete portrait of the concrete totality of capitalist societies. And if that is the case, it follows that this historical-materialist *Wissenschaft* contains a built-in epistemological demand for a next step through and beyond the abstractions of historical and social theory – a demand namely for a historical-materialist historiography devoted to articulating the concrete historical experience of really-existing human beings in their socio-cultural specificity.[53]

Concerned as he was with deciphering the exploitative logic of the capitalist production and valorisation process, Marx never did systematically articulate the place of historiography in a historical-materialist *Wissenschaft*. But we might assume that his and Engels's many historical forays in essays and journalistic commentaries were surely undertaken for more reasons than augmenting Marx's meagre income. And in an apparently little-known, but implication-rich comment in the *Urtext* of 'Toward the Critique of Political Economy', we find anticipatory evidence in support of Reichelt's and Psychopedis's evaluation of *Capital* as an abstract presentation of the capitalist production and valorisation process insofar as it corresponds to its necessarily abstract concept – and also the methodological imperative to proceed through and beyond the abstract

---

53 Further discussion of Marx and Engels on theory and history in Appendix 3.3.

presentation of the mode of production and toward the presentation of a given society in its concrete totality and historical specificity.

Like the discussion of 'the so-called originary accumulation' in *Capital*, this passage is also concerned with the 'historical stage of the development of economic production' on which 'the free labourer appears' and 'whose existence is the result of a protracted historical process in the economic formation of society'. The historical appearance of the free-labourer, Marx insists, *precedes* the historical stage at which capitalism appears and is 'the prerequisite for the becoming [*Werden*] of capital as such'. Thus, he insists further, although the structure and functional logic of the capitalist mode of production *can* be understood without considering this essential historical prerequisite, the historical situatedness of capital, its historicity, *cannot* be comprehended without understanding its genealogy. And in a brief sentence of the utmost importance, but that unfortunately seems to have remained unfamiliar, he summarises: 'This is the point that clearly shows *how the dialectical form of presentation is only correct when it knows its boundaries and limits*'.[54]

In Marx's hands, then, 'the dialectic' has no transhistorical pretensions. And while the dialectically developed conceptual presentation in *Capital* is necessary to explain the exploitative logic of the capitalist mode or production and to outline the general contours of capitalist social geography, it cannot alone paint a complete portrait of, nor can it give concrete historical content to, really-existing capitalist societies in their structurally similar, yet historically diverse manifestations; it can neither reach nor articulate the particular idiosyncrasies characteristic of capitalist valorisation at different sites, each geographically and culturally specific, each with its own particular historical clock. The remainder of this section is therefore devoted to suggesting why and how historical-materialist inquiry must turn to *Geschichtsschreibung* or 'historiography' in order to move beyond the boundaries and limits of 'the dialectic', to provide the abstract presentation of the essential with concrete historical content, and to write the histories of really-living individuals who

---

54   The '*Urtext*' of the *Grundrisse* in which Marx made this extremely important comment is not included in the Nicolaus translation. The source is Karl Marx, *Urtext 'Zur Kritik der Politischen Ökonomie', Abschnitt I. Drittes Kapital: Das Kapital* in Marx, no date given, *Grundrisse der Kritik der politischen Ökonomie* (Frankfurt: Europäischen Verlagsanstalt), p. 945; my translation and my italics. The sentence in original: '*Es zeigt sich an diesem Punkt bestimmt, wie die dialektische Form der Darstellung nur richtig ist, wenn sie ihre Grenzen kennt*'. *Grenzen* can be translated as 'borders' or 'boundaries' or 'limits'. Although a border or boundary need not be a limit, it seems fairly clear that Marx means a border or a boundary that is a limit beyond which the dialectic is ineffective. For that reason, therefore I have translated *Grenzen* as 'boundaries and limits'.

make their own histories, even if not always as they please – a move in the direction of the concrete totality that is of the utmost significance for reasons of both knowledge production and political praxis.

A healthy suspicion of the notion of 'totality' is certainly warranted, but paranoia is not. As noted above, a Hegelian or Lukácsian 'expressivist' (to borrow Althusser's term) and 'totalising' kind of totality that treats all its moments as centred around and wholly determined by an 'essence' or 'base' must be avoided.[55] Marx's notion of totality, however, is grounded in the assumptions that the dialectical presentation of categories remains abstract, and that concrete histories of really-existing societies cannot simply be subsumed under the necessarily centred logic of an abstract conceptual presentation. His is a rather decentred or (in a figurative, not a geometrically literal sense) elliptical notion of totality. For, while his notion of 'social totality' is grounded in the self-evident fact that all individuals exist within specific social forms, each of which is structured by the contradictory, antagonistic relations between the classes imbricated in the dominant mode of economic production and social reproduction, he also recognised, as evidenced by his many and insightful historical essays and journalistic commentaries, that no socio-historical totality is reducible to an expression of that dominant contradiction. If therefore social theory, or the abstract presentation of the essential structure of a social form, is a necessary step in deciphering the structure and exploitative logic of the mode of production, and in charting the major sites in social topography delineated by the dominant contradiction, it is only a first step in the open-ended task of writing the history of a particular society in its concrete totality. The next steps must be taken by a historical-materialist historiography. And in order to explain how crucial that historical-materialist historiography is to a historical-materialist *Wissenschaft*, I enlist the assistance of Dipesh Chakrabarty's insightful discussion of 'Two Histories of Capital' in his *Provincializing Europe*.

Although my tripartite division of the dimensions of a historical-materialist *Wissenschaft* (historical theory, social theory, historiography) might at first glance seem incompatible with Chakrabarty's depiction of capital's 'two histories', I would argue that our two positions overlap significantly. Chakrabarty prefaces his discussions of capital's 'two histories' with the epistemological assertion that 'an intellectual comprehension of the structure of capital is the precondition of … historical knowledge' – knowledge, that is, of 'the actual

---

55 There will no doubt be disagreement over this attribution of an 'expressivist' notion of totality and causality to Lukács. But I return to this matter and address it in some detail in Chapter 11.

process of history' that gave rise to capital, of the concrete histories of really-existing capitalist societies.[56] The work of comprehending intellectually 'the structure of capital' – of delineating capitalism as a historical phenomenon, explaining its antecedents, preconditions, and systemic logic its structure and logic – Chakrabarty designates 'History 1'. And the next step, that he calls 'History 2', is the work of explaining 'the actual process of history' (in Marx's formulation, the 'forms of its own life-process').[57]

Of Charkrabarty's 'Two Histories of Capital', History 1 is an abstractly general portrait of the logic of the capitalist production and valorisation process in its pure, and purely conceptual form, that is: as it would exist if unencumbered by any inconvenient 'empirical' factors (e.g. the lives of really-existing individuals,

---

56 Chakrabarty 2000, p. 63. Following citation in this paragraph, ibid; Chakrabarty's citation of Marx is from the latter's *Theories of Surplus Value*.

57 Although it may at first glance seem that my outline of a three-step mode of knowledge production differs from Chakrabarty's two-step position, I do not think I misrepresent Chakrabarty's 'two histories' in suggesting that they correspond directly to the second and third dimensions of my schema, to what I call, respectively: social theory or the critique of social form; and historiography. And if Chakrabarty's two histories correspond to what I view as the second and third dimensions of a historical-materialist *Wissenschaft*, it is fairly easy to reconcile apparent differences on the number of steps involved in knowledge production by considering the different purposes behind Chakrabarty's work and mine. Whereas my purpose is to outline the structure, logic, analytical objects, and tasks of a *Wissenschaft*, Chakrabarty's is to 'provincialize' Europe or, more specifically: European capitalist 'modernity', with at least two interrelated goals in mind: to deconstruct the particularist narrative that hypostatises European capitalist 'modernity' into the universal measure of human history, that evaluates the histories of colonial and post-colonial capitalist regions accordingly, and that justifies imperialist subjection by judging them as 'backward' or 'underdeveloped' regions not having made sufficient progress along the high road to 'modernity'; and, by thus emancipating the concrete histories of colonial and post-colonial capitalist regions from a provincially European narrative, to allow the complex and nuanced histories of those regions to be written. Given this two-fold purpose, there was no necessary reason for Chakrabarty to address the matters of historical theory that have occupied me in this first part of this book. But although he had in this book no need explicitly to articulate his stance on a materialist conception of history, that conception arguably serves as the implicit foundation of his work. Chakrabarty clearly does take *Capital* as the essential to the History 1 of the capitalist era – 'a work such as [his]', he insists, 'cannot afford to ignore Marx' whose 'writing constitute one of the founding moments in the history of anti-imperial thought' (Chakrabarty 2000 p. 47); and the first part of his book explaining what he means by History 1 and History 2 is, as he puts it, 'organized, as it were, under the sign of Marx' (Chakrabarty 2000, p. 18). It therefore seems fair to assume that he would agree with the historical-materialist assumptions (elaborated in Chapters 1 and 2) that underlay, and made possible, Marx's critique of capitalist social form – in which case Chakrabarty's 'History 1' and 'History 2' correspond to what I call the second and third dimensions of a historical-materialist *Wissenschaft*.

historical influences, cultural forms) that cannot be subsumed under the conceptual presentation. This corresponds to what I elaborated above, following Reichelt and Psychopedis, as the necessary yet necessarily abstract presentation of the essential structure and logic of the capitalist mode of production insofar as it corresponds to its concept, that is to say in its abstract purity, as an ideal type – the value of which, as Giovanni Arrighi concisely explains, is in presenting what 'defines the essence of capitalism', '[w]hat remains constant through all [its] adaptations', which 'is best captured by Marx's formula of capital M–C–M'.[58] Although that 'essence of capitalism' remains more or less constant, its 'adaptations' that further frame the lives of really-existing individuals do, of course, vary significantly and meaningfully. And Chakrabarty's History 2 or, as he aptly pluralises, 'History 2s' are devoted to analysing the histories of the specific 'life forms' and 'life-worlds' of really-existing individuals.[59] Chakrabarty's History 2s thus correspond to what I call historical-materialist historiography. And what he has to say about the relation between History 1 and 2 is certainly of relevance to a historical-materialist historiography.

Charkrabarty notes that in 'certain ambiguities' and 'underdeveloped ideas' in *Capital*, Marx expressed, albeit unsystematically, the need to move from the abstract critique of socio-economic form that is History 1 to concrete History 2s.[60] This move, he rightly insists, must be made through the theoretical critique that is presented in History 1 and that establishes the broad range of possible History 2s. Yet recognising also that the concrete content of those History 2s lies beyond the reach of the History 1, Charkrabarty insists further that History 2s must not simply be subsumed under the History 1. For, although History 1's portrait of the essential logic of the capitalist mode of production does provide indispensable insight into its inner workings, it is drawn in an abstract-conceptualist genre, and remains a colourless sketch of a particular *form* – an invaluable 'cartoon' in the fine arts sense, a preliminary drawing that outlines the contours and establishes the general form of the intended work, but also one whose strokes are literally too formal to capture, in all their subtle detail, the concrete historical contents that belong to the different clear and distinct portraits of historically diverse capitalist-based societies.

However much the logic of capital strives toward monolithic homogeneity, really-existing capitalist societies will, Chakrabarty maintains, always be heterogeneous. Although History 2s are 'not pasts separate from capital', and

---

58 Arrighi 2009, p. 92. My rendering reorders the sequence of Arrighi's sentence.
59 On the plural 'History 2s', see Chakrabarty 2000, pp. 64–6. On 'life forms', Chakrabarty 2000, p. 71; 'life-worlds' ibid, Chapter 3.
60 Chakrabarty 2000, pp. 65, 66.

although 'they inhere in capital', they nevertheless 'interrupt and punctuate the run of capital's own logic. ... There is nothing ... to guarantee that the subordination of History 2s to the logic of capital would ever be complete'.[61] Difference in the histories of capitalism, both among the metropoles and between the metropoles and colonial and postcolonial nations, is 'not something external to capital. Nor is it something subsumed into capital. It lives in intimate and plural relations to capital ranging from opposition to neutrality'. Thus 'History 2 does not spell out a program of writing histories that are alternatives to the narratives of capital. That is, History 2s do not constitute a dialectical Other of the necessary logic of History 1'. History 2 is, instead 'better thought of as a category charged with the function of constantly interrupting the totalizing thrusts of History 1'. A historical-materialist *Wissenschaft* must and, in my elaboration at least, does have 'room' for Chakrabarty's 'two kinds of histories', both for the '*analytical* histories' of History 1 that elaborate in general or abstract terms the historically specific logic of a given mode of production, and the History 2s that write 'more *affective* narratives of human belonging where life forms, although porous to one another, do not seem exchangeable through a third term of equivalence such as abstract labor' that would describe workers only from the standpoint of capital rather than as really-existing individuals living in concrete socio-historical contexts.

In an essay entitled (for the present discussion most appropriately) 'Reading *Capital*, Reading Historical Capitalisms' included in his volume entitled (most appropriately here also) *Only People Make Their Own History*, Samir Amin succinctly makes a similar point. Complementing his comment (cited above in the Introduction) that Marx is '*boundless*, because the radical critique that he initiated is itself boundless and always incomplete', Amin explains that '[t]o move from the reading of *Capital* (and particularly of Volumes 1 and 2) to that of historical capitalisms at successive moments of their deployment has its own requirements, even beyond reading all of Marx and Engels'. And he rejects the claim that Marx's work is 'outdated', 'not because [he] make[s] Marx into an infallible prophet, but simply because *Capital* allows us to grasp the essential foundations of capitalism beyond its historical forms and development. In this sense reading *Capital* will continue to provide us with guidance to perceive the diversity of forms in which the history of capitalism is expressed, but nothing more. *It is still necessary to interpret historical capitalism, something that is not found in Capital*'.[62]

---

61 Chakrabarty 2000, p. 64. Following citations in this paragraph, ibid., p. 66; p. 66; p. 66; p. 64; p. 74.
62 Amin 2019, pp. 176–7; my italics. This essay on *Capital* and capitalisms was written in

Chakrabarty's and Amin's highlighting of the variations in different 'History 2s' all framed by a given History 1, of the different historical trajectories of the diverse societies subject to the gravitational pull of capitalism, recalls Marx's above-cited caution in *The German Ideology* when, after having clearly delineated the limits of theoretical speculation, he then warns that 'our difficulties begin only when we set about the observation and the arrangement – the real depiction – of our historical material, whether of a past epoch or of the present'. One of the greatest dangers, for both analytical as well as political reasons, is the temptation to avoid these difficulties by taking the easy way around and collapsing the History 2s of diverse capitalist societies into a monolithic and homogeneous History 1. While all societies in which the capitalist mode of production prevails will obviously exhibit certain fundamental characteristics, *au fond* the exploitative valorisation process, their concrete histories will vary in degrees ranging from what we may very loosely call 'quantitative' (e.g. differences among nations of the capitalist metropole or among postcolonial capitalist nations) and 'qualitative' (e.g. differences between metropole and postcolonial capitalism). Thus, while it is absolutely necessary to move from History 1 (the abstract theoretical presentation of the logic of capitalist production and valorisation) to History 2s (the concrete histories of diverse societies) it is equally necessary to maintain what I have called the epistemological tension between theory and historiography in order to keep at bay both the potentially tyrannical abstractions of theory and the potentially entropic dispersal of local histories.

Ascertaining the necessity of moving from the critique of socio-economic form to historiography, however, divulges only the general framework of that historiography, but little about its specific contents. Yet, if we consider what Marx had to exclude temporarily in order to grasp the essential logic of capitalist socio-economic form, combined with Chakrabarty's reflections on the relations between History 1 and 2s, we can identify at least five crucial matters that can only, and must, be properly addressed by moving through and beyond social theory to concrete historical analysis. Two of these are matters of social-geography: completing the mapping of social topography and repopulating social geography; a third, the 'clocking' of different historical temporalities; the fourth, the portrayal or the super-structural institutions and cultural forms of a given society; and finally, the analysis of the forms of consciousness of really-existing individuals.

2016. See also Amin's 2011 essay on 'The Trajectory of Historical Capitalism and Marxism's Tricontinental Vocation' (in ibid. pp. 87–109).

Although analyses of these matters are absolutely essential if a historical-materialist *Wissenschaft* is to proceed from theoretical abstraction to an understanding of the concrete histories of really-existing individuals, I cannot here, for obvious reasons of space and time, even begin to address these matters in the detail they deserve. But neither would it do to ignore them completely. So, I will here utter a few words to intimate at least what is involved in each, to indicate why they can only be grasped in sufficient detail and depth, complexity and nuance by means of concrete historical analysis, and why the analysis of these matters is not only among the obligatory tasks of an open-ended historical-materialist *Wissenschaft*, but is also crucial if that *Wissenschaft* is contribute to an emancipatory politics.

To complete the social-cartographic project, it is first necessary to acknowledge that although class-divided social totalities are structured by and around a dominant binary (exemplified in the opening of the *Communist Manifesto* as that between 'freeman and slave, patrician and plebeian, lord and serf, capitalist and wage-labourer'), their complete topography will inevitably be more complex, containing sites other than those inherent in the dominant binary. It is therefore necessary to delineate the social sites and integrate the social classes and groups that in the abstract conceptual analysis were, for methodological reasons, temporarily ignored in order to decipher the structural logic, and delineate the dominant contradiction, of a given social form, that is: to map the social sites that are somewhat 'anomalous' in relation to the dominant contradiction, but whose inhabitants are not at all insignificant in the history of a given social form. By 'anomalous' I mean those socio-economic classes existing within, but not properly 'of', a given socio-economic form (e.g. the merchant class within the land-based Greek πόλις, the bourgeoisie developing within, bringing the monetary economy to, and ultimately overturning a feudal social order literally grounded in landlords and enserfed peasants; or the petite bourgeoisie – e.g. artisans, family farmers, small merchants – in capitalist society sandwiched between capital and labour). In order to integrate these 'anomalous' classes that give a social totality its elliptically particular form, it is necessary to think of any such totality, not in terms of a single binary, even if dominant, contradiction, but as a more complex set of differential relations among various social elements, some of which may neither derive from nor be wholly fashioned by the dominant contradiction, but whose situation necessarily comes to be mediated through it.

In their own voluminous historical writings, Marx and Engels demonstrated how to proceed in integrating such 'anomalous' social classes into historical portraits of existing capitalist societies. In *Capital*, for example, Marx performed a temporary methodological reduction of capitalist social geography to the binary of capital and labour, thus fully, but quite self-consciously, overlooking the 'middling classes', the *petite bourgeoisie* or *Mittelstände*, as not necessary to decipher the dominant structural principles and logic of the capitalist mode of production.[63] Yet in the concluding chapter of Volume I, Marx distinguished between 'personal' and 'capitalist' private property, and thereby points to the need to consider both the space in capitalist society inhabited by these market-oriented owners of small parcels of 'personal' private property in capitalist society, and also their politics (see Chapter 13.5 below). As we all too painfully know, this heterogenous, but still identifiable class has played, and continues to play, a not insignificant role in the history of fascist and fascistoid movements – a role Marx more or less anticipated in his historical analysis of *The Eighteenth Brumaire* that exposed the politically crucial role of the allegedly disappearing, but never disappeared *petite-bourgeois* class, and also that of the *Lumpenproletariat*, in the *coup* of Louis Napoleon.

Although a necessary first step in depicting the real life-processes of really-existing individuals, even the detailed mapping of social topography does not alone suffice to remove all the 'the difficulties' that arise in moving from the abstractions of theory to 'the study of the actual life-process and the activity of the individuals of each epoch ... in their actual, empirically perceptible process of development under specific conditions'.[64] If the first step in presenting the concrete history of a given society is to depict the lay of the social land, it cannot be the last. Just as a topographical map provides a general, but still very abstract view of the landscape, situating the peaks and valleys through the proximity and density of its monochromatic lines, but not depicting what the landscape actually looks like, a purely conceptual analysis (e.g. *Capital*) can only provide a general and rather featureless social topography.

In order to give concrete social-demographic content to social topography, it is necessary to repopulate the temporarily evacuated social terrain with the 'really living individuals' who, in the abstract critique of the structural logic of the mode of production and for methodological reasons, were treated only abstractly as the generic bearers of economic categories – a task as indispensable to historical-materialist *Wissenschaft* as it is vast and challenging (and its importance helps to explain Marx's lengthy historical discussions in *Capital* in which he goes beyond theoretical critique and paints detailed portraits of capital's adverse consequences for the lives of really existing wage-labouring

---

63   For further comment on Marx's analysis of the petite bourgeoisie and 'personal private property', see Chapter 13.5 and Appendix 13.5
64   This citation is a composite of two very similar passages that I took the liberty of merging. Both passages are from Marx 1845 in Tucker 1978, p. 155.

people; see Chapter 14). To meet that challenge, historical-materialist historiography must answer the kind of crucial questions that Heidi Hartmann posed, namely: who inhabits which spaces? why are certain groups of people more or less explicitly forced into certain socio-geographical spaces?[65] This historiography must therefore illuminate how the hierarchical categorisation of people based on extra-economic factors (though not without economic motivations or economic consequences) mediates the distribution of people so categorised in the social spaces delineated by the relations of production.

Really-living individuals come, of course, in various sizes, shapes, and skin colours, sexes and sexual orientations, ages and abilities. And the investment of such differences with social meanings that then serve as justifications to incarcerate certain groups of people in, if not utterly uninhabitable, certainly inhumane and inhospitable spaces in social geography has been a rather transhistorical constant. It is therefore the responsibility of a historical-materialist historiography not only to repopulate the socio-economic form under analysis, but to map its social geography – to portray how, and explain why, different socially-delineated groups of people are distributed in social space.

Hypothetically (that is to say: *theoretically*) speaking, a mode of production, capitalism, for example, can be *imagined* such that the only basis of differentiation in the social relations would be based on class. *Hypothetically* (or *theoretically*) speaking, capitalism *could* exist as Marx described in his abstract conceptual presentation in *Capital* through which he deciphered the logic of the capitalist valorisation process – and as it appears in the liberal imaginary: a society in which all supposedly have free and equal political and legal rights, including that to private property which will result in some being large property holders and others, with no property of their own, forced (through no fault, as Locke put it, other than that of their own quarrelsomeness and contentiousness, their lack of industriousness and rationality) to sell themselves (their 'labour-power') for part of the day in return for wages – to become, in Locke's terms, 'servants'. *Historically* speaking, however, it has not. *Historically* speaking, nowhere has any really-existing capitalist socio-economic form ever fully 'corresponded to its concept'.

Nor is any ever likely to do so – even though the world-wide diffusion of capital's quantitative logic (sketched in Chapter 12) seems to behave like a hyperbolic function, having set contemporary capitalist societies on an asymptotic course, ever converging on a conceptual axis that they will never quite reach.

---

65 See Hartmann 1997. See also Gayle Rubin (1997, esp. pp. 31–4) for an elaboration of Engels's intimations in *The Origin of the Family, Private Property, and the State* that those antagonistic relations can also be based in what Rubin calls a sex-gender system.

Thus, while the hypothetical or purely conceptual presentation of a socio-economic form (e.g. *Capital* or Chakrabarty's 'History 1') is a necessary dimension of a historical-materialist *Wissenschaft* and a crucial first step toward grasping the history of a given society in its concrete and multifaceted totality, it does not go beyond an ahistorical level of abstraction – and simply cannot, therefore, be the last step. To progress beyond the abstract presentation of the essential logic of the capitalist mode of production, to move toward the historical-materialist portrayal of really-existing capitalist societies in their historical specificity, it is absolutely essential to address what Cedric Robinson identified as 'racial capitalism', to address also gendered capitalism – to address, in short, each and every form of singling out and stigmatising groups of people, and confining them in socially specific sites subject to exploitation and oppression, be it on the basis of race, gender, sexual orientation, or any kind of 'otherising' category.[66]

In a richly suggestive passage from *Re-enchanting the World* Silvia Federici focuses on the kinds of matters that must be addressed in repopulating social geography. And although her particular concern in this work is to survey variations in the histories of capitalist societies, the lens that she crafts offers insights into what must be involved in moving beyond the abstract critique of any socio-economic form to the reintegration of the temporarily evacuated really-existing individuals:

> [A]n essential aspect of the capitalist project has been the disarticulation of the social body, through the imposition of different disciplinary regimes producing an accumulation of 'differences' and hierarchies that profoundly affect how capitalist relations are experienced. We, therefore, have different histories of originary accumulation, each providing a particular perspective on capitalist relations necessary to reconstruct their totality and unmask the mechanism by which capitalism has maintained its power. ... This means that the history of originary accumulation past and present [and of capitalism more generally] cannot be fully comprehended until it is written not only from the viewpoint of the future or former waged workers, but from the viewpoint of the enslaved, the colonized, the indigenous people whose lands continue to be the main target

---

66 On 'racial capitalism', see Robinson 1983. For comment on the logical and abstract, yet historically most significant meaning of Marx's reference in the *Grundrisse* to slavery in capitalism as an 'anomaly', and an attempt to reconcile Marx's position and Robinson's, see Appendix 12.7. Studies on women and class include: Angela Davis 1983; Johanna Brenner 2000; Heather A. Brown 2012; Vogel 2013; Giménez 2018.

of enclosures, and the many social subjects whose place in the history of capitalist society cannot be assimilated into the history of the waged.[67]

The forms and contents of 'the disarticulation of the social body' (or in terms I have used above: the social distribution of bodies into unequal social spaces) both on the basis of economic power or lack thereof, and also on the basis of the hierarchical valuation of corporeal differences, whether in physiognomy or physiology, obviously long precedes capitalism. And I take Federici's comment to be valid for the analysis of any social form characterised by hierarchies of power and therewith exploitation and oppression. To generalise her statement accordingly: an analysis of any society so characterised *must* expose 'the imposition of different disciplinary regimes producing an accumulation of "differences" and hierarchies that profoundly affect how [social] relations are experienced' and *must* produce 'different histories' of the genesis and structural logic of inequalities, 'each providing a particular perspective on [unequal social] relations necessary to reconstruct their totality and unmask the mechanism[s] by which [a ruling class] has [established and] maintained its power'. And to generalise Federici's conclusion accordingly, this means that 'the history of [any class society] cannot be fully comprehended until it is written from the viewpoint of [all exploited and/or oppressed social groups]'.[68]

In order to write such comprehensive histories, it is also imperative to address prejudicial divisions and grasp the often-hostile heterogeneity *within* socially delineated groups defined by class or race or gender. These include: racial divisions within the working class, such as those between black and white, or brown and white workers, between English and Irish workers, or Northern and Southern European workers, or gender divisions between male and female workers; racial and class divisions among feminists; class conflicts within racial- or gender-defined groups. Moreover, it cannot be emphasised enough that *none* of these analyses is subsidiary, and that *all* are essential to

---

67 Federici 2019, pp. 16–17.
68 One of the most important recent contributions to the ongoing discussion is that made by theorists of 'intersectionality' who also insist on the necessity of explaining all forms of exploitation and oppression, and who fault historical-materialist approaches for allegedly privileging class and establishing a hierarchy that ranks class exploitation over all other forms of exploitation and oppression. Although I cannot address intersectionality theory to the degree that it deserves, I do attempt, in Appendix 3.4., to situate my notion of historical-materialist *Wissenschaft* in relation to it. For an excellent overview of intersectionality see Collins and Bilge 2019. For insightful perspectives on the relation between historical-materialism and intersectionality, see: Bannerji 2005; McNally and Ferguson 2015; McNally 2017; Clark et al. 2018.

the repopulation of social geography with really living individuals – and therefore to the historical-materialist aspiration to paint accurate portraits of the various histories of capitalist societies in their concrete totalities.

Equally important in the writing of History 2s is to come to terms with 'the problem of temporality'[69] – a problem that Marx and Engels broached in several of their historical commentaries, including Marx's *Eighteenth Brumaire of Louis Napoleon* and his long study of the Russian road to capitalism and possibly socialism. And one of Chakrabarty's principal concerns is to ensure that we do not cast all societies in which capitalist relations of production prevail into the same bucket of historical abstraction and thereby dissolve the richness and texture of particular concrete histories into 'homogenous empty time' (Walter Benjamin[70]). To impose the abstract logic of *Capital* onto the concrete histories of all capitalist nations, from the capitalist metropole to the capitalised colonial and postcolonial world would be to posit a unilinear universal history of capital, with the histories of all nations stuck in a single evolutionary rut, some just further along, more 'advanced' than others. Such a one-dimensional take on history underlies not only Whiggish developmental histories, but also those Marxist approaches that take the particular historical path of 'the West' to, and presumably through, capitalism and on to socialism, as the single road of history along which all nations must pass.

Chakrabarty rightly takes issue with the theoretical reductionism of this approach. He does not at all deny capital's relentless and seemingly irresistible drive to remake the world in its own image – a drive briefly but powerfully portrayed in the opening pages of the *Communist Manifesto*, and to which the global ubiquity of McDonald's, adapted of course to local tastes with ethnically 'authentic' menu-variations, lends tasteless und unhealthy credence. (A sampling of the McDonald's World Menu reveals: the McVegan for Finland and Sweden and Big Vegan TS for Germany; the Dosa Masala Burger and McSpicy Paneer for India; Spicy McWings and the Double Chicken Burger for China; the Green Curry Chicken Burger with a Mango McFlurry for Malaysia; the Samurai Pork Burger for Thailand; the Bulgogi Burger for South Korea; Ebi Burger for Hong Kong; Big Brekkie Burger for Australia; McPollo Italiano for Chile; the McArabia Chicken for Saudi Arabia, etc.). Chakrabarty, however, insists on the obvious but all too often neglected point that although both the economic logic and flood-level historical current of capital is to expand, to recreate the world in its own image, that dominant current is diverted into different channels in

---

69 Chakrabarty 2000, p. 92.
70 Benjamin 1968, p. 261.

different societies: 'No historical form of capital, however global its reach, can ever be a universal. No global (or even local, for that matter) capital can ever represent the universal logic of capital, for any historically available form of capital is a provisional compromise made up of History 1 modified by somebody's History 2s'.[71] Each society in which the capitalist mode of production comes to prevail will nevertheless and necessarily have its own particular history, its own particular historical 'temporality'.

What prevents capital from realising its universalising intent are two kinds of resistance that act against and divert, if not block, the fulfilment of capital's drive to remake the world in its image: one is the weight of the histories and traditions that acts as a form of resistance in regions within which capitalism develops or on which capital attempts to impose itself, and disrupts capital's totalising tendency; and the other is the active political resistance of various anti-capitalist forces. The particular strength of these resisting forces in a particular society is a formative factor of the 'provisional compromise' that constitutes its particular historical temporality. This is evident in the rather obvious difference in historical temporality between the European metropoles and the colonial/postcolonial worlds. And although Chakrabarty does not explicitly address it, his argument is equally applicable to the 'local' variations in the historical temporalities within and among both Western metropoles and postcolonial capitalist societies.

The move from the abstract presentation of the essential logic of a social form to the historically specific presentation of a society in its concrete totality also requires also reintegration of non-economic 'superstructural' elements including political institutions, legal codes and administrative systems, social organisations, and cultural forms. Taken together, these elements constitute the national variations among, the unique and different histories of, societies grounded in the same mode of production. Because 'culture' has for almost a century dominated discussion, first among 'Western Marxist' thinkers beginning in the postwar period, then for the last half-century or so among semiotically-oriented 'cultural turn' theorists, I will here suggest a direction for a historical-materialist approach to culture that both borrows from and goes beyond both of those theoretical traditions – a direction I follow below (Part 4) in an anatomy of capital's quantitative culture.[72]

---

71   Chakrabarty 2000, p. 70.
72   Cultural-turn and Western-Marxist approaches to culture are discussed further in, respectively, Chapters 9 and 11. In Chapter 9, I argue that cultural-turn approaches are invaluable in deciphering the internal logic of semiotic systems, but that their assumption of the 'arbitrariness' of cultural forms prevents them from grasping the social mediation of cul-

A comment that Marx made in the Afterword to the second German edition of *Capital* to differentiate his dialectical method from Hegel's suggests how a historical-materialist *Wissenschaft* might approach the study of cultural forms – and in a manner consistent with Charkrabarty's notions of History 1 and History 2s. Whereas Hegel saw 'the life-process of the human brain, i.e., the process of thinking', as 'the demiurgos of the real world, and the real world [as] only the external, phenomenal form of "the Idea"', Marx approached 'the ideal [as] nothing but the material world reflected by the human mind, *and translated into forms of thought*'.[73] Although this statement seems clear and harmless enough, it (along with similar statements Marx made about the relation between ideas, culture, and the material world) can be interpreted in both a strong and a weak manner that have radically different methodological consequences. A clarification, possibly a qualification, is therefore in order here.

The strong rendering of this statement is determinist in the strong sense, that is: reductionist. It treats cultural forms and their content as mere epiphenomena, as reflexes of the economic base. This version is, of course, to be rejected. The modest version, however, understands the material base as a determination of cultural forms, with the emphasis here on *form*. Societies with similar modes of production will exhibit similar forms of mental representations: we would not expect to find animistic cultural forms (with the unique exception of the fetishised animation of the commodity form) in capitalist societies, nor a mechanistic view of nature and 'modern' science in gathering and hunting societies (an observation that would be platitudinous had not the notion of the arbitrariness of cultural forms become axiomatic).[74] Nor should we expect

---

ture. And in Chapter 11, I suggest a historical-materialist approach to culture that is grounded in Western-Marxist theories, but is critical of the way in which those theories take a methodological shortcut in their treatment of the relation between culture and the forms of consciousness, and ultimately and illegitimately reducing the latter to a mirror of the former.

73 Marx 1990, p. 102, my italics.
74 In conceiving of cultural forms and contents as relatively motivated by, as well as relatively autonomous from, the mode of production, a historical-materialist approach to culture would map a course between those of structuralist and poststructuralist analyses. In so doing, it could learn from the strengths of both, while avoiding the weaknesses that result from the binary opposition of structuralist universalism vs. poststructuralist arbitrariness. Like structuralism, a historical-materialist *Wissenschaft* would acknowledge the similarity of cultural forms underlying the difference or 'arbitrariness' of contents, though it would dispense with structuralism's universalist claims and limit the similarity of cultural form to societies with similar modes of production. (Although his differentiation between capitalist and pre-capitalist social forms might resemble Levi-Strauss's distinction between 'hot' and 'cold' societies, Marx also makes further qualitative distinctions

that cultures with the same general form also share the same contents. Given the diverse geographies, ecologies, and histories of societies with the same general form (e.g. hunting and gathering, capitalist), we should rather expect even radical variation in the contents of cultural forms that emerge in similar socio-economic contexts.

If we accept these seemingly rather obvious points and approach culture as a set of mental representations of the material world translated into, and objectified in, socio-historically specific forms of thought, then the study of culture requires investigation *not only* into the internal logic of cultural sign systems, but also into the process through which the material world is 'reflected' or, more accurately, 'refracted' in culture, that is: the particular translation process that produces the particular mental representations that make up the particular contents of a given culture. This is another way of saying that a historical-materialist methodology not only acknowledges, but also seeks to understand *both* the relative motivation involved in the production of cultural *forms* and the specific, highly variable *content* of those forms; it insists that cultural differences between populations with similar social forms be analysed as a result of the particular history, the particular social practice over time, of a given group population in a geographically and ecologically specific site.

In order to avoid imputing a false homogeneity to a given culture, a historical-materialist approach must not only delineate the specific sites of cultural and counter-cultural production, but also acknowledge and elaborate both the differences between, and the points of overlap of, hegemonic and alternative or oppositional cultures. To develop the socially diverse contents of a given cultural form, historical-materialist inquiry must reconstruct the process through which, and the social conditions within which, variously defined social groups (e.g. groups based on such factors as race, ethnicity, gender, sexual orientation, etc.) appropriate, modify, or expropriate cultural objectifications. In a synthesis of Marx and Walt Whitman: historical-materialist inquiry must reconstruct how the objects of people's material practice call forth from diffusion their meanings and give them shape; or in a more prosaic synthesis of Marx

---

among pre-capitalist social forms, each distinguished by its particular 'inner bond'.). And like poststructuralism, a historical-materialist *Wissenschaft* would not treat the variable contents of a specific cultural form as inessential manifestations of an essential structure, though it would reject the notion that that variation is merely arbitrary. The analysis of cultural forms, in short, cannot dispense with an understanding of a society's mode of production, its material 'base'. But nor can it simply 'develop' or derive the specific and highly variable content of cultural forms from an understanding of the material base. These issues are treated further in Chapters 8 and 9.

and Chakrabarty: historical-materialist inquiry must move from History 1 to History 2s.

The final matter mentioned above as belonging to the realm of History 2s concerns the forms of consciousness of really-existing individuals. Although the analysis of cultural forms is obviously most pertinent to the analysis of forms of consciousness, the two are not to be conflated. There has, however, been an in my view unfortunate tendency, in both poststructuralist approaches and certain historical-materialist approaches, to take a misleading methodological shortcut in the analysis of the forms of consciousness, namely: to derive the forms of consciousness of really-existing individuals from the purely conceptual critique of sociocultural forms. Because I address below, and in some detail, the misleading consequences of this methodological shortcut in the analysis of the forms of consciousness in structuralist and poststructuralist analyses (Chapter 9) and also in Lukács and those who adopted his method for the analysis of consciousness (Chapter 11), I will here note only what should be the obvious point, namely: that despite their intimate relation, it cannot simply be assumed that the study of cultural forms alone suffices to understand how those forms are received, interpreted, modified, adapted, appropriated by, and mediated through the concrete experiences of, really-existing individuals. As Marx insisted in *The German Ideology*, the historical-materialist analysis of the forms of consciousness must begin with 'the real living individuals themselves' and treat consciousness 'only as *their* consciousness', derived from their own 'real life process' and their 'actions' as individuals.

Given the immensity of these historiographical tasks – completing the mapping of social topography, repopulating social geography, clocking historical temporalities, deconstructing superstructural institutions and cultural forms, and reconstructing forms of consciousness – I should in concluding render more precise my evaluation ending the previous section where I dubbed *Capital* an albeit central, but nevertheless a single chapter of an open book. It would be rather more accurate to say that it is the first of a set of (many still unwritten) volumes devoted to illuminating the concrete histories of societies in which the capitalist mode of production prevails – volumes that collectively are but a part (for obvious political reasons a most pressing part) of a rather extensive and open-ended *oeuvre*, whose research strategy and programme were outlined by Marx, and the writing of which is the ongoing responsibility of a historical-materialist *Wissenschaft*.

3.5 Concluding Considerations on Chapter 3 and Part 1

My goal throughout the three chapters of Part 1 has been to sketch a kind of prolegomena outlining the dimensions and steps of historical-materialist knowledge production, beginning with a presentation of the fundamental assumptions of a historical-materialist *Wissenschaft*, to a reconstruction of its conceptual scaffolding and an articulation of its guiding threads, and an elaboration of the methodological resolution of the epistemological dilemmas arising from a materialist conception of history. As I argued in the first chapter, the foundation of this *Wissenschaft* is human corporeal organisation as the 'first fact' of Marx's materialist conception of history. From that foundation Marx derived a rather abstract, but nonetheless necessary set of the essential, corporeally grounded 'moments' of history – moments that I categorised in the second chapter as the production of material, social, and semiotic artefacts – the particular constellation of which gives each society its particular form. Having elaborated the materialist conception of history up from its corporeal foundations, I turned in Chapter 3 to its consequences for historical-materialist knowledge production. I attempted to show that in Marx's scattered passages on the methodology and content of a historical-materialist *Wissenschaft* we can find an outline of a mode of knowledge production, exemplified in his own intellectual practice, and consisting of three distinct but interrelated dimensions, three distinct but interrelated steps: a mode of knowledge production that begins with the abstractness of historical theory, and moves to and through still abstract social theory, to the concreteness of historical analysis. Each of these steps is necessary, each alone necessarily insufficient – and each, accordingly, having its particular and limited, but nevertheless indispensable methodological place-value. With this reconstitution of historical-materialist *Wissenschaft* as a process of moving from the abstractions of historical and social theory to concrete historical analysis, Marx solved the epistemological dilemmas raised by a materialist conception of history, effected what amounted to an epistemological break with traditional Western philosophical modes of knowledge production, and therewith completed his *Aufhebung* of philosophy.

Because historical-materialist historiography has too often been neglected, ignored, or dismissed in favour of privileging 'theory' as, if not the sole, at least the primary concern of a historical-materialist *Wissenschaft*, I conclude with a few comments about the respective roles of, and the relations between, theoretical work and historical-materialist historiography. Clarity is essential here: my point is certainly not to denigrate theoretical work. For, while a materialist conception of history does set needed limits on the place-value of theoretical work, it does not at all cancel its indispensable role as the essential first step in the study of a given social form – which is to decipher the logic of a given mode of production. And the next necessary step is toward historical-materialist historiography as the indispensable means of giving concrete content to, and of correcting, the abstractions of theory – and the neglect of which will almost inevitably lead to misleading and even dangerous shortcuts in both understanding the world and formulating political strategies. Before commenting further on the relation between theory, historiographical analysis, and political practice, however, it is worth making explicit another contribution that is implicit in the abstract theoretical presentation of *Capital* – and that itself also reinforces the need to supplement theory with historical analysis.

There has been a great deal of controversy over how to understand Marx's stirring rhetoric in *The Communist Manifesto* and in the section on 'the historical tendency of capitalist accumulation' that concludes the chapter on originary accumulation in *Capital*. His vivid pronouncements that 'the knell of private property sounds' and that 'the expropriators will be expropriated' are certainly prophetic in tone.[75] But precisely because of the necessarily abstract, purely conceptual character of *Capital*, we should perhaps be a bit more circumspect about reading such comments too literally as statements on the inevitable workings of some allegedly inexorable 'natural' laws of history. Because *Capital* is very consciously an *abstract* presentation, any apparent prediction found in it must be understood in the future conditional tense, as a statement of the historical *tendency* depicting what will happen *if* that tendency continues unabated – and also what could happen *if* those who are to expropriate the expropriators do what they might. Such statements are made, *not* in the modality of 'logical necessity, therefore historical inevitability', but rather in the modality of 'historical possibility and practical necessity', that is: the tendency of capitalist valorisation toward ever greater crises exposes the system's own irrationality, and reveals the possibility of building a rational system of production beyond capital. Thus, although socialism is by no means a foregone conclusion, it is certainly a historical possibility – and for the exploited, and the sake of the future, it is a practical necessity, that is: *if* the exploited are to emancipate themselves, it is practically necessary for them to take advantage of the historical possibility and, through their own political action, to supplant capitalism with socialism.

But as Walter Benjamin put it so poignantly, 'a storm is blowing from Paradise', leaving in its wake 'piles of debris growing skyward'.[76] While capital has

---

75   Marx 1990, p. 929.
76   Benjamin 1968, p. 257.

managed, thus far at least, to survive several rather calamitous crises, and to emerge in many ways even stronger from the human disasters it has begotten, those piles of debris continue to grow ever higher skyward to the point of threatening the future of the planet. And whether first uttered by Engels or Rosa Luxemburg, the alternative of 'socialism or barbarism' is a real one with no predestined outcome.[77] While Marx's rhetoric might sometime seem to exude too much optimism about a socialist future, there is also a warning embedded in his abstract presentation of capital's immanent logic that will, if not countered, relentlessly assert itself. This can be elucidated by considering another take on Chakrabarty's claim, cited above, that '[n]o historical form of capital, however global its reach, can ever be a universal', that '[n]o global (or even local, for that matter) capital can ever represent the universal logic of capital'.[78] This claim has certainly been correct up through our present – and for the sake of the future, we should assure that it remains so. But although the abstract conceptualism of *Capital* cannot tell the history of any really-existing capitalist society, it does illuminate what might be called the 'objective intent' or, in Chakrabarty's terms, 'the totalizing thrusts', of capital.

In contrast to all other socio-economic forms, capitalism is not parochial, but rather evangelical. Whereas traditional societies at war, be they gatherer-hunter or imperial, if they did not wipe the vanquished off the face of the earth, tended to exact tribute and/or slaves, but otherwise left the vanquished society and culture relatively untouched, the immanent logic of capitalism, its never-ending need for profit, as Marx and Engels noted in the impassioned rhetoric of the first pages of the *Communist Manifesto*, drives it to try to reproduce itself on ever greater scale. And by exposing those 'totalizing thrusts', *Capital* warns us of where the logic of capitalism leads, of what capitalism does in, with, and to the world: of its desire and drive to remake the world in its own image, and at all costs – except of course production costs which, in its *Heißhunger* (Marx) for profit, capital constantly seeks to minimise by 'capitalising' nature and human beings, by transmogrifying them into quanta of 'raw materials' and 'labour-power' (see Part 4 below). And it thus warns us of what capital, absent forces of resistance, *will* do – until the planet and its people are used up.

In heeding that warning, it is certainly worth appreciating the value of concrete historical analysis, not only to a historical-materialist *Wissenschaft*, but

---

77 For related discussion on how to understand Marx's seeming declaration of historical law concerning the expropriation of the expropriators, see Francis Wheen's comments cited in Appendix 12.8.
78 Chakrabarty 2000, p. 70.

also to the resistance and the emancipatory politics to which that *Wissenschaft* aspires to contribute. And one way of doing so is to take another look at Marx's comment that 'people make their own history, but not as they please' slightly rephrased, as suggested above, as 'people don't make their own history as they please, but they do make it'. Although it may at first glance seem platitudinous, this dictum offers a surprisingly parsimonious resolution to the seemingly interminable 'either/or' debate over the relation between structure and agency with a 'both/and' rejoinder.

The first two theoretical steps of a historical-materialist *Wissenschaft* that attempts to write the concrete history of really-existing human beings 'up from the body' delineate, respectively, the species-specific corporeal and the historically-specific socio-economic structures, that together frame and limit the possibilities for people to make their own history – but that neither deprive individuals of agency nor determine the specific histories that people, within those structural limits, do themselves make. And the final, most concrete, and absolutely necessary step of a historical-materialist *Wissenschaft*, therefore, is the concrete historical analysis of the histories that people do, within those limits, make – and those that they could make. Put briefly: historical and social theory address structural frameworks, the range of the possible; historical writing addresses agency, which of the albeit limited possible histories people actually make their own. Just as theoretical work is necessary to decipher the 'material conditions of life' under which 'real individuals live', so too is historiographical work necessary to comprehend the concrete experience of those 'real individuals and their activity', the histories they make within the given material conditions that frame, but do not determine their lives.[79]

Without writing such concrete histories, historical-materialist *Wissenschaft* would remain entrapped in the rarefied air of the abstract dimensions of historical and social theory that, although essential to explaining why people do *not* make their own histories as they please, are in themselves necessarily insufficient; for, the abstractions of theory alone cannot explain how really-existing people nevertheless do make their own particular histories. The failure to make the next crucial move from the abstractions of historical and social theory to concrete historical analysis makes it rather difficult to resist the temptation of doing precisely what Marx warned against, namely: imposing abstract theory as a 'recipe' or 'schema' on the concrete history of really living individuals – or, as historian William Hagen quipped decades ago in a graduate seminar, 'letting the theoretical tail wag the historical dog'.

---

[79] *MEW*, Vol. 3, p. 20; Tucker 1978, p. 149.

Such theoretical wagging would subsume and thereby disappear the complexities, intricacies, and uniqueness of the histories of diverse societies, even if grounded in similar modes of production. It would therefore undoubtedly lead to mistaken, because overgeneralised analytical conclusions that, by ignoring the specific and diverse contexts in which people make their own history, would also have adverse, even dangerous consequences for the formulation of an emancipatory political praxis. If political praxis is determined on the basis of abstract theory *alone*, then the resulting strategies and tactics will almost inevitably be misplaced and misdirected. If interpreting the world is to be a means of changing the world, then a historical-materialist *Wissenschaft* must be sure to interpret the world accurately – which requires analysis and understanding of the concrete experience and histories of the really-existing individuals to whom it seeks to appeal.

That Marx recognised how essential concrete historical analysis is to understand the crucial 'contingent' factors (specified in the previous section) that are, for methodological reasons temporarily excluded from the abstract conceptual critique of social form, but that shape the concrete conditions in which particular people make their own histories, is evidenced by his view of their political importance. As noted above and worth repeating here, there is in Marx's vocabulary perhaps no higher compliment to these 'contingent' elements, and to their historical analysis, than his insistence that the understanding of such 'contingencies' is of absolutely crucial importance to a socialist politics. And this is exactly what he wrote into the statutes of the First International where he noted that because of historical differences that produced different sets of institutions, laws, and cultural forms, each national section of the International has its own historically specific row to hoe – the recognition of which is not unimportant to determining strategies of national politics nor to overcoming misunderstandings that might undermine attempts to build international solidarity.[80]

It is not necessary either to disparage theoretical inquiry, or to insist that everyone engaged in historical-materialist knowledge production be a historian, in order to acknowledge the limits placed on theoretical knowledge by the materialist conception of history.[81] These limits are a consequence of the

---

80 See Marx 1964, p. 57.
81 The inverse is (as I hope should be obvious from my entire argument) also true, that is: just as theory must be complemented and completed with historical analysis, so too must historical analysis acknowledge its dependence on some theoretical framework, whether explicit or implicit. Historical analysis that would claim to be without a set of unspoken theoretical assumptions about history and society, and concerned only with 'the facts',

historical-materialist situating of the mind firmly within the body, and of intellectual labour firmly within the social division of labour, that together complicate the nature of knowledge production and reduce, but do not at all cancel, theory's methodological place-value. Precisely because it is presented in necessarily abstract concepts, theory, as Marx recognised in his methodological comments in the Preface to *Capital*, can only treat people only as personifications or bearers of economic categories. To temper the broad, sometimes self-aggrandising powers attributed to 'theory', it is therefore imperative that those who speak about, and seek to speak for, others recognise the importance of historical analysis to historical-materialist knowledge production, avoid treating people (as does capital) simply in abstract theoretical terms as bearers of economic categories, and treat people instead as really-existing individuals whose concrete experience deserves to be understood through concrete historical analysis – and must be understood if historical-materialist *Wissenschaft* is to contribute to building a meaningful emancipatory movement.

A brief but telling example of the hypostasis of theory as the indispensable guide to, and of theoreticians as the indispensable leaders of, properly emancipatory politics is the rather imperious sentiment expressed succinctly and rather simplistically in the slogan, not uncommon in Marxist intellectual circles, 'without theory, no revolution'. That slogan condenses and decontextualises Lenin's comment that '[w]ithout revolutionary theory there can be no revolutionary movement' – an idea, he continued, that 'cannot be insisted upon too strongly at a time when the fashionable preaching of opportunism goes hand in hand with an infatuation for the narrowest forms of practical activity'.[82] Lenin made this declaration in *What is to be Done?* as part of his polemic against what he considered the impoverished theory of, the 'eclecticism and absence of principle' in, contemporary social-democratic *parties*. There is no need here to rehash the debate between Bolsheviks and Mensheviks. But it does seem (to rephrase slightly Voltaire's trenchant witticism) that history played a pack of tricks on the dead Lenin. For, when taken out of context and sloganistically reduced to 'without theory, no revolution', this comment lends itself all too easily to privileging theory as the only viable guide to properly emancipatory political praxis – and to privileging theoreticians as its only viable leaders.

In 'track[ing] down idealism in its last hideout', Norman Geras noted (in a critique aimed specifically at Althusser, but applicable to any similar priv-

---

would be based on self-deception – which is why Marx in *The German Ideology* not only exposed the unacknowledged assumptions of 'the Germans' who claimed to be 'devoid of premises', but also clearly articulated his own. (Marx in Tucker 1978, p. 155 ff.).

82 This and following citation from Lenin 1969, p. 25.

ileging of theory) that Lenin's comment can be, and has been taken, to mean that 'the relation between Marxist theory and the working class movement as one of exteriority: the former is produced outside the latter, and must be imported into it, failing which this movement can only arrive at conceptions which are ideological, and bourgeois-ideological at that'.[83] These notions, 'however "Leninist" one may care to think them', are, Geras concludes, 'erroneous'. For, their 'final effect is to make the relation between Marxist theory and the working class a unilateral and purely pedagogic one: the intellectuals "give" the class the knowledge it needs'. And echoing Marx's third thesis on Feuerbach, Geras concludes rather emphatically that this 'is only the final consequence of every idealism: élitism. When knowledge celebrates its autonomy, the philosophers celebrate their dominance'.

The easiest and most meaningful manner to avoid those epistemologically deceptive and politically dangerous illusions is a bit of epistemological modesty on the part of knowledge producers who must remember that although theory is essential to deciphering capital's exploitative logic, its conceptual and therefore abstract nature precludes a treatment of really existing individuals in any but an abstract theoretical manner, as anything more than personifications of economic categories. Theory necessarily remains exterior to, and thus cannot alone grasp, the concrete experience of those who experience exploitation where abstract concepts cannot reach, namely: on their bodies (see Chapter 14). Theory can only effectively guide an emancipatory praxis if the producers of theory also learn to see the much that remains invisible to theory – recognise, that is, the much that they can and must learn from the people about whom they write and for whom they claim to speak. And such recognition requires that historical-materialist *Wissenschaft* to be not only concerned with theory, but also engaged in the attempt to reconstruct the concrete experience and the actual (rather than theoretically 'ascribed') forms of consciousness of really-living individuals.[84] Antonio Gramsci noted that Marx 'plants himself squarely in history ... He is a historian, he is an interpreter of the documents of the past, *of all the documents*, not just a part of them'. This must of course apply to a historical-materialist *Wissenschaft* as well.[85]

---

83 This and following citations in this paragraph from Geras 1971, pp. 83–4.
84 See Chapter 11 for a critique of Georg Lukács's notion of the 'ascribed consciousness'.
85 Gramsci, 'Our Marx', in *Il Grido del Popolo*, May 4, 1918; cited in Gramsci 2000, p. 37. My thanks to Max Novick for calling this passage to my attention.

PART 2

Toward a Historical-Materialist Cartography of Human Corporeal Organisation

∴

Introduction to Part 2

Part 2 consists of four chapters in which I undertake a historical-materialist cartography of human corporeal organisation. Chapters 4 and 5 are preparatory to this cartographical project; Chapter 6 is the mapping project itself; and Chapter 7 reflects on the consequences of that cartography for the relation between corporeality and cognition.

Chapter 4 considers three kinds of 'False Turns and Half Turns Toward, and Turns Away From, Corporeality'. These are: what under the guise of a 'corporeal turn' in poststructuralist and postmodernist analyses is actually a semiotic or discursive turn toward the body; the half-turn toward corporeality involved in recent Marxist attempts to counter poststructuralist/postmodernist denials of a 'human nature'; and the insightful but ultimately dismissive glimpses of a 'hidden bodily problematic' in Martin Heidegger's *Being and Time* and Hannah Arendt's *The Human Condition*. The dual purpose of this chapter is to glean what needs to be learned from these approaches, but also to expose their limits, and in so doing, by way of contrast, to set my approach in relief. Common in varying degrees to these three approaches is an acknowledgement of corporeality, an indication that corporeality is a necessary prerequisite of human existence. But acknowledgement without articulation amounts to little more than a perfunctory passing nod that reduces corporeality to a simple and irrelevant prerequisite that can be dismissed or neglected altogether. Whether dismissed or neglected, the elimination of corporeality from historical consideration severely narrows historical understanding. In contrast to these approaches, therefore, I shall in the following three chapters of Part 2 suggest how to approach corporeality as the 'first fact' of history.

Chapter 5, 'Toward a Historical-Materialist Mapping of Human Corporeal Organisation' addresses methodological issues that must be resolved before embarking on my cartographical undertaking. I begin with an introductory discussion of the various challenges involved in this cartographic attempt at a historical-materialist mapping of human corporeal organisation. These include: finding or developing the historical-materialist principles to guide the inquiry and a conceptual apparatus to organise the material; fashioning a mode of presentation with principles of selection and narrative that render it coherent, efficacious and, I would hope, readable and interesting; and ascertaining the place and value, the methodological place-value, of the resulting map, that is: determining what kind of, and how much, work it can do for us. This chapter therefore will be devoted to devising methodological solutions to these dilemmas of scope, content, and organisation and to addressing the consequences of those choices.

Chapter 6 is the lengthy attempt to draw a map of human corporeal organisation. Because this cartographical project could justifiably include all anatomical and physiological aspects of human corporeal organisation, I must obviously be selective for this chapter-length sketch. Accordingly, I focus on those corporeal aspects – the needs, the capacities, and the dexterities – that are most pertinent in establishing the range, the extent and limits, of the three modes (material, social, and semiotic) of human objectification. I adopt a loosely evolutionary framework as the organisational principle for the narrative. I begin with the earliest form-determinant of human experience, namely the third planet in a solar system whose situation establishes a whole range of temporal rhythms, a certain amount of gravitational pull, etc. all of which fundamentally frame human life and the possibilities of human experience. From there I proceed through the separation of plant and animal life, heterotrophy and locomotion, the emergence of bilaterally symmetrical vertebrates and warm-bloodedness, sexual reproduction, the evolution of the brain, the visually dominant primate constellation of sensory apparatuses, hominid bidpedality and body size, the relative hairlessness of the 'functionally naked ape', hominid social behaviour including sexuality, and I conclude with the biological foundations of speech and language. Given that scope, range of topics and space limitations, it should be obvious that this chapter is not intended as a definitive explanation of any of those topics, but instead as a suggestive essay that might aid us in avoiding what Gould called the 'insidious bias' of neglecting things that everyone knows about in principle. Although necessarily incomplete, this sketch should serve, though not as a template, certainly as much more than a backdrop to the elaboration of a corporeal semiotics in Chapter 10: it is intended to focus historical vision on the fact that, and the ways in which, corporeal organisation forms the interior structure of artefacts.

As its title and subtitle suggest, Chapter 7 concludes Part 2 with a set of reflections 'On Corporeality and Cognition: The Corporeal Constitution of Subjectivity and Subjecthood'. Here I draw the implications of my cartographic sketch of human corporeality for understanding the general forms of human cognition and subjecthood. These reflections are based on the assumption that although these general forms are always subject to socio-cultural mediations, they are nevertheless general forms of *human* consciousness – precisely because they are rooted in the 'universal', that is species-specific form of human corporeal organisation. For orientation purposes I begin with glances at two contrasting positions on the question of subjecthood. I first cast a glance at the language-centred conceits concerning the constitution of cognition and subjecthood that ultimately derive from the Saussurean *Course in General Linguistics* and that have become commonplace since the linguistic and cultural 'turns' of the twentieth century and into our own, namely: that thought without language is 'only a shapeless and indistinct mass', a 'vague uncharted nebula' and accordingly that human subjecthood is constituted solely by and through language. I then take a brief look at some non-'linguistocentric' approaches to cognition and subjecthood that point in the direction of my undertaking. Following these introductory glances, the main part of the chapter is devoted to articulating three dimensions of the 'wisdom of the body'. These are: human corporeal organisation itself as a body of materialised knowledge of the world from the particular perspective of the human organism; what Michael Polanyi calls the 'tacit knowledge', the corporeal logos, embedded in human corporeal organisation itself; and Mark Johnson and George Lakoff's notion of a 'cognitive unconscious' consisting of corporeally-rooted 'image schemata' as a means of articulating the link between human corporeal organisation and the forms of human cognition that are, of course, always refracted through socio-cultural mediations.

In a brief conclusion to Part 2, I offer a diagram of some of the fundamental, species-specific and thus corporeally rooted and generated patters of human experience that in-form all of the diverse and seemingly incommensurate human cultures. Finally, following summary reflections on the issues addressed in this chapter, I conclude with an excursus on Ernst Bloch's 'principle of hope' as a corporeally-rooted image schema.

CHAPTER 4

The Body Is Not a Tabula Rasa: Clearing a Path toward a 'Hidden Bodily Problematic'

4.1   Introductory

The narrative presented in this chapter is a bricolage doubtless more contrived than most. It begins with a critique of what I call 'ultra-constructionist' approaches to the body – those poststructuralist/postmodernist approaches that explicitly dismiss the significance and deny the socio-cultural efficacy of the very material, very real corporeal organisation of human beings, while valuing only the semiotic (linguistic and/or cultural) meanings invested in, or disciplinary techniques exercised on, bodies. It then moves to a critique of Marx-oriented attempts to construct a historical-materialist notion of 'human nature' that sought to counter the arbitrariness and relativism of ultra-constructionist analyses by taking a corporeal turn, but which prematurely veer off that path. Finally, it follows Martin Heidegger and Hannah Arendt to the trailhead of a path toward what Heidegger called a 'hidden bodily problematic' – yet from which they turned away.[1] I construct this unusual, somewhat eclectic constellation of analytical approaches, not to devalue the many insights that they produced, but in order to differentiate (what I take to be) a historical-materialist 'corporeal turn' from other approaches that claim to address the body, but that, in my view, come up short by failing to give human corporeal organisation its well-deserved due. A survey of the terrain covered collectively by these approaches will delineate also the remaining, still blank but essential space, surrounded yet untouched by their analyses, but whose mapping and exploration are crucial to Marx's winnable wager on writing history 'up from the body'.

As noted in Chapter 1, a venerable pillar of the Western philosophical tradition at least through Hegel is a dismissiveness toward the body viewed as but a simple prerequisite of human life and treated as an unruly and unwelcome disruptor of the quest for knowledge. And although the poststructuralist/postmodernist wave over the last half-century has imagined itself as a fundamental

---

[1] Heidegger 1962, p. 143. The term 'hidden bodily problematic' is my summary of Heidegger's statement: 'This "bodily nature" hides a whole problematic of its own' that, he continues, 'we shall not treat here'.

critique of that tradition, it has, at least in the crucial matter at issue here, similarly neglected the body – even while claiming to have turned toward it. The outpouring of such work ostensibly on 'the body' and thought to have constituted a 'corporeal turn' is more accurately described as a semiotic turn toward the body whose purpose is to deconstruct the ways in which bodies are linguistically, discursively, or culturally invested with meaning. Because of the sheer volume of such analyses, and also because of their invaluable contributions to exposing and interpreting semiotic inscriptions on the body, it would be difficult to clear a path for my undertaking without differentiating the corporeal turn that I am taking from a semiotically-driven linguistic/cultural turn toward the body. It is therefore necessary to situate my approach in relation to it – and to do so such that its contributions can be preserved, yet also expanded by integrating them into the more broadly conceived corporeal semiotics that I seek to develop in this project.

There have of course been many and sometimes vehement responses to this constructionist perspective coming from the more traditionally inclined, the sociobiologically inclined, and also from the historical-materialistically inclined. My concern here is with the latter – with historical-materialist attempts to counter the constructionist dissolution of the materiality of the body and its extreme cultural relativism by seeking to delineate a historical-materialist view of human nature. These attempts were also provoked by Louis Althusser: Althusser's 'anti-humanist' Marxism verges in at least one crucial sense on an ultra-constructionist position – namely in his denial of all transhistorical constants including, and for this project most importantly, what Marx referred to as 'human corporeal organisation'. Although not always directed at each other, Marxist attempts to counter both Althusser's anti-humanism by elaborating what they consider Marx's view of human nature and also poststructuralist denials of all human universals (species-specific corporeal attributes are generally acknowledged, but immediately ignored as always already culturally constructed) can, and for my purposes here will, be considered two antagonists in a debate that has in my view become an intellectual quagmire. The purpose of the following rather brief presentation and critique of these two positions is to expose how each gets bogged down by short-sighted intellectual vision, and also to explain why we must, and how we might, get out of this quagmire. Not only is this debate unresolvable in the terms with which it is carried out, but it also occludes the possibility of a whole new excavation of human corporeal organisation – one that begins with a 'universal' or transhistorical constant, the species-wide and species particular human corporeal organisation, as the 'first fact' of history, and therewith necessarily of cultural production as well.

After having differentiated my project from both the 'ultra-constructionist' linguistic/cultural turn toward the body and its antagonist, the attempt to develop a historical-materialist notion of human nature, I turn to Heidegger and Arendt, both of whom at least recognised the possibility of a very meaningful bodily problematic before turning away. Both viewed this bodily problematic as intimately related to labour. But because they were more concerned with the making of philosophical meaning, respectively the meaning of Being and the 'human condition', neither paid much attention to actual work and the making of meaningful material objects. Heidegger divorced made-objects from their making and showed interest in them only when breaking; and Arendt relegated work and labour to lower levels of human significance. Through reflecting on how they came to recognise the existence of a hidden bodily problematic, why they turned away from it, and how their neglect reduced artefacts to mere facticity, awaiting investment with meaning, but having no meaning themselves even as made-objects, I explain why they should have followed the path toward the 'hidden bodily problematic' that they both recognised. And my purpose in pointing out the blindnesses toward corporeality, not only in Heidegger and Arendt, but also in ultra-constructionist approaches to the body and in historical-materialist attempts to define human nature is to carve a new historical-materialist path toward that 'hidden bodily problematic'. In order to map and lay out this path, the present chapter engages in critiques of several approaches to the study of bodies. The purpose of these critiques is not to dismiss or even diminish the insights offered into so many matters pertaining to bodies by the authors (or the analytical traditions of which they are a part) whom I address in this chapter. My purpose rather is to open a path that is broad enough to include those insights, especially those into cultural constructions of corporeality, and also one that leads deeper into a more radical inquiry into the corporeal roots and the corporeal constitution of cultures – the outlines of which I attempt to elaborate in the following chapters.

4.2 The Ultra-constructionist Reduction of Corporeality to a *Tabula Rasa*

In the Introduction, I noted that although poststructuralist and postmodernist authors have often claimed to have emancipated the body from the logocentric chains of traditional Western philosophy, they end up treating the body as a simple prerequisite, as a silhouette or *tabula rasa* awaiting signification, inscription, discipline, or a role to perform. I indicated that such approaches are tantamount to a linguistic/cultural turn toward the body that denies, negates, neglects, and/or ignores the body's culture-creating capacities, and insists that for the 'human sciences' the only thing worth knowing about what they call the 'natural body' is its cultural and/or social constructedness. I therefore refer to such approaches as 'cultural ultra-constuctionism', the most succinct paradigmatic expression of which, adduced in the Introduction, but worth repeating here, is Anthony Synnott's description of the basic assumptions underlying his book, *The Body Social*:

> The thesis of this book is that the body and the senses are socially constructed. ... The body is *not* a 'given', but a social category with different meanings imposed and developed by every age, and by different sectors of the population. ... Like the organs and parts of the body, the attributes of the body are eminently social.
>
> The body, therefore, with all its organs, attributes, functions, states and senses, is *not so much* a biological given as a social creation of immense complexity and *almost limitless* variability, richness and power. ... The body social *negates* the body physical.[2]

The substitution of 'cultural' and 'culturally' in this passage for 'social' and 'socially' would provide a perfectly appropriate definition of 'cultural' constructionism – and it seems to me also to describe more accurately Synnott's undertaking which is devoted to cultural constructions of, and inscriptions on, the body. But whether it goes by the name of 'the body social' or 'the body cultural', the 'negation' of 'the body physical' is the ground of ultra-constructionism. Once the 'body physical' is negated and the body thereby reduced to a *tabula rasa*, ultra-constructionists can ignore the materiality and the culture-creating capacities embedded in human corporeal organisation and focus their energies instead on 'deconstructing' any and all works grounded in the assumption that there is any such thing as a 'body physical', or at least that it is of any analytical relevance to the study of society and culture.

Before proceeding, it is worth pausing a moment to consider the ever so important matter of the political implications of ultra-constuctionism (a matter that will recur often in the following, especially in Chapter 9). The denunciation of the 'body natural' and concomitant celebration of its alleged supplanting by the 'body social and/or cultural' has become commonplace among ultra-constructionists in Western academies; and deconstructive critiques have effectively exposed attempts to parade particular bodies (e.g. white, Western,

---

2 Synnott 1993, p. 1, p. 3, p. 5, my italics.

male) as universal norms. But an uncritical corporeal relativism, grounded in the 'negation' of the 'body physical' that ultra-constructionists take as the 'first fact' on which their enterprise is based, is not free of risks. For, the negation of a universal (that is species-wide and species-specific) physical body, the denial of a uniquely human corporeal organisation, easily slides into the denial of the universality of human being – a denial that, as Cameroonian political philosopher Achille Mbembe reminds, has for centuries served as the Western justification for extending its brutal rule over those whose all too human bodies have superficial phenotypic differences: 'Each time it came to people different in race, language, and culture, the idea that we have, concretely and typically, the same flesh, or that, in Husserl's words, "My flesh already has the meaning of being a flesh typical in general for us all," became problematic. The theoretical and practical recognition of the body and flesh of "the stranger" as flesh and body just like mine, the *idea of a common human nature, a humanity shared with others*, long posed, and still poses, a problem for Western consciousness'.[3] Mbembe's reminder is another reason why the necessary deconstructive critiques of false universals should not, and need not, base themselves on a falsely universalist claim that would negate the 'body natural' and categorically deny it any social or cultural relevance.

The general deconstructionist practice is to find the telling metaphor, the seemingly peripheral offhand statement, the loose thread that, when pulled, disassembles the whole fabric and exposes that which is presented axiomatically as the illegitimate universalising of particularist assumptions. But ultra-constructionist texts can themselves be subjected to deconstruction, and for precisely the same reasons: loose threads that, when followed, expose problematic universalist assertions. Just a quick glance at Synnott's language, for example, reveals several loose threads, the pulling of which exposes the untenable general assumptions he makes: Is not the statement that the body social 'negates' the body physical a groundless assumption presented as an axiom? And there is much unravelling even in his own wording: Is the body 'not' a given, or 'not so much' a given? Even if social and/or cultural constructions of the body are infinite, does this necessarily mean that they are even close to being 'almost limitless'. These are not trivial distinctions, for it is precisely the limits to social

---

3 Mbembe 2001, p. 2. To avoid confusion, it should be emphasised that Mbembe's reference to 'a flesh typical in general for us all' is to be taken literally – he uses 'typicality', not as a normative evaluation, but as, well, typical, in general, that is: as the flesh, the corporeal organisation, that makes all human beings, whatever their phenotypic differences, immediately recognisable as human beings.

and/or cultural constructions of the body that establish the very real species-specific 'boundaries of humanity'[4] and of human worlds in their potentially infinite, but not at all unlimited variation.

Before attempting to deconstruct the deconstructors, however, I must emphasise that my purpose in doing so is *neither* to rehabilitate a view of human nature *nor* to deny the validity of their deconstructions. Though such deconstructions are (as Derrida said of his own) a 'limited work', they are part of an absolutely essential undertaking.[5] The problem is not the deconstructions themselves, but the fundamentalist assumptions that ultra-constructionists seem to think necessary to ground their deconstructions. Understandably fearful of falling into the 'universalist' trap, they counter with the exaggerated, and what must be rightly called the 'universalist' claim that social and/or cultural constructions 'negate' the physical body. This apodictically presented assumption, however, is an all too human conceit – and one that bears a remarkable resemblance to the 'negation' of the body effected by the traditional 'logocentric' thought that ultra-constructionism considers its primary antagonist: both sever the corporeal foundations of the 'culture-producing animal' from the cultures that it produces; both reduce corporeality to at best a simple prerequisite of the production of cultures, and and fail to see corporeality as the 'interior structure' that in-forms social and cultural artefacts.

Ultra-constructionism catches itself in a counter-trap of its own making: with its categorical negation of 'the body physical', it counterproductively subjects itself to self-imposed but unnecessary limits. That negation of the 'body physical' is completely unnecessary for those deconstructions to expose illegitimate universalisings of particulars (e.g. deconstructing the universalised version of the Western male as 'man'). The problem, however, is that that negation limits the ultra-constructionist project to the deconstruction of 'always already' *given* social/cultural constructions; it prevents ultra-constructionism from going beyond the exposure of false universalisms and from explaining anything about the 'why' and 'how' behind the given constructions – matters not irrelevant either to the meaning of the constructions themselves or their political implications. Contrary to popular claims, hindsight is not always 20/20. There is also a myopia born of hindsight: the given, when viewed looking backward from the present, occludes sight of its genesis and genealogy, of why and how it came to be. Genesis and genealogy do not completely explain the given and its effects – but neither are they irrelevant.

---

4 To borrow the title of the essay collection edited by Sheehan and Sosna 1991.
5 Derrida 1981, p. 63.

The purpose therefore of the following partial deconstructions of ultra-constructionist positions is twofold: to show that they could be even more effective without their negation of human corporeality; and to raise the questions that that negation negates. There is obviously no room here for a comprehensive presentation and critique of the numerous variations of the ultra-constructionist position. Here I have chosen a few examples of studies from areas such as medicine, feminism, and sexuality in which there has been much concern about deconstructing cultural constructions of the body. Despite the important insights yielded by these works, the same problems that appear in general form in Synnott's comments are to be found in all of the specific analyses considered below: although of diverse content, the negation of the body physical imposes unnecessary limits that unfortunately prematurely block off promising avenues and force the inquiry back into itself, thereby breeding terminological muddles.

That diversity of cultural forms has led one philosopher to insist that cultures should be accorded species status. In so doing, John Dupré goes beyond the metaphorical, and advocates replacing an 'essentialist' biological taxonomy *Homo sapiens* with a relativist culture-based taxonomy of the many human species:

> We are inclined to suppose that because *Homo sapiens* is undoubtedly a perfectly respectable biological species, its universal properties must provide the fundamental insight into the nature and behaviour of its members. But such taxonomic paralysis is just a form of essentialism, a traditional philosophical view almost uniformly rejected by contemporary theorists of biology. If we reject essentialism, it is open to us to conclude, from the centrality of culture to human ethology and the great variability of culture, that for most purposes *Homo sapiens* is much too broad and coarse a category for understanding human beings. We might more usefully think of humans not primarily as constituting one biological species but rather as composing many, no doubt overlapping, cultural species.[6]

Few, if any, cultural constructionists would, I think, disagree with the statement that *Homo sapiens* is by reason of biology a culture-producing animal. And precisely because of this biological fact, it is impossible to imagine a human body that is not inscribed by cultural meanings. But for this very same biological

---

[6] Dupré 1991 in Sheehan and Sosna 1991, p. 130.

reason, though invisible to deconstructions that posit the body as the product of culture, *Homo sapiens* is *by corporeal definition* a culture-producing species, that is, it has a corporeal organisation that enables it to produce culture. Yet as comparison with the results of those researches into culture in other animal species immediately shows, though human beings produce various, sometimes seemingly incommensurate cultural forms, they are all specifically and unmistakably *human* cultures – immediately and directly related to *human* corporeal organisation.

Although it might be useful to read Dupré's statement that human beings 'are not a biological, but many cultural species' metaphorically, with all the flexibility that metaphor should entail, it cannot be taken literally. If it were to have literal value, it must at least be qualified as: Human beings are the biological species *that can make itself into* many 'cultural species' – but even then, the term 'cultural species' is only loosely analogical. Whereas cross-species interbreeding is biologically relatively rare, that which, following Dupré's logic, might be called 'cross-cultural interbreeding' in the forms of acculturation and assimilation is rather common. Even in those cases in which diverse cultural forms *seem* incommensurable and mutually exclusive to the ultra-constructionist eye, any human being can in principle assume a new cultural identity and reproduce that identity in his/her offspring. This is apparently what Dupré intends with the comment about 'no doubt overlapping' cultural species – but if so, then the term 'species' reveals itself as a misplaced metaphor.

Dupré's rejection of the notion that the 'universal properties' of *Homo sapiens* as 'a perfectly respectable biological species ... must provide the fundamental insight into the nature and behaviour of its members' is partially correct and wholly misguided: partially correct in its rejection of sociobiological reductionism that reduces human behaviour solely to genes whose form and function are governed solely by the logic of natural selection; yet misguided in rejecting human corporeal organisation as the fundamental fact of human being whose understanding can provide fundamental insights not only into the nature and behaviour of its members, but also into their cultures. The fundamental fact about *Homo sapiens* is that the species is, by virtue of its corporeal organisation, a culture-creating species; and however much cultures vary, there are, as I shall argue in the following chapters, certain 'universal', species-specific corporeal properties that are to be found in refracted form in all too human cultures.

Although they do not explicitly use the term, Frances E. Mascia-Lees and Patricia Sharpe effectively agree with Dupré's taxonomic division of *Homo sapiens* into a number of 'cultural species'. Introducing the purpose of their volume on

Tattoo, Torture, Mutilation, and Adornment with its subtitle, 'The Denaturalization of the Body in Culture and Text', they too decree that 'the body is always culturally constructed'.[7] They 'question traditional notions of the body as prior to, or outside of, culture' and approach the body, 'not as simple materiality', but rather as constituted in culture and text. The very notion of a 'natural' body is to be exposed as a Western cultural construct that 'ignores the particular meaning that both the body and the specific modifications to which it is subjected have for the people being represented. It resolves all bodies into the Western notion of the body as prior to culture and, thus, as natural'. But the notion that 'the unadorned, unmodified body is an unspoiled, pure surface on which culture works ... dehistoricizes and decontextualizes the body'. Their understandable fear of false universalisms even raises a concern about their own undertaking; for it 'implies a residual belief in the existence of a natural body it seeks to deconstruct, a body outside of culture, a physical norm that grounds human commonality in the face of vast "surface" or cultural differences'. But they need not worry, for what they want to 'deconstruct' is not the 'simple materiality' of the 'natural body' (for that they would need scalpels not words), but the 'Western body', 'the Western notion of the body', 'traditional notions of the body' – in short, what they seek to deconstruct are particular 'Western' linguistic (and artistic) *representations* of the body that are falsely universalised into a 'physical norm'.

Aimed primarily, and justifiably, at denaturalising Western notions of the white, male body as the universal 'physical norm', Mascia-Lees and Sharpe stake a political claim. Noting that in the context established by contemporary medical technology and the introduction of artificial body parts, they insist that 'the very question of what the body is is *up for grabs*, and the contest over the right to define the body's meaning has high stakes'.[8] The authors are of course correct in insisting that the contest over 'the right to define the body's meaning' has been the high-stakes object of social contention – although just as certainly incorrect in limiting that contention to the mod-

---

7   Mascia-Lees and Sharpe 1999, p. 2, p. 3. Following citations in this paragraph, ibid., p. 3; p. 3; p. 2; p. 2; p. 146; p. 3; p. 2. Mascia-Lees and Sharpe attribute this exposure to 'contemporary theorizing, whether feminist, postmodernist or anthropological, [that] has contributed recently to exposing "the natural" as a Western cultural construct'. It seems to me, however, that the differentiation of the cultural and the natural, the human world from the world around humans, is not exclusively a 'Western' construct natural and cultural, or the human world and the natural. What is more likely a Western construct is that the differentiation takes the form of a diametric opposition.

8   Mascia-Lees and Sharpe 1999, p. 5, my italics.

ern West, for the body has always and everywhere been a high-stakes contest. But that is another issue. My concern is with their confusion of the historicity of the contextualisations of the body with the historicity of the body.

Seeking to denaturalise the 'Western' (read: white, male) body as the universal 'physical norm', the physical epitome of humanity, the authors aim at a most deserving target. But their offensive against the 'simple materiality' of the 'natural body' is misplaced. The problem is not their claims about the efficacy of cultural constructions, but their myopic neglect of an entire corporeal problematic that bears directly on the matter of the meanings that are invested in bodies. Their unidirectional focus leads them to see only half of the question, and they do not even glance at the perhaps more important questions of where cultural constructions come from in the first place, and how cultural forms, including the meanings invested in the body, are produced. It should be rather obvious, for example, that the purpose of 'artificial body parts' is either to replace faulty body parts or enhance bodily capacities. The same is true of the adornments of bodies – the tattoos, piercings, cosmetics, etc. that are discussed in the various essays in their collection. And marking and/or mutilating the body to induct it into society or as a sign of social, cultural, sexual and/or gender identity treats the body as something 'natural' that must be acculturated. These practices may be quite literally fanciful, but they are not in the least arbitrary. On the contrary, their very *raison d'être* is inescapably related to the 'natural body' itself: whether their purpose is to enhance what are considered the body's attractions and capacities, to shield its vulnerability, to hide what are considered its defects and limits, or to induct it into culture, it is the 'natural body', *human* corporeal organisation, that underlies, motivates, and in-forms cultural constructions – *regardless* of how much, and precisely because, those constructions might aim to 'negate' it.

One need not deny that all human bodies are culturally constructed, inscribed, and adorned in order to argue that there is much more that matters about bodies than cultural adornments and inscriptions alone – and much more about bodies that matters *to* cultural adornments and inscriptions. Although Mascia-Lees and Sharpe are quite right to insist on the historicity of, and the social contentiousness over, meanings invested in the body, they are quite wrong to insist that 'the very question of what the body is is up for grabs'. What they neglect are the different temporal/historical horizons of the cultural meanings invested in the body on the one hand, and of the 'natural body' itself on the other. What is 'up for grabs', though in a not unlimited manner, are the representations of, the meanings invested in, the adornments inscribed on, the body – representations, meanings, and adornments whose placement and particular meanings are in-formed by the very corporeal organisation on which they are invested or inscribed, and that has made their production possible.

The 'natural body', however, also has a history and is for that reason not just 'up for [cultural] grabs': inscribed by evolution on an evolutionary timescale, the 'natural body' is much more stable than the various, diverse, and changing meanings invested in it. Macias-Lees and Sharpe are absolutely right in contesting falsely universalised 'physical *norms*'. But it is possible, even necessary, to contest those falsely universalised norms without denying the simple fact that there is a physical *form*, a corporeal organisation, that grounds human being and gives a peculiarly human logic underlying even the most diverse human cultural forms – including, as should be obvious, representations of the body.

The hypostatising of culture and cultural incommensurability is also evident in deconstructive critiques of 'Western' medical discourse which has very understandably been the target of deconstructions exposing its mechanistic assumptions about the body in general and its normative assumption of a male body.[9] One such is *The Culture of Pain* by David B. Morris.[10] Exploring the 'historical, cultural, and psychosocial construction' of pain, Morris seeks to deconstruct the ways in which 'our culture – the modern, Western, industrial, technocratic world – has succeeded in persuading us that pain is simply and entirely medical problem'. Pain, he acknowledges, 'is certainly the result of a biochemical process', and he is emphatically '*not* suggesting we reject our hard-won biomedical knowledge about pain: that way lies folly'. But he essentially reduces the biochemical process to a simple prerequisite of pain that, once acknowledged, can be ignored. For, he insists, pain 'is always more than a matter of nerves and neurotransmitters', and 'our biochemistry is inextricably bound up with the personal and cultural meanings that we carve out of pain'. He therefore wants instead to 'supplement [biomedical knowledge] and enrich it' with alternative forms of medical knowledge in order to 'recover some of the individual control over pain that as a culture we once possessed and too hastily gave up'. Deconstructing 'the mechanistic assumptions of traditional modern [sic] medicine' that understands pain as 'something like the wheeze and cough from a broken motor', Morris insists that once we break down Western medicine's stranglehold, we can 'tak[e] back responsibility for how we understand pain [and] recover the power to alleviate it'.

---

9   Other works devoted to deconstructing the discourse of Western medicinal science include of course Foucault 1973, and also Schiebinger 1993, Duden 1987; Martin 1992.
10 D. Morris 1991. Following citations in this paragraph, ibid., p. 1; pp. 2–3; p. 14; p. 2; p. 5; p. 5; p. 20; p. 5.

Morris calls for a 'a dialogue between doctors and writers (between medical and nonmedical voices)', which he sets up as 'a neglected encounter between pain and meaning'.[11] The participants or, more accurately given his formulations, the antagonists in this discussion are 'traditional Western medicine' that 'has consistently led us to misinterpret pain' as 'no more than a sensation, a symptom, a problem in biochemistry' and the neglected voices addressing the relation between pain and meaning and 'captured and created in writing from Homer to Beckett'. One suspects that this (very Western) dialogue will be monological – and rather more literary than medical.

This suspicion is quickly confirmed with a neo-Berkeleyan axiom that 'pain, after all, exists only as we perceive it. Shut down the mind and the pain too stops', and elsewhere: 'We experience pain only and entirely as we interpret it'.[12] I cannot refrain from asking whether the pain of an injured or infected body itself (its location, intensity, texture, duration, etc.) has anything to do with the fact that we experience it as pain??? and whether that experience has anything to do with how we interpret it??? Uninterested in those questions, Morris exemplifies his claims about the anaesthetising power of mind with an anecdote told by Immanual Kant who suffered 'excruciating' attacks of gout, yet alleviated his pain by 'taking responsibility'. Kant's method for 'taking responsibility' and exorcising his pain was to concentrate on a single object, e.g. 'the Roman orator Cicero, and of everything that could be thought in connection with Cicero'. Kant was 'so successful in banishing his pain that in the morning he sometimes wondered whether he had simply imagined it'.

Let us ignore the obvious questions that should be posed here (e.g. did Kant actually mean this comment so literally? Was his imagination playing tricks on his memory? Was his memory playing tricks on itself?). Let us focus instead on the not insignificant fact that Morris neglects to mention, namely: that although Kant may have wondered whether the pain was real or imagined, its reality was confirmed by 'the sign of the glowing red toes of the left foot'.[13] J.H. van den Berg, from whom Morris borrowed this anecdote, is somewhat less highbrow, claiming that Kant's method of diverting pain 'was effective [and] is still effective, as long as the one condition, which is mentioned by Kant is fulfilled. The condition is to concentrate oneself with effort on any chosen, if indifferent, object, regardless of what it is'.[14] And (obviously not imagining that

---

11 D. Morris 1991, p. 5. Following citations in this paragraph, ibid., p. 5; p. 3.
12 D. Morris 1991, p. 4; p. 29. Following citation, ibid., p. 7. I cannot refrain from saying here: would that it were so easy to shut down the mind and 'stop' the pain ...
13 Kant, 'Der Streit der Facultäten', http://gutenberg.spiegel.de/buch/3509/1.
14 van den Berg 1974, p. 227. Following citation ibid., p. 228.

pain can be so painful as to destroy the mind's ability to concentrate on anything but the pain), Morris concludes: 'Pain can be made to disappear by concentrating on something. Literally by attaching oneself to something; which means by creating a connection with something. Everybody can find out for himself how true this is. If we are bothered by a pain or an ache, we take a book, if possible an exciting book, a book which absorbs our attention – the word is literally correct – and the pain diminishes or even disappears altogether'.

Morris's definition of pain as a matter of perception resembles the semantic play in the brain teaser about whether a tree falling in the woods makes noise if there is no one there to hear it. If the mind is 'shut down', whether numbed by pharmaceutical means or by a Kantian-like 'force of concentration', is there pain? Even if one were to accept Kant's claim that he no longer was conscious of feeling the pain, there are still some serious questions to be raised about Morris's presentation of this anecdote.

First of all, Morris's admiration of Kant is imaginative: Kant 'did not merely distract himself, as if watching a sitcom. Nor did he sit fretting about his health. He employed the full force of his mind ... [,] employed a resource for opposing pain that we have almost completely forgotten how to use'. But for all the condescension in this distinction between Kant's concentration on Cicero as an example of the 'active' employment of the full force of his mind in opposing pain in contrast to those who might take a sitcom for their object of contemplation as being passive and merely distracting themselves, the fact of the matter is that Kant too, in Morris's own portrayal, simply distracted himself from his pain by thinking about something else. With his 'high culture' dismissal of those who prefer sitcoms to reading Kant, Morris ignores the comment that he had just cited from van den Berg who insisted that what mattered was not the particular object of concentration, but the concentration itself. If the desired result is the shutting down of the mind in order to block the perception of pain, does it really matter, as long as it works, whether one is absorbed with Cicero, a sitcom or with the 'Virtual Reality Therapy' recently hailed in the *New York Times* (30 April 2019) as 'the new kid on the block for pain management'?

Furthermore, assuming for the sake of argument that Kant did win his battle against the *perception* of pain, does that mean that he succeeded in 'banishing' the pain? This semantic difference can have rather painful consequences. Here Morris's portrayal of Kant's activity is telling: Kant, he says, did not 'sit fretting about his health'. While he may not have fretted about his health, it is safe to assume that he did 'sit', that he was not engaged in anything physically taxing while contemplating Cicero. But what of those in pain who literally cannot sit? Injured professional athletes, for example, are often given the alternative between the 'Western' solution of using pharmaceuticals to numb pain or the (non-Western???) 'Kantian' solution of focusing so intensely on the game that they can 'play through pain'. Whichever of these two methods is chosen, if the injured athlete ignores the perception of pain and plays the game, the odds are that the injury, the wound, will get worse. Or what if Kant had not been a respected (and presumably adequately paid) philosopher who earned his livelihood by thinking (while sitting and presumably also during his regular evening stroll through Königsberg), but a peasant or factory worker who could not afford to sit and contemplate his way to distraction. The 'meaning' of that pain, the ability to shut it out and/or the ability to work despite it, will vary greatly depending on how one makes a living. Poverty has a way of increasing people's tolerance of pain – but often, and not surprisingly, of causing thereby greater injury, worsening the wound and inflicting greater pain.

To say that pain is all in one's head, and exists 'only as we perceive it', is a condescending dismissal of all of those whose wounded bodies are in pain, and especially of those who, when in pain, must perform physically-taxing work. With his idealist positing of the mind as the locus of pain, Morris rather cavalierly renders irrelevant what the body suffers. 'Shut down the mind', he counsels, 'and pain stops'. Would that it were so easy. He could at least have said more modestly 'shut down the mind and the perception of pain stops'. For there is something very real and embodied that causes pain. The source of that pain, the 'biochemical process', 'those electrical impulses speeding along the nerves' that Morris acknowledges only to dismiss, is an injury, a laceration, a wounded body in pain, whether the mind perceives it or not.[15] The mind can be so numbed with Cicero, sitcoms, narcotics, or other means that it ceases to notice pain. But the mental ignoring of pain does not heal the body's wound, the aggravation of which could lead to the death of the (non)perceiving subject – a rather pyrrhic victory of mind over matter.

This reduction of pain to a matter of perception, moreover, also undermines by shortcutting Morris's analysis of his own chosen topic: diverse cultural understandings of pain. Though the neurological locus of our perception of pain may be in the mind, we 'feel' pain as residing in our leg, arm, hand, heart, spleen, liver, etc. – wherever the wound is. And if, as Morris argues, pain is as we perceive it, then the bodily sites of the wounds perceived to be the locus of pain are not unimportant for cultural constructions of pain. His focus on the mind as the 'real' locus of pain prevents him from even asking some very interesting questions pertaining to diverse cultural meanings attached to the specificity of pain, questions such as: how are different pains resulting from the wounding

---

15   D. Morris 1991, p. 5.

of different body parts or regions perceived? what different meanings are given to pains resulting from different wounded body parts? what are the different cures developed for different wounds in different body parts? Again, my point here is not to reject Morris's very important critique of certain aspects of Western medicine – especially of its refusal to recognise certain kinds of especially 'chronic pain' that seem to be much more than a matter of a single somatic cause, and yet whose millions of sufferers are often told by doctors that there is nothing wrong with them, that (given Morris's argument, with painful irony) it is all in their mind. Nor is it to reject his very important exploration of 'the historical, cultural, and psychosocial construction of pain'. But he can easily do all of this without the exaggerated claims that render his argument in some cases dismissive and condescending, in other cases silly, and in all cases falling rather short of his own goal of understanding culturally-specific approaches to pain.

One need not defend 'Western medicine' to acknowledge that there are rather significant differences between ignoring pain, 'mak[ing]' sense' of it and accepting its 'place in human life' on the one hand, and curing it on the other. And the attempt to cure the somatic sources of pain is certainly not limited to 'Western medicine' – most people, Kant included, seem to want to displace bodily pain from human life. But only amid the flood of such ultra-constructionist negations of the body physical does the obvious point made in the introductory statements to a volume on *Pain as Human Experience* seem profound: Rejecting the either/or for the both/and, Arthur Kleinman et al. assert that 'pain is a ubiquitous feature of human experience. ... It is thus reasonable to assume that pain is a universal feature of the human condition' – and also that 'at the same time, the cultural elaboration of pain involves categories, idioms, and modes of experience that are greatly diverse'.[16]

Deconstructing normative assumptions about gendered bodies has been a powerful feminist tool of analysis and politics. Here I consider a psychoanalytically and a performatively ultra-constructionist approach to bodies. These studies by, respectively, Elizabeth Grosz and Judith Butler provide much-needed deconstructions of the cultural and performative constructions of bodies, but avoid questions that from a historical-materialist perspective are crucial, namely: where do the constructions to be deconstructed come from? Why

---

16   Delvecchio Good 1992, p. 1. For a discussion of the 'dynamics' of 'complementary pairs', the 'both/and' rather than the either/or, in the 'quantum world' and 'ordinary day-to-day experience', see Kelso and Engstrom 2006. My thanks to Maxine Sheets-Johnstone for this reference.

these constructions rather than those? More specifically, what role does the 'natural body' or human corporeal organisation play in the cultural construction of bodies?

'If feminists are to resuscitate a concept of the body for their own purposes', Elizabeth Grosz argues (while imposing a rather rigid litmus test), 'it must be extricated from the biological and pseudo-naturalist appropriations from which it has historically suffered'.[17] To perform this extrication, Grosz suggests an incisive feminist deployment of psychoanalytic theory which 'has enabled feminists and others to reclaim the body from the realms of immanence and biology in order to see it as a psycho-social product, open to transformations in meaning and functioning, capable of being contested and re-signified'.[18] '[S]purred at least in part by psychoanalytic theory itself, feminists have sought to re-evaluate the body beyond biologistic, essentialist and universalist presuppositions'. Psychoanalytic 'insights provide a challenge to the domination of biology in discourses of the body' and have revealed 'the generic category "the body" [as] a masculinist illusion'. Instead, as she states elsewhere:

> The specificity of bodies must be understood in its historical rather than simply its biological concreteness. Indeed, there is no body as such: there are only bodies – male or female, black, brown, white, large or small – and the gradations in between. Bodies can be represented or understood not as entities in themselves or simply on a linear continuum with its polar extremes occupied by male and female bodies (with the various gradations of 'intersexed' individuals in between) but as a field, a two-dimensional continuum in which race (and possibly even class, caste, or religion) form body specifications.

Grosz's purpose in arguing (and acknowledging) that *'the body* [my italics] is plastic, malleable, and amenable to social re-inscription' is to show 'that *the female body* [my italics] is *a priori* capable of being seen and understood outside the notion of castrated privation' – or for that matter 'outside of any oppressive prevailing system of meaning and value'.[19] Challenging the domination of sociobiological-based discourses that treat the body only as biological and that reduce culture to a mere epiphenomenon of the natural laws governing bodies is of course crucial. And lurking, no doubt, behind this insistence that the

---

17   Grosz 1994, p. 20.
18   Grosz 1999, p. 270. Following three citations in this paragraph, ibid., p. 271; p. 270; Grosz 1994, p. 19.
19   Grosz 1999, p. 270. Following citations in this paragraph, Grosz 1994, p. 23; p. 41.

body is always already culturally constructed is a fear of reverting to some kind of biologically or economically determinist 'master narrative'. Going even beyond Synnott's notion that the body social 'negates' the body physical (yet all the while speaking of '*the* body'), she claims: 'The body is not opposed to culture, a resistant throwback to a natural past; it is itself a cultural, *the* cultural, product'. And: 'The biological body, *if it exists at all* [sic; my italics], exists for the subject only through the mediation of an image or series of social/cultural images of the body and its capacity for movement and action'. But exposing the fallacies in certain reductionist discourses need not be grounded in the equal and opposite reductionism that counters the treatment of culture as an epiphenomenon of economy (economist versions of Marxism) or of biology (sociobiology) by treating biology as an epiphenomenon of culture.

Almost as if she recognises her exaggeration in calling it a creation of culture, Grosz tries to lend the body a degree of agency. But even this attempt subverts itself through her formulations. She writes: 'Far from being an inert, passive, noncultural and ahistorical term, the body may be seen as the crucial *term*, the *site* of contestation, in a series of economic, political, sexual, and intellectual struggles'.[20] Of course the body is, and always has been, a crucial 'term' and a 'site' of contestation. But Grosz's claims to the contrary notwithstanding, the exposure of cultural constructions of the body does not automatically avoid a treatment of the body as inert and passive. This is evident in her own determinations: to treat the body only as a 'term' or a 'site', as an object or a place of 'contestation' is to render it inert and passive. Such *de facto* treatment of the body as passive fully ignores not only the constitutive role of human corporeality in the production of cultural forms, but also the obvious facts that the topography of the field on which and over which battles are fought is the species-specific corporeal organisation itself in its diverse but all very human forms. And that corporeal topography substantially in-forms those battles.[21]

---

20 Grosz 1994, p. 19, my italics.
21 Grosz seems to be striving to avoid falling into a mirror-inversion of materialist and biological determinism. This is evident in her notion of a 'body image' that 'does not map a biological body onto a psychosocial domain, providing a kind of translation of material into conceptual terms; rather, it attests to the necessary interconstituency of each for the other, the radical inseparability of biological from psychical elements, the mutual dependence of the psychical and the biological, and thus the intimate connection between the question of sexual specificity (biological sexual differences) and psychical identity'. (Grosz 1994, p. 85). But to follow through on this definition, that does at least recognize the body's agency and the constitutive role, she would have to ignore various of her own insistence that the body is 'a cultural, *the* cultural product'. And the whole argument becomes more muddled when she relies on Merleau-Ponty in developing the notion of a body image.

It is no secret that human bodies come in different colours and sizes, sexes and genders. And while such phenotypic variation (all of which can be invested with culturally specific significance) makes it literally true that one cannot speak of a human 'body as such', this does not mean that it is impossible to speak of a species-specific corporeal organisation that itself frames and limits possible phenotypic permutations. Nor is it necessary to deny the natural bodies of human beings in order to deconstruct 'discourses of the body' and expose linguistic and cultural constructions of racial or gendered bodies. Grosz is absolutely right to insist that we focus on 'the specific types of *body* [sic; my italics], concrete in their determinations, with a particular sex, race, and physiognomy'.[22] But it is certainly fair to ask whether what she calls those 'specific types of *body*' are different bodies or whether they are phenotypicly different attributes of the species-specific 'natural body' of *Homo sapiens*??? The irony here, of course, is that Grosz herself cannot avoid speaking of the relation between bodies and their social constructions in very biological and non-arbitrary terms. Her own reference to 'the specific types of body', whether bodies are 'male or female, black, brown, white, large or small', is very much a matter of simple 'biological concreteness'; what is 'historical' are the different meanings culturally invested in the phenotypic variations among diverse, but all very human bodies. It is simply not necessary to deny the simple 'biological concreteness' of bodies in order to expose falsity of culturally-constructed meanings. Grosz is absolutely correct in arguing that the body can easily be amenable to cultural re-inscription, but what is plastic and malleable are the modes of inscription and not the body. Or more precisely: the body is exponentially less malleable; for while socio-cultural inscriptions may be amended on the scale of historical time, the very material corporeal-kinetic organisation of the human primate was amended on an evolutionary timescale.

As described in her subtitle, Judith Butler's *Bodies that Matter* addresses 'The Discursive Limits of Sex'.[23] Borrowing a theme from Foucault, she insists that '[t]he category of "sex" is a regulatory ideal whose materialization is compelled'. Specifying her analytical target and its political import, she writes that 'the regulatory norms of "sex" work in a performative fashion to *constitute the material-*

For Merleau-Ponty is very much committed to explaining the body's constitutive role in knowledge production (ibid., pp. 89 ff.).

22   Grosz 1994, p. 19.
23   Butler 1993. Following citation in this paragraph, ibid., p. 1; p. 2, my italics; p. 2.

ity of bodies and, more specifically, to materialize the body's sex, to materialize sexual difference in the service of the consolidation of the heterosexual imperative'. 'In this sense, what constitutes the fixity of the body, its contours, its movements, will be fully material, but materiality will be rethought as the effect of power, as power's most productive effect'.

Butler rejects 'gender-construction' models that treat gender simply as a cultural inscription on a passive surface that is itself biologically sexed; nor is she content with 'radical linguistic constructivism' through which '"sex" becomes something like a fiction, perhaps a fantasy, retroactively installed at a prelinguistic site to which there is no access'.[24] She proposes instead 'a return to the notion of matter'. But she has a somewhat unusual (in the combination of what she adds to and what she neglects in her) notion of 'matter' that she construes 'not as site or surface, but as *a process of materialization that stabilizes over time to produce the effect of boundary, fixity, and surface we call matter*'. To explain the materialisation of 'sex', not as a moment, but as a process of repeated instantiations, Butler borrows the notion of 'performativity' from speech act theory. 'Performativity', she writes, is 'not a singular "act", for it is always a reiteration of a norm or set of norms, and to the extent that it acquires an act-like status in the present, it conceals or dissimulates the conventions of which it is a repetition'. And 'a performative' is 'that discursive practice that enacts or produces what it names'.

Wanting to avoid 'the exasperated debate [between essentialism and constructivism] which many of us have tired of hearing', Butler seeks to carve a path beyond the field of tension created by this binary. She provides a modest explanation of the deconstructionist position, explaining that '[t]o claim that discourse is formative is not to claim that it originates, causes, or exhaustively composes that which it concedes'.[25] And she seeks to distance herself from radical constructivism by stating that she does not mean 'to dispute the materiality of the body'. Her point is rather that 'there is no reference to a pure body which is not at the same time a further formation of that body. In this sense, the linguistic capacity to refer to sexed bodies is not denied, but the very meaning of "referentiality" is altered. In philosophical terms, the constative claim is always to some degree performative'. Or again more explicitly in describing the first two essays of her book: 'together they constitute partial and overlapping genealogical efforts to establish the normative conditions under which the materiality of the body is framed and formed, and, in particular, how it

---

24 Butler 1993, pp. 4, 5. Following citations in this paragraph, ibid., p. 9; p. 12; p. 13.
25 Butler 1993, p. 10. Following citations in this paragraph, ibid., p. 17; p. 11; p. 17; p. 23.

is formed though differential categories of sex'. Against essentialism and constructivism, Butler's study of the performative materialisation of the body as a regulatory ideal seeks to provide 'the occasion for a radical rearticulation of the symbolic horizon in which bodies come to matter at all'.

Butler's insightful critiques of the performative reiteration of sex and sexuality that materialises those 'differential categories of sex' in, on, and through the body are not in question here. Her claim that the *category* of "sex"' (my italics) is 'materialized' on the body as 'a regulatory ideal' seems to me indisputable. For that reason, her further claim that 'the regulatory norms of "sex" work in a performative fashion ... to materialize sexual difference in the service of the consolidation of the heterosexual imperative' also seems undisputable. Her introduction of the active element of performativity is a most valuable step beyond those 'older' forms of cultural constructionism that treat the body only as a *tabula rasa*, as a passive site of cultural inscriptions. And the performative materialisations of the *categories* of 'sex' as regulatory *ideals*, that then become re-incorporated in discourse as 'representing' a 'natural' reality, are without question in need of precisely the kind of deconstructive critique that Butler levies.

Her third claim, however, that those norms also 'constitute the materiality of bodies' and 'materialize the body's sex', is unnecessary to substantiate the first two claims, which together are sufficient for her much-needed 'radical rearticulation of the *categories* within the *symbolic horizon* in which bodies come to matter *at all*' (emphasis added). And from the corporeal perspective under construction in this book, this third claim raises the question of whether the introduction of performativity as that which constitutes the materiality of bodies alone suffices to circumvent treating bodies as pure matter, as a blank slate, in and on which particular socio-culturally prescribed sex-texts are inscribed – even if performatively, that is: with and through the active participation of the body itself as both actor and enacted, as socio-culturally disciplined performing subject and performed object. From my perspective, the notions of 'the constitution of the materiality of bodies' and 'the materializing of the body's sex' can be understood in two distinct ways: as matters not only of socio-cultural, but also of bio-evolutionary performativity. Dismissing the 'natural body' can be just as misleading as universalising it. And my argument throughout this work is that if we avoid unnecessary and misleading dismissals of the 'natural' body, and instead give human corporeal organisation its due, then these two modes of materialisation will prove to be both complementary and mutually enriching.

To explain that her use of the term 'bodies that matter' is 'not an idle pun', Butler provides an etymological argument, adducing 'classical contexts' in which 'to be material means to materialize, where the principle of that materialization is precisely what "matters" about that body, its very intelligibility. In this sense, to know the significance of something is to know how and why it matters, where "to matter" means at once "to materialize" and "to mean".[26] But there is about this seemingly clear statement a bit of fog arising from her focus on two, while ignoring the third, of three distinct meanings of 'matter'. She addresses 'matter' in the sense of the material force of words and symbols, and also in the sense of something that matters, is an issue, a concern. These two notions of 'matter' certainly matter. Yet, although she does not actively dispute, she does effectively ignore a third, very corporeal matter: the fleshy materiality of bodies. And consideration of this fleshy 'matter' would point to rather different (but not incompatible) notions of both the '*bodies* that matter' and also *how* those bodies matter – with, that is, rather different (but, again, not incompatible) notions of both the meaning and the 'materializing' of bodies.

When Butler describes her focus on the mattering 'materialization' of the body in terms of its 'very intelligibility', it certainly seems as though her focus is on *how* the body matters, on the 'materializing' of the body in and through thought ('intelligibility', it is worth interjecting, is rendered possible and framed by the intelligence of the creature to which, and that makes, something intelligible, an object of knowledge, that is: by the creature's corporeal means of knowledge production – its perceptual organs and cognitive apparatus; see Chapters 6 and 7). And there is a strong hint of at least *de facto* dismissal of the relevance of the 'natural' flesh and blood body in the final words of her description of her project as a 'radical rearticulation of the symbolic horizon in which bodies *come to matter at all*'. Butler's project of radically rearticulating the symbolic horizon in which bodies matter is without a doubt a necessary undertaking. But their fleshy materiality is also most pertinent to the mattering of bodies.

Bodies always matter – and not only within 'symbolic horizons'. It is one very important matter to decipher how embodied behaviours materialise through performativity and assume a material form that *matters culturally, symbolically*. But it is another, altogether different, but also important matter to claim that the 'materiality', the corporeal organisation, of performing bodies themselves (and the range of roles they can perform) is constituted through socioculturally prescribed performativity alone. Although Butler does not mean 'to dispute the materiality of the body', her designation of the 'symbolic horizon' as the site where 'bodies come to matter *at all*' certainly seems to justify the

---

26   Butler 1993, p. 32.

neglect of human, species-specific corporeal organisation. And when, whether by design or default, the corporeal organisation of always already animate and acting human bodies is effectively treated as form without content, as a silhouette awaiting its turn on the stage where it enacts culturally-prescribed performances, where it ever dances to the same regulatory tune, performatively incorporating into itself a prescribed script, the bottom line is a reduction of living bodies to 'simple (even if animated) prerequisites' – to bodies whose active participation in the process of their own 'materialization' is limited to their not wholly volitional acquiescence to performing socio-culturally prescribed roles in a symbolic play.

This is unfortunate, and for two reasons. One is that the erasure, or simple neglect, of the biological body (the foundation of the 'radical constructionist' position that Butler seeks to avoid) is completely unnecessary; for, her critique of the performative materialisation of *embodied behaviour patterns* (and corresponding forms of consciousness) is perfectly capable of sustaining itself without the claim that the 'materiality of *bodies*' is thereby constituted. The other is that the claim that the 'materiality' of bodies only 'comes to matter *at all*' when constituted by socio-culturally prescribed performative processes occludes a different, but potentially complementary approach to the materialising, the materiality, and the meaning of bodies. It is not at all necessary to defend an essentialist position in order to suggest that Butler's focus is on the processual matter of the disciplining of bodies through which is 'materialized' a set of socio-culturally-imposed, corporeally-enacted, performatively-constituted behaviour patterns – and therefore to conclude that what she insightfully deciphers is the materialisation of *behaviourally disciplined* bodies: bodies not formed, but 'reformed' by enacting, by performatively repeating, and thereby 'materialising', in the sense of ritualising, 'naturalising', socio-culturally prescribed behaviour patterns grounded in socio-culturally particular determinations of how bodies matter. And if it seems trivial to note that her focus is on the 'materializing', not of flesh and blood bodies themselves, but on socio-culturally prescribed, corporeally-performed behaviour patterns, then I would recall Gould's warning (cited in the Introduction) against the insidious bias of neglecting things that everyone knows about in principle.

Butler herself provides reason to consider the corporeal organisation that is subject and object of its own performance. Later in her explanation of how bodies matter, she speaks of the 'referent' in simple but significant terms as 'the "that which" which makes its demand in and to language'; and she adds that while '[l]anguage and materiality are fully embedded in each other', they are 'never fully collapsed into one another, i.e. reduced to one another, and yet neither fully ever exceed the other'.[27] I fully agree (and rely on this notion of the referent in Chapter 8 and beyond). And I would therefore argue that the natural, material, sexually dimorphic (in terms of the two poles that establish and limit the range of permutations of human sexes; see discussion of Anne Fausto-Sterling below) corporeal organisation of *Homo sapiens* is 'the "that which" which makes its demand not only in and to language', but also in and to all symbolic horizons – 'the "that which"' which in-forms, establishes the range of and limits on, the permutations of performative scripts to which those very material 'natural' bodies are subjected.

What matters to me in this regard is that the unnecessary dismissal of the 'natural body' closes off what I consider the potentially rich approach, rooted in Marx's wager on corporeal organisation as the 'first fact' of history – an approach that does not counter, but welcomes Butler's analyses, and that opens avenues for the analysis of related and rather relevant issues, the understanding of which would not only complement, but also give corporeal depth to the 'symbolic horizon' within which is performatively materialised the categorial 'effect of boundary, fixity, and surface [she] call[s] matter'. A corporeally-grounded historical-materialist *Wissenschaft* that takes human corporeal organisation as the first (but by no means the last) fact of history recognises that the materialising, the materiality, and the meaning of bodies are also matters of evolutionary biology. The embodiment of socio-culturally prescribed behaviour patterns materialises through performativity, and assumes the material form that matters socio-culturally, on a scale of historical time. But the materialising of human bodies, a biological process taking place on the longer scale of evolutionary time, is also a matter of performative materialisation: it is a matter of the performative forming of the form and fleshy content, the capacities and limits, of performing human bodies through the interaction between organisms (in this case anthropoid primates) and their environment; it is a matter of the materialising of a creature with a species-specific corporeal organisation, with a corporeally-framed range of possible behaviour patterns and corporeally equipped with culture-creating instruments and capacities; it is a matter of the bio-evolutionary materialising of a corporeal organisation that frames and informs the range of the socio-culturally specific meanings that are inscribed discursively on, and performatively into, it. The matter of human corporeal organisation is, as I argued in the Introduction, the point where Marx met Darwin, where evolutionary theory meets historical theory, where the biologically materialised body does become the object of socio-cultural materialising – but

---

27 Butler 1993, pp. 68–9.

nevertheless remains, as I argue throughout this work, not just relevant, but essential to the construction, and thus also to the deciphering, of the form, content, and meaning of cultural inscriptions on, and performative scripts enacted by, human bodies.

To grant that all bodies, and even sex and sexuality, are objects of social/cultural construction does not at all require us to dismiss the 'undisputed fact' of a species-specific human form of corporeal organisation as irrelevant to human cultures.[28] And just as there is no reason not to focus on a deconstruction of those social/cultural constructions, neither is there any reason to deny the cultural relevance of the 'undisputed facts' about bodies. One way of recognising that the 'natural' body and the 'cultured' body are two ways of looking at the same body, and in so doing to indicate how the perspective being developed here could complement Grosz's and Butler's arguments, while allowing them to dispense with unnecessary denials of the 'natural' body, is by asking the obvious question of where categories like those of sex and sexuality come from. However differently defined, deployed, or materialised, sex seems to be cross-cultural and universal. And it was certainly not immaculately conceived without a corporeal referent – without, as Butler put it, a '"that which" which makes its demand in and to language' and culture. Linguistic categories and cultural meanings do not just spring arbitrarily and fully grown out of pure language for no particular reason.

Definitions of bodies and sex and sexuality are certainly, as ultra-constructionists claim, contextual. But it is neither trivial nor culturally irrelevant to note that the most immediate context for both is the 'undisputed fact' of bodies with particular sex organs, not in infinite variation but according to the sexual dimorphism of the species. Bodies can of course be, as Grosz claims '*represented* or *understood* not as entities in themselves or simply on a linear continuum with its polar extremes occupied by male and female bodies (with the various gradations of "intersexed" individuals in between [my italics])'. But, however 'represented' or 'understood', it seems a rather 'undisputed' biological fact that the representations and understandings are limited to the permutations of a set of two, of male and female.

Like all 'facts', this 'undisputed one' has also been disputed – or at least the conceptual representation of that fact has been disputed. Anne Fausto-Sterling's 1993 essay, 'The Five Sexes' undertakes to explain 'why male and

---

28 The term 'undisputed facts about bodies' is Thomas Laqueur's in *Making Sex* (1990, p. 13). For Comment on Laqueur's *Making Sex* and how to deconstruct cultural constructions of the body without negating the 'body physical', see Appendix 4.1.

female are not enough'.²⁹ She acknowledges 'the concept of the intersexual body', but insists that the practice of 'us[ing] the term intersex as a catch-all for three major subgroups with some mixture of male and female characteristics' is inadequate. She therefore advocates naming those three 'subgroups' (true hermaphrodites as 'herms', male pseudohermaphrodites as 'merms', and female pseudohermaphrodites as 'ferms') and categorising each as itself a 'sex'. And she 'would argue further that sex is a vast, infinitely malleable continuum that defies the constraints of even five categories'. In revisiting 'The Five Sexes' seven years later, however, she rejects the seemingly 'natural' view that 'regard[s] intersexuals and transgendered people as living midway between the poles of male and female' and concludes rather that 'male and female, masculine and feminine, cannot be parsed as some kind of continuum', that 'sex and gender are best conceptualised as points in a multidimensional space'.³⁰ Fausto-Sterling prefers to situate the points in 'a multidimensional space' rather than along a continuum, because the non-linearity of the former might avoid viewing intersexuals in terms of their proximity to the male or female pole. My concern here, however, is not with situating the points, whether along a linear continuum or within a multi-dimensional space, but in delineating the boundaries, the number of poles, that set limits to the possible permutations of sex.

Fausto-Sterling implicitly recognises the sexually dimorphic limitations on possible sexes in stating that 'one can find levels of masculinity and femininity in almost every possible permutation'.³¹ But this statement acknowledges that the number of possible permutations of human sex organs is limited to a set of two, of the male and female biological poles of human species, each pole of which contains subsets of chromosomes, genitals, and secondary sex characteristics. If any sexually reproducing species were to have three, four, or any number beyond two sexes, that is, to have three or more sets of chromosomes, genitals, and secondary sex characteristics, then the number of possible permutations, though still limited by the number of its sexual poles, would be exponentially greater.³² And if, as Fausto-Sterling rightly insists, 'gender iden-

---

29   Fausto-Sterling 1993, p. 21.
30   Fausto-Sterling 2000, p. 22.
31   Ibid. Following citation, ibid.
32   Though not involving a different set of sex organs, Gerald Durrell (2004, p. 79) tells of a Corfiot Lepidopteran species, the China mark-moth (so named because its markings were thought to resemble those on Chinese pottery), that has two female corporeal forms: one of which is fully winged like the male is is aerial following its acquatic hatching, while the other female has no wings and continues to live under water, using its legs to swim. It is not difficult to imagine how such a tripartite distribution of human corporeal forms would further complicate already complex human gender constructions.

tity presumably emerges from all of those *corporeal aspects* [my italics] via some poorly understood interaction with environment and experience', then the greater number of qualitatively distinct corporeal aspects pertaining to sex would presumably produce a commensurably greater number of gender identities. However many entities it contains, any set will have limits. Sex/gender may be performative, but the kinds of performativity that a given person will enact, and regardless of whether that person wants to be man, woman, homo- or hetero-, trans- or bi-sexual, etc. will depend on which combination of the dimorphic human sex organs that person's body actually has, and which ones and/or which identity that person desires among the possibilities established by, and between, the two biological poles of male and female. And as the set of permutations of human sex organs is limited by those two biological poles, so too is the set of possible gender permutations. Although those permutations may not be situated along a rigidly 'linear continuum', their range is limited to the sphere circumscribed by the two poles of a sexually dimorphic species.

In differentiating a currently oppressive from a potentially emancipatory discourse, Fausto-Sterling addresses an absolutely essential dimension of an emancipatory politics. My point is not to challenge that but to complement it by suggesting that these cultural constructions and power relations are not arbitrary, but are rather discursive and political refractions of a seemingly indisputable, *quantitative* biological fact of the predominance of polar male-female dimorphism in our species. Recognising in *non-evaluative* terms the purely *quantitative* 'normality' or 'typicality' of male-female sexual dimorphism is not at all irrelevant to understanding the power relations and cultural constructions that *evaluate* intersexuals in *qualitative* terms as 'abnormal' and 'atypical' – and discriminate accordingly.

As this brief 'deconstruction' of an eclectic sample indicates, ultra-constructionism tends to succumb to some of the temptations it sought to resist. Rejecting the theoretical abuses that the body has suffered at the conceptual hands of Western thought, the ultra-constructionist reaction, understandably but problematically, too often takes the form of an equal and opposite reaction, several examples of which have been encountered above: the body social negates the body physical; there is no natural body; pain exists only as we perceive it; human beings are not one biological, but several cultural species; the body is *the* cultural product; performativity materialises the effect of boundary, fixity, and surface we call matter. Not only are such universalising anti-universalist claims thoroughly unnecessary as justifications of the much-needed deconstructive critiques, but they are also short-sighted and prematurely foreclose avenues of inquiry. Whether they conceive the production process as one of inscription, discipline, or performativity, ultra-constructionists agree that the 'natural body' is a product of culture and has itself no significance for cultural analysis.[33] Simply negating traditional philosophy's answer to the question about the body by no means guarantees an escape from idealism.[34] Making only a linguistic or cultural turn toward the body, and subjecting the 'natural body' and its efficacy in the production of (freely, culturally specific) meaning to the insidious bias of neglect, ultra-constructionism fails to escape the idealism it criticises – differing only in countering 'logocentric' truth claims with proclamations of the arbitrariness of all meanings.[35]

---

[33] The fundamental agreement on this crucial point is itself made possible by an even broader assumption about the relation of linguistic signs to the objects of the world. The reason why ultra-constructionists are so unconcerned about the baby's natural body when emptying the bathtub is that the 'baby' in their bathtub is what Saussure called 'the referent'. Concerned with deciphering, how signs work, Saussure methodologically bracketed the referent to which signs refer as unnecessary to understanding the anatomy of signs and the logic of signification. The excluded referent has in semiotic-based analyses never been rehabilitated. And its exclusion allows for all variations on Synnott's claim that the body social negates the body physical. This semiotic ostracism of the referent and my rehabilitation of it will be developed in detail in Chapter 9.

[34] See McNally (2001 pp. 1–2; p. 7) for a critique of postmodernist treatment of body as a 'new idealism'. The 'linguistocentrism' of ultra-constructionist approaches produces a recurring theme in the form of an obsessive concern with what cannot be said or known. Regarding the body, this concern is perhaps most succinctly summarised by Gayatri Chakravorty Spivak who emphatically noted that 'If one really thinks about the body as such, there is no possible outline of the body as such. There are thinkings of the systematicity of the body, there are value codings of the body. The body, as such, cannot be thought, and I certainly cannot approach it' (quoted in Butler 1993, p. 1). But the reply to this is the same as that with which Hegel responded to Kant's notion of the *Ding-an-sich*, which he defined as the unknowable essence of a given thing. But as Hegel pointed out, it was Kant himself who posited both the *Ding-an-sich* and its unknowability. The joke here is that lurking behind the curtain veiling the Ding-an-sich was only Kant himself in the form of his own proposition. The same is true of Spivak's statement. While she and others are of course right that, as Grosz put it, 'there is no body as such: there are only bodies – male or female, black, brown, white, large or small – and the gradations in between', this does not mean that we cannot say anything about species-specific 'natural bodies', nor does it mean, as this entire work aims to show, that we cannot say anything that is culturally meaningful about species-specific natural bodies. The outline of a species-specific 'body as such' is directly related to the kinds, the rather broad, but nevertheless limited range of the social behaviours and cultural forms available to *Homo sapiens*.

[35] This denial of the 'natural body' is in my view what separates them from the theoretician whose focus on the body and attempts to inscribe and discipline it and its sexuality did perhaps the most in focusing attention on the body. That is of course Michel Foucault – and it might come as a surprise, precisely because of his central role in body studies, that I do not include him in this overview, nor do I consider him an ultra-constructionis. My take on Foucault is elaborated in Chapter 11 where I argue, probably unexpectedly, that

While a large dose of cultural relativism is certainly a much-needed antidote to the universalising tendencies of traditional Western thought, the thoroughgoing and arbitrary relativism inherent in ultra-constructionist approaches precludes as many important questions as it addresses. Nor should it be forgotten or ignored that cultural relativism can be, has been, and is still being used just as effectively as universalism in ideological justifications of not only oppressive, but also genocidal practices against some group designated as 'different', 'other', 'inferior', 'dangerous'. The exclusive focus on cultural analysis, combined with the narrow focus on the linguistic or semiotic dimension of cultures, hypostatises the astonishing diversity of human cultures into, as Dupré put it, incommensurate cultural species. The myopic consequence of this focus is that the central corporeal facts of human being, including the corporeal organisation that makes all human beings and human cultures identifiably human in form, fall completely outside the range of poststructuralist vision. Focused so intently on the very real phenotypic diversity of human bodies that becomes the referential material and material referent for the production of linguistic and cultural signs, ultra-constructionists either cannot see, or fail to recognise, the importance of the obvious fact that *Homo sapiens* is but one corporeally-specific and corporeally unique animal species amidst the splendorous diversity of corporeally-specific and corporeally-unique animal species – which leads to a treatment of intraspecies differences among human cultures as of greater significance than the interspecies differences through which each species is defined. To cultural ultra-constructionist vision, it is not through an evolutionary process, but only through a 'symbolic horizon' of some kind that human bodies are formed and, as Butler put it, 'come to matter at all'. Viewing the body as what Maxine Sheets-Johnstone calls a 'somatological *tabula rasa*'[36] ultra-constructionist vision sees in the body nothing of meaningful import until it is inscribed by language, culture, discipline, and/or performances.

The inability to see clearly the absolutely fundamental importance of species-specific corporeal organisation in the histories of any species is itself a consequence of a greater blindness. In addition to having allegedly overcome

---

he and Marx were both writing within a shared historical-materialist horizon. Here I will just say that Foucault does not deny the 'natural body' because he doesn't need to in order to carry out his critique of cultural constructions, inscriptions, and disciplining of the body. This is a crucial and fundamental difference from the ultra-constructionist position. Whereas ultra-constructionists are atheistic on the question of the body, Foucault is agnostic.

36 Sheets-Johnstone 1994, p. 109.

logocentric universalism, another of the self-proclaimed accomplishments of linguistic or 'cultural' ultra-constructionists is that their turn toward the body has overcome the legacy of Cartesian mind-body dualism. But although their conception of human beings as 'embodied minds' might at first glance seem to denote a unity of body and mind, closer inspection shows that it only supplants an untenable dualism with an equally untenably monism.

Studies in 'embodied epistemology' claim to recall from exile the ostracised 'natural body' that has been supplanted by cultural constructions grounded in the assumption that 'the specific types of body, concrete in their determinations, with a particular sex, race, and physiognomy' (Grosz) produce a body-specific form of 'embodied knowledge'. The resulting deconstructions of racist and sexist discourses are without question both theoretically and practically valuable, as are too the new understandings of how gender and/or race can produce different ways of knowing. Nevertheless, in terms of the question of the mind-body relation, it must be recognised that there is a conceptual sleight of hand at work here. Though the term itself denotes a unity, it is clear, both grammatically and in the practice of 'embodied epistemologies', that the substantive noun takes precedence over the adjective, that is: although these approaches treat the mind as residing in a (culturally constructed) gendered, racial, or ethnic body, the term 'embodied mind' still puts the primacy on the mind; and the body remains passive, functioning exclusively as a site that 'particularises' thinking. As Sheets-Johnstone summarises, the term 'embodiment' is just 'a lexical band-aid put on a three-century old metaphysical wound'. It is therefore not surprising that 'the program of "embodied knowledges" actually takes the body itself for granted in its entire epistemological enterprise; functioning as an indexical, the body is simply the place one puts one's epistemology', 'an epistemological receptacle'.[37]

Ultra-constructionist critiques of 'logocentric' thought from the standpoint of embodied epistemologies have succeeded very well in decentring Western universalist claims. But insofar as they treat the body only as 'an epistemological receptacle', they do not escape the privileging of mind over a passively conceived body. Insofar as they take only a cultural turn toward the body, they limit themselves to the deconstruction of 'always already' *given* social/cultural constructions, and thus do not (and cannot) explain anything about the 'why' and 'how' behind the given constructions – matters not irrelevant to the meaning of the constructions themselves. And were they to take instead a corporeal

---

37 Sheets-Johnstone 1994, p. 66.

turn toward culture, they would recognise that although the social and/or cultural constructions of the body are potentially infinite, they are neither limitless nor arbitrary.

4.3   Some Limitations of Marxist Debates on 'Human Nature'

Among Marxist theoreticians we find, perhaps surprisingly, another version of treating the body as a 'somatological *tabula rasa*', which has a quirky history. Well before the high tide of poststructuralism, Louis Althusser's 'anti-humanist' Marxism provoked a heated and still unresolved debate on the question of Marx's view of human nature. Those who, following Althusser, deny that Marx's materialist conception of history is grounded in a view of human nature have it fairly easy: they need only read all too literally the sixth of Marx's 'Theses on Feuerbach' which states that the human essence 'is no abstraction inherent in each single individual ... [but] the ensemble of social relations'. Interpreting this thesis as a categorical denial of any and all transhistorical human constants, they need not waste time thinking about how humans make their own history, but can focus exclusively on the structures that prevent them from doing so as they please.[38]

Those who defend a notion of human nature or insist on some kind of human constants have, however, a rather more difficult time of it – unless, of course, they are content with a reductionist reading of Marx's definition of the first historical act as the satisfaction of needs, which gives rise to new needs and the means to satisfy them, etc.,[39] the result of which is a simplistic view of *Homo sapiens* as *Homo economicus* whose history can thus be (mis)understood as a straightforward dialectic of needs and technology.[40] But those seeking a ten-

---

38 For a critique of the 'structuralist fetish' (e.g. Althusser) of Marx's 6th thesis on Feuerbach, see Archibald 1989, pp. 25–6. But as Oskar Negt (1988, p. 230) shows, that thesis need not be fetishised and can rather be understood, not as an *a priori* denial of human constants, but as 'a research direction in relation to the Subject'.

39 See Marx 1845a in Tucker (1978, p. 156). The problems with Marx's formulation were addressed in Chapter 3.

40 This *Homo economicus* view of human nature and technologically determinist view of human nature is attributed (undeservedly???) to Engels and deservedly to the official Marxism of the Second and Third Internationals. G.A. Cohen (1978) defends a much more sophisticated version of this dialectic of needs and technology. In different ways Theodor Adorno and Jean Baudrillard attributed this view of human nature and history to Marx – the former with his accusation that Marx wanted to turn the world into a workhouse and the latter by with the accusation that Marx was imprisoned within the categories of bourgeois political economy. See Adorno (1975, pp. 241–2) and Baudrillard (1975).

able, because sufficiently nuanced, historical-materialist definition of human nature have a longer path to tread and more imposing obstacles to confront. For not only must they show that Marx's materialist conception of history rests on a view of human nature, but they must also define the attributes of that nature. In so doing, they must negotiate a variety of dilemmas, not the least of which are the following: they must determine the relation between the natural/biological and social/cultural; they must speak of universals, yet avoid universalising a particularist notion, and still be able to account for how one species can produce a seemingly endless variety of cultural forms; they must be able to account for historical change without falling into a transhistorical Whiggishness, and to discern the directions of historical changes without falling into teleologies; and if they manage to avoid all of these traps, they must still determine the methodological place-value of human nature in historical-materialist theory and analysis.

The challenge that Althusser's structuralist Marxism posed to the notion of human nature (which is not unlike that issued by anti-essentialist poststructuralists) prompted several authors to respond with an attempt at a historical-materialist account of human nature, among them: John McMurtry, *The Structure of Marx's World View*; Gyorgy Márkus, *Marxism and Anthropology*; Kate Soper, *On Human Needs*; Norman Geras, *Marx and Human Nature*; W. Peter Archibald, *Marx and the Missing Link: Human Nature*; Richard Lichtman, 'The Production of Human Nature by Means of Human Nature'; and Sean Sayer's *Marxism and Human Nature*.[41] Though they travel on different paths, all of these works are headed in the same general direction and share the common goal of overcoming the obstacles mentioned above in order to provide a historical-materialist definition of human nature. It is my contention that, though heading in the right direction, these works have gotten bogged down while attempting to negotiate those theoretical obstacles, and have become entangled in seemingly endless battles with their antagonists. While all of the above-named works might be read as counterarguments to the poststructuralist denial of human constants, Sayers' book, is explicitly and self-consciously so. I will therefore concentrate on it as an example of why such attempts at a historical-materialist view of human nature have fallen short. Although Sayers and the others are certainly heading in a corporeal direction, they seem

---

41 See McMurtry 1978; Markus 1978; Soper 1981; Geras 1983; Archibald 1989; Lichtman 1990; Sayers 1998. For comment on why I think these works are not materialist enough and thus come up short in their attempts to counter denials of any human universals by Althusserians and poststructuralists more generally, see Appendix 4.2.

to have stalled – the reason for which, in my view, is that they are not materialistic enough, that is: they did not reach far enough in attempting to grasp Marx's materialist conception of history by its corporeal roots.[42]

Acknowledging the 'controversy and ... confusion' generated by the question of human nature, Sayers seeks 'to restate, and to clarify and defend, a fundamental and central strand of Marxist philosophy': its 'historicist account of human nature'.[43] Convinced that this historicist account of human nature will enable him to carve a path between and beyond the poles of such conceptual binaries as essentialist universalism vs. relativism and natural vs. sociocultural, he promises to go 'out of [his] way to bring [his historicist account of human nature] into relation and dialogue with other contemporary philosophical positions and to show its relevance within the context of the wider current

---

42 A much more recent, and in my view, far superior attempt to address the question of human nature, and one that does grasp a materialist conception of history by its corporeal roots in Marx is John G. Fox's *Marx, The Body, and Human Nature* (2015). I became acquainted with Fox's book only fairly recently, and well after I wrote this chapter. But I should explain what I see as the relation between our two similar-sounding projects. When I first encountered the title of Fox's book, I thought he might have pre-empted my undertaking. Having read the book, and having conversed with him on the telephone and in email, I think the best way to describe the relation between his work and mine is that we start from the same point and are heading in the same direction, but with different stops along the way, with different points of emphasis, that result in each of us emphasising and elaborating some points that the other acknowledges, but does not elaborate. The only somewhat significant difference that I find is terminological. Fox uses the term 'human nature' in his title and throughout the work. And although he does have a chapter title with the term 'species-being' in it (though none with 'human nature'), he does seem to use the terms interchangeably. For reasons discussed in Part 1, I avoid the term 'human nature', mostly because of the essentialist philosophical baggage it carries. And although the term 'species-being', that can be understood as a description of the way a species *is* in the world (where it lives, how it makes its living, etc.), is less susceptible to essentialism, I think Marx was right when, after having posited 'human corporeal organisation' as the 'first fact' of history in *The German Ideology*, he refrained from using the term. Fox certainly avoids the problem of essentialism, and not least because he does take so seriously 'the body' as the 'first fact' of a materialist conception of history. But one way of illustrating our different points of emphasis along similar paths is to construct a categorial continuum as follows:
   human nature – species-being – human corporeal organisation
I think it would be accurate to say that Fox primarily uses the first, occasionally the second, and rarely the third; whereas I primarily use the third, occasionally the second, and avoid the first. This difference of terminological emphasis leads us into different discussions; and it helps to explain our different yet (I think) parallel paths, and the different but (I think) complementary contents of our respective undertakings. Further comment on Fox's book in Appendices 0.1, 1.3 and 10.2.

43 Sayers 1998, p. 13. Following citations in this paragraph, ibid.

philosophical debate'; in so doing he aims 'to show how Marxism involves ... an unfamiliar and ... illuminating approach to problems which appear intractable from within a more traditional and familiar philosophical perspective'.

Sayers's overly Hegelianised (and by no means unfamiliar) historicist account of human nature, however, casts only a translucent light. While attempting to resolve these binary oppositions, he does effectively wield against several of Marx's critics the historicism that he attributes to Marx. He exposes the obvious problems with essentialist absolutism and arbitrary relativism, with the ahistoricism of analytical Marxism, the myopic utopianism of André Gorz's vision of the liberation from work, and with the inflated charges of those environmentalists who accuse Marx of Promethean productivism. But he fails to resolve the problems posed by the binary oppositions, and therefore does not succeed in the most important matter: the construction of an efficacious, historical-materialist conception of human nature. Consequently, as Terry Eagleton has relentlessly shown, the problems remain as intractable at the end of the book as they were in the beginning.[44] Here I want to focus on what I consider the fundamental problem – one that has beset not only Sayers's book, but virtually all attempts to construct a historical-materialist view of human nature. And that is the problem resulting from the invocation of a human nature in order to avoid relativism combined with a reticence about defining that nature (except as historicistically becoming) in order to avoid essentialism.

Sayers chooses to stake his theoretical claim on the field already surveyed by Kate Soper (1981), who insisted (specifically regarding a Marxist theory of needs, but also applicable to Sayers's undertaking) that 'all theorisation ... must necessarily live in the field of forces created by the antithetical poles of relativism and essentialism'.[45] One should not, indeed cannot, avoid engaging relativism and essentialism in the attempt to develop a notion of human nature. But the choice to fight the theoretical battles on the conceptual terrain delimited by these two poles enhances the risk of becoming entrapped between them – when what is necessary is to carve out a position beyond them. And this is Sayers's greatest dilemma. Unable to escape the conceptual space delineated by these antithetical poles, he attempts to hold the middle ground. Caught between universalist essentialism and arbitrary relativism, his strategic problem is that he commits himself to fighting a two-front battle on the conceptual terrain determined by his binary antagonists; and his tactical problem is that

---

44   Eagleton 1999, pp. 150–61.
45   Soper 1981, p. 123.

while he engages his antagonists one at a time, he yields to the temptation of alternately borrowing the conceptual weaponry of each to attack the other. So, against the universalists, naturalists, and essentialists he argues that there is no universal human nature or essence. But against the relativists and extreme social constructionists he argues that since *Homo sapiens* is the species whose nature is to create its own nature, that the essential human nature is in the process of (progressively) becoming. Trapped in a defensive position, Sayers remains so preoccupied arguing that there is such a thing as human nature that he never delineates it sufficiently to win the battle.[46]

While Sayers is tautologically correct in stating that the nature of humans is to make their own nature and their own histories, the fundamental problem is that he fails to explain what it is about human beings that enables them to do so. He justifies his hesitation to define human nature with the quite correct insistence that human universals, such as biological needs, are malleable and always socio-culturally mediated, and thus can only be discussed with a certain degree of abstraction. But abstractions, as Marx very consciously wielded them, can be both meaningful and methodologically invaluable. Moreover, the particularity of their manifestations does not abrogate the universality of needs: if some people will not eat what others consider a delicacy, the fact is that both have a minimum nutritional requirement. Because he refuses to define (in consciously abstract terms) such universal needs as a first step to analysing the

---

46   See for example Sayers's (1998) back and forth between the natural and social dimensions of human nature (Sayers 1998, pp. 151–6), the conclusion of which is that 'in short, there is both a universal and a particular, a natural and a social, aspect to human nature' (ibid., p. 153). This is of course true, but it leaves the relation between the natural and social completely unresolved. And without establishing what that relation is, it is, as these pages show, impossible to escape the conceptual ground delineated by the binaries. Soper too succumbs to the same two-front battle. She writes: 'For who was it, if not Marx himself, who showed us that individuals do not inherit their needs (except to a minimal degree, and even then only in the most abstract conception) in the form of a natural, biological patrimony, but acquire their needs (including the content of their "basic" physiological and psychological needs) eccentrically, and independently of their wills, through their encounter with the objective social patrimony into which they are born and through which they live out their lives?' (Soper 1981, pp. 194–5) And she summarises, that Marx himself constantly insists that 'it is on pain of mouthing the most "dumb generalities" ... that one reduces [needs] to their basis in the individual, and fails to take account of the way in which social institutions have always operated upon natural "givens" so as to create the distinctive, cultural existence that is human existence' (ibid., p. 195). While we must of course avoid 'dumb generalities', we must also avoid the trap of taking about the body, in this case, its biological needs, as a 'simple prerequisite' – which is what happens if we focus only on the socio-culturally specific mediations of needs and neglect the needs themselves that are mediated.

different forms given them by different cultures, Sayers produces by default a philosophy of history consisting of a formless species that somehow forms itself while making its own history.[47] Unable to figure out how to ground historical theory in human nature, he ends up having history produce human nature. In a definitional sleight of hand, he introduces us to a human nature – but one that resembles an invisible ink drawing on an apparent *tabula rasa*: the sketch is there, but its form and contents can only be brought forth by the light of its own history. Without having explained, however, what it is about humans that enables them to create their own nature and to make their own histories, how that human nature also affects the histories they make and prevents them from making the histories they please, Sayers methodologically reduces the human nature on which he so emphatically insists to the status of what Marx – depicting the political economists' treatment of use-value – called merely a 'simple prerequisite'.[48]

Seeking to establish an efficacious, but not essentialist notion of human nature, Sayers's only recourse is to appeal to a future-perfect historicism. And this traps him in a difficult place; for he can only argue in effect that since human nature is in the process of becoming, there is no human nature until it will have become; and until it will have become, it cannot be described except in what he considers empty abstractions. This methodological insistence on an essentially formless human nature that forms itself in the course of its history results in a kind of teleonomic progressivism: history has no teleological pur-

---

47 On this matter Sayers relies heavily on Lichtman (1990). On a purely formal level, I agree fully with Lichtman's statements that nature is 'the condition of embodied practice', that human beings are 'self-constituting, that we are simultaneously the subject and object of our own activity', that human nature provisionally understood is 'the structure of capacities, tendencies, and sensibilities that humans bring, incompletely formed to their life world' and that 'the self-constitution of human nature means the production of a variety of fundamentally different human natures' (Lichtman, pp. 14–18). But at least two of his particular formulations have unfortunate implications. One is the perhaps unintended Whiggish progressivism embedded in his notion that we are born 'incomplete' (ibid., p. 15, p. 18), that 'as we appropriate the world, we come to appropriate ourselves and produce ourselves as distinctly human' (ibid., p. 21). This is obviously true ontogenetically, the case of a child growing into culture, which is the situation that Lichtman most often addresses explicitly in his essay. But if applied phylogenetically, which Sayers explicitly does, the notion that we are born incomplete imposes a Whiggish curve on history as ascending from the 'primitive' to the 'truly human'.

48 'einfache Voraussetzung' which I have translated as 'simple prerequiste'. The Nicolaus translation (Marx 1973 [1857–58], p. 320), reads 'simple presupposition'. The difference might be a simple matter of preference. But I prefer 'prerequisite' because seems more strongly to suggest an existing 'precondition', whereas 'presupposition' seems to me to be more suggestive of something tacitly assumed in an argument.

pose, but it is a one-way street: since human nature is to cultivate itself, and since this self-cultivation is cumulative, history is the progressive development of human nature – the measure of which is the mutually reinforcing expansion of human needs and human productive capacities.[49]

While I doubt that Sayers would agree with any of the following positions, the problem is that the progressivism that follows from his argument (whether by design or default) must view history as an ascending arrow and it measures historical time by its great leaps forward. Though it frees the future from *a priori* essentialism, it imprisons the past in 'primitivism'. According to this logic, past and present 'underdevelopment' can only be understood as various, perhaps necessary, but nevertheless still incomplete stages in the progressive process of human self-cultivation and self-creation. The complex histories of 'pre-capitalist' socio-cultural forms are reduced to one-dimensionality and considered only in terms of their contribution to the self-production of human nature. Such an approach resembles the Whiggish progressivism of Marx's philosophical materialism of the *1844 Manuscripts* which, as noted above, only lets us measure what we have gained, not treasure what we have lost; and it can only treat the barbarism of what, according to this itinerary, should have been the most civilised of centuries, the twentieth, as atavistic remnants of a primitive past, rather than a product of 'civilised' human productive capacities.

These problems resulting from the simultaneous appeal to relativism to avoid essentialism, and to the historicist becoming of an essential human nature to avoid relativism, are not peculiar to Sayers's analysis, but remain unresolved in most historical-materialist accounts of human nature. Insofar as they attempt to avoid the binary extremes of dogmatic essentialism and arbitrariness, these works are headed in the right direction. But they have ultimately fallen short. As mentioned above, the reason for this is that they are not materialist enough. Although such historicist accounts of human nature as becoming all insist that the body is the material foundation and starting point of historical materialism, the failure to follow through and elaborate thoroughly why Marx designated corporeal organisation as the 'first fact' for the study of history inadvertently results in a treatment of the body as simple prerequisite – as a silhouette in form and a *tabula rasa* in content.

---

49 There are, to be sure, several passages throughout Marx's writings that seem to entail this progressivist view of human nature. But, as I argued above in Part 1, Marx had, at least by the *Grundrisse*, eliminated the last vestiges of a speculative philosophy of history while establishing the guiding threads and research programme of his materialist conception of history.

4.4 The Reduction of the Artefactual to Facticity: Martin Heidegger and Hannah Arendt

Although they turned away to pursue something they felt more philosophically sure of, both Martin Heidegger and Hannah Arendt in their studies of *Dasein* or human Being-in-the-World understood well enough to take seriously, even if only briefly and dismissively, the matter of made-objects and their making. And they both acknowledged a path leading toward what Heidegger called a 'hidden bodily problematic', a unique logic of a bodily nature that is inextricably imbricated in the using of tools to make things and therewith in the very fabrication of human worlds and worldliness. Neither, however, followed this path, preferring instead to turn toward weightier matters of greater philosophical import. Heidegger's and Arendt's ultimate dismissiveness of the body, fabrication, and made worlds does not require us to dismiss their insights about them. Here therefore I intend to follow Heidegger and Arendt through the phenomenological woods to the clearing where my corporeal path diverges from theirs; and by reviewing what I consider the insights and blindnesses in their works, it will be possible to differentiate between their philosophical ontology and the kind of corporeally-grounded social ontology peculiar to historical materialism.

Setting out in *Being and Time* to elaborate an ontology of Dasein, an account of human Being-in-the-World, Heidegger reproached traditional philosophy, especially since Descartes, for its mind-body dualism that results in a merely theoretical contemplation of the world and its objects. Whereas Plato considered those toiling in chains in his dark cave only as a backdrop for the one among them who 'was freed' and allowed to ascend, only in order to establish a *chiaroscuro* contrast with the enlightened, Heidegger at least insisted that one has to go through, not just out of, the cave or, in his case, the forest, in order to attain knowledge – that the everyday consciousness of the toilers must be understood, even if only in order to get at what is obscured by it. And if we imagine Heidegger walking among (decidedly not working with) the labourers in Plato's allegorical cave, we find that his philosophical reflections on this led him to the threshold of another, rather different path. Entangled in the discussion that led him to this threshold are some rather interesting insights about a corporeal logos – insights that he quickly dropped in his pursuit of Being, but that can help to illuminate the intimate and animate relation between bodies and artefacts.

In the early stages of his analysis, Heidegger presents his 'Preparatory Fundamental Analysis of Dasein', in which he turns his phenomenological gaze onto Dasein's 'dealings' [*Umgang*] with its environment [*Umwelt*]. In its everyday world, Heidegger insists, 'the kind of dealing which is closest' to Dasein is 'not a bare perceptual cognition, but rather that kind of concern which manipulates things and puts them to use' – which refers of course to labour. This practical kind of dealing has 'its own kind of "knowledge"' involving the use of the equipment ready-to-hand in the environment for the purpose of producing a 'work'.[50] The equipment used in this production is 'known', not in any merely theoretical sense that treats it 'as an occurring thing'. Rather, equipment is, appropriately, used, and 'can genuinely show itself only in dealings cut to its own measure (hammering with a hammer, for example)'. In our choice of the hammer for hammering, 'our concern subordinates itself to the "in-order-to" which is constitutive for the equipment we are employing at the time; the less we just stare at the hammer-Thing, and the more we seize hold of it and use it, the more primordial does our relationship to it become, and the more it is unveiled and encountered as that which it is – as equipment'.

Once we seize hold of the hammer and initiate the act of 'hammering', we find that this act 'itself uncovers the specific "manipulability" of the hammer'. The German term for 'manipulability', *Handlichkeit*, renders even more graphically the fittedness of the tool to human 'bodily nature' or corporeal form. Heidegger's instinct here is right on target. His example acknowledges the forming of the human world and its objects in correspondence with human corporeal form and dexterities. As '*handlich*' or 'handy', a hammer is formed in accordance with the human hand; itself constructed by human hands, it is made to fit and to be used by a creature with an opposable thumb that can grasp, and with a weight and balance corresponding to the strength and length of a human arm. When fabricated according to the dimensions of human corporeality, our relationship to, our use of, the hammer is primordial, immediate, non-conceptual. It fits, we use it, and together we produce a work. Our 'knowledge' of the hammer reveals itself in our practical activity; it is manifested in the efficacy with which we use it, in the way in which our dexterity in handling it turns it into an extension of our body, and also in the object that we make with it.

In a distinction that resonates with Michael Polanyi's notion of our 'tacit knowledge', of the fact that 'we know more than we can tell' (see Chapter 7), Heidegger distinguishes between traditional philosophical knowledge that

---

50 Heidegger 1962, p. 95, p. 99. Next two citations in this paragraph, and the citation in next paragraph: ibid., p. 98. Heidegger at least took labour seriously as something that is uniquely human, in contrast to Arendt for whom labour is animal as opposed to work; the product of the former consumed, while that of the latter is free-standing and thus human. This completely overlooks the fact that labour, both agricultural and industrial, produces the goods whose consumption (*re*)*produces* the human body, human life.

treats the object only as an object of theoretical knowledge and practical activity which presupposes a kind of 'knowledge'. In practical activity, '[i]nterpretation is carried out primordially not in a theoretical statement but in an action of circumspective concern – laying aside the unsuitable tool, or exchanging it, "without wasting words"'.[51] Against those who would banish from the domain of thought the silent syllogisms inherent in the process of making, he cautions: 'From the fact that words are absent, it may not be concluded that interpretation is absent'.

And it is not only the labour-process with its tacit corporeal logos beyond language that is suffused with meaningfulness. The product of labour, the made-object or, in Heidegger's terms, the 'work', is the teleology that gives meaning to the equipment that goes into its making – both the tools which will produce it and the materials out of which it will be produced: the work 'bears with it that referential totality within which the equipment is encountered'; it is 'the "towards-which" of such things as the hammer, the plane, and the needle'.[52] However, the constellation of meaning that the work gathers around itself is not limited to tools and raw materials. For, 'the work to be produced is not merely usable for something'. On the contrary, 'the work produced refers not only to the "towards-which" of its usability and the "whereof" of which it consists: under simple craft conditions it also has an assignment to the person who is to use it or wear it. The work is cut to his figure; he "is" there along with it as the work emerges' (and, Heidegger adds, that this is true even under conditions of mass production, though in that case it points to the 'random, the average' individual). 'Thus along with the work, we encounter not only entities ready-to-hand but also entities with Dasein's kind of Being [that is: other people] – entities for which ... the product becomes ready-to-hand; and together with these we encounter the world in which wearers and users live, which is at the same time ours'. Implicated in the labour-process, then, are humans' relations not only to nature, but also to one another (albeit on a socially rather superficial level of the relation between producer and consumer).

Immersed in what David Krell calls the 'intricate contexts of meaning' whose form is not that of conceptual cognition, Dasein is at home in this familiar and known world of work and others.[53] Heidegger, however, exposes this familiarity as an 'inauthentic' Being-at-Home because this 'knowledge' has the form only of unreflected immediacy. And Dasein is forced beyond this immediacy only when the inevitable occurs, when our everyday 'dealings' are interrupted

---

51   This and next citation, Heidegger 1962, p. 200.
52   Citations in this paragraph, Heidegger 1962, p. 99; p. 99; p. 100; p. 100.
53   David Krell, 'Introduction' to Heidegger 1962, p. 20.

by some 'disturbance' in our equipment.[54] When there is a misfit between tool and body, when the tool breaks, when the hammer is too heavy or the light bulb burns out, then we become cognisant of the attributes of the tool that we have been using or need, then 'the context of equipment is lit up, not as something never seen before, but as a totality constantly sighted beforehand in circumspection' – and then: 'the world announces itself'.[55] When some malfunction disturbs our everyday immediate at-homeness, then the world becomes 'unhomely' [*unheimlich*]. And only then can we begin to understand the nature of our Being-in-the-world which was hitherto obscured by the immediacy of our 'dealings' with the world. Whereas for Novalis, philosophy was the yearning to be everywhere at home, Heidegger insisted Dasein's odyssey could only begin when it broke with its at-homeness in its immediate environment; only by passing through a stage of homelessness could Dasein grasp its authentic Being as Being-toward-Death and then (in a rather morbid inversion) truly be at home in the world (*Heimat*).

In his passing, phenomenological interest in the nature of Dasein's everyday practicality, even if only in order to transcend it, Heidegger glances intently, if only externally and thus superficially, at the mundane workaday world. He recognises that Dasein's silent activity, the unreflected yet meaningful immediacy of bodily movements in labour, constitute a form of knowledge beyond language. In addressing Dasein's self-orientation in, and ability to navigate, the world – and this applies also to the kinaesthetics of labour – Heidegger notes that Dasein's 'spatiality' and 'directionality' are 'marked out in accordance' with its 'bodily nature'; and 'this "bodily nature"', he adds (unsurprisingly, in a parenthesis), 'hides a whole problematic of its own'.[56] His glance on the threshold of this hidden bodily problematic offers a glimpse of what is hidden, undisclosed, when we approach and apprehend artefacts only in their

---

54   Citations in this paragraph, Heidegger 1962, p. 105; p. 105.
55   Heidegger's example is taken from artisan production. But in my view, the significant factor is the breakdown of the means of production, regardless of whether a hammer, a jack-hammer, or an assembly-line. In glancing at the broken tool, Heidegger made an insightful, tantalising, and provocative allusion to a 'hidden bodily problematic' – which he promptly ignored, in favour of contemplating the abstract meaning of Being that reveals itself when the daily work routine is interrupted, and leads him toward a philosophical/idealist conception of Being-toward-Death. He had no interest in interrogating the consequences of the broken machine for the lives of the producers and those whose lives depend on the products. And he thus ignored the fact that the breakdown of the tool, whether a hammer or an assembly line, prevents workers, whether artisans or proletarians from earning a living and forces them to confront, quite literally: to live, Being-toward-Death.
56   Heidegger 1962, p. 143.

facticity – a glimpse of a non-conceptual, corporeal mode of knowing, what I would call a corporeal logos that, if pursued, would lead to a corporeal semiotics aimed at deciphering the corporeal contexts of meaning in both the act of making and in the made-object.

But little more than a glimpse, for Heidegger skirts the issue, quickly withdrawing from it, implicated as it is in the immediacy of everydayness that obscures Dasein's 'authentic' Being. Distracted from his reflections on this hidden bodily problematic by the breakdown of the tool, now just being there, lying inertly in its facticity, Heidegger's glance is quickly attracted to the philosophical (ontological) possibilities that open up with this disruption of practical activity. Only when the tool has ceased to function does it become philosophically interesting, no longer as a material tool of mere practical activity, but as a conceptual 'tool' of philosophically meaningful ontological knowledge. The broken tool that signifies the inauthenticity of the world of labour and artefacts provokes Dasein out of its everydayness and helps drive the phenomenological odyssey toward authentic Being-towards-Death (which, one might assume, should have something to do with a 'bodily problematic') – and away from what we might, in Heideggerian form but with historical-materialist content, call the 'Being-toward-Life' involved in human worldmaking.

In this way, and despite having arrived on that threshold, Heidegger's separation of practical from philosophical knowledge remains firmly within the bounds of traditional philosophical idealism. In this respect his treatment of the 'hidden bodily problematic' resembles Hegel's of the master-servant relation. Both cast insightful glances at the labour-process that they then submerge in a purely philosophical perspective. For Hegel, the true meaning of work as gleaned from the master-servant relation is understood only by *Geist* for whom that relation, specifically the work done by the servant, provides food for thought; while the servant continues his servitude and produces real worldly goods for the master, *Geist* appropriates the chapter's lessons, the 'product' of labour idealistically conceived as concepts, and moves on to the next phenomenological challenge. Similarly, after having cast several insightful glances at, and pointed toward, a whole 'hidden' corporeal problematic, Heidegger opted for the realm of thought as the locus of his practice and ultimately advocated a philosophical attitude adjustment acknowledging Being-towards-Death as Dasein's authentic posture which alone will result in authentic Being-in-the-world, real at-homeness.

But as the philosopher wanders off in pursuit of the structure of Being, leaving the artefact, the tool, lying inert, reduced to mere facticity, the practical activity, the labour, of producing and reproducing the world must go on unabated – the alternative being, of course, death. Ironically, Heidegger might

THE BODY IS NOT A TABULA RASA   257

agree with Michael Polanyi's statement that '[W]e endow a thing with meaning by interiorizing it and destroy its meaning by alienating it'.[57] But even as he acknowledged that whole hidden corporeal problematic and tacit corporeal knowledge so intimate that we can know something without having to 'waste words' on it, Heidegger was not at all interested in pursuing them. For the kind of knowledge that he sought could only be attained by the alienation of the artefact from the body, its deanimation or death, its reduction to facticity. Only through, if not the death, then at least the paralysis of the artefact could Dasein's authentic Being-toward-Death be revealed.

Hannah Arendt, we might metaphorically say, followed Heidegger into the interpretive woods where she came across the broken tool lying where he had left it – at the intersection of the two paths, one leading toward a 'bodily nature' which 'hides a whole problematic of its own' and that leading in the opposite direction toward a clearing whose illumination would reveal the alleged authenticity of human being. Although she had no doubts about which path she would tread, she did feel obliged to explain why her choice was the superior one. To do so, she took a few steps down the path indicated by the tool, and her glimpse of this realm contains thoughtful and helpful insights gained from her first enthusiastic glances at the new landscape. The problem, however, is that after having taken only a few steps and barely able to see around the first bend, Arendt nevertheless felt that she could map the entire terrain. But this corporeal territory is vast and topographically complex. And mapping this difficult terrain was not made any easier by her conviction, even as she pursued her topographical task, that this path was a dead end that would lead to little of philosophical significance. Although she recognised that this path leads to matters essential to human *life*, she concluded that such corporeal matters are not the essential attributes of properly *human* life. Deceived by the simple appearance of this complex bodily path, and thus convinced she had seen enough, she hurried back to the clearing where the paths diverged and more confidently followed the one Heidegger had already trod, leading not to bodies and artefacts, but to minds and 'bodies of thought'.

Arendt's study of 'the human condition' aims not at what humans *are*, which in any case 'seems unanswerable', but at what humans *do*.[58] She is concerned therefore 'only with the most elementary articulations of the human condition, with those activities that traditionally, as well as according to current opin-

---

57   M. Polanyi 1969, p. 146.
58   Arendt 1958, p. 10. Following citations in this paragraph, ibid., p. 5; p. 5; p. 7; p. 2.

ion, are within the range of every human being'. She finds human activity to be of two kinds, belonging either to the *vita contemplativa* or the *vita activa*. Like her philosophical predecessors, she designates the mind as the uniquely human organ and the *vita contemplativa*, 'the contemplative activity of thinking' as 'the highest and perhaps purest activity of which [human beings] are capable'. Yet despite having designated the *vita contemplativa* as the only commensurately human activity, she leaves it out of her analysis of the 'human condition' precisely because it is *not* an activity 'within the range of every human being'. Her analysis of the human condition focuses instead on the *vita activa* (apparently to explain why human beings, some philosophers excepted, have failed to live up to their humanity). In any case, she subdivides the *vita activa* into three 'fundamental' kinds, each corresponding to 'one of the basic conditions under which life on earth has been given to man'. These are in ascending order (an order determined by their proximity or distance from the 'other living organisms' to which 'man' is related): labour, work, and (political) action. These three forms of the active life are infected in varying degrees by their dependence on the body that she, like her philosophical predecessors, views as the merely animal side of human being, as the site of mere life through which 'man remains related to all other living organisms'.[59]

Labour is the most basic (and base) activity 'which corresponds to the biological process of the human body, whose spontaneous growth, metabolism, and eventual decay are bound to the vital necessities produced and fed into the life process by labour. The human condition of labour is life itself'.[60] Because labour is subordinated to necessity, Arendt finds the term depicting the labourer, *animal labourans*, 'fully justified' as opposed to the 'very questionable use of the same term in *animal rationale*'. Rooted in the bodily needs that must be satisfied to sustain life, labour, in both process and purpose, is the most corpor-

---

59   Because my concern here is Arendt's interesting and insightful, but ultimately dismissive discussion of 'labour' and 'work', I will not address political action other than to comment on why Arendt views political action as the highest activity on the lower plane of human existence. To act as a free citizen or, in Rousseau's terms, 'to obey a law that one makes for oneself', is the freest, most human dimension of the *vita activa*. Despite that ideal, politics *qua* activity cannot free itself from the reach of the body. In an argument analogous to, if not drawn from, Plato, Arendt views politics as not free from special interests which ultimately emanate from the body's needs and desires leads individuals to see politics more as a sphere to assert their special interests. Thus tainted with traces of corporeality, politics remains consigned to the lower sphere, and only the *vita contemplative* qualifies as a properly human 'activity'.

60   Arendt 1958, p. 7. Following citations in this paragraph, ibid., p. 84; p. 110; p. 145; p. 121; p. 98; p. 143.

eal and, therefore, the most animal of human activities. Accepting the Greek (and later Locke's) distinction between 'the labour of the body and the work of the hands', she writes: 'There is no doubt that, as the natural process of life is located in the body, there is no more immediately life-bound activity than labouring'. The thoughtlessness, that is, the unhuman character of labour is evident in the fact that it 'requires for best results a rhythmically ordered performance'; and despite 'enormous improvement in labour tools', human labour is only quantitatively, but not qualitatively different from the foraging of animals. Since its purpose is to satisfy the constantly recurring bodily needs, labour is an endless activity, 'part of the cyclical movement of nature and therefore endlessly repetitive;' labour 'always moves in the same circle, which is prescribed by the biological process of the living organism and the end of its 'toil and trouble' comes only with the death of this organism'. As a means to sustain life, the product of labour is destined to be annihilated in consumption. The *animal labourans*, like all other animals, must consume the product of its activity in order to sustain itself so that it can begin ever anew the laborious process of finding sustenance: 'Labour [...] produces for the end of consumption, but since this end, the thing to be consumed, lacks the worldly permanence of a piece of work, the end of the process is not determined by the end product but rather by the exhaustion of labour power, while the products themselves, on the other hand, immediately become means again, means of subsistence and reproduction of labour power'.

Work, on the other hand, 'is the activity which corresponds to the unnaturalness of human existence, which is not imbedded in, and whose mortality is not compensated by, the species' ever-recurring life-cycle. Work provides an "artificial" world of things, distinctly different from all natural surroundings. Within its borders each individual life is housed, while this world itself is meant to outlast and transcend them all. The human condition of work is worldliness'.[61] Work is the productive activity not of the human *animal labourans* but of *Homo faber*. The determination of what productive activity counts as work is first of all derived teleologically from the purpose of the product: 'The world, the man-made home erected on earth [through work] and made of the material which earthly nature delivers into human hands, consists not of things that are consumed but of things that are used'. In work, consequently, the nature of productive activity and the relation of the producer to the product have a logic of their own: 'The work of our hands, as distinguished from the labour of our bodies – *homo faber* who makes and literally "works upon", as distin-

---

61   Arendt 1958, p. 7. Following citations in this paragraph, ibid., p. 134; p. 136; p. 139; p. 139.

guished from the *animal labourans* which labours and "mixes with" – fabricates the sheer unending variety of things whose sum total constitutes the human artifice'. The work of *Homo faber* is 'fabrication', the production of durable products which she calls 'reification'. Through the fabrication of the durable human world, *Homo faber* lifts itself above the merely animal, bodily dimension of the human condition: 'The *animal labourans*, which with its body and the help of tame animals nourishes life, may be the lord and master of all living creatures, but he still remains the servant of nature; only *homo faber* conducts himself as lord and master of the whole earth'.

Herein lies both the peak and the limits of *Homo faber's* accomplishment. For though work creates worldliness, the activity of work is narrowly utilitarian. In work aimed at a 'definite, predictable end', the end not only 'justifies the means', but 'does more, it produces and organizes them'.[62] The end 'justifies the violence done to nature to win the material ... Because of the end product, tools are designed and implements invented, and the same end product organizes the work process itself ... During the work process, everything is judged in terms of suitability and usefulness for the desired end, and for nothing else'. The 'anthropocentric utilitarianism' of *Homo faber*, who is 'nothing but a fabricator and thinks in no terms but those of means and ends which arise directly out of his own activity', renders him 'just as incapable of understanding meaning as the *animal labourans* is incapable of understanding instrumentality'. Worse yet, *Homo faber* 'instrumentalizes, and his instrumentalization implies a degradation of all things into means, their loss of intrinsic and independent value'. The understanding of meaning is reserved for the higher activities of action, which attains only a partial understanding, and contemplation which alone can fully grasp meaning.

On the basis of these distinctions Arendt insists that Marx's biggest problem was one of conflation. Arendt found Marx profoundly insightful in understanding labour and its relation to the reproduction of both one's own life and the species.[63] But, she insists, he hypostatised labour and defined that which is uniquely human with 'the very content of the definition of man as *animal labourans*'. In so doing, he reduced the human condition to the performance of what in Arendt's hierarchy is the basest, most animalistic of human activities – to labour and the mere preservation of life. Arendt finds this conflation of labour and work in what she considers Marx's muddled notion of objectifica-

---

62 Arendt 1958, p. 143, p. 153, p. 153. Following citations in this paragraph, ibid., p. 153; p. 155; p. 156.
63 See Arendt 1958, p. 106. Following citations in this paragraph, ibid., pp. 99 note 36; 102, note 41. See also Chapter 10, note 52.

tion (*Vergegenständlichung*). Because he failed to make the proper teleological distinction between the product as 'material' to be consumed and the product as 'reified' and durable 'thing', Marx allegedly inaccurately attributed to *animal labourans* what in Arendt's view is the property of *Homo faber*. But it is first of all worth noting that what Arendt lists as attributes of work (preconceived image, subordination of tools and materials as means to an end) are equally applicable to labour. The problem is that although she applies the term 'labour' to any activity whose products are aimed at biological life, she is clearly thinking of certain kinds of 'mindless' labour – pushing or pulling a plough, assembly line labour, etc. But while labour of preparing a meal, clearing a field, growing crops, etc. may involve hard and/or repetitious work, it is simply inaccurate to claim that it has no mental content.

More importantly, Arendt's use of the durability of the product as the means to differentiate those products of work whose condition is 'worldliness' from those products of labour whose condition is 'mere' biological life quickly proves to be a rather shaky foundation on which she erects a structurally weak edifice. The criterion of durability seems to work all too self-evidently in the case of food production whose product is immediately consumed. But even this case is deceiving for in order to grow food crops, fields must first be cleared and cultivated; and the clearing and cultivation of fields is certainly a durable transformation of nature. Moreover, some of those durable products of *Homo faber* such as clothes, beds, houses, and countless other things are just as important to biological life; these are not consumed in the sense of immediate using-up, annihilation, but their albeit slow consumption is essential to the perpetuation of biological life. Shelter, whether a tent, igloo, house, or palace – is essential to human biological life as the means of maintaining body temperature within the proper range. Houses, especially in the form of palaces, long outlast 'individual life', and can also be a form of architectural aesthetic and/or display of power or status. But though palaces may also be signs of status and power, houses, regardless of whether palaces or hovels, certainly pertain to biological life; houses are thus both sustainers of life and part of the 'artificial world of things'.

Most importantly, however, durability is not just a quality of things, but also of bodies – the durability of which would, from a historical-materialist perspective at least, be called *life*. Arendt fails to see the permanence of the living body throughout the lifespan of its existence, and its ability to reproduce itself in procreation, thereby guaranteeing the permanence of the species, as of any importance to the other activities of which the human condition is comprised. Having in a sense turned her back on the generations of 'begatted' living bodies chronicled in the Hebrew *Bible*, she instead fully accepted the Greek conception of the bodily as the realm of enslavement to necessity and therefore animal rather than human; and she elaborates her category of labour such that the durability of individual bodies and of the species contributes nothing more to the higher activities of work, politics, and contemplation than its mere existence. But the labour that sustains life is the absolutely fundamental prerequisite, and goes fundamentally into the making, of 'worldliness'.[64] So concerned with the durability of artefacts, Arendt dismisses as a 'simple prerequisite', having no other effect on 'worldliness' than by virtue of its mere existence, the durability of the lives that (not to mention the bodily capacities that enable humans to) produce those artefacts and engage in those higher activities. As a kind of existential Ozymandias, she seems to overlook the significance of the simple fact that the production of the fabricated world is directly related to the biological life of the species, and that the durability of the fabricated world will not long outlast the durability of the species. Only on the basis of a very one-dimensional understanding of durability is it possible to draw such an uncrossable border between biological life and artefactual worldliness.

The philosophical dismissal of corporeality, finally, leads to a narrow and ultimately dismissive attitude towards artefacts. Arendt does acknowledge the 'worldliness' of durable artefacts, and she does glimpse in their interior structure 'objectified' the bodily skills, capacities, and dexterities requisite to make them. But almost as promptly as she dismisses labour as a merely bodily activity of the human animal, so too does she dismiss the work that produced worldliness (with the exception of the work that produces works of art) as a narrowly focused, 'anthropocentric utilitarianism', as an 'instrumentalization [that] implies a degradation of all things into means'.[65] Though she seriously addressed the very historical-materialist issues of the relation between the body, life, and making, she could not take any of these matters very seriously because of her pre-established hierarchical ranking of what she posited as ontologically distinct activities. And even work, though in her view far superior to labour, is still subordinated to the narrow world of matter, objects, 'things'. Having denigrated the body as the locus of mere life, she is not in the least interested in the inextricable relation between the life of the body, the sentience of artefacts, and the life of the mind. Instead, she values only the higher activities of politics (subjects/minds directly encountering each other) and contemplation (a purely mental matter) that, she supposes, are untainted by bodies.

---

64 Lurking behind, and mirrored in, Arendt's *vita contemplativa* (of the 'symposium') and her tripartite division of the *vita activa* is the class-based division of activities in classical Greek society, now ontologised as human conditions.

65 Arendt 1958, p. 155; p. 156.

4.5 A Critique of Philosophical Ontology and a Note on a Historical-Materialist Ontology of (Social) Being

Discontent with what he saw as the lifelessness of traditional philosophy's view of the world and its inhabitants as merely objects of knowledge, Heidegger sought to inject life into philosophy by focusing on how humans 'are' in the world. Although he began with everyday practical life and the process of making from the standpoint of which he glimpsed the 'hidden bodily probelmatic' and about which he developed some valuable insights in passing, he quickly concluded that practical activity, although essential to human being, is inauthentic and thus a distraction to the search for the meaning of human Being. But in turning his back on the practical world and the bodily problematic of really living individuals making things, sustaining their lives while producing human worlds, Heidegger saw in corporeality only its mortality and treated it only as a limit-concept. He thus turned Being-toward-Death into an object of knowledge, into an abstraction that shrouded the concrete, 'practical' meaning of Being-toward-Death for really living individuals. And a complete, that is corporeal understanding of Being-toward-Death would require an understanding of its complement, namely: Being-toward-Life – the kind of Being, that is, that animates human animate form and motivates it to produce the means to satisfy its corporeal needs and wants and to build the worlds that it inhabits

Although Heidegger glimpsed the bodily problematic involved in making, he turned away and instead found meaning by reflecting on and beyond the broken tool. But the tool is other and more than a philosopher's stepping-stone. For those socially condemned to the lower dimensions of Arendt's *vita activa*, to labour and work, the broken tool has lost all meaning. For them the broken tool cannot be abandoned; and their contemplation of it would be guided by the practical necessity of repairing it; of discovering what is wrong with it in order to repair it, to allow it again to serve its purpose – and thereby to restore its meaning. What the philosopher (mis)takes as a stepping-stone on the path to the meaning of Being is, for those whose life's labour is intimately tied to it, the means of their practical activity through which they produce the artefacts that maintain human life and make up human worlds. For those engaged in productive activity, whether 'labour' or 'work', the broken tool must be repaired so that life (both theirs and that of others who benefit from their labours) can be sustained; from their perspective, therefore, there is a taint of mortality about the philosopher's choice to leave the tool lying inert – which is quite literally Being-toward-Death. Thus, Heidegger's superficial complexity puts in relief the profound superficiality of Marx's first condition for history – namely that there be living human beings who sustain their lives by producing the means to satisfy their needs. Humans producing and reproducing the conditions of human being is thus the nature of 'human being', the condition of the human condition.

When considered not as an object of philosophical reflection, but 'up from the body', Being-toward-Death assumes a much different form – a much more real, *because* much more immediate, form. The activity aimed 'merely' at perpetuating life, both 'the labour of our bodies' and 'the work of our hands' is in its very ontological meaning the activity of forestalling death; producing the goods to satisfy needs is, from a historical-materialist viewpoint, obviously a mode of 'Being-towards-Death', of being toward our corporeal mortality. Satisfying needs (indeed, the concept of need itself) is a clear *de facto* recognition that death is the alternative. The production and reproduction of life in the labour that satisfies our needs and in the work that builds our homes and fabricates the worlds in which we 'dwell', in short: a mode of Being-toward-Life, is not just a necessary, but also the only 'authentic' mode of truly Being-toward-Death. Without it, there is not Being-toward-Death – only death, the 'meaning' of which is to cease to be. Whereas the notion of Being-toward-Death exudes all the dramatic elements of a philosophical tragedy, the very real corporeal and all too human tragedy of high occurrences of death among the impoverished (in a world with the technical capacity to end poverty) is all too often treated with all the sensitivity of statistics.

In Heidegger's philosophical ontology, it is 'conscience manifest[ing] itself in the call of care' that eventually forces Dasein to confront its Being-toward-Death and challenges Dasein to behave 'authentically' in accordance with this ontological truth.[66] For a historical-materialist ontology of social being, that voice of care would emanate from corporeality, and it would speak of its needs, desires, and its labours; in this way, it would speak the voice of life and death, not as an object of knowledge, but as corporeal reality. In thus articulating corporeality's knowledge of what it needs to live, to avoid death, and how it can satisfy those needs, that voice would express the tacit corporeal knowledge of Being-toward-Death. 'Authentic' Being-toward-Death, in short, is not an abstract category of a philosophical ontology, but a very real category deriving from human corporeal organisation and entailing both a corporeal logos of needs and wants and the corporeal wherewithal to satisfy those needs and wants through the production of the made-objects that sustain life. And it is this corporeal logos that, as Elaine Scarry puts it, imparts a 'sentience' into artefacts which is completely overlooked in philosophies such as Heidegger's

---

66   Heidegger 1962, p. 322.

and Arendt's. The deciphering of the corporeal logos embedded in 'sentient' artefacts through a corporeal semiotics will be addressed in Part 3. But it is first necessary to address that 'hidden bodily problematic' and determine the particularly human corporeal logos that imparts a particularly human form of sentience into the artefacts it produces.

4.6   Concluding Remarks

Whether in the form of an ultra-constructionist hypostasis of culture, a Marxist historicist approach to human nature, or a philosophically ontological version of human *Dasein*, any approach that treats the body as a *tabula rasa* and/or as a 'simple prerequisite', ends up in a theoretical *cul-de-sac* (noted by Ernst Mayr) that leads to treating human histories as though Darwin never existed, that (in Sheets-Johnstone's words) prevents us 'from taking evolution seriously'.[67] In whatever form, the turning away from the 'bodily problematic' prematurely forecloses potentially rich avenues of historical inquiry. Sheets-Johnstone's simply, but eloquently formulated summary of the failure of 'cultural reductionism', or what I have been calling cultural ultra-constructionism, to take evolution seriously is applicable to any and all approaches that fail to recognise corporeality as the 'first fact' of history:

> [Cultural reductionism] in fact quickens the passing of natural history. It precludes our recognizing that, our individual and great historical-cultural diversities notwithstanding, we humans are basically the same. Though we speak in different tongues, speaking tongues are part of our evolutionary heritage; though we explain the world indifferent ways, explaining the world is part of our evolutionary heritage; though we dance, sing, tell stories, and paint differently, such creations are part of our evolutionary heritage. Similarly, though we eat different foods, we all eat – we all bite, we all chew; though we laugh at different things, we all laugh – we all grin, we all smile. Similarly too, though we all have different hands, different beds for sleeping, different walking gaits, and the like, we all use our hands to make things, we all lie down to sleep, we all walk the earth, and in the same binary patterning of our feet. When we ignore these ties that bind us in a common humanity and that articulate a very human repertoire of 'I can's', we put ourselves out of reach of our own history, insulating

---

67   Sheets-Johnstone 1994, p. 328.

ourselves from corporeal matters of fact and the archetypal forms latent within them. We proportionately distance ourselves from our own human nature.[68]

Any theory, she continues, that fails 'to take the evolutionary body into account', will 'not only ignore the relational ties that that historical process describes and that bind us to certain corporeal acts, dispositions, and possibilities, and to a certain related intercorporeal semantics; they also put us on the edge of an unnatural history. It is as if we humans descended *deus ex machina* not just into the world but into a ready-made culture, a culture that, whatever its nature, can only be the product of an immaculate linguistic conception'.[69] In order to begin to understand cultural forms and the 'roots of thinking' in general, it is, Sheets-Johnstone insists, necessary to begin with that 'natural body' that is 'the product of a natural history' – that is:

> a Darwinian body, a body not just shaped in morphological ways by evolution but shaped semantically – which means kinetically, gesturally, spatially, behaviourally. Because we are all natural bodies in this sense, we ourselves have a history. Our fundamental human habits and beliefs have an evolutionary past ... Fundamental aspects of our humanness cannot be written off as mere cultural inscriptions. They have to do with a history more ancient than we, a history in which the body is precisely not a surface on which any culture can leave its marks – arbitrarily and willy-nilly – but *a three-dimensional living natural form that itself is the source of inscriptions – meanings.* ... [T]his natural form is in fact our original semantic template; it cannot be 'discoursed' out of existence. In a concrete phylogenetic sense, it is a carrier of meanings, an emitter of signs, but the richness and complexity of its intrinsic, ancient semantics cannot be acknowledged until the conception of the body *exclusively* as a surface is recognized as the myopic cultural conception it is, that is, until the surface is seen to be the literal outer skin of a far deeper and denser body, and indeed, in a fundamental sense, to depend upon the inscriptions of that deeper, denser body.[70]

Sheets-Johnstone advocates accordingly a 'corporeal turn' that would allow us 'ultimately to map our pan-culturally invariant corporeal heritage, thereby

---

68   Ibid.
69   Sheets-Johnstone 1994, p. 69.
70   Sheets-Johnstone 1994, pp. 62–3; my emphasis.

coming to know the idiosyncratic ways in which cultures have specifically reworked that heritage – by exaggerating, suppressing, neglecting, or distorting aspects of it'.[71] As she insists, '[o]nly by a concerted turn toward the animate do we have the possibility of elucidating the essentially corporeal terrain on which the relationship of culture to nature – and mind to body – is forged. Clearly, as with the linguistic turn earlier this century, in turning toward the animate, we turn toward something we have long taken for granted, and in so doing give living bodies – animate forms – their living due'. The myopia in the above-discussed approaches lies in their failure to see that bodies *always* matter – and this because, as Wilhelm Reich put it (in a phrase echoing Marx's insistence that corporeal organisation is the first fact of history): 'we don't have bodies, we *are* bodies' – and human bodies are not a *tabula rasa*. Like all other bodies, whether organic or inorganic, human bodies have shape and form, contours and texture, mass, volume, and density. And like all other organic bodies, human bodies have a species-specific set of bodily instruments, capacities and dexterities, needs and limits. The next step to be taken in the following chapter therefore is to take the kind of corporeal turn that will give living bodies their living due – and begin to map the species-specific corporeal organisation of *Homo sapiens*.

[71] Sheets-Johnstone 1999, pp. 357, 353. Following citation, ibid., 357.

CHAPTER 5

Toward a Corporeal Cartography: Methodological Preliminaries

5.1   Introductory

The cartographic project I am proposing is daunting in its anatomical and physiological breadth and evolutionary depth. One means of illustrating that breadth and depth is by way of contrast with the idealist approach to historical anthropology characteristic of Western philosophy from Plato to at least Hegel. The starting point of an idealist mapping of the history of human being is fairly easy to determine.[1] Given its definition of the truly human being as the knowing being, a cartographic undertaking from the standpoint of traditional philosophy need focus only on the mind and thus 'only' go back to the origins of human consciousness – in paleoanthropological terms: to the emergence of the putative knowing human, *Homo sapiens*, some quarter-of-a-million or so years ago. From there, it would then proceed (more or less as did Hegel in his encyclopaedic *Phänomenologie des Geistes* and voluminous *Enzyklopädie*) to trace the steps through which the developing proto-linguistic consciousness of what we now call 'anatomically modern *Homo sapiens*' cleanses itself of all traces of the body and emerges as fully and properly thinking human consciousness capable of preventing 'his' rationality from contamination by the prejudices and superstitions deriving allegedly from the body's instincts, emotions, desires, etc. Were an idealist like Hegel to engage in the kind of anatomical and artefactual questions with which this project is concerned, the only organ of interest would be the brain, and the only artefacts of interest would be those that Hegel called 'objective mind', that is: art, religion, and philosophy.[2]

---

1   Neo-idealist poststructuralists and postmodernists, who focus exclusively on the allegedly arbitrary cultural constructions of bodies and insist that there is no such thing as a 'natural' body, do not consider the question of the evolutionary emergence of the human species at all relevant to the study of human being, beings, and cultures.
2   '*objektiver Geist*'. The usual translation of *Geist* as 'spirit' is in my view rather misleading in implying a non-material subject, a de-theologised deity. 'Mind' is in my view the better translation not only because it does not misleadingly suggest some metaphysical entity, but also because the development of mind, of its progressively successive forms of thought, is the analytical object of the *Phenomenology*.

A historical-materialist cartography, however, does not have the luxury of focusing only on the mind as the properly human organ while dispensing with the body as a 'simple prerequisite' of human being. Because it takes human corporeal organisation as its first fact and redefines the subject as the objectifying corporeal subject, it confronts a much more imposing task. The full scope of a historical-materialist investigation would include all the *Leitfaden des Leibes* linking most, if not all, aspects of human corporeal organisation to the worlds of human material, social, and semiotic artefacts.[3] Such an investigation thus confronts an excessive wealth of legitimate and fascinating candidates for inclusion in a fully-detailed historical-materialist cartography.

The problems created by the evolutionary depth of the project, moreover, are even greater than those resulting from its anatomical breadth. Although a historical-materialist cartography is in principle concerned, like its philosophical counterpart, with the species classified as 'anatomically modern *Homo sapiens*', its starting point cannot be so clearly demarcated nor dated so recently. The complexity arises precisely because we are, as Maxine Sheets-Johnstone put it, 'Darwinian bodies', 'products of natural history'. And Ernst Mayr is by no means the only biologist who, in Philip Lieberman's words, 'has pointed out time and again that the structure and physiology of any living organism necessarily reflects its evolutionary history'.[4] Precisely because many of the key attributes of human corporeality originated in various of our proto-human predecessors and some too in our distant and definitively non-human ancestors, a historical-materialist cartography must reach much deeper into the evolutionary past.

To introduce a different set of terms in order to indicate the two dimensions of depth of this cartographical project: it is both, and must integrate, an archaeological and a genealogical investigation of human corporeal organisation. Its primary concern is with an 'archaeological' investigation of the corporeal depths of human being and history. However, because of the pre- and proto-human origins of what have become peculiarly human aspects of our corporeal organisation, this mapping must also delve into its genealogical depth far back beyond the emergence of hominids. Even if limited only to tracing that genealogy (that is, without attempting to explain the evolutionary causes), the vast dimensions of human corporeal organisation make for an impossibly vast cartographic undertaking. For it to be at all effectual, it will be necessary to make a number of choices: to find historical-materialist principles to guide the inquiry;

---

3 On Nietzsche's notion of '*Leitfaden des Leibes*', see Introduction, note 38.
4 Lieberman 1991, p. 11.

to construct a conceptual apparatus to organise the material; and to fashion a logic or mode of presentation with principles of selection and narrative that make it coherent, efficacious and, I would hope, readable and interesting. Making such choices will require too reflection on their consequences for the place and value, the methodological place-value, of the resulting map. This chapter therefore will be devoted to devising methodological solutions to these dilemmas of scope, content, and organisation and to considering the consequences of those choices.

Finally, a word (as Marx put it) to avoid possible misunderstandings. My focus in the following two chapters on human 'uniqueness' might well provoke accusations of 'anthropocentrism'. If I hesitate to acknowledge 'anthropocentrism', it is because of the term's acquired connotations. But I would admit to 'anthropocentrism' if, *and only if*, understood in the specific and limited sense that I use it here – a sense almost diametrically opposed to that which is meant by the usually epithetic use of the term.

I proceed on what should be the tautological assumption that each and every species is, by corporeal definition, not only unique, but also and necessarily 'species-centric'. 'Species-centrism' results from the fact that each animal species 'has' the world in a unique and particular manner; each species 'has' a world that appears to it from, and as mediated through, the unique and particular viewpoint and perspective afforded it, and limited by, its unique and particular species-specific corporeal organisation. The ways in which the members of each species navigate, apprehend, comprehend, dwell in, and procure nourishment from, the world, the ways in which members of each species communicate with conspecifics, and modify the world in the ongoing process of satisfying their bodily needs and desires, all depend on, and are fashioned by, the range of the capacities of the locomotive, sensory, cognitive, and communicative organs embedded in the anatomy and physiology that constitute its unique corporeal organisation. From the corporeal perspective developed here, in short: species-uniqueness and species-centrism are corporeal facts. Human animals cannot be any more or less 'anthropocentric' than spiders can be anything other than 'arachnocentric'. Yet although each species is the centre of *its* world, each has, because of the limitations embedded in its corporeal organisation, a necessarily particular take on, a necessarily limited or 'decentred' view of, the world. Defined in this way, 'anthropocentrism' does not elevate *Homo sapiens* above, but rather situates it as one among, all other, decentred species-centric animals.

If I focus here on the uniqueness of human corporeal organisation, it is for the simple reason that this is a book about the histories made by the human animal. However, this focus on one particular species does not preclude recognition that each and every animal species has its own unique corporeal organisation and its own unique modes of material, social, and semiotic objectification; nor does it preclude recognition of the fact that all species, albeit in degrees varying according to their corporeal capacities and limits, use their bodily instruments to re-make the environment in the process of building their niches, their worlds. For that reason, a corporeal cartography of the uniqueness of the human animal, such as the one I undertake here, could be done to portray the uniqueness of any animal species. Were I attempting (as an animal ethologist might) to write the histories made by any other species, whether fish or fowl, whether frogs, hogs, or dogs, I would proceed in the same manner: I would begin by mapping the unique corporeal organisation and the behaviour possibilities and patterns of the species under analysis – which of course is nothing more than elaborating what it is that makes a species a species. This obvious but overlooked tautology that each species is in a class by itself is acknowledged in the modest simplicity of the (redundant) title that anthropologist Robert Foley gave to his book on human evolution: *Another Unique Species*.

My interest here, therefore, is not to indulge in what is generally considered the 'anthropocentric' conceit of differentiating the 'human' from the 'animal'. It is rather to inquire first into the particular, and peculiarly anthropomorphic corporeal foundations of the human animal, and then into the particular worlds that it 'anthropocentrically' builds. And if a decentred species-centrism is an inescapable, corporeally-determined fact of all animal life, then it might be worth concocting the somewhat awkward, but not inappropriate term 'anthropo*ego*centrism' or 'anthropohubrism' to signify the self-centred presumptuousness and imperious pride commonly associated with 'anthropocentrism'.

5.2   Historical-Materialist Principles and Corporeal Categories

Other than his very brief comments on human needs, Marx barely indicated, and never systematically elaborated, what he meant by 'human corporeal organisation' – leaving perhaps the impression that he too treated the body solely as the locus of needs or as only a 'simple prerequisite'. I argue, however, that a systematic and foundational corporeal logic is present behind the numerous passages on human corporeal organisation scattered throughout his writings. In *Capital*, for example, corporeally based categories such as use-value and concrete labour were crucial to his deciphering of the logic of capitalist exploitation; and throughout the long chapters on the production of absolute and relative surplus value, he measured the degree of workplace-produced immiseration in terms of the deformation of the body, the flip-side of which is that the free cultivation of bodily attributes and capacities is essential to any historical-materialist notion of freedom.[5] Although (and also because) Marx never systematically elaborated the very corporeal foundations of human being in which he rooted his critique of capitalism, it is a task well worth undertaking.

To ensure that this mapping follows Marx's corporeal turn and proceeds along a historical-materialist path, it is first necessary to fashion an appropriately historical-materialist conceptual apparatus. The construction of this set of categories must itself be guided by historical-materialist principles. The most general and foundational historical-materialist principle that could best serve as the guiding thread to such a taxonomic endeavour is Marx's oft-repeated aphorism about human beings and their histories, namely that 'people make their own history, but not always as they please'. Marx generally intended this aphorism to refer to socially-determined capacities of people to make their own history and to social limits and constraints on people doing so as they please. But underneath the changing social capacities (e.g. the specific character of technology) lies the foundational set of species-specific corporeal capabilities that establishes the possibilities for humans to make their own histories; and beyond the changing limits of inherited socio-cultural conditions, it is the set of corporeal constraints, the needs and limits embedded in human corporeal organisation, that prevents humans from making their histories as they please, that imposes limits on human malleability and on the variability of human cultures. A map constructed according to this principle, that provides a delineation of species-wide human corporeal organisation depicting *both* the capacities *and* the constraints embedded in human corporeal organisation, would thus establish the range, the infinite but not unlimited possibilities, of all too human worlds.

If this aphorism about people making their own history though not as they please, provides the fundamental principle and general direction, the next step is to determine what aspects of human corporeal organisation are most pertinent to historical-materialist cartography. The desideratum of such an undertaking would be a map of the entirety of human corporeal organisation; and given world enough and time, it would include narrative chartings of anatomy and physiology of each and every corporeal attribute in relation to the (culturally diverse) constructions derived from and the (culturally diverse) mean-

---

5 These claims about the corporeal roots of Marx's categories in *Capital* are elaborated in Chapters 13 and 14.

ings invested in it. A fascinating charting of the spleen or bile, for example, in relation to its metaphorical usages and extensions in everyday speech or in Baudelaire's poetry is easily imaginable. Although the charting of every corporeal attribute should be included in this mapping, here choices must be made – and not just for reasons of space but, more importantly, for reasons of organisation and coherence that are directly related to the matter of differentiating a historical-materialist cartography from a textbook in anatomy or physiology.

What is unique about the specifically historical-materialist path toward the body, and what therefore provides the criteria for determining the more important corporeal attributes for inclusion in what must perforce be a rather abbreviated sketch, is that it is aimed at explaining the corporeal foundations of human history-making. As elaborated in detail in Chapter 1, the fundamental historical-materialist concept denoting human history-making is the concept of objectification [*Vergegenständlichung*]. As the dialectical category depicting the interaction of subjects with the world, both natural and social, objectification refers to the ways in which humans (or any species for that matter) living in distinct social groups work over, rework, remake, and transform the given (the 'natural' as well as the pre-existing socio-cultural) into human worlds made (as I shall argue here) in their own corporeal image.[6] Although the instances of objectification are many and varied, they can effectively be subsumed under the three modes of objectification elaborated in Chapter 2, namely: material, semiotic, and social objectification that collectively result in the production of human worlds consisting of material, semiotic, and social artefacts. As its contents, therefore, a historical-materialist mapping of human corporeal organisation would include those corporeal aspects most pertinent to these three modes of objectification and the production of these three kinds of artefacts.

Although the principles and criteria thus far established delineate the field somewhat, it remains rather undefined topographically. The next step in giving historical-materialist definition to the corporeal landscape is the development of a properly historical-materialist conceptual apparatus, of the set of categories to be used in demarcating and arranging the material. To develop this conceptual apparatus, we might begin by considering a term that appears irregularly in Marx's works, but always in the context of defining the general attributes of human being – which makes it a promising candidate to assist both

---

6 Interpreting 'The Organism as Subject and Object of Evolution', Levins and Lewontin (1985, pp. 85–106) insist that all species are capable of objectification; for, whether instinctually or intentionally, all species create their own environments, their so-called 'niches' by transforming what is naturally given into worlds made in the image of their own needs and capacities (e.g. beaver dams, spider webs, beehives, etc.).

in demarcating the corporeal landscape as seen from a historical-materialist standpoint and in bringing categorial order to the cartographic undertaking. This term, *Anlage*, generally refers to a 'facility', 'arrangement', 'installation', or 'disposition'.[7] For my purposes appropriately, it also carries a specific biological application meaning the 'natural tendency' or, in the plural *Anlagen*, the 'hereditary factors' that predispose an organism to act in certain ways. Given this definition *Anlagen* may serve as the generic category for the 'predispositions' inherent in human corporeal organisation and thus as the ordering principle for a historical-materialist mapping of *Homo sapiens*.

As the generic category encompassing all attributes of human corporeal organisation, *Anlagen* must be subdivided into sets of subcategories that can cover the range of Marx's references to the body and also include dimensions of human corporeal organisation that he did not address, but that nevertheless belong to a historical-materialist map of *Homo sapiens*. If the guiding thread of a materialist conception of history is that people make their own history, but not as they please, then, the two major categorial subdivisions of *Anlagen* or corporeal dispositions would accordingly have to be the *capabilities* and *constraints* embedded in human corporeal organisation, that is: the corporeal capabilities that enable people to make their own history, and the corporeal constraints that prevent them from doing so as they please.[8]

Surveying Marx's scattered comments about corporeal capabilities, we find the following: In the *1844 Manuscripts* he devoted some of his most powerful prose in praise of the human capacity to apprehend the world sensually through employment of what Marx called the theoretical powers of the senses, or what J.J. Gibson would later call the body's 'perceptual systems'.[9] Discussing the bodily prerequisites of labour in the *Grundrisse*, he wrote: 'No production

---

7   Perry Anderson calls attention to a passage in the *Grundrisse* in which Marx wrote of 'needs, capacities, wants, and productive powers of individuals' [*Bedürfnisse, Fähigkeiten, Genüsse, Produktivekräfte etc. der Individuen*] and then uses the term 'creative dispositions' [*schöpferische Anlagen*]. From this passage it would appear that Marx used the term *Anlagen* to refer to those attributes that enable humans to make their own history, and that limiting factors are not to be considered *Anlagen*. I shall argue, however, that those limiting factors (needs, wants, bodily limits and constraints) should be considered *Anlagen* since they also 'predispose' humans to find food, shelter, satisfy desires, take care not to overstep bodily limits that would result in death, etc. See Marx 1857, p. 387; Anderson (1988).
8   This focus here on the corporeal capabilities and constraints that are attributes of *Homo sapiens* does not, of course, preclude recognition that their functioning is always socio-historically mediated; and establishing the modes of mediation is essential to the concrete analysis of any specific socio-cultural form.
9   See Marx 1844 in Tucker 1978, pp. 86–92; and J.J. Gibson 1966.

[is] possible without an *instrument* of production, even if it is only the hand. No production without stored-up, past labour, even if it is only the *dexterity* gathered together and concentrated in the hand of the primitive through repeated practice'.[10] In *Capital*, when discussing the labour-process in general, he spoke of labour as an embodied process and about embodied instruments of labour. In the labour-process humans set in motion 'the natural *powers* belonging to [their] embodiment', and all labour involves the labourer's use of a means of labour, the most original (in the temporal sense) and the most immediate (in the spatial sense) of which were the labourer's own '*bodily organs*'. Echoing Marx's reference to the hand, Engels, in his essay on 'The Role of Labour in the Humanisation of the Ape',[11] pointed to bipedality as the decisive step in human evolution since its result was that 'the hand had become free and was able constantly to develop new *dexterities*' – the hand therefore is 'not only the organ of labour, it is also its product'. Engels, like Marx (in this case, Groucho) and not afraid of risking a bad pun, concluded that the development of the sense organs and the production of cultural artefacts went 'hand in hand' with the development of the hand through labour: 'through the constantly renewed application of this hereditary refinement [of the hand] to new, increasingly complicated tasks, the human hand attained that high degree of perfection on the basis of which it could conjure forth the paintings of Raphael, the statues of Thorvaldsen, the music of Paganini'.

From these passages we can glean two subdivisions within the set of bodily attributes enabling humans to make their own histories. The references to the hand and other bodily organs as instruments of labour may be subsumed under the category of 'bodily instruments'.[12] In addition to the human hand whose opposable thumb, flexible digits, and prehensile grasp were so appreciated by Marx and Engels, the most obvious of these bodily instruments are the human perceptual systems, the flexible human supra-laryngeal tract which is the absolute prerequisite for all human languages, and of course the human brain. Here it is worth reiterating the crucial point that from a historical-materialist viewpoint, *Homo sapiens* is a mindful body, rather than, as is so current today, an embodied mind; while the latter treats the body only as a site for thinking, the former situates the mind where it belongs: in the brain, perhaps the most for-

---

10   Marx 1857 in Tucker 1978, p. 7. All words in *italics* in this paragraph are my emphasis.
11   Engels in *Marx-Engels Werke* Vol. 20, pp. 445–7.
12   This term is John McMurtry's (1978, p. 34). Though Marx may not have used the exact term 'körperliche Instrumente' (I know of no such precise usage), McMurtry is surely justified in using the term 'bodily instruments' to refer collectively to Marx's scattered references to the body's tools.

midable, but nevertheless only one of the many indispensable, interdependent, and uniquely human, bodily instruments.[13]

The obviously unique capacity of the human mind (on our planet, at least) for making (and breaking) worlds obscures another point that should be so obvious as to verge on the banal were it not occluded by a narrow-sighted focus on the mind, namely: the mind alone cannot even exist let alone carry out its projects; the mind is embedded in a body itself endowed with certain instruments, capacities, dexterities, etc. that enable it to realise its mental projections as objects, as artefacts in the world. As noted above in the Introduction, the aptness of Norman Geras's quip, 'no fish could be Mozart' is not just because of the size of a fish's brain, but also because it takes human hands to play a piano, to write sonatas and symphonies – the same point Gramsci made in response to his son's musing about what life would be like if human brains were as big as those of elephants by asking: what good would a larger brain be without hands?[14] Whereas Anaxagoras explained in a good materialist, corporeal manner that humans are the most clever of creatures because of the uniqueness of human hands, Aristotle, the good idealist, imagined that he had refuted Anaxagoras's materialism with his inverse and evolutionarily dubious teleological explanation that: 'man has hands because he is the most clever being. For the hands are a tool, and nature, like a clever man, distributes each thing to him who understands how to use it'.

These uniquely human bodily instruments are deployed in an astonishing variety of ways, giving rise to what Marx called bodily 'dexterities' (which, of course, change according to socio-cultural form, though not always in a

---

13 My reasons for using 'mindful body' will be elaborated in Chapter 7. The positivist Marxist theory of consciousness, the economically reductionist, mirror theory of mind, was developed primarily by Second International Marxists in the late nineteenth century and perpetuated by Third International Marxists of the twentieth. This mirror theory was a great gift to critics of historical materialism who cling to it as an excuse not to take Marx seriously. Though my claim for the primacy of human corporeal organisation can easily be misread as fitting into that reductionist tradition, a corporeal emphasis does not require a mirror theory of consciousness. Though Marx's aphorism that 'consciousness [*das Bewußtsein*] can never be anything else but conscious existence [*das bewußte Sein*]' (Tucker 1978, p. 154) can be read in a reductionist manner, it should be understood more modestly, meaning simply that human beings are thinking bodies, integrated structures, all elements of which, and not just the mind alone, are indispensable to human being, and that the specific forms and contents of consciousness of 'really living individuals' are inevitably related to the very embodied existence of those real individuals living at specific historical moments and in specific socio-cultural forms.

14 Geras 1983, p. 109. Gramsci, 1973, p. 271. Following citation of Anaxagoras and Aristotle in Katz 1989, p. 253.

progressive manner – as evidenced by his graphic descriptions in *Capital* of the atrophy of so many corporeal dexterities effected by the capitalist labour-process). Arguably the most consequential dexterity in human evolution is bipedality which freed the hands for, and therewith the mouth from, carrying – thus opening the possibility of the development of speech organs capable of producing an extraordinary range of the nuanced sounds, of those 'mouthy little noises we call words'.[15] This is but one corporeal example of the species-specific particularity of *Homo sapiens*: the extraordinary flexibility of bodily instruments that enables humans to develop an even more far-ranging set of dexterities; and these, in turn, give human production that 'universal' – i.e. adaptable and diverse – character that Marx in the *Manuscripts* contrasted to the one-dimensional, instinctual production of other species.[16] These bodily instruments and the corporeal dexterities grounded in them enable humans to produce the means necessary to break out of a narrow ecological niche of the kind inhabited by other species and to adapt to the most varied of niches from desert to polar regions and to create artificial instruments that allow us to develop the capacities embodied in other species such as moving through the air, on and under the water, for digging underground passages, building dams, etc. Few (if any) other species in the animal kingdom have made themselves at home almost everywhere under the sun, in so many and such diverse ecological 'niches' ranging from polar ice to desert sand – and everywhere in between.

Though the possibilities opened up by human bodily instruments may seem infinite in contrast to other species, they are by no means unlimited. Beyond the changing limits of inherited socio-cultural conditions, it is the set of constraints, the needs and limits embedded in human corporeal organisation, that ultimately prevents humans from making history as they please, that imposes limits on the infinite variability of human cultures and on human malleability. The corporeal constraints that most preoccupied Marx are systems of bodily needs whose satisfaction is the absolute precondition of human existence and which provide the impetus and telos of production. In this regard it is, as Agnes Heller argues, useful (though, as I shall soon argue, insufficient) to characterise the biological or, as she calls them, the 'natural needs' of *Homo sapiens* as 'not a group of needs but a limit concept: a limit beyond which human life is no longer reproducible as such, beyond which the limit of bare existence is passed'.[17]

This 'limit of bare existence' of course, corresponds to Marx's insistence that we take seriously the seemingly obvious fact that human beings must first be

---

15   Langer 1974, p. 61.
16   Marx 1844, in Tucker 1978, p. 76.
17   Heller 1976, p. 32.

able to live in order to be able to 'make history'; and it points specifically to the physiological imperative for the daily survival and reproduction of the body. When Marx referred to these needs as 'eating and drinking, as habitation, clothing and many other things', these are shorthand forms of saying that the body needs a certain amount of nutrition to reproduce its cells, a certain amount of liquid to prevent dehydration, a certain amount (variable according to climatic conditions) of clothing and shelter to maintain its temperature within a fairly narrow range.[18] Under 'still much else' we might include the equally obvious bodily needs for a certain amount of oxygen, rest and sleep, no doubt too for a certain amount of exercise. Looked at in this way, the set of bodily needs surely does represent quite literally a vital 'limit concept', the limits of human being.

Every species has its 'limit concept' – and humans are no exceptions. For each species, of course, the contents of, and the range covered by, that limit concept varies. And the peculiarly human limits emerge when we begin to define those contents and delineate those ranges: how many calories, what kind of vitamins and minerals, what range of body temperature, how much rest and sleep (and when)? While the elasticity of physiological adaptation (to, for example, the reduced oxygen levels at high altitudes) necessarily results in a degree of fuzziness at the borders which makes it impossible to define those limits with quantitative precision, we can determine with certainty the qualitative biological needs whose satisfaction is an absolute prerequisite of human existence.

Despite countless universalist accusations to the contrary, Marx endlessly insisted that human biological needs are always satisfied in socio-culturally specific ways. Were it not for the all too common ultra-constructionist insistence that there is no 'natural' body and therefore that the only relevant analytical aspect is the culturally specific mode of satisfying bodily needs, it would be platitudinous to state the obvious point, namely: the fact that needs are always satisfied in socio-culturally specific ways does *not* abrogate the biological character of those needs. Accordingly, we might speak of biological needs and their socio-cultural mediation or refraction: the biological needs providing the limit concept for our taxonomic sketch of *Homo sapiens*, and the category of socio-cultural mediation or refraction pointing to both the necessarily abstract character of the map and therewith to the absolute necessity for historical-materialist analysis of the culturally specific ways of satisfying biological needs.[19]

---

18   Marx 1845, in Tucker 1978, p. 156.
19   These socio-culturally mediated needs are themselves supplemented by socio-cultural

In order to complete the inventory of corporeal constraints, it is necessary to supplement the category of needs with two related categories. These are bodily limits and constraints: limits such as those of the human sense organs or, most definitively, human mortality; constraints such as human terrestriality and diurnality or those resulting from needs (e.g. the need for oxygen which makes it impossible to live without artificial support above certain altitudinal limits or underwater). However, those corporeal factors that prevent us from making our history as we please – that which we lack and which we need, want, or desire, that which constrains and even limits our capacities – should not be understood exclusively in negative terms as merely passive limits. First of all, constraints and limits give definition and form to an organism that would otherwise be the living contradiction of a shapeless form. Constraints and limits force the organism to focus its energies, to direct them in relation to its predispositions or *Anlagen*, to exercise and develop the capacities and dexterities that it does have.[20] And although Heller is right to see corporeal needs, limits, and constraints as 'limit concepts' that establish the boundaries of human being, they also present challenges that provoke the production of artefacts ranging from material goods to symbolic forms. It is the very elasticity of, and the creative capacities embedded in, our universal human corporeal organisation that can turn bodily limits into socio-cultural opportunities that lead to the creation of a great variety of human worlds. As Marx noted in his double definition of the prerequisite of human existence, the 'first historical act' consists of satisfying needs and producing the means to satisfy those needs. As alluded

---

        determined wants and desires whose pertinence to the body is not always immediate. At the level of abstraction involved in this historical-materialist mapping, it is not (yet) necessary to discuss the content of those socio-culturally refined needs nor of those socio-culturally determined wants and desires. But it is necessary to recognise the complex of, and the range of possible relations between, needs and wants and desires. On the one hand, post-modern cultural studies are right to point out that the cultural determination of what properly satisfies, say, hunger and of what is considered too disgusting to eat can result in a situation that a starving person in need of food will not eat some form of nourishment because of cultural taboos. We may admire the power of culture to elevate mind over body, but we should not forget that rejection of food because of cultural taboos might well ultimately lead to the pyrrhic victory of the body over mind, namely: death. The tasks of determining the forms of socio-cultural mediation of biological needs that produce socio-culturally specific wants and desires falls to concrete historical-materialist analysis of specific socio-cultural forms. Here, however, it suffices to establish the nuanced range of sub-categories (biological needs, socio-culturally refined needs, socio-culturally determined wants and desires) that fall under the general heading of corporeal constraints. On needs and wants, see Archibald (1989, pp. 83–97) and Márkus (1978, pp. 9–12).

20   Stephen Jay Gould makes this point in two essays (1980, 1994) that focus specifically on the significance of limits and constraints for evolutionary direction.

to above, the far-ranging capabilities made possible by our bodily instruments and corporeal dexterities enable us to turn natural constraints into limits to be overcome, problems to be solved, by human artifice – by building airplanes or oxygen canisters to overcome our terrestrial limits, by developing means of artificial lighting to compensate for our diurnality, etc.

Moreover, our bodily limits such as mortality, terrestriality, diurnality, etc. also provide us with food for thought, that is: the material of cultural forms which humans living in different socio-cultural contexts transform into a corporeally consistent variety of metaphors, symbolic forms and other semiotic artefacts. One need only think of the corporeally-based unitary logic underlying the various culturally-specific symbolic meanings attached to natural phenomena: how our terrestrial constraints provide the underlying logic beneath the culturally varied meanings attached to the sky and sea; how our diurnal constraints provide the logic underlying culturally varied meanings attached to night and day, to the sun and moon; how the limit of our corporeal lives, our death, underlies the variety of meanings attached to mortality and immortality.

Or consider the important cultural usages of temporary disruptions of our corporeal equilibrium. As Andre Leroi-Gourhan notes, 'if we bear in mind that in all cultures many unusual motor or verbal phenomena occur as a result of individuals being "transported" to a mental state other than their normal one, we must acknowledge that disturbances of the rhythmic balance do play an important role'.[21] Leroi-Gourhan gives examples of disruption of the visceral sensibility such as fasting, sexual abstinence, and prolonged periods without sleep. To these can easily be added several other examples of rituals and practices that pray or play on the disruption of vestibular sensibility. From the aesthetic-religious sublime of Balinese trance dancers and Sufi whirling dervishes to the banal but thrilling sensory overload of riding a roller coaster, not to mention the use of substances that alter the mind's chemistry, whether for insight, thrills or both – all of these, and many other, cultural practices consciously exploit the distortion of vestibular sensitivity for a brief walk on the unbalanced side. But it is precisely the abnormality, the transitoriness, that is the seduction – and the return to normalcy quite literally the salvation. We simply could not live (long) with permanent disruption of vestibular sensitivity – or if our bodies were so constituted that we could live in such a state, we would be different beings with vastly different cultural forms. These rather basic examples clearly indicate that although cultural forms are certainly relative, they are not arbitrary; they are inextricably linked to human corporeal

---

21 See Leroi-Gourhan 1993, p. 284.

organisation and mediated through social practice. In this way the body may be seen as the interior structure of semiotic artefacts as well.

At this point, the construction of the categorial framework for a historical-materialist mapping is complete. It begins with the generic category of *Anlagen* denoting the general predispositions embedded in human corporeal organisation. It then moves to the two sub-categories that together establish the range of those corporeal predispositions: one delineating those aspects of human corporeal organisation that allow us to make our own history – the bodily instruments, capacities, and dexterities that enable us to produce a perhaps infinite, but certainly not unlimited variety of human worlds consisting of material, semiotic, and social artefacts; and the other delineating those bodily attributes that prevent us from making our history as we please – bodily needs, (socio-culturally mediated) wants and desires, and bodily limits and constraints which themselves could be transformed into challenges that humans solve through the production of artifice.[22]

Anlagen
(Corporeal Predispositions)

Corporeal Capacities:	Corporeal Constraints:
Bodily Instruments	Biological Needs
Corporeal Dexterities	Corporeal Limits

Having constructed the framework for this mapping, the next question is: What is its methodological place value? That is: what can it do? What can it not do? How should it be used?

---

22   Through her corporeal reading of Husserl's notions of 'I-cans', Maxine Sheets-Johnstone has constructed a complementary vocabulary that, when supplemented by historical-materialist categories in the same vein, is helpful here. She reformulates the term as 'bodily I-cans' that enable, and fundamentally in-form our knowledge of the world gained through touch and movement – to which I would add that these 'bodily I-cans' in-form, as their interior structure, the artefacts we produce. To adopt this term for my project would require the addition of a few related categories. The needs (food, sleep, warmth) and limits (terrestriality, diurnality, mortality) embedded in corporeal organisation require us to consider (what for the sake of categorial symmetry I would call) 'bodily I needs' (themselves the locus of desires or 'bodily I wants') and 'bodily I cannots' – which taken together establish the range, the extent and limits, of possible cultural forms. See Sheets-Johnstone 1998, pp. 70–1. This issue is addressed further in Chapter 7 below.

5.3 The Methodological Place-Value of a Historical-Materialist Cartography of Human Corporeal Organisation

Perhaps the most serious of the potential dangers and abuses of Marx's 'breathtaking' historical-materialist wager to write history 'up from the body' is the risk of universalising a particularist definition of 'the body' and illegitimately imposing it on all bodies. The means to avoid this risk lies in a proper understanding of the use and limitations of historical-materialist abstraction. It is therefore absolutely crucial to define very carefully the capacities and limits, that is: the methodological place-value, of what will very intentionally be a very abstract mapping of human corporeal organisation.

The question of the methodological place-value of necessary abstractions was discussed in Chapter 3 as part of the elaboration of the methodology of a historical-materialist *Wissenschaft*. There, based on the work of Reichelt and Psychopedis, I argued that *Capital* was an 'abstract presentation of the essential' logic of the capitalist mode of production, a presentation of capital 'insofar as it corresponded to its [necessarily abstract] concept'. And I argued that in order to present the general logic of the capitalist mode of production and of its valorisation and exploitation process, Marx was obliged to abstract from really-existing capitalist societies in their historical, national, and cultural specificities, and from really-existing individuals whom he consciously, yet temporarily, treated as bearers of economic categories.

In like manner, and in order to construct the categorial framework for a historical-materialist mapping of human corporeal organisation, it is necessary here to abstract from commensurate kinds of corporeal specificities, from phenotypic differences in human corporeal form and from the diversity of cultural constructions of the body. The methodological purpose of these abstractions is to determine what it is that defines the species-specific possibilities and limits of human being, that establishes the infinite possibilities and ultimate limits of the diversity of cultural forms and human histories. *Capital* is not a depiction of any existing capitalist society, nor will this map be a depiction of any existing human body. Both are conscious abstractions necessary for certain purposes, but necessarily insufficient for others.

In this regard, it is essential to recall Marx's warning in *The German Ideology* against confusing an abstraction with reality and imposing the former on the latter. There, while developing the overall framework of his materialist conception of history, he delineated in no uncertain terms the methodological place-value of the 'general results, abstractions which [arose] from [his] observation of the historical development of people': such abstractions, 'viewed apart from real history [...] have *no value whatsoever*. They can only serve to facilitate the arrangement of historical material, to indicate the sequence of its separate strata. But they by no means afford a recipe or schema, as does philosophy, for neatly trimming the epochs of history [my emphasis]'.[23] And later, in the Introduction to the *Critique of Political Economy*, he referred to such abstractions as the 'guiding threads' of his study. Similarly, a historical-materialist map understood as an abstract presentation of human corporeal organisation can provide a direction and the guiding threads for historical-materialist research and analysis; it can, among other things, lead us to consider the bodily dimensions of human history and sensitise us to the corporeal roots of cultural forms. But only by acknowledging its abstract character and obeying the methodological imperative to move from an abstract mapping of the essential to the analysis of 'real history' consisting of real bodies can we avoid the deterministic and reductionist consequences of confusing the abstraction with reality and imposing it as an *a priori* recipe or schema on real bodies in their concrete cultural specificity.

At this point, I must run the risk that a brief comment on crucial and complex topics may be a greater injustice than no mention at all, and confront the greatest danger facing such an attempt to map human corporeal organisation, namely: the risk of occluding crucial issues of race and gender and disabilities. That risk notwithstanding, I will venture two comments on these issues precisely because a delineation of the relation between an abstract mapping of human corporeal organisation and the multiplicity of really-existing racialised and gendered bodies helps to establish the limits of such a map – and therewith its value within its proper limits. As I have argued throughout, the reason for talking in the singular about human corporeal organisation as the object of a historical-materialist map is to define what it is about members of the species *Homo sapiens* that not only allows them to make their own histories, but that also delineates the corporeal possibilities and limits of the histories they can make, and differentiates the diverse but all uniquely human histories from those of all other species. As should be obvious, the same set of culture-creating corporeal instruments, capacities and dexterities (human hands, a human brain, human perceptual systems, a human supra-laryngeal tract) is common to all races and sexes. This is why any visitor to a zoo can, without knowing their sex or race, differentiate human beings from other species. And this is why it is possible to speak generically (that is: abstractly) of a species-specific human corporeal organisation recognisable regardless of sex and race – a 'species-being' [*Gattungswesen*] as Marx put it in the *1844 Manuscripts*.

---

23   Marx, 1845 in Tucker 1978, p. 155. Following reference to 'guiding threads' from Marx 1859 in Tucker 1978, p. 4.

This is not to suggest that there is one human body that could be described in concrete detail and taken to represent all human bodies. A single detailed portrait, anything more than a silhouette, of 'the human body' is obviously rendered impossible by the kind of phenotypic differences that have come to be designated as 'racial' and 'sexual', and by those who are blind, deaf, mute, or bearing some other quantitatively atypical corporeal attribute.[24] But at this level of analysis the concern is with the species typical attributes that enable human beings to produce the diverse yet all too human worlds that they do – the genotypical body whose phenotypic diversity all too often serves as the source of discriminatory and oppressive cultural evaluations that are enforced by the discriminatory use of social power. Those matters are crucial to any analysis of a given socio-cultural form in its historical specificity. But at this still very abstract (but necessary) level, the key task is establishing, in abstract form, the species-specific attributes of human beings and differentiating human corporeal organisation from that of other species.

The kinds of histories that different groups of humans make will of course vary according to social form and technology, demographic composition, geo-ecological environment, the legacy of the group's own past, and the particular kind of cultural forms it develops. In the production of those cultural forms, sexual dimorphism and phenotypic differences, real or imagined, such as skin colour can become objects of socio-cultural mediation in the construction of socially efficacious symbolic forms.[25] Though race is a cultural construct, if all

---

24   Lest there be misunderstanding, I mean atypical only in a quantitative sense. If any such attribute (e.g. blindness) were a quantitatively typical trait of the majority of our species, all human cultural forms would obviously be radically different. Specific cultural evaluations of such atypical traits, what kinds of meanings are invested in them, is a crucial question; but it is, at this stage of the analysis, a premature question.

25   An anonymous reviewer of the essay in which I originally made these comments (Fracchia 2005a) insisted that 'it is a mistake to suggest ... that such [phenotypic] differences are just out there waiting to be socially mediated' into racial constructions. Noting pseudo-scientific attempts in England and the US to differentiate the Irish as a distinct race on the basis of 'alleged differences in brain size, morality, religion and level of "civilization"', this reviewer rightly points out that classifications of race have also been constructed on the basis of *imagined* phenotypic differences. Two points here. One is that while I don't doubt that imagined phenotypic differences have been the source of racist taxonomies, I think the more common case is the construction of such taxonomies on the basis of real phenotypic differences, most obviously skin colour. And there is a sense in which the racist construction of the Irish as a distinct race can be explained (which is *not* to say justified). If we consider the Greek word for nation, εθνος, that refers both to the common family heritage, the ethnicity, of a group and also to that group's socio-political organisation, it is not difficult to see how such imagined racial differentiations could be constructed on the basis of 'nationality'.

human beings had identical phenotypic attributes, were of the same colour and had the same physiognomy, there would be no foundation for its construction. Though gender is a cultural construct, if humans were, like some species, asexual and asexually reproducing creatures, there would be no foundation for its construction. The problem lies not in the recognition of physiological differences, but in the issuance of hierarchical verdicts on their significance that both produce and support exploitation, oppression, and discrimination. The particular content of those semiotic forms cannot be predicted by any general theory. But it can be analysed in a historical-materialist manner and understood as the particular product of people living within a specific set of social relations inscribing particular meanings onto what are constructed as racialised or gendered bodies. This abstract mapping must recognise its limits in order to avoid the deterministic and reductionist confusion of the abstraction with reality and imposing it as an *a priori* recipe or schema on real bodies in their concrete gender, racial/ethnic, and cultural specificities. But if those limits are honoured, the concern with human corporeal organisation might serve to remind us that although gender, racial, and ethnic categories are certainly culturally constructed, they are not randomly arbitrary. Real people with specific physiognomic attributes are made to suffer for them. And we can only make sense of those distinctions by seeing them as cultural impositions, motivated by perceivable (but not species-defining) physical differences among really-existing bodies.

As a final aid in determining the methodological place-value of this cartographic undertaking, I enlist Franco Moretti whose *Graphs Maps Trees* inspired my choice of a 'map' as the metaphorically appropriate term for my abstract presentation of the foundational attributes of human corporeal organisation. In his meditations on the value and limits of the 'literary maps' he constructed to aid his investigations, Moretti responds to his own question of what such maps can do:

> First, they are a good way to prepare a text for analysis. You choose a unit – walks, lawsuits, luxury goods, whatever – find its occurrences, place them in space ... or in other words: you *reduce* the text to a few elements and *abstract* them from the narrative flow, and construct a new, *artificial* object ... And with a little luck, these maps will be *more than the sum of their parts*: they will possess 'emerging' qualities, which were not visible at the lower level.[26]

---

26   Moretti 2005, p. 53.

As Moretti conceives it, the literary map 'offers a model of the narrative universe which rearranges its components in a non-trivial way, and may bring some hidden patterns to the surface'.[27] As an abstract and 'artificial object', the literary map is not a re-presentation of reality, but rather a heuristic device – a new set of lenses opening the eyes to a different way of seeing and thus affording fresh insights. The literary map, however, is most emphatically 'not itself an explanation' and any explanatory deployment of it results in a simplistic reductionism.[28]

What Moretti says of the literary map can also be applied to the map of human corporeal organisation that will emerge from the cartographic explorations of human corporeality in the next two chapters. This map will be an artificial object produced through abstraction; it aims to reveal emerging qualities not otherwise visible (or perhaps visible but too easily neglected or reduced to a 'simple prerequisite'). And although this map of human corporeal organisation should (as this entire book argues) be an indispensable component of historical explanation, it does *not* in itself bear any explanatory power. This undertaking makes no claims to completeness, nor is it an explanation, but, to echo Moretti's hopes, it will, 'with a little luck' produce an 'artificial object' that will be 'more than the sum of [its] *parts*' and that will make visible '"emerging" qualities' essential to the histories of human worldmaking. The qualities intended to link corporeality with cognition and culture(s) will emerge in the course of my cartographical project in the form of corporeally grounded patterns of human experience that are refracted in varying ways in different socio-cultural forms.

---

27   Moretti 2005, pp. 53–4.
28   In this way, Moretti's understanding of the methodological place-value of the literary map has affinities with Marx's purely conceptual presentation of the capitalist mode of production in *Capital*. As Kosmas Psychopedis argued (see Chapter 3 above), the methodological place-value of *Capital* is to be understood as an 'abstraction presentation of the essential'. The model of capitalism presented in purely conceptual form in *Capital* is constructed by temporarily abstracting from the concrete, site-specific, and contingent aspects of 'really-existing' capitalist economies in order to make visible the essential structure and logic that are definitive of, and common to all, capitalist modes of production despite their historically specific idiosyncrasies. As with Moretti's approach, this process of abstraction creates 'an artificial object' that is neither 'real' nor 'true', but is instead a heuristic device whose purpose is to make visible fundamental factors, the neglect of which will render any explanation partial at best, misguided at worst. Yet though a crucial part of it, this abstract artificial object is *not* in itself an explanation. And the history of Marxism contains enough examples of the simplistic theoretical reductionism and the disastrous political consequences that follow from the explanatory deployment of the abstract presentation.

5.4 Challenges: A Mode of Presentation and a Knowledge Deficit

Although Moretti's invocation of the 'little luck' needed to turn such maps into 'more than the sum of their parts' may have been added as a rhetorical gesture, certainly a great deal more than a little luck will be needed to overcome the two remaining and major obstacles that must be confronted in order to sketch a usable map of human corporeality in the very limited space available here. One obstacle is that although the choices regarding guiding principles and categories have certainly narrowed the field of inquiry and demarcated its topography, there still remains the rather imposing problem of how to survey a still vast field and present it (especially in the very limited space of one chapter) in a coherent, effective, and readable manner. And that obstacle is compounded by the further problem that such an undertaking requires me to range widely across disciplines with which I am rather unfamiliar. There are fortunately two forms of assistance available to augment luck in solving these two problems. These are: a logic of presentation, a principle to hold the narrative together; and what Marx called 'the most solid form of social wealth'.[29]

While both the construction of the conceptual apparatus around the general notion of *Anlagen* (and divided into capacities and constraints) and the delineation of the modes of objectification are crucial to organising the material, both would be ineffective as a means of organising the presentation. A mapping of human corporeal organisation charted according to the categories of *Anlagen* or the modes of objectification would result in long listings of body parts, each annotated by brief anatomical and physiological descriptions and followed by descriptions of correlations between body parts and culture. Lengthy, tedious, and prone to endless expansion, such listings could easily fall into what Hegel called the 'bad infinity'. They would amount to a glossary of the items of human anatomy, but would not provide a meaningful cartographic profile of human corporeal organisation; nor would they be of any help in elaborating the generative relations between corporeality and culture(s).

A more effective mode of organisation may be based on two terms introduced above as a means of describing the two dimensions of this cartographic undertaking: the 'archaeological' and the 'genealogical'. As stated above, the purpose of this undertaking is 'archaeological'; it is aimed at sketching a map or the *Bauplan* of human corporeality.[30] As also noted above, the pre- and protohuman roots of so many essential attributes of the human *Bauplan* necessarily

---

29 Marx 1973 [1857–58], p. 540.
30 On *Bauplan*, see Gould and Lewontin 1979.

give this cartography a 'genealogical' dimension. And that genealogical dimension may be enlisted to serve as the mode of presentation. Accordingly, the 'archaeological' map will be presented in a 'genealogical' form, that is: I shall trace (but, I hasten to add, with no pretensions of explaining) the evolution of the *Bauplan* of anatomically modern *Homo sapiens*.

I should also add here that although I avoid evolutionary explanation, I do freely and eclectically indulge in the 'evolutionary subjunctive': 'what would humans be like if ...?' We have already encountered Norman Geras's quip that no fish could be Mozart, and Gramsci's son's inquiry about what life would be like if human brains were as large as those of elephants. Significant for purposes of this chapter is that contrasts based on the evolutionary subjunctive retrieve, from the insidious bias of neglect, things that everyone knows about in principle, but that are instead ignored or (what amounts to the same) reduced to 'simple prerequisites'. The use of the evolutionary subjunctive puts into sharper relief the peculiarly human instruments and capacities, the fundamental corporeal prerequisites of human ways of worldmaking. It will help to indicate how different human cultures would be if our bodily form and instruments could not do what they can, and could do what they cannot, and thereby to illuminate how peculiarly human all human cultures are.

As a further and final refinement of the genealogical mode of presentation, I will borrow and give an evolutionary rendering to the Linnaean taxonomy of *Homo sapiens*. Linnaeus proposed a systematics in the form of a vertical hierarchy of consisting of seven nested levels of taxa, namely: Kingdom, Phylum, Class, Order, Family, Genus, and Species.[31] Though not an evolutionist, Linnaeus certainly did consider *Homo sapiens* a species of animal, the classification of which as a vertebrate, mammal, primate, hominid, homo, and sapiens provides a blueprint of the human *Bauplan* and thus suggests the steps of an archaeological excavation of human corporeal organisation. And to transform Linnaeus's vertical hierarchy into a genealogical sequence of evolutionary stages is only a matter of metaphorically turning it ninety degrees. With this 'horizontal' rendering, the taxonomic sequence from animal kingdom to our own species can be read temporally, as a narrative outline of a genealogical retracing of the evolution of the corporeal organisation of anatomically modern *Homo sapiens*, the creature biologically outfitted to make its own histories, but whose histories are inescapably both informed and constrained by its corporeal organisation.

---

31 There have been, of course, countless refinements of and additions to Linnaeus's taxonomic categories, but for my organisational purposes in this limited space, his are more than adequate.

Having established the evolutionary sequence as the general principle of narrative organisation of the following cartographical sketch, I must immediately admit that I shall on occasion violate that principle in the interests of narrative clarity. These violations will occur with some attributes of corporeal organisation that have a more primitive origin, but that appear in the discussion of a period rather later than that of their emergence – in the period, that is, in which that attribute becomes definitive for the process of 'becoming human'.[32] For example, although all of the five apparatuses of external sensation are much more primitive, they will all be discussed in the section on our primate heritage, for this is the point at which the particular sensory constellation later bequeathed to *Homo sapiens* acquired its definitive form. The purpose of these violations is to reduce repetition and thereby to condense the narrative and enhance the clarity of presentation.

Regarding the challenge of traversing so much unfamiliar intellectual terrain, I have, if not luck, certainly the good fortune of having access to more social riches than I could possibly expend. 'Knowledge' [*Wissenschaft*], wrote Marx in the *Grundrisse*, 'is the most solid form of social wealth'. I take this quite literally and will avail myself of the accumulated social wealth in the knowledge that no one person could amass in a lifetime. That is to say: I make no claims of originality here. All of the content presented comes from far outside my own field of history. I have borrowed it from, and am fully dependent on, a wide variety of anatomical, physiological, psychophysical, evolutionary, and paleoanthropological studies. My main goal is to take what is more or less universally accepted as valid about human corporeal organisation and its evolution and re-frame it in a historical-materialist context, that is: to treat corporeal organisation, not as just a 'simple prerequisite', but as the 'first fact' of human histories, and the starting point for their reconstruction. All that is new, if anything, is the way I shall use, and position in my argumentation, the 'social wealth' that I have borrowed from the work of others, to whom I am indebted and grateful. Such extensive borrowing, especially from areas with which one is only distantly familiar, necessarily runs the risk of misunderstanding and/or misusing the work of others. If I do so, it will be a consequence not of my intention, but of my ignorance – for which I offer an anticipatory apology.

Finally, as befitting its self-consciously abstract character and given the spatial constraints, this attempt to map human corporeal organisation cannot possibly be anything more than that: an (albeit very long) attempt, *un essai, ein*

---

32   To borrow Nancy Makepiece Tanner's title: *On Becoming Human: A Model of the Transition from Ape to Human & the Reconstruction of Early Human Social Life* (Tanner 1987).

Versuch, whose goal is to indicate the great breadth and depth of the problematic revealed when human corporeal organisation is taken as the 'first fact' of historical theory – and in the process to provide analyses of just a few of the great many issues involved. It will be a necessarily abbreviated experiment in synthesising Darwin and Marx which is, of course, a shorthand expression for synthesising the evolution of human corporeal organisation with a materialist conception of human histories. It will be the most cursory of elaborations, the sketchiest of portraits, and overall embarrassingly inadequate.

It does aim, however, at creating an 'artificial object' in Moretti's sense, one that 'rearranges its components in a non-trivial way and may bring some hidden patterns to the surface'. And it attempts to do so through a story (through a narrative of genesis, if one will) whose purpose is not to explain human evolution, but simply to describe the formation of human corporeal organisation, the moulding of the instruments in the human bodily toolkit that establish the possibilities and limits of possible human cultures. If somewhat successful, this 'artificial' map will portray in briefest outline some of the most definitive aspects of human corporeal organisation that frame definitive patterns of human experience, that establish the range, that is the extent and limits, of *how* human beings can experience the world around them, and the extent and limits of *what* of the world human beings can experience. This mapping project, then, seeks to outline the boundaries and establish the range of peculiarly human worlds; to delimit those aspects of the universe that are (possible) components of human experience; and thereby to approach the infinite but not unlimited diversity of human cultural forms as variations on, and permutations within, a set of corporeal themes. Thus, if successful, this cartography will set up Part 3, where I undertake the elaboration of the inseparable link between the history of human 'natural technology' in the form of corporeal organisation and the histories of material, social, and semiotic artefacts, where I seek to articulate the body as the interior structure of all human artefacts. My hope is that this abbreviated mapping of human corporeal organisation will at least be interesting, provocative, and suggestive of a potentially rich historical-materialist manner of looking at bodies and artefacts. In any case, its inadequacies alone will suggest how much more remains to be done if a materialist conception of history is to win its 'breathtaking' wager – a wager that may ultimately be unwinnable, but that is not at all a foolhardy one.

Nor is it a wager without political implications. In the previous chapter I cited Achille Mbembe's reminder that the denial of the species-specific universality of corporeal form can easily slide into the kind of denial of the humanity of others that has long served as a justification of imperialist conquest and domination. And it is worth recalling his words here as I am about to embark on this attempt to map, in abstract form, the essential, species-specific contours of human corporeal organisation. Writes Mbembe: 'Each time it came to people different in race, language, and culture, the idea that we have, concretely and typically, the same flesh, or that, in Husserl's words, "My flesh already has the meaning of being a flesh typical in general for us all," became problematic. The theoretical and practical recognition of the body and flesh of "the stranger" as flesh and body just like mine, the *idea of a common human nature, a humanity shared with others*, long posed, and still poses, a problem for Western consciousness' – and, he might have added, it obviously poses still a problem for politics as well.[33] Here I take Mbembe's profoundly simple statement of the theoretical and political importance of humanity's common flesh as more than sufficient reason to undertake a cartographical sketch of the organisation of the flesh that, by corporeal necessity, makes all human beings all too human.

33   Mbembe 2001, p. 2.

CHAPTER 6

A Historical-Materialist Cartography of Human Corporeal Organisation (in Outline): On the Corporeal Constitution of Patterns of Human Experience, Behaviour, and Realities

6.1   Cosmic and Planetary Form-Determinants

A corporeally-grounded, historical-materialist response to the Delphic injunction to 'know thyself' would have to begin by acknowledging the cosmic conditioning of human corporeal organisation – which is, of course, intimately related to the formation of our solar system.[1] When it first formed on earth, organic matter did not have at its feet a planetary blank-slate on which it could arbitrarily imprint or inscribe itself. Rather, the corporeal organisations of the new life-forms were themselves already subject to a particular set of cosmic inscriptions on the planet on which they emerged. It is of course commonplace that our planet, the third in our solar system, is well-situated for life. This obvious fact is not simply a simple prerequisite, but fundamentally 'in-forms' (the term 'information' primarily means 'giving form to'[2]) earthly life-forms. A contrasting glance at our two planetary neighbours provides some basic perspective.

Some 67 million miles distant from the sun, Venus has an orbital year of 224 earth days. The planet's rotational period, its 'day', however, lasts 243 earth days; a Venetian day, in short, lasts longer than a Venetian year. Rotating in a direction opposite that of the earth, its sunrise is in the west and sunset in the east. The planet has an average temperature near 850 degrees Fahrenheit, and an atmosphere constantly churned by hurricane-force winds reaching up to 360 kilometres/hour. With an atmosphere 93 times that of the earth, its surface-level gravitational pull is equivalent to that at a one-kilometre depth in earth's ocean. Venus has no moon. Mars, on the other hand, some 150 million miles from the sun, has a rotational speed similar to earth's. Mars rotates in the same direction as the earth and a Martian day lasts about half hour longer than ours.

---

1   For comment differentiating this mapping of human corporeal organisation that begins with the formation of the solar system from 'deep history' approaches, See Appendix 6.1.
2   See Lorenz 1977, pp. 22–3.

But its orbital year is nearly twice as long, with a duration of 687 earth days. It has an average temperature of minus-30 degrees Celsius. With a surface gravity only 37% that of earth's, basketball nets would have to be placed at perhaps twenty feet, for a human could jump three times higher in such an atmosphere. The planet's polar ice-caps consist of frozen carbon dioxide ('dry ice') that in the 'summer' months 'sublimes' (passes directly from solid to gaseous state, bypassing the intermediate liquid 'watery' phase), causing winds gusting up to 400 km/h. Mars has two moons.

Earth, as we know, resides at a distance of 93 million miles from the sun; our orbital period, or year, is 365 days; our rotational period, or day, lasts twenty-four hours. The earth's tilt of some twenty-four degrees on its axis defines our climatic zones and seasonal cycles, its west-to-east (seen from the North Star, counter-clockwise) rotation provides us directional orientation. A planetary instance of the so-called 'Goldilocks Principle', earth is neither too near nor too far from the sun, which provides an average surface temperature of fifteen degrees Celsius (fifty-nine Fahrenheit), and therewith a supply of H_2O in its liquid, as well as solid and gaseous state. Earth's gravitational pressure keeps our human feet terrestrially planted, firmly yet flexibly – making it possible for tall, long-legged and springy humans to dunk a ball in a basket at an elevation of only ten feet or a bit more. Our single moon defines our lunar months and circadian tidal cycles.

Familiarity with our planet's vital statistics should not lead us to neglect their foundational significance for earthly life-forms including our own species and *all* its members living in diverse, yet all too human cultures. Our solar system is situated in the outer reaches of the Milky Way galaxy that contains some 200 billion stars – not all of which are visible, but we glimpse enough to gain a sense of their seemingly infinite number. Visible stars have been the objects of human usages and means of navigating the world in forms ranging from astrologies, psychologies, philosophies, and sciences, to land and sea travel, and to literary imagination. Closer to home, imagine what kind of temporal measurements and metaphors would be constructed in a world like Venus, whose day is longer than its year and that, bereft of a moon, would have no lunar cycles – and no months. A less radical tilt of the earth's axis (like, say Venus or Jupiter of only three degrees in place of our twenty-three) would flatten out the seasons, alter the annual rhythms of agriculture, and deprive poets of seasonal metaphors of a time to sow and a time to reap, of the springtime and autumn of life, of death and regeneration. A more radical tilt on the other hand (even Neptune's twenty-eight degrees, not to mention Uranus's ninety-seven degrees) would intensify seasonal fluctuations and lengthen the winter and summer. If, like Venus, our planet spun from east to west, we would not orient ourselves toward the 'orient' as that part of the heavens in which the sun and other celestial objects 'rise', nor toward the 'occident' as that in which those celestial objects 'set'.[3] And we would perforce put a westward spin on Horatio's greeting of 'the morn, in russet mantle clad, walk[ing] o'er the dew of yon high eastward hill' – and also on Romeo's metaphorical exclamation 'But, soft! What light through yonder window breaks? It is the east, and Juliet is the sun'. But on Venus, Romeo could not have continued with his heavenly metaphors, for Venus has no moon – whether 'envious', 'already sick and pale with grief', or otherwise – that he could have bidden the 'fair sun' to 'arise' and 'kill'.[4]

Speaking of moons: were our planet, like Venus, without one, or encircled by multiple moons like Mars (two), Saturn (sixty-two known, several more under consideration), or Jupiter (seventy-nine known ones and counting[5]), the effect on human life and cultural forms would be profound: tidal cycles would be non-existent with no moon, and more frequent and complex with multiple, thus altering significantly the kinds of marine life, life rhythms of coastal people, and, with moon-lit nights rather more bright, perhaps altering too the now diurnally oriented circadian rhythms of our species. Human poetics could hardly remain unaffected: the possible permutations in the metaphorical deployment of tidal rhythms would increase proportionally with the number of moons – as would the construction and use of lunar metaphors: with multiple moons, Shakespeare might not have reached so deeply into the heavens, and could have written instead of a pair of 'moon-cross'd lovers' who took their lives.

And water: Earth's mild surface temperature, averaging 15 degrees centigrade, 59 degrees Fahrenheit, allows for the existence of H_2O in all of its states. 'To be provocatively simplistic', says Philip Whitfield, 'the presence of water, plus a physiologically mild temperature, led to the start of the evolution of life on Earth at least 3.5 billion years ago'.[6] To be equally provocative and profoundly simplistic, imagine how dried-out cultural forms would be without attributions of significance to water: to oceans and seas (no Moby Dick), to lakes, rivers, and ponds, (no 'Lake poets', no Huckleberry Finn, no Walden); also no H_2O in its frozen form in certain regions or climatic zones (Thomas Mann's *Magic Mountain* without snow). Not to mention water's significance for human

---

3 Definitions from *Oxford English Dictionary*, on-line edition.
4 William Shakespeare, *Romeo and Juliet*, Act 2, Scene 2; *Hamlet*, Act 1, Scene 1. I might add here that behind the reference to the 'envious moon' obviously lies the fact of human diurnality. See below.
5 See 'Jupiter Has 79 Moons. For Now', *New York Times*, 24 July 2018, p. D4.
6 Whitfield in Ayensu and Whitfield 1982, p. 17.

corporeality itself: envisage how dried-out we ourselves would be without our sixty-percent watery composition – which prompted the silicon-crystal entities, encountered by Captain Jean-Luc Picard and his crew on one of the voyages of the Federation Starship Enterprise, to refer to humans as 'ugly bags of mostly water'.

Such metaphors, whose form is based on and derived from cosmic and planetary form-determinants (and taken eclectically from some of the few cultures with which I am familiar), could be multiplied endlessly, and, although differing perhaps significantly in specific content, I would venture to guess also cross-culturally. Were the hypotheticals suggested above actually the case for our planet, the contents of all natural or animistic theologies (which have of course been a universal characteristic of the histories of all cultures) would have been radically different because of a radically different underlying referential logic. However much human cultures have varied and continue to vary cross-culturally, the limits and logic of that variation are established by those cosmic constants that frame the place of our planet in the universe and determine its vital statistics – and that, in turn, establish fundamental patterns of human life and experience, and therewith the range of their cultural refractions. Of immediate importance here are the effects of these cosmically constructed rhythms on human biorhythms.

The significance of biorhythms for cultural production is of course denied in all variations on Anthony Synnott's pseudo-axiom that 'the body social negates the body physical'. It would seem that such a notion would already be refuted by the cultural meanings invested in the rhythms (and their variation according to emotional state) of the beating human heart. But if that does not suffice, Gilles Deleuze and Félix Guattari propose an irreverent counter to notions such as Synnott's in their depiction of human beings as 'desiring machines', each of which 'breathes, heats, eats, shits, and fucks' and 'doubtless ... interprets the entire world from the perspective of its own flux, from the point of view of the energy that flows from it'.[7] While Deleuze and Guattari take a rather earthy step toward corporeality with this description, and also recognise the species-centrism of all forms of animal life, each interpreting 'the entire world' from its particular perspective, the very abstractness of their reduction of human beings to desiring *machines*, combined with the intentional crassness of their formulation, seems to point more to an effort to *epater* not just *le bourgeoisie*, but idealists of all stripes, than to address the unique biological form-determinants that establish the range of life-possibilities of (not

---

7   Deleuze and Guattari 1986, p. 1, p. 6.

just) human life. And the obvious point here is that the functions they list are performed not only by human 'desiring machines', but also by all other sexually-reproducing 'desiring machines' or species, each in its unique, corporeally-constituted species-specific and, in the case of humans, socio-economically and culturally mediated manner.[8]

Although Deleuze and Guattari are not incorrect in appealing to physics, their metaphor seems misplaced; for, the physics involved is not the mechanics of machines, but the cosmic physics of planetary motion. In contrast to the mechanical work-rhythm of machines that are oblivious to daily, seasonal, and annual cycles, the biorhythms of earthly life-forms are patterned in essential ways by planetary rhythms. So, the first step would be to replace 'machines' with 'organisms'. And the second would be to replace the arbitrariness entailed by Deleuze's and Guattari's formulation of how and when 'desiring organisms' perform these functions with the understanding that the particular ways in which each species of 'desiring organism' performs these same functions varies according to its particular corporeal organisation. And the third step, finally, is to recognise that although each such species has its own rhythms of performing these biological functions, those various biorhythms are directly related to a set of cosmic constants. For the 'sobering, unflippant fact', says Whitfield, is that 'the intrinsic organization of almost every living thing on Earth ... conforms to a pattern of design dictated by the motions of the Earth and moon in space. ... Each of us on Earth, each of the 10 million species that have evolved on and now swarm over its surface, carries the time signature of the planetary motion of our world indelibly stamped within it'; and 'woven into the structure, physiology and behaviour of [earth's] animals and plants is a remarkably precise inventory containing not only information about the conditions that exist on Earth, but also several vital facts about the nature of our solar system' which has produced a 'rhythmical environment that has made us rhythmical creatures'.[9]

---

8 In a much different context, a theorising of the 'postcolony' in Africa, Achille Mbembe (2001, p. 14) describes the 'life-world' as 'the field where individuals' existence unfolds in practice ..., where they exercise existence – that is, live their lives out and confront the very forms of their death'. Because of this focus on the real life-experience of really living individuals, he rejects 'theories that – by proclaiming not only "the death of God" and "man" but also of "morality" and the "subject" at the risk of bringing about the disappearance of any axiological reference and any object other than "oneself" – reduce individuals to mere flows of drives and networks of "desires," to libidinal machines' (ibid., pp. 14–15). Although Mbemebe makes no explicit reference here to Deleuze and Guattari, his critique, even if not aimed directly at them, does certainly seem applicable to their position.

9 Whitfield 1982, p. 15.

A HISTORICAL-MATERIALIST CARTOGRAPHY

In a similarly chronobiological study of the *Rhythms of Life*, Russell Foster and Leon Kreitzman modestly focus on 'The Biological Clocks that Control the Daily Lives of Every Living Thing'. But for anthropo*ego*centric conceit, it should be no surprise that the rhythms of life, the biorhythms, of each and every organism (human organisms included) are planetary specific. Nor should it surprise that the rhythms of the lives of all organisms inhabiting a given planet might be stamped by certain planet-specific form-determinants: 'We [human beings] and just about every living thing on the planet – animals, plants, algae, bacteria – have a biological clock that was first set ticking more than three billion years ago'.[10] They continue:

> The climate changes; mountain ranges form and continents are remodelled. But the one constant in this ever-changing environment, since the earth and the moon locked into their orbits, is that the earth will turn on its axis, within a minute or two, every 24 hours; that every 365.25 days, Sirius the Dog Star will rise with the sun; the moon will wax and wane every 29.5 days; and twice a day the tides will roll over the shore. It is small wonder that these basic rhythms are etched into living creatures .... Through these internal timing processes, organisms have adapted to maximise their chances of reproduction in a temporal environment that changes daily with unfailing regularity.

These rhythms – circadian, circalunar, circannual – 'are generated within us'. Circadian rhythms 'are orchestrated by a central clock to keep our bodily systems working in harmony':

> Like the conductor of an orchestra, the clock keeps the ensemble of the human body beating to a collective time. It keeps everything from happening all at once and ensures that the biochemistry of the body runs on time and in order. Biological clocks synchronise the times of activity and rest of both diurnal and nocturnal organisms and those that are crepuscular (active at dusk and dawn, to ensure that peak activity occurs when food, sunlight or prey is available). They enable us and other living things to anticipate the predictable rhythmic changes in our environment: light, temperature, humidity, and ultraviolet radiation.
>
> Biological clocks impose a structure that enables organisms to change their behavioural priorities in relation to the time of day, month, or year.

---

10   All quotations in this paragraph from Foster and Kreitzman 2004, pp. 2–3.

> They are reset at sunrise and sunset each day to link astronomical time with an organism's internal time.

There are obviously species-specific variations in responses to these planetary constants, but the 'big difference between [humans] and other living things is that to some extent we can cognitively override these ancient hard-wired rhythms. Instead of sleeping as our bodies dictate, we drink another cup of coffee, turn up the radio, roll down the car window and kid ourselves that we can beat a few billion years of evolution'. While jet lag, for example, effects a temporary disruption of the circadian rhythm, one wonders what consequences a lifetime of night-shift work must have on people who are subjected to biologically unsound sleep patterns and to chronic Vitamin D deficiency. In any case, there are among humans, to state the obvious, variations in geo-cultural responses to human biorhythms (coastal dwellers and tides), but an earth day is an earth day and all species are, each in its own way, corporeally accustomed to the length of the day (and night), lunar cycles, seasonal changes, annual cycles. If cosmic conditioning establishes the general framework for everything from directional orientation and perspective on the 'universe' to circadian, circalunar, and circannual rhythms, the particular patterns of human biorhythms (that underlie their cultural usages) are further refined by the various legacies of our diverse ancestry; and these will be addressed below, each on the evolutionary site where it becomes definitive for human being.[11]

6.2 Locomotive Organisms with Backbone

Skipping casually over the billion years from the formation of our solar system to the emergence of those first prokaryotic organisms, the human discovery of which wreaked havoc with the Linnaean binary division of all life into plant and animal kingdoms (current taxonomies include up to six kingdoms subdivided into domains, superregna, superkindoms, and empires), and leap-

---

11 It is impossible to cover everything here, but it should at least be mentioned there are several other biorhythms not directly linked to planetary specifics, but essential for the rhythm of human life and also refracted in various cultural forms. These include the rhythm of the heartbeat, of respiration, of food intake, digestion and excretion, etc. Noteworthy is one biologically necessary activity, the reproductive cycle, that has a circannular rhythm in most other mammal and primate species, but not in *Homo sapiens* for which conception can take place all year long – although only during a certain, roughly circalunar, period.

ing also over the next three billion years, we shall take up the thread of this narrative relatively recently when measured on a cosmic timescale: with the emergence of animal life. Animals share with plants three of the four most fundamental dimensions circumscribing the lives of all organic species, namely: the reproduction of the individual's life through acquisition of sustenance; the reproduction of the species through procreation; and a life-cycle culminating in the inevitable extinction of the individual's life – whose trinitarian formula for *Homo sapiens* might be rendered in more familiar, peculiarly human terms as 'food, sex, and religion'. A crucial fourth dimension of animal life, not shared with plant life, is one revealed by the expansion of knowledge of microorganisms (the inconclusiveness of contemporary taxonomy notwithstanding) and that establishes a very distant, but certainly curious and unexpected affinity between human beings and, of all things, bacteria. Though the English language contains the term 'bacteria culture', it is still most unexpected, and certainly deflating to idealist and ultraculturalist notions, to encounter evolutionary biologist John Bonner's quite literal claim that the first corporeal step toward culture was taken by bacteria, specifically: with the capacity for 'motility' that first appeared in bacteria.[12]

Whether or not we care to trace our family tree back to bacteria, locomotion is, according to paleoanthropologist Andre Leroi-Gourhan, the 'determining factor' of human biological (and social) evolution that fundamentally differentiates the 'being-in-the-world' of animals from a rooted, sessile plant-like existence.[13] Within the animal kingdom Leroi-Gourhan differentiates two fundamental kinds of locomotive being-in-and-toward-the-world proceeding from two kinds of corporeal morphology. The more sedentary of the two are those species (e.g. jellyfish) whose mobility is barely voluntary, but are driven by winds or waves and tides; and the more dynamic, in terms of both movement and evolutionary potential, are the volitionally mobile species. Noting that the sedentary species have shown little evolutionary change, whereas mobile species have undergone a great deal, he designates mobility 'the significant feature of evolution toward the human state'.

It does not at all diminish the evolutionary significance of organismic motility to ask what should be the obvious questions that it begs – those concerning the wherefore and the whereto: why do some organisms move and where are they going? Motility is neither random nor an end in itself. If motility might be

---

12 Bonner 1980, p. 54 and throughout Chapter 4.
13 Leroi-Gourhan 1993, pp. 26–7. Next citation, ibid., p. 26.

seen as a basic means of differentiating between the plant and animal kingdom, it certainly did not evolve without reason. Kinaesthetic bodies have a *raison d'être*, a purpose that points toward an even more fundamental distinction between animals and plants.

That most basic factor differentiating the animal kingdom (including the relatively sedentary species) from the plant kingdom is 'economics', or what is more accurately captured by that term's etymological ancestor, namely: the Greek οἰκονομία that carries the basic and literal sense of the procurement of the indispensable means to go on living, the nourishment required to satisfy the organism's corporeal needs for its daily reproduction. As Leroi-Gourhan puts it, '[a]nimals differ from plants in that their nourishment involves the intake of food in units that must be mechanically processed before any assimilative chemical process takes place'.[14] Plant species are (with few exceptions) autotrophic; capable of producing their own food internally,[15] they are (again, with few exceptions) rooted to the spot, sessile. Animal species, however, are heterotrophic and require an external supply of energy. Those organisms that need to procure food tend to be motile and kinaesthetic, whereas those that produce their own food internally tend not to be.[16] Heterotrophism not only produces a fairly rhythmic cycle of ingestion, digestion, and excretion (and all the associated profanity, humour, taboos, notions of cleanliness, manners, etc.), but it quite literally *moves* organisms. Because 'nutrition in animals is to a considerably greater degree than in plants connected with the search for food', it 'therefore involves the use of mobile capturing organs and of a detection mechanism' – that is to say the organs and mechanisms that make up the motor and sensory systems of a species.[17] Because heterotrophs are condemned to search

---

14 Leroi-Gourhan 1993, p. 26. Next citation, ibid., pp. 26–7.
15 There are of course exceptions, e.g. the carnivorous heterotopic plant *Dionaea muscipula* commonly known as the Venus Flytrap.
16 No sooner is the general rule pronounced than do the expected exceptions to it beg recognition. For, strictly speaking, mobility is not the definitive attribute of all animal species. Even given the seeming infinite possibilities of ways of moving about, there were heterotrophic organisms that were apparently not at all enthusiastic about doing so. There are those species which, 'without adopting the purely chemical nutritional processes of plants, have adapted themselves to capturing food while remaining immobile' (Leroi-Gourhan 1993, p. 27). There are, as Leroi-Gourhan notes, numerous invertebrate species (sponges, hydras, sea anemones, etc.) which are essentially sessile, and many others (worms, mollusks, echinoderms, or crustaceans) for which 'the sedentary habit of adults is a secondary phenomenon' (ibid.). And also those (e.g. sea sponges) whose movements are not volitional, but which are moved by currents, tides, or winds.
17 Leroi-Gourhan 1993, pp. 26–7.

for external nourishment, 'it is no surprise to see that most animals have well-developed nervous, sensory, and movement systems to allow them to sense and acquire food'.[18]

In their most primitive form, animal sensory-motor systems may accurately be described, based on their two most essential attributes, as tactile-kinaesthetic bodies. We have already noted Leroi-Gourhan's accentuation of the role of motion in animal evolution; and Ashley Montagu has eloquently paid tribute to the primacy of touch and the organ of touch, the skin:

> The skin, like a cloak, covers us all over, the oldest and the most sensitive of our organs, our first medium of communication, and our most efficient of protectors. The whole body is covered by skin. [...] In the evolution of the senses the sense of touch was undoubtedly the first to come into being. Touch is the parent of our eyes, ears, nose, and mouth. It is the sense which became differentiated into the others, a fact that seems to be recognized in the age-old evaluation of touch as 'the mother of the senses'.[19]

Although it would be difficult to doubt its chronological primacy, Montagu's further insistence that touch is 'the most sensitive' and also 'perhaps next to the brain ... the most important of all our organ systems' is rather more controversial. For, each of the other four 'classic' senses has persuasive advocates of its primacy. These five senses will be addressed below in the appropriate places where they assume their essentially human form. In anticipation of the emergence of the other senses, the important matter here is to consider corporeal organisation not just as a 'tactile kinaesthetic', but more broadly as a heterotrophic 'sensory kinaesthetic' body.

In 1962 Little Eva performed a 'No. 1' hit song, 'Do the Loco-motion', written by Gerry Goffin and Carole King and ranked by *Rolling Stone* as number 359 among 'The 500 Greatest Songs of All Time'. To 'swing your hips now ... jump up, jump back ... move around the floor in a loco-motion' – that all takes backbone. Who could have guessed the cultural portent of the evolution of a phylum called *Chordata* because characterised by a spinal cord, or of its subphylum, the vertebrates? There are three phyla of *Chordata*, two of which along with the twenty or so other invertebrate phyla make up approximately ninety-five percent of all animal species. Thus, even though vertebrates are the largest and

---

18   Relethford 1994, p. 195.
19   Ashley Montagu 1978, p. 1. Next citation ibid.

the 'the major group' of the three *Chordata* subphyla (with various estimates hovering around some 60,000 species), creatures with backbone and capable of 'doin' the loco-motion' are rather rare in the animal kingdom. Vertebrates are, as Michael J. Benton put it, 'a minor twig on the Universal Tree of Life'.[20]

The absence or presence of a vertebral column differentiates between 'two types of dynamic organization': animal bodies are either radially or bilaterally symmetrical; and each type has consequences for both locomotive capacity and sensory apparatus, the way a given organism moves about in, and navigates, the world.[21] All chordates 'possess at some point in their life a notochord, a flexible internal rod that runs along the back of the animal ... and acts to strengthen and support the body'.[22] The extent of the notochord and the timing of its presence in a vertebrate's lifecycle vary: 'the notochord becomes surrounded by skeletal vertebrae during embryonic development – in higher vertebrates it is present in the early embryo only and is later completely replaced by the vertebrae'.[23] The evolutionary appearance of the notochord and then the spinal column of vertebrae was crucial in the emergence of larger and more complex organisms. It not only gave organisms the 'backbone' with which to venture onto land, but it is also an obvious prerequisite of the eventual emergence of the upright ape; and it provided *Chordata* species with 'the special vertebrate characteristics includ[ing] a range of features that make up a true head: well-defined sensory organs (nose, eye, ear) with the necessary nervous connections, the cranial nerves, and the olfactory, optic, and auditory (otic) regions that make up a true brain'.[24]

That bony but 'flexible internal rod that runs along the back of the animal' is called the 'backbone'. Strictly speaking, however, that designation is appropriate only for evolutionarily-tardy terrestrial bipeds; if that rod must be named with a locational designation, it would be more accurately called a 'topbone' for quadrupeds and a 'centrebone' for fish. Whether back, top, or centre, however, that internal rod is the definitive structural factor in the vertebrate *Bauplan*; for it establishes the bilateral symmetry characteristic of vertebrates; it divides the vertebrate organism into two sides (known as the right and left in English) that are mirror images of each other. In contrast to radially symmetrical species (e.g. jelly fish, sponges, sea anemones, polyps), the backbone of vertebrates not only

---

20   Benton 2005, p. 2.
21   Leroi-Gourhan 1993, p. 27.
22   Relethford 1994, p. 195.
23   'notochord', *The Columbia Encyclopedia*, Sixth Edition, 2008, Encyclopedia.com. 20 July 2009, http://www.encyclopedia.com.
24   Benton 2005, p. 14.

gives them greater support and the capacity to grow larger, but it also creates the orientation axes: right and left, front and back.

Also common to bilaterally symmetrical animals is what Leroi-Gourhan calls 'the normal design of animal bodies' – the 'design whereby the entire organism is placed behind the aperture for ingesting food'.[25] This 'anterior polarity of the mouth and of the organs of prehension of mobile animals is', Leroi-Gourhan elaborates, 'so obvious a biological and mechanical fact that to dwell upon it would be ridiculous, except perhaps in order to stress that it is this fact and no other that represents the fundamental precondition for evolution toward higher life forms'. For these higher, or more complex, life-forms to develop, certain preconditions must be met, preconditions that are at first fairly generalised and met by a large number of species, yet that become increasingly restrictive. The first of those is a general attribute of bilaterally symmetrical organisms: 'Mobility implies that for purposes of nourishment the organs that ensure orientation, adjustment of position, and the coordination of the organs of food capture with those of food preparation must also be situated in front of the body. From the first acquisition of mobility to the present time, the general structure of an animal – whether insect, fish, or mammal – has not changed. The polarization of certain organs has thus led to the formation of the *anterior field* within which the complex operations of animals with bilateral symmetry take place'.[26]

A surprising number of the building blocks of human corporeal organisation can be traced to our vertebrate heritage. These include 'a range of features that make up a true head: well-defined sensory organs (nose, eye, ear,) with the necessary nervous connections, the cranial nerves, and the olfactory, optic, and auditory (otic) regions that make up a true brain'.[27] That 'true head' would house an enlarged area of nerve tissue at the front end of the spinal cord which of course is the early vertebrate brain – and one already definitive enough that vertebrates have been called 'craniates' for their 'specialized head features (the cranium, the skull)'. Of all the phyla and subphyla, vertebrates have the most differentiated brain consisting of a hindbrain, a midbrain, and a forebrain: 'In most vertebrates, the hindbrain is associated with hearing, balance, reflexive behaviours, and control of the autonomic body functions such as breathing; the midbrain is associated with vision; and the forebrain with chemical sensing such as smell'.[28] This advanced sensory apparatus made vertebrates rather

---

25   Leroi-Gourhan 1993, p. 27. Next citation ibid.
26   Leroi-Gourhan 1993, pp. 27–8.
27   Benton 2005, p. 14. Next citation ibid.
28   Relethford 1994, p. 204. Information in the next two sentences from ibid, p. 196.

adept in moving about the world in their heterotrophic pursuits. Crucial too, especially for human manipulative capacities, is the basic vertebrate skeletal pattern (shared by humans, whales, and birds) that includes limbs, each consisting of a single upper bone and two lower bones with five digits at its end. Though the primitive five digits were lost in many mammal species (e.g. the horse has one toe/hoof at the end of each leg), they were retained among our primate ancestors.

6.3　The Mammalian Corporeal Heritage

The first primitive creatures that Linnaeus would in 1758 dub *Mammalia* were tiny shrew-like creatures with total body lengths of less than 150 mm that evolved from early reptiles, appearing during the Triassic period (230–195 mya) of the early Mesozoic Era. Throughout the Triassic and Jurassic (195–141 mya) mammals remained rather small, the largest growing to the size of a house cat. And they stayed quite literally in the shadows, generally being habitually nocturnal and avoiding the daytime that was the dinosaurian domain.[29] Only in the late Mesozoic, during the Cretaceous Period (141–65 mya), did the placental and marsupial mammalian species 'of the modern aspect' emerge; and only with the mass extinction of dinosaurs on the border of the Mesozoic and Cenozoic (65 mya) did they came into their own.

As characterised in one introductory text on evolution, mammals are 'warm and furry, and they suckle and care for their young'.[30] This depiction points to the most striking and unique adaptations characteristic of the class of mammals – adaptations pertaining to the apparatus, process, and aftermath of their reproduction process and to their warmbloodedness. But other adaptations, especially in skeletal structure and the jaw and dentition, and above all the brain, are not only definitive of mammals in general, but are also fundamental building blocks of the peculiarly human form of corporeal organisation.

Let us begin with the 'warm and furry'. The most striking mammalian characteristic, not immediately visible in itself but certainly manifest in its corporeal and behavioural consequences, is that mammals are *homiotherms*, warm-blooded. Mammals can and must maintain a constant body temperature, with but a couple degrees leeway, in order to remain healthy, functioning, and alive. Mammals have developed several complementary means of keeping their body

---

29　All information in this paragraph from Dodson and Dodson 1985, pp. 472–4.
30　Dodson and Dodson 1985, p. 472. For further comment on the taxon 'mammalia', se Appendix 6.2.

temperature where it belongs. The most visible of these is of course the fur that insulates warm-blooded mammals (with the exception of the 'functionally hairless' human ape; see below). Another is the ingestion of large quantities of food; mammals need a more extensive and more regular menu than cold-blooded animals and have a more difficult time surviving in environments with limited food supplies. But given an adequate food supply, mammals show an impressive range of environmental flexibility. The ability to convert food energy into heat, and to regulate body temperature through various adaptations such as sweating and the temporary dilation or contraction of blood vessels to increase or decrease heat loss, enables mammals to make themselves at home in a large range of environments. If cold-blooded creatures that need not maintain a constant body temperature could develop language and speak, notions of hot and cold would not have much in the way of linguistic or metaphorical value. For warm-blooded creatures, on the other hand, that must maintain a fairly constant body temperature, heat and cold are existentially significant factors; and it is no surprise that the experiential patterns of heat and cold provide a rich source of metaphorical projections.

Because warm-blooded creatures have a very high energy requirement, and must spend a good part of the waking lives foraging for food, both for themselves and also for their offspring during the latter's extended period of dependency, efficient means of locomotion would no doubt facilitate the foraging process. It should therefore be no surprise that the mammalian *Bauplan* included adaptations for greater mobility. Unlike their cold-blooded reptilian ancestors whose limbs come out from the side of the body, mammalian limbs slope downward from the hips and shoulders; this structure conveniently tucks the limbs underneath the body and allows for more efficient and quicker movement. This development contributed significantly to that liberation of the head from the ground which Leroi-Gourhan deemed a crucial prerequisite of the evolution of what Maxine Sheets-Johnstone called a 'mindful body'.[31]

The satisfaction of the dietary requirements of warm-blooded mammals could also be facilitated by more efficient means of processing that food once found or captured. And those dietary requirements are themselves inscribed in the mammalian dental apparatus. In contrast to the uniform sharp-sided teeth of reptiles, amphibians and fish whose function is to hold and kill prey that are generally eaten whole, mammals have a rather varied dental toolkit. It includes four different types of teeth each suited for a particular task: the flat incisors located in the front of the jaw are used for cutting and slicing; the canine teeth

---

31 Sheets-Johnstone 2011.

located behind the incisors, generally long, sharp, and projecting (though small in humans), are in most mammals used as weapons or to kill prey; and the large, thick and heavy premolar and molar teeth are used for grinding. This variety of teeth enables mammals to enjoy a varied diet that could include the plants, fruits, and nuts for which reptilian teeth are useless. Moreover, the ability to chew food, to grind down large pieces with the molars, makes it more easily digested.

The mammalian mode of reproduction was characterised by two peculiar attributes would become definitive also for human mammals. 'After sexual reproduction', writes Wenda Trevathan, 'the next adaptations of concern in the evolution of the human reproductive strategy are the steps of internal fertilization and internal gestation, or the evolution of viviparity from the primitive oviparous baseline. Each step resulted in a further reduction in numbers of offspring that can be reproduced with each generation'. Species reproduction patterns have come to be categorised as either 'r-selected' species that 'produce large numbers of offspring but provide little care to them' (e.g. fish, insects, rodents and rabbits) and K-selected species that have 'few offspring but provide much more care to each of them'.[32] Although both r- and K-selection are found among mammals, the fact that the mammalian lineage of hominids was K-selected would be a crucial factor in structuring their life-cycle and social behaviour. Generalising about K-selected species, Relethford notes that 'the more K-selected the species, the more intelligent it is and the more it relies on learning rather than instinct. Extensive parental care requires increased intelligence and the ability to learn new behaviours in order to provide maximum care for infants. The increased emphasis on learning requires in turn an extended period of childhood during which to absorb the information needed for the adult life. Furthermore, the extension of childhood requires more extensive care, so that offspring are protected during the time they need to complete their growth and learning'.

These 'warm and furry' mammals also suckle and care for their young; and the close mother/child relations characteristic of K-selection are enhanced by the nature of mammalian birth. Mammalian birth is 'viviparous', that is: offspring are 'born', they emerge from the mother's body alive (rather than in the egg-form in oviparous birth). The two forms of live birth differentiate the two basic mammalian subclasses. Viviparous birth is the more common form

---

32   Relethford, 1994, p. 198. Next citation, ibid., 205. The theory of r- and K-selection is attributed to Robert H. MacArthur and Edward O. Wilson's *The Theory of Island Biogeography* (MacArthur and Wilson 1967).

of live birth, practiced by some 4,000 extant species of placental mammals. Less common, though not quite rare, is the ovoviviparous birth practiced by approximately 300 species of extant marsupial mammals. Ovoviviparous birth refers to the embryo forming in eggs that are hatched within the body of the mother, followed by a relatively short intrauterine period of ten to thirty days; and when the extremely underdeveloped foetus is born, it is then either housed in a maternal pouch or clings to the mother's underside for two to five times that long.[33] Although our concern is with placental mammals, of which *Homo sapiens* is one, it is worth noting in passing the vastly different bodies, experiences, and metaphors pertaining to conception, the womb, birth, the umbilical cord, etc. that would have been developed in all diverse human cultures were we ovi- or ovoviviparous creatures.

The viviparous birth of placental mammals is a rather extensive process stretching from well before to well after the actual birth. The length of time between their conception and birth is inordinately long. During its extended stay in the womb, the mammalian embryo/foetus imbibes nutrients through the umbilical cord that attaches it to the placenta which is a rather more efficient means of protecting and feeding the foetus, thus giving placental mammals better chances of surviving than have egg-laying reproduction or non-egglaying mammals. Once born into the world, the mammalian offspring suckles at the mammary glands embedded in its mother's breasts for another extended period. And even after weaned, the offspring remains in a state of extended dependency, childhood, which demands a great deal of parental, usually maternal, time and commitment to gather food for and protect the young. The provision of sustenance and protection during the protracted phase of dependency (which is also a period of instruction and learning; see below) requires a large investment of time and energy on the part of mammalian parents, especially, of course, the mother.

The development of the mammalian brain was a crucial building block of the human brain. A tripartite brain is common to all vertebrates, but those parts vary in size, relative proportions and functions. The hindbrain is generally linked to hearing, balance, reflexive behaviours and control of the automatic functions of the body such as breathing; the midbrain is associated with vision, and the forebrain with the chemical senses of smell and taste.

---

33 To be all-inclusive it is necessary to mention also the now rare and unusual primitive mammalian order of Monotremata, egg-laying mammals found only in Australia (the platypus) and New Guinea (the echidna).

Fish have larger forebrains, and reptiles that rely on vision and hearing have enlarged mid- and hindbrains. The atypical but significant development in the mammalian brain is a 'greatly enlarged forebrain that is responsible for the processing of sensory information and coordination. In particular, the forebrain contains the cerebrum, the outermost layer of brain cells, which is associated with learning, memory, and intelligence'. The folds or convolutions of the cerebrum allow for huge numbers of interconnections between brain cells. With this more developed and differentiated brain, learning and flexible responses become part of the mammalian behaviour repertoire; 'behaviour patterns are less instinctual and rigid' and 'previous experiences become more important in responding to stimuli. As a consequence, mammals are more capable of developing new responses to different situations and are capable of learning from past mistakes. New behaviours are more likely to develop and can be passed on to offspring through the process of learning'.[34]

Built on the foundation of its evolutionary past, the mammalian brain thus takes what amounts to a quantum leap beyond it. As Don Tucker explains in his analysis (of the development of) *Mind from Body*, 'a remarkable feature of the vertebrate brain is that it evolved through the progressive elaboration of certain basic structures'.[35] The evolution of the mammalian brain, he suggests, can be explained with the help of the principle of 'terminal additions', that is: evolution 'through the progressive elaboration of certain basic structures' in which 'newly evolved structures are added on top of the old ones at the end (termination) of the embryological process'. This principle explains 'why, in every mammal brain, we find the major circuits of a fish brain within the brain stem ... and then the reptilian circuits on top of that' and 'only then do we find the mammalian circuits on top of these'. There are, in short, 'multiple learning systems in the mammalian brain, and, as they become mature, they are stacked vertically, one on top of the other'. Mammals thus retain the immediate stimulus-response mechanism of their aquatic and reptilian ancestors, but also develop a much more complex mental mechanism with vastly greater cognitive capacities and a wider and more flexible range of responses.

More specifically, there is in the learning and memory systems of mammals 'a hierarchic structure' which makes expectancy-based learning 'integral to mammalian behaviour'; and though human learning processes are obviously more advanced, Tucker theorises that 'the mammalian adaptive controls that lead to expectant engagement of the world may be integral to ... human

---

34 All citations in this paragraph, Relethford 1994, pp. 204–5.
35 All citations in this paragraph from D. Tucker 2007, pp. 124–5.

structures of intelligence'.[36] Characteristic of this mammalian learning process is that 'an increasing representational capacity acts to separate stimulus and response':

> Just as stimulus-response associations cannot explain mammalian learning, expectancy may be both a necessary explanation and a requisite development in human intelligence. It is not enough to delay responses based on an extended memory capacity and greater recruitment of networks of relevant meaning. People, like other mammals, need to act in the world rapidly, using their powerful memory capacities as effective guides, not as drags on response speed. The evolutionary solution seems to have been expectancy, which creates memories of the future that reach out to oncoming events based on predictions built up from previous learning.

Studies of animal learning principles have found that 'mammals represent their worlds'; they 'continually represent their desired future worlds, and these expectant cognitions are the guides for learning'; and they 'also determine what constitutes information'. In contrast to fish and reptiles whose behaviour is shaped by 'the simple association between stimulus and response', learning in mammals is 'contextual and inextricably bound with an animal's expectancy for what should happen in a given situation'. Mammalian consciousness thus has a 'forward bias': '[t]o be conscious is to lean into the future' and to 'meter our awareness of the world by our expectations of it'.

But the same separation of mammalian brain mechanisms into perceptual systems that take in information and motor systems that create actions, the separation into distinct stimulus and response systems that makes possible this 'lean into the future' and provides time for reflection about the best course of action, also provides time for doubt and uncertainty. And that new separation in the mammalian brain, combined with the lingering fish/reptilian mechanisms of immediate response, is the corporeal foundation of a much-debated philosophical/moral quandary: whether discretion, as folk wisdom would have it, is the better part of valour; or whether Hamlet, ruing that 'the native hue of resolution is sicklied o'er with the pale cast of thought', was correct in concluding with an axiom of self-disgust that 'conscience doth make cowards of us all'. Underlying and in-forming human conscience and wisdom, and even enabling

---

36   D. Tucker 2007, pp. 125–6. Further citations in this paragraph, ibid., p. 126; p. 126, p. 130, p. 130; p. 131.

us to pose one of our mostly lofty philosophical/moral dilemmas of bravery vs. cowardice, spontaneity/impulsiveness vs. wisdom, is a 'base' corporeal foundation, an organisation of the brain that distances the sensory from the motor apparatus and provides us, for better or worse, not only with food for thought, but also with time for reflection.[37]

Beyond their common mode of reproduction and warm-bloodedness, mammalian species exhibit a good deal of variation in their corporeal organisation. For our purposes, the best way to categorise this variation is between species with a more specialised corporeal form and those whose bodies retained more 'primitive', generalised anatomical organs.[38] Significant here is that the retention of generalised 'primitive' traits in some mammals opened evolutionary paths that were closed to others in which selection had bred specialisation. Whereas the first of the class of mammals, like their vertebrate and reptilian ancestors, had five digits at the end of each limb, most of their descendants, lost that primitive pentadactyly as the digits gave way new, more specialised forms. The advantages and limits of this specialisation are well-exemplified in the relation between predatory carnivorous mammalian species and their 'classmates' and prey, the grazing ungulates. This antagonistically symbiotic relationship initiated a cycle of selection for quicker and more efficient movement enabling the predators to pursue and the prey to flee. This selective cycle resulted in at least two key anatomical modifications, both specialisations aimed at speed. One was that '[b]oth carnivores and ungulates have lost clavicles, which brings their shoulders closer together and is an aid to running';[39] and the other transformation of the pendactyl (five-fingered) limb-endings or 'hands' and 'feet' into hooves, paws and claws specialised for speed, sure-footedness and/or tearing. While both of these modifications enhanced speed, they also locked carnivores and ungulates into using their forelegs and forepaws for rapid terrestrial mobility. With all four feet planted firmly on, and adapted to, the ground, these mammalian species were locked into their specialisation, their niche, and a kind of evolutionary stasis in terms of modification of corporeal organisation.

---

37 See Appendix 11.2. for comment on Judith Butler's critique of Louis Althusser's theory that attempts to explain that and how 'conscience doth make subjects of us all' (the title of Butler's article). In this article, Butler presents a critique of Althusser's attempt to explain how ideology produces what might be called 'subjected subjects'.

38 *Oxford English Dictionary* (Online): ORIGIN late Old English, via Latin from Greek *organon* 'tool, instrument, sense organ'*,* reinforced in Middle English by Old French *organe*.

39 Dodson and Dodson 1985, p. 477.

Other mammalian orders, however, whose bodily structure was less specialised and thus retained the more general primitive characteristics, remained 'capable of revolutionary adaptations'.[40] And those most 'revolutionary' of species from which evolved 'forms with the most advanced cerebral features' are, with a certain evolutionary irony, the more primitive and 'least specialized groups', those that maintained the key primitive attributes that were specialised out of existence in carnivores and ungulates. Thus, the retention of the clavicle, while not conducive to the greatest speeds, did facilitate arboreal locomotion, and would provide the foundation for the differentiation and disarticulation of the fore- and hindlimbs such that they would work in different branches of the division of corporeal labour. Even more portentous, however, was the retention of pendactly, the pair of five-digit 'forefeet', of proto hands, that were also immediately valuable in arboreal locomotion, grasping fruit and eventually in making and using tools. The freeing of the hand is, in Leroi-Gourhan's view, the crucial step in the evolutionary process that resulted in *Homo sapiens*: those animals 'whose body structure corresponds to the greatest freeing of the hand are also those whose skull is capable of containing the largest brain, for manual liberation and the reduction of stresses exerted upon the cranial dome are two terms of the same mechanical equation. For each species a cycle is established between its technical ability (its body) and its ability to organize itself (its brain)'. And it is from among the mammalian species that retained the primitive trait of pentadactyly that the primate order with its protohands and larger brain would emerge.

---

40   Information and citations in this paragraph from Leroi-Gourhan 1993, p. 60. The tragic (if that isn't too anthropomorphic a term) evolutionary irony of specialisation is exemplified by various species of mole that dug themselves into an evolutionary hole. Once digging mammals began to burrow underground, natural selection resulted in increasing adaptations to underground life; and beyond a certain point, those animals lost the ability to function aboveground. Subterranean adaptation includes reduction of the eyes and ears, with the consequence that highly specialised burrowers are functionally blind and often hear low-frequency sound better than they do the higher frequencies that travel better in air. These changes result in a sort of dead-end adaptation, where emerging from the burrow aboveground is essentially impossible, and so adaptation tends to proceed toward ever-increasing underground specialisation. Examples of this oft-repeated pattern are: moles (family Talpidae), marsupial moles (family Notoryctidae), golden moles (family Chrysochloridae), mole rats (family Bathyergidae), tuco-tucos (family Ctenomyidae), gophers (family Geomyidae), bamboo rats (subfamily Rhizomyinae), and mole voles (genus *Ellobius*). My thanks to geologist Samantha Hopkins for this insight and information.

6.4 The Primate Corporeal Heritage

'Humans could not have evolved from any creatures other than apes'.[41]

∴

Towards the end of the Mesozoic Era (~252–66 mya), during the dinosaur-dominated Cretaceous (~145–66 mya) period, a number of shrew-like mammals took to the trees.[42] These mammals, rarely larger and generally smaller than a domestic cat, were arboreal, nocturnal and quadrupedal insectivores whose limbs were well-suited to climbing; and as they 'peered nervously from behind some branches', they must have seen the last dinosaurs whose extinction made way for primate primacy.[43] Having outlived the dinosaurs, these 'proto-primates propagated slowly until well into the Cenozoic era. The appearance of flowering plants and trees in the late Paleocene and early Eocene (~55–37.5 mya) provided the ecological framework for extensive radiations of what would come to be considered 'true' or 'modern' primates occurred. And it was during the period of its primate ancestry that the most immediate and definitive foundations of human corporeal organisation took shape, the corporeal foundations that frame the ways in which *Homo sapiens* navigates and apprehends the world – and that make obvious why humans 'could not have evolved from any creatures other than apes'.

Although (or because) some three-hundred living species are classified as primates, it has not been easy to define primate attributes precisely, and the lists of attributes vary greatly in both content and length. Richard Klein re-

---

41 Davidson and Nobel 1993, p. 52.
42 The earliest fossils conveying information about primate evolution are those of the Paleocene mammalian order *Plesiadapidae* of North America and Europe. Their ambiguous status as proto-primates is accurately, if coincidentally (and somewhat ominously) captured in the naming of the oldest Plesiadapform fossil after the site where it was found: *Purgatorious*, found on Purgatory Hill in Montana; and also by the disagreement over whether they were 'the last of the early ground-living primates' or whether the strong claws on their digits are an adaptation for tree-climbing. But whatever the exact status (primate ancestor or offshoot) and habitat (terrestrial, arboreal, or both), and despite much dispute over the question of why primates took to the trees, however, there is no doubt that the further evolution of primates took place in the trees.
43 Benton 2005, p. 366.

sponds to the difficulty by listing seven features 'generally possess[ed]' by living primates that differentiate them from other mammals. John Relethford opines that 'no single characteristic identifies primates; rather they share a set of features' that he elaborates under the headings of skeleton, vision, brain and behaviour, reproduction and care of offspring, and social structure – the latter two seemingly more generally mammalian traits. Paleontologist Michael Benton, on the other hand, notes some '30 or so' characteristics that 'relate to three major sets of adaptations', namely agility in trees, large brain and acute daylight vision, and parental care.[44]

Nevertheless, these and most authors commenting on the difficulty of determining the traits that set primates apart almost unanimously mention a characteristic that is not so much a specific trait, but a more generalised contrast; and that is the rather generalised nature of the primate bodily toolkit as opposed to that of other more specialised mammalian orders. David Pilbeam, for example, comments on the generality of primate characteristics by contrasting their lack of 'obvious anatomical specializations' to such specialised characteristics of other mammalian species as the hooves of ungulates or the incisors of rodents. Moving from anatomy to ethology, Pilbeam finds the same general pattern, noting that 'most primates have a rich repertoire of behaviour and live in social groups organized according to relatively complex patterns of interaction'; the primate order includes many and very diverse species that 'show a wide range of adaptations'.[45] And Anthony Smith, after listing 'the characteristics which distinguish the primates from the bulk of the mammalian stock – the improvement of visual acuity, the deterioration of smell, the development of limbs for grasping, the forelimbs for investigation, and an expansion of the brain for the agility and coordinated skills necessary for an active treetop existence' – makes the 'seemingly paradoxical' comment that perhaps the most notable characteristic of primates is their 'great lack of specialization. On the ground the mammals tended to concentrate on running, on digging, on hopping, on one particular activity and on eating only a small range of foods .... The early primates had simple teeth. They were capable of dealing with a wide selection of foods, and there was little specialisation in other parts of their body. They could survive in a wide variety of circumstances. Many mammals cannot do so, and perish when their precise habitat is suddenly destroyed'.[46] This anatomical and behavioural flexibility, gained 'seemingly paradoxically' by the retention of primitive traits, was enhanced in the course of anthropoid primate

---

44   See also: R. Klein 1989, pp. 40–1; Relethford 1994, p. 208; Benton 2005, p. 364.
45   Pilbeam, 'Human Evolution' in Harrison et al. 1988, pp. 27–30.
46   Anthony Smith 1968, p. 9.

evolution. This phase witnessed the formation of the unique forelimb complex of Hominoid primates, the first skeletal steps crucial to eventual human bipedality, and also the anatomical development of, and the interrelationships among, primate sensory systems.

Early primates were arboreal quadrupeds, the adaptations of whose limbs to life in the trees would have definitive consequences for human evolution. Climbing trees, hanging from branches, and springing from one branch to another all require a bone structure that allows flexibility of the limbs. Changes in the primate skeletal structure that facilitate life in an arboreal habitat include grasping hands and feet and a very mobile and flexible shoulder and arm structure. Though lacking the specialised anatomical structures that make for speed efficiency, the evolution of their limbs and limb-endings made for a much greater efficiency in locomotive dexterity that enabled most primates to be kinaesthetically at home not only in the arboreal canopy, but eventually on the ground as well.

The two major adaptations resulting in this dexterity are actually cases, not of the development of specialised structures, but rather of non-adaptation or adaptive retention of generalised ones. As Relethford notes, 'the arm and leg bones of primates follow the basic pattern of many vertebrates' – a more generalised limbic structure that could be adapted to an arboreal locomotive efficiency defined rather in terms of flexibility than speed. The retention of the clavicle and the five-digit extremities were obviously of great value in brachiation. So too was the retention of a more 'primitive' vertebrate bone structure in the limbs: each limb consists of an upper bone and two lower bones that are joined, and able to be bent, at roughly their midpoint which makes for efficiently flexible movement. This flexibility is enhanced and refined by the two bones in the lower limbs, 'wrist' and 'ankle', which enabled most primates to rotate those grasping extremities at limbs' end and facilitated arboreal mobility. When at the end of those flexible limbs are limber, five-digit, prehensile extremities one of whose digits is opposable, the result is that, in contrast to more specialised mammal species whose reach exceeds their grasp, the grasping range of (both sets of) primate limbs is virtually coextensive with its reach. Relethford suggests that we 'imagine trying to jump from one branch to another with your arms and legs made up of one long bone' or 'climb in a tree without the ability to move your hand into different positions'. The flexibility of primate limbs, 'obtained by the retention of a generalized skeletal structure', makes for such impressive flexibility in primate locomotion and in the tactile investigation and manipulation of things.[47]

---

47 Relethford 1994, p. 211. Citations in the following paragraph from ibid., p. 232; pp. 231–

This general skeletal flexibility became even more elastic in hominoid primates with increased range of mobility of the shoulders. Primate habitat and habits encouraged the development of a particular kind of climbing that differentiated them from their simian cousins: Hominoids 'are adept at climbing and hanging from branches. They are suspensory climbers and hangers'. Such activity requires 'three basic anatomical features': 'First, hominoids have a larger and stronger collarbone than monkeys. Second, the hominoid shoulder joint is very flexible and capable of a wide angle of movement. Third, the hominoid shoulder blades are located more toward their backs. By contrast, monkey's shoulder blades are located more toward the sides of the chest. Hominoid shoulder joints face outward, compared to the downward-facing shoulder joints of monkeys'. The particular upper body and shoulder anatomy that enabled hominoids to 'raise their arms above their heads with little trouble, whereas a monkey would find this difficult' is, according to Relethford, '[p]erhaps one of the[ir] most important characteristics'. Our arboreal heritage has served us well; for, although the human shoulder/forelimb complex has certainly been evolutionarily refined, its unique biomechanical flexibility is an essential part of our inheritance from our brachiating hominoid ancestors.

The key to the functioning and flexibility of the entire forelimb/forepaw become arm/hand complex is the shoulder that 'represents the first link in a mechanical chain of levers that extends from the shoulder to the fingertips. It is defined in a broad sense as the group of structures connecting the arm to the thorax'; as 'by far the most intricate joint complex in the body', the shoulder's 'combined and coordinated movements of four distinct articulations [...] allow the arm to be positioned in space for efficient function. The result is a range of motion that easily exceeds that of any other joint: the humerus can be moved through a space exceeding a hemisphere'.[48] Moving down the arm, '[t]he elbow-forearm complex represents the second link in a mechanical chain of levers that begins at the shoulder and ends at the fingertips'. This complex allows for the refining of movements initiated at the shoulder: 'The shoulder, as the first link, functions to permit the hand to be positioned anywhere within an imaginary sphere that represents the full excursion of shoulder motion. Elbow motion allows the height and length of the

---

2. Human hominoids, have retained, though seldom take advantage of, this suspensory climbing and hanging ability – the one exception being, as Relethford notes, children playing on 'so-called "monkey bars" at playgrounds' which, he corrects, 'should more properly be called "hominoid bars" [because] the ability to suspend by the arms and then swing from one rung of the bars to the next is a basic hominoid trait'.

48   Zuckerman and Matsen in Nordin and Frankel 1989, p. 225.

upper extremity to be adjusted, whereas forearm rotation allows the hand to be placed in the most effective position for function'.[49] And at the other end of the forearm, the wrist is responsible for even further refinement of hand movements: The wrist 'complex is capable of a substantial arc of motion that augments hand and finger function, yet it possesses a considerable degree of stability. The wrist functions kinematically by allowing for changes in the location and orientation of the hand relative to the forearm, and kinetically by transmitting loads from had to forearm and vice versa. Although the function of all joints of the upper extremity is to position the hand in space so that it can perform the activities of daily living, the wrist appears to be the key to hand function. Stability of the wrist is essential for proper functioning of the digital flexor and extensor muscles, and wrist position affects the ability of the fingers to flex and extend maximally and to grasp effectively during prehension'.[50]

These potential feats of arms would have been less pronounced if primate extremities had all remained feet, or even monkey hands. But the hands of our primate ancestors featured four fingers and an opposable thumb capable of prehensile grasping. While the human hand has a longer thumb, and shorter, flatter, yet more mobile fingers, the primate hand is certainly the prototype of its human descendant. Introducing the biomechanics of the human hand, which apply also to that of its primate predecessor, Fadi J. Bejjani and Johan M.F. Landsmeer first note that the reach of this 'final link in the mechanical chain of levers that begins at the shoulder' depends on 'the mobility of the shoulder, the elbow, and the wrist, all operating in different planes, [which] allows the hand to move within a large volume of space and to reach all parts of the body with relative ease'. But it is the final link that completes this musculoskeletal chain. For the 'remarkably mobile and malleable' hand is capable of a great variety of functions, from grasping objects of various shapes, to tactile exploration, to emphasising an idea being expressed.[51]

The astonishing range of capabilities of the five-digit human hand with opposable thumb has long attracted attention from students of human nature. But Aristotle's eloquent and worthy tribute to the human hand is marred by his inverse reasoning downward from the brain which led him rather contemptuously, and incorrectly, to dismiss the corporeal insight of his learned pre-Socratic predecessor:

---

49   Zuckerman and Matsen in Nording and Frankel 1989, p. 249.
50   Steven Stuchin in Nordin and Frankel 1989, p. 261.
51   Bejjani and Johan M.F. Landsmeer in Nordin and Frankel 1989, p. 275.

Anaxagoras indeed asserts that it is his possession of hands that makes man the most intelligent of animals; but surely the reasonable point of view is that it is because he is the most intelligent animal that he has hands. Hands are an instrument; and Nature, like a sensible human being, always assigns an organ to the animal that can use it. [...] We should expect the most intelligent to be able to employ the greatest number of organs or instruments to good purpose; now the hand would appear to be not one single instrument, but many, as it were an instrument that represents many instruments.[52]

Exemplifying that flexibility by describing its role in what the citizen-warrior knew best, Aristotle contrasts the military value of human hands to the fixed corporeal manual weapons of other animals. Because of the hand's flexibility, humans have available many means of defence and can change them at any time: the hand 'is as good as a talon, or a claw, or a horn, or again, a pear or a sword, or any other weapon because it can seize and hold them all'. Unfortunately (although, coming from one who considered emancipation from labour a necessary prerequisite for the pursuit of philosophy and truth, not surprisingly), while Aristotle extended his eloquence to the hands' elegance in aesthetic pursuits such as painting, and writing, he did not deign to acknowledge their absolutely essential role in making and using tools and building the worlds within which we live. Although he may well have appreciated the finished product, his contempt for, and condescension toward, labour went so far as to dismiss the sculpting that produced all those chiselled figures of marble, those much-admired artefacts of the 'Golden Age' of Greece, as 'a mechanical and vulgar craft'.[53]

However refined, the human hand owes its sophistication, its 'consummation of all perfection as an instrument', to the 'extraordinary degree of primitiveness' that it shows.[54] While most accurate, this is, marvels John Napier, nevertheless an 'astounding conclusion when one thinks of its specialised movements, its acute sensitivity, its precision, subtlety and expressiveness'.[55] While

---

52   Aristotle, On Animals, IV, 10, cited in David Katz 1989, p. 244 note 2.
53   Aristotle, *Politics* VIII. 2, 1337b8–15; Plutarch was equally dismissive, noting that even though well-sculpted marble 'delights with its grace, it does not necessary follow that the one who wrought it is worthy of your esteem'. Plutarch, *Life of Pericles* 2.1–2. My thanks to Carlo DaVia for contributing these passages.
54   This citation from nineteenth-century naturalist Charles Bell in his book *The Hand*, cited in Napier 1993, p. 44.
55   Napier, 1993, p. 10. The following summary of the evolution of the hands is drawn from Napier, Chapter 4.

hands as skilled as those of primates in general and humans in particular are biologically unique, their evolutionary origins are ancient – going far back beyond the primates and even mammals to the reptilian past. The earliest mammals all retained that five-digit reptilian foot. As noted above, however, evolutionary developments in the majority of mammalian orders led away from the primitive and generalised feet to feet specialised for speed and escape (the hooves of the ungulates), for speed and attack (the claws of canine and feline species), for scratching, digging, and climbing (the claws of rodents and squirrels). The retention of the primitive five-digit extremity among mammals is as peculiar as its primitive predecessor was pervasive; and the primate precursor of the human hand evolved in a habitat rather unfrequented by mammals: the arboreal habitat that was 'the only environment in which the major distinctions of the primate hand could have developed'.[56]

One of the first steps toward human hands was the development of the prehensility, 'the ability to seize or grasp an object and hold it securely in one hand'.[57] And the arboreal experience of primates, who 'climb by grasping', led to 'critical adaptations' such as 'flat nails rather than claws, and opposable, prehensile first fingers and first toes'.[58] According to Napier, the impetus for this adaptation was likely a 'dietary change' in response to the spread of angiosperms, fruiting plants and trees, during the Cretaceous period. Sketching a 'plausible chain of events', Napier, writes:

> Assuming that the habitat of the earliest primate insect-eaters was the deep litter and low shrubs of the forest floor, the first effect of a change of diet would eventually have been a change of habitat by exploitation of the trees where food was more prolific and of a different sort. Feeding in trees on fruits and leaves would have raised many problems concerned with life high above ground, not the least of which would have been the question of stability. Claws would have been reduced to nails and digital touch pads on the tips of the fingers would have become important. Divergence of the big toe probably preceded divergence of the thumb, but soon competition would have placed strong selection pressures on the increased mobility of the thumb and the manipulative capacity of sensitive touch pads. Thus, the forefoot would have become a foot-hand.[59]

---

56   Napier 1993, p. 84.
57   Napier 1993, p. 91.
58   Pilbeam in Harrison et al. 1989, p. 42.
59   Napier 1993, p. 82.

If prehensility was crucial to the emergence of the 'foot-hand' with its nails and digital touch pads, it was the opposable thumb that gave rise to the hand proper. Attributing to the 'movement of the thumb [...] all the skilled procedures of which the hand is capable', Napier compares the hand without a thumb to 'at worst, nothing but an animated fish-slice, and at best a pair of forceps whose points don't meet properly'.[60]

Despite the incomparable degree of manual flexibility, that fore-hand had become about as sophisticated in this regard as it could, as long as the forelimbs were still being used in locomotion. Among the higher primates, however, a new mode of motility would evolve from quadrupedalism, first into knuckle-walking in apes, eventually into the full bipedality of hominids that freed the foot-hands from the labour of locomotion. The eventual consequence was a unique arrangement of the hand's 19 bones and 14 joints that 'provide the structural foundation for [its] extraordinary functional adaptability'.[61] All these bones and joints provide the hand with the two degrees of freedom that allows the fingers to be flexed into a fist or spread like a fan.[62] The addition of an opposable thumb to these flexible digits gives the hand an extraordinary range of dexterity; it renders the hand capable of at several kinds of grasps, grips and pinches that enable it to hold large, small, and irregularly shaped objects.[63]

---

60 Napier 1993, p. 55. And he adds that evolution of the opposable thumb had essential consequences 'for the emergence of man from a relatively undistinguished primate background. Through natural selection, it promoted the adoption of the upright posture and bipedal walking, tool-using and tool-making which, in turn, led to enlargement of the brain through a positive feed-back mechanism. In this sense it was probably the single most crucial adaptation in man's evolutionary history' (Napier 1993, p. 55).
61 Bejjani and Landsmeer in Nordin and Frankel 1989, p. 275.
62 R. McNeill Alexander 1992, p. 20.
63 What may at first glance seem to be an infinite number of movements that the hand can perform in picking, grabbing, gripping, holding a great variety of objects can actually be reduced to two main and two subsidiary patterns. The two main patterns, made possible by the two degrees of freedom in the human thumb are: the Precision Grip which involves opposing the thumb to one or more of the fingers and is executed between the thumb and finger pad(s), and employed when delicacy of handling and accuracy of instrumentation are essential and power is a secondary consideration; and the Power Grip, 'executed between the surface of the fingers and the palm with the thumb acting as a buttressing and reinforcing agent' and 'under some conditions ... suppl[ying] directional grip' (Alexander 1992, p. 28). Two subsidiary grips are: hook grip which is 'a function of the flexors of the fingers; the knuckle-joints are straight and the two terminal joints acutely bent' and is used when carrying a suitcase or when grasping specialized tools such as pliers or wire-cutters; and the scissor grip, 'in which an object is grasped between the sides of the terminal phalanges of the adjacent index and middle fingers' – a common grip on a cigarette and occasionally used to pick up small, flat objects when the thumb cannot be

The fingers' flexibility, their softness, and their nails enable the manipulation of objects of various sizes and delicacy and the dexterity to pick at the strings and keys of violins and typewriters at astonishing speeds; and the tactile sensitivity of palm and fingers make the hand one of the most important sources of sensory information in the body.[64]

In a taxonomic order already consisting of the 'most touch-oriented of all mammals',[65] the manumission of the hands from their rough and callous-inducing perambulatory role not only enabled them to be fully devoted to manual tasks, making possible an unparalleled sophistication in manipulative capacities, but it also gave rise to a heightened and refined haptic sensitivity that opened up new 'worlds of touch'.[66] Although the manipulability and sensitivity of the hand that so enhanced the haptic powers of primates seem to provide reason enough to address the sense of touch here, that discussion will be postponed until touch assumes its fully and uniquely human form in the *Homo* line. For, despite its unique and impressive powers, the hand is only one instrument in the haptic toolkit of *Homo* species – a took-kit that will not be fully stocked until the emergence of the 'naked ape' whose uncovered skin makes the entire body into a uniquely sensitive tactile organ. Thus, although the haptic sensory apparatus was chronologically the first to appear in animal life, it will for this reason be the last discussed in this sketch of human corporeal organisation. There is nevertheless a constellation of pressing sensory matters

---

        brought into play (descriptions according to Napier 1993, pp. 62–4 and Alexander 1992, pp. 28–31). Of course, the extraordinary flexibility of the arm placing the hand and of the gripping fingers gave rise to a huge range of possibilities. 'There is no apparent need for more than three fingers to grip any single rigid object, but some of the tasks we perform with our hands involve holding several things at once, or several parts of a flexible object … Having five fingers rather than three enables us to do complicated things' like tie knots (Alexander 1992, p. 19).

64   By way of a graphic contrast with a crab attempting to grasp a metal bar with its hard-shelled claw, Alexander notes that '[o]ne solution to the problem of holding hard things is to have soft finger tips' (Alexander 1992, p. 18). And inviting the reader to imagine a crab holding an egg without breaking it, he reminds us that the same soft-tipped digits enable humans to hold both hard and delicate objects. On the value of fingernails, Napier writes: 'The principle function of nails is to provide both a rigid backing and a protective carapace for the pulpy fingertip which is of such critical importance for the manipulation of small objects and the discrimination of textures. The secondary functions are legion – from winding a watch to opening a cellophane-wrapped package. Habitual nail-biting may have many sinister temperamental overtones, but a far worse deprivation is the loss to the nail-biter of a built-in tool-kit of cutters, pliers, scrapers and screwdrivers' (Napier, 1993, p. 42).

65   Jablonski 2013, p. 98.

66   Katz 1989.

to be discussed at this point; for the sensory constellation – by which I mean the range of each sense and their contributions, both relative and absolute, to human sensory experience – of *Homo sapiens* was formed among our anthropoid primate ancestors.

6.5   The Theoretical Powers of the Senses

6.5.1   *Introductory*

After centuries of favourable reception, Descartes' anointing of sight as 'the most comprehensive and noblest' of our senses has in recent decades become rather incendiary, igniting poststructuralist/postmodernist attacks on what is supposed, from that perspective, to be the undeserved 'hegemony of vision' in the oppressive 'ocularcentric' regime of 'modernity'.[67] But in their haste to beat back 'ocularcentrism', such critics take a short-sighted look both at what Descartes actually wrote about the sense of sight and at the sense of sight itself – which results in a misplaced 'denigration of vision'.[68] Critics often counter Descartes' evaluation of vision by espousing the virtues of the other senses – as if he had ignored them. But even a glance at his comments on the senses more generally reveals that it is hard to attack Descartes on these grounds. For in the first part of the sentence that designates vision the noblest, Descartes states rather categorically that 'all the management of our lives depends on the senses', that is: on *all* of the senses. His designation of vision as the noblest in the human sensual hierarchy is neither a negation nor a denigration of the other senses. It is rather a statement of comparative nobility, that reserves for vision the 'royal' status of *primus inter pares* – a status that, I shall argue, accurately represents the sensual hierarchy of primates – human or otherwise.

Anti-ocularcentrics tend to take a rather dim view of the sense of sight, and focus exclusively on only one, and a rather particular use of primate vision: they focus on the stare or reifying gaze. Staring is of course a very common sociocultural usage of vision; and it certainly can be used to intimidate, to fix another as 'other'. It would, however, first of all be safe to assume that the main reason

---

67   Descartes' comment about vision as the noblest sense is from Descartes 1999, p. 167.
68   The term 'denigration of vision' is Martin Jay's in *Downcast Eyes*. For discussions of the attack on vision in French thought and by postmodernists more generally, see Jay 1993 and Levin 1993. As Jay notes, despite his encomium to vision, 'Descartes, like Plato before him, was never content with the sufficiency of mere sense experience, visual or otherwise' (Jay 1993, pp. 72–3).

for the efficacy of the primate stare is precisely because of the capacities and power of the visual apparatus embedded in the primate 'body natural' – among nearly blind moles, needless to say, the stare would be as little useful socially as it is for purely perceptual apprehension. More importantly, however, is the simple fact that there is much more to the sense of sight than just the stare – and it should be noted too that the stare can be used not only to distance and reify, but also, and very effectively, to attract. Their own insightfulness inhibited by a self-induced myopia vis-à-vis the 'body natural', the denigrators of vision can cast only a dull light on the social and cultural uses of vision that relegates the richness and multi-dimensionality of the human visual apparatus, and also of the social and cultural usages they seek to illuminate, to the shadows.[69]

As should be obvious, the positing of the primacy of vision must not be taken as implying that the other senses are irrelevant. Nor does it preclude the possibility that a given culture will evaluate the senses differently and construct a different hierarchy of the cultural significance of the senses. But I would argue that a deeper and broader understanding of socio-cultural uses and constructions of all the senses can be gained by mapping their capacities and limits and understanding their place in the primate sensory hierarchy. Accordingly, the tasks of the following cartography of the sensory apparatuses embedded in the human 'body natural' are: to review the patents of nobility of the various senses in the primate sensory hierarchy; to trace the ascendancy of vision in that hierarchy; and to elaborate the consequent reconfiguring of the sensory constellation that was bequeathed to the hominid descendants of the arboreal anthropoid primates. In so doing I will seek also to show that the sensory apparatuses are not just simple, but rather foundational prerequisites of socio-cultural constructions, that is: that the socio-culturally specific uses of, and meanings invested in, the senses are closely related to, and in-formed by, the capacities and limits of each sensory apparatus embedded in human corporeal organisation.

If ultra-constructionists were to admit that the body social or cultural does *not* negate the body physical, and if they were then to look carefully at the anatomy of human sensory apparatuses, they would find reliable indicators of the relative nobility of all the senses. Descartes' tribute to vision is really

---

69   For studies in the fairly new ultra-constructionist 'Histories of the Senses' that sees itself as a counter to the 'universalism' of the more 'traditional' psychophysical approaches, and that proceeds as though the anatomy, physiology and psychophysics of the senses were historically and culturally irrelevant and dissolves species-specific and very corporeal sensory apparatuses into exclusively cultural constructions of the senses –, see: Classen 1993, Jütte 2005, and Mark Smith 2007.

neither astounding nor outrageous – nor, considering the relative contribution of vision to human sensory apprehension, incorrect. For there is no doubt that anthropoid primate species, *Homo sapiens* included, are existentially dependent on vision.[70] Perception, as Peter Dodwell puts it, 'is the primary process by means of which [human beings] obtain knowledge of the world' – and estimates are that 'more than 80 per cent of it is accounted for by vision'.[71] Nevertheless, rather than quibble over the quantitative question of which sense is the noblest of senses (and not without reason do they all have their champions), I shall follow instead the lead of Giannozzo Manetti and Michel de Montaigne. In his paean to the 'Dignity of Man' Manetti sings the praises of the senses:

> For there is no human action – wonderful to say – if we pay diligent and close attention to its nature from which man does not draw at least some little pleasure. Nay, he at all times takes such deep and intense pleasure from each and every one of his external senses – sight, hearing, taste, smell and touch – that other interests meanwhile appear superfluous, excessive and unnecessary. It would be hard, indeed impossible, to describe the intense pleasures that possess man: they derive partly from the untrammelled vision of beautiful bodies, partly from listening to sounds and symphonies and even more delightful things, partly from smelling the odors of flowers and such like, partly from tasting various sweet and succulent viands and finally, partly from the touch of the softest substances.[72]

And despite his desire that the senses be governed by reason, Montaigne surrendered to them as 'our masters': 'Knowledge begins through them and is resolved into them. After all, we would know no more than a stone, if we did not know that there is sound, smell, light, taste, measure. ... The senses are the beginning and the end of human knowledge'.[73] Or as e.e. cummings put it in a more troubled twentieth-century vocabulary:

> My mind is
> A big hunk of irrevocable nothing which touch and

---

[70] The emphasis here is on *species*, for individual blindness obviously occurs. The indubitable point, however, is that were we as a species as (eye) blind as a bat, our lives and of courses our cultures would be radically different. Species blindness would also, and obviously, preclude the not uncommon human cultural deployment of blindness as the source of insight, of a means to a higher vision (see below).

[71] Dodwell in Gregory and Coleman 1995a, p. 1.

[72] Manetti 1966, pp. 76–7.

[73] Montaigne, cited in LeGuerer 1994, p. 156.

> Taste and smell and hearing and sight keep hitting and
> chipping with sharp fatal tools
> in an agony of sensual chisels I perform squirms of
> chrome and execute strides of cobalt

The point here, accordingly, is to address the wondrous qualities of each of the senses and to sketch the patterns of experience and knowledge that each makes possible. And one of the many lessons to be learned by reviewing the nobility of each of the senses is that a sensory system's contribution to an organism's life can be in inverse proportion to its psychophysical weakness – and this is especially true of human life in which cultural forms do not negate, but rather refract the 'natural'.

6.5.2 Matter That Sees: On the Ascendance of Vision and the Reconfiguring of the Sensory Apparatus of Anthropoid Primates

In the history of literature, the moment quite literally of 'insight' into one's world and/or one's self often comes with blindness, as for example with Sophocles's Oedipus, Shakespeare's Gloucester, Goethe's Faust. In what might be considered the origin myth of the Western philosophical tradition, Plato's 'Allegory of the Cave', the moment of insight comes when one is freed from the deception of perceptions provided by the body's eyes and emerges into the physical light of the sun – which is of course deployed metaphorically as illuminating that which the emancipated one can see in his 'mind's eye'. The perceptual apparatus of that 'noblest sense', however, is not the cyclopsian 'mind's eye' of philosophy that has been evoked from Plato through Descartes and well beyond. Philosophers' metaphorical attribution of vision to the 'mind's eye', the notion of a 'seeing mind', is an idealist fetish that has become so commonplace that the *Oxford English Dictionary* defines the verbal form of 'vision' as 'to display to the eye or mind ... to bring before the eye of the mind' – which presumably needs no physical light in order to 'see'.[74] But the Hebrew story of *Genesis* is far more corporeally insightful in this regard. For the first creative act of the immaterial deity was to 'let there be light' in order to be able, at the end of each of the following days of creation, to view the fruits of, the artefacts produced by, 'His' labour – and to *see* that 'it was good'.[75]

---

74 *Oxford English Dictionary*, 'Vision', Second Edition, 1989, 2 March 2009, http://www-oed-com.libproxy.uoregon.edu/view/Entry/223944?rskey=hBWDu4&result=2&isAdvanced=false#eid.

75 I borrowed this notion from Diane Ackerman 1991, p. 231. Because, however, the sun and

While visual percepts must be 'brought before the mind' in order to be seen, a 'mind's eye' would be of dubious value: as singular, it could only produce monocular vision, and is thus incapable of seeing objects 'clearly and distinctly' (that is, for Descartes, accurately and truthfully); and because the 'mind's eye' can 'see' only ideas, it is fully an-aesthetic, asensual and, among other things, incapable of colour vision. Vision is quite literally in the eyes of the beholder. It is not the 'mind's eye' that brings visual images before the mind, but rather the body's visual apparatus consisting of two frontally-set eyes capable of stereoscopic and colour vision that produces and allows us to perceive three-dimensional images of a colourful world. The ascendancy of vision in the primate sensory hierarchy was, in the eyes of many observers, responsible for the development of the human brain itself. Whether or not vision is the noblest, it is certainly the most informative of human senses. And human eyes establish a rich and sophisticated set of experiential patterns that are fundamental to the forms and contents of human consciousness and cultures.

Richard Gregory's reference to the emergence of eyes (that is: of matter that sees) as 'largely mysterious' seems rather an understatement; 'miraculous' seems much more appropriate. Nevertheless, given the existence of light-sensitive organs, the general moments of the evolutionary process leading to the particular form and capacities of human eyes are clear enough. To Gregory's genealogical glance, the anatomy of the eyes themselves allows itself to be read as an open book of their evolutionary history:

> It might be said that by moving from the centre of the human retina to its periphery we travel back in evolutionary time; from the most highly organised structure to a primitive eye, which does little more than detect movements of shadows.
>
> The edge of the retina is sensitive only to movement. ... The very extreme edge of the retina is even more primitive: when stimulated by movement we experience nothing, but a reflex is initiated which rotates the eye to bring the moving object into central vision, so that the highly developed foveal region with its associated central neural network is brought into play for identifying the object. The edge of the retina is thus an early–

'natural' light were not created until the fourth day, the nature of this primordial light is not exactly clear – perhaps it was a light visible to the mind's eye. Nevertheless, the use of visual criteria for the revelation of the cosmos is telling.

warning device, used to rotate the eyes to aim the sophisticated object-recognition part of the system on to objects likely to be friend or foe or food rather than neutral.[76]

The process began with a sensitivity characteristic of 'almost every living thing': the simple sensitivity to light. The 'first simple eyes' (which can hardly be classified as eyes at all and are more accurately termed 'photoreceptors') were 'light-sensitive spots on the surface of simpler animals', that 'responded only to light, and changing intensity of light'.

From 'so simple a beginning' (in Darwin's memorable phrase), and through a still unknown process, emerged 'the later image-forming eyes'. As Gregory reconstructs the likely sequence of the evolution of vision, these photoreceptors became recessed in uncovered pits which protected them from the direct glare of light and enabled them better to detect moving shadows which signalled danger or food. A still extant example is the *Nautilus*, a marine mollusk whose eye consists of but 'a pin-hole to form an image'.[77] This 'open-pit' eye is without a protective lens and is thus often temporaily blocked by floating debris which is then washed out by the sea. The next evolutionary step was the development of a transparent protective membrane which eventually, by way of 'chance mutations', thickened in its centre and became 'a crude lens'. The inside of this crudely-lensed *Ur*-eye was 'filled with specially manufactured fluids to replace the sea' – which leads Gregory to the primitive prototype of one of the two most profoundly and almost uniquely human expressions of emotions (the other being the smile): the shedding of 'human tears [that] are a re-creation of the primordial ocean, which bathed the first eyes'.

Lensed eyes evolved into a great variety of forms – from the many-lensed eyes of arthropods and insects that go along with few receptors and a simple brain to the single-lensed eye with thousands or millions of receptors tied to a more complex brain, typical of vertebrates.[78] The more limited concern here, however, is the practical ascendance of vision as certainly the dominant and most comprehensive of anthropoid senses. The visual apparatus that emerged among Eocene and Oligocene primates is essentially that which anatomically modern *Homo sapiens* inherited. The formation of the anthropoid visual apparatus, moreover, is important not only for its own sake, but also because of its crucial consequences for the entire complex of anthropoid (including human) senses. For not only was the anthropoid visual system formed during

---

76   Gregory 1990, pp. 70, 101. Next citation in this paragraph, ibid., 35.
77   All citations in this paragraph, Gregory 1990, p. 37.
78   Ibid.

this crucial period, but with it also the particular anthropoid constellation of the senses, the anthropoid mode of sensation (the anatomy, physiology, capacities and relative strength of the various sensory organs). Though perhaps not as miraculous as the initial emergence of matter that sees, the anthropoid visual system is at least in the category of wonders; and the degree of the visual patterning of anthropoid experience in general and the range of visual contributions in human cultural forms in particular should not be overlooked.

Even before delving into the fine points and powers of primate vision, an indication of its relative importance for primates can be read from an interesting divergence in primate facial morphologies, not only from that of most other mammal species, but also from the more intimately related prosimian primates. Like most mammals, prosimian primates (lemur, tarsiers, etc.) 'have larger and more projecting faces' than anthropoid primates with a 'globular' skull and flattened face. This, David Pilbeam explains, is 'partly related to the importance of olfaction' in the former, and to a 'reduction in the olfactory apparatus' in the latter.[79] The 'hegemony of vision', so freely denounced by the critics of 'ocularcentrism', is not, as those critics would have it, simply a cultural construction, a production of the Western intellectual tradition. It is rather an evolutionary consequence to be taken quite literally at face-value as a corporeal clue to the anthropoid primate realignment of the mammalian sensory order of things; for, objectified in the snout protruding outwards from the face of most mammals and prosimian primates, and sensibly held close to the ground, is a powerful olfactory apparatus. The biological fact of the 'hegemony of vision' in anthropoid primates, on the other hand, is objectified in their flattened faces and modest noses (Cyrano's and Pinocchio's notwithstanding). The hegemony of vision that began to emerge in tree-dwelling and eventually knuckle-walking primates would be reinforced and expanded with the evolution of that uniquely hominid trait, bipedality, that lifted the nose far off the ground. But that is jumping too far ahead, and it is first necessary to glance at the key aspects of the primate ocular apparatus, at the beholding eyes outfitted with binocular, stereoscopic, and colour vision – and also at the extremely rich, yet also extremely limited worlds that they reveal.

---

79   Pilbeam in Harrison et al. 1989, pp. 35–7. The larger, projecting prosimian face is, Pilbeam continues, also related 'to the biomechanical requirements of tooth use in mainly insectivorous forms which use their projecting incisors and canines as dental combs or gum scoops; and partly reflecting a small brain. The orbits are surrounded by a bony ring, are quite large, and face more forwards than sideways'. The 'globular' skull of anthropoid primates is likewise 'related, in part, to reduction in the olfactory apparatus, but also to biomechanical factors that involve moving the dentition backwards under the orbits'.

Given the breadth, depth, and richness of our visual world, it seems all but impossible to imagine that we actually can see only the tiniest fraction of all there is that could be seen. Electromagnetic radiation consists of radio waves, infra-red, light, ultraviolet, and x-rays, that are essentially the same, differing only in their frequency. Light waves are but a sliver of the total range of electromagnetic radiation, the spectrum of light visible to the human eye is but a sliver of that – only about one-seventieth of the total electromagnetic spectrum.[80] Or as Richard Gregory explains: 'Only a very narrow band of these frequencies, less than an octave in width, stimulates the eye to give vision and colour. ... Looked at in this way, we are almost blind'. In addition to the outer limits of our eyes' range, there are internal ones as well: 'only about 10% of the light reaching the eye gets to the receptors, the rest being lost by absorption and scattering within the eye before the retina is reached'.[81] Hence we cannot even see most of what is within our field of vision. Nevertheless, we should not let ourselves be overwhelmed by our blindness to so much of what there is to see; for, if we close our eyes to all that we *can* see, we will fail to see how much of human worlds is constituted through the visual apparatus that is the legacy of our primate ancestry. Were we, for example, able, like bees, to perceive ultraviolet,[82] the world would appear to us in shades of blue; or if we could detect infrared, the world would appear in shades of orange and red – like daytime landscapes seen through the haze of forest fires. Were the boundaries of our vision extended so that we could see a wider band of the electromagnetic spectrum, the Moody Blues need not have sung 'in search of lost chords', nor suggested the use of perception-intensifying substances in order to apprehend that which is

> all around if we could but perceive.
> To know ultraviolet, infrared and X-rays
> Beauty to find in so many ways[83]

But loss can also be gain, and the setting of limits can enhance capacities within those limits. And if Descartes' establishment of 'clarity and distinctness' as the criteria of truth may have been philosophical overreach, there is no doubt that

---

80   Geldard 1972, p. 28.
81   Gregory 1990, p. 29.
82   According to, but unspecified by, Frank Geldard, human eyes are apparently 'under some special conditions capable of responding to waves coming from the infrared and ultraviolet regions' (Geldard 1972, p. 21).
83   'The Word' written by Graeme Edge of the Moody Blues, *In Search of the Lost Chord* album.

the clarity and distinctness of primate visual perception is essential to human successes in apprehending and navigating the world

The two essential primate foundations of human vision are the binocular, stereoscopic vision and highly developed colour vision that emerged among the arboreal and diurnal primates ancestral to *Homo sapiens*. For those tree-dwellers striving toward rapid and agile movement through the arboreal world, it was an obvious advantage to be equipped with acute visual depth-perception. Moreover, colourful fruits, the key food source of arboreal primates would be more visually discernible by daylight than at night when, to paraphrase Hegel, all fruits are black. Thus, regardless of whether the move toward binocular and stereoscopic vision in primates began in a pre-arboreal nocturnal phase,[84] the arboreal phase and the diurnality that accompanied it were essential both in the fine-tuning of the primate visual apparatus and also in the addition of the qualitatively new dimension of acute colour vision, both of which would in turn be crucial to the development of the primate brain and the determination of its contents.

Although not uncommon among arboreal mammals and mammalian and avian predators, eyes situated frontally side-by-side and thus capable of stereoscopic vision are by no means the norm in any order except primates. Most mammal species have eyes on the sides of their heads aiming outwards in opposite directions, thus maximizing the visual field to virtually 360 degrees, and therewith the ability to detect potentially threatening movement (and a neck flexible enough to turn the head without moving the rest of the body). In doing so, however, the two sideways-facing eyes produce different, non-overlapping images. The result is a dual monoscopic vision that, relative to binocular vision, can detect motion in a much wider field of vision, but is less accurate in delineating objects and situating them in space. Such monoscopic vision can of course be hazardous when moving about in an arboreal environment. Rapid arboreal locomotion requires the capacity to perceive distance and depth in three spatial dimensions, adding height to the length and breadth dimensionality that terrestrial creatures confront; and it also requires the ability to obtain at a glance non-ambiguous information such as the distance to a

---

84 It could very well be, as Matt Cartmill hypothesised with his visual-predation theory, that the move among primates toward binocular and stereoscopic vision began in a pre-arboreal nocturnal phase. And it can readily be admitted that arboreal existence does not necessarily require excellent depth perception, superb hand-eye coordination, and a brain capable of rapidly processing a flood of incoming visual information. The rather languid locomotion of arboreal creatures such as the South American sloth mentions indicates that haste at least is not an absolute prerequisite of arboreal existence, nor are highly developed visual and mental powers. See Cartmill 1974.

branch, or its weight-bearing capacity, or how it is best grasped – all of which are matters of limb and life.

The migration of the eyes from the side to the front of the head was of immense consequence. On the one hand, it meant the loss of the ability to survey all 360 degrees of the visual world with only the most minute adjustments of the head. It meant that visual experience would be patterned more or less thoroughly by the bifurcation of front and back; and it gave rise to the need 'to have eyes in the back of one's head' to protect one's now clearly differentiated and functionally invisible rear. One need only imagine what it would be like to see the entire surroundings, the *Umwelt* (literally, the 'around-world': the world around us), 'back' as well as 'front', with only a slight turn of the head. It is a fascinating thought, and one that would dilute the meanings of 'back' and 'front' in human patterns of experience. But the view of the entire 360-degree world would lack the clarity and distinctness with which we perceive that part within range of our stereoscopic vision.

The frontal migration of the eyes that limited the field of primate vision was thus not without several compensating advantages – and ones that would become constitutive of human worlds. As Margaret Livingstone and David Hubel explain, the primate visual system contains two subdivisions: the 'magnocellular layer' and the 'parvocelluar layer'. The magno system, generically referred to as the 'where' system, is a general mammalian attribute and enables 'an animal that uses vision to navigate in its environment, catch prey, and avoid predators'. The parvo system, commonly called the 'what' system, is 'well developed only in primates'; and it 'seems to have added the ability to scrutinize in much more detail the shape, colour, and surface properties of objects, creating the possibility of assigning multiple visual attributes to a single object and correlating its parts' and is 'especially suited for visual identification and association'.[85]

Aimed at navigating the world, the 'where' system's capacities include situating objects in space and time and, if in motion, their trajectory as well. Establishing visually the 'where' of things, and the 'what' of things that are there, is best accomplished through binocular and stereoscopic vision whose corporeal foundations are frontally-situated, closely-spaced eyes facing in the same direction and with convergent eye sockets. One advantage of such vision, compensating for the loss of range, was a matter of survival for arboreal primates: the enhancement of the visual depth-perception required for rapid brachiation. More generally, stereoscopic vision, 'the ability of the visual system to

---

85   Livingstone and Hubel in Gregory et al. 1995, p. 64.

synthesize the slightly different images sensed by the two eyes into a single perception of solid objects lying in three-dimensional space', is 'one of the ways we obtain an awareness of the distance and solidity of objects'.[86]

This stereoscopic capacity of binocular eyes is the foundation of what O.J. Braddick and J. Atkinson elaborate as the 'higher functions' of vision.[87] The two main tasks that must be performed in order to provide that richer information are to recognise objects and to situate them in space.[88] And these can be further divided into the subtasks of: pattern recognition, or 'comparing a description derived from the sensory input with some stored definition or prototype'; perceptual segregation, or finding 'something in the visual image that corresponds to the boundaries between surfaces'; and scene analysis or determining which surfaces belong together and make up cohesive objects.[89] Situating objects in space includes determining their distance from the viewer, for which stereoscopic vision is perhaps the greatest and most reliable aid. But visual depth perception also makes use of: motion parallax (movements of the head or body causing relative displacements of objects at different distances in the visual field, which lead to a strong sense of depth); interposition (the information that one object occludes the view of another, which must be farther away); and the effects of perspective (objects of the same size have retinal images that get progressively smaller with increasing distance from the observer). As Matthew Alpern summarises: '[w]hat eyes do better than any other sense organ is resolve two objects in space'; the eyes and the 'six very quickly acting muscles (the fastest in the human body)' attached to them makes them 'better than all other [organs] at localising the precise positions of objects in space'.[90]

---

86   First citation in this sentence, Gregory 1990, p. 72. Second citation Braddick in Barlow and Mollon 1982, p. 192.
87   Braddick and Atkinson in Barlow and Mollon 1982.
88   In his study of 'Visual Acuity' psychologist Lorrin A. Riggs defines visual acuity in terms of 'at least four fundamentally different tasks' on which subjects were tested. He defines these tasks under the headings of detection, recognition, resolution, and localisation. Though divided and subdivided differently, his taxonomy of visual tasks covers the same ones listed by Braddick and Atkinson. Riggs in Graham 1965, p. 322.
89   Braddick and Atkinson in Barlow and Mollon 1982, pp. 218, p. 221, p. 222. Information in next sentence from ibid., p. 224.
90   Mathew Alpern 'Eye Movements and Strabismus' in Barlow and Mollon 1982, p. 201. It should be added that none of the commentators invoked here suggests that vision is infallible. It is no different from any other sense in that it too is capable of misperception, of producing the deception of perception. Having analytically defined the various tasks that go into the higher functions of delineating, recognising, and situating objects, Braddick and Atkinson immediately move to dispel the impression that these tasks are performed

The addition of these 'higher functions' of primate vision (delineating objects and situating them in space) to the *Urfunktion* of those light-sensitive patches of skin produced much richer insight into a kinaesthetic world. As reptilian and mammalian eyes developed in complexity and visual acuity, they retained their original purpose, the detection of movement. The frog's eye, for example 'signals only changing light patterns and moving contours and thus its brain is only fed with these limited kinds of information';[91] and even the infinitely more sophisticated eyes and brains of many mammals cannot clearly and distinctly delineate stationary objects. The world perceived by eyes unable to differentiate objects in the absence of motion would be rather static. It was 'only in the eyes of the highest animals', most notably primates, that the sophisticated visual capacity to send a 'signal to the brain in the absence of movement' emerged – signals that made possible the differentiation of objects in stasis.

The agility of primate/anthropoid kinaesthetic vision is heightened by two related capacities. One is the ability of primate eyes to hold the world visually stable when the eyes are themselves in motion (whether by shifting the focus of vision or by moving with persistent focus). Such a feat is obviously of particular importance to arboreal primates in rapid brachiation; and without this capacity the visual world would permanently resemble that blurry scene observed by those temporarily engaged in disrupting their vestibular sensitivity whether for sacred purpose (trance dancing or peyote use for religious insight) or profane ('getting high' or the cheap thrill of a roller coaster ride).[92] And the second is the flip-side of the sophisticated capacity to differentiate among static objects, namely: the ability to recognize a *moving* object as a moving *object*. As neatly depicted by Konrad Lorenz: 'The perceptual feat that permits us to see ... shape changes in the retinal images as movements and not

---

in an automatic manner by mechanical sense organs. Generalising about (visual) perception as a collection of 'selective processes', they conclude that in perceiving we form a 'perceptual hypothesis' about the object of perception 'which is consistent with the sensory evidence, but is by no means proved by that evidence' (p. 229). Like Gregory, they refer to perceptual puzzles and optical illusions to show that in some cases a 'correct' hypothesis about something can, if used as a basis for interpreting other sensory evidence, lead to 'incorrect' hypotheses about the latter, whereas in other cases (the Neckar cube) more than one 'correct' hypothesis is possible for the same sensory evidence. The conclusion of their studies and tests is that perception is a complicated process, liable to selective biases (and though they do not mention it explicitly, and as will be discussed below, to cultural construction), variable according to the temporal duration of the exposure of the perceptual system to the percept, and in all cases involves the flexible and active, though not conscious, hypothesis construction by the perceptual system itself.

91 Citations in this paragraph: Gregory 1990, p. 103; p. 101.
92 For a succinct explanation see Gregory 1990, pp. 106–8.

as changes in shape of the object, that *correctly* allows us to '*interpret*' them as movements and not shape changes, is so familiar and self-evident to us all that we no longer marvel at it'. This capacity of human eyes, Lorenz adds, also 'represents one of the most wonderful achievements of our brain. Just imagine the number and complexity of the "unconscious inferences" that must be made in order to take the vast number of different combinations of sensory inputs that can generate the image of [an object] in all its different spatial locations and that nevertheless are able consistently to "infer" the same, constant form of the object!'[93] Without this ability, our normal visual world might consist of images akin to Marcel Duchamp's *Nude Descending a Staircase*. In juxtaposing the various kinaesthetic moments of a nude walking down a flight of stairs, Duchamp sought to render motion in three-dimensional living onto the still-life of a two-dimensional canvas. Considered in the context of the evolution of vision, however, this aesthetically *avant-garde* painting might be viewed as a representation of a more primitive visual capacity – one that sees, in the different moments of a single moving object, a series of overlapping still shots of seemingly different objects.

Complementing the 'where' system in primate vision is the 'what' system 'especially suited for visual identification and association'.[94] And in determining the 'what' of things, colour vision plays a crucial role. The superior ability of the eyes to localise objects in space has led at least one ocular enthusiast to underestimate the importance of colour vision. While acknowledging that colour 'has a fascination for us perhaps not unrelated to the beauty it brings to our world', Alpern (cited above) insists that 'the important *business* of the eye has nothing to do with colour' and reduces colour to 'one of the hobbies of the human retina'.[95] Alpern may have ordered this demotion of colour vision to a retinal hobby because it was, in order of appearance, a latecomer to the primate visual apparatus, having emerged as arboreal primates became diurnal. But although a latecomer, colour vision should by no means be an afterthought; for, its value not only to biological survival, but also to human cultural production (and aesthetics, 'beauty') is impossible to exaggerate. And one can freely grant Alpern's comment on the psychophysical priorities of the eye without conceding the crucial roles of colour vision in either psychophysics or culture.

The multi-coloured world that even the most colour-blind human beings inhabit does make it hard to imagine that there is no such thing as colours-

---

93   Lorenz 1997, p. 59.
94   Livingstone and Hubel in Gregory 1995, p. 64.
95   Alpern in Barlow and Mollon 1982, p. 201.

in-themselves existing 'in nature'.[96] But colour too is in fact in the eyes of the beholder, a synthetic product of the dialectic between an organism's visual toolkit and the wave-length of light reflecting off objects. Although the capacity of the human visual apparatus to produce a colourful world ranks among the top in the animal kingdom, before priding ourselves on 'seeing' deeper into the nature of things than so many of our fellow species, it is worth putting that visual acuity in perspective.[97] The various colours that we see are a product of the eyes' ability to detect different wavelengths of visible light. However, even within that small band of light that we can perceive, there are countless subtle differences in wavelengths that are too fine to be detected by that visual apparatus. As J.D. Mollon puts it: 'We are all colour blind. Despite the seemingly endless variety of hues that we experience, the colour vision of typical observers differs only in degree from that of those labelled 'colour blind'. Mixtures of wavelengths that are physically very different may look identical to us. Our eyes cannot analyse the spectral composition of lights in the way that a

---

96   Jillyn Smith 1989, p. 70. Colour-blindness in humans refers to the inability to see some of the colours visible to the 'normal' human eye, not a return to monochromatic vision.

97   Gregory points out the strange situation that among mammals only primates produce and inhabit a colourful world, although this capacity is available to 'many lower animals' and is 'highly developed in, birds, fish, reptiles, insects such as bees and dragon flies' (Gregory 1990, p. 127). The variety and fineness of colours varies according to species and the degree to which their habitat is bathed in light. Because of the absorption of light rays by water, many fish living above a depth of 100 feet (Geldard 1972, p. 21) are equipped with colour vision, but one whose spectrum ranges only from what measured in human terms are violet through blue to green.

The anatomical indicator of the importance of depth-perception to eyes, and found in birds, tree-living apes and their descendants is, as Gregory also points out, the well-developed fovea, the central region of the retina in which both kinds of light-receptor cells, the rods and the cones, are tightly packed. Other animals with frontal eyes functioning together include cats, but these do not have the well-developed fovea for heightened depth perception; and '[s]tereo vision for movement is also provided by the paired compound eyes of insects, and it is highly developed in insects such as the dragon fly which catches its prey at high speeds on the wing. The compound eyes are fixed in the head, and the mechanism of their stereo vision is simpler than in apes and man where foveas are brought to bear on objects at different distances by convergence of the eyes' (Gregory 1990, p. 73).

Braddick and Atkinson (in Barlow and Mollon 1982) mention as other means of judging distance: motion parallax movements of the head or body that cause relative displacements of objects at different distances in the visual field which lead to a strong sense of depth; interposition, the information that one object occludes the view of another, which must be farther away; and effects of perspective, the knowledge of the size of objects and that the farther away they are, the smaller they appear.

spectroscope can'.⁹⁸ These humbling facts tell us that even that which we see clearly and distinctly is neither necessarily accurate nor all there is to see. But it should be added that capacities and limits are not exclusively antithetical. The thresholds of our visual apparatus establish not only limits, but also stability. Speaking of our 'absolute visual threshold', Geldard contends: 'the visual apparatus is apparently tuned to the highest possible degree consistent with the nature of light energy. If man's eyes were much more sensitive to light than they are, the "shot effect" in photon emission would be perceived, and "steady" light would no longer appear steady' – and the world we perceive would appear much wobblier and more muddled.⁹⁹

With the evolution of eyes capable of seeing 'in living colour', the Eocene world of seen by our primate ancestors underwent a fundamental change in colouration. And it takes some effort for those of us accustomed seeing the world in colour to imagine how dramatic was that millennia-long chromatic upheaval. As Gregory notes 'we attach such importance to our perception of colour – it is central to visual aesthetics and profoundly affects our emotional states – that it is difficult to imagine the grey world of other mammals, including our pet cats and dogs'.¹⁰⁰ The world perceived by eyes incapable of colour vision would be not unlike the visual world of those enchained in Plato's cave: a rather simple binary one of lighter and darker, of dark shadows in motion against a background without contours. It is, Richard Leakey urges, therefore 'worth pausing to consider the tremendous benefits that [colour] perception confers in discriminating objects against a monochromatic background, and as an aid in perceiving depth and distance. In a forest environment made up of kaleidoscopic shades of green, with occasional splashes of colour, the usefulness of monochrome vision is severely limited .... Even in the single, but clearly important, activity of searching for fruit, being able to perceive colour is an enormous advantage'.¹⁰¹

A direct consequence of the ability to differentiate among colours is an increased precision in the delineation of objects in general; to those capable of perceiving colour discontinuities the world appears as populated by a

---

98   Mollon in Barlow and Mollon 1982, p. 165.
99   Geldard 1990, p. 39.
100 Gregory 1990, p. 127. Commenting on the matadors' use of bright red capes in bull fights, Ackerman reminds us that because bulls don't have colour vision, it is the motion of the cape that arouses them. Though bulls are indifferent to the colour, not so the audience 'which finds the colour intrinsically arousing and also suggestive of the soon-to-be flowing blood of either the bull or the matador' (Ackerman 1991, p. 265).
101 Leakey and Lewin 1977, p. 45.

greater number of discrete objects. And to arboreal creatures who had already developed a rather sophisticated capacity for orientation in the spatially complex, multi-dimensional arboreal world, the addition of the capacity to differentiate objects by their colour could only heighten their sense of spatiality – of depth and distance, of spatial relations between objects. Explaining how stereoscopic and colour vision are mutually reinforcing in delineating the world of objects and spatiality in general, David Katz writes: 'Inasmuch as space is always presented in coloured form, it plays an important part in determining the colour-impressions which we receive. Without the spatial factor we should lack the wealth of spatially organized modes of appearance which colours assume, and inasmuch as colour is always presented in spatial form it exercises a corresponding influence on the impression of space'.[102]

The fact that visual immediacy does not require immediate proximity, that vision can apprehend things at vast distances, has a remarkable effect – an effect unique among the senses, yet seemingly invisible to those anti-ocularcentrists who myopically see in human vision only the staring gaze, and who thus fail to see its depth, breadth, nuance, complexity, and richness. One hardly need deny the significance of the distancing stare in competitive social interaction among primates (humans included; see below) in order to acknowledge that the social stare is neither the only mode of gazing, nor even the most used modality of vision. While focusing only on the distancing effect of the staring gaze, however, such critics completely overlook the opposite effect for which I shall coin the clumsy term *nearing*, that is: vision brings distant objects near; it brings objects that cannot be apprehended by any of our other senses into our perceivable universe, even if 'only' as light-images. Hans Jonas is quite literally correct in insisting that 'it would be incorrect to say that in sight the distant is brought near'.[103] But it is, on the other hand, most correct also to note that our visual capacity expands our perceptual reach infinitely farther than does any other sense, bringing objects at light-years distance into the folds of our intimacy: the planets and stars that we cannot smell or taste or touch, the spheres whose harmonious *musica universalis* we cannot hear (except perhaps as imagined by Willie Ruff and John Rodgers in their composition *The Harmony of the World: A Realization for the Ear of Johannes Kepler's Astronomical Data from Harmonices Mundi 1619*).

The intimacy born of vision can be delightful – as is, for example, stargazing on a moonless night over an Aegean island where the canopy seems

---

102   Katz 1935, p. 2.
103   Jonas in Spicker 1970, p. 327.

almost within reach; or from a high mountain peak where the universe seems to provide a glimpse of both its density (the countless stars, solar systems, and galaxies cluttering the sky), yet also its immensity (the countless stars, solar systems, and galaxies reaching endlessly into infinite space). But visual intimacy can also be painful – as it was for Lycenus, the tower warden in Goethe's *Faust*, who rued the range of his visual organs that condemned him to be a helpless spectator witnessing from afar the distant flames consuming the cottage of Philemon and Baucis: 'You eyes, must you behold this sight!/Must you see so very far!'[104] Yet if, as Baudelaire claimed (with, I would argue, a good degree of validity), 'genius is nothing more or less than childhood recovered at will', then the visual dimension of genius must be the ability to behold the universe and its contents, not with the distancing stare of the competitive individual, but (in the words of Albert Einstein that are said also to describe his own way of looking) with the gaze of inquisitive wonder and awed wonderment peculiar to 'curious children before the great mystery into which we were born'.[105]

Because of the powers of binocular eyes and stereoscopic and colour vision, human beings apprehend an expansive world richly populated with distinct objects, distant as well as near.[106] It is thus not fortuitous that Descartes elevated the visual categories of clarity and distinctness to the fundamental criteria for measuring the truthful functioning of the 'mind's eye'. In so doing,

---

104 *Faust*, Kaufmann translation 1963, pp. 448–51.
105 Baudelaire 1970, p. 8. In his biography of Einstein, Walter Isaacson (2008) wrote that '[t]hroughout his life, Albert Einstein would retain the intuition and the awe of a child. He never lost his sense of wonder at the magic of nature's phenomena ... which grown-ups find so commonplace. He retained the ability to hold two thoughts in his mind simultaneously, to be puzzled when they conflicted, and to marvel when he could smell an underlying unity'.
106 *Wahrnehmung* is generally translated as 'perception', and can also be rendered as 'cognition', but the interest here is in its literal meaning produced by the combination *wahr*, meaning 'true', and *nehmung* from the verb *nehmen*, 'to take', thus *Wahrnehmung* = 'to take' or 'to perceive' as 'true'. The taking of a percept as true can of course be mediated by environment. Colin Turnbull relates the experience of travelling to the savannah with an Mbuti companion who had lived his entire life in the forest where distance vision was limited to a few dozens of yards by the density of trees. When on the savannah the Mbuti man saw a herd of buffalo at a great distance, he asked 'what insects are those?' Not having had in the forest the opportunity to use the distant vision inherent in human eyes, he took the size that he perceived at a great distance to be the true size of the buffalo. See Turnbull 1962, p. 252. See pp. 247–53 for further discussion of this matter of surroundings, perception, and *Wahrnehmung*.

he simply, if inadvertently, acknowledged the fundamental contribution of the inherited primate visual system to human perception and knowledge, the tacit knowledge that is the foundation of conceptual knowledge. It seems, moreover, that Descartes was not so wrong about vision, about its capacities and the kinds of knowledge it provides. His catalogue of visually-apprehended 'qualities' lists 'six principal' ones, namely: 'light, colour, position, distance, size and shape'.[107] Although light and colour may be, as Descartes opined, 'the only qualities belonging properly to the sense of sight', primate vision, as W.E. Le Gros Clark explains in elaborating the visual *Antecedents of Man*, also enhanced the perception of the other qualities that Descartes enumerated: 'The visual sense is the most informative of the discriminative senses, for it provides a means whereby objects may be recognized near at hand or in the far distance in regard to their position, form, texture, and colour, and enables spatial properties to be defined with an accuracy which is hardly approached by the use of other sensory mechanisms'.[108]

Although the stereoscopic, kinaesthetic, and colour vision inherited from our primate ancestors frames the way objects meet the human eye, there is much more to this sophisticated visual perception than meets the eye. As impressive as the 'brute facts' of clearly delineated, coloured objects, whether in motion or stasis, are, they pale in comparison with their long-term significance for the development of the human brain and the constitution of human meaning. And if the two most crucial factors in the formation of the primate visual apparatus were arboreality and diurnality, it is not just these factors in themselves that are of significance. Primates were certainly neither the original diurnal nor arboreal creatures. It is rather the particular evolutionary sequences involving diurnality and arboreality that not only differentiated primates from other diurnal and arboreal creatures, but that were also so consequential. For, each step in the sequence from diurnality to nocturnality and back again deposited layers of objectified experience in primate corporeal organisation that would not only result in a particularly close relationship between primate vision and the sophisticated primate brain, but that

---

107   Descartes 1999, p. 167.
108   Descartes 1999, p. 167; Le Gros Clark 1960, p. 266. Noting the unique primate symbiosis of the senses of sight and touch, Le Gros Clark adds 'When the visual sense is developed in conjunction with the development of the tactile pads characteristic of the prehensile extremities in Primates generally, the combination of the two provides opportunities for exploring objects in the immediate environment, and for comprehending their significance, which is not possible in non-Primate mammals', p. 266.

would also establish a constellation of the primate senses in which vision would become hegemonic. This sequence is, according to Paul Shepard, crucial to understanding the 'animal' origins of human intelligence.[109]

Shepard explains the significance of the re-emergent diurnality of primates by contrasting what the diurnal primate eye knows with that which the primitive diurnal eye of certain reptilian and amphibian species knows. Amphibians and reptiles have a rather simple visual apparatus: they have 'fixed connections between eyes and brains and muscles', and their bodies are 'activated by just the right visual signals. For example, if the right-sized image moves across the retina of a hungry frog's eye, the frog reacts by eating it. If the image is not right, the "food" signal will never reach the frog's brain or trigger its foodcatching movements. The filtering device is located in the eye, not the brain'.

The nocturnal habits of the early mammalian descendants of those diurnal reptilian and amphibian species, however, entailed a shift from vision to hearing and smell as the primary means of obtaining information about food sources. This shift in mammalian ethology, moreover, was, as Shephard explains, also crucial because of its more immediate (on an evolutionary timescale) consequences both for the development of the increasingly powerful primate visual apparatus itself, and for its longer-term consequences for the development of the primate brain. The reliance on hearing and smell for information about the distance, movement, and direction of another creature requires 'successive stimuli' and '[p]erceiving these signals as a pattern meant ordering them in time rather than visual space, translating them into the all-at-once of a spatial map'. The result was a more complex sensory process and a brain able to interpret them:

> Sound and smell were analyzed and integrated cortically, not sensorially – in the brain rather than in the sense organ. Though hearing and smell are not basically spatial, their temporal analysis creates a kind of analogue to space. Because we descended from these sniffers and smellers, the first step in human-like intelligence was the encephalizing or deep-brain elaboration of tissues for storing information. The perception of patterns from signals coming at intervals meant holding what had gone before, putting it into a spatial code. And it meant the reverse: calling and marking by scent were actions scattered through time by which the individual conveyed information about its location and movements.

---

[109] All citations from Shephard in next three paragraphs from Shepard 1978, pp. 15–18.

In his summary of this process of sensory evolution, Shepard situates vision in its complex and sophisticated relation to the lesser nobles in the primate sensory hierarchy:

> (1) hearing replaced vision as a distance sense when mammals became nocturnal;[110] (2) this required a capacity to translate successive signals into spatial maps, to perceive sequences of sounds as wholes and to re-hear or re-cognize them simultaneously in space; and (3) with re-emergence into daylight activity and vision, the same kind of temporal encoding of visual imagery, creating a continuous visual world of objects. Our reptilian ancestor's hearing analyzer was deep in its head, its vision analyzer in the eye itself. Its descendants became night creatures, centering their attention on hearing. When, much later, as primates, they emerged once again to live in daylight, their new visual analyzer was connected to the deep-brain hearing centers.

The primate re-emergence in daylight and ascent to an arboreal habitat required a return to vision – a return, however, undertaken with a brain that had already learned to process auditory and olfactory stimuli in a manner meaningful to a nocturnal world. The newly diurnal primates had brought with them into the daylight 'a deep-brain integrating and storing ability, created through the interaction of the senses other than vision. It related time to space, a time-binding capacity. The kind of temporary storage that made melodies from tones now occurred in vision', and there emerged 'a new kind of vision organized in the brain instead of the retina, based on time-coding like that of sound'. And in what could easily be read as an evolutionary prolegomenon to Kant's analysis of the transcendental structure of the mind, Shepard describes a new perceptual apparatus that organised the world spatially and temporally and with an acute awareness of its contents/objects:

> A perceptual visual world was created in which distance could mean time or space, and those events distant in time were remembered as mental images in the space of the mind's eye. *The visual world became, as*

---

110   It is also worth noting that the 'interim of early mammalian evolution in the dark may have made later brain enlargement possible by the advantage it gave to body-temperature regulation. Keeping warm without sunlight may have been initially a physical or behavioural adaption, but out of it came the warm, constant internal environment or 'warm-bloodedness' necessary to higher brain activity' (Shepard 1978, p. 18).

it were, constant or continuous rather than an illuminated field punctuated by the right signals. ... The primates redefined the whole idea of the stimulus. It ceased to be simply a releaser and became entrained in sets, patterned as objects making a perceptual world, subject to autonomous re-presentation or recall. This recall of images establishes an imaged past and imagined future framing the present. *This capacity for visual presentation of objects from the past to one's self and the way it sensitizes us to a stream of time is not a general capacity*. Consciousness is a very highly specialized mode of modeling and learning, dependent on specific brain elements and functions. (my italics)

This new and complex perceptual process that appeared in visually-oriented primates and that enabled the organism to differentiate, hold and recall images made possible the 'special kind of attention for learning and communication, even for consciousness', and would 'in time become the imagination'. The origins of the imaginative forms of human consciousness can thus be traced back to a shift in the relations among the sense organs that rendered vision 'hegemonic': as a primate, *Homo sapiens* is 'the beneficiary of the shift of the deep mid-brain, nose-ear information storage into a time-binding visual coding process'. Having designated notions of space and time as two of the foundational and constitutive components of the 'transcendental structure of the mind', Kant could only explain them as '*a priori* intuitions'. Shepard's analysis suggests, however, that Darwin's trenchant rebuttal of Platonists claiming that 'our "imaginary ideas" [that] arise from the preexistence of the soul are not derivable from experience' with the simple suggestion to 'read monkeys for preexistence' is just as applicable to Kant's *a priori*: those foundational aspects of our consciousness are themselves corporeally constituted by means of the primate visual apparatus.[111]

Vision, writes Hans Jonas (in a formulation that also exposes the near-sightedness of those who would narrow the realm of vision to only the star-

---

111   Darwin 1980, p. 64. Konrad Lorenz (1977, p. 9, p. 14) also locates the origins of Kant's transcendental structure of the mind in the body's cognitive apparatus. Although Kant's stated doctrine denies the possibility of knowing whether our 'phenomenal world' actually corresponds to the 'real world', Lorenz has a 'heretical suspicion' that 'Kant himself ... was not so completely convinced that the two worlds were unconnected' (Lorenz 1973, p. 14). Lorenz's point is not that our knowledge is absolute truth, but that it is 'real' and 'objective' in that it derives from an organism's modes of apprehending the world that enable it successfully to negotiate the world.

ing gaze), is 'the freest' of the senses, sight is 'effortless', and 'seeing requires no perceptible activity either on the part of the object or on that of the subject'[112] While some senses, such as touch and taste, require physical contact, and others, such as hearing and smell, are strengthened by close proximity, vision operates relatively independently. We voluntarily look out at the world, and can freely control the opening and closing of our eyes and the direction and duration of a look and a mere glance provides an abundance of information. Unchained from proximity as a prerequisite of sensual apprehension, primate eyes freely traverse a perceptual field wider and deeper than that any other sense, and within which those eyes apprehend an abundance of objects both near and far; and it is the great extent of that field of vision that underlies Dodwell's claim (cited above) that 'more than 80 percent of human perception' (itself 'the primary process by means of which humans obtain knowledge of the world') is 'accounted for by vision'. Such a preponderance could not but have profound consequences for the nature of primate knowledge production, on both tacit knowledge and also the linguistically-expressed knowledge uniquely produced by *Homo sapiens* (one indication of which is the great preponderance of nouns signifying objects that we encounter visually). Accordingly, it is worth casting a brief glance at the relation of the visual apparatus inherited from our primate ancestors to thought and language.

The ascension of vision to a place of primacy in the primate sensual hierarchy had consequences that were not limited to the visual realm alone, but included also the realm of intelligence, reproduction, and therewith social behaviour. Here our concern is with the relation between primate vision and intelligence. The quantity and quality of the kind of information that eyes capable of differentiating a rich and nuanced world of chromatic things, both in motion and stasis, is directly related to brain capacity. And the richness of the 'food for thought' that primate eyes can deliver to the brain was of the utmost consequence for the evolution of the anthropoid primate brain itself:

---

112 Jonas in Spicker 1970, p. 324. Jonas adds that vision is the least, and touch the most 'realistic' of the senses and he speaks of the 'causal detachment of sight' which 'more than any other sense withholds the experience of causality: causality is not a visual datum' (ibid, pp. 324, p. 325). Though I agree with Jonas on sight being the 'freest' sense, both of these claims are in my view vastly overstated. The unreliability of touch will be addressed below in the section 'The "Functionally-Naked" Ape and the Humanising of Touch'. As for the question of causation: of the senses, only sight could perceive both clouds and rain, witness the correlation between dark clouds and rain, and thus provide the basis for imagining a causal link between them – even if, as Hume argued, the most that could be established is only constant conjunction and correlation but not causality.

'Partly because of the emphasis on vision, primate brains are larger than those found in other mammalian orders. This increase also reflects a greater "intelligence".[113]

Alone the quantity of visual information accumulated by primate vision activates the mind. Contrasting the serial nature of the more developed olfactory and audial systems of other creatures (which is generally true of the gustatory and haptic systems as well), Derek Bickerton notes that there 'is surely a limit on the number of things a creature can smell or hear *simultaneously*', but 'there is virtually no limit to the number of objects a creature with efficient vision can see at one time'. This, Bickerton concludes, has important consequences for brain development: 'Given an identical quantity of information, more apparatus is required to process it simultaneously than would be needed if processing were serial. Thus, reliance on sight should increase the relative size of brain areas devoted to the analysis of sensory data'.[114] Similarly, John Relethford on the hemispheric development of the primate brain: 'in non-stereoscopic animals, the information from one eye is received in only one hemisphere of the brain. In primates, the visual signals from both eyes are received in both hemispheres of the brain'.[115]

Moreover, the structure and logic of visual perception is essential to anthropoid primate reasoning and tacit knowledge production. Like Shepard, Gregory argues that the visual sense must have been a latecomer; for in contrast to touch and taste, that monitor the conditions immediately important for survival, 'visual patterns are only important when interpreted in terms of the world of objects. But this requires an elaborate nervous system (indeed almost a metaphysics) if behaviour is controlled by belief in what the object is rather than directly by sensory input'.[116] Considering the symbiotic relation between primate eyes and minds, Gregory speculates that the human brain probably 'could not have developed without senses – particularly eyes – capable of providing advance information, by signaling the presence of distant objects. ... [E]yes require intelligence to identify and locate objects in space, but intel-

---

113 Lewin and Foley 2004, p. 132. The authors' summary of the 'shift in a series of life-history factors' resulting from the 'enhanced encephalization' related to the hegemony of vision in the primate sensory constellation: 'animals with large brains or their body size tend to have a greater longevity and a low potential reproductive output. For instance, primate gestation is long relative to maternal body size, litters are small (usually one), and offspring precocious; age at first reproduction is late and interbirth interval is long. 'Primates are, in short, adapted for slow reproductive turnover' observes Martin' (ibid., p. 132).
114 Bickerton 1990, p. 148.
115 Relethford 1994, p. 212.
116 Gregory 1970, p. 12.

ligent brains could hardly have developed without eyes. It is not too much to say that eyes freed the nervous system from the tyranny of reflexes, leading to strategic planned behaviour and ultimately to abstract thinking. We are still dominated by visual concepts'.[117] The term 'visual concepts' suggests a rather intimate relation between primate vision and primate thinking.[118] And in addition to delivering a preponderance of visual sources of semiotic and/or conceptual referents, visual perception is, almost ironically, the foundation of at least two invaluable, visually derived yet non-visual dimensions of tacit knowledge production. These pertain to problem-solving and prediction, both of which involve a sense of temporality.

Rejecting the common analogy of the eye as camera, Gregory insists instead that 'the quite uncamera-like features' of visual perception are the 'most interesting'. Vision is less like the reproductive mechanics of the camera and more like the productive vision of the photographer – or of the scientist. Visual perception is 'a kind of problem-solving'; it entails the organisation of visual sense data into 'an object-hypothesis which fits current facts, and one that is also predictive'.[119] To describe perception as selecting 'object-hypotheses' is 'no vague analogy to the use of the word "hypothesis" in science. A scientific hypothesis must be capable of predicting future events for it to have any power. The same should be true of perceptual object-hypotheses; it is indeed their ability to predict which gives power over enemies and over nature. Prediction makes it possible to plan action before events'.[120] Accordingly, visual perception is essentially a process, and an essentially 'inductive' one (that as such is 'not limited to the human species').

---

117 Gregory 1970, p. 13. Gregory speculates that the evolution of written language from ideographic pictograms through hieroglyphics to the phonetic alphabet may be evidence of the developing capacity of the brain for abstract thought. In the pictograms of the earliest written languages, he argues, 'we see, pictured, [the] object-hypotheses – [the] units of seeing and thinking – [the] intelligent eyes' of the people who made them (ibid., p. 144).
118 Though decried by anti-ocularcentrists, the close relation between (human) vision and (human) knowledge is registered in many Indo-European languages. The notion that 'to know' is 'to see' (registered in the classical Greek εἰδέναι that signifies both) is, in evolutionary terms, not at all far-fetched.
119 Gregory 1970, p. 31.
120 Gregory 1970, p. 61; next citation, ibid., p. 162. Braddick and Atkinson similarly describe visual perception as a collection of 'selective processes' through which we form a 'perceptual hypothesis' about the object of perception 'which is consistent with the sensory evidence, but is by no means proved by that evidence' (Braddick and Atkinson in Barlow and Mollon 1982, p. 229).

Though he speaks of vision, indeed, sense perception in general as an inductive process, so that human beings, by virtue of their senses are equipped with the parts of a per-

This predictive component of visual perception as 'problem-solving' opens an entirely new horizon: that of the 'not-yet', a concept of the 'future'. In contrast to the very immediate threat of proximate objects detected by the more tactile senses with rather limited range, the 'eyes give warning of the future, by signaling distant objects'.[121] Primate eyes bring even distant objects into the realm of visual immediacy which, when combined with a brain capable of judging the distance of the possible threat and the time it would take to become immediate, provides the time to reflect on the best course of action before engaging motor responses. Reflecting on the epistemology of vision, Hans Jonas concludes: 'Knowledge at a distance is tantamount to foreknowledge'.[122] This could have equally appropriately been formulated as 'Sight at a distance is tantamount to foresight' – but either way, it portends the construction not only of a notion of the future, but also the formulation of a future tense and the very horizon of temporality itself. The ability of binocular and stereoscopic vision to recognise and situate distant objects and thus 'give warning of the future' brings about a *de facto* separation between sense perception and motor response. This produces time for reflection on the best way to confront the future, time to determine the situation, to put it in *perspective*, and the possibility of choice, of deciding which of the diverging roads to take into the future. In opening the realm of future possibilities, it opens also the realm of the conditional and, after the fact, reflection on what might have been had the road not taken been taken, that is: the realm of the counterfactual subjunctive.

---

ceptual problem-solving apparatus that need only be employed regularly for it to mature, Gregory by no means implies that this universal apparatus will be employed universally in like manner. He provides specific examples of cultural differences in perception. One example concerns the culturally different susceptibility to visual illusions. He mentions the Zulus who inhabit a 'circular culture': their houses are round; they plough in curved rather than straight lines; and few of their possessions have corners or straight lines. Probably because of their rounded environment, 'they experience the Muller-Lyer arrow illusion to only a small extent, and are hardly affect at all by other distortion illusion figures' (Gregory 1990, pp. 169–70). Referring perhaps to Colin Turnbull's account of his trip to the savannah with the Mbuti who had spent all their lives in dense forest, Gregory writes that when seeing distant objects across the savannah, forest dwellers see them not as distant, but as small (see note 106 above). Such examples could be multiplied many-fold. But the obvious point has been made, namely: that a species-wide visual perceptual system is bounded by certain absolute thresholds that can be more or less specified quantitatively. It is those thresholds, despite individual variations within the species, that differentiate human perceptual systems from those of other animals. But the application or employment of this universal visual capacity assumes many different forms and is powerfully influenced by cultural and geographical factors.

121   Gregory 1970, p. 13.
122   Jonas in Spicker 1970, p. 327.

The binocular eyes embedded in our corporeal organisation are much more intelligent than is captured by the philosophers' monocular metaphor of the 'mind's (colour-blind) eye'. One might with perhaps more justification invert the metaphor and assert that the primate mind is, although not exclusively, nevertheless very much 'the eyes' mind'.[123] But we might avoid a fruitless either/or discussion by concluding with Merleau-Ponty's judicious recognition of the symbiotic relation between human eyes and mind. The mind's 'symbolic function', he writes, 'rests on the visual as on a ground; not that vision is its cause, but because it is that gift of nature which Mind was called upon to make use of beyond all hope, to which it was to give a fundamentally new meaning, yet which was needed, not only to be incarnate, but in order to be at all'. Thus, 'one cannot say that man sees because he is Mind, nor indeed that he is Mind because he sees'. Rather, 'to see as a man sees and to be Mind are synonymous'.[124]

It may well be that the greatest capacity of the human mind involves its language facility. But Stephen Jay Gould presumably did not intend any disrespect to enhanced powers of the human mind effected by language when appending to his statement 'primates are visual animals, and we think best in pictorial or geometric terms' the comment that '[w]ords are an evolutionary afterthought'.[125] I take his point rather to be – in contradistinction to linguistic ultra-constructionists who deny such a claim – that the general foundation of human cognition, hitherto thought to be situated in a disembodied transcendental structure, preceded language, in short: that thought (still primitive compared to the loquacious *Homo sapiens*, but most sophisticated in comparison to the rest of the animal world) was and is possible without language. Similarly Richard Leakey:

> For the higher primates, with their ability to see the world in colour and in three dimensions, and, also to pick up and manipulate objects, the world

---

123   Primates are characterised by 'a unique neural apparatus for processing visual signals and enlarged visual centers in the occipital and temporal lobes of the brain' (R. Klein 1989, p. 41). And Gregory notes: 'The retina has been described as an 'outgrowth of the brain'. It is a specialised part of the surface of the brain which has budded out and become sensitive to light, while it retains typical brain cells functionally between the receptors and the optic nerve (but situated in the front layers of the retina) which greatly modify the electrical activity from the receptors themselves. Some of the data processing for perception takes place in the eye, which is thus an integral part of the brain' (Gregory 1990, p. 69).
124   Merleau-Ponty 1966, pp. 127, 137.
125   Gould 1995, p. 10.

becomes more than just a three-dimensional coloured pattern. It is also a world full of identifiable objects. ...

The implications of this new mental dimension are vast; indeed, they become essential as the background against which the development of the human mind is to be understood. The opportunities for learning about the world, rather than simply reacting to particular shapes in a pre-programmed fashion, are enhanced enormously. And, ultimately the ability to view objects as separate entities is an absolute prerequisite for the evolution of language, which is possibly the one unique human attribute. In a very real sense we owe our capacity for speech to the higher primates' reaching out to analyse their three-dimensional world.[126]

We will return to speech below and turn to language in Part 3. Here it is worth emphasising that the primacy and power of primate vision has had the most profound effect on the structure and contents of human languages, providing the foundation for, among other things: discrete objects and object-hypothesis reasoning; the notion of three-dimensional space; the notion of time with its grammatical tenses; causality; the predominance of visually-derived words, and cultural forms, metaphors, and symbols derived from the colourful three-dimensional world. Our primate, *Australopithecine* and *Homo* ancestors had acquired a wealth of tacit knowledge about, through their visual apprehension of, the world and had much to talk about long before they could give voice to it – and without which language would have had little to talk about.[127]

Regardless of language capacity, however, vision too has, in primate species at least, a communicative function: looking is not only a means of taking in information, but also of expressing it, most importantly, the expression of inner emotional states and in socially meaningful ways. Eyes are not only literally 'windows on the world', but are also so proverbially considered 'windows into the soul' that British essayist Max Beerbohm claimed to 'need no dictionary of quotations to remind' him of that. Variations on this theme are found in Cicero, the gospel of Matthew, and Shakespeare, among others; and Darwin frequently mentioned the use of eyes (and eyelids and brows) in his study of *The Expression of the Emotions in Man and Animals*. The broad range of ocular expression of emotion includes, but is certainly not limited to: surprise, delight, horror, rage, admiration, inquisitiveness, attraction, desire, repulsion,

---

[126] Leakey and Lewin 1977, p. 45.
[127] For an eclectic summary of visual imagery, see Ackerman 1991, pp. 230–1.

fear, aggression. As Jillyn Smith notes, 'pupil dilation may indicate taste differences too small for a subject to consciously notice and that pupil dilation can be used as a measure of the arousal value of a stimulus'. And the increase in our rate of blinking betrays us in moments of lost concentration or found boredom. Generally, she concludes, 'widening of the pupil indicates a positive response; constricting a negative response'. Providing an example for business history, she adds that the natural dilation of the eyes in response to emotions was centuries ago an important business signifier in China where jade salesmen allegedly watched their customers' eyes for dilation, indicating interest in purchasing their wares.[128]

The expression of inner states is of course often in response to, and directed in a socially meaningful way at, another subject. When registering my objection above to the too common conflation of vision and the 'gaze' or 'stare', my point was not to deny the reifying possibilities of looking, but to defer the discussion of it. For it was first necessary to undo the conflation of vision and the staring gaze in order to gain insight into the richness of vision as manifested in the richness of the world that we perceive visually, and also in the intimacy, produced by vision's 'nearing' effect, that we can feel with objects we see at a distance. Now is the time for that deferred discussion of the social/interpersonal uses of 'the look' – and I emphasise the plural 'uses', for while using 'the look' to distance and/or reify the other, it can also be used as a means of attraction.[129] (It is difficult to imagine the effect of the stare of an animal with side- rather than frontal-eyes being anywhere near as penetrating – whether in distancing or attracting.)

The distancing look and the reifying gaze that serves to establish hierarchy in people and other primates has a long heritage. Maxine Sheets-Johnstone begins her analysis of 'Optics of Power and the Power of Optics in Evolutionary Perspective' by citing descriptions of the primate stare in natural history literature.[130] A dominant male baboon's first reaction to annoyance is 'to stare at the offenders. The stare is long and steady, with the animal's whole concentration behind it'. The recipient of the stare generally understands its significance and can respond in one of two ways. As with many primates, 'on being threatened

---

128   Jillyn Smith 1989, pp. 88–9.
129   This discussion of the stare was prompted and informed by a paper written by Katy Pelissier, an undergraduate student in my course on Mapping Human Corporeal Organization, Winter 2009.
130   Sheets-Johnstone cites accounts of dominance and submission in macaque, baboon, and monkey societies written by Sarel Eimerl and Irven De Vore. The first two citations here are from Eimerl and Devore, cited in Sheets-Johnstone 1994, p. 34. The last quote is Sheets-Johnstone's commentary, ibid., p. 35.

by a definitely dominant monkey, a subordinate is likely to display submission. Confronted with a fixed stare, it will look away'. The breaking of the stare constitutes surrender and deflates the conflict at hand, while a returned stare can be seen as a challenge. In this regard, 'it is not a static proprietary stance of one individual toward another, but a dynamic ritual of intercorporeal behaviours repeated over and over again'.

It hardly needs mentioning that this anthropoid-primate staring ritual is also all too human. The staring gaze of a person in a dominant social position aimed at one in an inferior social position is also a means of reifying the other; and insofar as this staring gaze turns the other person into a thing, it is a dehumanising gaze. This is, as so many feminist critics have rightly noted, most common in the male stare that reduces women to sex objects and evaluates whether the object is worth being subdued, conquered, and/or possessed. As is always the case in unequal relations, the reified fight back. And one socially effective use of the eyes was to return, but manipulate the staring gaze. The apparent attractiveness of dilated pupils to the male gaze (or perhaps the ego reinforcement coming from being beheld by wide-eyed women) led women of the Middle Ages (and no doubt of the upper classes) to 'dilate their pupils with the drug belladonna ("beautiful woman" in Italian), perhaps to convince men they found them overwhelmingly interesting'.[131]

Finally, it is certainly worth mentioning another species-specific and culturally extremely significant attribute of the anatomy and physiology of human eyes, namely the ability to shed tears. Darwin had accentuated the rarity of weeping in other species by finding only two examples: a *Macacus maurus* in the London Zoological Gardens and Si E. Tennent's description of weeping Indian elephants.[132] But there is an ongoing debate over whether other animal species besides *Homo sapiens* actually cry. Those who find crying uniquely human suggest that those attesting to crying in non-human species confuse crying in the vocal sense with weeping; and they insist while many species can cry (vocally), it may be that only human beings have the bodily instruments and corporeal capacities actually to shed tears. Here it is not necessary to give a definitive answer as to whether the shedding of tears is uniquely human in order to establish that weeping is a universally human trait and is (obviously in various socio-culturally specific ways) of universal significance in human social relations and cultural values.[133]

---

[131] Jillyn Smith 1989, p. 89.
[132] See Darwin in *Darwin* (Wilson (ed.) 2006, p. 1355).
[133] For a natural and cultural history of tears, see Lutz 1999.

The ascension of vision in primates to the perceptual 'structure in dominance' (to adapt an Althusserian expression) necessarily effected a restructuring in the ranks of primate sensual nobility. Although the once dominant senses of smell and hearing fell in ranking to the lesser nobility, they should be no means be considered to have lost their noble patent; and while taste, along with smell and hearing, lost much of their importance to biological survival, their value to human cultures cannot be measured by biological criteria alone; for, as will be argued in the following, the less noble senses can have a cultural value in inverse relation to, and precisely because of, their lesser capacities. That having been said, it must also be acknowledged that the micro- and macro dimensions of the universe as *Homo sapiens* experiences them are established through vision. If our visual apparatus already allows us visually to apprehend countless things, both minute and distant, that we cannot hear, smell, taste, or touch, the development of artificial tools has extended the range of our vision far beyond that of our corporeal toolkit and established the expanding borders of our universe: microscopes that extend our vision into the world of the small, allowing us to see into atoms and genes; and telescopes that let us peer into the distant worlds of deep space.

6.5.3 Matter That Hears: From Gill Bars to Jawbones to Ears That Transform Vibrations into Sound

Depending on the criteria selected (primordiality, survival value, aesthetic value, psychophysical range, etc.), strong cases can be, and have been, made for the superior nobility of each of the senses. In a letter to his friend Karl Amenda, Beethoven announced the great deterioration of his hearing, which he proclaimed, in a very un-Cartesian fashion, the 'noblest faculty'.[134] Philosopher Bruno Liebrucks pronounced the ear 'the first organ of mind' and the faculty of hearing 'the true sensory faculty of the mind' because it assembles 'all the senses into the world of language'.[135] In the realm of contemporary psychophysics, E.F. Evans singles out hearing as 'arguably the most important sense for man. For what marks out *Homo sapiens* from other species is his ability to express ideas and concepts, and these he communicates to his fellows chiefly by means of language. This communication occurs first by means of sound, and oral communication remains foremost throughout life. It has been said that a blind person is cut off from the world of *things*, whereas one who is deaf is cut

---

134 Beethoven, letter to Karl Amenda, 1 July 1801, http://www.lvbeethoven.com/Bio/BiographyDeafness.html.
135 Liebrucks 1964, pp. 99, 71: 'Das Ohr ist das erste Organ des Geistes'; 'Das Gehör als der eigentlich geistige Sinn ist der der Versammlung aller Sinne in die Welt der Sprache'.

off from the world of *people*'.¹³⁶ This comment is generally attributed to Helen Keller, but the exact source has not been found. Keller, however, did express that sentiment in a letter, writing that 'the problems of deafness are deeper and more complex, if not more important, than those of blindness. Deafness is a much worse misfortune. For it means the loss of the most vital stimulus – the sound of the voice that brings language, sets thoughts astir and keeps us in the intellectual company of man'.¹³⁷ And reflecting on 'a lifetime in silence and darkness' she concluded that 'to be deaf is a greater affliction than to be blind ... Hearing is the soul of knowledge and information of a high order. To be cut off from hearing is to be isolated indeed'.¹³⁸

There are of course critics of such audiocentrism. In a moody existentialist half-truth Erwin Straus finds the auditory to be the most servile of senses: in contrast to seeing, in which one is an actor who casts one's eyes upon something, in hearing, one is passive, a receiver, subject to the 'overwhelming power of sound'. Taking the common derivation of the terms for 'hear' and 'obey' (in German, respectively: *gehören* and *gehörchen*) as etymological evidence, Strauss concludes that '[i]n hearing, obedience is foreshadowed'.¹³⁹ But rather than continue to review this by now familiar scene of arguments over pre-eminence in the sensory nobility, we shall proceed in the by now familiar manner, and recognise that although hearing too was in the course of primate evolution superseded by vision as the greater supplier of images to the brain, it certainly retained its 'noble' status, providing unique qualities of experience without which human existence – particularly those two human universals: language and music – is quite literally unthinkable.

Although we generally are not at all surprised when hearing beautiful music produced by a skilled violinist, the truth of the matter actually sounds much more fictional, namely: that a tactile encounter of the bow causing strings to vibrate creates a mechanical disturbance, a wave motion, that produces an auditory experience in an organ capable of registering it. But as Frank Geldard

---

136   Evans in Barlow and Mollon 1982, p. 239.
137   Helen Keller, letter to Dr. Kerr Love, 1910, reprinted in Brian Grant, ed., *The quiet ear: deafness in literature, an anthology* (London: Andre Deutsch, 1987), pp. 36–7. Cited in http://library.gallaudet.edu/Library/Deaf_Research_Help/Frequently_Asked_Questions_(FAQs)/People/Helen_Keller_quotes.html.
138   Christie 1987, Vol. 2, p. 125. Christie does not say when or where this was originally said, but newspaper clippings in the Gallaudet University Archives show that it was said on 21 June 1955, in a pre-75th birthday interview at her home in Arcan Ridge, CT. From: http://library.gallaudet.edu/Library/Deaf_Research_Help/Frequently_Asked_Questions_(FAQs)/People/Helen_Keller_quotes.html.
139   Straus in May et al. 1958, p. 159.

summarises: '[s]ound is generated only by vibrating bodies and is transmitted by wave motion of a material medium'.[140] This curious mechanical origin of sound raises the curiouser question of what is it that enables the mechanical disturbance of a material medium, air, for example, to be translated into and received as sound – and not just sound, but an array of sounds ranging from those loud noises that shatter our ears and jar our entire bodies, to the great variety of articulated linguistic sounds, 'those mouthy little noises we call words', to the perfume-sweet sounds of oboes heard by Baudelaire. The obvious answer is: a sensory apparatus that receives vibrating wave motion and transforms it into sound – and whose evolution is another strange, convoluted tale.

The evolution of hearing and, therewith, the evolution of sound, is in one respect even more astonishing than that of the emergence of eyes. At least in the case of the eye, the transformation of light-sensitive receptors in the skin into an organ with great powers to discern size, shape, colour, and distance had the constant function of sensitivity to light. Because lacking a great deal in detail, Jillyn Smith's narrative of the evolution of ears has a fairy-tale-like, once-upon-a-time quality, but one that, in this case, is perhaps appropriate as a register of her justified claim that 'the evolutionary sequences associated with hearing have been even more dramatic':

> Over millions of years of evolutionary modification a breathing structure was transformed into a feeding structure and finally into a hearing structure. The vertebrate hearing apparatus has its origin in the gill bars of early jawless fishes. The gill bars eventually became jaws, structures to help dismember and consume prey. The jaws in turn became reduced into the small ear bones in the premammalian reptile line, and other bones took over the function of jaw hinge.
>
> Premammalian ears probably were first ears to the ground, functioning to detect substrate vibrations. Later they received low-frequency sounds transmitted through the air. The sense of hearing continued to elaborate (as, presumably, did vocalizations used in challenging and courting), the reptiles and birds evolving in one direction, the mammals in another. A few modern reptiles make good use of hearing, and some birds have clever hearing adaptations, ... but it is within the mammals that we find examples of hearing as the highest technology: the high-frequency echolocation of bats, the exquisite elaboration of the sense in whales and

---

140 Geldard 1990, p. 154.

dolphins, and the uncanny sensitivity of cats. In our own group we find incredible discriminative capacity for one of the more complex waveforms – human language.[141]

If the anatomical shift from jawbones to ears as the locus of sound-wave reception were not sufficiently unexpected, then we can heighten the surprise factor with Anthony Smith's comment that 'the so-called auditory organs of the earliest vertebrates were probably quite unconcerned with hearing; they were more probably totally concerned with the detection of changes in spatial orientation'.[142]

In principle, writes E.F. Evans, 'any vibration, transmitted to the ear via the air or directly via the bones of the head, is ... capable of generating auditory sensations. In practice, because of the limitations of the hearing mechanism, and the complex transformations that such vibrations undergo in the ear, only a restricted range of sounds is audible'.[143] Compared to the high-tech auditory systems of most mammals, primates, especially human primates are even more restricted in the range of sounds they can hear. Whereas tree shrews, for example, have a high-frequency boundary of some 60,000 Hz. (hertz or cycles per second), that upper limit for humans is around 20,000 Hz., and the lower about 20 Hz. From the viewpoint (or 'soundpoint') of bats or dogs, humans would seem to be wandering through the world wearing ear plugs. To us predominantly visual creatures, watching someone blowing on a 'silent' whistle and dogs responding is a disconcerting sight, precisely because we cannot hear the sound we know is there. The same is true of receiving 'ultra-sound' treatment to heal some injury – ultra-sound to us so silent that it is simply difficult to believe that it is not applied for a placebo effect. Ironically, we even produce music that our ears cannot hear: the lowest frequencies used musically, the 16 Hz. waves generated by the largest organ pipes, are unheard by humans and 'make their contribution to [human] musical enjoyment as tactual rather than as auditory stimuli'.[144] There is thus literal and metaphorical, as well as evolutionary truth in George Rochberg's hypothesis that music is closely related to the logic of the central nervous system and that therefore 'we listen with our bodies'.[145] The rock-and-roll generation was by no means the first to realise that

---

141 Jillyn Smith 1989, pp. 22–3.
142 Anthony Smith 1968, p. 387.
143 Evans in Barlow and Mollon 1982, p. 242.
144 Geldard 1990, p. 156.
145 Cited in Ackerman 1991, p. 212.

'high decibel music activates the peripheral nervous system by low frequency sound waves beating against the body' produces a kind of high from a rush of adrenalin.[146]

If listening with our bodies helps us to hear, those creatures with more astute auditory systems use them to 'see'. What humans do with eyes, other creatures do with their ears by means of echolocation. For humans, the task of locating things in space is primarily a visual one. Though human ears have some capacity to situate objects in space, they are, *by contrast* with other species, woefully inadequate; and much of their ability to do so results from visual supplements – memories of the seen distances of the sources of sounds that then aid the ears when the source cannot be seen.[147] Whales and dolphins 'see' to navigate and forage through their sound-perceiving organs: 'The sound picture a dolphin "sees" of a fish or a scuba diver probably would resemble an Xray to us'.[148] And bats click a frequency – at approximately 50,000 cycles per second – ten or twenty times a second at their prey, then wait for these sounds to bounce back to them. Judging by the returning sound's delay and intensity, they are thus able to locate their prey in reference to themselves. Through this audial cartography, bats are able to 'build a complete echo picture of its world, a canvas on which all the objects and animals reveal themselves in detail, down to their texture, motion, distance, and size'.

The relatively impoverished range of vibratory disturbances that human ears can detect is not without its advantages. As noisy as our industrialised,

---

146   Jillyn Smith 1989, p. 39.
147   Caitlyn Baxter, an undergraduate student in my course on Mapping Human Corporeal Organization (Winter 2009) contributed this: 'Another example of precise sound localization can be found in the barn owl, *Tyto alba*. Although the barn owl has extremely acute vision, it is completely nocturnal and can hunt successfully in complete darkness. This is due to its precise sound localization system. The barn owl has asymmetrical ear canals, which allows it to localize sound both horizontally and vertically. Horizontally, the barn owl uses the same interaural timing difference cues that we do as humans to determine which direction the sound is coming from. However, vertical localization is where their asymmetrical ear canals come into play. The key is that one ear canal points up and one points down, meaning that sounds coming from above are louder in one ear than the other. A sound that is equally loud in both ears indicates that the source is directly in the middle. This precise method of localization in both horizontal and vertical planes allows the barn owl to pinpoint prey from sound cues alone. Human ears, by contrast, are able to differentiate horizontal location fairly well, through comparisons of timing and sound pressure level differences between either ear. However, our ability to discern the elevation of sounds is poor, and based on learned frequency/elevation correlations that may or may not reflect reality. For example, a sound of a certain frequency may seem like it is coming from above no matter the location of its actual source'.
148   Jillyn Smith 1989, p. 32. Next citation, Ackerman 1991, pp. 196–7.

urban world is, it would quite literally be incomprehensibly more so were we endowed with a more sensitive hearing apparatus.[149] Imagine being able to hear those 'silent' dog whistles and all the other sounds that make up the world of more audibly-abled creatures. Or what Jillyn Smith calls the 'whole noisy worlds of animals ... communicating with each other just outside our tuning'.[150] The limits of our ears protect us from a sensory overload that would hinder our ability to make sense of our world – and not just in terms of noises, but also in terms of our ability to communicate with one another. As Frank Geldard writes, 'if man's ears were any better attuned they would be assailed by noises coming from the "dance of the molecules" in the very air in which he lives'.[151] The limitations of human hearing have their virtues in specific purposes, both of preventing sensory overload and in enabling a refinement of the ability to hear fine sound nuances within the range audible to the ear.

However impoverished human hearing may be when compared to dogs and other more auditory-abled species, our audio system does give 'sound-shape' to human worlds.[152] As Anthony Smith notes, '[t]here are three properties of any sound, and human speech is also associated with these three – loudness, pitch, and quality'.[153] And as Hegel recognised, 'Just as sight is connected with physicalized space, with light, so hearing is connected with physicalized time, with sound. For in sound, corporeality has become posited as time'.[154] And Erwin Straus fine-tunes Hegel's observation by differentiating among 'the very forms of temporality': while vision patterns our notion of persistence, hearing delivers our sense of duration. He exemplifies this with a clock, 'the sight of which persists', but whose 'unbroken ticking [is] a constantly renewed happening'. And he summarises that motion is 'perceived in the optical field as a place-

---

149 There is, of course, a great deal of physiological adaptation to particular environments that affects the range of sounds that we can listen to comfortably. Ear specialists in Sudan noted that the ears of groups of people living in the remote hinterlands and rarely hearing anything much louder than human speech suffered ear pains when subjected to the noises of urban life (Anthony Smith 1968, p. 390). And Ackerman notes that inhabitants of the Arctic regions, accustomed to the polar quiet, often suffered deafness when they first began using rifles for hunting, the sharp blast of the gun exploding on unaccustomed ears (although I would suspect that would be true of any pre-firearms people first becoming acquainted with firearms). Ackerman, PBS broadcast, 'The Natural History of the Senses'.
150 Jillyn Smith 1989, pp. 27–8.
151 Geldard 1972, p. 39.
152 'Sound-shape' from Waugh and Jakobson, 1979; this is addressed further below, Chapter 6.6.6. on 'The Biological Foundations of Speech and Language'.
153 Anthony Smith 1968, p. 341.
154 Hegel in Houlgate 1998, pp. 288–9. My translation of *Körperlichkeit* as 'corporeality'; Houlgate uses 'corporeity'.

change of something identical', but 'in the acoustic field as a time-sequence of changing data – e.g. as a sequence of tones in a melody or in what the English language characteristically calls a "movement" in music'.[155] And speaking of music and language: were we like functionally-deaf invertebrates, we would be bereft of the hearing through which human worlds are enlivened with the harmonious sounds of music, of speech and poetry, the song-speech of birds and bees and crickets, and with the cacophonic, but sometimes stirring buzz of urban life.

6.5.4 *The Chemical Senses: Smell and Taste*

The sense of smell has not fared well in the Western intellectual tradition whose canonical representatives from Plato to Hegel turned up their philosophical noses at the body's olfactory capacities. While both Plato and Aristotle found a certain aesthetic value in smell, they were more than a little wary of it because of what they sniffed as its potential to enhance carnal cravings beyond the bounds of moderation, the latter designating it 'the most undistinguished' of all the senses.[156] With the rise of German idealism came another decline in the philosophical fortunes of smell. For Kant, smell, though the 'most necessary' of the senses, is also 'the most unproductive'.[157] And Hegel's contrast of the animal and human nose was certainly not to the advantage of the sense of smell. The animal nose is a slave to the 'practical', and the protruding animal muzzle 'the expression of pure and simple utility, devoid of any spiritual ideality'; whereas, the modest human nose, as captured in the Greek profile representing the 'ideal form of the human head', expresses the triumph of the mind over nature 'which is thrust totally into the background'.[158]

Though few, there were some sensualists within that tradition who were more appreciative of smell. As noted above, Manetti found it 'impossible to describe the intense pleasure' afforded by 'smelling the odors of flowers and such like'; and Diderot seemed to revel in his designation of smell as the 'most voluptuous' of the senses.[159] That sensualist critic of Cartesianism *avant la lettre*, Montaigne, also gave a privileged place to smell – the only sense that merited a chapter of its own in his *Essays*. Though Montaigne seems to have been abnormally averse to unpleasant odours ('I particularly loathe bad [odours], which I can detect at a greater distance than anyone else'), he 'very much like[d]

---

155   Straus, 'Aesthesiology and Hallucinations' in May et al. 1958, p. 158.
156   LeGuérer 1992, p. 141.
157   LeGuérer 1992, p. 174.
158   LeGuérer 1992, p. 177.
159   Manetti 1966, p. 77; Diderot, cited in LeGuérer 1992, p. 166.

to be regaled with good smells' and, 'want[ed] to smell as much as possible'.[160] Sensing an intimate connection between body, mind, and spirit, he suggested that physicians should 'make greater use of scents than they do, for I have often noticed that they cause changes in me, and act on my spirits according to their qualities'. And he opined that the 'so ancient and widespread a practice among all nations and religions' of using incense and perfume in worship 'was for the purpose of raising our spirits, and of exciting and purifying our senses, the better to fit us for contemplation'.[161]

The sensualists' appreciation of the olfactory was more auspicious than the idealists' misplaced disdain – not only because the decreased role of smell in primate life and the commensurate decline in snout size were anatomical prerequisites for the evolution of the primate brain and its eventual human form, but also because smell, even in its relatively diminished capacity, continues to play a profound (if somewhat illusive) role in human thinking and social and cultural life. The ascending importance of vision among arboreal primates had anatomical correlates. The (relative) decline of the use of smell was accom-

---

160 Montaigne 1958, p. 134.
161 Montaigne 1958, p. 135. The post-Hegelian Western tradition has been somewhat more appreciative of our sense of smell and of its role in cognition that either its idealist predecessors or neo-idealist, post-linguistic turn successors. Feuerbach's philosophical sensualism, which helped dissolve the philosophical idealism of his predecessors, lent smell an 'autonomous and theoretical significance and dignity' (cited in LeGuérer 1992, p. 180). And Nietzsche, apparently willing to philosophise with the nose as well as with a hammer, immodestly shattered the pretentions of traditional philosophy with his claim that 'all my genius is in my nostrils' (cited in ibid., p. 184). 'The nose', he insisted, 'of which no philosopher has ever spoken with veneration and gratitude – the nose is, albeit provisionally, the most delicate instrument at our disposal: it is an instrument capable of recording the most minimal changes of movement, changes that escape even spectroscopic detection' (cited in ibid., p. 184). Granting to his own nose at least the powers of an epistemological detective, Nietzsche claimed to be 'the first to have discovered the truth by virtue of the fact that I am the first to have sensed, to have had the flair to scent out, falsehood as falsehood' (cited in ibid., p. 185). And Sartre, echoing both Montaigne and Nietzsche in their apparent attraction to the powers of smell, yet ambivalence about olfactory products, wrote: 'When we smell another's body, it is that body itself that we are breathing in through our mouth and nose, that we possess instantly, as it were in its most secret substance, its very nature. Once inhaled, the smell is the fusion of the other's body and my own. But it is a disincarnate body, a vaporised body that remains whole and entire of itself while at the same time becoming a volatile spirit' (cited in ibid., p. 24). As LeGuérer comments on Sartre's existential take on smell, the 'inhalation [of a body] provokes a spontaneous and instinctive reaction that can be either positive or negative, one of acceptance or refusal. The olfactory sense is the prime means we employ for discriminating between the pleasant and the unpleasant, the known and the unknown. It can inspire either recognition or rejection' (ibid., 24).

panied by a decrease in the size of the snout and in the number of olfactory receptors. The reduction of snout size initiated a process of facial restructuring tending toward a flatter face, a rudimentary forehead, and a more modest dental apparatus, a 'reduction in the number of incisors and premolars [...] combined with a relatively simple and primitive cusp pattern on the molars'.[162] These anatomical modifications helped clear the corporeal path that would lead to increased cranial capacity and the sophisticated supralaryngeal tract capable of speech. Evolution along this pathway sped up when our primate ancestors descended from the trees and moved out onto the savannah where they eventually began to walk on their own two feet, and by which time they were outfitted with a sophisticated visual apparatus that served them well.[163] And that bipedality, which increased the distance between the nose and the ground, was the last step in establishing ocular hegemony and reducing the powers of smell.

Ever a source of refreshingly useful enthusiasm, Diane Ackerman insists that smell was 'the first of our senses'. While the honour of chronological primacy must, it seems, belong, as Ashley Montague insists, to the sense of touch, Ackerman explains her claim in terms of the anatomically intimate relation between smell and brain. The sense of smell, she argues, 'was so successful that in time the small lump of olfactory tissue atop the nerve cord grew into a brain'. Noting that 'our cerebral hemispheres were originally buds from the olfactory stalks', she makes another exaggerated, but impressionistically useful claim that, put in Cartesian form, would read: 'we smelled, therefore we thought'.[164] Although the human sense of smell does play an important, if subtle role in human thinking, this contrasts with other animals whose minds are quite literally filled with smells.

Reflecting on E.O. Wilson's speculation that 'somewhere on other worlds are civilizations that communicate entirely by the exchange of chemical substances', Jillyn Smith adds that 'chemical communication and smell are not insignificant here on earth. The social insects, with chemicals that communicate about colony membership, sex, and other useful things such as trails to food, provide a close approximation to that in the here and now. Every kind

---

162 R. Klein 1989, p. 41.
163 Because unnecessary for my purposes, I again sidestep an evolutionary chicken-egg debate – here between partisans of the older view that bipedalism developed on the savannah and their more recent critics insisting that bipedal capacity was already developing in the arboreal phase. Representing the former position, Dart 1925, pp. 195–9; and the latter, Thorpe et al. 2007, pp. 1328–31.
164 Ackerman's comment is 'we *think* because we *smelled*' (1991, p. 20), the Cartesian rendering is my doing. The limits on the usefulness of this comment are addressed below.

of vertebrate animal has a chemical sense, testimony to its widespread usefulness. In contrast, some vertebrates have lost the ability to perceive sound, and some have lost the ability to perceive light'.[165] But 'among the vertebrates in general, through bony fishes, amphibians, reptiles, and most mammals, smell provides a main source of information. Through chemical memories, salmon seem to find the waters of their origin for spawning. Smell brings the Ridley sea turtles back to the islands where they were hatched in order themselves to lay eggs. A rat remembers a food that previously made it sick and avoids it. A wolf identifies territory marked by another wolf'. Dogs 'can detect odors at concentrations nearly 100 million times lower than we can'; and 'salmon detect scent particles of their birth waters in concentrations as low as 3×10^{-18}'.[166] As E.B. Keverne summarises, the very acute olfactory sense in most mammalian species plays a fundamental role in 'sexual behaviour, defensive and territorial behaviour, mother-infant interactions, and feeding behaviour'.[167] It is therefore not 'surprising to find that in most mammalian species a relatively large area of the brain is given over to the analysis of chemical stimuli'.[168]

The major exception to this general relation between mammalian olfaction and brain development is, of course, the anthropoid primate line. Compared to the olfactory feats performed by most mammalian species, primates in general and humans in particular are grossly inept. Their noses no longer to the ground, and their perceptual needs better met by their visual sense, primates lost the olfactory (and audial) acuity of their mammalian ancestors and cousins. The relative impoverishment of the human olfactory apparatus is exemplified by

---

165 Jillyn Smith 1989, pp. 94–5; next quotation from ibid., p. 99. The intimate relation between smell and thought that Wilson addresses by way of the subjunctive and Ackerman by way of a claim about evolutionary origins, suggests respectively a potential future and a once-upon-a-time that physician Lewis Thomas situates in the here and now. In his compilation *Late Night Thoughts on Listening to Mahler's Ninth Symphony* (1983) Thomas insists that this inseparable link between smell and thought is constitutive of our cognitive process: '[t]he act of smelling something, anything, is remarkably like the act of thinking itself. Immediately, at the very moment of perception, you can feel the mind going to work, sending the odor around from place to place, setting off complex repertoires throughout the brain, polling one center after another for signs of recognition, old memoires, connections'. This, he supposes, 'is as it should be ... since the cells that do the smelling are themselves proper brain cells, the only neurones whose axones carry information picked up at first hand in the outside world' (Lewis Thomas 1983, p. 42). Or as Rachel Herz puts it, the olfactory receptors, unlike the receptors in any other sensory system, are directly exposed to the outside world' (Herz 2007, p. 20).
166 Herz 2007, p. 22.
167 Keverne in Barlow and Mollon 1982, p. 409.
168 Ibid.

contrast with that of bloodhounds which boasts around 220 million scent receptor cells, while humans possess a mere 20 million. In an attempt to indicate how much of the odoriferous world humans are missing, Ackerman asks us 'to imagine the stereophonic world of aromas we must pass through, like sleepwalkers without headphones'.[169] Ackerman's accent on the relative weakness of human olfaction (to continue in concert with her somewhat cacophonic metaphor) rings loud and clear. Nevertheless, as Anthony Smith reminds, although 'from our less efficient point of view, a dog's powers of smell are nearly miraculous', there are advantages to our inferior olfactory apparatus. The most important of these, and the one most crucial to 'mankind's success in the world' is that while a good chunk of a dog's brain is devoted to 'record and interpret olfactory stimuli', in humans the 'disregard for smells' enabled the 'development of that part of the brain for other purposes'; and he reminds us that even though canine olfactory ability is 'over a million times' that of humans, our olfactory capacities are still 'incredible'.[170]

Crucial here is that the importance of human olfaction cannot be understood simply in terms of comparative weakness in relation to the other senses. Although 'the area of our brain that is devoted to olfaction is very small, about 0.1 percent of our total brain size', the human olfactory tract does contain 'more receptors for smell than ... for any other sense except vision'.[171] This large number of receptors is embedded within what psychophysicist Frank Geldard calls our 'remarkably elaborate olfactory tract'.[172] A legacy of the evolutionary past, our olfactory system is 'a bequest from our animal ancestors, whose noses were much closer to the ground and for whom olfactory decisions were often life or death affairs'. Its complexity results from a peculiar evolutionary process that preserved the old foundations while integrating new sets of relations between the olfactory apparatus and the areas of the brain processing smells. And it is

---

169 Ackerman 1991, p. 31.
170 Anthony Smith 1968, p. 371.
171 Herz 2007, p. 21.
172 Geldard 1990, p. 447; next citation ibid. E.B. Keverne also takes issue with those who suggest that the olfactory chemical sense is relatively unimportant for man and infra-human primates. He says this as an unwarranted reaction to the relatively small olfactory areas in the primate/human brain combined with the smaller area of *olfactory epithelium* (the primary receptor surface for smell). This view was reinforced by the long-held belief that the olfactory sense is an exception in that it does not have access, via the thalamus, to neocortical areas – a mistaken view as shown by the discovery by T.P.S. Powell and his collaborators in Oxford that 'olfactory pathways do in fact project to the neocortex via the thalamus now provides an anatomical basis by which the old "smell brain" has access to these integrative capacities of the neocortex' (Keverne in Barlow and Mollon 1982 p. 410).

precisely this combination of an elaborate olfactory perceptual apparatus and a weak processing centre that establishes the subtle, in many ways ineffable, yet most fundamental role of olfaction in human social and cultural life. Although primate olfaction is no longer as crucial for survival as in other primates, its impact on our sense of smell on memory, emotion, and social and cultural behaviour is profound; it has retained duties pertaining to emotion, sex, etc. and is responsible for the certain ineffability of smells that plays a subtle and concrete role in human life. As a concrete example of the realm of sensory freedom beyond that of sensory necessity, Keverne writes that '[e]ven our aesthetic preferences among chemical stimuli, our preferences for wines or perfumes, are in part determined by our cultural background. Thus, although it may have been the development of the neocortex that freed man from dependence on the chemical senses, it is also the development of the neocortex that has permitted such finer appreciations of the trained nose or palate'.[173]

This corporeal downgrading of the sense of smell may have been necessary for the emergence of the knowing and loquacious *Homo sapiens*. Nevertheless, we must avoid Hegel's anthropocentric disdain of the olfactory lest we myopically overlook the fact that smell, though perhaps demoted to the lesser orders, still ranks among the sensory nobility and continues to play a subtly substantive role in primate and especially in human life. In contrast to the many animals whose world is 'above all, a word of smells', and that 'build their perception on smell and hearing', using sight 'only to confirm the perceptions thus perceived', humans, writes Leroi-Gourhan, 'build their perception on sight and hearing'. Yet although 'the world of odour serves only as a secondary practical reference', this is not, he insists 'a negligible one'. All but directly invoking Proust's search for time lost through remembrances of things past, he elaborates: 'Aesthetically, the sense of smell is closely connected with the visual and auditory system; a particular odour, unperceived for many years, will suddenly evoke scenes forgotten since childhood'. What differentiates smell, however, and lends it its subtle and indefinable powers, is that although 'we do not recollect odours as we do events ... [,] olfactory perception, precisely because it activates physiological areas unrelated to reflection, bestows considerable depth and intensity upon reflective images'.[174] And it is by no means just as an afterthought that

---

173 Keverne in Barlow and Mollon 1982, p. 409. By 'cultural background' Keverne clearly means the general species-wide capacity for culture, not the particular olfactory and gustatory discriminations of particular cultures.

174 Leroi-Gourhan 1993, p. 294. The title of Proust's great work, *A la recherche du temps perdu* translates literally as 'in search of time lost'. The usual English rendering of the title as

Smith appends to her list of vertebrate olfactory feats that even the notoriously weak human nose well 'remembers a tasty food, a love-filled night'.[175] Here it might be worth giving a corporeal twist to Marx's comment that the realm of freedom is beyond the realm of necessity by noting that the emancipation of smell from the realm of necessity (of feeding, protection, and reproduction) to which it (along with the other chemical sense, taste) had hitherto been chained enabled its eventual refinement and established its subtle yet pervasive role in human social and cultural behaviour. One might even argue, as I shall in the following, that the surprising complexity of the human olfactory system, standing as it does in intimate relation to the memory and emotional centres of the brain, has actually made it possible for smell (and its chemical fellow traveller, taste) to acquire an even greater nobility in the realm of social hierarchy – if nobility is a matter not of biological survival, but, as Bourdieu put it, of social distinction. It is therefore necessary to address (to borrow from and paraphrase the subtitle of Montagu's book on touch) the 'human significance of smell'.

The relative weakness of the olfactory receptors combined with the relative complexity of the olfactory apparatus gives a distinct structure to human olfactory perception and to the world of smells that humans perceive. The sense of smell is not at all as discrete as vision and hearing. Although the human nose is so modest compared to that of other mammalian species, Montaigne rightly judged as wrong anyone 'who reproaches nature for failing to furnish man with the means of bringing smells to his nose' – this of course because smells 'bring themselves'.[176] Cyrano's protuberance is thus an appropriate metaphor for the human olfactory system. The olfactory receptors of even the rather modest human snout

> protrude into the environment directly from the olfactory bulb of the brain, guarded only be a layer of mucus. They encounter an ever-changing stream of molecules containing complex information, and they make sense of it. The sense of smell has fewer limitations than the senses of vision and hearing. For vision, light and a clear path are necessary to transmit the image, making vision of limited use at night. Sounds are good for nocturnal communication, but again open environments are important for sound transmission. Sounds can be distorted and deflected by obstacles.

'remembrance of things past' is not only literally incorrect, but it shifts the goal of Proust's search to its means – although as the means, 'remembrance of things past' would make a decent subtitle.

175   Jillyn Smith 1989, p. 99.
176   Montaigne YEAR, p. 135.

Olfaction, however, requires only chemicals traveling up the nose. Signals for vision and hearing are immediate. Chemical signals linger.[177]

Like hearing, but more so, smell is rather passive and unavoidable. The nose and ears are more immediately open to the world than the other senses. We can effortlessly close our eyes and, by simply not acting, avoid touching or tasting something. In contrast, we must not only act, but also employ something foreign to the sensory apparatus itself, in order to plug our ears or nose and prevent audial or olfactory sensation. Except in times of a cold or sinus infection, the nose is constantly vulnerable to smells. Because our olfactory glands are exposed to the passages through which we respire, as long as we live and breathe, we submit ourselves to smells. And we do so continually: 'Each day we breathe about 23,040 times and move around 438 cubic feet of air. It takes us about five seconds to breathe – two seconds to inhale and three seconds to exhale – and, in that time, molecules of odor flood through our systems. Smells coat us, swirl around us, enter our bodies, emanate from us. We live in a constant wash of them'.[178] While we can choose to seek out particular scents such as those added to shampoos, candles, and perfumes, we are also passively subjected to whatever smell happens to be present in our environment. As a result, not only is our perception of scents inescapable, but it is more often than not unintentional as well.

The unintentional character of smelling pertains to a second reason for its invisible importance in human life, namely, the nature of the smells as filtered through the human olfactory apparatus. Because we are without those olfactory headphones that Ackerman mentioned, the general role of smells in human life is not overt. We are constantly smelling, but we do not always comprehend what we apprehend. It is hard not to smell, but in part because of the comparative weakness of our olfactory apparatus and its mediated links to the brain, it is often harder to put our mental finger on what comes through our nose. Ackerman refers to 'some researchers' who 'believe that we do indeed perceive, through smell, much of the same information lower animals do'; the difference is that 'we do not have a trigger response. We're aware of smell, but we don't automatically react in certain ways because of it, as most animals would'.[179] Because of the comparative weakness and layered complexity of our olfactory apparatus, compounded by our mammalian legacy of increased separation between the sensory and motor apparatuses, we may register, without reacting

---

177   Jillyn Smith 1989, p. 95.
178   Ackerman 1991, p. 7.
179   Ackerman 1991, p. 37.

to, all but the strongest and most intrusive of smells. The unavoidable immediacy of smells to our comparatively weak nose gives them an ambiguous quality, both lingering and fleeting. A sudden gust of wind from another direction and they can be wiped completely off our faces. But until they are (or until we have endured them awhile), we cannot get them out of our noses – nor, for that reason, out of our heads. It is perhaps this curious ambiguity of smells, their lingering yet evanescent and ephemeral quality, that makes them so difficult to name and describe though they often affect us with an immediacy greater, and a power stronger, than that of thought – and certainly stronger than language.

'The physiological links between the smell and language centers of the brain', are, as Diane Ackerman unambiguously puts it, 'pitifully weak'.[180] Although our 'sense of smell can be extraordinarily precise, yet it's almost impossible to describe how something smells to someone who hasn't smelled it'. Because the attempt to explain smells linguistically renders us inarticulate, Ackerman dubs it 'the mute sense, the one without words'. Despite living in a 'constant wash' of smells, when we attempt to describe them 'words fail us like the fabrications they are'. The relative weakness of our olfactory apparatus produces the rather ineffable character of odours filtered through it. While we have a rich visual vocabulary to describe seen objects 'in gushing detail, in a cascade of images', 'who can', Ackerman rhetorically inquires, 'map the features of a smell?' And she points out that our most common method of speaking of smells, our use of 'words such as smoky, sulfurous, floral, fruity, sweet', is actually a substitute description of smells 'in terms of other things (smoke, sulfur, flowers, fruit, sugar). Smells are our dearest kin, but we cannot remember their names. Instead we tend to describe how they make us feel. Something smells "disgusting", "intoxicating", "sickening", "pleasurable", "delightful", "pulse-revving", "hypnotic", or "revolting"'. Like Ackerman, Smith notes that 'smell wafts away from us by its inarticulateness. Smells have no names, except those of the objects they come from'.[181] And the very weak links between smell and language present a major obstacle to researchers seeking to classify and develop a nomenclature for them.

---

180 All citations in this paragraph from Ackerman 1991, pp. 6–7.
181 Jillyn Smith 1989, p. 106. Though even the relatively limited human sense of smell is susceptible to a great range of odours, these do not easily submit to either conceptualisation of classification. For that reason, perhaps, philosophers and scientists have tended to avoid sustained consideration of smells. Plato divided odours into pleasant and unpleasant, while Aristotle divided smells into good ones that are good for us, and bad ones that are bad. Linnaeus suggested a seven-class system; Hendrik Zwaardemaker, 'the founding father of olfactory physiology' and inventor of the olfactometer for the meas-

It may be their defiance to language that leads us to attach so many diverse and indefinite connotations to smells. As Smith put it, 'the sense of smell seems an ethereal, mystical sense, transcendent as perfumes, capable of evoking nebulous ideas and forgotten scenes as well as strong, sudden emotions'.[182] 'It is therefore quite true', Smith continues, 'that odours play a subliminal, subtle role in our lives'. Yet the opposite is also quite true, and indicative of the ambiguous complexity of smells in human being, namely: because of the immediacy of smell, its connection to the parts of brain controlling emotion, its being 'inside of us' (the percepts deriving from touch, vision, and hearing largely and hearing to some extent are 'external' to us, but smells, like tastes are very much inside), strong odours can also play an overt, passionate, volatile, and even violent role in our lives. Because of their resistance to classification, conceptualisation, and linguistic formulation, the products of the human olfactory apparatus could never fulfil the (visual) criteria of clarity and distinctness that Descartes established as the measure of truth. On the other hand, and this is why I prefer Smith's characterisation of smell as the 'inarticulate sense' over Ackerman's 'mute' sense. It may be the 'inarticulateness' of smells that makes them not inimical, but rather so beguiling to thought, and that causes us to expend so many words trying, unsuccessfully, to articulate them.

This suggestion would be anathema to those who follow the 'linguistic turn's' narrowing of the notion of thought – expressed most succinctly by Jacques Lacan's insistence that 'it is the world of words that creates the world of things – the things originally confused in the *hic et nunc* of the all in the process of coming-into-being – by giving its concrete being to their essence, and its ubiquity to what has always been'.[183] However appalling it might sound to adherents of Lacan's verbal creationism, it seems eminently plausible to suggest that the estranged relation between smell and language not only does not interfere

---

        uring of olfactory sensibilities, modified it with nine taxa in 1895; in 1916, Hans Henning attempted to chart the topography of smells with a six-cornered, three-dimensional prismatic scheme that represented the six major smells in their degrees of proximity. But as, S. Howard Bartley notes, although the 'various attempts on the qualitative level ... to classify odors ... may have some practical use, they have no satisfactory basis in physiology or chemistry' (Bartley in Dill et al. 1964, p. 98). For a brief overview of efforts at, and the difficulties of, the classification of smells, see Jillyn Smith 1989, pp. 106–11; also Bell and Watson 1999.

182 Smith 1989, p. 95. Following citation in this paragraph, ibid.
183 Lacan 1984, p. 39. This neo-idealist matter of the alleged linguistic constitution or 'creation' of things will be addressed in detail in Chapter 8. Here the concern is with what the relation between smell and thought can tell us about language and what the relation between smell and language can tell us about thought.

with, but perhaps enhances the intimacy and expansiveness of, the relation between smell and thought. If the content of our thought were limited only to what can be expressed in language, conceptualised, our mental worlds would be rather more impoverished; and the apparent fact that smells resist language does not preclude their playing a most important role in human cognition.

This, at least, seems to be the conclusion offered by Proust's monumental investigation of the *'mémoire involontaire'* – his several hundred pages of inconclusive thought rendered superfluous by one inexpressibly meaningful whiff and taste of a madeleine that unlocked lost times and retrieved things past. Meditating on the twin chemical senses, Proust wrote movingly and insightfully (should we perhaps coin the awkward but appropriate neologism 'insmellfully'???): 'but when from a long-distant past nothing subsists, after the people are dead, after the things are broken and scattered, taste and smell alone, more fragile but more enduring, more unsubstantial, more persistent, more faithful, remain poised a long time, like souls, remembering, waiting, hoping, amid all the ruins of all the rest; and bear unflinchingly, in the tiny and almost impalpable drop of their essence, the vast structure of recollection'.[184] As Proust's olfactory odyssey seems to suggest, perhaps it is precisely their inarticulateness, their resistance to conceptualisation, that makes smells such intrusive, yet illusive and obscure objects of cognition – particularly, as this passage implies, in regard to memory and emotion.

Though the link between smell and the brain's language centre are weak, this is not at all the case with the mutually reinforcing links between smell and memory and also between smell and emotion. We have already encountered Montaigne's advice to physicians and his deciphering of the not-so-secret reasoning behind the use of incense in worship, both based on his understanding of the close relation between smells and emotions. And Ackerman appropriately refers to the link between the smell and the memory centres as 'a route that carries us nimbly across time and distance'.[185] The same intimacy, Rachel Herz explains, exists between smell and the brain's emotional centres, an intimacy so strong, that odours not only 'trigger emotions, they can also *become* emotions'.[186] Although the association of smell, emotion, and memory is commonplace, it does not attract the scientific interest devoted to what are often con-

---

184 Proust 1981, pp. 50–1; cited in LeGuérer 1992, p. 200.
185 Ackerman 1991, p. 7.
186 See Herz 2007, p. 11. All further citations from Herz in this paragraph from ibid., p. 67. See ibid., pp. 64–6 for description of the few investigations of smell and emotion. Herz's scientific publications whose findings she summarises here are: 'The Effects of Cue Distinctiveness on Odor-based Context-dependent Memory', *Memory & Cognition*, 25: 375–

sidered the more 'noble senses'. Intrigued by the question, however, Herz took it up herself to develop procedures to compare memories triggered through the various sensory systems. Physiologically speaking, the emotional power of smell derives from the fact that '[s]mell and emotion are located in the same network of neural structures, called the *limbic system*. The limbic system is the ancient core of the brain, sometimes called the *reptilian brain* because we share it with reptiles, and sometimes called the *rhinencephalon*-literally, the "nose-brain". The key limbic structure to interact with our olfactory centre is the *amygdala*. The amygdala is the brain's locus of emotion. Without an amygdala we cannot experience or process emotional experiences, we cannot express our own emotions, and we cannot learn and remember emotional events'.[187]

Based on her comparative studies of memories provoked by the various senses, Herz found that 'in terms of their accuracy, detail, and vividness, our recollections triggered by scents are just as good as our memories elicited by seeing, hearing, or touching an item – but no more so'.[188] In one important way, however, in terms of their 'emotionality', the memories triggered by scent are 'distinctive': 'We list more emotions, rate our emotions as having greater intensity, report our memories as being more emotionally laden, and state that we feel more strongly a sense of being back in the original time and place when a scent elicits the past than when that same event is triggered in any other way'. By way of explanation, she found that the 'amygdala, the wellspring of emotion in our brain, is more highly activated' when a memory is provoked by scent rather than by any of the other sensory systems. She therefore concludes that 'scent-evoked memories are *different* from other types of memory experiences. They are uniquely emotional and evocative – in our minds and in our brains'.

The unique effect of smells in our minds and brains requires further specification. And Charles Fourier, who conceived 'all of creation' as conceived by the 'aromal copulations of the stars', even imagined such a science.[189] But as the 'founding father of olfactory physiology' and Dutch contemporary of Proust, Hendrick Zwaardemaker, recognised, a scientific study of smell cannot but be rather impressionistic. In contrast to the 'world of light and sound', the world of smell 'yields us no distinct ideas grouped in regular order, still less are they fixed in the memory as a grammatical discipline'. Olfactory sensations make only 'vague and half-understood perceptions', but these are 'accompanied by very

---

80; 'Emotion Experienced During Encoding Enhances Odor Retrieval Cue Effectiveness', *American Journal of Psychology*, 110: 489–505.
187   Herz 2007, p. 3.
188   Herz 2007, p. 67.
189   LeGuérer 1992, p. 197, p. 203.

strong emotion' that 'dominates us' even though 'the sensation which was the cause of it remains unperceived'.[190] Seeking to isolate the uniqueness of smell, English essayist and psychologist, and another Proust contemporary, Havelock Ellis, differentiated smell as the 'sense of the imagination' from the other 'senses of intellect'. Elaborating, he writes that whereas sight is the 'most intellectual' human sense, smell has 'ceased to be a leading channel of intellectual curiosity. Personal odours do not, as vision does, give us information that is very largely intellectual; they make an appeal that is mainly of an intimate, emotional, imaginate character'.[191] And we have already encountered that very Proustian insistence (expressed by Leroi-Gourhan who was born into Proust's milieu and ten years of age when Proust died) that '[w]e do not recollect odors as we do events, but olfactory perception, precisely because it activates physiological areas unrelated to reflection, bestows considerable depth and intensity upon reflective images'.

These impressions of the complicated, multi-layered ways in which smells impress on us are confirmed by cognitive scientists. Using a choreographical metaphor, Rachel Herz explains: 'What we think a certain scent is, its connection to language and concept, what the scent means to us, what it makes us feel, and what it reminds us of – all interact in a complex multifaceted dance and determine our *perception* of that scent. Odour sensation happens at the level of our nose and olfactory bulb, but olfactory perception occurs in our mind, where our personal experiences take over'.[192] Insisting that 'the mechanisms of experience are largely unconscious', while 'only the surface of meaning is conscious', Don Tucker argues that 'when meaning cannot be fully grasped through concepts differentiated with specific referents in the world, then it may need to be approached with more intuitive concepts. These are more diffuse, inarticulate ideas that represent the world through feelings, hunches, and qualities of the common sense'. This, Tucker continues, is 'the visceral basis of mind – gut-level experience'. Olfaction, therefore, 'may be essential to the holistic experience of a place, even though it is usually a subtle component in the inventory of awareness. We may not notice how a certain smell colours the quality of a time or place until an unexpected encounter at some future time brings back a vivid memory of a unique episode of personal history. ... The nature of holistic memory is that it is organized through the self. ... The nature of smell is that it pervades both the emotional responses and the holistic experience of a

---

190   Zwaardemaker 1895, cited in Bell and Watson 1999, p. 5.
191   Ellis, cited in Bell and Watson 1999, p. 5.
192   Herz 2007, p. 29.

place and time'. Because it 'fuses many elements into a single, undifferentiated concept', this kind of olfactory experience 'can be called *syncretic*' – or, as Herz put it, 'a dance'.¹⁹³

Perhaps the best way to characterise smells is as 'ineffable'. Smells are 'inarticulate', because they are ineffable – in the sense of that which 'cannot be expressed or described in language; too great for words; transcending expression; unspeakable, unutterable, inexpressible'.¹⁹⁴ Although 'ineffable' is generally used to signify divinity, the sublime, that which is so far superior to human beings whose paltry language is wholly inadequate to the grandeur of that which it would signify (e.g. 'the name of Iehouah' that is 'not to be uttered'), smells too are ineffable – but not because they are divinely sublime, too 'great' in the sense of above and beyond human being, because rather they are profanely sublime, that is: all too human contents of thought that are 'greater' in the sense of richer, than names, linguistic concepts. Smells are ineffable, not because they are 'irrational', but because they cannot easily (if at all) be categorised and conceptualised. They are only speakable in metaphorical terms – a good metaphor being both as precise and as ineffable as smells themselves.

To redress the categorial impoverishment of what she calls the 'cartography of smell', Ackerman hopes (against her own characterisation of smell as the 'mute sense') for 'sensual mapmakers to sketch new words, each one precise as a landform or cardinal direction'.¹⁹⁵ But given the limited power and range of smells perceivable by the human olfactory apparatus, this is probably a vain hope, for the products of human olfaction, both vague and ineffable, simply do not lend themselves to conceptualisation. A 'cartography of smells' would resemble those earliest maps containing inaccurate contours and much blank space. But that does not at all mean that smells resist language altogether. It simply means that indirect, metaphorical means are required to speak of smells, and that the relation between words and smells will always be evocative and associative. If conceptual/philosophical language is thoroughly informed by vision which provides us with clear and distinct referents for indi-

---

193   Tucker 2007, pp. 66–7.
194   *Oxford English Dictionary*, on-line: http://www.oed.com.libproxy.uoregon.edu/view/Entry /94904?redirectedFrom=ineffable#eid. It is worth noting the negative connotations of 'ineffable' when applied to human beings, specifically to non-rational behaviour and corporeal attributes or appendages. The OED provides the following examples: 'a thoroughly bad citizen, as well as an ineffable fool' and an 'ineffable bungler'. In an 1823 prototype of Victorian vocabulary, ineffable assumed a colloquial meaning as a 'humorous euphemism', synonymous with 'inexpressible' and 'unmentionables', as in the observation that 'our lower garments, or Ineffables, sit but awkwardly'.
195   Ackerman 1991, p. 8.

vidual verbal signs, we might ask whether poetry is in-formed by smell??? It would obviously be too much to claim that our sense of smell is the source of poetry. But smell clearly seems more closely linked to poetry than to conceptual thought. The emotionally intense, but intellectually indefinable, ineffable images delivered by our olfactory apparatus lend themselves to the imagination and aesthetics rather than conceptualisation and philosophy.[196]

While taking care to avoid monocausal reductionism, it is worth giving a hearing to Leroi-Gourhan's suggestion that the emergence of the imagination was a peculiarly odoriferous affair. He argues that among animals that mark territories through the secretion of glandular contents or that exude odours to indicate hostile or receptive states, or even in the human use of 'perfumes, aromatic oils, and deodorants', 'the process of figurative representation has come into play'. More so than the other senses, with smell there can be a great gap between the olfactory sign and its referent. The object of vision disappears with it or with the disappearance of the light that makes it visible; though touches, tastes, and sounds might leave a lingering afterimage (the warmth of the touched skin, the savoury taste, an echo), these quickly fade. But the lingering of smells conveys meanings to those animals (including our own mammalian ancestors) with the olfactory apparatus to perceive them over considerable distances in space and time and long after the bearer of the signifying smell has passed. For better noses than ours, smells can signify territorial boundaries or sexual receptivity; to its potential prey, the predator's smell that exceeds its grasp signifies danger and gives warning. This must be what Leroi-Gourhan meant in claiming 'the sense of smell stands at the threshold of the imaginary in the strict sense'.[197]

Our lesser olfactory acuity might not enable us to sniff out territorial signs or (at any distance) signs of danger or desire; but following Gaston Bachelard's argumentation, human olfaction, even in its reduced capacity, still brings us to the 'threshold of the imaginary'. Although the borders of our olfactory range are near and narrow, smell opens pathways deep into distant pasts and is thus key to recovery in a Proustean search for time lost. Whoever 'would wish', says Bachelard, 'to penetrate into the zone of indeterminate childhood, into the

---

196 That unorthodox philosopher Albert Camus made a noteworthy comment on the relation between mental images (rather than concepts) and poetic metaphor, that might be applied also to the contributions of smell to our imagination. Upon imagining a physicist explaining atoms as 'an invisible planetary system in which electrons gravitate around a nucleus', he wrote in response: 'You explain this world to me with an image. I realize then that you have been reduced to poetry'. See Camus 1955, p. 15.

197 Leroi-Gourhan 1993, p. 293.

childhood without proper names and without a history either, would no doubt be helped by the return of the great vague memories like the memories of odors from the past'. For 'Odors!' are 'the first evidence of our fusion with the world'; odour 'is a root of the world, a truth of childhood. The odor gives us the universes of childhood in expansion'.[198] Odours activate the *mémoire involontaire* and imaginatively 're-present' to us things past.

Here Bachelard's seemingly Proustean project takes not a prosaic, but rather a poetic turn. After volumes of unfulfilled prose, Proust still 'needed the dough of the madeleine to remember' (i.e. to re-present in the imagination). Bachelard suggests instead that 'the odor has remained in the *word*' – but he means the poetic word: 'What a lot of memories come back to us when poets tell us their childhood!' – yet with so little verbal expenditure: 'When poets lead us into this domain of vanished odors, they give us poems of great simplicity'.[199] According to Bachelard's logic here, the poetic word is not a merely a matter *internal* to the sign, not merely a relation between a *signifier* that arbitrarily *represents* (stands in for, signifies) a *signified* idea. The poetic word is rather a *sign* that, by association, metaphor, imaginatively *re-presents* a *referent*. The power of the poetic word to re-present the referent lies in its associative, metaphorical character. Metaphors of course abound in prose, but poetry is their natural element. The logic of metaphor is not to be conflated with that of the sign's internal anatomy, the relation between its internal components, the signifier and signified, that Saussure compared to two sides of a sheet of paper, neither one of which can exist without the other.[200] A metaphor, however, transfers meaning from one sign to another, different sign; and the associations carried from the one to the other give to something that is seemingly indefinable, ungraspable, and ineffable a presence that is, if not definable and graspable, at least effable, graphic, *bildmalerisch* – a sensual presence.

In contrast to the ultra-constructionist reduction of the world of things to the world of words, of thinking and being to nothing more than the effects of semiotics, Bachelard's aromatic sensualism treats the poetic symbol as a semiotic attempt to re-present a referent, something outside itself, in the world of things – a rather challenging attempt, but one that, in the hands of a good poet, can succeed. In reading a poem by Edmond Vandercammen, Bachelard discovered that 'a whole childhood is evoked by the memory of an isolated fragrance'. Vandercammen's line, 'My childhood goes back to that of wheaten bread', provoked Bachelard's *mémoire involontaire* and evoked 'an odor of warm

---

198 Bachelard 1969, p. 136, p. 138.
199 Ibid.
200 Saussure 1959, p. 113.

bread [that] invaded the house of my youth. The custard and round loaf returned to my table. Festive occasions are associated with this domestic bread. The world was in joy for the celebration of the warm bread. Two cocks on a single spit were cooking before the scarlet hearth. "A well-buttered sun was roasting in the sky"'. Acknowledging smell as an equal partner in the determination of taste, he concludes, 'In days of happiness, the world is edible'.[201]

'[T]he world is edible'. We understand the sense of the sentence easily enough. But the literal sense is literally non-sense, and our 'behavioural response' (Umberto Eco; see Chapter 9) will not likely be actually to attempt to take a bite out of the world. The literal sense alone does not allow us to understand the meaning of the metaphor – which we can only understand if we are also sensually acquainted with the smell and taste of warm bread, if we have in our repertoire of sensual experience that which allows us to recognise the synesthetic similitude between the odour of warm bread coming out of the oven, the sight of the brightness and the feel of the warmth of the 'well-buttered' yellow sun 'roasting in the sky' ('baking' would perhaps have been a better choice here), and the taste of a warm well-buttered slice of bread. Because of its sensuous source, what Tilley (echoing Peirce's insistence that acquaintance with the object or referent of a sign is a prerequisite of knowing it) says of 'material metaphors' is true too of (also material) verbal metaphors, namely: that '[m]aterial culture as image metaphor requires phenomenal experience for its understanding. Words provide no substitute for the power of the thing, for it acts synaesthetically and simultaneously along a whole series of dimensions such as sight and sound and touch and smell'.[202]

The linear nature of signifying words lets us know that /odour/ is not /sound/, that /warm/ is not /cool/, that /bread/ is not /fish/, that /butter/ is not /syrup/, that /yellow/ is not /blue/, etc. But that is only the abstract knowledge of dictionary definitions. The signified idea, although not non-sensical, is, by definition, non-sensual. And the idea signified by the sign-sequence, 'the odour of warm bread', is without sensual depth; it has no odour (nor, given its intimate relation to smell, no taste either). It is only our own remembered sensual experience (assuming we have had it and found it pleasing), not of the signified ideas that in any case cannot be sensually experienced, but of the referents of the signs he deployed, that enables us to understand Bachelard's account of his experience: that enables us to follow in the direction he was moved, to sense that to which he refers, and what he means, by the sign-sequence 'odour of

---

201 Bachelard 1969, p. 141.
202 Tilley 1999, p. 267. The matter of signs and referents will be addressed further in Chapters 8 and 9.

warm bread' – an odour that we can recognise and tacitly know, that we can, because of our own sensual experience, associate with the 'well-buttered sun' and the edibility of the world, yet that we cannot articulate – except perhaps in poetry and by means of metaphor.

Perhaps it is precisely the inarticulateness of the sense of smell, the impossibility of creating even an illusion of exact correspondence between words and the smells of things, that forces us to realise the inadequacy of the world of words when confronted with the world of things, that forces us to find alternative verbal means to describe smells, that, in short, forces us into metaphor – and that, perhaps leads us, as it seems to have led Bachelard, to wonder whether smell is the biological parent of poetry? If poetry is the preferred medium of metaphor, are poems then like smells? Something that you can't put your verbal finger on, can't grasp, can't name, but that unlocks 'universes'? Is this the secret of Baudelaire's 'Correspondences'?

> Perfumes there are as fresh as children's bodies, springs
> Of fragrance sweet as oboes, green and full of peace
> As prairies. And there are others, proud, corrupt, intense,
>
> Having the all-pervasiveness of infinite things,
> Like burning spice or resin, musk or ambergris,
> That sing the raptures of the spirit and the sense.[203]

An intriguing line of inquiry. But we must take leave of these necessarily inconclusive musings prompted by Leroi-Gourhan's provocative suggestion and the persuasive eloquence of Bachelard's reverie on the relations between the ineffable, inarticulate sense of smell and poetic production. And we might end with the following in place of a conclusion: that although it would seem too much to claim that smell is the biological parent of poetry, we need not establish such direct lineage in order to appreciate that the isomorphisms (if not homologies) between smell, the imagination, and poetry give us a strong whiff of the intricate, subtle, and all too human significance of our relatively weak olfactory powers.[204]

---

203 Baudelaire 1989, p. 12.
204 Ackerman (1989, p. 49) made an analogous suggestion in terms of music: 'Perfumery is closely related to music. You will have simple fragrances, simple accords made from two or three items, and it will be like a two- or three-piece band. And then you have a multiple accord put together, and it becomes a big modern orchestra. In a strange way, creating a

Although the above musings may only be of interest to those of poetic inclinations, the most universally human significance of smell probably lies in its affective power over human interactions. While smell plays a powerfully immediate and 'instinctual' role in the social behaviour and sex life of most vertebrate species, the olfactory perceptions play a more mediated and subtler role in anthropoid primate, and especially human, social behaviour and sexuality – again due to the combination of the relative weakness of the receptors and the complexity of the system. The human nose may not be as discerning as that of other species; but whether 'right' or 'wrong' in its determinations, nasal discrimination between 'the foul and the fragment' certainly plays a definitive role in the social imagination.[205]

The determination of the foul or fragrant odours of other people is explained scientifically in terms of our immune systems that contain a cluster of genes that scientists call the 'major histocompatibility complex' or MHC. With the exception of identical twins, all individuals have a 'unique set of MHC genes', the 'external manifestation' of which 'is your body odor' which produces an 'odorprint as unique as your fingerprint'.[206] 'Odorprints' of course provoke greater affective reactions than fingerprints. The relation between smells and sex attracted scientific attention in 1886, when Auguste Galopin explained that '[t]he purest union that can exist between a man and a woman is that created by the sense of smell and sanctioned by the brain's normal assimilation of the animate molecules emitted by the secretions produced by two bodies in contact and in sympathy and in their subsequent evaporation'.[207] With Galopin and contemporaries such as Wilhelm Fliess and his pupil Sigmund Freud inquiring into sexual power of smells, science finally began to recognise what had been commonplace in literature from Petronius to Proust.[208]

More recent scientific studies have uncovered interesting findings about the specifics of smell and sexuality: several tests and studies have concluded that

---

fragrance is similar to composing music, because there is also a similarity in finding the "proper" accords. You don't want anything being overpowering. You want it to be harmonious'.

205   Corbin 1986. It should go without saying that, as Corbin's subtitle, 'Odor and the French Social Imagination', suggests, what counts as 'foul' or 'fragrant' is socio-culturally constituted. Ackerman (1991, p. 23) provides several examples of cultural variations in determinations of the foul and fragrant. See also LeGuérer 1992, Chapters 1–2; and Herz, 2007, Chapter 6.
206   Herz 2007, pp. 125–6.
207   Auguste Gaolpin, *Le Parfum de la femme et le sens olfactif dans l'amour*, cited in LeGuérer 1992, p. 11.
208   See LeGuérer 1992, pp. 12–13.

individuals tend to find most erotic the smells of others most different from their own – a finding that swings to the opposite among women taking birth control pills. As fascinating as these findings are, of crucial importance here is that what one thinks of and feels about another is fundamentally linked to nasal discrimination. Smell may not the final factor in deciding on a life-long mate, but it is a bottom line in sexual behaviour: intimacy in general and sexual intimacy in particular are difficult when one cannot abide the smell of the other. But smell is of course not just a factor of repulsion, but also of attraction. Herz recounts the case of a woman who was in part attracted to her husband by 'his wonderful, sexy smell'; but after having lost her sense of smell, she was no longer 'attracted to', 'less interested in being intimate with', him and unable to love him 'the same way [she] used to'.[209]

The irony is that as more smells are eliminated through washing, disguised with deodorants, and enhanced by perfumes, the more powerful the effect of what have come to be considered foul body odours and the greater our concern with how we smell to others. This 'modern' obsession with our own bodily odours and their social consequences is diametrically opposed to dominant attitudes from the European Middle Ages into the modern period. Until the later nineteenth century, bathing was in European socieites 'actually widely regarded as a health hazard'; 'getting wet and soapy [...] was thought to make the body soft and moist and hence vulnerable to the prevailing unhealthy, "smelly" air, which people believed to be directly related to disease'.[210] And before the sanitising obsession with pasteurisation, the body's natural odours were considered sexually stimulating – by Napoleon at least who wrote to his Empress Josephine asking her '"not to bathe" for two weeks before he returned from battle so that he could enjoy all her natural aromas'.[211]

In the course of the nineteenth century, however, body odours came to be deemed an olfactory offence, leading to the ostracism of those who exuded them. In the latter half of the century, Louis Pasteur's scientific work on the germ theory of disease prompted the hygienic practices of purifying public places and private parts. But even 'before Pasteur's theories triumphed', 'the increased attention to social odors', writes Alain Corbin, 'was the major event in the history of olfaction'.[212] In terms of physical geography, Corbin's study is of France, but in terms of social geography, it is a study of bourgeois life which, in terms of olfactory hygiene and the social verdicts based on it, varied

---

209 Information and citation in this paragraph from Herz 2007, p. 138.
210 Herz 2007, p. 165.
211 Ackerman 1991, p. 9.
212 Corbin 1986, p. 142.

little throughout Europe during this period. And though the hygienic regime of cleanliness imposed in earnest in the wake of Pasteur's triumph may have diminished the capacity of the nose to discern social class, it by no means reduced the power and vehemence of verdicts against those deemed olfactory offenders; it may even have augmented the effrontery of the offence, since with the proper hygienic regime made known and with the technological means to abide by it widely available (at least to those who could afford it), what excuse could there now be to allow foul odours to escape from one's body? This is graphically illustrated in Herz's interviews with the newly anosmic woman who had become extremely anxious about how *she* smelled. She was obsessed to the point of paranoia about whether or not her body odour was bad and if her clothes smelled unclean. She admitted: 'if anyone ever gives me an odd look, I immediately assume it must be because I smell. I've started showering at least twice a day, and I wash my clothes as soon as I've worn them'.[213]

Not only in the personal and private spheres is the discriminatory role of smell efficacious, but also in the public sphere – and often with political consequences. Despite his strong sympathies with workers, but doubtless because of what he himself described as his 'lower-upper-middle class' upbringing (i.e. one in which the family's 'gentility' was inherited, but not its prosperity), George Orwell writing in the late 1930s (when indoor plumbing and regular hot baths were even far more exclusive than they are now) could not avoid perceiving class in olfactory terms.[214] Well-aware that the culture and values of his class-of-choice were a world apart from those of his class-of-birth, and seeking to bridge that abyss, Orwell recognised that 'to get rid of class-distinctions you have got to start by understanding how one class appears when seen through the eyes of another'.[215] His advocacy of cultivating the visual ability to see through the eyes of those inhabiting very different places in social geography is of course insightful. But it is a telling shift of perceptual modality from his comment shortly before that the crucial class difference and the biggest obstacle to bridging class oppositions was what the 'respectable' classes took as a 'fact', namely that 'the lower classes smell'.[216] And Orwell's appeal to enhance under-

---

213   Herz 2007, p. 149.
214   Orwell 1937, p. 153. The comment about gentility and prosperity is cited from the George Orwell *Wikipedia* entry.
215   Orwell 1937, p. 163; next citation from Orwell, ibid., 159.
216   This idea was contributed by Daniel Friedman, an undergraduate student in my seminar on Mapping Human Corporeal Organization (2009). In his paper entitled 'Corpo-reality' Friedman set these two passages together, thereby making 'visible' Orwell's shift in modality from sight to smell.

standing by expanding the visual capacities of the mind's eye is undercut by his own argumentation that posits the alleged 'stench of the poor' as that which turns a social gap into an unbridgeable abyss.[217]

Such olfactory barriers are not only erected between social classes. Odours attributed by racists to 'races' can have the same effect. Earlier twentieth-century social theorists such as Georg Simmel and Ernst Bloch reflected on the olfactory obstacles to racial reconciliation; and a glance at many if not all tracts advocating genocide, most notably Hitler's *Mein Kampf*, immediately reveals a good deal of ink spent in describing what they take to be the offensive odours of the 'other'.[218] For the racist, smell is the most damning sense. Because of its close links between the olfactory apparatus and the memory and emotional centres of the brain, the perception of different odours that are received as foul ones is emotionally powerful and lasting. When those odours are linked to a group of people, and one portrayed as both inferior and a threat to the social well-being and biological health of another, smell can be a powerfully 'subtle component in the inventory of awareness' – and one that can be taken as confirmation of what people consider the justice of their prejudices.[219]

Although the weakened human olfactory apparatus is no longer as essential to survival as it was to our quadrupedal mammalian ancestors, it still plays essential roles in human experience, in memory and emotion, in social behaviour and cultural values. An inkling of the imperceptible importance to our lives of the ineffable sense of smell can be gleaned from the accounts of those afflicted with anosmia and have suffered the loss of a once-functional olfactory system (and here it must be emphasised that the following refers to those who had, but lost their sense of smell, and not to those whose never had a functioning olfactory system and who nevertheless orient themselves in the world through their other senses). Without smell, Ackerman writes, 'we feel lost and disconnected';[220] and she illustrates her point with the chronicle of a thirty-three-year-old man who suddenly lost his sense of smell after an accident. In a seven-year period 'he had failed to detect the smell of smoke when his apartment building was on fire, he had been poisoned by food whose putrefaction he couldn't smell; he could not smell gas leaks'.

---

217 Corbin 1986, p. 142.
218 And what the bigot designates as offensive odours need not be body odours per se. In Germany (also, I imagine, in much of Northern Europe and North America) peoples from the Mediterranean region, esp. Italians and Greeks, have been disparagingly referred to as *Knoblauchfresser* or 'garlic munchers' as a euphemism for smelly and stinky.
219 D. Tucker 2007, p. 66.
220 Ackerman 1991, p. 40. Next citation, ibid., p. 41.

Anosmia not only cuts the sufferer off from the things of the world. The woman whom Herz interviewed (see above), whose anosmia also resulted from a car crash, lost 'touch' with others, lost her intimacy with her husband, and became obsessed about how she smelled to others. Unable to situate herself in relation to others, she came to feel 'disconnected from her *self*'.[221] And because the sense of smell is so closely related to emotion and memory, its loss deadens the emotions, all but erases the pre-anosmic past, and severely cripples memory production. The accident not only destroyed the thirty-three-year-old man's gourmet taste, it also destroyed his *mémoire involontaire* – the memories and associations provoked by a chance encounter with an evanescent odor that are such an intimate and integral part of a smelling person's life. Speaking of his life without the 'scents and odors to provide him with heart-stopping memories and associations', he felt 'empty, in a sort of limbo'.[222] As Smith puts it, 'People who can't smell don't call up memories with present smells, and they aren't making new smell memories'.[223] Though the olfactory sense was demoted in the primate sensory nobility in the wake of the ascent of vision, it is actually very difficult to grasp the magnitude of the formative psychological impact of this, psychophysically speaking, weak sensory system on human existence. Cutting off one's nose will not only spite one's face, but cut the individual off from the things of the world, from others, from one's past, from one's self as a person with a past and, of course, one's ability to enjoy food. Perhaps the worst thing about the situation of the man rendered anosmic by an auto accident is that before the accident he was 'not just a gourmet but a wunderkind', able 'to taste a dish and tell you all its ingredients with shocking precision' – a gustatorial 'perfect pitch';[224] afterward, however, his broad and discerning palette was reduced to experience only the basic five (salty, bitter, sour, sweet, and umami).

The psychophysics of this tragedy lies in that fact that it is not the gustatory, but the olfactory system that adds flavour to tastes. The confusion that generally leads us to ascribe to taste sensations that belong to smell is 'a natural one'; for '[u]nless one takes the trouble to block off the nostrils and make the test to determine what the tongue by itself can do to identify food flavors, one may never discover how poor the sense of taste is and what a great richness and vari-

---

221   Herz 2007, pp. 7–8.
222   Ackerman 1991, p. 41.
223   Jillyn Smith 1989, p. 125.
224   Ackerman 1991, p. 40.

ety of experience are contributed by smell. The sense of taste, unassisted, fails utterly to encompass the full flavor of meats, fruits, butter, and coffee. These, together with nearly all other foods, depend for their appreciation mainly on their appeal to the sense of smell'. Olfaction 'furnishes the most elaborate of experiences connected with food, for it is the receptor system situated high in the nostrils that supplies the overtones for the fundamental tastes, that adds 'aroma', that transforms sheer acceptance of food into appreciation of flavor'. Were we all anosmic, none of us could hope to be, as Ackerman's interlocutor once was, a gourmet; gustatorily speaking, the anosmic is tasteless, reduced to a mere 'consumer of nutriments'.[225] The physiological intimacy between our smell and taste, and the dependency of the latter on the former, is disconcertingly clear in the sudden blandness of food whenever we suffer a sinus cold which can suddenly reduce discrete and appealing flavours to homogeneous and unappetising tastes. And because it plays such a definitive role in discriminating flavours, the sense of smell also bequeaths its inarticulateness to taste.

Like its chemical counterpart smell, the sense of taste is primitive, and its survival value in humans has long since been superseded by vision and hearing.[226] Like the olfactory, the gustatory system fares badly in cross-species comparisons; the human tongue has far fewer receptors per taste bud and these are, like the olfactory receptors, linked to the limbic system, the oldest and most primal section of the brain. And given that much of human taste perception depends on the comparatively weak olfactory receptors, humans are, comparatively speaking, rather lacking in taste.[227] The human tongue has 2,000–8,000 taste buds, and each bud possesses an average of 30–50 cells. Rodent taste buds

---

225 All citations in this paragraph, Geldard 1990, pp. 438–9.
226 S. Howard Bartley in Dill et al. 1964, p. 98.
227 The relative weakness of our sense of taste is weakened further by its dependence on our sense of touch as well. As Frank Geldard notes, '[f]oods and beverages, once taken into the mouth, make at least a dual, usually a triple, appeal. The tissues of the mouth, throat, and nasal cavity are so innervated, and so disposed in relation to one another, that any or all of three sensory systems go into operation simultaneously in response to the same stimulus. The cutaneous sensibilities of the mouth region are inevitably brought into play. They not only report on texture of foods but contribute the "biting", "burning", or astringent elements of certain of them and the "coolness" or tingle of others. The sense of taste is obviously involved, end organs in the tongue and palate accounting for a limited but basic repertory of sense qualities' (Geldard 1990, p. 438). Geldard adds that temperature, a sensation of touch, is also 'one of the important and interesting variables' in taste: 'As a practical matter it has long been known that the taste of food is partially determined by its temperature. Good cooks salt foods when they are neither too hot nor too cold. In making iced tea the sourness of lemon is not apparent until the tea has cooled down. Confectioners know

have double the number,[228] and a catfish tastes much better with its some 200 receptors per bud.[229] Taste is, according to Leroi-Gourhan, 'the lowliest of the human senses, as it is of all animals'; and our taste buds are 'the simplest of our sensory systems [...] which in biological terms are mere alarm signals' whose purpose is to differentiate between the poisonous and the nutritious.[230] Likewise Geldard, who calls taste the 'poor relation' in the family of senses, because '[g]ustatory phenomena do not loom large in the world of human affairs, not so large as the number gourmets and gourmands in it would seem to imply'. Nevertheless, although taste has 'only a restricted set of qualities to contribute to the sum of human experience', Geldard concludes that 'fully as intriguing mysteries exist here as in other senses fields'.[231] As with smell, the emancipation of taste from the realm of biological necessity opened up a wide range of aesthetic/sensual possibilities.

While there is obviously a great deal more to be said about taste, here I shall address only one issue, and that very briefly: the role that the intimate chemical senses of smell and taste plays in social life. It is perhaps curious that despite its intimacy with smell, taste is linguistically speaking (in English, at least) associated, in some ways appropriately, with the most tangible sense. Etymologically, 'taste' derives from the Latin *tangere*, meaning to touch, and *taxare*, meaning to touch sharply. It first appeared in Middle English as *tasten* meaning to examine by touch.[232] The earliest definitions in the *Oxford English Dictionary* link the noun 'taste' to two different sensory systems and used in two ways. In sensory terms, taste referred both to perceiving the flavour of a thing, but also to touching, feeling with the hands. In addition to perception, taste also pertained to evaluation through a trial, test, or examination. A 'taste test' could be conducted by either the tongue or the fingers. Although the older meaning of manual sensing is long lost, 'taste' has maintained both its sensory and its evaluative dimension – the latter eventually becoming associated with aesthetic judgement, manners, with that which is 'classy'.

---

that candy made for use in the tropics must not be over-sweetened lest it taste insipid' (ibid., 491). Similarly, S. Howard Bartley explains that 'flavor' should be used for 'the end result of putting something in the mouth', the 'complex experience' in which 'olfaction and the temperature and pressure senses as well as pain may be involved', while 'taste' is properly reserved for the now five 'classical qualities' (Bartley in Dill et al. 1964, p. 97).

228   Taylor and Roberts 2004, p. 58.
229   Cagan 1989, p. 3.
230   Leroi-Gourhan 1993, p. 291.
231   Geldard 1990, p. 480.
232   Ackerman 1991, p. 128.

It is curious that all of the senses except taste are used to determine what has taste and class, what is tasteful and classy: hearing determines whether a person's voice is appropriately pitched, or too loud, shrill and/or boorish; vision whether a person's clothes are fashionable or garish, matched or mismatched – whether, in short, the person has a taste for fashion; touch determines whether a texture is coarse and crude or fine and tasteful; and smell differentiates fragrantly tasteful perfumes from their foully cheap imitations. But when it comes to a taste-test of food quality, the gustatory depends on the olfactory to refine taste with flavour. And this is even more so the case in the evaluation of social taste and refinement, in which the sense of taste itself plays no role at all. As in our gustatory, so too in our social experience, the olfactory, not least because of its links to emotion and memory, plays an essential, and a most visceral role in discerning taste and determining 'class'. Because of the relative weakness of our sense of smell and the proximity we therefore require for olfactory apprehension, the determination of whether other people seem, to the nose of the olfactory beholder, to smell good or bad may not be the most prevalent or immediate factor in determining their 'taste'. But precisely because of that requisite proximity, smell can be the most intimate and perhaps most powerful one. And olfactory hierarchies based on hygienic regimes can be rigid and ruthless in their evaluations of class and taste. While smell does not determine class, the sense of smell is often deployed to discern what has 'class'. Yet in contrast to the perceptual hierarchy, in which taste is all but tasteless without smell, the socially-constituted olfactory hierarchy of modernity rests on an ironic inversion: here, those who do smell or who can only afford to use cheap cloying perfumes to disguise their smells are considered to have no taste and thus no 'class', whereas those who do not smell, have both taste and class.

6.6 The Hominid Corporeal Heritage

Having flourished during the Oligocene (~37.5–22.5 mya) and the early Miocene (~22.5–10.5 mya) epochs, later Miocene arboreal primates were confronted with a climatic challenge. Drier weather in East Africa during the middle-Miocene (~14 mya) resulted in the disappearance of large swaths of tropical forests with their abundant fruit tries and their transformation into woodlands and savannahs. The environmental changes provoked by the drier climate brought both hardship and opportunity. And despite the aura of simplicity surrounding a one-sentence condensation of a lengthy and complex process, Richard Klein's summary is apt: 'one of the more terrestrial [primate] forms' exploited the new situation and 'began to alter its habitual pattern of ground locomotion to emphasize an energetical efficient form of bipedalism and the hominid lineage emerged'.[233] If the hominid shoulder/upper-limb complex was formed in the arboreal habitat of our primate ancestors, and through brachiating, the hip/lower-limb shows the unmistakable inscriptions of the terrestrial environment in which the uniquely bipedal primate became accustomed to standing upright and walking on two feet.

Although science-fiction books and films give no explicit indication that there might be a link between a mode of locomotion and (human) intelligence, they almost invariably portray any species with intelligence and language (often mistakenly taken as synonymous; see Chapter 7) as bipedal. But science-fiction is not the only genre afflicted by this reduction of bipedality to a simple and neglected prerequisite of (at least) human intelligence. The cranialcentrism essential to idealist philosophy had its paleoanthropological counterpart in a 'brain-first' theory of evolution which produced a general and long-lived indifference toward the evolutionary significance of bipedality. This bias, that persisted into the latter half of the twentieth century, was most apparent in the surprising longevity of the Piltdown fraud (1912–1953), in which a human skull was planted with an ape-like jaw and whose 'discovery' was long taken as evidence that the evolution of *Homo sapiens* was brain-driven. The 'brain-first' bias was so strong that it produced scepticism toward and dismissal of the find that should have laid the Piltdown fossil to rest: the 1925 discovery of the skull of a small-brained biped by Raymond Dart.

It took some three decades and the exposure of the Piltdown fraud before Dart's discovery was fully accorded its due. Dart named his fossil *Australopithecus africanus* or the Southern Ape of Africa; and though the name remains in dispute,[234] it is generally agreed that the small-brained bipeds exemplified by Dart's find were the first Hominids. The *Australopithecines* seem to have emerged some four million years ago during the Pliocene (5–1.8 mya) and gone extinct about one-million years ago during the Pleistocene. The lack of fossil finds anywhere else suggests that *Australopithecine* habitat was limited to the African savannah.

---

233   R. Klein 1989, pp. 85–6; p. 98.
234   The naming of these hominids is still unsettled. Noting that the *Australopithecines* had the face and brain case of apes, but the teeth structure and, decisively, the bipedality of hominids, Relethford calls them 'basically bipedal apes'. He does agree that 'perhaps a better term could be coined now', but yields to scientific habit, stating that change would bring 'confusion and inconsistency' (Relethford 1994, p. 317). Differences in classification lead to differences in the number of species designated *Australopithecine*, estimates ranging from 'may have been four or more' (ibid., p. 317) to 'as many as eight' (Benton 2005, p. 378).

To be fair, aside from the small cranium that provoked idealist incredulity, other anatomical attributes raised questions about the *Hominid* status of the *Australopithecines*. Pilbeam notes, for example, that '[s]ome features of hand, wrist, elbow, and shoulder joints suggest better climbing and suspensory abilities than for *Homo*'.[235] Klein too notes that '[p]ostcranially, *Australopithecus afarensis* also possessed some remarkably apelike features, including the longest arms relative to legs of any known hominid, the patently cranial orientation of the glenoid cavity on the scapula, curved (vs. relatively straight) food and hand phalanges, and relatively long toes' – all of which indicates that *A. afarensis* was 'adept at climbing trees, perhaps to obtain food or to avoid predators'.[236] In fact, the only unmistakably hominid aspects of *Australopithecine* anatomy were the adaptations of the hind limbs and pelvis that clearly indicate habitual bipedalism.

That Australopithecines were hominid in hip and leg only was doubtless the source of that still prevalent 'strange feeling' that Leroi-Gourhan noted a decade after the final exposure of the Piltdown Fraud in 1953: a feeling 'almost of embarrassment' that humans have in the presence of fossilised *Australopithecine* skulls. And although the granting of hominid status to the *Australopithecines* on the basis of their bipedalism suggests a victory of the 'feet-first' over the 'cranial primacy' evolutionary scenario, even Dart's naming of the fossil betrays, Leroi-Gourhan insists, an inadvertent bias: because 'pithecus' means ape, the term *Australopithecus* suggests that these beings were recognized as only hominoid, 'superior monkeys', rather than being accorded the status (befitting their habitual bipedality) of the first hominids.[237] The uneasy feelings and inadvertent biases before these, our progenitors, stems in Leroi-Gourhan's view from the fact that they were 'humans with a braincase that defies humanity'. This was a rather unwelcome fact to those cranialcentrists who 'were prepared to accept anything except to learn that it all began with the feet'. Leroi-Gourhan, however, points to that habitual bipedality as a genus-defining fact and the reason why it should be called '*Australanthropian*' which unambiguously signifies its status as the earliest of our hominid ancestors. Putting the obvious fact that 'once humanity has been achieved, the brain plays a decisive role in the development of human societies' in evolutionary per-

---

235   Pilbeam in Harrison et al. 1989, p. 114.
236   R. Klein 1989, pp. 142–3.
237   Leroi-Gourhan 1993, pp. 64–5. Following citations in this paragraph, ibid., p. 65; p. 19. Leroi-Gourhan argues that the taxonomic name should be *Australanthropians* which explicitly situates the species in the hominid line, instead of *Australopithecines* which puts it among the apes.

spective, he notes that in strict evolutionary terms the brain 'is undoubtedly a correlative of erect posture and not, as was thought for a long time, primordial. The situation of the human, in the broadest sense, thus appears to be conditioned by erect posture'.

In line with Leroi-Gourhan's reasoning, Stephen Jay Gould also insists that the steps taken by those two *Australopithecine* feet opened the evolutionary path to *Homo sapiens*.[238] Countering the 'cerebral primacy' prejudice that rapid encephalisation made us human, Gould suggests 'a diametrically opposite' explanation, namely that '[u]pright posture is the surprise, the difficult event', and the 'subsequent enlargement of our brain is, in anatomical terms, a secondary epiphenomenon, an easy transformation embedded in a general pattern of human evolution'. Bidpedalism, he continues, 'is no easy accomplishment. It requires a fundamental reconstruction of our anatomy, particularly of the foot and pelvis'; and it represents furthermore 'an anatomical reconstruction outside the general pattern of human evolution'. Gould cautions that his analysis concerns 'a pure problem in architectural reconstruction' that does not at all disparage our large brain whose effect 'has far outstripped the relative ease of its construction'. Nevertheless, the *Australopithecines* took what he calls the 'greatest evolutionary step' toward *Homo sapiens*: 'By the time we became upright as *A. afarensis*, the game was largely over, the major alteration of architecture accomplished, the trigger of future change already set. The later enlargement of our brain was anatomically easy'.[239]

---

238   Gould 1980, p. 131. Further quotations in this paragraph from pp. 132–3.
239   The extraordinary nature of that 'greatest step' is eerily captured in volcanic ash at Laetoli: the fossilised footprints, some seventy prints in all, in two parallel trails about thirty metres long, found by Mary Leakey's team in 1976, prints that dated hominid bipedalism back 3.5 million years. Leakey's reaction to this 'most significant of finds for which I have been responsible' (Leakey 1984, p. 213) is worth reading: 'The discovery of the trails was immensely exciting – something so extraordinary that I could hardly take it in or comprehend its implications for some while. It was a quite different feeling from the discovery of a major hominid fossil ... because that happens to you all at once, and within a short time you know exactly what you have found. The Laetoli hominid trails were something that grew in extent, in detail and in importance over two seasons. But then again, there *was* an immediate impact in the vastness of our discovery because from a very early stage it was clear that we had before us unique evidence, of an unimpeachable nature, to establish that our hominid ancestors were fully bipedal a little before 3.5 million years ago. ... The Laetoli Beds might not have included any foot bones among the hominid remains they had yielded to our search, but they had given us instead one of the most graphic alternative kinds of evidence for bipedalism one could dream of discovering. The essentially human nature and the modern appearance of the footprints were quite extraordinary' (ibid., p. 177).

While encephalisation may at this point have become 'anatomically easy' in principle, the actual process was likely more nuanced. A new twist on Ludwig Feuerbach's materialist aphorism, *'man ist, was man isst'* ['one is what one eats'] was advanced by biologist Richard Wrangham, who suggests that the path to the larger brain may have passed through the hominid 'kitchen'. Wrangham's evolutionary explanation of *Homo* encephalisation inverts Levi-Strauss's view of cooking as a metaphor for culture, and treats cooking instead as culture's 'precondition'.[240] In brief, his argument is that cooking 'breaks down collagen, the connective tissue in meat, and softens the cell walls of plants to release their stores of starch and fat' – thus making digestion easier and more energy-efficient: 'The calories to fuel the bigger brains of successive species of hominids came at the expense of the energy-intensive tissue in the gut, which was shrinking at the same time'. Cooking, moreover, 'freed up time, as well; the great apes spend four to seven hours a day just chewing, not an activity that prioritizes the intellect'. (It is, however, parenthetically worth noting that although the term would likely not be used by the participants to describe their intellectual dialogue and exchange of ideas at academic conferences and symposia, it would not be amiss to refer to it as 'chewing the fat' – and most appropriately, both literally and figuratively, to Plato's *Symposium*.)

As with virtually every paleoanthropological issue, this one too solicits the usual disagreement over the 'who?', 'when?', 'where?', 'why?', and 'how?'. In this case, sceptics note that the brain enlargement of *Homo erectus* preceded the domestication of fire. But evidence of fires long since extinguished is, by nature, ephemeral: ashes might be scattered by winds, buried by shifting sands, or washed away by rain, and charred bones chewed by carnivores. Wrangham therefore considers the dating inconclusive and the issue still unresolved. Nevertheless, it is certainly appropriate and perhaps telling that the recognition (cited above) of Wrangham's hypothesis as what we might consider a historical-materialist inversion of Levi-Strauss's reduction of cooking to a cultural metaphor was the work of Michael Pollan – a chef.

Returning from that culinary byway to the evolutionarily winding high road of this cartographic peregrination: although bipedalism laid the foundation for the process of hominid encephalisation, the full emergence of the large brain and the re-functionalising of the vocal tract into one capable of speech were the last of the anatomically reconstructive steps in the production of human corporeal organisation. Bipedality effected fundamental transformations in virtually all parts of the post-cranial skeleton (generally defined as that

---

240   This and all following citations in this paragraph, Adler 2013. See Wangham 2010.

part of the skeleton 'behind', or more appropriately in the case of bipeds: *below*, the skull).[241] The major transformations addressed here include: the spine; the limbs and their extremities; pelvis, genitalia and reproductive apparatus; and the skin of the 'functionally naked ape'.[242]

6.6.1 Bipedality and the Vertical Primate

Despite the obvious fact that *Homo sapiens* exhibits socio-culturally diverse '*ways* of walking',[243] they are all, it should be equally obvious, variations on the peculiarly human *way* of walking – different gaits of the upright bipedal primate. And to attain the bodily instruments required for walking on two feet with the torso perpendicular to the ground, the anatomy of the quadruped ancestors of the hominid line had to undergo a 'rapid and fundamental reconstruction'[244] that 'led to anatomical changes in all parts of the body':[245]

> The foot became a flat platform structure with a non-opposable big toe and straight phalanges in the toes. Apes and monkeys have a grasping foot with curved phalanges and an opposable big toe. The angle of the human knee joint shifts from being slightly splayed to being a straight hinge, and all the leg bones are longer. The hip joint faces downwards and sideways and the femur has a ball-like head that fits into it. The pelvis as a whole is short and bowl-like as it has to support the guts, and the backbone adopts an S-shaped curve. In apes, the pelvis is long and the backbone has a C-shaped curve to brace the weight of the trunk between the arms and legs.

Elaborating the 'many anatomical correlates of bipedalism', that include 'body proportions, muscle mass and its distribution, joint structure and orientation, and muscle orientation', David Pilbeam explains:

> Important are control of pelvic tilt and pelvic rotation to minimize centre of gravity displacement, a linked pattern of hip, knee, and ankle flexion and extension, and a particular pattern of weight transmission through the foot. The pelvis and hip region has been radically remodeled, pro-

---

[241] The idealist bias is obvious in the nomenclature. Were our conceptual apparatus consistently constructed in terms of corporeal organisation, it would be more accurate to speak, not of the body as 'post-cranial', but of the skull as 'post-skeletal'.
[242] Jablonski 2013, p. 35.
[243] See, for example, Ingold and Vergunst 2008, my italics.
[244] Gould 1980, p. 132.
[245] Benton 2005, pp. 375–7.

ducing low and broad iliac blades with outwardly oriented, small gluteal muscles permitting controlled rotation and tilt of the pelvis. The hamstrings have a short moment arm. The foot has a parallel and stout big toe, short and straight lateral toes, and a wide heel.[246]

The lower-limb anatomy of bipedal hominids is remarkably flexible:

> The hip joint is a ball and socket: the socket is in the pelvic girdle and the ball on the femur, the bone of the upper leg. The knee is a hinge between the femur and the tibia, which is the principal bone of the lower leg, but a much more slender bone (the fibula) lies alongside the tibia. The ankle is a universal joint: you can tilt your foot toe up or toe down, and side up or side down. Thus there are three degrees of freedom of movement at the hip, one at the knee and two at the ankle, a total of six between trunk and foot. This is the minimum need for us to be able to place our feet where we want (within limits) on level or tilted surfaces. [...] However, the fibula cannot rotate on the tibia as the radius rotates on the ulna, so the leg lacks the extra degree of freedom that is found in the arm.[247]

In contrast to chimpanzees that are 'unable to extend their knee joints – to produce a straight leg – in the stance phase' and must thus exert muscular power in order to support the body, the 'human knee can be "locked" into the extended position during the stance phase, thereby minimizing the amount of muscular power need to support the body'.[248]

> The striding gait of human bipedalism involves the fluid flow of a series of actions – collectively, the swing phase and the stance phase – in which one leg alternates with the other. The leg in the swing phase pushes off using the power of the great toe, swings under the body in a slightly flexed position, and finally becomes extended as the foot again makes contact with the ground, first with the heel (the heel-strike). Once the heel-strike has occurred, the leg remains extended and provides support for the body – the stance phase – while the other leg goes through the swing phase, with the body continuing to move forward.[249]

---

246   Pilbeam in Harrison et al. 1989, p. 66.
247   R.M. Alexander 1992, p. 47.
248   Lewin and Foley 2004, p. 242.
249   Lewin and Foley 2004, pp. 242–3.

This lower-limb flexibility is also responsible for the efficiency and the grace of the bipedal gait: During this swing phase, 'the center of gravity of the body must be shifted toward the supporting leg (otherwise one would fall over sideways). In humans, because of the inward-sloping angle of the thigh to the knee (the valgus angle), the two feet at rest are normally placed very close to the midline of the body. Therefore, the body's center of gravity need not be shifted very far laterally back and forth during each phase of walking'.[250] Human corporeal organisation thus makes it possible both comfortably to stand upright and still and also to walk great distances in a 'bee-line'.

Though not at all the swiftest mode of locomotion, the bipedality of the *Australopithecines* and their descendants *Homo* is, in terms of energy expenditure, a most efficient one. The hominid body during bipedal walking (in contrast to that of quadrupeds) has, Pilbeam explains, 'frequently only one support at a time'; the body's 'centre of gravity', accordingly, 'is moved in as undeviating a line as possible during locomotion, to minimize energy expenditure [and] human bipedal walking is energetically not more costly than that of typical mammalian quadrupeds'.[251] Similarly Klein who notes that 'the short, broad, backwardly extended iliac blade' of the *Australopithecine* pelvis ('very similar' to that of 'modern people') that 'centers the trunk over the hip joints' was most effective in 'reducing fatigue during upright, bipedal locomotion'.[252] And from a biomechanical perspective, R. McNeill Alexander notes that '[t]he peculiarities of human stance and gait suggest that we should be remarkably economical of energy. Our erect trunk and straight knees enable us to stand with little or no activity in the large muscles of our thighs. These muscles should therefore use little metabolic energy. In walking, kinetic and potential energy changes are largely balanced, over a wide range of speeds. Therefore, the muscles have little positive and negative work to do and might be expected to use little metabolic energy'; and in terms of comparative rates of oxygen consumption, humans are while running, 'less economical than chimpanzees and most other mammals, but rather more economical than other species while walking'.[253]

Although 'bipedal running is twice as costly' in energy expenditure, 'humans are good endurance runners and the cost of locomotion does not vary with speed'.[254] This gives bipedal humans at least one significant advantage over swifter quadrupeds. Foley estimates that a bipedal hominid could travel up

---

250   Ibid.
251   Pilbeam in Harrison et al. 1989, pp. 65–6.
252   R. Klein 1989, pp. 142–3.
253   R.M. Alexander 1991, pp. 263–4.
254   Pilbeam in Harrison et al. 1989, p. 66.

to 11 km for the same level of energy expenditure as a similar-sized chimpanzee over 4 km.[255] Acknowledging that it is 'somewhat surprising', D.A. Carrier explains that *Homo sapiens* is 'among cursorial mammals [...] one of the best distant runners': '[w]hile game animals are faster over short distances, they generally have less endurance than man'. And he provides examples of human hunters from several different cultures (e.g. Kalihari Bushmen, Native Americans in Mexico and the US Southwest, Australian Aboriginal peoples) who 'run down prey (e.g. zebras and wildebeests, deer and antelope, kangaroos) by dogged pursuit often lasting one or two days'.[256] The speed of the animals is nullified by the stamina of the hunters which keeps their prey from having the opportunity to graze and feed; and eventually the animals collapse from hunger and exhaustion and are then killed by hand.

The efficiency of bipedal locomotion is not only a quantitative matter. And for insight into the qualitative dimension, it is worth lingering a moment over Isaac Asimov's description of human walking. To his own question, 'What makes it possible for human beings to walk *comfortably* on two legs?', Asimov responds: 'It is that the spinal column, just above the pelvis, bends backward in human beings. It assumes a shallow S-shape in us, and can therefore remain generally vertical without trouble. It adds a little spring and bounce to the human walk. No other organism has that backward bend to the spine in the small of the back, so that while some tailless animals can walk bipedally at need, none do so comfortably, let alone preferably'.[257] Although a slow-motion description of the physics of bipedal walking can, as Relethford admits, sound rather clumsy, the net effect of these physiological exertions is rather more 'graceful'.[258]

Like any definitive aspect of the corporeal organisation of a species, upright posture is more than just an anatomical fact or simple prerequisite – which is why R. McNeill Alexander's matter-of-fact summary of the two basic peculiarities of human stance and gait, namely that 'we keep our knees remarkably straight while our feet are on the ground, and we carry our trunks remarkably vertical',[259] is deceptive in its succinct accuracy. For bipedality is not just a mode of locomotion. Or better: *as* a mode of locomotion, bipedalism is also a mode of being-in-the-world: the facts that 'we keep our feet on the ground' and

---

255 Foley in Smith and Winterhalder 1992, p. 140.
256 Carrier 1984, p. 83.
257 Asimov 1988, p. 125.
258 Relethford 1994, p. 253.
259 R.M. Alexander 1991, p. 256.

'carry our trunks remarkably vertical' establish a particular and certainly rare, sensory-kinaesthetic orientation toward the world that requires elaboration.

Although there is no denying that hominids have two feet and keep them on the ground, there is some dispute over how best to describe the path that led to this state of affairs. The common notion is that bipedalism 'freed the hands'. But this, Graham Richards vigorously argues, is a 'misleadingly dramatic formulation'.[260] The spurious character of this formulation, he notes, is rendered obvious by the very illustrations that advocates of the 'bipedal-freeing-of-the-hands' theory often choose to accompany their written arguments: 'On becoming terrestrial the hand was never then "freed" from branch-holding, it brought the branch with it, as innumerable artist's impressions testify, along with the appropriate co-ordination schema'. With the reminder that the hind 'feet' of arboreal primates were also capable of grasping and 'manipulating' objects, he suggests that it would be more accurate to return to a term once 'felt apter for the living great apes' and refer to them not as 'quadrupedal', but as 'quadrumanous'. For, the only differences in hand-usage between arboreal primate grasping of branches and early bipedal hominid clutching of tools and spears lie in the specific activity undertaken and the object manipulated, 'the detached stick replacing the attached branch, rocks and stones supplementing fruit and nuts as objects to be picked up, knocked, thrown and broken, skinning of carcasses supplementing stripping of bark'. The significant consequence of the development of hominid bipedality, Richards therefore concludes, was not the 'freeing' of the hand, but the 'enslavement of the foot', 'its loss of 'manual' functions' and the 'subsequent subordination of its morphology' (and that of the lower limbs as well) to locomotion.

But one could just as easily see in this development, not the *enslavement* of the legs and feet, but rather their *emancipation*. Liberated from also having to do the work of the hands, the *lower* (no longer 'hind') limbs could concentrate on what they do best: fulfilling 'the twin functions of ensuring stability of stance and facilitating bipedal walking'.[261] For although the capacities and activities of the lower limbs and extremities may have become quantitatively more restricted, the division of labour was most advantageous for the hominid line; and their qualitative value is captured in the verbatim metaphors based on the literal facts that hominids 'stand on their own two feet', are 'upright' with their 'feet planted firmly on the ground' (which is of course what Marx, by turning the upside-down idealist Hegel upright and putting him on his feet, intended to

---

260 Richards 1986, p. 143. Following citations, p. 146; p. 144; pp. 146–7; p. 148, p. 147.
261 Richards 1986, p. 147.

do to the Western philosophical tradition). As Richard Griffith points out in his whimsical 'Anthropodology', '[t]he foot 'sub-stantiates' man, man is a-foot'.[262] Footing himself in etymology, he notes that 'the very word 'exist' is from the Latin *existere*, meaning to stand forth, to arise, to set out, to stand out – from the ground, the underground'. And we metaphorically ground our mental missteps in their literal corporeal counterpart, such as 'losing my way' or 'losing my footing' in an argument, or making a verbal 'slip'. As Rebecca Solnit summarises after providing several more ambulatory metaphors in *Wanderlust*, her delightfully insightful *History of Walking*: '[w]alking and traveling have become central metaphors in thought and speech, so central we hardly notice them'.[263]

The limbic division of labour effected by habitual bipedality was accompanied by a restructuring of the morphology of the lower limbs: 'Most hominoids have longer front limbs than back limbs. Modern humans are an exception to this'.[264] The now lower limbs of the human species are longer than the upper limbs which not only facilitates walking, but gives human locomotion its particular form of grace. And if the flexible human legs and arms, each attending to its proper labours, may result in, for example, a lack of swiftness compared to quadrupeds, their working in concert yields an extraordinary and rather unique range of dexterities. But what hominids lack in specialised skills, they make up for in breadth. Hominids are, as Konrad Lorenz formulates through fusing terms from Ernst Mayr and Arnold Gehlen, 'exploratory animals'.

Such animals, observes Konrad Lorenz, are 'open to the world' – an openness stemming from the fact that their 'knowledge of the objects or processes that make up their environment is not specified in innate release mechanisms containing a wealth of information and characteristics, but is acquired by objective investigation'.[265] Exploratory animals tend therefore to be 'comparatively little specialized representatives of their taxonomic groups – "specialists in non-specialization"'. It is, Lorenz continues, 'also significant that among the higher animals only such "non-specialists" can become cosmopolitans. Certainly a rat or a human being may, physically speaking, perform less efficiently on occasion than an animal highly specialized in that particular field, but both will outstrip their closest zoological relatives in the versatility of their motor skills'. Giving a concrete example of the great dexterities and capacities of the upright bipedal ape with its upper and lower limbs, he writes: 'If human beings were to challenge the entire animal kingdom to a test of versatility, consisting, say, of walk-

---

262 Griffith in Spicker 1970, p. 275. Following citation ibid. p. 277.
263 Solnit 2001, p. 73.
264 Relethford 1994, p. 232.
265 Lorenz 1977, p. 148. All Lorenz citations in this paragraph, ibid., pp. 148–9.

ing twenty miles, swimming fifteen metres underwater at a depth of five metres and simultaneously retrieving various specified objects, then climbing several metres up a rope – all of which any average person can do – there would not be a single other mammal capable of doing all these three things'. (It may or may not be telling that if 'one scaled down the requirements to suit its size, the only real rival in all three tests would be the rat'.) By turning *hind* limbs and paws into *lower* limbs consisting of legs and feet, and *front* into *upper* limbs consisting of arms and hands, habitual bipedality effected a division of limbic labour – relegating the former to locomotion while 'freeing' the latter for manipulation (and with both activities cooperatively coordinated, e.g. in wielding a pick or hoe, or throwing a 100-mile/hour fastball). This opened an expansive range of corporeal capacities and dexterities for bipedal hominids that, though perhaps not excelling at any individual event, became the undisputed masters at triathlons, pentathlons, decathlons, etc. And it laid the foundation for a whole new range of range potential metaphorical projections based on the differentiation of arms from legs.

The fact that bipedal hominids carry their trunks 'remarkably vertical' is definitive of hominid being-in-the-world; and that upright posture has been the object of poetic and philosophical tribute and the recipient of a patent of nobility. Admiring the graceful form of Adam and Eve in *Paradise Lost*, Milton writes:

> Two of far nobler shape, erect and tall,
> Godlike erect, with native honour clad.[266]

And Erwin Straus insists that 'because he enters into his own through his upright posture in and over against the world', 'Man is "the first freedman of creation"'.[267] Though Straus's enthusiasm for human erectness leads to some evolutionary shortcuts, it is still worth listening to what he has to say about value of upright posture for human experience:

> Everything in the structural plan of the human body is organized for and by the upright posture. Upright posture enables the development of the

---

[266] Straus cited in Spicker 1970, p. 339. See also Ovid's contrast of humans with all other animals: 'And while all others are bent, head down/and fix their gaze upon the ground, to man/he gave a face held high; he had/man stand erect, his eyes upon the stars'. Cited in Lollini 2011, p. 123. See also Lollini's discussion of Vico's notion of the 'status erectus', ibid., pp. 122–4.

[267] Milton, cited by Erwin Straus in Spicker 1970, p. 338. Following two citations, ibid., pp. 338–9; p. 339.

fore extremities into the human shoulder, arm, and hand, and the development of the head into the human skull and face. Moreover, to the modification of structure correspond not only the variations of functions and accomplishments; with the upright posture a particular mode of being-in-the-world is simultaneously given. The animal organized to stand erect becomes the *animal rationale*; it takes its stand and wins a stance in the world it makes.

The centrality of the upright posture of the bipedal ape is, Straus continues, expressed in language 'through terms like "upright" and "upstanding" and antonyms like "fall", "stumble", and "collapse". In denoting the freedom and jeopardy of human existence, language links the human world with the human figure'.

But that link is not just to a static human figure, but rather to an animated terrestrial one in bipedal locomotion moving fairly freely about the earth. For, the grace in hominid bipedalism lends a kin-aesthetic to locomotive activities that is most evident in the very ancient and universally human art-form of dance. To her own question, 'What is it about dance that makes two and only two feet intuitively and even empirically requisite if not imperative', Maxine Sheets-Johnstone replies that '[i]f we reflect upon the nature of bipedally moving bodies, we readily see that such bodies have greater movement possibilities than quadrupedal, sextupedal, or octopedal ones'.[268] While 'quadrupedal animals have a variety of gaits including those with air-borne moments – galloping, running, cantering and so on – [...] any and all gaits are constrained anatomically by the need to support a horizontally-elongated torso, i.e., a spinal column that is not freely moving but directly tethered to its quadrupedal supporting structure'. Bipedal creatures, however,

> have freely moving or potentially freely moving parts: wings and arms are not weight-encumbered, for example, and can move independently of the base of support, as in tilting forward or leaning to the side. While specific morphologies certainly constrain movement in distinctive ways for all moving bodies, bipedal or not, bipedality clearly engenders a greater range of movement possibilities; torsos can twist and bend; heads can swivel and fall in any direction; arms can swing and throw; and so on. Moreover, a single base of support suffices at times, not simply as it might

---

268   Sheets-Johnstone, '"Man Has Always Danced": Forays into an Art Largely Forgotten by Philosophers', in Sheets-Johnstone 2009, p. 316. Following citations in this paragraph, ibid.

in shifting weight from one foot to the other, but in wheeling about on one leg, for example, or in stamping and kicking.

Sprinting quadrupeds such as deer, antelope, mountain lions, etc. are a graceful sight to behold, and the same might be said of dressage horses. Gazelles are certainly elegant racing across grasslands. But on a dance floor??? There they cannot match the agile, intricate and graceful steps performed by two-legged human dancers. Because bipedality 'clearly maximizes movement possibilities', it is 'in this sense integral to the art of dance'. And 'in maximizing possibilities, it simultaneously opens a palette of qualitative possibilities, a freedom of movement aptly labelled by noted Russian physiologist Nicolas Bernstein "degrees of freedom"' that are 'from an aesthetic viewpoint … a springboard to the creative dynamics that constitute the art of dance; that is, they emanate not just from anatomy but from the qualitative structure of movement'.[269] It should be noted that while literally true, the 'not just' in this sentence can be a bit misleading; for it is precisely that 'anatomy' that makes possible the 'qualitative structure of movement' of all human locomotion, including dance.

Because bipedal locomotion is arguably the key stepping stone in becoming human, and because of the intimate relation between bipedality and dance, we can certainly understand Susanne Langer's claim that dance was 'the first true art'. Although we will probably never be able to substantiate this claim for dance's ordinal primacy, we can nevertheless agree with Charles Olson on its ubiquity – that people 'everywhere dance' and that there 'are no human societies in which they do not'.[270] Drawing the deeper corporeal prerequisite of Langer's and Olson's claims, Sheets-Johnstone explains that 'if man has always danced, he was necessarily, from the beginning, attuned to the qualitative dynamics of movement. How else would he come to the experience of movement that is the bedrock of dance?' It is, in short, the relatively great range of freedom of movement embedded in human corporeal organisation, combined with the bipedal hominid's proprioceptive awareness of its body – that is, of itself – in motion (locomotion being, as noted above, an essential attribute of heterotrophic chordates), that makes dance not only possible but ubiquitous in human societies, assuming vital functions in various branches of life ranging from courtship and love, to the religious and sacred, to art and amusement.

---

269   Sheets-Johnstone 2009, p. 316.
270   Citations of Langer and Olson, in Sheets-Johnstone 2009, p. 306. Following citation in this paragraph, ibid., p. 318. The comment on vital functions is taken from Sheets-Johnstone's gloss on Havelock 1976 essay on 'The Art of Dancing'; see ibid.

If being able to move about in the world is a key prerequisite of freedom, it is alone insufficient. For in order to be free, one cannot be lost, but must instead know where one is in the world (a possible exception being the purposeful but temporary losing of oneself in the world – permanent loss of one's bearings, however, could very well lead to madness). And in this regard, too, bipedality and upright posture have certainly contributed to human emancipation.[271] Commenting generally on the relation between upright form and spatial orientation, J.J. Gibson writes: 'The pointing or directing of [the] perceptual organs depends on the upright posture of the head and body. The perception of external space, the dimensions of the vertical and horizontal and the third dimension, distance, is an accompaniment of the fact of body posture and equilibrium – that is, of orientation to the constants of the earth that have existed over millions of years of life'.[272] In the discussion of primate vision we encountered Straus's insight into the relation between upright posture and vision as beholding, as bringing near (as opposed to the distancing gaze). In effect elaborating Gibson's point, Straus explains how the visual metamorphosis from seeing to beholding characteristic of the upright primate is intertwined with *Homo's* spatial orientation: 'Upright standing man ... is quasi an embodiment of the Euclidean dimensions that extend forwards, backwards, and sidewards into the unbounded. Man looks and moves in a direction perpendicular to the length axis of his body. In the upright posture the skull becomes head, upheld by the trunk. The muzzle, turned mouth, has receded beneath the line of sight; in the human "face" the eyes are directed at the things themselves, no longer exclusively devoted to in-corporation, desire and aversion, approach and withdrawal. ... While the surround encloses the animal body, the world is opened up for the human look. The vertical is bounded only as a perpendicular downwards; upwards it rises like a flame beyond the crown of the head'.[273] Suggesting a thought experiment to perceive the world as a quadruped, Straus imagines crawling around on all fours inside a tent where 'we are down, next to the ground. Our gaze is directed forward-downward, along the axis of the trunk. [... But] as soon as we get up in front of the tent, the curtain before our eyes soars up; the horizon opens and expands'. And more relevant here: 'For the first time the back is turned backwards, the figure shut in on three sides and point-

---

271   The inseparable link between knowledge, self-knowledge, and freedom has been the mainstay of the mainstream of (at least) the Western philosophical tradition. The antagonist of this hegemonic position is that of Romantic philosophies advocating spontaneity and arguing that self-knowledge lies in self-expression and creativity.
272   Gibson 1966, p. 72.
273   Straus in Spicker 1970, p. 341; Following two quotes from Straus in this paragraph, ibid.

ing downwards becomes a form polarized forwards and backwards, upwards and downwards, striving away from the ground. The cardinal direction points upwards, counter to gravity. But the direction of the gaze is forward, at a right angle to the long axis of the body. Thus vision becomes the distance sense par excellence'; and 'the eye of man, emancipated from the bondage of catching, grabbing, and gobbling, can dwell on the things themselves'. From head to toe, then, hominids' being-in-the-world is fundamentally shaped by bipedality and upright posture. Bipedality completed the differentiation between arms and legs, hands and feet – and opened whole new worlds of capacities and dexterities and, once language appeared (if not before), new horizons of metaphorical projection.

Straus's enthusiastic praise of vision would likely turn the outrage among the host of recent 'anti-ocularcentrists' into blind rage.[274] But it would be myopic not to see Straus's insight about the relation between upright posture and the primacy of primate vision in framing both the world that *Homo* can experience and the way that *Homo sapiens* navigates that world. Although Steven Pinker is certainly correct in observing that '[o]rganisms are not symmetrical up and down because gravity makes up different from down', this does not mean that all bilaterally symmetrical species have the same spatial orientation and experience.[275] In transforming hominid corporeal organisation, upright posture differentiated the 'up' of a bipedal hominid from that of a quadruped, thereby transforming hominid spatial experience and orientation. Quadruped bodies generally (giraffes excepted) have a longer horizontal than vertical axis: their heads are situated in front of their bodies and their 'backbones' on top. With their noses closer to the ground than those of bipeds, it is not surprising that the quadruped olfactory apparatus is superior. The placement of the quadruped head in front of the body and the 'backbone' on top produces more of a right/left, front/ back spatial orientation, with 'back' being, because of their long necks and side-eyed monocular vision, more accessible than it is for (human) bipeds. The relative proximity of the quadruped head to the ground, combined with the more powerful nose would seem to make a downward orientation more pervasive than upward. Hominid bipedality, however, means upright posture, and upright posture means: a body whose vertical axis is longer than its horizontal axis and whose head is balanced on top of the body, specifically on top of the spinal column or 'backbone', which truly is a *back-bone* – as opposed to the quadruped 'topbone' or the piscatorial 'centrebone'.

---

274   See Jay 1993. That denigration is not limited to 'French thought', but is true also of cultural ultra-constuctionism more generally. See for example Levin 1993, and note 68 above.
275   Pinker 1994, p. 303.

While the buttocks actually are the posterior of a quadruped, it is an evolutionarily anachronistic and corporeally inaccurate metonymic reduction that lets 'posterior' or 'rear *end*' signify only the human buttocks rather than the entire backside.[276]

6.6.2 *Bipedality, Verticality, and Body-Size*
Bidpedality was accompanied not only by qualitative anatomical transformations, but also by quantitative increases in the size of both the cranial and post-cranial skeleton that had qualitative consequences. Hominid encephalisation seems initially to have preceded the increase in body size. Although paleoanthropologsts are almost unanimous in concluding that their bipedalism guarantees *Australopithecines* membership in the *Hominid* family, that 'strange feeling, almost of embarrassment' (Leroi-Gourhan) evoked by the combination of the ape-like facial features and humanity-defying braincase of *Australopithecines* seems not to have been completely eliminated even by the discovery of fossils of a later bipedal species with an enlarged cranial capacity. This new larger-brained biped, given the species name *habilis*, is accorded the (perhaps dubious) honour of being classified the first *Homo* species. But there seems to be some (seemingly inadvertent, but therefore suggestive) taxonomical hesitation. Whether because the lifespan of *Homo habilis* stretched from ~2.4–1.5 mya, and thus overlapped with the later *Australopithecine* species, or because the morphology of *habilis* seems closer to its *Australopithecine* ancestors (and perhaps contemporaries), or for some other unknown reason, it is in any case noteworthy that *habilis* is often treated in paleoanthropological texts in the same chapter or section as its ancestral *Australopithecines*, and not with its descendent *Homo* species.[277]

The main anatomical difference between *habilis* and the *Australopithecines* is in cranial capacity. *Australopithecine* brain size was similar to that of chim-

---

276 Though dripping with hyperbolic existential determinism, Erwin Straus's contrast of hominid bipeds with canine quadrupeds is descriptively valuable: 'The animal moves in the direction of its length, of its gastrointestinal tract, with its muzzle as entrance and its anus as exit. Its locomotion is in the service of bodily incorporation. The animal is confined to the limits of its own body. Vertical extension is amputated, as it were, from the cardinal directions: upward-downward, forward-backward, left-right. The animal lifts itself from the ground only to return at once. The space sidewards, which our arms broach, is not opened to its grasp. The "backward" movement of a dog is not back-wards, it is actually tail-wards, just as the forward movement is mouth oriented. The zone term "behind the back" when referring to the human body is displaced upwards for the dog, enclosing the entire region above its body. While a human being can re-turn to the field left behind, he animal remains turned away from the "above." The horizon of animal interest is pulled down very low and limited to a narrow territory just ahead'. Straus in Spicker 1970, pp. 340–1.
277 E.g. R. Klein 1989, Relethford 1994, and Benton 2005.

panzees. As estimated from endocasts, the brain volume of *A. afarensis* averaged from 400 to 415 cubic centimetres.[278] *A. africanus* shows a size increase with an average endocranial capacity of 440 cc – a clear advance, perhaps 10 percent greater than its predecessor's brain volume, but still very primitive. Measurements of fossilised *habilis* skulls range from 510–750 cubic centimetres, with the average being somewhere around 650. This encephalization seems to be the only basis for classifying *habilis* as genus *Homo*. Yet though half again as large as that of the *Australopithecines*, *habilis* cranial capacity was still only roughly half that of anatomically modern *Homo sapiens* which averages approximately 1350 cubic centimetres.

This still small brain sat atop a still rather diminutive body. It is, as Klein put it, 'particularly striking' that encephalisation 'was accompanied by little, if any, increase in body size, compared with the australopithecines'.[279] Pilbeam estimates the range of body weights of *A. afarensis* from less than 25 to over 50 kilograms. Klein's survey of data delineates their height and weight range from 'perhaps 33 kg (73 lbs.) and a height of 1 m (3' feet 3" inches) to a weight of perhaps 68 kg (150 lbs.) and a height of 1.7 m (5 feet 7 inches)'. A younger *Australopithecine* species, *africanus*, whose appearance is dated to approximately three-million years ago, is a bit larger. According to Klein, most recent estimates of body weight suggest that adult weight probably ranged between 33 and 67 kg (72 and 142 lbs.), with a mean perhaps near 46 kg (101 lbs.). Average stature was probably around 1.45 m (4 feet 9 inches).[280] Fossilised skeletons of *Homo habilis* also fall within this height and weight range. What Klein refers to as 'the least equivocal postcranial bones of *Homo habilis*' are of an individual 'probably only about' one metre tall, and with arms 'remarkably long relative to the legs'.

---

278   Pilbeam in Harrison et al. 1989, p. 113; Klein 1989, p. 140. Figures concerning *A. africanus* provided in the remainder of paragraph from Klein 1989, p. 148.
279   R. Klein 1989, p. 157. Next citation from Pilbeam in Harrison et al. 1989, p. 113.
280   Figures from R. Klein 1989, p. 146. The great variation in the size within each of the species is usually attributed to great sexual dimorphism. Both Klein (1989, p. 146) and Pilbeam (1989, p. 113) suggest that a high degree of sexual dimorphism accounts for the great range in size. But Klein notes that if the great range in size is a case of sexual dimorphism, 'it equals or exceeds the known degree of dimorphism in other hominids and raises the possibility that *A. afarensis* actually consists of two (or more) species' (Klein 1989, p. 146). And Niles Eldredge and Ian Tattersall in *Myths of Human Evolution* (1982) argue that the positing of a high degree of sexual dimorphism might all too often and easily be substituted for a discriminating study of the fossils and be adduced as evidence of a preconceived adaptationist notion that posits a relatively straight-line view of hominid evolution and does not considered the possibility of a plurality of hominid species and, therewith, evolutionary possibilities.

It might therefore be surprising that the most striking feature of *Homo erectus*, the immediate descendant of *H. habilis*, is its body size. The fossil record indicates that *H. erectus* was much taller than its various hominid ancestors and within the size-range of *H. sapiens*: male and female averages in the 5'8" to 6' range, and size dimorphism seems greatly to have diminished in relation to the Australopithecines.[281] Yet, the trend of notable increase in cranial capacity with relatively constant body size that held from the *Australopithecines* through *H. habilis* seems to have been reversed with *Homo erectus* whose post-cranial body size reached modern human proportions, but the same could not yet be said of facial structure and cranial capacity. Brain volume ranged from 850–900 cc. in the earliest erectus to 1050–1100 in the latest – still some twenty percent smaller than anatomically modern *Homo sapiens*.[282]

Body size is, perhaps even less often than bipedality, seldom considered as anything more than an anatomical feature. This led J.B.S. Haldane to begin his 1927 essay, 'On Being the Right Size', with an expression of surprise that 'in a large textbook of zoology ... I could find no indication that the eagle is larger than the sparrow, or the hippopotamus bigger than the hare'. Insisting on what should be obvious, he adds: 'But yet is easy to show that a hare could not be as large as a hippopotamus, or a whale as small as a herring' – in short, that 'for every type of animal there is a most convenient size, and a large change in size inevitably carries with it a change in form'.[283] The body size alone of *H. erectus* must be considered an important factor in its survival: standing upright, the taller *H. erectus* enjoyed an enhanced version of one of the many advantages of bipedality: the higher eyes made for a better vantage point for seeing further over tall herbage. The fact that 99.9 per cent of animal species were smaller 'probably meant that during the early stages of man's evolution in the Pleistocene era ..., there were few animals that he could not hunt and kill when

---

281 Pilbeam in Harrison et al. 1989, p. 126. Klein 1989, pp. 201–2, notes that older assumption that they were rarely over five feet, six inches, seems to be refuted by the discovery of a probably 12-year-old male skeleton already that tall and who would probably have grown to around six feet. On the less pronounced sexual dimorphism in body size, Pilbeam suggests that selection perhaps favoured larger females who 'would be at an advantage in carrying and giving birth to infants with larger brains and bodies than preceding species' (Pilbeam in Harrison et al. 1989, p. 129). The fossils show a more pronounced sexual dimorphism in facial structure, the male face being bigger with massive brow ridges. According to Pilbeam this implies that intra-male competition was perhaps more 'biologically' mediated than in humans and perhaps that relationships between the sexes were more like those in non-human species than in humans (Pilbeam in Harrison et al. 1989, p. 129).
282 Klein 1989, p. 196.
283 Haldane in Maynard Smith 1985, p. 6. See also McMahon and Bonner 1983, esp. pp. 22–3.

operating in a cooperative group'.[284] *H. erectus* must have been a formidable presence to quadrupedal predators who may have been as heavy, but not as imposingly tall (the suggestion to stand erect, 'make yourself tall', to ward off a threatening cougar is the standing advice given to members of our own species venturing into the wilds today).

More portentous for our purposes, however, are the comments of those who have taken up Haldane's insight and addressed the relation between human body-size and the human cultural capacities. Accentuating the fictional character of those whom Gulliver encountered in his travels by explaining their biological impossibility, Derek F. Roberts points out that

> When Swift wrote *Gulliver's Travels*, his biology was greatly at fault. No human beings could possibly be as small as those in Lilliput or as tall as those in Brobdignag. There could not, indeed, be human beings only 1 ft. tall or 10 ft. tall. ... A dwarf only a few centimeters high would have a head too small to accommodate the complex neural equipment needed to be an adult, whereas a giant would be incapable of moving, because the weight of structural and muscular material necessary to support and operate a massive body of human shape would be too great to move. The heart reaches the limits of its capacity in modern Man subjected to all-out physical effort. Hence, to support even moderate activity in an erect giant would require a much more powerful cardiovascular system. There are no bipedal creatures today that are much larger than Man. Only bipedal birds and the giant carnivorous dinosaurs have attained the same or greater sizes, and these were assisted, respectively, in movement by their wings and in support by their large tails.[285]

An increase in height would bring a disproportionately high ratio between the increase in weight and the strength of the body-weight bearing legs. Thus, although already 'a rather slow animal', 'were Man any larger he would be slower still, and if much larger, he would be a fixture'.

The body size of the *Homo* line is essential not only to internal physiological functioning of human corporeal organisation itself, but also to the relations between *Homo* species and the world that they have so radically transformed. Complementing Roberts' account of the anatomical impossibility of diminutive or giant hominids, Richard Lewontin explains the biological impossibility

---

284 Ayensu and Whitfield 1982, p. 35.
285 Roberts in Walcher and Kretchmer 1981, p. 129. Next citation in this paragraph, ibid.

of the cultural achievements of Swift's Lilliputians by highlighting the inextricable link between the corporeal fact of human body size and material culture. Like Haldane, Lewontin argues that '[i]f one were to choose a simple biological property of human beings that was of supreme importance, it would be our size. The fact that we are somewhere between five and six feet tall has made all of human life possible as we know it'. Therefore,

> The Lilliputians, who were said to be six inches tall, could not, in fact, have had the civilization that [Gulliver] ascribed to them because six-inch-tall human beings, no matter how they were shaped and formed, could not have created the rudiments of a technological civilization. For example, they could not have smelted iron, because a six-inch-tall being could not get sufficient kinetic energy from swinging a tiny pickax to break rocks. ... Nor could the Lilliputians have controlled fire, because the tiny twigs that they could bring to a fire would burn up instantly.[286]

Arguing that human body size is as essential to human mental culture as it is to material culture, Lewontin continues: 'Nor is it likely that [Lilliputians] could have thought about mining or have been able to speak, because their brains would be physically too small. It probably takes a central nervous system of a certain size to have enough connections and enough complexity of topology for speech. Ants may be terribly strong and terribly clever for their size, but their size alone guarantees that they will never write books about people'.[287] As Gould summarises: 'humans have to be just about the size they are in order to function as they do'.

---

286 Lewontin 1991, p. 122. Although humans did not necessarily have to reach the size of *H. erectus* in order to control fire, that control was one on the impressive list of accomplishments of *H. erectus*. The control of fire made possible the occasional occupation of caves and was perhaps the essential factor allowing migration out of Africa (Pilbeam in Harrison et al. 1989, p. 128). But perhaps more importantly the control of fire indicates a fundamental change in human learning capacity, a step in supplanting the domination of behaviour by instinct by learned behaviour and culture. As John W.K. Harris (1983) notes, 'Only humans have learned to overcome a fear of fire that is instinctive amongst animals. Thus, in very real terms, the controlled use of fire by early hominids would have had an important adaptive advantage as a means of protection against larger animals, and, more particularly, carnivores. On the one hand, it would have facilitated moves into new and unfamiliar habitats and, on the other, occupation and more efficient exploitation of drier and more open grassland habitats where bush and tree cover were more restricted'.

287 Lewontin 1991, p. 122. Follwing citation, Gould 1977, p. 180. Gould elaborates: 'Our skills and behaviour are finely attuned to our size. We could not be twice as tall as we are, for the kin-

In addition to the essential contributions of human body size to survival and the production of material culture, there is a fundamental relation between size and the longevity of human life – and not only because human body size served to protect and defend. The 99.9 per cent of species smaller than humans also have a shorter average life-cycle. As biologists have long recognised, 'there is a direct relationship between size and longevity or generation time'.[288] And although that longer 'generation time' means it takes humans awhile longer to reach sexual maturity which limits the natural rate of increase of the species (becoming, on this overpopulated planet, a greater necessity with every passing day), it also 'allows for developmental possibilities and perceptions of the world forever barred to such "boom and bust" reproducers'. The biological fact of a relatively long life frames the human sense of time: 'the intellectual reward of human longevity is that it endows us with the long view':

> Emotionally and instinctively we never measure out our lives in minutes or seconds. The pattern of days is only the most immediate and fleeting aspect of our world view of time. Our natural milieu is the grand progress of seasons and years so that, if asked to describe the pattern of our lives, most of us naturally fall into a discussion of periods of this duration. For man, such a perception of time is a mental creation, but it is also rooted in fundamental biological processes which are only partly conceived in cerebral terms. Physiologically we respond to the changing seasons much as other large, long-lived organisms do.

The eventuality that these large, long-lived hominids would eventually come to write books about themselves (and in which the human life-cycle is often rendered metaphorically in terms of the 'grand progress of seasons') would of course have to await the further anatomical restructuring of the head of *Homo*. Nevertheless, bipedality had already stimulated the development of a whole new set of bodily instruments, corporeal dexterities, and modes of behaviour that define hominid/human being-in-the-world. Although a delayed

---

etic energy of a fall would then by 16 to 32 times as great, and our sheer weight (increased eightfold) would be more than our legs could support. ... At half our size, we could not wield a club with sufficient force to hunt large animals (for kinetic energy would decrease 16 to 32-fold); we could not impart sufficient momentum to spears and arrows; we could not cut or split wood with primitive tools or mine minerals with picks and chisels. Since these all were essential activities in our historical development, we must conclude that the path of our evolution could only have been followed by a creature very close to our size' (Gould 1977, p. 181).

288   All citations in this paragraph, Ayensu and Whitfield 1982, p. 35.

consequence of the bipedal manumission of the hands, the liberation of the mouth from carrying gave it the potential to become a key organ in a sophisticated vocal apparatus. And although it would still be a long while before the development of speech and language enabled hominids to write books about themselves, the genus was already developing, in the wake and as exaptations of bipedalism, the corporeal prerequisites not only for the eventual development of speech and language, but also, and more proximately, of the behaviour patterns that would supply much of the content of books that would eventually be written, namely: work and social production, reproduction and familiality, sensuality and sexuality.

6.6.3 Bipedalism and Its Consequences

One way to avoid the still endless and fruitless debate that pits language against tool-use as competitors for the title of the 'uniquely human' attribute is to view language as itself a *tool* – or, since that term raises linguistocentric hackles, perhaps as 'a means of semiotic objectification'. And were we so to consider language (for doing which there are, as implied in Part 1 and to be elaborated here and in Part 3, many good reasons), then we could conclusively claim that tool-use is the crucial factor that has separated the *Homo* genus from all others and allowed it radically to transform the entire planet by building worlds in its own image(s). But the discussion of the origins of speech and language-use will have to await its evolutionary turn; for well before language became a part of the hominid toolkit, *Homo* species were busily manipulating other kinds of tools.

Above we encountered Graham Richards's protests against the 'misleadingly dramatic' account of the 'bipedal freeing-of-the-hands' that obscured the fact of the 'enslavement of the feet'. Richards is certainly correct in pointing out that bipedality meant the harnessing of what had been the lower foot-hands of arboreal primates to foot traffic. His protests notwithstanding, however, a new division of limbic labour, made possible by the manumission of the forepaws from locomotive responsibilities, would allow primate hands to assume human form and became adept at manipulating and manufacturing. The degree of tool-use in hominid evolution is correlated to the degree of bipedality: the greater the degree of bipedality, the more the forelimbs-become-arms can be devoted to the use of tools in working and making. As Mary Leakey reflected upon her discovery of the famous Laetoli footprints: 'One cannot overemphasize the role of bipedalism in hominid development. It stands as perhaps the salient point that differentiates the forebears of man from other primates. This unique ability freed the hands for myriad possibilities – carrying, tool-making, intricate manipulation. From this single development, in fact, stems all modern technology'.[289] And the division of limbic labour among hominids would become further specialised with the evolution of 'monodexterity' or handedness – a development that appears to have been closely linked with the use of implements (other than the body's own instruments) as tools.

While there is some debate whether the *Australopithecines* used tools, there is no doubt that tool use is characteristic of the *Homo* line.[290] As indicated by the general agreement that the first *Homo* species deserved the taxonomic epithet *habilis*, these beings were not only tool-users but also tool-*makers*. The earliest discovered remnants of stone-tool technology date back 2.5 million years and were found in association with *habilis* fossils. They were made in what has become called the 'Oldowan tradition', so-named because discovered in Olduvai Gorge by the Leakey expedition in the 1930s. Compared to later generations of technology, Oldowan tools were extremely simple and made by using a second stone to strike 'several flakes off a rounded stone to give it a rough cutting edge'.[291] They had a variety of uses including chopping, scrapping and hammering; they could cut through bone and muscle, thereby making up for the hominid lack of claws and sharp teeth and allowing meat to become a regular dietary fare; they could be used to sharpen sticks into digging tools, hunting and scavenging devices, and weapons; they could be used to scrap hides to make primitive articles of shelter and protection from the elements.[292] Such tools could certainly give a variety of advantages to a creature otherwise lacking in both defensive and offensive bodily instruments and dexterities.

The production of even these fairly simple tools 'appears to take more skill and ability to work with complex three-dimensional shapes' than has been found among modern apes, whether in the wild or in laboratories.[293] The fact that many of the tools were found at sites a good distance from where they were made suggests 'longer habitual transport distances, as well as longer attention spans for keeping potential tools for future use'. The concentration of tools at

---

289   Mary Leakey cited in Solnit 2001, p. 41.
290   The lack of evidence, however, is also not conclusive. *Habilis* hands probably differed little from *Australopithecine* hands. Both had hand bones implying 'an ape-like ability for underbranch suspension' (Klein 1989, p. 157) and 'well-adapted for precision grasping, facilitating tool use and manufacture' (Klein 1989, p. 169). And tools made of wood are not very susceptible to fossilisation. This all suggests the possibility at least that *Australopithecines* made and used tools such as the wooden termite fishing sticks of modern chimpanzees. R.L. Susman (1994) makes the case that australopithecine anatomy included sufficiently flexible hands with the manipulative ability to produce stone tools.
291   Relethford 1994, p. 335. Shick and Toth 1993, p. 68.
292   Relethford 1994, p. 336.
293   All citations in this paragraph, Schick and Toth 1993, pp. 219–21.

specific sites indicates greater organisation in 'their use of the environment' and the development of 'a special spatial focus', a greater sense of space as place. That concentration also indicates 'production sites' and therewith 'a new cognitive plateau ... that emphasized planning and foresight'. The preferential right-handedness of *habilis* fossils suggests increased lateralisation of the brain – with the left hemisphere devoted to tasks such as 'time sequencing, language, and controlling the dominant right hand for manual activities like hammering and tool use; the right hemisphere devoted more to spatial perception and mental mapping of the environment'.

Crucial to note is that these mental capacities so fundamental to human thought were forming, along with tool-making, some two-million years prior to language. Schick and Toth hypothesise that *habilis* tool use probably meant increased communication skills; but by this they do not mean language, but 'merely a more highly developed set of vocal symbols to communicate more elaborate meanings from one individual to another'.[294] But if, as Frank Wilson states, 'handedness *is* uniquely human, ranking with speech and tool use as a distinctive behavioural trait of *H. sapiens*', it seems safe to assume that since handedness and brain lateralization are common to both tool use and speech, their emergence along with tool use established part of the mental scaffolding for language use.[295] Leroi-Gourhan, at least, was convinced on the 'essential point' that making tools and symbols both 'derive from the same process or, rather, draw upon the same basic equipment in the brain' which leads him to conclude 'that language is as characteristic of humans as are tools'; 'as soon as there are prehistoric tools, there is a possibility of a prehistoric language, for tools and language are neurologically linked'.[296]

Handier than its *habilis* ancestor, *Homo erectus* is considered the founder of the more advanced 'Acheulian industry'. In body size *H. erectus* was significantly larger than that of *H. habilis*, reaching into the lower range of modern humans.

---

294 Schick and Toth 1993, p. 221.
295 F. Wilson 1999, p. 150. Tools – defined in the broadest sense as external implements enhancing corporeal capacities and used to some purpose – would also include sticks and stones and bones (e.g. *2001: A Space Odyssey*) hurled by hominids whether in pursuit of prey, self-defence, aggression, and/or play (in which case, 'tools' become 'toys'). For discussion of William H. Calvin's hurling theory of brain lateralisation (1983), see Appendix 6.3.
296 Leroi-Gourhan 1993, pp. 113–14. He notes that language and tools both 'are the expression of the same intrinsically human property, just as the chimpanzee's thirty different vocal signals are the precise mental counterpart of its use of several sticks to pull down a banana hanging overhead' (ibid.).

Although its cranial capacity was still twenty percent smaller than that of its modern descendants, the brain of *H. erectus* was sufficient to render it proficient in fashioning and using the more complex Acheulian technology, whose toolkit, though still stocked with stone tools, shows a variety of more complex bifacial implements. However rudimentary, the Acheulian toolkit was sophisticated enough to enable *H. erectus* to become the first hominid capable not only of extending its habitat throughout Africa, but also of venturing out of Africa into the Middle East and Asia, to inhabit somewhat different climes, to create somewhat different ecological niches, and thus to become the first hominid (to put it in terms recalling Marx's notion of human 'species-being') whose production of artifice enabled it to break through the narrow niche commensurate with its corporeal organisation alone; or as Schick and Toth put it, inadvertently echoing Marx in a paleoanthropological vocabulary: the first species capable of replacing 'biological organs with organic synthetic, artificial tools' and thus capable of 'techno-organic' evolution – which, they suggest, 'is probably as profound an evolutionary step as the first self-replicating life, or the first eukaryote cells, amphibians, reptiles, or mammals'.[297]

Homo erectus seems to have been long content with having put only one foot into 'techno-organic' evolution. For, once the significant step toward the production of bifacial implements was made, the technological level remained rather constant; and there was little change in the Acheulian took-kit over the next million years. This extremely slow pace of technological change indicates 'a distinctly non-human kind of behaviour, one buffered by biological constraints. Learned behaviour patterns in *Homo erectus* were clearly less flexible than they would become in *Homo sapiens* – which implies that capacities for symbolic behaviour, including language use, were less developed'. Thus, despite the more complex and broader range of behaviour from tool-making to control of fire to an omnivorous diet, 'this was not human behaviour. Prolonged anatomical and archaeological stability points to a successful adaptation, but one which in its durability is unrecognizable to us humans. It was one where behavioural flexibility was constrained, where the mix of "biology" and "culture" in behaviour was different, the "biological" component being greater'.[298] The *longue durée* of the at best proto-linguistic *Homo erectus* suggests the obvious – that it was the development of language that enabled its user, *Homo sapiens*, to tilt the ratio at an ever-growing rate in favour of the cultural component. But although the brain lateralization that accompanied tool-use was an essential, it

---

297   Schick and Toth 1993, p. 186.
298   Pilbeam in Harrison et al. 1989, pp. 129–30.

was not the exclusive, prerequisite of language. Anatomical alterations to the face and, strange as it may seem, to the pelvis would be required before the loquacious hominid would appear.

As noted above, the ascension of vision to *primus inter pares* in the primate sensory constellation had facial consequences, most notably the facial flattening accompanying the diminution of the nose that gave exceptional status to the protrusions of the self-effacing Cyrano and the fibbing Pinocchio. With habitual bipedality and upright posture, this process proceeded apace as *Homo* species evolved from their still somewhat ape-like *Australopithecine* ancestors. The more primitive ape-like 'prognathic' face with its forward-jutting jaws and large supraorbital torus or brow receded into the more 'orthonathic', or straight and upright face with a smaller but higher supraorbital torus – giving objectified form to the highbrow pretensions of *H. sapiens*. The corresponding reduction in the size of the teeth suggests improving facility in food-preparation.[299] And the smaller 'modern' canines provided the contrasting basis for fanciful images of the long-fanged half-human, half-animal forms such as the wolfman or TV-versions of Dracula. The combination of the relatively large frontal surface area on the uprightly flat hominid face and the flexible musculature underlying it would increasingly, in inverse proportion to the decreasing visibility of hominid hirsuteness (see below), become a primary and articulate means of expressing emotions. Here it remains only to note that the crowning glory of these anatomical transformations of the head of *Homo* was the increase in the size of the brain behind the high brow. But before we become too carried away with its mental accomplishments, it is first necessary to consider the major corporeal challenge presented by the encephalising process that led toward the knowledgeable primate *Homo sapiens*.

In the course of his phenomenological genealogy of *Geist* (mind) Hegel mocked what he viewed as the materialist fallacy in phrenology's assumption that analysis of the physical structure of the skull could reveal the mental structure of the mind; and he did so by reducing that fundamental assumption to the oxymoronic aphorism '*Das Sein des Geistes ist ein Knochen*': 'The being of mind is a bone'.[300] Commenting shortly thereafter on how 'self-consciousness' at this still rudimentary stage of development had not yet grasped the full meaning of *Geist* and had become infatuated with the co-incidence of the 'high' and the 'low' (by which he essentially means mind and body), Hegel likens this

---

299   Pilbeam in Harrison et al. 1989, p. 129.
300   Hegel 1974, p. 260. Next citation ibid., p. 262 my translation.

co-incidence to that which 'Nature naively expresses in its conjunction of the organ of greatest perfection, the organ of procreation, and the organ of pissing'. Had he taken a less androcentric viewpoint, he might have realised that the relation between 'high' and 'low', between mind and bone, particularly the (female) pelvis, is much more intimate than he imagined. His mind's eye was as myopic as phrenology's was presumptuous. And evolutionarily speaking, the joke is on Hegel as well. For, the procreative process is not consummated until the foetus exits the womb. But in the *Homo line*, both the exit and therewith the exiting would become antomically complicated. And the grain, not of truth, but at least of unintended correlative plausibility in phrenology's claim lies in the fact that the development of the human mind was inextricably linked to two particular bone structures whose evolutionarily contemporaneous growth engendered a corporeal dilemma.

Encephalisation, and the corresponding increase in the size of the brain-bearing skull, posed a major problem concerning human 'coming-to-be-in-the-world' – or human birth. This problem arose precisely because encephalisation was contemporaneous with another evolutionary alteration of *Hominid* anatomy that would profoundly affect the birthing process in the *Homo* line: the restructuring of the pelvis bone in bipedal primates, and most profoundly among the habitually terrestrial *Hominid* bipeds. These two osseous processes were, as Wenda Trevathan explains, 'in direct conflict with each other when it comes to childbirth'.[301] The enlarging head of *Homo*, in short, had to negotiate a shrinking birth canal. And this conflict between the pelvis and the cranium created a biologically-induced, universal (i.e. species-wide) birthing dilemma that found a virtually universal solution – even if culturally diverse in the details.

Any universal claim, even one about birth, is, in our allegedly postmodern times, bound to be met with incredulity. Thus, for example, in a volume on 'birth rites in cross-cultural perspective', editor Lauren Dundes notes, with apparently unintended understatement, but in a well-meaning attempt to appreciate cultural variations in the birthing process, that 'the array of cross-cultural customs surrounding birth through infancy includes practices that are both fascinating and instructive'. While cross-cultural variation in birth practices is of course 'both fascinating and instructive', as are also the volume's various essays depicting those variations, Dundes's hypostatising of these differences creates a straw woman. It is possible, she acknowledges, that '[o]ne

---

301   Trevathan 1987, p. 21. This entire discussion (the idea, the sources, and the general structure of the argument and presentation) is taken from a paper written by Adrien Wilkie, an undergraduate student in my seminar on Mapping Human Corporeal Organization.

might logically but incorrectly assume that human birth is essentially a "natural" phenomenon, biologically and physiologically determined to a degree that would make the details of parturition more or less universal, meaning virtually identical in all cultural contexts'. The 'theoretical difficulty' with this assumption, however (as she explains in what has long since become a cliché in epistemological clothing), 'is that "nature" can never be identified or perceived except through the lens of culture', and 'the visions of nature afforded by diverse cultural spectacles offer a rich panoply of hues and textures'.[302] But, one might ask, does not the very existence of variation in the hues and textures of cultural constructions presuppose something that is variously hued and textured across cultures? And there are certain rather essential aspects of the particularly human birthing process that are 'natural' and 'universal' because determined by anatomical and physiological aspects of human corporeal organisation. The unique pelvic structure and the birth canal of females of the genus *Homo* establish the universally human birth dilemma and, therewith, the general form of its cultural refractions, and the range of the culturally specific yet all specifically *human* birthing practices developed in response to that dilemma.

The primate pelvis, and particularly that of the primate female, has had an interesting history. Trevathan illuminates that history by comparing 'three locomotor categories', namely the quadrupedalism characteristic of most monkeys, the brachiation of apes, and the bipedalism of humans. The purpose of her comparison is to demonstrate 'how mechanical requirements of locomotion place limits on the size of the birth canal'; for 'in general, the size, shape, and rigidity or flexibility of the pelvic girdle relates directly to the mode of locomotion'.[303] Referring to W. Leutenegger's studies of the *Australopithecine* pelvis, Trevathan explains that 'efficient, habitual quadrupedalism favours a short distance between the sacroiliac and the hip joints, a relationship that results in a narrow pelvic opening. This, in turn, limits the size of the foetal head at birth for quadrupedal primates'. For brachiates, on the contrary, 'a decreased distance between the two joints is not necessarily disadvantageous, so that selection for larger cranial size at birth can proceed without sacrificing locomotor efficiency. In other words, with the evolution of brachiation in primates, the constraint on foetal cranial size at birth has relaxed, with the expected result of larger neonatal brains in brachiates, including apes, gibbons, and New

---

302 All citations in this paragraph from Dundes 2003, p. 1.
303 Trevathan 1987, p. 17. All following citations in this paragraph ibid., pp. 17–18. Trevathan reference in the following sentence is to Leutenegger's study 'Newborn and pelvic dimensions in *Australopithecus*'.

World spider monkeys'. The absence of locomotive-rooted hindrances to the increased size of the pelvis of brachiating primates opened up a corporeal avenue toward encephalisation and the well-known intelligence of primates. That avenue, however, was not without its evolutionary curves.

Attempting to map those curves in retrospect, Trevathan and Karen Rosenberg begin by asking a question about the evolutionary origins of what in their view is an almost cross-cultural universal of human behaviour and unique among mammals and even primates. Mammalian species universally give birth alone; and while the birthing process is more of 'a challenge' for primate species, all primate females except those of *Homo* species typically use their own hands to assist in the delivery of infants.[304] Human beings, by contrast, 'are the only primate species that regularly seeks assistance during labor and delivery' which for Trevathan and Rosenberg begs the question: 'when and why did our female ancestors abandon their unassisted and solitary habit' of giving birth alone?[305] The answers, they suggest, 'lie in the risky nature of human birth' which is itself a consequence of the anatomical modifications that enabled efficient bipedal locomotion in hominids, yet made it difficult for the mother to use her own hands to guide the child out of the womb.

Against ultra-constructionist formulations that sever all relations between the 'biological body' and allegedly arbitrary socio-cultural constructions, Trevathan insisted in an earlier essay that 'the evolutionary transformation of a nonbipedal prehominid into a bipedal hominid first transformed birth from an individual to a social enterprise'.[306] Notwithstanding romanticised fictional accounts of women giving birth alone and easily, 'human birth is seldom easy and rarely unattended'; 'even among the Kung of southern Africa's Kalahari Desert, who are well known for celebrating solitary birth as a cultural ideal, women do not usually manage to give birth alone until they have delivered several babies at which mothers, sisters or other women are present'.[307] Acknowledging 'rare exceptions', Trevathan and Rosenberg conclude that 'assisted birth comes close to being a universal custom in human cultures'.[308] They then proceed to explain a universal, corporeally-determined pattern of human experience, related to the anatomical reconstruction of the pelvis effected by bipedalism, that exposes the corporeal logic underlying the rather diverse socio-cultural rituals surrounding the birth process.

---

304 Trevathan 1996, p. 288.
305 Rosenberg and Trevathan 2003, p. 80.
306 Trevathan 1996, p. 288.
307 Rosenberg and Trevathan 2003, p. 82.
308 Ibid.

The bipedalism of *Australopithecines* was quite literally the first step toward complicating what had been, among brachiating primates, a much less complicated affair. Transformed by a pelvis realigned for bipedal locomotion, the *Australopithecine* birth canal is 'a flattened oval with the greatest dimension from side to side at both the entrance and exit' – a shape that 'appears to require a birth pattern different from that of monkeys, apes, or modern humans'.[309] Specifically, 'the evolutionary modifications of the human pelvis that enabled hominids to walk upright necessitate that most infants exit the birth canal with the back of their heads against the pubic bones, facing in the opposite direction as the mother'; this makes it difficult 'for the labouring human mother – whether squatting, sitting, or lying on her back – to reach down and guide the baby as it emerges'. As Trevathan explains elsewhere, among nonhuman primates the infant emerges from the birth canal facing the mother who can help by pulling it 'up toward her along the normal flexion of its body', while the infant 'may pull itself out of the birth canal by climbing up along the mother's abdomen'; and primate mothers 'have been observed licking or wiping the mucus and foetal membranes from the infants' noses and mouths, which clears a breathing pathway even before the body has emerged'.[310] The restructuring of the birth canal in bipedal primates, however, specifically required the baby to rotate its head and shoulders 'sideways to squeeze through the birth canal'.[311] This need to rotate in order to exit the birth canal introduced 'a kind of difficulty in australopithecine deliveries that no other known primate species had ever experienced'. Even so, the authors estimate that depending on whether the baby rotated its head to the front or back, it had 'about a 50–50 chance of emerging in the easier face-forward position'; and if backward, 'the austraolpithecine mother – like modern human mothers – may well have benefitted from some kind of assistance'.

The fifty-fifty odds among *Australopithecines* are still decent compared to what happens in the *Homo* line. The process of encephalisation increased the odds of a difficult birth by requiring the emerging infant to undergo series of rotations and emerge facing away from the mother, which in turn necessarily modifies how the mother reacts to the infant: 'If she pulls the infant up toward her abdomen or chest, against the normal flexion of its body, she does so with the risk of injury or even paralysis, especially in the neck region. This position also hampers her ability to manipulate the umbilical cord if it is wound tightly around the neck, or to clear a breathing pathway for the infant after

---

309   Rosenberg and Trevathan 2003, p. 83. Next citation ibid., p. 82.
310   Trevathan 1988, p. 678.
311   Rosenberg and Trevathan 2003, p. 83. Next two quotes in this paragraph, ibid.

emergence of the head'.³¹² Although hominid females certainly 'can and have given birth unassisted for millennia', it is rather obvious, given the peculiar complications and challenges of hominid birthing, that 'with some assistance from other adults, mortality is reduced'.³¹³ Thus, Trevathan concludes, 'as selection favoured further assistance during birth, the behaviour [of 'obligate midwifery'] became a part of the normal parturition in hominids'. And, she notes elsewhere, the pronounced helplessness of human infants at birth 'added to the advantages of having another person present at delivery'.³¹⁴ Whether with early or late *Homo* species, 'beginning with the origins of bipedalism approximately 5 million years ago, having someone present to help during the final stages of delivery, especially to help guide the infant from the birth canal and assist with neonatal respiration, probably made the difference between life and death for many mothers and infants'.

This difference was of evolutionary significance, for '[e]ven a slight reduction in mortality would lead to selection for the behaviour of seeking companionship at birth'.³¹⁵ If non-assisted birth increased the chances of the infant's death on arrival, then it seems that the few cultural exceptions (themselves qualified, as among the Kung, by previous birth-experience) confirm a universal corporeal rule. Therefore, when drawing the cultural consequences of the corporeal challenges involved in the human birth process, Trevethan not surprisingly concludes that '[t]oday [birthing assistance] is almost universally distributed in our species'. And in a concluding methodological note on the species-specific and species-wide corporeal organisation underlying even the most diverse cultural forms, Trevathan argues that 'only by understanding human birth in its evolutionary context can we appreciate the historical basis for the myriad cultural constructions of authoritative knowledge about birth'.³¹⁶ Important here is her insistence that all these culturally diverse forms

---

312   Trevathan 1988, p. 678.
313   Trevathan 1987, p. 225. Citation in next sentence, ibid.
314   Trevathan 1996, p. 289. Following citation, ibid.
315   Trevathan 1988, p. 678. Following citation, ibid.
316   Trevathan 1996, p. 289. To put this in perspective, consider a highly unusual, but nonetheless telling counterfactual of the 'proud mother' who is actually a male: were the human reproductive process similar to that of seahorses which consists of the *female* depositing up to 1,500 eggs in the *male's* brood-pouch on the ventral, or front-facing side of the tail, who then carries the eggs for nine to 45 days as they mature and until they hatch. Once a birthing cycle is completed, 'the male often mates again within hours or days during the breeding season, while female seahorses take "time-outs" from the reproductive cycle 1.2 times longer than those of males'. This means of course that male seahorses polygamously seek new mates and thus 'have the potential to produce 17% more offspring than females in a breeding season'. It should not be difficult to imagine how different our socio-sexual

of knowledge are *authoritative*, that is: diverse forms of efficacious knowledge concerning a corporeally-constructed, universal human experience.

The corporeal constitution of culturally-refracted universals only begins with the birth process. For the same dilemma following from the 'narrowed birth canal required by a bipedal animal' and the encephalised hominid cranium is also constitutive of both the early stages of hominid life and social relations between parents and child.[317] The divine Athena may have sprung from the head of Zeus fully grown, well-armed, and mature, but the mere mortal neonate must be pushed through a restricted birth canal and arrives in the world underdeveloped, vulnerable, and immature. Proportional to the 228-day gestation period in chimpanzees and 256 days in gorillas, both with a 35–40 year life span of chimps and gorillas, one would expect a human gestation period of nearly twice as long. Instead, however, the human gestation period is barely two weeks longer than that of gorillas. To explain this unexpected similarity, Trevathan turns to suggestions by Montagu and Gould that 'the human gestation period actually may be about 18 months, but that the foetus must be delivered half way through that period in order to be born at all because of the restriction placed on neonatal cranial size by the narrow bipedal pelvis. Extending the gestation period for human beings by 6–9 months would bring it more in line with the other developmental stages. Montague has suggested the term *exterogestation* for the period following birth when human neonates are functioning in many ways more like a foetus than an infant'.[318] Because of their larger brains and smaller birth canals, hominids must be born premature with a not yet fully-formed head.

The profound consequences of the restructuring of the anatomy and physiology of hominid sex on hominid being-in-the-world were by no means limited

---

behaviours and cultural values pertaining to sex and parenthood were we humans outfitted with the same corporeal set of reproductive instruments as seahorses, that is: if Eve delved and Adam span, if human females impregnated, and pregnant males carried the unborn offspring. First citation, Foster and Vincent 2004; following citation, Vincent 1994, pp. 153–67. I found both citations in the Wikipedia article 'Seahorses'. I first encountered the strange reproduction regimen of seahorses in Durrell 2004, p. 99.

317 Trevathan 1987, p. 34.
318 Trevathan 1987, p. 17. According to Noble and Davidson (1996, pp. 158–9), the benefit of this delayed development and for mothers in early *Homo* species was to counter the extra energy requirements of encephalised/large-brained offspring. An elongated period of infancy which allowed the brain to develop slowly 'reduces the need for the mother to provide so much energy so soon, both before and after the baby's birth'; moreover, 'just as ... with hairlessness and bipedal walking, so too prolonged infant dependency increased the opportunity for joint attention in human development and likely facilitated the evolutionary emergence of language'.

to reproduction itself. That restructuring also gave new form to much older sets of relations between parents and offspring, between the parents themselves, and between family and society. Those consequences include moreover the introduction of new, yet foundational attributes of hominid life and life-cycle, whose uniqueness in the animal kingdom and the monumentality of whose role in both the biological and cultural dimensions of human life lies in inverse relation to the brevity of their treatment here: sexuality, love, and death.

Birth (it must be said in our age of alleged arbitrariness) is the beginning of a 'universal' and species-specific life-cycle that can be divided into four more or less clearly differentiated biological stages. The transition from one stage to another will vary among individuals; some individuals will die prematurely without completing the 'normal' cycle; and different social and cultural forms will create various subdivisions and/or invest each division with variations of meaning. But the life-cycle that seems to have universally in-formed social and cultural forms begins, obviously, with birth; and the relatively abbreviated human gestation period results in the birth of a functionally premature infant and means an inordinately prolonged period of helplessness and dependence. Although the utter helplessness and dependence of infants in other mammal species is, by contrast, a relatively brief matter, its prolonged persistence in human infants is a universal fact that all social forms must accommodate, and with which all cultural forms must come to terms. Having learned to walk and talk, the infant enters childhood, a period of continued dependence, but also one of developing physical and mental faculties and capacities; then adulthood and the maturation of those faculties and capacities; and finally, their decline in old age.

The dividing lines between the stages vary according to socio-economic form. Puberty is a more or less universally recognised marker of the end of childhood. But into what? In hunting and gathering and agricultural societies, the onset of puberty and sexual maturity generally signifies the transition to young adulthood and entails economic responsibilities to be followed soon thereafter by marriage and familial responsibilities. Among the trading classes in 'pre-modern' societies such as Imperial China, puberty meant for some sons of the merchant classes a transition into what might be viewed as the prototype of modern adolescence: the beginning of their studies intended to raise the family's and thus too their own fortunes by achieving Mandarin status. Similarly in Renaissance Italy, where sons like Petrarca were sent by their fathers to the university to study law to help the family business – but who, like some of his contemporaries and many of our own, eschewed law and business for a pursuit of arts and letters. And in consumer capitalism of course, a period of prolonged adolescence, lasting at least until the attainment of an age determined by law as the 'age of maturity', the 'age of reason', has become second nature.[319] Socio-economic determinations of the exact dividing lines between the arcs of the human life-cycle vary, as do, and probably more so, the culturally specific determinations of their meanings.[320] But underlying all of those variations is the biological determination of the species-specific life-cycle that begins with infancy, proceeds through childhood and adulthood, in some cases to old age, but in every case, to death.

6.6.4 Bipedality, Reproduction, Sexuality, and Mortality

The transformation of the reproductive physiology that (to reword slightly Niles Eldredge's formulation) enabled 'human females [to be] continually sexually receptive and [able to] conceive twelve months of the year, albeit only for a few days each month', fundamentally restructured hominid life.[321] In contrast to 'ultra-Darwinist' approaches in sociobiology and evolutionary psychology that focus solely on the question of reproductive success of genes by means of the life of organisms treated as their 'survival machines',[322] Eldredge insists instead that 'life is not 'about' evolving [but] about living', and 'living' requires organisms to be 'both economic "machines" and reproducers'.[323]

---

[319] The two most common responsibilities that can be assumed when attaining this maturity are the right to vote (Voting age and maturity: Brazil 16, Indonesia 17; most countries 18–21) and the right to drink legally (and thus get drunk rationally???).

[320] As prolific as they have been, the various tables of taxonomic categories seeking to classify all living things seem to have become far exceeded by taxonomies of the human life-cycle. This seems surprising at first glance, but it shouldn't be, for only specialists would dare to devise a taxonomy of all life-forms. But all socio-cultural forms develop at least one narrative taxonomy of the human life-cycle. And in our contemporary world with its obsession with classification, it seems that every organisation, private business or public office, has a vested interest in devising a 'stage theory' of human life that suits their own purposes, be they the taxonomies of sociologists and psychologist, of officials charged with organising a public-school system, of devious insurance representatives devising policies, or of those in advertising and marketing trying to delineate their targets. But although we might need to alter it slightly to fit the human condition and again to fit the contemporary world, it would be hard to surpass the description of the human life-cycle in the Greek version of the riddle of the Sphinx: 'Which creature has one voice and yet becomes four-footed and two-footed and three-footed?' The necessary transhistorical alteration is to divide the two-legged phase into still-dependent childhood and mature adulthood; and the alteration appropriate to our world would be the addition of 'no footed' to account for the use of wheelchairs for the aged. Nevertheless, there is only one species that fits the description.

[321] Eldredge 2004, p. 147.

[322] The coinage is Richard Dawkins's (1989).

[323] Eldredge 2004, p. 227.

While it is obvious that '[w]ithout reproduction, life would long ago have ceased', economics 'is essential to mere existence', to the very 'survival of individual organisms'.[324] Organisms, in short, 'do not live to reproduce, but if they are relatively successful at living, they may also reproduce; those best at making a living in general are more likely to reproduce'. The changes in reproductive physiology and sexual behaviour that made sex and reproduction into year-round affairs created a wholly new and unique constellation of sex, reproduction, and economics. Acknowledging that 'there may well have been some reproductive adaptive value for being able to make babies year round', Eldredge confesses that he has 'no idea what that advantage would be'. It 'makes more sense', he suggests instead, 'to think that access to continual sex evolved not for reproductive purposes but rather as a kind of 'food for sex, sex for food' arrangement that led to the creation of more stable pair bonds'. Sex, in short, 'has become decoupled from reproduction in human life, forming the "human triangle" of sex, reproduction, and economics'. This decoupling not only gives new and unique twists to a dimension of the life of all sexually reproducing species, but it also adds new and unique dimensions to hominid living.

The very new twists to a traditional dimension of the lives of sexually reproducing species pertains to the relations between hominid parents and offspring and between the parents themselves. The 'notorious' helplessness of human infants, who cannot begin to walk for about a year, cannot talk for another two years, and who 'simply cannot fend for themselves until, as a rule, their teens or (in some situations in some societies) even later', requires more parental 'investment' than in any other species.[325] As Nancy Tanner suggests, because of the immaturity of hominid infants at birth and their prolonged period of dependence, 'increased maternal care (both initially and for a longer time) was necessary. Mothers probably carried their infants with them wherever they went. Contact between mothers and their offspring was necessarily intense and

---

324   Eldredge 2004, p. 227. Following citations in this paragraph, ibid., p. 228; p. 147; p. 148; p. 231. In commenting on his inability to figure out the reproductive adaptive value of being able to make babies year-round, Eldredge explains, 'All but the largest families on record could just as easily have been produced with a single seasonal period of estrus, given the nine months it takes for a human fetus to develop fully' (ibid., pp. 147–8). The decoupling of sex from a particular seasonal cycle and the resulting fact of human birth days on all days of the year gives the human birthing cycle a much different pattern from that of any other species; imagine how different social rhythms (not to mention astrology) would be if all human babies were born within the same seasonal period.

325   Eldredge 2004, p. 148.

of increased duration'.³²⁶ The intensity and duration of this mother-child relation could not but intensify affective feelings.

Something similar was occurring in the relations between parents. For corporeally unspecialised and vulnerable hominids, social organisation for purposes of both production and protection was a practical necessity. In the relatively close-knit quarters of even a fairly fluid *Australopithecine* social grouping, a significant degree of sociability would be a requirement for both the daily economic reproduction of individual lives and for the biological reproduction of the group. Tanner hypothesises that the key to the sociability of early *hominids* lies in the changes in sexual behaviour following from 'the reduced visibility of [the estrous swellings of the female ape genital areas] as a result of bipedalism': '[w]ith the loss of an anatomical signaling device (estrous swellings), females necessarily communicated to males an interest in sex through behavioural and nonverbal cues'.³²⁷ Moreover, she continues, '[f]emales' increasing reliance on voluntary cues to initiate sexual activities would also intensify female choice of sexual partners' – a choice increasingly based 'on greater maternal investment' which increasingly meant that females' choice of recipients of their sexual clues would incline to the more sociable males thought capable of both a more stable pair bond and more cooperative community bond. And she concludes that '[o]verall, females apparently were choosing males who were sociable, cooperative, willing to share, and protective'.

Eldredge similarly elaborates the close relation between human 'familial' and 'social', or biological and economic relations. He starts from what he sees as 'one ineluctable truth about social systems generally – a truth often glossed over in most sociobiological studies', namely: '*social systems among nonclonal animals are fusions of the economic and reproductive interests of their component individuals.* ... In other words, social groups are fusions of economic and reproductive life, mergers of the eating and baby-making adaptations of species'.³²⁸ The particularly human form(s) of this fusion are framed by the need 'to provide the economic support for such a labour-intensive job as raising a human child' for which 'stability of the support system is crucial'. In this context, the behavioural consequences following from the restructuring of human reproductive anatomy and physiology are formative: '[s]exual gratification is the carrot on the stick (so to speak), not just to keep the guys around (as has

---

326   Tanner 1987, p. 209.
327   All quoted passages in this paragraph, Tanner 1987, pp. 209–10.
328   Eldredge 2004, p. 106. 'non-clonal' = offspring that are not clonal copies of parents, as is the case (aside from mutations) with asexually reproducing species. Next two citations in this paragraph, ibid., p. 148.

most commonly been supposed, since guys are supposedly the main breadwinners) but also to keep women interested in the arrangement'. And the formation of more exclusive mating patterns to accomplish the 'labour-intensive' task of child-rearing is 'an arrangement with clear reproductive advantages, since pair bonds would presumably have led to a more protracted and stable "family" life, in which economic necessities were looked after by both parents and care of offspring particularly (if not exclusively) was the domain of the mother'.

The voluntary behavioural and non-verbal cues with which hominid females communicated to males an interest in sex could, as Tanner elaborates, 'be given at any time and therefore differed significantly from the ape ancestors' hormonally clocked, overt morphological signal'.[329] The liberation of reproduction from a particular time of the year, combined with the liberation of sex from reproduction, created an entirely new state of affairs in the animal kingdom. Acknowledging the profundity of the obvious, Eldredge writes 'Humans have sex for lots of reasons, only some of which have to do with making babies and thereby passing along their genes'.[330] 'Though, as in all animal life, there can be no reproduction without both sex and economics, sex in human life exists also for its own sake and has, as well, intricate connections with the economic world quite apart from reproduction'. Sex 'is now free to have its own life in human affairs'. Although perhaps a bit hyperbolic in its monocausal formulation, Eldredge's conclusion – that it is 'not the reproductive imperative, but rather the diffusing influence of taking sex away from its strictly reproductive function, that ... really drives human existence' – points to a fundamental biological fact refracted variously in all human socio-cultural forms. The decoupling of sex from reproduction effected by the adjustments of reproductive anatomy and physiology to bipedal existence was the foundation for the emergence of human sexuality itself – a uniquely and, its diverse cultural refractions notwithstanding, a universally human form of sexual behaviour that differs qualitatively from the essentially reproduction-bound sexual behaviour of other animal species. Given its crucial importance to 'species, parenthood, survival' (not to mention its pleasurableness), it is no surprise that sex is in every society the subject of some of its most important prescriptions and taboos, the specifics of which vary radically across cultures. But the obvious truth (really a platitude – but one that is rendered profound by the recent and ongoing ultra-constructionist denial of the 'natural' or 'biological' body) is that precisely

---

329 Tanner 1987, p. 209.
330 This and following three citations in this paragraph, Eldredge 2004, p. 168; p. 231; p. 149; p. 149.

because of its corporeal organisation, and despite great variation in specifics, human sexual behaviour is (need it be said???) uniquely human. Broad cross-cultural variation in sexual mores and taboos notwithstanding, sex in the human species is decoupled from purely reproductive matters to such an unmatched degree in the faunal world that the term 'human sexuality' is effectively redundant.[331]

Bipedality not only restructured the entire corporeal logos of hominid sexual interaction, but by decoupling sex from reproduction, it also reconfigured and repurposed, by eroticising, certain corporeal instruments in the human bodily toolkit. Freud, not surprisingly, made some interesting observations on this matter. The 'diminution' of the olfactory sense, which 'seems itself to be a consequence of man's raising himself from the ground, of his assumption of an upright gait' had two (in Freud's rendering rather androcentric) consequences: in terms of sex, 'the diminution of olfactory stimuli by means of which the menstrual process produced an effect on the male psyche'; and in terms of self-consciousness, the new visibility of the genitals of the upright (in keeping with Freud's language: male) hominid rendered them 'in need of protection, and so provoked feelings of shame in him'.[332] Acknowledging that it is 'only theoretical speculation', Freud, in a rather compact, if not completely consistent genealogy of civilisation, suggested what is tantamount to a direct line from bipedality to Victorian society by way of visually-induced shame: from erect posture 'the chain of events would have proceeded through the devaluation of olfactory stimuli and the isolation of the menstrual period to the time when visual stimuli were paramount and the genitals became visible, and thence to the continuity of sexual excitation, the founding of the family, and so to the threshold of human civilization'. We need not accept *in toto* Freud's andro- and ocularcentric speculations on what he calls 'the fateful process of civilization' in order to accept the point most relevant here; for even though visual sexual clues were/are certainly not unique to bipedal hominids (estrous swelling and colouration are common among mammals and primates), the olfactory in hominid sexual matters, if not eliminated as a kind of base determination (see discussion of smell above), was certainly superseded by the visual. And the diminution of the olfactory in sexual stimulation combined with the frontal replacement of the genitalia opened new horizons of visual eroticism.

---

331 Eldredge 2004, p. 130.
332 Preceding and following citations in this paragraph, Freud 1962, pp. 46–7n; p. 46n.

Representations of male and female sexual (and sexualised) organs, the upright penis and forthright breasts, in painting and the plastic arts from ancient to modern bear witness to the enhanced eroticism of the visual. After the anatomical restructuring of the bipedal hominid generally made face-to-face encounters the initial site of the expression of sexual attraction, sexually inquisitive hominid eyes no longer looked exclusively, or even primarily, to the backside for signals of sexual receptivity or repulsion. But once hominids began wearing clothes, the now frontally-situated corporeal instruments of sexual intercourse would no longer provide a visible clue or offer a visible cue. Fortunately for the future of the species, there were and are other means of visual attraction. As noted above, the eyes themselves, enhanced by belladonna, could be deployed as sexual cues. Also, as Relethford rather matter-of-factly formulates the visible fact of female anatomy, 'human females have relatively large breasts' – and like most primates, human females have only two of them (pigs have eighteen, and the Virginia opossum thirteen, one of the few with an odd number).[333]

Explanations of the biological oddity of the relatively large breasts of human females vary widely: from the rather fanciful androcentric-based claim that they developed to resemble the buttocks that had been the male preference, and would thus attract males to a female's front; to the claim that large breasts were a byproduct of the evolution of fat in human females, stored reserves for reproduction in times of food shortage; to a byproduct of hormonal changes accompanying increased fat reserves. But whatever the reasons, what is important here is the fact stated by Linnaeus when naming the class of *Mammalia*, namely that 'all females have lactiferous mammae of determinate number'.[334] And the fact that for human females that determinate number is two has not been insignificant for human aesthetics from the sublime to the obscene, from the representational to the surrealistic. To emphasise the obvious, were the breasts of human females similar in number to those of most of our mammalian relatives and in size to those of our primate ancestors, representations of women, whether realistically, metaphorically, or allegorically, in images ranging from the erotic, to the reproductive, to the religious would have a radically different figure. And the strange truth is that the 'emancipation' of sex from reproduction combined with the replacement of olfactory by visual stimulation in sexual matters establishes a bio-basis for the frontal visual erotics that has run in a no doubt unexpected and certainly long, but fairly direct line from

---

333 Relethford 1994, p. 256.
334 Schiebinger 1993, p. 46. See Appendices 0.2 and 6.2 for further comment on Linnaeus and the naming of mammals.

the corporeal combination of bipedality and primate vision, to Pompeiian frescoes and statuary of bare-breasted women and of men erect in the double sense, and eventually to the photos of the same in *Playboy* and other forms of visual pornography.

The fascinating evolutionary process by which bipedalism effected the restructuring of hominid anatomy and behaviour and produced a constellation of unexpected relations stretching from bipedality to narrow pelvises and large brains, to infant dependence, to more stable and emotional attachments between parents and between parents and children, to the decoupling of sex and reproduction, did not end up in a pornographic cul-de-sac. It is also responsible for putting Eros (love) into eroticism (sexual excitement), and into human affective relations more generally – which in turn laid the corporeal foundations for all kinds of questions hitherto treated as 'philosophical'. The practice of non-reproductive sex between creatures outfitted with a highly sensitive organ of pleasure stretching from head to toe (that is: the skin; see below on the 'functionally naked ape') and the practical consequences of infant dependency and increased parental contact with and caring for offspring not only intensified hominid sociability but in so doing contributed to the formation of self-consciousness through interaction with and consciousness of other selves – and therewith to the formation of what for Freud were those complementary opposites: Eros and Thanatos, feelings of love and awareness of death.

It seems safe enough to say that habitual companionship combined with both sexuality and parental responsibility could encourage the development of that emotional attachment called love. And it seems equally safe to say that with love comes the awareness of a point when the absence of the beloved other would no longer be temporary, but permanent which, in turn, brings one to the recognition of the finitude of one's own life. Already among *Australopithecines*, Nancy Tanner argues, the 'process of dying and the fact of death would attract attention'. She notes that *Australopithecines* 'could not yet conceptualize well enough to develop rituals to deal with death, but it was doubtless already posing even more of a problem both socially and emotionally for them than for the ancestral population'. This 'problematic quality of death was related directly to the early hominids' greater capacity (and necessity) for affective interrelationships, which were, in turn, a product of immaturity at birth, longer development in a highly social context, and dependence on socially mediated learning'.[335] Awareness of the termination of life, then, is directly related to the conditions of hominid birth that infected human Being-

---

335   All citations in this paragraph, from Tanner 1987, p. 210.

towards-others with enhanced affectivity, or in less clinical, more human terms: love – that made the loss of the beloved an immediately intimate and personal matter. And in the awareness of human finitude lies doubtless the origin of all religion. It is therefore not inappropriate to consider, by way of summary and conclusion to this section, two perspicacious and prescient texts that foreshadow these paleoanthropological insights by well over three millennia.

The Hebrew recounting of the story of Adam and Eve from their creation through their expulsion from the Garden touches on, or at least alludes to, affective relations and the consciousness of self and other selves, all wrapped up in a story of sexuality, love, and death. Having 'fashioned the human, humas from the soil, and [blown] into his nostrils the breath of life', and then having warned him that the penalty for gaining knowledge of good and evil is death, the Lord God recognised that 'it is not good for the human [Adam] to be alone'.[336] In modern terminology, even though Adam had at best the most rudimentary self-consciousness (lacking awareness of his own nakedness, of good and evil, and of death), the Lord was nevertheless sympathetically concerned about the adverse effects of loneliness and therefore 'built' for Adam a 'sustainer beside him'.[337] And although 'the two of them were naked, the human and his woman, … they were not ashamed' – their shamelessness obviously because, as we soon find out, they did not know of, could not see, their own nakedness. But Eve '*saw* that the tree was good for eating and that it was lust to the *eyes* and the tree was lovely to *look* at' [my italics], and she succumbed – and seduced Adam into succumbing as well. Having eaten of the fruit of the tree of knowledge of good and evil, 'the *eyes* of the two of them were opened'. And having tasted the knowledge of good and evil, having 'become as gods', the first thing that they know as evil and that causes them shame is (of all possible evils) knowledge (sight) of their own nakedness. This rather unusual and somewhat unexpected first and foundational item of knowledge of good and evil prompts them to hide when they hear the sound of the Lord walking in the garden in the time of the evening breeze. Caught by the Lord who deduced their

---

336   *Genesis* in Alter 2004, pp. 21–2. As Alter explains in a note, the Hebrew etymological pun is *'adam*, 'human', from *adamah*, the 'soil'. All following citations from the Book of Genesis, Chapters 2 and 3 in ibid., pp. 21–8.

337   Alter 2004, p. 22. Alter's reasoning for his decision to refer to Eve as a 'sustainer' rather than the 'help meet' of the *King James Bible* is that 'help' is 'too weak because it suggests a merely auxiliary function, whereas [the Hebrew] *'ezer kenegdo* connotes active intervention on behalf of someone' (ibid.). He also notes that 'though [*built*] may seem an odd term for the creation of woman, it complements the potter's term, "fashion", used for the creation of first human' (ibid.). Two millennia later, Pico della Mirandola (1948, p. 224) would refer to God as 'the best of artisans'.

transgression from the fact that Adam and Eve could now see, know, that they were naked, and thus must have eaten the apple from the tree of (moral) knowledge, Adam and Eve are forced to confess – whereupon the Lord condemns Adam to live by the sweat of his brow, and Eve to the pain of childbirth and obedience to her human lord. This fate could perhaps could have been overcome, if they had been allowed to remain in the Garden. For having attained knowledge of good and evil, Adam and Eve differed from the Lord only in their mortality – which could be remedied by eating of the 'tree of life' which was not forbidden them; and once immortal, they presumably would not have to worry about working, nor even, perhaps, about bearing children. In any case, to prevent them from becoming gods, the Lord banished them from the Garden. To the religious reader, this is a story of the fall from grace and to the moralist, a fall from innocence. But to the paleoanthropologically inclined, it may, as I shall explain momentarily, be read as an allegory of the evolutionary emergence of *Homo sapiens*.

First, however, let us delve another millennium or so deeper into the past where we find a story with different characters but familiar reflections on the process of becoming human – and one narrated more as an ascent than a fall. A kind of early *Bildungsroman*, the *Epic of Gilgamesh* chronicles the adventuresome learning processes of the legendary King of Uruk. Our focus, however, will be on the story of Enkidu who would become for a time Gilgamesh's companion in their epic adventures. Enkidu initially appears as a creature with a bipedal human body, but the behaviour and mentality of a pre-human animal (an *Australopithecine*, perhaps). We first encounter him running wild, eating grasses with gazelles, jostling with the other animals at the watering hole to slake his thirst with mere water – and freeing his animal companions from traps set by humans. A trapper, on his father's advice, goes to King Gilgamesh and asks for assistance. Gilgamesh tells the trapper to bring the harlot, Shamhat, with him to the watering hole. Shamhat will overcome Enkidu by 'tak[ing] off her robe and expos[ing] her sex'.[338] When Enkidu arrives at the watering hole where Shamhat waited, she 'unclutched her bosom, exposed her sex', whereupon Enkidu 'took in her voluptuousness' and 'he lay upon her, ... his lust groaned over her; for six days and seven nights Enkidu stayed aroused and had intercourse with the harlot until he was sated with her charms'.

At some point during his week-long satiation of what began as lust, Enkidu clearly crossed a threshold between copulation and 'making love' – and toward

---

338 *The Epic of Gilgamesh* 1989, p. 9. Following citations p. 9; p. 9; p. 9; p. 16 note 2; p. 16 note 2; p. 10; p. 12.

the consciousness of both himself and another self. The immediate consequence of this was that his strength was gone and he could no longer run with the animals, who in any case now shunned him. But having 'known' Shamhat, having been initiated through her performance of 'the task of womankind', 'his understanding had broadened'.[339] The harlot clothed him and taught him how to eat bread for 'it is the way one lives' and drink beer 'as is the custom of the land'; and 'becoming aware of himself, he sought a friend'. That friend would be Gilgamesh who himself anticipated Enkidu's coming in dreams that, his mother explained, were of 'a man' whom you will 'love and embrace as a wife'.

These remarkable stories address many of the elements identified by paleoanthropologists as crucial to the process of becoming human. Both stories focus on the gaining of self-awareness which is, in both, associated with both corporeal and social awareness. The importance of affectionate affective relations with others appears in the form of the Lord's concern about Adam's loneliness and Gilgamesh's desire for a friend. Adam's and Eve's sudden recognition of their nakedness suggests not just sexual desire, but a consciousness of that desire, self-consciousness. And whether Enkidu's sojourn with Shamhat be called 'having sex' or 'making love', it certainly was, or became, something other than the immediate satisfaction of an instinctual urge in copulating animals – anticipating Eldredge's analysis of the decoupling of sex from reproduction and the emergence of sexuality and that affective emotion we call love.

The taming, the humanising, the civilising of Enkidu, his awakening to self-consciousness, moreover, is gained not antagonistically through disobedience to a deity's command, but by having been seduced into a week of copulation-*cum*-love-making; and the consequence is not a fall from grace, but learning to live according to 'the custom of the land' – an awareness of the necessarily social being, the interdependence, of humans. And it should be noted that the humanised Enkidu uses his remaining strength – no longer what it once was, but, with the exception of Gilgamesh, certainly superior to that of his new human companions – not in an antagonistic, but in a sociable way: he 'routed the wolves and chased the lions so that the shepherds could eat' and 'the herders could lie down'.[340]

Both stories chronicle the increased importance of the visual in both eroticism and epistemology: Adam and Eve saw and thus knew that they were

---

339 N.K. Sandars's translation (1978, pp. 64–5) renders this as: by means of 'the woman's art', 'wisdom was in him'.

340 This is in notable contrast to bourgeois myths of the isolated antagonistic individual whose self-awareness is gained, in Hegel's rendering, through a 'struggle for recognition' and the successful subduing of the other self – a rendering that has countless social-

naked; Enkidu 'took in' the 'voluptuousness' of Shamhat's 'exposed sex', and sex 'broadened' Enkidu's 'understanding'. Although not as explicit, the link between sex and consciousness of both self and other is also contained in what has become the euphemistic rendering of sex, derived from when Adam 'knew Eve his woman' and she 'conceived', as 'knowledge in the Biblical sense' – the kind of knowing that, as we also euphemise, 'conceives' a child.[341] Finally, both stories are tales of the life-cycle of the human individual, specifically its culmination.

The pervasive presence lurking below and hovering over both the *Epic of Gilgamesh* and the Hebrew *Torah* is that of mortality. After an all too brief life of adventure and fraternal love with Gilgamesh, Enkidu must die. On his deathbed, Enkidu curses the harlot and all those responsible for making him self-conscious and thus aware of his own demise. However, when the deity Shamash reminds him of all that he had come to experience and appreciate, and of which he would not otherwise have *known*, he rescinds the curse. But he could not stop bemoaning his mortality. Nor could Gilgamesh, who in his friend's fate recognised his own: 'Am I not like Enkidu?! I am going to die!'; and he 'began to fear death' for 'the issue of Enkidu, my friend, oppresses me'.[342] Finally, after spending the rest of his life vainly searching for immortality, he realised that fame and leaving a name to posterity are no compensation for the transitoriness of life.

The Hebrew resolution of the dilemma that death poses for life was of course the covenant. The Hebrew covenant did not (like the later Christian version) promise resurrection, but did guarantee an afterlife through progeny, that (generically) one (specifically: a man) would live on in and through his 'seed'.[343] In these two early texts we see diverse cultural refractions of the self-conscious confrontation with the universal corporeal fact of death, with one's own mortality. And the different meanings invested in that corporeal fact were not without social consequences. It seems too much to suggest, as some have, that the demise of ancient Sumerian culture was a result of its inability, exemplified by its legendary king Gilgamesh, to find meaning in death.[344] That need

---

Darwinistic counterparts in science, social science, and pseudo-science. It is of course true that Enkidu and Gilgamesh engaged in a 'struggle for recognition'; but it ended neither in the kind of lordship/bondage relation that Hegel posited, nor in the possessive individual of bourgeois lore but, in a friendship so profound that Enkidu's death so changed Gilgamesh that he spent the rest of his life trying to come to terms with his own mortality.

341   Alter (ed.), *The Five Books of Moses* 2004, p. 29.
342   *Epic of Gilgamesh*, Kovacs translation, p. 75; I have inverted the order of the two sentences; Next citation, ibid. p., 85.
343   Alter (ed.), *The Five Books of Moses* 2004, p. 82.
344   A counter-example is provided by the hunting and gathering Hadza of eastern Africa who

not prevent us, however, from recognising that the promise of an 'everlasting covenant' establishing an unbreakable relation between the deity, a patriarch and his family, and their descendants over endless generations has had cohesive consequences for a 'nation' (in the traditional sense invoking family, ethnicity) spending most of its history in a diaspora – as well as exclusionary consequences among some in its contemporary nation-state. Be that as it is, the broader point for our purposes is that well before the achievements of evolutionary science in our Darwinian world, the *Epic of Gilgamesh* and *Genesis* were prescient in having anticipated the inextricable links between the social being of the bipedal primate and its capacity for self-consciousness that made *Homo sapiens* capable of love – and conscious of death.

6.6.5 *The 'Functionally-Naked' Ape and the Humanising of Touch*

The evolutionary prescience of *The Epic of Gilgamesh* does not end there. When readers first encounter Enkidu at the watering hole, 'his whole body was shaggy with hair'.[345] Among the customs of the land that Shamhat teaches Enkidu following their week of amorous activity is bathing. After having drunk seven jugs of beer, Enkidu 'splashed his shaggy body with water, and rubbed himself with oil, and turned into a human' – and then 'put on some clothing'. Although dramatically condensed, these few lines summarise an eons-long process that produced among bipedal hominids an exterior rather unique among primates, and even among mammals. If the terrestrial 'where' of hominid primates encouraged the restructuring of rear limbs to lower limbs, the reshaping of the spine, and their upright posture, the diurnal 'when' of their bipedal locomotion effected a further crucial and uniquely human anatomical transformation: a transformation in their skin covering.

To force acknowledgement of a rather familiar and crucial, though generally overlooked fact about the uniqueness of *Homo* species among primates, Desmond Morris coined his non-specialist, but very graphic taxon 'the naked

---

on the death of their fellows do not make 'a lot of fuss. They dig a hole and place the body inside. A generation ago, they didn't even do that – they simply left a body out on the ground to be eaten by the hyenas. There is still no Hadza gravemarker. There is no funeral. There's no service at all, of any sort. This could be a person they had lived with their entire life. Yet they just toss a few dry twigs on top of the grave. And they walk away'. See Finkel 2009, p. 118. As Finkel had earlier (2002) been dismissed from his position as writer for the *New York Times* after it was discovered that the figure about whom he wrote a biography was actually a *bricolage* of the lives of several people, his testimony might be questionable. But the lack of funeral rites and a belief in the afterlife among the Hadza is corroborated by Marlowe 2009, pp. 247–75.

345   *Epic of Gilgamesh*, Kovacs translation, p. 6.

ape'. Though empirically accurate in contrast to the hirsuteness of other primates, Morris's notion of the 'naked ape' is, of course, exaggerated; for although it has but relatively few noticeable patches of hair, the human body does have as many hairs as the chimpanzee body; those hairs (with the exception of those few patches) just happen to be much finer often unnoticeable to a passing glance. It would therefore be more appropriate to enlist Nina Jablonski's less graphic but more accurate, and certainly awkward-sounding reformulation of Morris's epithet as the 'functionally naked' ape.[346]

It is difficult to pinpoint when the 'functionally naked ape' appeared; the fossil record is obviously of little help in this matter. But in an explanation that 'centers on the importance of sweat', Jablonski's elaboration of the 'why' and 'how' of hominid 'hairlessness' also suggests the 'when'.[347] Her argument, briefly, is that because sweating alone is not sufficient to keep the body cool, most mammals develop other forms of somatic cooling (e.g. panting). For hair-bearing primates with only the one embodied cooling apparatus, sweating, but with a layer of hair insulating the skin from the sun and heat, and with an ethological predilection for shade-seeking, this was sufficient. And it remained sufficient even for the earliest Hominids, the *Australopithecines*, whose skeletal features, Jablonski argues, indicate that they were 'not yet naked apes': though their legbones show they were good walkers, there are no 'anatomical signs of high-energy, long distance sojourns'; and their long arms and grasping toes indicate arboreal dexterity and thus time spent in the shady canopy.

The early members of the genus *Homo*, however, 'were taller and more long-legged than their ancestors, with relatively shorter arms'; they had 'the long legs of powerful long-distance walkers and runners' – anatomical features indicating that members of this diurnal genus spent more hours moving about on the sun-drenched savannah.[348] Jablonski refers to what she takes as general paleoanthropological agreement that our *Homo* ancestors 'were active, striding bipeds who ate eclectic diets and walked great distances in search of materials for making tools'; and she consults recent studies in comparative paleoanthropological anatomy demonstrating that 'long-distance running may have been the activity that influenced the shape of the modern human body more than any other'. On this basis, she concludes that for a creature so active under the hot savannah sun, a coat of hair loses its cooling function: 'a hominid with a thick coat of hair would have a hard time keeping cool when it was highly act-

---

346 Jablonski 2013, p. 35.
347 Jablonski 2013, pp. 38–42, p. 43.
348 Jablonski 2013, p. 77. Following citations in this paragraph: ibid., pp. 47–8; pp. 45–6; p. 46; p. 46. Citation in first sentence of next paragraph, ibid., pp. 2–3.

ive because its wet hair would act as blanket, impeding the loss of heat from the skin's surface. The body's efforts to produce more sweat in a vain attempt to keep cool would then result in rapid fluid loss'. The selective solution was twofold. One was to 'remove most of the body hair and the problem of evaporating sweat from the surface of the skin disappears'. Complementing (functional) hairlessness was the development of a more efficient cooling system that could produce a much greater volume of coolant in the form of sweat than could 'animals with heavy fur coats [that] produce only 10 to 20 percent as much sweat as a competent human "sweater" under conditions of high heat or strenuous exercise'.

The result of this adaption to bipedal and diurnal life under the savannah sun was a skin with three particular attributes: it is 'naked and sweaty'; 'it comes naturally in a wide range of colours'; and 'it is a surface for decoration ... [,] a potentially ever-changing personal tapestry that tells the world who we are or who we want to be'. To be added to these three attributes is a fourth, namely that the 'functionally naked' skin turns the entire body into an extremely sensitive sensory apparatus and a source of tactile experience. Though the first of the senses to develop among the earliest sentient beings, touch was the last to assume its peculiarly human form. Whereas the other four systems in the human sensorium had already been more or less fully formed in the arboreal primate phase, the humanising of touch followed in the wake of a move to a new habitat and a new circadian rhythm. Moving about in the daytime on the hot savannah eventually resulted in the loss of a now dysfunctional thick furry covering – a loss that would turn the entire body into a source of tactile experience; the largest of human sense organs, the 'naked' skin produces the multidimensional breadth and sensual depth of the human world of touch. Here, then, a consideration of Jablonski's study of three consequences of human 'hairlessness' and the corresponding patterns of experience organised by it will serve also as an entry into a discussion of the various dimensions of the peculiarly human sense of touch.

Jablonski explains that '[f]or an active primate living in a hot environment, having a functionally naked and actively sweating skin is [not only] the best way to maintain a steady body temperature[, but also] – and literally – to keep a cool head'.[349] She points to the fact that since the appearance of the 'functionally naked ape' some two-million years ago, 'the size of the human brain has expanded significantly, to the point where we now have the largest brain

---

349 Jablonski 2013, p. 43. Further quotes from in this paragraph, ibid., p. 49; p. 49; p. 49; p. 55; p. 49.

of all animals relative to body size'. That large brain, however, is also rather 'costly to maintain'; and 'with increased brain size, the importance of having a hard-working and efficient whole-body cooling system comes into play more than ever before'. Though generally ignored, if not disdained, the 'humble sweat gland', Jablonski lobbies, 'must assume pride of place in human evolution. Without plentiful sweat glands keeping us cool with copious sweat, we would still be clad in the thick hair of our ancestors, living largely ape-like lives'. In noting that 'behind every large human brain, there is a potentially very sweaty human body', she essentially establishes the corporeal prerequisite of the Cartesian *cogito* that might be rendered as 'I sweat, therefore I [can] think'.

In addition to its key role in keeping the head cool and maintaining a large, culturally capable brain, the social and cultural roles of sweat itself are not insignificant. The diverse but universal cultural constructions and usages of sweat ranging from the healing to the repellent (and the huge and commercial industry richly profiting from 'anti-perspirants' aimed at masking the odours signified as repugnant) derive from selection's solution to a problem in hominid corporeal thermodynamics. Thus, Jablonski (obviously oblivious to the often pathetic hyperbole of sports announcers) concludes, although 'no one has composed paeans or odes to celebrate the glories of sweat, ... well they should'; for 'it is plain old unglamorous sweat that has made humans what they are today'.

A further adaptation pertaining to the problem of cooling is the retention of 'a strategic mass of thick hair on top of the head'. Hair plays a dual role in keeping a cool head. As is immediately, sometimes painfully obvious to those with hairless heads, hair protects the scalp from the damaging rays of sun. And it aids in brain cooling because the heating of the surface of the hair 'leaves a barrier of slightly cooler air next to the scalp' that 'can then lose heat efficiently into the barrier layer through radiation and evaporation'.[350] This fine-tuning of the solution to the problem of *Homo*'s corporeal thermodynamics is also the object of diverse, but universal cultural constructions and usages. The remaining patches of hair on the otherwise naked ape are imbricated in systems of social and cultural signification. And in contrast to ubiquity of hair among the 'hirsute apes', though in keeping with the predominance of vision in the primate sensory hierarchy, these strategic patches stimulate a highly-developed visual eroticism. Although the particular role of hair certainly varies greatly across cultures, it seems to play – whether as an object of attraction and/or proscription – a universally important role in human sexuality.

---

350 Jablonski 2013, p. 50.

The functional loss of all but a few patches of hair is also of species-wide significance in the expression of emotions. Common to hirsute creatures of all kinds is the raising of hairs that 'occurs when an animal is angry, frightened, or thrilled and serves to make the animal look larger and more threatening'.[351] The purpose of this 'piloerection' is to communicate emotion. Because piloerection actually does occur among the still impressive wealth of hairs that we have on our bodies, the linguistic metaphors for the emotion of fear – describing situations as 'hair-raising' or as 'making the hair on the back of the neck stand up' – are literally true. But they are rendered only metaphorically valid by the functional invisibility of human piloerection – which prevents our standing but unnoticed hairs from effective service as a means of expressing and communicating emotion.

To compensate for the loss of hair, *Homo* species had to develop alternative means of communicating emotions, perhaps the culturally most important of which is, as Jablonski explains, 'our repertoire of facial expressions, which are the most complex and varied in the animal realm. Our sensitively expressive faces permit us to convey subtle nuances of information about what we are feeling. Through these expressions, we not only have compensated for lacking body hair that can fluff and bristle but also have developed ways to convey more information'.[352] While humans are not the only creatures capable of facial expressions, no species has the facial form and flexible facial muscles that enable such a wide range of facial expression (such that entire conversations to be carried on with facial signifiers).

A third consequence of hairlessness, the socio-cultural constructions of which have been the impetus for all too much injustice and violence, concerns the skin. Human skin is unique, one of the few ways in which the genetic makeup of humans differs (some 98% of which, as is well known, differs not) from that of chimpanzees.[353] The hairless and unprotected human skin is both sensitive and vulnerable, yet also tough and valuable in supplying nutrients to the human organism: it has the 'amazing ability not only to serve as a protective shield against the damaging effects of sunlight but also to utilize some of that same sunlight to the body's advantage, by beginning the process of producing vitamin D right there in our skin' (the importance of vitamin D ranges from reproductive health, bone, cartilage, and skeletal health and inhibition of cancer cells). This combination of vulnerability and value 'is a comprom-

---

351   Jablonski 2013, p. 19.
352   Jablonski 2013, p. 20.
353   Jablonski 2013, p. 4; next two citations in this paragraph, ibid., pp. 10–11.

ise hammered out at the negotiating table of evolution. Its complex properties reflect a balance, brought about through natural selection, between conflicting needs – in this case: protection against harmful solar radiation and production of an essential vitamin'.

The key mediator in this compromise is melanin, a chemical compound produced by the body itself and 'a superb natural sunscreen'.[354] Adaptation to their functional nakedness required an increase in melanin production among our early African ancestors, hence a darkening of their skin. The migration of some of their descendants into regions of less sunshine and cooler climes meant further adaptations, this time toward reduced melanin to be able to take greater advantage of less intense sunlight. Another result of hairlessness then, and a very distinctive attribute of human skin, is its variation in colour. Whereas our hirsute hominoid and hominid forebears 'likely ... had light skin covered with dark hair', human skin 'comes naturally in a wide range of colours, from the darkest brown, nearly black, to the palest ivory, nearly white', thus making up 'an exquisite sepia rainbow [that] shades from darkest near the equator to lightest near the poles'. There is, in short, biological or, more specifically, bio-geographical meaning behind the variations in skin colours.

Like the spectrum of light visible to humans, that 'exquisite sepia rainbow' of skin colours can be, and in different socio-cultural forms has of course been, varyingly divided – into 'races'. Such variations in the division of the colour spectrum, whether of light or skin, are not arbitrary in the strong sense of random and without referents. Racial categories are rather socio-culturally mediated refractions of bio-geographically meaningful variations in a phenotypic characteristic: refractions of the quantitative variations in melanin content that result from the geographically diverse relations between functionally naked human skins and the star known as our sun. Were all human inhabitants of this planet bathed in an equal amount of sunlight, variations of skin colour (genetic disorders such as albinism excepted) would be minimal. And were the human race monochromatic, the differences in skin tones taken as the basis of the socio-cultural constructions establishing what W.E.B. DuBois called 'the colour line' would obviously be non-existent – as would, we might presume, its attendant racism.

The problem, of course, is not the existence of the 'sepia rainbow', but rather the malignant socio-cultural metamorphosis of bio-geographically meaningful phenotypic differences in skin colour into essentialised, hierarchically eval-

---

354 Jablonski 2013, p. 66. Following citations in this paragraph, ibid., p. 38; p. 3.

uated 'racial' differences between imagined 'racial' communities that then serve as the justification for hostile and discriminatory practices of all kinds. The investment of those bio-geographically meaningful differences in skin tones with differential semiotic meaning and hierarchical value is certainly arbitrary in the sense that the socio-culturally constructed meanings and values attached to 'racial' categories are mistakenly imagined to be biologically determined. But it is neither random nor without motivation; for, racism and discrimination are intimately related to concrete matters of social power – or lack thereof. As Kimberlé Crenshaw, put it so succinctly, 'the problem is not the existence' of racial categories derived from phenotypic differences, but lies rather in 'the particular values attached to [those categories], and the way those values foster and create social hierarchies' – hierarchies that have served as the basis of and justification for unequal treatment, segregation, internment, and/or murder.[355]

Last, but by no means least, the functional nakedness of hominids opened new horizons to the sexuality that developed in the wake of the decoupling of sex from reproduction. 'Although we don't usually think of it as such', the skin is, says Jablonski reminding us of the often neglected obvious, 'the largest sexual organ of the human body'.[356] 'Much of the pleasure of sexual intimacy', she elaborates, 'comes from the exquisite expectation of touch and the delight and relief of skin-to-skin contact with another person, before, during, and after the sex act itself. Certain parts of the body are especially sensitive to sexual touch; this heightened sensitivity may result from a greater density of nerve networks closer to the surface of the skin. Caressing, stroking, or lightly brushing these erogenous zones increases sexual pleasure and arousal'. While the origins of grooming among mammals and primates may well have been hygienic, it is also a clear expression of affective affinities. Among hominids, however, the affective dimension of tactile encounters eclipses the hygienic; and the drastic reduction of the sexual role of the olfactory among bipedal hominids, moreover, made way for an increased role not only of the visual, but also the tactile. The decoupling of affectionate tactile encounters between hands/lips and skin from hygienic grooming developed, one would imagine, homologously with, and as part of, the decoupling of sex from reproduction. The practice of delicately touching functionally naked skin with relatively soft hands and/or lips opens onto the much more expansive and eroticised practices of caressing and kissing, each of which is both a tactile expression and

---

355 Crenshaw 1991, p. 1297.
356 This and following citations in this paragraph, Jablonski 2013, pp. 119–20.

a means of tactile stimulation of sexual desire. These new kinds of tactile encounters, decoupled from reproduction, are, in short, part of the emergence of that peculiarly human sexuality.

Touching is the title of Ashley Montagu's prose ode to the 'Human Significance of Skin' (as his work is subtitled). Montagu's study, that we might call a kind of 'Phenomenology of the Mind of the Skin', is perhaps the most sustained and eloquent discussion of both touch and the human significance of skin. Touch, like all the other senses, has its advocates for primacy in the sensual hierarchy – and Montagu is among the foremost. According touch ordinal primacy in evolutionary emergence and cardinal primacy in importance, Montagu avers:

> The skin, like a cloak, covers us all over, the oldest and the most sensitive of our organs, our first medium of communication, and our most efficient of protectors. The whole body is covered by skin. ... In the evolution of the senses the sense of touch was undoubtedly the first to come into being. Touch is the parent of our eyes, ears, nose, and mouth. It is the sense which became differentiated into the others, a fact that seems to be recognized in the age-old evaluation of touch as 'the mother of the senses'. Touch is the earliest sensory system to become functional in all species thus far studied, human, animal, and bird. Perhaps next to the brain, the skin is the most important of all our organ systems. The sense most closely associated with the skin, the sense of touch, is the earliest to develop in the human embryo.[357]

Neuroscientist Saul Schanberg opined that 'if touch didn't feel good, there'd be no species, parenthood, or survival'.[358] The life-giving force of touch is, as Renee Weber points out, perhaps most powerfully represented in Michelangelo's visual rendering of the *Genesis* tale of God's creation of Adam by presenting touch, and not breath, as that which gives life[359] – a narrative supported by more recent studies of the relation between touch and healthy child development (see below).

Other advocates of the primacy of touch attribute to it epistemological and ontological powers, arguing that through touch we come to know what is real. While acknowledging that touch does not provide all the subtle nuances or the remote sensitivity available through vision, David Katz nevertheless insists on

---

357 Montagu 1978, pp. 1–2.
358 Schanberg cited in Ackerman 1991, p. 77.
359 R. Weber 1990, p. 16.

the 'precedence of touch over all other senses' – and this because 'its perceptions have the most compelling character of reality. Touch plays a far greater role than do the other senses in the development of belief in the reality of the external world. ... What has been touched is the true *reality* that leads to *perception*; no reality pertains to the mirrored image, the mirage that applies itself to the eye'.[360] Theological corroboration of this view is provided in the *New Testament* when doubting Thomas needed to touch Christ's wounds in order to know their reality – a touching scene touchingly rendered visual in Caravaggio's *The Incredulity of St. Thomas*. Rembrandt, according to art historian Svetlana Alper, would concur, having 'represent[ed] touch as the embodiment of sight'.[361] Samuel Johnson's famous kick of the rock to refute Bishop Berkeley, while perhaps not convincing to philosophical idealists, certainly exemplified a persuasively performative materialist metaphysics of touch (and one which, if the kick was hard enough, would have required a physician to address the somatic pain). And Roland Barthes, though wisely avoiding the debate over precedence in the sensual hierarchy, argues similarly that the tactile sense provides our sense of reality: while sight is, he opines, the 'most magical' of the senses, touch is 'the most demystifying'.[362] In the same vein Ortega y Gasset writes: 'It is clear that the decisive form of our intercourse with things is in fact touch. And if this is so, touch and contact are necessarily the most conclusive factor in determining the structure of our world'.[363] And again Montagu: 'in the final analysis we do not believe in the reality of anything unless we can touch it; we must have *tangible* evidence'.[364]

Impressive arguments all, and impressively supported by Montagu's impressionistic evidence that 'touch' is the longest entry in Oxford English Dictionary whose many pages of definitions and chronicles of the usages of the word 'touch' attest to its wide-ranging multi-dimensionality.[365] But here too, it must be noted, we are dealing with a rather excessive enthusiasm that has produced much eloquent, but at times untenable exaggeration. Montagu's claim that touching is universally considered the touchstone of reality is countered by the simple fact that much of the world's population believes in the reality of some kind of spiritual divinity that is, by definition, immaterial and therefore intangible, literally untouchable. The mainstream of traditional Western philo-

---

360 Katz 1935, p. 240.
361 Svetlana Alper cited in Ackerman 1991, p. 94.
362 Barthes 1972, p. 90.
363 Jose Ortega y Gasset cited in Montagu 1978, p. 101.
364 Montagu 1978, p. 100.
365 Montagu 1978, p. 102.

sophy from Plato and Hegel (and well beyond) viewed the tangible and finite material world as only contingently real, and situated the really and truly real in the intangible world of ideas. An aphoristic claim for the onto-epistemological primacy of vision is expressed in 'seeing is believing'. And popular wisdom allegorises the unreliability of touch in the story of the blind men and the elephant. But here too, I shall put aside the unhelpful argument over primacy and focus instead on the particular patent of nobility belonging to touch, on the unique patterns of experience given to humans by the nature and range of their tactile organs.[366]

To situate my treatment of touch, I quibble a bit with Montagu, not to win an argument, but to help explain why this is, for my purposes, the best place to address the sense of touch. Montagu stakes his claim for the primacy of touch in the order of importance on its primacy in the order of appearance. He appeals to what he calls a 'general embryological law which states that the earlier a function develops the more fundamental it is likely to be'.[367] But this 'law' must surely have almost as many exceptions as exemplifications, for it seems to imply that earlier traits cannot be rendered weaker and less important (or even disappeared) in the process of maturation. Be that as it may, the main point is that my concern here, like Montagu's, is with the uniquely refined sense of *human* touching and the 'human significance of skin'.

Questions about its genealogical primacy and its noble pedigree aside, touch is doubtless the most indispensable of the senses and a fundamental prerequisite of daily life. Although deprivation of sight, hearing, smell and/or taste certainly complicates the task of living, adaptation to the loss of one of more of these senses has proven successful, often through the increased acuity of the remaining sense organs. To be deprived of touch, however, is an infinitely greater challenge. As Montagu summarises:

> The skin as the sensory receptor organ which responds to contact with the sensation of touch, a sensation to which basic human meanings become attached almost from the moment of birth, is fundamental in the development of human behaviour. The raw sensation of touch as stimulus is vitally necessary for the physical survival of the organism. ... Basic needs, defined as tensions which must be satisfied if the organism is to survive, are the needs for oxygen, liquid, food, rest, activity, sleep, bowel and bladder elimination, escape from danger, and the avoidance of pain. ... [T]he

---

366 Some thoughts on the close relation between sight and touch, see Appendix 6.4.
367 Montagu 1978, p. 3.

evidence points unequivocally to the fact that no organism can survive very long without externally originating cutaneous stimulation.³⁶⁸

Because of its indispensability to daily life, the sense of touch is especially difficult to study. 'Scientists', writes Ackerman, 'can study people who are blind to learn more about vision, and people who are deaf or anosmic to learn more about hearing or smell, but this is virtually impossible to do with touch'; or as psychologist William T. Greenough puts it bluntly, we know very little about touch because although 'we can deprive an animal of most sound and all vision, ... how do you deprive an animal of touch?'³⁶⁹ But aside from the difficulty of finding 'experimental subjects', the study of touch must confront two interrelated challenges inherent in this multi-dimensional sense, namely: the delineation of the haptic organ(s); and the determination what kinds of percepts are properly haptic.

The delineation of the touch organ(s) is rendered difficult by their scope and multiplicity. It was precisely because touch, unlike the four 'classical' senses (vision, hearing, smell, taste), does not have a specific organ associated with it that Aristotle called it the 'fifth sense'. In praise of, rather than perplexity at, the multi-dimensionality of the tactile apparatus, Erasmus Darwin noted that the other sense organs 'are confined to a small part of the body, as the nostrils, ear, or eye, whilst the sense of touch is diffused over the whole skin, but exists with a more exquisite degree of delicacy at the extremities of the fingers and thumbs, and in the lips' – and he could have added the tongue and sexual organs (perhaps also the ear touched by sound waves) to his por-

---

368 Montagu 1978, p. 317.
369 Ackerman 1991, p. 77; Greenough 1990, p. 119. In contrast to the relatively common occurrence of blindness or deafness, there are fewer than ten reported cases of complete sensory neuropathy (excluding cases of paralysis). The most cited case is that of a young man who lost all sensation below the neck at the age of nineteen: 'He has no awareness of where his arms, legs, and body are in space unless he is looking at them. ... Walking, standing, even sitting are under strict visual, exhaustively conscious control. He cannot walk in a crowd or on uneven terrain because he is unable to make the on-line adjustments needed to remain upright in response to a jostle or an awkward footfall. Indeed, he cannot make the necessary adjustments to remain standing should he sneeze or simply if the lights go out; he immediately falls to a heap on the floor. Actual walking is quite deliberate: he leans forward and downward to keep his legs and body in view, swinging each leg stiffly from the hip, slapping each foot down as a whole, using an abnormally wide stance to enhance stability'. Cited from Carello and Turvey 2000, p. 28. This comment and citation are from a paper written by Elizabeth Sedlak, an undergraduate student in my seminar (2009) on 'A Historical-Materialist Mapping of Human Corporeal Organization'.

trait.³⁷⁰ This multi-dimensionality of receptors leads Frank Geldard to question whether the sensations of pressure, temperature, pain, contact etc. all pertain to a single sense of touch; he views the skin as instead 'housing three more or less separate systems of sensitivity, one for pressure reception, one for pain, and one responsive to temperature changes' while acknowledging that some cutaneous receptors will answer to more than one form of energy.³⁷¹ Anthony Smith expands the 'fifth sense' into 'five senses on its own'.³⁷² Sidestepping (or perhaps prestidigitating) the problem of many senses in one, David Katz, more likely prompted by his fascination with the hands rather than frustration with the multiplicity of haptic organs, focused in a 'bold stroke' on 'the importance of purposive [i.e. 'active'] touch in exploration' and proposed, *contra* Aristotle, that the hand is an organ 'quite as unitary as the organs of the other senses'.³⁷³ Intrigued by Kant's depiction of the hand as 'man's outer brain', and in all but the actual minting of the tactile counter-metaphor to the ocularcentric 'mind's eye', Katz treated touch as the 'mind's hand' – which is an apt description of the diagnostic touch of a medical doctor and the healing hands of a massage therapist or acupressurist.³⁷⁴ Strongly influenced by Katz on this point at least, J.J. Gibson elaborates the 'active, exploratory touch' of the hands as the kind of touch that 'permits both the grasping of an object and a grasp of its meaning'.³⁷⁵

---

370   Erasmus Darwin, cited in Montagu 1978, p. 202.
371   Geldard 1990, pp. 259–60.
372   Anthony Smith 1968, p. 398.
373   Lester E. Krueger, Editor's Introduction to Katz 1989, p. 5.
374   Katz 1989, p. 28. To make his own case for the nobility of the hand, Katz cites Gerhart Hauptmann's novel, *Die Insel der grossen Mutter*: 'The hand replaces all instruments, and through its congruence with the intellect it vouchsafes the latter a universal mastery. – The social structure of Europe and its inherent morality should be illuminated by this new orb of thought. ... It cannot be overestimated what would happen if the hand, now looked down upon, were elevated to the highest nobility' (ibid., p. 30).
375   Gibson 1966, p. 123. This is semantically grasped by the German verbs *greifen*, to grasp an object, and *begreifen*, to comprehend or to grasp the meaning of an object. But two reminders are required here. One is the latest iteration of a recurring theme: while manual exploratory touch is a universal human behaviour, the constructions of the meanings grasped can and of course do vary widely across cultures. And the other concerns the kind of hands with which 'one may lay hold of the surroundings merely to obtain information' and which 'can grope, palpate, prod, press, rub, or heft' thereby grasping tactilely many properties of an object. Unspoken but assumed in this accurate description is the kind of hands that can do these things. They are not the paws or claws of a creature that can rip or dig into an object, nor the flat palms that can be laid on one side of an object. The flexible and dexterous instrument described here is the set of humanly-refined primate hands with two opposable thumbs and eight very flexible fingers that together make possible a variety of grips (power, precision, hook, and scissor), a variety of ways of grasping

Although this brief overview of a few attempts to categorise the tactile organs certainly adds breadth and perhaps also depth to the world of touch, it does not bring order. So perhaps the best starting point here is simply to accept that the anatomical diversity of the haptic apparatus makes it rather difficult to establish a neat taxonomic table of the tactile organs and the kinds of sense perceptions – a starting point all the more acceptable here where the point is not to establish taxonomic clarity, but to suggest how human experience is framed by the many and varied capacities, and also by the limits, of our organs of touch. And as good a stepping-stone into this discussion as any is Gibson's all-encompassing yet succinct summary that 'the tactile sensory apparatus, unlike the other perceptual systems, includes, the body, most of its parts, and all of its surface'.[376]

Avoiding the problem of clearly and cleanly categorising the tactile organs, however, only brings us to a similar problem at the next step. As with smell, the complexity of touch is registered in the lack of agreement on the categories of tactile perceptions. But whereas the difficulty in cataloguing smells lies in their inarticulateness, their resistance to conceptualisation, the difficulty in cataloguing touch results both from the plurality of haptic organs and the often-overlapping multiplicity of the kinds of sensations perceived. Several binaries have been suggested as the first step in categorising sensations according to the kind of touch that produced them; these include: active and passive touch, touch in feeling and doing, and the one that will be adopted here to facilitate our inquiry: Katz's 'bipolar' categorising of what he considers the unique two-dimensionality of tactile sensory experience.[377] In contrast to vis-

---

an object, the hands that (having been liberated from and relieved of the wear and tear of, the locomotive process) are possessed of a uniquely delicate sensitivity that provides a textured feel of, feeling for, and therewith a multi-faceted tactile knowledge, of material objects.

376 Gibson 1966, p. 99.
377 Although he does not use the term, Gibson discusses two other 'bipolarities' in categories pertaining to touch. One is that that between 'active' and 'passive' touch: whether tactile stimulation is, respectively, initiated or imposed, whether one *touches* or *is touched*. Although active touch is generally associated with 'objective', and passive with 'subjective' tactual perception, this 'bipolarity' is not at all as rigidly bipolar as it may seem. In actively touching something, one might focus either on how the 'something' makes one feel (subjectively) or on how it feels (objectively); alternatively, when one is touched, one might attend to either how it makes one feel or what the object that touches one feels like. (See Gibson 1966, pp. 32, 123; Montagu 1978, p. 240). The other 'bipolarity' peculiar to the sense of touch is that, with at least two sources of tactile experience, the 'equipment for *feeling* is anatomically the same as the equipment for *doing*'; the hands and mouth are both 'exploratory sense organs' and 'performatory motor organs' (Gibson 1966, p. 99).

ion that 'never gives even a glimmer of what we readily know to be a state of our own bodily self', tactual phenomena are immediately two-dimensional: 'a subjective component that refers to the body seems inescapably linked with a second component that refers to the properties of objects'.[378] Likewise Gibson: 'in touching a solid object one can attend either to the external resistant thing or to the impression on the skin. [...] It is as if the same stimulating event had two possible poles of experience, one objective and the other subjective'.[379] Following Katz and Gibson, then, I shall touch on these two 'poles' or 'dimensions' of tactile experience.

Whether exploratory and active or imposed and passive, 'objective' touch refers to the perceived qualities of the object touched. Yet again faced with multiple possible organising principles, I once again borrow from Gibson whose subsuming of the tangible qualities of (material) objects under three categories is perfectly sufficient for present purposes.[380] These categories are: '(1) *geometrical variables* like, shape, dimensions and proportions, slopes and edges, or curves and protuberances; (2) *surface variables* like texture, or roughness-smoothness and (3) *material variables* like heaviness or mass and rigidity-

---

Confusion can arise here from that fact that the verb *to feel* can be either active and transitive (I feel the object) or intransitive and fairly passive, describing a state of the individual (I feel cold). The confusion would arise if one were to associate feeling exclusively with the later meaning. This could produce an antithesis of feeling and doing when for Gibson, both feeling and doing are active, the difference being that the former explores the object whereas the later transforms it. These 'bipolarities' can become a problem if one were to take them as establishing rigid antitheses between the poles of each of the pairs subjective/objective, feeling/doing, passive/active, and link 'passive', 'feeling', and 'subjective' on the one hand as opposed to 'active', 'doing', and 'objective' on the other. The problem with such bipolarities is that haptic experience can just as easily be of a hybrid nature – can simultaneously be *both* active and passive, doing and feeling, objective and subjective. In any tactile encounter, I can just as easily attend to the qualities of the object as I can to my subjective experience of the encounter, how it makes me feel – or both.

378   Katz 1989, p. 41. Such categorical claims as Katz's and Gibson's on behalf of the unique dual nature of tactile sensation would doubtless be contested by the advocates of the other senses. And it does seem that smell, taste, and hearing all have a very subjective component, perhaps in part because they have a tactual component of odours touching the nose, tastes the tongue, and sound the ear drums. And as graphically portrayed by Impressionist painters, even vision has a moving subjective dimension. That having been said, it is certainly worth pursuing the particular two-dimensional experience of touch.

379   Gibson 1966, p. 99.

380   Anthony Smith (1968, p. 398) associates each of his 'five senses' with 'a particular kind of objective tactile perception: touch, pressure, pain, heat and cold' – and he immediately adds that these five sensations can become blurred and not traceable to five distinct kinds of receptors.

plasticity', and also 'relative temperature'.[381] The variety of these variables already suggests the great range of the immediate experience of objective touch. Their reach, however, extends well beyond the immediacy of sensation and opens onto mediated horizons of tactile experience.

We encountered above Marx's notion of the senses as 'theoreticians'. And in the view of many reputable advocates, the tactile sense is richly endowed with 'theoretical powers'.[382] David Katz, for example, argues that the experience of the 'material variables' of objects provides 'the psychological roots for the physical concepts of impenetrability, resistance, and strength', thereby substantiating J. Petzoldt's[383] claim that 'mechanics originated from the sense of touch just as optics originated from vision'.[384] Katz moreover would add a whole new modal category of 'volume touch' perhaps best exemplified by the important role it plays in medical practice in the form of palpation or feeling 'the internal organs through the skin and cushions of fat in order to detect pathological changes in them'. And Bertrand Russell points out that '[n]ot only our geometry [shapes and dimensions, slopes and curves] and our physics [mass, heat, energy] but our whole conception of what exists outside us, is based upon the sense of touch' – thus extending the theoretical powers of touch to horizons ranging from mathematics and physics to ontology and metaphysics.[385]

Again, as examples from the sacred (the widespread belief in the reality of intangible deities, spirits, etc.) to the profane (the blind men and the elephant) remind us, touch is not necessarily the touchstone of conceptions of reality, nor is it impervious to deception. Nevertheless, it is difficult to argue that objective touch, through which we feel the shape, texture, temperature, and above all the resistance of the 'not-I', of objects outside ourselves, does not provide us with a (perhaps mistaken, in any case limited) sense of the material reality of the world – and perhaps also with the possibility of signifying the existence of the intangible by conceiving of it as the opposite of the tangible. At the very least, a strong case can be made that by providing us with tangible sensation of something outside of ourselves *and* outside of language, the tactile sense compels acknowledgement of the material world in general and of the referents of signs in particular. And semiocentric ultra-constructionists might consider whether signs could be produced without a belief in the (perhaps only seem-

---

381 Gibson 1966, p. 123 (my italics).
382 This formulation is intended to recall Marx's comment in the *1844 Manuscripts* on 'the theoretical powers of the senses'.
383 J. Petzoldt, cited in Katz 1989, p. 52.
384 Katz 1989, p. 52. Following citation ibid., p. 53.
385 Russell, cited in Montagu 1978, pp. 6–7.

ing) reality of the world derived from tactile experience (and regardless of great variation in the way in which that seeming reality is culturally refracted). As noted above, Samuel Johnson's attempt to refute Bishop Berkeley's idealism by kicking a rock may not have been philosophically satisfying, but the rock's resistance to the objective touch of Johnson's foot certainly provided a corporeal sign of the real, thereby lending credence to Johnson's claim.

As for subjective touch, common metaphors and idioms indicate how much we take for granted the relation between tactile perception and proprioception, between our ever so touchy haptic organ coextensive with our bodies and our sense of self, viz: 'I nearly jumped out of my skin'; 'I saved my skin'; a person is 'thick-' or 'thin-skinned'; a person who annoys me 'gets under my skin'.[386] A most graphic illustration of this metonymic association of skin and self is captured in Nina Jablonski's description of 'the reaction of students in her anatomy classes about to perform their first dissection of a human body', most of whom 'approached the task with hesitation, and some with great fear'. Jablonski explains that for many it was not just a reluctance to touch a dead person for the first time: '[m]uch of their reserve' derives rather 'from a sense of trepidation about trespassing a boundary they had not considered crossing. The intact skin of the cadaver, especially the skin of the face, was associated with a real person who had lived a real life of laughter and tears – a person like them, who had felt joy and sorrow'. Once they had removed the skin, however, that reticence diminished: Even though 'the body was no deader without skin, the partially flayed cadaver lacked the covering ... associated with dynamic personhood. The veil of personality and individuality had been removed, revealing the muscles, nerves, and sinews of the human species'. Jablonski's account of her students' association of skin is of a visual association made by an observer viewing the self from the outside, as an object, and *ex post facto*, i.e. after the expiration of the self.

The subjective sense of self, however, begins at the other end of the life-cycle, with birth and develops first through tactile experience. And that tactile experience is 'bipolar'; i.e. it is very intimately both subjective (an awareness of one's own body and being) and objective (an awareness of the self in relation to other entities, whether material objects or other selves, social touch).

The formative role of touch in developing a subjective sense of self begins already in the womb. Just six weeks after conception, according to Montagu, the embryo has a layer of skin sensitive to cutaneous stimulation.[387] And some

---

386 All citations in this paragraph: Jablonski 2013, p. 4.
387 Montagu 1978, p. 2.

seven-and-a-half months later, the new-born infant enters the world with an accumulated fund of tacit tactile knowledge, objective as well as subjective, acquired in the womb. In Erasmus Darwin's words, the 'first ideas we become acquainted with are those of the sense of touch; for the foetus must experience some varieties of agitation, and exert some muscular action, in the womb; and may with great probability be supposed thus to gain some ideas of its own figure, of that of the uterus, and of the tenacity of the fluid that surrounds it'.[388] From the immediate moment of birth through the prolonged period of human infant and childhood dependency, cutaneous stimulation is crucial to the 'healthy' maturation process. Montagu claims that the 'raw sensation of touch as stimulus is vitally necessary for the physical survival of the organism' and that tactile stimulation must therefore 'be added to the repertoire of basic needs in all vertebrates, if not in all invertebrates as well'[389] – and especially so for mammals and primates.[390]

---

388   Erasmus Darwin, both passages cited in Montagu 1978, p. 202.
389   Montagu 1978, p. 317; it is questionable whether the range of taxonomic classes touched by touch is as broad as Montagu claims: such a basic need in r-selected species among which parental investment is necessarily limited both because of the number of offspring and because of the rather brief period of infancy, nor in oviparous species in which the mother does not have the foetus inside its own body.
390   The human need for social touch and cutaneous stimulation is much older than our primate past, a legacy of our mammalian heritage. The results of several experiments with our mammalian and primate contemporaries 'strongly suggest', according to Montagu, 'that cutaneous stimulation is an important biological *need*' for both the 'physical and behavioral development' of young mammals. (Montagu 1978, p. 28). The most well-known of these studies, Harry Harlow's oft-cited primate experiment, showed that infants monkeys fed by a surrogate mother built out of wire but covered with a cloth skin matured far more normally than those feed by the mother built out of wire alone without the soft covering to which the infants could cling and against which they could gently rub (ibid., pp. 29–34). Generalising about the results of Harlow's and other experiments on touch and monkey behaviour, Stephen J. Suomi concludes that 'the stimulation provided through tactile contact with conspecifics seems crucial for normal development to take place' within 'species-normative social environments' (Suomi in Barnard and Brazelton 1990, p. 156.) The human species, of course, is unique in having a broad range of socio-cultural environments, and what Suomi says of monkey species – that 'tactile contact stimulation comes from a wide range of sources and takes a substantial number of different forms' (ibid., p. 156) – is even more true within the human species. Nevertheless, though the range of healthy tactile stimulation for humans may be broader, and though the forms may be even more varied, what Suomi concludes is true of monkeys is shown by Montagu's cross-cultural analysis to be true of humans as well, namely, that when species-normative tactile contact is prevented or 'abnormally' restricted, 'certain systematic problems in social development seen to follow, many of which are clearly profound and often permanent' (ibid., p. 156).

In most mammal species the new-born's initial cutaneous experience is immediate, intense, and multi-faceted, consisting of fondling, inspection, grooming, manipulation, and licking.[391] While licking the new-born is uncommon in primates and almost unheard of in humans (except where water is scarce such as the Polar regions and Tibetan highlands), the metaphorical references to motherless human children as 'unlicked cubs' is perhaps telling. Montagu finds a human substitute for licking during the protracted human birth process in which 'the contractions of the uterus provide massive stimulations of the fetal skin' and 'serve much the same functions and end-effects that licking of the new-born does in other animals'. The abnormally long human birth process, he suggests, serves to ignite the self-functioning of the new-born's respiratory, circulatory, digestive, eliminative, and endocrine systems that are no longer supported by the mother's body.[392] 'When the skin has not been adequately stimulated, the peripheral and autonomic nervous systems are also inadequately stimulated, and a failure of activation occurs in the principal organ systems'. The adverse consequences of this are borne out, he argues, by studies contrasting full-term vaginal deliveries with premature and caesarean births: premature babies tend toward short attention spans, shyness, hyperactivity, hypersensitivity to sound, anxiousness, etc., while caesarean babies have higher mortality rates, tend to be more lethargic, have decreased reactivity, and show biochemical imbalances.

Montagu has no qualms about asking a 'universal' question about human 'species-being': whether all human infants must 'undergo, in the course of early development, certain kinds of tactile experiences in order to develop as a healthy human being'.[393] Nor does he have qualms about answering in the affirmative – great cultural variation in attitudes toward, and the practices of, cutaneous stimulation notwithstanding.[394] For, he concludes his long

---

391 Montagu (1978, pp. 12–14) provides several examples, provided by animal breeders and researchers, of the calming effects of gentle touch in various species including rats and dogs, cows and dolphins. And the main purpose of washing and grooming, whether performed by the animal on itself or by others, does not seem to be cleanliness; rather the 'proper kind of cutaneous stimulation is essential for the adequate organic and behavioural development of the organism' (ibid., p. 15). Support and additional evidence for Montagu's claims may be found in a volume of the papers presented at the Johnson & Johnson Pediatric Round Table entitled *Touch: The Foundation of Experience*. See Barnard and Brazelton 1990.
392 Montagu 1978, p. 38. Following citations and paraphrasings from Montagu 1978, p. 50, pp. 51–2, p. 53.
393 Montagu 1978, p. 12.
394 Montagu 1978, Chapter 7, 'Culture and Contact', provides a lengthy discussion of cultural variations.

study of its human significance with the insistence that 'the skin as the sensory receptor organ to which basic human meanings become attached almost from the moment of birth, is fundamental in the development of human behaviour. In that sense it may be postulated that the need for tactile stimulation must be added to the repertoire of basic needs in all vertebrates, if not in all invertebrates as well'.[395] Perhaps the most 'basic human meanings' for the social animal, *Homo sapiens*, is an awareness of self in relation to others; social touch should contribute to the understanding that 'the I is a we' (Hegel).

Tactile experience plays a primary role (by both ordinal and cardinal measures) in the development of the sense of selfhood, in ego-formation which necessarily includes a sense of other things and other selves. Essentially summarising Freud on ego-formation, Montagu explains: 'The infant is at first not only lacking psychic structure but also in psychic and somatic boundaries. He is unable to distinguish between inside and outside, between 'I' and 'not-I'; in brief, he is in a state of psychic nondifferentiation'.[396] Differentiation begins, in Freud's terms, when the infant's psyche is forced beyond the pleasure principle toward the reality principle by the recognition that the still obscure objects of its desire are not part of its own self, but can, like the mother's breast, be taken away. Through the tangible experience of desired objects and the intangible experience of their absence, the infant learns of an 'external reality' consisting of things outside the self and not subject to its desires. It is thus through touch that the infant begins to differentiate itself from other objects, both animate and inanimate, of the world and thereby to establish the contours of the self. But precisely because of the subject-object dialectics of touch, the differentiation of external objects is at the same time the delineation of the contours of the self. As Walter Ong puts it, 'by the very fact that [touch] attests the not-me more than any other sense, touch involves my own subjectivity more than any other sense. When I feel this objective something 'out there', beyond the bounds of my body, I also at the same instant experience my own self. I feel other and self simultaneously'.[397]

The extended infancy of human babies provides a variety of, and ample time for, 'bipolar' tactile experiences – for human forms of grooming, inspection, manipulation, and cleaning, for holding, caressing, fondling the child which is

---

395   Montagu 1978, p. 317.
396   Montagu 1978, p. 201.
397   Ong, cited in Montagu 1978, p. 100.

doubtless more pronounced and prolonged in humans than other mammals, and for that uniquely mammalian experience of breastfeeding. Breastfeeding is, of course, an integral part of that process; and like sex and other interpersonal tactile encounters, it is both subjective and objective. While passively experiencing the pleasure and healthy consequences of motherly touch, the new-born engages in its own initial acts of exploratory touch. The primary organs of these first tactile forays are not the hands but the lips and mouth and the objects of this active oral touch are of course the mother's breasts. And the initial tactile experience of breastfeeding is, Erasmus Darwin argued, the source of that particularly important and peculiarly human expression of emotion, the smile: 'In the action of sucking, the lips of the infant are closed around the nipple of his mother, till he has filled his stomach, and the pleasure occasioned by the stimulus of this grateful food succeeds. Then the sphincter of the mouth, fatigued by the continued action of sucking, is relaxed; and the antagonist muscles of the face gently acting, produce the smile of pleasure'.[398] Finding this explanation 'as good a theory of the origin of smiling as any that has been offered', and noting Darwin's recognition that 'some nations are more remarkable for the gaiety, and others for the gravity of their looks', Montagu agrees that 'the fact that the smile universally constitutes an evidence of pleasure, of friendliness, may at least partly be due to the organs of smiling in the infant's oral-tactile pleasures at the maternal breast'. Alternatively, the opposite oral motion from sucking the breast inward, sticking the tongue out, has connotations opposite those of sucking, meaning 'I don't love you' or 'I don't care for you'.[399] And once the infant attains language, those same gestures can be expressed in a wide range of terms and phrases, including: 'rubbing' people the wrong way as opposed to 'stroking' them the right way; a person has a 'happy' or a 'soft touch'; we get in 'touch' or 'contact' with others; some people must be 'handled carefully', with 'kid gloves' because they are 'touchy' and 'tactless'; others are callous (from the Latin *callum* meaning hard skin); sympathy or a kind act is 'touching' and one is 'touched' by it.[400] As important as breastfeeding may be, its lack may be compensated for, Montagu contends, if the infant is often lovingly touched, carried, or caressed. Pointing to the very high death rate of infants in the nineteenth century, especially among orphans

---

398 This citation from Erasmus Darwin and following commentary by Montagu in Montagu 1978, pp. 74–5.
399 Montagu 1978, p. 102.
400 These examples are from Montagu 1978, pp. 5–7.

in institutions, from a disease called *marasmus* (from the Greek word meaning 'wasting away'; known also as infantile atrophy or debility) that stemmed from the cutaneous sterility and emotional aridity of the infant's environment, Montagu concludes that '[e]xtreme sensory deprivation in other respects, such as light and sound, can be survived, as long as the sensory experiences at the skin are maintained'.[401]

If Stephen Suomi's experiments with rhesus monkeys are any indication of human behaviour, there appears to be, not surprisingly, a direct correlation between mother-infant tactile contact and the willingness of the infant to explore the environment and its contents. Habitual tactile contact with the mother through grooming 'establish[es] and maintain[s] a secure base for ever increasing exploration of their immediate physical and social environment'; and with a secure base where the infant receives tactile stimulation upon returning, the exploratory forays grow 'increasingly frequent, longer in duration, and greater in distance from the mother'; isolated infants experimentally denied access to tactile contact with their mother ceased to explore and avoided social contacts.[402] Humans are, in this regard at least, not so different from rhesus monkeys. The recognition of 'the unequivocal short- and long-term benefits to the baby' of loving cutaneous stimulation has led some American and European hospitals to introduce massage as part of 'normal infant care', and also with autistic children who generally do not like being touched but do seem to like deep massage, after sessions of which they relate better to caregivers and sleep better.[403] Knowing where one is in the world, being on familiar terms with, and thus at home in, one's world is not only

---

401 Montagu 1978, p. 77; p. 79. Montagu also mentions the experiment initiated by the thirteenth-century German emperor Frederick II: to see whether infants possessed and innate language and if so what, he forbade nurses infants to do anything more than feed and bathe orphaned infants, but not speak or prattle to them – an activity that usually is accompanied by holding and caressing the infant. The chronicler of this experiment records that all the children died and noted that 'they could not live without the petting and joyful faces and loving words of their foster mothers' (ibid., p. 81). As a counter example, Montagu cites the 1930s case of Isabelle, an illegitimate child who was secluded with her mother in a dark room where they could not embarrass the rest of the family. When found at the age of six, she suffered from light deprivation and poor nutrition resulting in physical deformation. However, despite all expectations, within a few years she was able to participate normally in school activities with her own age group – which Montagu attributes 'almost certainly ... to the fact that she had been adequately loved by her mother, handled, held, caressed, and fondled' (ibid., p. 81).
402 Suomi in Barnard and Brazelton 1990, p. 139, p. 147.
403 Jablonski, 2013, pp. 106–7.

(in Novalis's view) the desire behind philosophy; it is also, in a variety of formulations, the foundation of freedom. And if the loving tactile experience in infancy that encourages exploration of the world is crucial to an adult sense of being-at-home-in-the-world, then it might be equally crucial to a sense of freedom.

Feeling 'at home in the world' is not just a matter of feeling at home in the physical/material world, but in one's social world as well; and a willingness to explore the social world is the foundation of learning to be in the world with others. The readiness for social exploration is also tied to infant tactile experience which is certainly a case of simultaneous objective and subjective tactile experience. 'Objective' tactile qualities of soothing, caressing, contact of skin, etc. produces subjective feelings, of contentment, closeness, and, perhaps most important, trust, the ability to avoid immediate feelings of vulnerability when touched by others. 'Tactical failure in infancy', Montagu concludes, restricts social exploration and 'results only too often in estrangement, uninvolvement, lack of identity, detachment, emotional shallowness, and indifference – all marks of the schizoid or schizophrenic personality'.[404] And fear of falling, whether actually from a great height or metaphorically in love, has been linked in more than one study to 'those who have not been lovingly and securely held in infancy'.

Delicate, loving tactile stimulation not only is pleasing to the infant recipient of such touch, but also provides clues to the social world – the first glimpse of other selves; and if those initial tactile glimpses/senses are pleasing, reassuring during this process of separation and ego-formation, they help to counter the infant's potential shock of recognising a world outside its own control with the reassurance that it is not (necessarily) a hostile world. If Edith Wyschogrod is correct, and touch is both the structural model for, and a key means of enhancing, the intersubjective emotions of sympathy and empathy, then early and reassuring tactile experience would also cultivate cooperative social behaviour.[405] Similarly, and although the modern Western medical establishment might discount its efficacy, the seeking of some form of therapeutic touch as a means of alleviating pain – be it physical, mental, or emotional – seems a rather universal desire. And the exercise of some form of therapeutic touch – whether the 'laying on of hands', the 'king's touch', acupressure and massage, the therapeutic benefits of a nurse's care (deified in the Greek

---

404 Montagu 1978, p. 107. Citation in next sentence, ibid., p. 217.
405 Wyschogrod 1981, p. 41.

pantheon as *Hygeia*, the goddess of 'the gentle hands'[406]) or the consoling touch of a friend – seems equally widespread.

'Inadequate tactile experience will', Montagu insists, 'result in [...] a consequent inability to relate to others in so many fundamental human ways'.[407] The lack of loving touch might produce the kind of adverse reactions described in Erwin Straus's one-dimensional and rather moody existentialist rendering of the feeling of being touched: 'In the passivity of being touched, I am aware of my body in its sensitiveness, its vulnerability, its powerlessness, and its nakedness. The more powerfully the *Other* presses in upon me, the more I am overpowered by it – the more I sink back into the forsakenness and forlornness of my existence'.[408] Straus is certainly correct in situations when passive touch is unwanted, when touch is a violation of the self, whether in the form of being beaten, raped, or 'just' the recipient of unwanted touch. But the one-dimensionality of Straus's point lies in the fact that, in being touched, it is not only the act of touching that matters, but also the *how* of touch: whether it is aggressive or affectionate, combative or caring, painful or pleasurable. And, of course, even the *how* of the touch can be trumped by the desire for it and/or its consequences: a painful initiation process, a curing injection or healing surgery, the exhilaration of contact sports, or a masochist's pursuit of erotic pleasure in pain are but a few examples of the voluntary experiencing of pain as the means to a desired end.[409]

---

406 Meehan in Barnard and Brazelton 1990, p. 376. Meehan's essay and also that of Renee Weber on 'A Philosophical Perspective on Touch' (in Barnard and Brazelton 1990) address the debate between the contemporary medical establishment and the proponents of therapeutic touch. Weber cites Dolores Krieger, one of the 'pioneers' in the study of 'therapeutic touch' and coiner of the term itself, who also called it an 'evolutionary emergent'. Weber herself finds this a 'stimulating' idea and ventures her 'own tentative conjecture' that 'the healing capacity of touch has been latent in our species all along, awaiting only the right cultural and intellectual climate' – which she now thinks is at hand with increasing 'Western awareness of Eastern philosophy' and 'contemporary physics, with its field theory and its novel notions of space, time, matter, and energy' (ibid., p. 35).
407 Montagu 1978, p. 319.
408 Straus 1958, p. 161.
409 Be that as it may, though one-dimensional, Straus's description is not inaccurate for adverse or undesired, tactile encounters. Doubtless because of their immediacy and intimacy, adverse tactile encounters are perhaps the most unpleasant of sensual experiences – especially if the encounter is painful as well as unpleasant, in which case the immediacy of the experience might linger as long as the pain. As much as smelling their odors, tactile experience with despised others is considered abhorrent and contaminating. This is evident in the common expression of needing to wash one's hands or take a

Straus's glum tactile phenomenology is nowhere more out of touch than in the realm of desired sexual encounters. Sexual touch certainly involves the nakedness and sensitiveness of the body (so sensitive because of its functional nakedness). Yet, although sexual touch can provoke feelings of vulnerability and powerlessness, it by no means must. Just as the diminished role of the olfactory in sexual stimulation opened greater horizons for the visual in the expression and stimulation of sexual desire, so too for the tactile. Straus either forgets or ignores the fact that the 'functionally naked' skin is not only the largest sensory organ, but also 'the largest sexual organ of the human body' (Jablonski) – and underlies what Herbert Marcuse called the 'polymorphous perversity' of treating the entire skin-covered body as the sexual organ that it is.

And passive touch, being touched, can just as easily be the source of intense individual pleasure, of trust, of being beloved, of being a very corporeal desiring and desired subject. As in Nietzsche's rendering of the Dionysian, or Gustav Klimt's painting of *The Kiss*, the pleasure of passionate sexual touch, at once both active and passive, objective and subjective, can have the contrary effect of submerging what Straus depicts as the vulnerable, powerless, forsaken and forlorn self in the self-transcending intoxication of merging with another into a union beyond what Schopenhauer bemoaned as the 'pain of individuation'. The encounter of two desiring subjects, each actively desiring to touch and be touched, to feel both the self and the other, is clearly a most complex, intimate, and pleasurable kind of tactile/cutaneous experience. An obvious corollary of Schanberg's claim that there would be no species, parenthood, or survival 'if touch didn't feel good' is that if sexual touch didn't feel good, there would be no sex. But it does, and there is – and in humans, of course, not just (nor any longer even primarily) for reproductive reasons.

Noting that 'different cultures vary in both the manner in which they express the need for tactile stimulation and the manner in which they satisfy it', Montagu insists that 'although the form of its satisfaction may vary according to time and place', 'the need [for tactile stimulation] is universal and is everywhere the same'.[410] However diverse culturally-prescribed kinds of general social and particularly sexual touching may be, the constant factor underlying, structuring, and circumscribing all of the peculiarly human worlds of

---

shower after having touched or been touched by a 'slimy' person; and it was socially institutionalised in the Indian caste system in which the 'outcasts' were not only called, but also considered 'untouchables' whose touch is polluting.

410 Montagu 1978, p. 318.

touch is the corporeal organisation of the 'functionally naked' ape that is outfitted, in consequence of its diurnal bipedalism, with a unique and extensive bodily toolkit for both subjective and objective touch: arms for reaching out and embracing; uniquely flexible hands and fingers, the latter with uniquely sensitive tips, for grasping, stroking and caressing; the highly sensitive 'naked' skin that turns the entire body into both an apparatus of tactile apprehension and a sexual organ.[411] In a burst of existential enthusiasm over this fact that 'the body as a whole is a tactile field', Wyschogrod finds in its polymorphous 'sensitivity to pressure, temperature and surface qualities, together with kinesthesis, its felt respiratory movements, its pulse, the hand's capacity for manipulative endeavor, its motility' – in all of these she finds: the 'primordial ground of existence as incarnate'.[412]

I remain agnostic on the existential claim. Nevertheless, the tactile body is certainly a 'primordial ground' of rather diverse cultural forms. Tactile sensations of the shape and mass of objects are foundational, Russell claimed, for geometries, the physics of matter in motion, thermodynamics, and even for metaphysics and ontologies. Tactile sensations of pleasure and pain, including those pains associated with the aging body's approach to death, are arguably at the root of virtually all philosophical inquiries into the nature of human life and also of all theologies, most explicitly those offering visions of *postmortem* heavenly pleasures or hellish pains. Social touch, whatever its culturally-specific expression provides the foundation of healthy human experience from infancy through adulthood. And the tactile sensations are the foundations of metaphorical projections, at least as wide-ranging and extensive as human touch itself, that humans use to make sense of and to depict aspects of our worlds. This multi-dimensionality of tactile experience and its vast array of metaphorical projections explains why 'touch' is the longest entry in the *Oxford English Dictionary*.

---

411   See Napier 1993, pp. 56–7: 'Although opposition of the thumb is one of the hallmarks by which man can be authenticated as it were, it is not a movement unique to him. What is unique is the broad area of intimate contact between the finger-tip pulps of the opposing digits that results. The advantage of intimate contact concerns both function and feeling; the greater the surface area of highly sensitive papillary skin available, the more effective is the handling of small and delicate objects'.

412   Wyschogrod 1981, p. 26.

6.6.6 *The Biological Foundations of Speech and Language*

> Thanks to words, we have been able to rise above the brutes; and thanks to words, we have often sunk to the level of demons.
> ALDOUS HUXLEY[413]

∴

6.6.6.1 Introductory

In addition to the taxonomic epithet, *sapiens*, bestowed, probably satirically,[414] by Linnaeus, a good number of other monikers has been coined for our species, each indicating what its coiner considered the definitive human attribute: *zoon politikon* (Aristotle), *Homo faber* (Benjamin Franklin), *Homo economicus*, *Homo metaphysicus* (Arthur Schopenhauer), *Homo laborans* or *animal laborans* (Hannah Arendt), *Homo socius* (Peter Berger and Thomas Luckmann), *animal symbolicum* (Ernst Cassirer), *Homo ludens* (Johan Huizinga), *Homo pictor* ('man the artist', Hans Jonas), *Homo viator* ('itinerate man', Gabriel Marcel), *Homo patiens* ('suffering man', Victor Frankl), etc.[415] Each of these epithets pointing to some easily recognisable human attribute sounds appropriate, but none more so, at first hearing at least, than that coined by Johan Gottfried von Herder who named the species for its unique capacity of speech: *Homo loquens* – an epithet that Henri Bergson rendered (for our time certainly appropriately, and especially for internet voices that are at once mute and mind-splittingly loud) as *Homo loquax*, the 'loquacious' or 'chattering' man. Although it could easily be argued that the capacity for speech and language use is the single most important and consequential one embedded in human corporeal organisation, and although the isolation and exclusive focus on speech or language is a perfectly legitimate methodological move for analytical purposes (but not free of analytical traps; see Chapter 8), it would be mistaken to imagine that the nature and purpose(s) of speech and language can be fully understood in isolation from the corporeal organisation and ethology of the hominid that speaks.

---

413 Aldous Huxley, cited in Corballis 1991, p. 107.
414 Broberg 1983, p. 194.
415 http://en.wikipedia.org/wiki/List_of_alternative_names_for_the_human_species.

The intimate relation between human corporeal organisation and speech and language was recognised long ago in an extraordinary formulation voiced by a fourth-century Christian creationist, the perspicacious philosopher-monk Gregory of Nyssa: 'So it was thanks to the manner in which our bodies are organized that our mind like a musician, struck the note of language within us and we became capable of speech. This privilege would surely never have been ours if our lips had been required to perform the onerous and difficult task of procuring nourishment for our bodies. But our hands took over that task, releasing our mouths for the service of speech'.[416] Elaborating in rather graphic detail, he continues:

> Yet it is above all for the sake of speech that nature has added hands to our body. If man had been deprived of hands, his facial parts, like those of the quadrupeds, would have been fashioned to enable him to feed himself: His face would have been elongated in shape, narrow in the region of the nostrils, with lips protuberant, horny, hard, and thick for the purpose of plucking grass; the tongue between his teeth would be very different from what it is, fleshy, resistant, and rough, so as to crush his food together with the teeth; it would be moist, capable of allowing food to flow down its side, like those of dogs or other flesh-eating animals, which allow food to flow through the interstices between their teeth. If our body had no hands, how could the articulated voice form inside it? The parts around the mouth would not be so constituted to meet the requirements of speech. In such a case man would have had to bleat, bark, neigh, low like the oxen, or cry like the ass, or roar as the wild animals do.

Gregory is by no means the only commentator who gave the hands all the talk, while ignoring the feet that did the walk, thus relieving the forepaws of locomotive responsibilities. Nevertheless, he is most astute in understanding the corporeal prerequisites of speech, in recognising what should be the obvious fact (ignored by 'brain-first' theories of human being, whether Aristotle's teleological explanation of the hands as a consequence of human intelligence or evolutionary versions of the same) that human hands, in assuming responsibilities that other species fill with the mouth, made the mouth available for other endeavours, most notably speaking. Although it is probably not incorrect to say that speech and language are the final building-blocks and definitive attributes of *Homo sapiens*, it is incorrect to isolate them as the only ones and

---

416 Gregory of Nyssa, cited in Leroi-Gourhan 1993, p. 25. Next passage citied in ibid., p. 35.

to insist, as many have, that they are the sole determinants of human cognition. For speech and language are themselves dependent on a long-evolving set of corporeal attributes and cognitive capacities that enabled and in-formed them – but whose absolutely essential enabling role too often remains unrecognised, seemingly having been occluded by that key human grammatological invention that separated language from its user, namely: writing.

It has long since become commonplace to treat language as a semiotic system, a system of signs. But it should be as unsurprising as it is seemingly trivial to say that not all signs are linguistic; nor that the ability to interpret and also to produce signs (whether that production be incidental, e.g. an animal necessarily leaving a footprint in the sand or a scent of its passing, or purposeful even if only 'instinctually' and not consciously intentional) is certainly not unique to *Homo sapiens*.[417] In addition to the vocally and behaviourally produced signs just mentioned, signs can be produced through gesture, facial expression and even rudimentary tool-making to name a few. What Terry Eagleton says of human labour, namely that 'it works Nature up into human meaning' and is therefore 'a signifying activity'[418] can be said of the bees and spiders (which Marx mentioned as also labouring creatures) and to any organism that, in producing its own niche, creates a world of artefacts (however modest) in its own corporeal image – giving apic or arachnidic meaning to its nook of the world.

There are, however, two unique aspects of linguistic sign production and interpretation. One is that whereas biosemiotic signs (human or otherwise) are generally iconic or indexical signs with fairly unambiguous meanings (e.g. danger, sexual readiness) and relatively tied to time and place, the meaning of linguistic signs, by contrast, is *relatively* arbitrary.[419] The meaning of signs, at least in the majority of cases, is not indicated by the sound (but see below

---

417 Thomas Sebeok insists that 'communication' defined as 'the transmission of any influence from one part of a living system to another part, thus producing change', those transmitted influences being 'messages' which are 'the subject matter of semiotics', is 'present in the humblest forms of existence, whether bacteria, plants, animals, or fungi, and, moreover, in their component parts, such as subcellular units [...], cells, organelles, organs, and so forth' (Sebeok 1991, p. 23). In anticipation of the discussion of language and communication below, I shall note that in recognising both the essentially communicative nature of language and also the absolute uniqueness of linguistic sign systems, Sebeok is one of those who has little trouble holding two allegedly discordant thoughts in his head at the same time without succumbing to cognitive dissonance.

418 Eagleton 2011, p. 232.

419 Even when some biosign is used to lie and deceive (e.g. signalling predator when one isn't there, adult birds feigning a broken wing in a seeming attempt to escape that is intended to lure a predator away from their nesting young), the success of the deceit depends on the clarity of meaning. On biosemiotics, see Sebeok and Umiker-Sebeok 1991.

on 'the sound-shape of language'); and interpretations of the linguistic signs (whether oral or written) can vary widely from place to place (geo-cultural specificity), from time to time (Shelley's 'Ozymandias'), and/or person to person (idiosyncrasy).[420] And the other is that the human corporeal capacities for semiotic objectification have enabled the species, for better or worse, to impose human meanings on the entire planet – and, whether in the form of anthropomorphic deities or the projections of human science, even on the heavens, on celestial bodies, on the universe(s).

There is of course no doubt that the invention of writing played a role beyond quantifiable magnitude in the various forms of 'humanising' the universe. But the invention of writing created a new mode of 'languaging' (a now rarely used verb meaning 'to express in language, put into words; to tell, describe, report') that made possible two methodologically valuable, ontologically untenable separations.[421] Languaging in written form facilitated, even encouraged, that development so much regretted by Plato and Rousseau, yet welcomed by Derrida: the separation of language from speaking (and therewith the drifting apart of the hitherto synonymous meanings of Latin term *lingua* into the polysemic senses of 'tongue' and 'language').[422] If 'speaking' [*parole*] is, as Saussure's *Course* calls it, 'the executive side' of speech [*langage*], the invention of writing made it possible for humans visually to encounter and to find meaningful the graffiti of language [*langue*] left behind by a no longer present executor. Writing, in short, not only separated language from speaking, but in so doing made it possible for the products of written languaging, scriptural artefacts, to have a graphic existence independent of their author.

This separation might seem analogous to the olfactory biosemiotics that, as Leroi-Gourhan suggested, brings the olfactory-abled to the 'threshold of the imaginary'; whereas audible linguistic signs are fleeting, vanishing when the speaking executor holds his/her tongue, written words to the visually literate (in braille: the tactually literate), like smells to the olfactorily-attuned, linger long after their executor has disappeared.[423] But although the written sign

---

420 For reasons elaborated in detail in Chapter 8, 'arbitrary' can carry either a strong meaning of completely random or a weaker meaning of contingent but not inexplicable, relatively arbitrary or, alternatively, relatively motivated.
421 To avoid charges of phonocentrism in using the term, it is worth both emphasising that languaging is a matter of *verbal* expression, and also reminding that 'verbal', though often misused to mean 'spoken', refers to 'words', regardless of whether spoken or written. (Definitions of languaging and 'verbal' from *Oxford English Dictionary*, on-line edition).
422 See Derrida 1976, esp. Part One, Chapter 2, 'Linguistics and Grammatology' that includes discussions of Plato and Saussure, and Part II on 'The Age of Rousseau'.
423 See discussion of the olfactory sense above.

might invoke its author/producer in much the same way as olfactory-gifted animals can perceive and interpret lingering olfactory signs as invoking an imaginary i.e. absent referent, it need not. The development of mechanical and computer technologies capable of virtually infinite reproduction of written words aside, the relative arbitrariness of linguistic signs combined with the transportability of scriptural artefacts from place to place and their durability over generations and epochs makes it possible for them to take on a life of their own, independent of their producers. And rather than invoking its producer, the life of the text is gained by the 'death of the author'. The demise of the author paves the way for the apotheosis of language, elevated from a means of expressing meaning to the actual producer of meaning.

There are (as mentioned in Chapter 2 and addressed in detail in Chapter 8), necessary reasons for a (temporary) methodological isolation of language from its producers and users in order to understand how language functions as a system of signification. And Derrida justifiably objected to the Saussurean 'phonocentric' condemnation of the 'tyranny of writing'.[424] Yet, it would be equally objectionable to swing to the opposite extreme and fall into a 'graphocentrism' that effects an unjustifiable ostracism of speaking/*parole* and enables language/*langue* to reign supreme and tyrannise over the realm of speech/*langage* or languaging. At this point, our interest is not an 'abstract objectivist' one that would treat language/*langue* as 'a ready-made object' with its own *raison d'être*.[425] The concern here is rather with languaging (which we might Heideggerianise as the Being-of-Language-in-the-World), that is: with an interlocutory behaviour involving interlocutors and language. For present purposes at least, the fact that languaging was phonic long before it became also graphic is crucial; and to ignore this fact is to ignore the corporeal prerequisites of speech and languages and thus to efface the very corporeal locus and human significance of speech. Human speech as we know it is not only, and obviously, unspeakable, but it is also unthinkable without phonics. Accordingly, the mode of speech production, or speaking, and the means of speech production, language (itself a product of speech), are in-formed by the vocal and audial apparatuses that are essential to speech and language production. And these are the main matters that will be considered here as the next (and last) step in this historical-materialist sketch of human corporeal organisation. The debates over language are as convoluted as the matter is complex, and this essay will include a good

---

424 Derrida 1976, p. 38.
425 Vološinov 1973, pp. 52–61 *et passim*. Vološinov was referring specifically to the Saussurean *Course in General linguistics*, but the term is applicable to any such hypostatising of *langue*.

number of seeming digressions that are intended to establish categorial clarity and delineate exactly what I am, and what I am not, claiming. As for a starting point: because hominids *were becoming*, long before they became, 'languagers', we begin with a glance at hominids becoming 'linguistically-abled'.

6.6.6.2 Hominid 'Languaging'

Although there is, unsurprisingly, a good deal of variation in dating the origins of speech (the previously accepted estimate of 30,000 years ago has now been pushed back to some 200,000 years ago), this is, in terms of evolutionary time, a rather negligible difference.[426] And there is, surprisingly, a rare moment of seeming concord among students of human evolution on the (somewhat tautological) proposition that fully human speech and language capacity developed relatively recently with anatomically modern *Homo sapiens* – the only species with a thoroughly modern vocal and audial apparatus that allows it to produce and 'consume' language. Researchers of non-human animal species like Donald Griffin, who has found surprisingly sophisticated cognitive capacities in animal minds, and Sue Savage-Rumbaugh, whose accomplishments in training apes to understand and communicate using human language are astonishing, would certainly insist that the minds of *Homo sapiens* are not as far removed from the minds of other animal species as many would like to believe (which was perhaps Linnaeus's point in establishing the taxonomic affinity between *Homo sapiens* and *Simia sapiens*). But neither would say that apes or any other creature has acquired 'human' language. No one attributes to *Australopithecines* a kit of corporeal instruments capable of producing and consuming language. David Pilbeam, for example, opines that although *Australopithecines* 'almost certainly used some very rudimentary form of verbal communication, [...] their small cranial capacity, protruding facial structure, and ape-like vocal apparatus meant a much more limited repertoire of sounds than in modern humans and consequently a necessarily limited "vocabulary"'.[427]

General agreement seems also to hold in analyses of the speech apparatus and capacities of the early *Homo* species. The earliest of the *Homo* line, *Homo habilis*, had only the 'rudiments of a spoken language' (Falk), a 'proto-language' (Bickerton), possibly 'a developing capacity for articulate speech' as indicated by an increase in average endocranial volume and a restructuring of the brain

---

426 Stephen Pinker (1984, p. 353) argues that 'the date most commonly given in magazine articles and textbooks for the origins of language: 30,000 years ago' is 'demolished' by the fact that modern *Homo sapiens*, which includes language capacity, is now thought to have emerged about 200,000 years ago.
427 Pilbeam in Harrison et al. 1989, p. 118.

(Klein), etc.[428] Nevertheless, *Homo habilis* exhibits the beginnings of anatomical developments that would be the prerequisites of language. Falk among others interprets traces of the appearance of brain lateralisation and Broca's area (the motor area for speaking) found in endocasts of *Homo habilis* skulls as evidence of 'the rudiments of a spoken language'.[429]

The gradual evolution of the cranial prerequisites of speech and language, brain size and organisation, and of speaking itself seems to parallel the development of tool-use – in both its growth spurts and slack periods. Robert Nadeau writes for example that 'The evolutionary success of our species is commonly expressed in terms of our larger brain size'; brain size 'became an evolutionary advantage at the point at which the excess neuronal capacity allowed us to invent a new tool. [...] *Homo habilis* may have been the first of our ancestors with enough excess neuronal organization, or hardware, to invent the first rudimentary elements of human language ... During the million-year transition from *Homo habilis* to *Homo erectus*, the neocortex, which became the principal centre for association and thought, more than doubled in size'.[430] Philip Tobias formulates this as a succinct equation: 'increase in brain size = gain in neuronal organization = rise in complexity of nervous function = progressively amplified and enhanced cultural manifestations'.[431] And S.L. Washburn specifies: 'Tools, hunting, fire, complex social life, speech, the human way and the brain evolved together to produce ancient man of the genus *Homo*'.[432] Slightly more nuanced, but reaching the same conclusion is Leroi-Gourhan's claim that 'though they started out with the same formula as primates, [humans] can make tools as well as symbols, both of which derive from the same process or, rather, draw upon the same basic equipment in the brain. This leads us to conclude, not only that language is as characteristic of humans as are tools, but also that both are the expression of the same intrinsically human property ... One essential point that we can establish ... is that as soon as there are prehistoric tools, there is a possibility of a prehistoric language, for tools and language are neurologically linked and cannot be dissociated within the social structure of humankind'.[433] Specifying this a bit more, Philip Lieberman views the corporeal prerequisites of tool use in moulding raw materials into finished products – sophisticated motor control, the automatisation of motor processes, and the cognitive

---

428   See Falk 1992; Bickerton 1995, pp. 28–33; pp. 169–70; R. Klein 1989, p. 157.
429   Falk 1992, pp. 169–70.
430   Nadeau, cited in Bickerton 1995, p. 9.
431   Tobias, cited in Bickerton 1995, p. 9.
432   S.L. Washburn, cited in Bickerton 1995, p. 9.
433   Leroi-Gourhan 1993, pp. 113–14.

capacity for intentional thought processes – as also prerequisite for moulding sounds into words and sentences, from which he concludes: 'the brain mechanisms that control speech production probably derive from ones that facilitated precise one-handed manual tasks'.[434]

But the parallel development of speech and language, tool-use and the brain, was not a whiggish arrow of progress. The still primitive Acheulian toolkit produced and used by *Homo erectus* was a great advance over the much more limited Olduwan toolkit of *Homo habilis*. And most seem to agree that *Homo erectus* had a somewhat more developed speech capacity and language than *habilis*.[435] Lieberman, for example, who focuses on supra-laryngeal vocal tract as the indispensable prerequisite of speech production, finds in *Homo erectus* 'the first major change from the nonhuman vocal tract that characterizes all other living terrestrial mammals'. Nevertheless, he (like most) doubts that the airway of *Homo erectus* was adequate to produce the variety of sounds characteristic of modern languages and required for in-depth conversations.[436] Speculating about the linguistic exchange of *Homo erectus*, and judging from the persistence of Aechulian stone technologies that remained unchanged for millennia, Desmond Clark concluded: 'I don't know *what* they were saying, but I bet it was the same things over and over again'.[437]

In short, despite a good deal of often contentious quibbling over the details, most would agree that a primitive 'proto-language' first emerged with *Homo habilis*; that *Homo erectus* took a significant quantitative step in speech and language use, but once attained, these showed little progress, remaining as constant and steady and rudimentary as the species itself; and that only with anatomically modern *Homo sapiens* did 'uniquely human' language appear. Thus, few if any would disagree that the *Homo* line only reached mature speech and language capacity after certain corporeal prerequisites were fulfilled, most significantly: the development of a supra-laryngeal tract capable or articulating the range of sounds essential to human speech; and a brain of sufficient size and organisation to produce and comprehend verbal signs, words.

6.6.6.3   The Corporeal Prerequisites of Speech

Speaking is of course as much a corporeal activity as it is social. And when it comes to situating its place in relation to the 'science of language (*langue*)', the 'Saussurean' *Course* treats the corporeal prerequisites of speech and the phon-

---

434   Lieberman 1991, p. 4.
435   On the co-evolution of the hominid supralaryngeal tract and the brain, see Appendix 6.5.
436   Lieberman 1991, pp. 53–77.
437   Desmond Clark, cited in Schick and Toth 1993, p. 280.

ological production of signifying sound images in much the same way as it does the 'social' side of speech, namely, as a simple prerequisite: although '[t]he production of sounds [is] necessary for speaking', the 'vocal organs are as external to language/*langue* as are the electrical devices used in transmitting the Morse code to the code itself; and phonation, i.e., the execution of sound-images, in no way affects the system itself'.[438] Phonology, therefore, 'is only an auxiliary discipline and belongs exclusively to speaking'; and 'even after we have explained all the movements of the vocal apparatus necessary for the production of each auditory impression, we have in no way illuminated the problem of language/*langue*'.[439]

Although the temporary neglect of phonological matters is a necessary methodological move, it must not be granted permanent status. The permanent dismissal of such matters ignores the phonational contribution to the texture, the 'sound-shape', of languages and the formation of meaningful linguistic signs.[440] But before those matters can be considered, it is first necessary to address the corporeal prerequisites that make what Darwin called 'phonational movements' possible and that in-form not only speaking/*parole* but also language/*langue* itself. It is worth noting parenthetically that Darwin, in contrast to the sterile notion of language following from its permanent isolation from speaking bodies, had a very corporeal, visceral take on the significance of the 'phonational movements' that were the 'means of development of the voice'; their 'primeval use', he declared, was in the relations between 'the sexes of many animals incessantly call[ing] for each other during the breeding-season' – in which case 'the use of the vocal organs will have become associated with the anticipation of the strongest pleasure which animals are capable of feeling'.[441]

A synthesis of Raymond Tallis's graphic image of words as 'sculptured puff(s) of air' and Susanne Langer's equally apt reference to those 'little mouthy noise[s] we call word[s]' suggests that speaking is a process of 'verbal sculpting' – which points clearly to what should be obvious: that sound is an inescapable dimension of speech and language, and that the product will be a synthesis of the properties of the material of human speech production, air, and of the means of speech production, the supralaryngeal tract.[442] Making the same point about the audial dimension of speech/*langage* in an almost tauto-

---

438 Saussure 1959, p. 18.
439 Saussure 1959, p. 33.
440 The 'sound-shape of language' is the title of a book by Linda Waugh and Roman Jakobson (1979). See below.
441 Darwin, *The Expression of Emotions* in Wilson (ed.) 2006, p. 1308.
442 Tallis 1995, p. 124. Langer 1974, p. 61.

logical statement that has been rendered profound by the general neglect of its content, Roman Jakobson notes that '*we speak in order to be heard*'; and '*it is in order to be understood that we seek to be heard*'.[443] Moreover, the way in which we make ourselves heard, the phonatory speech act, itself plays an essential role in meaning production. Citing Poe's use of the word 'nevermore' in *The Raven*, Jakobson explains that '[t]his expression's value *is not entirely accounted for in terms of its purely semantic value*, narrowly defined, i.e. its general meaning plus its contingent, contextual meanings' [my italics]; and, he emphasises, it is 'certain that variation of its phonic qualities, such as modulation of tone, stress and cadence, the detailed articulation of the sounds and of the groups of sounds, that such variations allow the emotive value of the word to be quantitatively and qualitatively varied in all kinds of ways'. Similarly, Lecercle cites the 'test that [Russian actor/director Konstantin] Stanislavsky imposed on trainee actors: pronounce a simple word – e.g. the exclamation "Good!" – in sixty different ways in order to give the utterance thus produced sixty different meanings'.[444] This prosodic dexterity of the human vocal tract allows us, as Anne Karpf put it, to 'colour our voices with pitch, volume, and tempo' and thus vary the meanings conveyed in and through the speech act itself.[445]

These various modulations and modifications are all effected in the phonatory act; the differing ways of speaking the *same* string of phonemes effects in turn meaningful variations in the emotive value and thus the meaning of the word. And these vocal modulations that modify meaning are made possible by the unique vocal apparatus of *Homo sapiens*. Were the human vocal

---

443 Jakobson 1978, p. 25. Following citation from Jakobson, ibid., p. 2, my italics.
444 Lecercle 2009, p. 115. Lecercle points to Vološhinov as one who made the role of intonation in meaning-production or signification 'not a curiosity or an exception, but the starting-point of analysis' (ibid., p. 109) and as 'one of the few linguists or philosophers to take an interest in the phenomenon of intonation [...] whose contribution to the meaning of an utterance is of the first importance' (ibid., p. 115). See Vološhinov 1973. Rejecting what Vološhinov called the 'abstract objectivism' of the Saussurean-based synchronic structuralist linguistics, and pointing to issues of the life and meaning of signs to be addressed in Part 3, Lecercle adds that 'every sign is multi-accentuated not only because it contains a multiplicity of possible meanings, realised by the use of the sign in concrete interlocution, but in that it is history-laden, in that it sediments the meanings which these realisations have imparted to it' (ibid., p. 109). Similarly arguing against the semiocentrism of the post-Saussurean tradition, Langer writes: 'Of course a word may be used as a sign, but that is not its primary role. Its signific character has to be indicated by some special modification – by a tone of voice, a gesture [...], or the location of a placard bearing the word'. See also Langer 1974, p. 61.
445 Karpf 2006, p. 33. Prosody = patterns of stress and intonation, e.g. an ironic tone can undermine the conventional understanding of a sign's content; or tone alone might communicate emotional states that contrast directly with the content of one's utterances.

apparatus as undexterous as that of our fellow primates, it could only produce a rather limited range of sounds and at best a monotonous because monotonal and therefore meaningfully impoverished language. 'All meaning interchange, whether linguistic or not, depends', as anthropological linguist Mary LeCron Foster reminds, 'upon bodily movements or the result of those movements'. The exchange of meanings in the form of complex verbal messages 'involves nothing more than interaction between surfaces in the mouth and throat' – a feat we are so accustomed to performing that we rarely 'wonder at it'; nor do we often 'consider the subtlety of these movements or the complexity of coordination of gesture, sound and sense that is involved'.[446] But before becoming so accustomed to and adept at producing those mouthy little meaningful noises, early hominids underwent 'a whole set of physical adaptations'.[447] The ability of human beings to speak what we know as language(s), and of interlocutors to hear and comprehend spoken language(s) obviously depends on a corporeal set of language-related instruments and capacities that Eric Lenneberg called 'the biological foundations of language'.

Lenneberg approaches the question of language's biological foundation by reformulating it. He feels that the two major antagonists in the debate over language (whom he delineates as linguists focusing on the unique and arbitrary nature of human language vs. animal researchers studying vocal communication in other species) have faulty vision.[448] He doubts neither that human speech and language have a biological foundation nor that they are unique in the animal world; he recognises *both* that communicative speech is an essential dimension of language *and* that 'there is nothing unbiological about recognizing language as unique in the animal kingdom'.[449] And he phrases his ques-

---

446 Le Cron Foster in Sheets-Johnstone 1992, p. 211, p. 209.
447 McCrone 1991, pp. 159–60.
448 Lenneberg's (1967, p. 2) summary of the poles of the debate is not unlike my discussion below of 'inclusionists' and 'exclusionists'. Among the 'linguists' (exclusionists), Lenneberg refers specifically to 'Wittgenstein and his followers' who were the target of Gustav Begmann's coining of the term 'linguistic turn' (see Chapter 8). But the term has been extended to refer to more recent poststructuralist and postmodernist positions that also view language as a cultural convention, as a word game likened 'to the arbitrary set of rules encountered in parlour games or sports'. Lenneberg finds this view short-sighted, for although there is some 'superficial resemblance' between the rules of natural languages and those of parlour games, he points out the 'major and fundamental differences' between them, namely that 'the former are biologically determined [whereas] the latter are arbitrary'. On the other hand, researchers seeking language in animals are engaged in a farsighted inquiry, seeking only the resemblances between languages and animal signalling systems, but neglecting their vast differences.
449 Lenneberg 1967, pp. 265–6.

tions so that both extremes (i.e. the significatory and also the communicative dimensions of language) find a place in the overall framework of his study. He acknowledges that *Homo sapiens* 'is not the only vertebrate that makes noises for communicative purposes'.[450] But rather than asking 'In what respect is learning to speak similar to conditioning or operant learning as studied by animal psychologists?', a question that will lead to an 'endeavour to discover analogies between stimuli, responses, rewards, and the temporal and spatial relationships between them', Lenneberg frames his 'biological inquiry into language' with a more precise question: 'Why can only man learn to speak a natural language?' And in seeking 'to discover biological principles that explain why a single species displays behaviour that is unique in the animal kingdom', he turns 'to anatomy, physiology, and developmental studies for an answer (all of which are biological disciplines)'.

Lenneberg's 'fundamental thesis is that behaviour, in general, is an integral part of an animal's constitution', an 'integral part of the organic whole', and is related to structure and function, one being the expression of the other'.[451] He rejects the analogy that would reduce anatomy and physiology to simple prerequisites by comparing them to the physical nature of the tool, while likening behaviour to the use to which the tool is put; and he argues instead 'that behaviour has the same history and the same origin as form and physiological processes'. Behaviour that is common to all individuals of a species must have a biological foundation; and he aims 'to show how dependent speech- and language-production are on specific physiological propensities' that are 'inextricably intertwined' with 'universal, that is, supracultural, features of language'. While readily admitting the possibility of 'infinitely many variations' in natural languages whose 'outer form [...] may vary with relatively great freedom', he nevertheless insists that the biological foundations of language and human cognition 'set strict limits to the range of possibilities for variations'; beneath the great variation in languages, there is a biologically structured 'underlying type' that 'remains constant'.

The morphological and physiological foundations of speech reside in the uniquely human anatomy and capacities of the facial, laryngeal, and cranial regions that make possible, and in-form, speech. The corporeal toolkit that has 'a decisive influence upon speech sounds' includes: the 'complexity, size, and number of muscles originating particularly in the corner of the mouth [that] greatly facilitate oral motility'; and the 'peculiar anatomy of the lips

---

450   Lenneberg 1967, p. 76. Following citations in this paragraph, ibid., p. 2; p. 4; p. 2.
451   Lenneberg 1967, p. 3. Following citations in this paragraph, ibid., p. 3; p. 76; p. 375.

and the shape of the mouth [that] make possible rapid and air tight closure and sudden explosive opening, both being prerequisite for speech articulation'. The changes in the primate skull that accompanied bidpedalism (its greater size and volume, and the shift in the centre of gravity of the head with the emergence of upright posture) 'affect the entire configuration of the sound-producing structures' by altering 'the internal geometry of all resonating chambers'.[452] Human speech, Michael Kenstowicz notes, has often been described as 'movements made audible by the vocal apparatus': 'after air has been expelled from the lungs into the trachea or windpipe, six separate *articulators* may modify it in linguistically significant ways. These articulators are the *larynx*, the *tongue root*, the *velum*, the *tongue body*, the *tongue blade*, and the *lips*'.[453] These are the key features of the *supralaryngeal vocal tract* that was, in Philip Lieberman's passionate elaboration, decisive for 'the particular form that human language has taken'.[454] The supralaryngeal tract is 'the top half of the airway that leads from the lungs into the atmosphere'. Its most important parts are 'the pharynx and oral and nasal cavities. The tongue, lips, the larynx (which can move upward or downward), and the velum, the soft flexible part of the palate that can close off the nose to the mouth, work together to change the shape of the supralaryngeal vocal tract'.

A contrast of the human vocal apparatus with that of our familiar 'closest primate relatives' reveals that the human supralaryngeal apparatus is just as unique as human speech itself – which is perhaps all the more astounding considering that 'the voice is produced by a system biologically designed not for speech, but for eating and breathing'.[455] Although also capable of emitting complex sounds, the mouths, tongues and laryngeal position of our primate cousins 'are adapted to moving food and drink efficiently into their stomachs'; and the anatomy that enables 'nonhuman mammals [to] simultaneously breathe and drink' also prohibits refined vocal production.[456] In monkeys and apes 'the edges of the vocal folds constitute a somewhat more loosely coupled vocal lip' that enables their vocal cords to vibrate extremely rapidly and to

---

452 All above citations in this paragraph, Lenneberg 1967, p. 34; p. 37; p. 39.
453 Kenstowicz 1994, p. 14.
454 Lieberman 1975, p. 181. Following citations in this paragraph, Lieberman 1991, p. 39. On the anatomy and physiology of speech production see also Kenneth N. Stevens 1998, Chapter 1, pp. 1–53.
455 Karpf 2006, p. 23. Karpf cites French physician Alfred Tomatis: 'We were given a digestive apparatus and a respiratory apparatus, but no specific oral-language apparatus. What ingenious adaptation and unlikely combination was necessary to attain that goal!' (ibid., p. 22).
456 Lieberman 1991, p. 54.

'achieve fundamental frequencies much higher than those of the most talented soprano', but does not contribute to clear and distinct articulation.[457] Moreover, the coupling of the nasopharynx to the vocal tract and the inability to close off the nasal passage in sound production make it difficult for chimps to produce 'fully nonnasal sounds which would handicap an animal considerably in terms of phonetic range'. Because the supralaryngeal tract is in other primate species more one-dimensionally harnessed to eating and drinking, 'the animal's larynx', as Lieberman describes, 'rises like a periscope; air goes through the raised larynx to the lungs, while food and water goes [sic] around it to the stomach'; and 'in correlation with the high position of the larynx, animals have long, thin tongues positioned entirely in their mouths'.[458] Given the anatomy of their nose, mouth, and throat, non-human anthropoids 'are unable to produce the voluntary muscular movements that underlie human speech' and 'have difficulty in the *intentional*, voluntary control of their vocal signals'.

In the adult human airway, by contrast, 'a round, "fat" tongue projects down into the throat. Half of the tongue forms the lower boundary of the mouth, half the anterior boundary of the pharynx. The human larynx cannot reach the opening to the nose because it is positioned at the lower end of the tongue'. With this configuration, 'air, liquids, and solid food make use of the common pharyngeal pathway, sliding past the laryngeal opening to the lungs'. Humans, accordingly, 'are more liable than other terrestrial mammals to choke when they eat because food can fall into the larynx, obstructing the pathway into the lungs. The human configuration is also less efficient for chewing because the palate ... and mandible ... are relatively shorter than in nonhuman primates and archaic hominids'. The crowding of the teeth in the smaller human jaw presents 'the possibility of infection from impacted wisdom teeth – a condition that was usually fatal until the introduction of anaesthesia in dentistry in the nineteenth century'. What made these adverse consequences evolutionarily worthwhile is that 'the only thing to which the adult supralaryngeal vocal tract is better suited in humans than in other animals is the production of the sounds of human speech'. As Darwin had already noted, 'a system that was initially adapted for breathing and eating was preadapted for a new function – speech – by changes in the shape of the tongue, the position of the larynx, and the supporting skeletal structures'.[459] And Lieberman similarly concludes: 'The human larynx is ... adapted for efficient phonation at the expense of respiratory

---

457 This and following citation, S. Anderson 2004, pp. 176–7.
458 Lieberman 1991, p. 54. Following citations in this paragraph, p. 51; p. 52.
459 Except the last, all citations in this paragraph from Lieberman 1991, pp. 54–6. Last citation, Lieberman 1975, p. 27.

efficiency. ... The human vocal tract in a sense represents the most recent stage of a long evolutionary process in which various anatomical specializations have been added to the respiratory system making it a more effective instrument for communication'.[460]

Though the use of the supralaryngeal tract for vocalisation is not an 'optimal' system, it is one that 'works', and obviously does so in an incomparably superior manner.[461] The 'relatively small mouth and the highly mobile powerful lips', Lenneberg explains, 'allow instantaneous building up of air pressure followed by sudden release employed in the labial stops p and b ... If the release of the lips is less sudden and closure sustained in the presence of vocalization, the sound m is produced. The intricate muscular anatomy around and in the corners of the mouth also comes regularly into play during the production of all vowels and labio-dentals such as f, v, w, and wh'.[462] Moreover, although human internal vocal organs have the same bones, muscles and soft tissues of other primates, the changes in the skull ('the increase in volume of the brain' and 'the change in posture and the concomitant shift of the centre of gravity of the head') that alter 'the internal geometry' of the vocal tract's 'resonating chambers' enhance the clarity and distinctness of human phonation.[463] Also contributing to that clarity and distinctness is the acoustically productive 'round human tongue'. In contrast to the less nimble chimpanzee tongue that all but fills up the entire oral cavity and renders impossible the production of sounds that require rapid tongue movement, the 'round human tongue', 'moving in the right-angle space defined by the palate and spinal column[,] can generate formant frequency patterns that define quantal sounds'.[464]

The term that perhaps best characterises the anatomical means of human speech production is flexibility – to which considerations of human speech physiology lead us quickly and admiringly to add: a *controlled* flexibility that is the physiological foundation of the human phonation factory and the disciplined creativity of human speech production. Because human vocal cords are stiff at the edges, their tension 'is rather precisely controllable by the intrinsic muscles of the larynx'.[465] And because its air passages can be separated from the nasal cavity, the human supralaryngeal tract can produce a great variety

---

460   Lieberman 1975, p. 27.
461   Lieberman 1991, p. 56.
462   Lenneberg 1967, pp. 38–9.
463   See Lenneberg 1967, p. 39.
464   Lieberman 1991, p. 57. On 'quantal sounds', see below.
465   S. Anderson 2004, pp. 176–7. This section is based on research by Erica Hadley, an undergraduate student in my senior-level seminar on 'A Historical-Materialist Mapping of Human Corporeal Organization'.

of clear and distinct nasal and nonnasal sounds that are more easily identifiable by listeners.[466] Jillyn Smith notes that '[a]s a source of musical sounds, the human voice is most versatile of musical instruments in its possible variations of pitch (roughly corresponding to frequency), loudness, and the quality of sounds that it can produce'.[467]

That flexibility of the human vocal tract stands in sharp contrast to that of our closest relatives, chimps and gorillas. In a musical rendering of that contrast, McCrone likens the 'short and poorly controlled' vocal tract of the latter to 'a rasping bugle', whereas the human voice is a 'richly varied trumpet'. Humans, he explains, 'can make hundreds of different noises because their voice box, or Adam's apple, has dropped deep down the back of the throat and the roof of the mouth has become arched, giving the human air passage the necessary shape and length to make a wide range of sounds. Furthermore, humans have developed a mobile tongue, powerful throat muscles, and strong lips, which allow us 'to "bite" the flow of air into the rapid series of vowels and consonants that make up speech'.[468] Similarly resorting to musical analogy, Lieberman compares the vocal tract's production of human speech with a woodwind instrument's production of music: the puffs of air emitted from the larynx, like those produced by the reeds of the instrument, are 'a rich source of acoustic energy. The airflow enters the supralaryngeal vocal tract which acts as a filter much as does the tube of a woodwind instrument. The musical quality of the notes produced by the instrument depends on the length and shape of the tube, which lets more acoustic energy through at certain frequencies'.[469] The combination of flexibility and control is responsible not only for the musical qualities but also the linguistic capacities of the human vocal instrument. Whereas the more rigid and less controllable chimpanzee vocal tract 'is incapable of producing most of the vowel sounds of human languages ([a], [i], and [u] are beyond its capacity), as well as many consonants (such as the velar sound [k], [g]) [and] distinct nasal and nonnasal sounds ([m] as opposed to [b])', the controlled flexibility of the human supralaryngeal tract enables the production of 'most of the distinctions in vowel and consonant quality that typify human speech' and also the 'high data transmission rate that distinguishes human speech from other vocal signals'.[470]

---

466   Lieberman 1991, p. 44; Lieberman, 1975, p. 61.
467   Jillyn Smith, 1989, p. 24.
468   McCrone 1991, pp. 159–60.
469   Lieberman 1991, p. 41.
470   Lieberman 2006, p. 77.

As creative and productive as the surpralaryngeal phonation factory is, it is intricately enmeshed in a wider physiological ecology involving the respiratory, articulatory, and coordinative aspects of speaking, with whose 'physiological peculiarities' the 'supracultural, features of language appear to be inextricably intertwined'.[471] Pointing to examples such as panting in dogs as a means of cooling, air intakes that change an animal's sound-making or shape during fighting, and the respiratory needs of migratory birds during flight, Lenneberg finds it fairly obvious that 'locomotion, activity cycles, forms of hunting and feeding, the geographical extent of an individual's animal's hunting territory, etc., are all dependent on special adaptations of respiratory patterns'. Speech is one of those 'activity cycles' that requires special respiratory capacities. Perhaps unique to this activity is that '[d]uring speech respiration is not simply a matter of supplying oxygen to the organism in support of some other activity', but is rather a means 'used to perform work' and thus crucial to the mode of speech production itself. This work is characterised by 'the marked increase of thoracic muscular activities, the buildup of subglottal pressure, and the driving of air against a resistance of flow'. 'Since more work is done under these circumstances, it is not surprising that the rate of air-exchange per minute is also increased during speech'. What is surprising, however, is 'the manner in which this is accomplished'; for, 'it is a marked alteration of silent breathing patterns observed under no other conditions but speech. The number of breaths per minute is drastically reduced ...; while inspiration is slightly accelerated, expiration is markedly slowed down, and breathing becomes much deeper'. The 'peculiar changes' (as Lenneberg calls them) that breathing undergoes during the animation of language in speech, perhaps most notably the 'astonishing' human ability to 'tolerate these modifications for an apparently unlimited period of time without experiencing respiratory distress', have clearly affected political culture – 'as is well demonstrated by the interminable speeches with which many a statesman embellishes his political existence. Cloture is dictated by motor fatigue and limited receptivity in the audience – never by respiratory demands'.

Though we are by now used to computers able to convey information at rates infinitely greater than that of oral communication, the biologically conditioned rate at which humans can articulate thoughts and convey meanings is proportionally astonishing in the animal world. In his study of the 'rate of articulatory events', Lenneberg found that the average speaker utters six syllables contain-

---

471 Lenneberg 1967, p. 76. Next citation ibid., p. 77. All following citations in this paragraph, ibid., p. 80.

ing a total of fourteen phonemes per second. In the beginning, before the word, or at least before the word could be spoken with such seeming effortlessness, a rather complex and multi-faceted corporeal logos had developed that was the fundamental and formative prerequisite of speech. While acknowledging that we cannot know exactly how many muscles are involved in and necessary for each speaking second, Lenneberg provides a minimalist description: '[i]f we consider that ordinarily the muscles of thoracic and abdominal walls, the neck and face, the larynx, pharynx, and the oral cavity are all properly coordinated during the act of speaking, it becomes obvious that over 100 muscles must be controlled centrally. Since the passage from one speech sound to another depends ultimately on differences in muscular adjustments, fourteen times per second an 'order must be issued to every muscle', whether to contract, relax, or maintain its tonus'. Lenneberg thus sums up the rate that individual muscular events must occur in speaking as 'of an order of magnitude of several hundred events every second'.[472]

In addition to the corporeal instruments, capacities, and dexterities behind the production, consumption, and comprehension speech, the corporeally constructed nature and rate of speech articulation have a formative impact on the nature of human language, that is: speech is not just a vehicle for the transmission of language, but also a formative factor in language itself. Crucial here, Lieberman explains, is that speech, a system of discrete and meaningful sound distinctions, 'allows us to transmit phonetic "segments" (which are approximated by the letters of the alphabet) at the remarkable rate of up to 25 per second. By contrast, it is impossible to identify non-speech information at rates greater than seven to nine items per second'.[473] Non-speech transmission such as Morse Code is so slow and cumbersome that the memory requires assistance supplied by the written recording of sound-clusters as letters.

---

472 This and previous citation, Lenneberg 1967, pp. 91–2. Lieberman summarises several other relevant pre-cognitive processes that go into speech production under the term 'automatization', the process that 'converts a series of *learned* motor instructions into a 'subroutine' that is stored in the motor cortex and executed as a complete whole', that allows us rapidly and unthinkingly to execute the 'complex voluntary articulatory maneuvers involving the tongue, lips, velum, larynx, and lungs' that allow us to produce in rapid succession differentiated and meaningful sounds. See Lieberman 1991, pp. 48–51.
473 Lieberman 1994, p. 134. Lieberman notes with a tone of astonishment that 'until the 1960s ... it was not realized that speech is itself an important component of the human ability to use language' (ibid., p. 134). As discussed above, the Saussurean dismissal of phonology played a crucial role in that neglect. And since the 1960s, the semiotic-based linguistic turn has again dismissed the possibility that corporeality and the bodily activity of speaking might have any formative influence on meaning.

If our comprehension of a sequence of 'those mouthy little noises we call words' required the same kind of supplementary assistance as deciphering Morse Code, we would, without it, have difficulty remembering the beginning of a long and complex sentence before hearing its end. As it is, 'within one minute of discourse as many as 10 to 15 thousand neuromuscular events occur'; and this 'production of speech and the understanding of language may be sustained for several hours without any interruptions longer than a few minutes' – thus laying the corporeal foundations of, among other things, the filibuster and Fidel's philippics.[474] If we could not speak as rapidly as we do, our languages would doubtless be rather simple since the listener would not be able to remember the significance of the sounds at the beginning of a long sequence. And if we could speak even more rapidly than we do, and beyond the limits of our audial system to receive the ideas signified, the result would be even more chatter with even less art. As Lieberman concludes, 'The high transmission rate of human speech is thus an integral part of our linguistic ability, as it allows complex ideas to be transmitted within the constraints of short-term memory'.[475] That high transmission rate, in turn, is dependent on the kind of sounds that 'can be related to some of the species-specific properties of the human supralaryngeal tract': the 'sounds of human speech have some rather special properties that make rapid acoustic communication possible, given the temporal limitations of the human auditory system'; these therefore and 'no other sounds will do for humans if they wish to communicate at the rates typical of normal human speech'.[476]

Before continuing this inquiry into human speech production, however, it is necessary to turn our attention to the endless and often acrimonious debate over the relation between speaking and language that draws participants from across the disciplinary spectrum (often seemingly under the misguided assumption that disciplinary 'integrity' or 'honour' is at stake). I could not hope to resolve the debate; but in reviewing it, I can delineate my path between and beyond its antagonistic poles.

6.6.6.4 Languaging, Language, and Communication: Interlocution and the Social Side of Speech

Paleoanthropological debates, bogged down as they are by a sparse fossil record that provides little firm footing, are not only contentious, but also swampy; and

---

474 Lenneberg 1967, p. 107.
475 Lieberman 1994, p. 134. On Lieberman's discussion of the capacity of speech production and the human brain, see Appendix 6.6.
476 Lieberman 1975, pp. 67–8.

the argument over language origins is an enormous conceptual quagmire.[477] This is largely because of the wide field of contestants drawn not only from the natural sciences (evolutionary biologists, paleoanthropologists, archaeologists, paleoanatomists,), but also from the social sciences (anthropologists, evolutionary psychologists, cognitive scientists, linguists) and even the human sciences (philosophers and literary critics are eager to contribute). The discussion of language origins is mired down by the fact that the inevitable interpretive differences are intensified by disciplinary specialisation and cross-disciplinary incomprehension resulting from fundamental differences in the definitions of the key terms used in the debate. The question of language origins is not the issue here, but terminological clarity certainly is.[478]

Though some psychologists view the simultaneous holding of antithetical ideas as a cause of 'cognitive dissonance', I would, with one amendment, agree with F. Scott Fitzgerald's rather different position that '[t]he test of a first-rate intelligence is the ability to hold two opposed ideas in mind at the same time and still retain the ability to function'.[479] My amended version considers that ability more modestly as a test, not of 'first-rate intelligence', but of common (dialectical) sense. Be that as it may, the more important point here is that two ideas too quickly assumed to belong to different universes might turn out to be perhaps distant and opposite, but nevertheless related poles of a single planetary continuum. While simultaneously holding two irreconcilably opposed ideas can no doubt cause cognitive dissonance, the failure to distinguish between, and the hasty conflation of, 'difference' and 'contradiction' can also, and just as easily, cause cognitive dogmatism – of a kind that (tied as it is to vested intra- and inter-disciplinary interests) has raised the temperature of debates surrounding language often to fever pitch.

---

477 For a delightful account of the almost soap-operatic drama over (as described by its subtitle) *Controversies in the Search for Human Origins*, see Lewin 1987.

478 To recall my comment on my terminological practice established in Chapter 2: because of the prevalence and clarity of the Saussurean vocabulary in semiotic approaches to language, and because of the easy confusion of those terms in English, I continue my practice of following the English term with its French counterpart in cases of possible ambiguity. In Part 3 I shall argue strenuously for an alternative elaboration of the methodological place-value and consequences of these terms. For now, however, these definitions suffice for the attempt to bring some clarity to a definitional matter that has been the subject of verbally violent battles and that, because of its relevance to a mapping of the corporeal foundations of speech, must be addressed here in a bit more detail: the struggle over *language* and *communication*.

479 F. Scott Fitzgerald, 'The Crack-Up', *Esquire*, February 1936.

The problem, it seems to me, is that the antagonists in these debates about language speak different disciplinary dialects and thus often talk past each other – each referring to the relations between signals and language, communication and signification, in disciplinarily appropriate terms that, however, are too easily wielded parochially. Such conceptual dissonance can foster the cognitive dogmatism that, in turn, promotes an unnecessary polarising of the debate into an incommensurable, untenable, and dysfunctional either/or. What matters for my purposes here is how the key terms of the debate – 'language', 'signals', 'signification' and 'communication' – are defined, and the relations among them delineated. The two diametrically opposed positions that I shall sketch here are not the only ones; but the pre-eminence in their fields of the proponents of each and the often-contentious din of their pronouncements have dimmed other voices. And the purpose of this brief sketch is to suggest how to introduce some categorial order that in turn will help establish the importance of, and place for, a study of the biological foundations of speech, of the corporeal instruments for 'languaging'.

One way to classify the antagonists in this rather cacophonic debate (and the one that suits my purposes) is to differentiate the 'inclusionists' who include communication as part of the definition of language and the 'exclusionists' who exclude it. Inclusionists are most often found among paleoanthropologists, paleoanatomists, paleoarchaeologists, and animal behaviourialists. Inclusionists are generally 'gradualists'; their research focuses on what they view as a long and slow evolutionary process (a kind of dialectic of quantitative changes producing qualitative change or speciation) whereby a particular primate separated itself from its fellow primates, by virtue of its bipedal locomotion, brain development, and capacities to use tools and language. For 'inclusionists', communication is the successful passing of information from one organism to another – a broad enough definition to encompass both signalling and languaging. This inclusion of communication in the definition of language is not (exclusionist accusations notwithstanding) a reduction of the complexities of language to simply an advanced form of signalling. Rather, while acknowledging the vast differences between signalling and languaging, inclusionists view both as not unrelated forms of communication; they thus take a long view that includes consideration of the corporeal and cognitive prerequisites of both signalling and language use. Given these interests, their focus is understandably not on the internal complexities of language as a system of signification through which meaning is expressed – which they do not deny, but do normally neglect.

The understanding of how meaning can be expressed through language is, of course, precisely the concern of the 'exclusionists' who (in general) are found among linguists in the Saussurean and Chomskyan traditions. The insights of this approach into the structure and functioning of language are not in question. The problem, however, is that exclusionists unnecessarily establish a mutually-exclusive binary opposition between signals and communication on the one hand, and language and signification on the other. And this differentiation is then taken as the starting point for a rather circular syllogism that runs something like this:

- The essential property of signals is to communicate information; that of linguistic signs to signify meaning.
- Signalling systems and linguistic sign systems are therefore fundamentally different, incommensurable.
- Since language and communication share no essential properties, language is not (essentially) communicative.

'Exclusionists' obviously do not doubt that language can be used communicatively, but argue rather, with Umberto Eco, that because communication is an exchange of signals rather than signs, then language as a sign system must be essentially something other than (even if it may also function as) communicative.[480] That argument, however, assumes the form of a circular syllogism, based on incommensurately constructed definitions of signals and language and deploying a disproportional correlation: whereas the pair *communication/signals* is a relation between an action and the code that is its means, the pair *language/signs* is redundant, both referring, the latter in general, the former in specific terms, to the code. A construction of action and means properly parallel to *communication/signals* would rather be *speaking (or writing)/language*. This sleight of syllogistic hand results of course in a foregone conclusion that conveniently allows one to acknowledge communication as a possible use of language while abdicating any responsibility to articulate what that means for

---

480   Eco's argument seems to be that a signal triggers a necessary and automatic, reflex-like response which makes it impossible for a signal to lie – the possibility for which Eco sees as the distinguishing feature of a sign: 'Thus semiotics is in principle the discipline studying everything which can be used in order to lie' (Eco 1979, p. 7). This issue of mendacious signs will be addressed in detail below in the Conclusion to Part 3. Though excluding mechanical systems and 'limiting' it to living organisms, Thomas Sebeok has a much broader notion of communication as an exchange, not only of signs, but of signals as well. He insists that 'communication' defined as 'the transmission of any influence from one part of a living system to another part' is 'present in the humblest forms of existence, whether bacteria, plants, animals, or fungi, and, moreover, in their component parts, such as subcellular units ..., cells, organelles, organs, and so forth'; and his list includes DNA as well. And he insists that those transmissions, regardless of whether in the form of signals or language, are 'messages' which are 'the subject matter of semiotics'.

both speech and language. In so doing, exclusionists posit an abyss between language and the communicative signalling of other animal species and verge (by default if not intent) on treating language as *sui generis*.

Whether by intention or default, the poles of the debate have been established with the inclusionists acknowledging the similarities in difference between animal signalling and human language, while the exclusionists hypostatise difference into absolute incommensurability. Neither side seems able (or willing) to hear the qualifications made by the other – and not least because both the pertinence of this definitional debate over language and communication to the debate over the evolutionary origins of language, and the often-inflated disciplinary stakes that its antagonists wager, help to raise its temperature. The evolutionary argument, though not irrelevant, is addressed briefly in an albeit lengthy appendix.[481] But to orient my venturing into questions of the corporeal prerequisites of speech, it would be helpful to get a sense of how the stakes are inflated.

Inclusionists fear that the digging of an abyss between communication and language would be tantamount to digging an abyss between *Homo sapiens* and other animal species. Their fears are justified; for in order to preserve the purity of language from communicative contamination, exclusionists essentially treat language as precisely that which differentiates humans *from* animals. This exclusionist position is expressed rather explicitly by one of Chomsky's admirers, Derek Bickerton, who tried to rescue the master's teachings from his own 'an-evolutionary' inclinations.

In seeking the key to the evolution of language, Bickerton claims to have discovered a 'Rubicon' between what are, on his presupposition, incommensurables, namely: communication and language. Contrasting the expression of meaning through language with the 'mere' instrumentality of signalling communication, Bickerton writes: '[i]f one envisages language as no more than a skill used to express and communicate the products of human thought, it becomes ipso facto impossible to regard language as the Rubicon that divides us from other species'.[482] Having imagined a vast riverine divide between

---

[481] For an overview of 'gradualist' and 'salatationist' positions on the evolution of language that fairly closely correspond to what I call the 'inclusionst' and 'exclusionist' positions, see Appendix 6.7.

[482] Bickerton 1995, p. 9. Here a brief explanation of why I spend much more time on Bickerton's 'exclusionist' argument than I have on the 'inclusionist' position. Although it seems at first glance impossible to exaggerate the significance of language, Saussurean-based structuralist and poststructuralist/postmodernist analyses (as I argue in Chapter 8) have managed to do exactly that in attributing to language (elevated by Saussure to the status of '*patron général*') powers of immaculate conception; and (as I argue in Chapter 9) the same

communication and language, and having postulated a taxonomical chasm between humans and (other) animal species, Bickerton finds our hominid ancestors stuck on the communicative bank, and capable only of signalling.

But Bickerton's antithetical pairing of communication and language is another conceptual thimblerig. Communication and language are certainly incomparable – but not for the reason Bickerton advances. Though qualitatively different, apples and oranges are also comparable as separate but equal species of, siblings within, the 'fruit' family. Communication and language, however, belong to altogether different orders of things, different taxonomic phyla: communication is an *act*, a *mode*, of expressing and exchanging meaning; language is a system of signs, a *semiotic means*, through which, if used, meaning can be expressed (and exchanged). Neglecting that not irrelevant matter, Bickerton (mis)allocates the *act* of communicative expression and the linguistic *means* of expression to the same taxonomic plane and, without further contextualisation, proceeds with his evaluation. The unsurprising, because foregone, conclusion of his comparison is a contrast of incommensurables. The significance of the great linguistic leap forward in the *Homo* line can hardly be exaggerated, and it is certainly not in question here. What is, rather, in question here is how Bickerton explains language evolution with another circular syllogism enabled by a sleight of definitional hand that establishes a 'Rubiconical' divide between 'animal' communication and 'human' language. It might therefore prove useful to look more closely at Rubicons, both real and metaphorical.

The actual Rubicon is a rather modest river: only 50 miles long, narrow, and shallow. The metaphorical Rubicon obviously acquired its momentous significance not from its unimposing physical attributes, but from its geo-political significance as the border separating the Roman Republic proper from the territory Cisalpine Gaul, the region south of the Alps governed in 49 B.C.E. by Julius Caesar – a border across which provincial governors were forbidden to bring their armies. The metaphor is based on the epoch-making historical significance of Caesar's crossing that initiated a 22-year period of struggle marking the end of the Republic and the emergence of its (alleged) antithesis, the

---

power has been conferred in much semiotic analysis of culture. Though poststructuralists and postmodernists would no doubt be aghast at what they would consider Bickerton's 'humanism', his analytical line, that treats language not only as *sui generis*, but also, and quite literally, as that which, allegedly untainted by communication, alone creates meaning and thus alone turned hominids into humans, runs parallel to theirs. Clarifying this not immediately obvious parallelism, and the conceptual muddle surrounding the discussion of communication and language, of signals and linguistic signs, not only contributes to the critique of 'linguistocentrism' that runs through this entire work, but also helps create the conceptual clarity that better puts my own argument in relief.

Empire. The metaphorical significance of Caesar's crossing of the river thus derived, not from its physical difficulty, but from its political consequences.

Bickerton initially seems to have mistaken the magnitude of the metaphor as the measure of the actual distance between river's banks, thus swelling the tiny tributary into a non-traversable expanse – the crossing of which then appears an all but impossible physical feat. It is therefore a bit curious that he assiduously whittles away, shrinking the divide between communication and language – but maintaining all the while his conviction that it remains unbridgeable. He finds 'proto-languages' and 'pidgins' (forms that contain 'arbitrary, meaningful symbols but lack any kind of syntactic structure') on the far evolutionary bank, while situating 'creoles' (which also use arbitrary, meaningful symbols and have, in addition, 'features of universal grammar') on the near bank – and he insists that 'the differences between them are both wide and deep'.[483] By the time he is finished, he has effectively reduced the metaphorically-implied great distance between the banks of this metaphorical river to the rather modest span of the actual Italian river. Nevertheless, he retreats into the metaphor, now repurposed to imply 'impassability' rather than 'momentously significant' – on the basis of which he continues to insist that there can exist no purely semiotic logic that could get us across the river. There remains an unbridgeable abyss between incommensurables. The twain never had met, nor ever shall; for, 'between protolanguage and language, we find nothing'.[484] *Hic Rubiconus, hic saltus.*

The unwillingness to acknowledge the possibility of evolutionary links between incommensurables produces some odd explanations. Having created a riddle by establishing his metaphorical Rubicon as a rift that cannot be bridged, but that has somehow been crossed, Bickerton constructs an overly creative solution. The effect of his reflections on proto-languages and pidgins is to narrow the gap such that it might now be crossed with a metaphorical mini-leap of monumental consequence. And at this point Bickerton introduces a *deus ex machina* that effects a kind of 'punctuated equilibrium' in language evolution. But his is a punctuation measured not in geological, but rather in ontogenetic time – and one that genetically transports our communicative hominids across this now shrunken gap to the linguistic bank of the river. It seems likely, he explains, 'that the development that gave us language took place in a single individual at a not very remote periods and that the progeny of this individual spread throughout the then inhabited world and superceded previous hominid

---

483   Calvin and Bickerton 2000, p. 257, p. 250; Bickerton 1990, p. 126.
484   Bickerton 1995, p. 71.

populations in all parts of it'.[485] As Steven Pinker rather bluntly but not inaccurately satirises Bickerton's 'jaw-dropping suggestion', 'reminiscent of hurricanes assembling jetliners': what got the *Homo* line across the Rubicon was 'a single mutation in a single woman, African Eve, [that] simultaneously wired in syntax, resized and reshaped skull, and reworked the vocal tract'.[486] Pinker counters with the modest and (in my view) much more plausible suggestion that 'the languages of children, pidgin speakers, immigrants, tourists, aphasics, telegrams, and headlines show that there is a vast continuum of viable languages systems varying in efficiency and expressive power' which, he adds, is 'exactly what the theory of natural selection requires'.

Having amplified the magnitude of challenge in crossing the riverine referent and thereby altering the meaning of the metaphor to signify an impassable barrier between communicative signals and meaningful language, Bickerton then redeploys it. On the basis of this allegedly insurmountable distance between communication and language, he digs a taxonomic abyss and sets communicatively signalling animals and linguistically-abled humans on opposite sides of an unbridgeable divide. Following this circular path, he is then able to conclude what he had already presumed, namely: that language and communication must be incommensurable. For, if language were contaminated by communication, it would no longer be a uniquely human attribute – and such contamination of language by communication would, in this circle of circles, leave us no means of differentiating humans from animals. It is, however, not necessary to deny the admittedly vast and qualitative difference between the expressive power of language and the limited range of signals in order to acknowledge that they might be genealogically more closely related than exclusionists imagine – nor (as should be obvious) need the very corporeally-rooted human capacity for language be mistaken as a sign that *Homo sapiens* is not an animal species.[487]

---

485   See Bickerton 1990, p. 174.
486   This and following citation, Pinker 1994, p. 366.
487   Bickerton's logic that because signals and language are qualitatively different, they cannot be genealogically linked leads him to a kind of evolutionary creationism: that language must have sprung fully grown from the womb of a linguistic African Eve. That qualitatively different entities can be genealogically linked certainly should not be surprising to anyone who accepts a Darwinian explanation of the origin of species. The German language makes a distinction between '*Genesis*' and '*Geltung*'. *Geltung* is a notoriously difficult term to translate into English; German-English dictionaries offer 'validity', standing, and 'worth' among other possibilities. In this context, however, it is not illegitimate to articulate the difference as that between the 'genesis' or genealogy of an entity and its 'being' or 'nature'.

Bickerton would, presumably, not deny that humans are animals. However, the same logic that refuses to recognise language and signals as rather distinct, but not unrelated genera of the family 'communication' would also fail to see the *Hominidae* familial link between chimpanzees and humans. The problem here too is that an exclusive focus on the uniquely human attribute of language subjects human belonging to the animal kingdom to the oft-encountered insidious bias of neglect: for if language were considered the only uniquely human characteristic, then the entire and very unique corporeal organisation (in which the corporeal instruments of speech production are embedded) that consigns humans to the animal kingdom must be considered irrelevant to human being.

Because of its corporeal organisation, every species is, as I have often noted, species-centric. But in order to avoid the 'anthropo*ego*centrism' or 'anthropo-hubrism' noted above, and to understand the uniquely human significance of language, we must rid ourselves of the intertwined intellectual conceits that animals merely react whereas humans think, and that animals only "communicate" whereas people only 'significate'. If the best we can do is insist that only language separates us from (other) 'animals', if we fail to recognise human corporeal organisation as that which differentiates the human animal from all other species (in this respect we are, of course, not unusual, since each and every species has its unique species-specific corporeal organisation), and as that which also enables that human animal to engage in 'languaging' – if we cannot grasp this, it is doubtful that we might heed the Delphic injunction to know ourselves. Thus, before pencilling the final strokes in this sketch of the corporeal instruments and capacities for speech and language use, it is necessary to clear away the major definitional obstacle that has, in my view, hindered that self-knowledge – and to do so by forging an alternative to the cognitive dogmatism resulting from an unnecessary either/or relation in definitions of communication and language and by replacing it with a both/and.

Jean-Jacques Lecercle in *A Marxist Philosophy of Language* presents a conceptual wrinkle to the communication question that might assist in resolving this dilemma – at least for my purposes here. In his book with which I otherwise agree almost completely, Lecercle delivers a rather categorical critique of the notion that 'language/*langage* is an instrument of communication'.[488] Lecercle's very understandable problem with the term 'communication' is that it has become inextricably intertwined with the capitalist communication industry – an industry advertising 'enticing promises' for the flourishing of the

---

488 Lecercle 2009, p. 212. French original Lecercle, *Une philosophie marxiste du langage*, p. 197. Citation of Cameron 2000, pp. 214–15. Lecercle's reference is to Cameron 2000. Worth not-

individual subject by virtue of its ability to convey clear and useful information that would allow the individual to gain control, sovereignty, over his/her own life. Lecercle borrows Deborah Cameron's term 'verbal hygiene' to expose how the communications industry sanitises its practice of prohibiting freedom of expression among its employees and limiting it as much as possible among its customers by convincing them that buying their products will develop their individuality. But just as adamantly as he (like 'exclusionists') rejects the communicative understanding of language, Lecercle (unlike the 'exclusionists') not only insists that language is a 'social practice', an act of interlocution, but treats it essentially as such. Recalling Nietzsche's aphoristic warning that 'only that which has no history can be defined', we should cast an etymological glance at 'communication' and also at Lecercle's preferred term, 'interlocution'.

According to the *Oxford English Dictionary*, both interlocution and communication derive from Latin: the former a combination of *inter* meaning 'between' and 'loqui' to speak, thus speaking between people; 'the action (on the part of two or more persons) of talking or replying to each other', 'the action of sharing in something', 'talk, conversation, discourse, dialogue'. And communication derives from 'communicatio', 'the action of sharing or imparting'; typical fourteenth-century Anglo-Norman usages include the 'fact of having something in common with another person or thing; affinity; congruity', 'interpersonal contact, social interaction, association, intercourse' (the latter both social and sexual). In short, the two words were virtually synonymous.

Contrast these with their current usages provided in the Wikipedia on-line dictionary: the meaning of interlocution has changed little; an interlocutor is 'one who takes part in a dialogue or conversation' implying that interlocution is a dialogue or conversation. The meaning of 'communication' has by contrast narrowed noticeably and become in fact a one-way street: 'the imparting or exchanging of information of news'; and the Wikipedia Thesaurus lists as synonyms: 'transmission, conveyance, divulgence, disclosure; dissemination, promulgation, broadcasting'. Given Wikipedia's ubiquity, it seems that Lecercle is right, that the communications industry has, at least temporarily, won the definitional battle over the meaning of 'communication'. I will therefore in the following adopt Lecercle's use of 'interlocution' to signify that language use is not a relation between a transmitter and a receptor, but 'communicative' in an older sense: a social practice necessarily involving interlocutors, that is: speaking and listening human beings.[489]

---

ing, too, are the affinities between his notion of communication and Herbert Marcuse's concepts of 'repressive desublimation' and 'one-dimensional' language.

489 A further comment is in order here. As a Marxist, Lecercle, not surprisingly, insists on the

By adopting Lecercle's notion of 'interlocution' (and by using 'communication' in the following as synonymous with it[490]), it is possible to bring together the important points raised by each side that (passionate partisanship notwithstanding) need not be considered incommensurable opposites. The 'exclusionist' emphasis on the unique properties of linguistic meaning-production will be addressed in Part 3. Pertinent here, however, is the 'inclusionist' consideration of the corporeal prerequisites of (vocal) communication and of the forms of cognition underlying language use. The interlocutory process requires speakers and listeners (that is: bodies with appropriate instruments to speak and hear) and a world about which is spoken (even if the things to which speaking refers can be apprehended only in refracted form). While language should not be reduced to just an exercise of the vocal cords in communicative speech acts, it is myopic to claim that vocalisation and interlocution, in short, speaking (*parole*), is not as integral a part of the faculty of speech (*langage*) as language (*langue*). If, as is rightly claimed, there is more to languaging than 'just' communication, it can with at least equal justice be claimed that there is more to the human significance of speech (*langage*), and even to language (*langue*), than just syntactical structure and semantic contents. The exclusivist focus on the verbal code or semiotic system results in a rather one-dimensional notion of the human capacity for speech and use of language, and in an equally one-dimensional view of our species as, depending on hypostatising nuance, *Homo linguisticus*, *Homo grammaticus*, or *Homo significus*, but not as *Homo loquens*.[491] My interest here, however, is in the latter, whom John McCrone dubbed 'the ape that spoke' or, more appropriately: 'the apes who spoke' –

---

inevitable role of class and, as somewhat of an Althusserian Marxist, on the interpellation of subjects through language use: 'inter-subjectivity emergences from interlocution, which has a relationship of mutual presupposition with social relations, the relations of labour and the division of labour, which are power relations' (Lecercle 2009, p. 186). It is interesting to note that despite the numerous similarities between the two, Rossi-Landi eschews the term 'intersubjective' and insists that 'we must use the terms "collective" or "communitary" rather than "intersubjective", since the latter presupposes 'the simultaneous presence of independent subjects' (ibid., p. 38). These matters are of course important, but must be passed over for now; for what is at issue here is establishing the social, interlocutive nature of language use in speech acts – which, as I shall argue in Part 3, has crucial consequences for determining the relation between sign and referent.

490   This synonymous treatment of the two terms is necessary because several of the authors I cite in the following use 'communication' in the same way that Lecercle uses 'interlocution'.

491   To avoid charges of 'phonocentrism' such as those Derrida levied on Saussure, it is worth remembering that though often mistaken to mean 'spoken', 'verbal' refers, as the *Oxford English Dictionary* registers, to 'words', regardless of whether spoken or written.

dialogically, that is: to one another – which presumes not only the social character of interlocution, but also apes possessing the corporeal instruments that enabled them to produce speech.[492]

That speech/*langage* in general, and its two component parts, language/*langue* and speaking/*parole*, are 'social' is universally acknowledged. What that means, however, is less often articulated. Again, we can take the Saussurean *Course in General Linguistics* as a paradigmatic case – this time of depopulating the social: 'In separating language [*langue*] from speaking [*parole*] we are at the same time separating: (1) what is social from what is individual; and (2) what is essential from what is accessory and more or less accidental'; language (*langue*) 'is the social side of speech'. Since the presumably social interaction of speaking, of interlocuting speakers, is 'dispense[d]' with in order to make 'the science of language ... possible', we are left wondering what could possibly be meant by the claim that *langue* is the 'social side of speech'.[493] The *Course* does allude to two diachronic moments of the 'social side of speech': one pertains to origins: 'speaking is necessary for the establishment of language and historically its actuality always comes first'; and the other pertains to history, the changes in languages over time. Both of these moments require speakers speaking; but as diachronic and contingent, they are excluded from a synchronic science of language.[494] With the very social acts of speech production and interlocution eliminated, the 'social side of speech' is incorporated into language in a very disembodied manner: 'every means of expression used in society is based, in principle, on collective behaviour or – what amounts to the same thing – on convention'[495] Here, while the presence of the social *qua* convention is acknowledged 'in principle', the 'social' is deprived of any meaningful presence by the dissolution of the speakers responsible for originating, using, and changing linguistic meanings into the anaemically abstract category of 'convention'. With the very social acts of language production and language use dismissed,

---

492   The use of 'dialogically' here is obviously a reference to the notion, first expressed by Mikhail Bakhtin (1981), of the dialogic character of language and literature – with which I fully agree. Roman Jakobson, among many others, seconded Bakhtin's suggestion and approached language as dialogical, insisting also that not only interlocution among people, but also monologue and inner speech are dialogical in nature. See Jakobson 1990, pp. 94–102.

493   Saussure 1959, p. 18; See Part III, 'Diachronic Linguistics' for discussion of linguistic changes.

494   The rather problematic claim that the diachronic must be excluded, not only temporarily, but once and for all, in order to establish a (synchronic) science of linguistics will be addressed in Chapter 8.

495   Saussure 1959, p. 68.

the 'social' wafts through language/*langue* as an inert and inefficacious entity whose *raison d'être* is simply 'being-there' – but without occupying any real space worthy of articulation.

From a historical-materialist perspective, however, the problem is not the bracketing of interlocuting subjects in order to focus on the internal logic of linguistic sign systems; such bracketing is just as necessary to deciphering language as a semiotic system as was Marx's self-consciously temporary abstraction from both real people and 'really-existing' capitalist societies to his deciphering of the structure and logic of the capitalist system of production. The problem lies not in the isolation of language/*langue* as an object of study, but rather in turning what should be only a temporary isolation for analytical purposes into an ontologically permanent one that excludes all the crucial diachronic factors pertaining to the actual life of language in the world. From a historical-materialist perspective, the human significance of speech and its components, language and speaking, cannot be fully understood if the interlocuting creators and users of language, and also their various reasons and usages, are precluded from consideration. A permanent (as opposed to a methodologically temporary) divorce of language from interlocution abstracts language from the social context without which, it seems fair to say, language (as we know it) could not be used, and thus in all likelihood, as even the *Course* admits, would not have evolved.

While hominid sociability established the interlocutive context for language evolution, it is also true that that sociability existed well before the language capacities of anatomically modern *Homo sapiens*. And the more proximate prerequisite of language-use was the development of the corporeal means of, and capacity for, speech production – capacities whose exercise was dependent on restructuring and refunctionalising the corporeal instruments of human vocalisation. The first corporeal fact to note here is that languaging (unlike seeing, smelling, tasting, or hearing) possesses no *single* organ; not only does it require bodily organs like the ear and larynx that 'are not specialist organs' devoted only to speech, but moreover 'the organs in question ... *do not belong to the same individual*'.[496] Thus the organs of linguistic intercourse (like its sexual counterpart) render it a social practice; in languaging, interlocutory intercourse is effected by undulating waves of sound: As Anne Karpf explains: 'Ear and voice complement each other: both are activated by the movement of air. Just as air makes the larynx vibrate, so it's the air in the form of sound waves that causes

---

496 Lecercle 2009, p. 39. Lecercle's comments are, not surprisingly, consistent elaborations of Marx's reflections on the social character of language. For some perspectives on the social character of language, see Appendix 6.8.

the eardrum to vibrate – the basis of hearing. To listen to someone's voice is therefore "a partnership of vibration". The ear has even been called a "sonic mouth", since some of the same organs in the body form them both. By ensuring that the ear canal resonates at the same frequencies as the vocal tract, nature has thoughtfully matched the reception organ with the production one, and developed a human ear with the precise properties best needed to hear the human voice'.[497] While acknowledging that the ear of the interlocutor is essential to the very social practice of languaging, the primary concern here is with the means of speech production: the vocal apparatus.

6.6.6.5 Vocal Learning and Communication

'The most significant motivation for human communication is', Ian Cross et al. argue, 'the sharing of experience; that is, wanting another to see, feel, think, or know what I see, feel think, or know'.[498] Most mammals are well endowed with multiple means of expression and can communicate their emotions through various kinds of bodily gesture (facial, manual, postural) as well as vocally. Humans are quite adept and dexterous in using all those modes of expression, but, like songbirds, excel in vocal communication. While the vocal communication of songbirds is one-dimensional, hominids have of course expanded their expressive universe through the development of speech and language. Nevertheless, because singing and speaking are modes, and song and language forms, of oral expression and communication, it is worth lingering a bit over the affinities between these two most developed forms of learned vocal communication.

Although communication by means of emitting a fixed and innately acquired repertoire of sounds is widespread in the animal kingdom, few species are capable of vocal *learning*. Vocal learning is a rather more complex affair of knowing when to do and when not to do, that is: of controlling expression. While 'we share many of our repertoire of screams and groans, growls and whimpers with apes, monkeys, and other creatures', what differentiates learned from instinctual vocal expression is the ability to control *when* to express, when, for example, to submit to cultural proscriptions on uninhibited vocal sounds that 'only survive in rituals or reappear when we're *in extremis* – for example in pain or grief'. In this sense, then, 'human beings are not only vocal learners

---

497 Karpf 2006, p. 27. The quotations within this passage are Karpf's citations of Alfred Tomatis, an ear, nose and throat doctor who developed effective techniques in treating singers with vocal problems whose source he traced to hearing difficulties.
498 Cross et al. in Arbib 2013, p. 548.

but also vocal unlearners: an important part of acquiring social skills is learning to suppress emotional expression in the voice'.[499] The 'ability to regulate the expression of emotion [...] may differentiate humans from other species' – and without which extended and coherent speech would be impossible.[500]

Although several mammalian species exhibit some vocal learning capacity (whales and dolphins, seals and sea lions, bats and perhaps elephants), hominids are the only primates with such skills.[501] And the only other creatures in the same vocal-learning category with humans, albeit in a very distant second place, are songbirds. Although perhaps surprising, the link between humans and songbirds is not fortuitous. Whether the medium is music or language (or both), research has shown that songbirds and humans have a similarly structured forebrain region that is dedicated to vocal learning – that 'indeed birds may have similar brain structures for generating song as humans have for learning vocalization'.[502] Darwin recognised that humans and songbirds are in a vocal-learning league of their own, and hypothesised that the lineage of languaging might be traced back to singing: 'some early progenitor of man probably used his voice largely [...] in producing true musical cadences, that is in singing; we may conclude from a widely-spread analogy that this power would have been especially exerted during the courtship of the sexes, serving to express various emotions as love, jealousy, triumph, and serving as a challenge to their rivals'.[503]

Taking an 'ornithomorphic perspective', cognitive biologist W.T. Fitch and neurobiologist E.D. Jarvis offer a 'birds-eye view' on song and speech.[504] Despite the

---

499   Karpf 2006, p. 51.
500   Ian Cross et al., in Arbib 2013, p. 550.
501   See Fitch and Jarvis in Arbib, 2013.
502   Karpf 2006, p. 50. Karpf bases herself here on the research of Erich D. Jarvis et al., 'Behaviourally Driven Gene Expression Reveals Song Nuclei in Hummingbird', *Nature*, 406, 10 August 2000. See also Dina Lipkind et al., 'Stepwise Acquisition of Vocal Combinatorial Capacity in Songbirds and Human Infants', *Nature*, 498, 6 June 2013, pp. 104–8, who find that the 'babbling of pre-lingual human infants showed a similar pattern' of development to that of songbirds.
503   Darwin, *The Descent of Man* in Wilson (ed.) 2006, p. 810.
504   See also Hockett in Wang 1982. Hockett employs a 'comparative method modelled on that of the zoologist' whose 'frame of reference must be such that all languages look alike when viewed through it, but such that within it human language as a whole can be compared with the communicative systems of other animals, especially the other hominoids, man's closest living relatives, the gibbons and great apes'; the focus must be on 'the basic features of design that can be present or absent in any communicative system, whether it be a communicative system of humans, of animals, or of machines'. Hockett's study

profound differences between language and music, [both] take the vocal output mechanism as their default in all cultures (via song or speech), and in both domains the cultural transmission and elaboration of songs or words requires an inborn capacity for vocal learning. Song and speech thus share a core similarity: reliance on vocal learning. From a bird's eye view, song and speech can be seen as different manifestations of the same underlying fundamental ability: to hear a complex sound in the environment and then produce a close imitation yourself.[505]

'Ornithomorphically' glancing at hominids 'from a neural or comparative viewpoint', Fitch and Jarvis find that a 'strong distinction between learning and production of human speech and song breaks down ... because both behaviours may be different ways of expressing the same specialized evolved mechanisms for vocal learning'; and they conclude that 'complex vocal learning in humans is also a necessity for the culture-specific flexibility required to produce human speech and song'.[506]

In a concluding co-authored essay by several contributors (including Fitch and Jarvis) to a Strüngmann Forum volume on *Language, Music, and the Brain*, the authors 'propose' that, 'rather than discrete domains', music and language 'constitute a continuum' that 'can be interpreted in terms of at least two dimensions, the first running from definite to indefinite meanings and the second from greater to lesser affective potency':

> Music's power to form complex patterns (enabled by its generativity), its frequent repetition of elements (in comparison with language), together with its iconicity (i.e., its exploitation of biologically significant aspects of sound) endow it with an ambiguity and an immediacy that can be emotionally compelling. Language's capacity to formulate and exchange

---

yielded '13 design-features' for which 'there is solid empirical justification for the belief that all languages of the world share every one of them'; and although 'at first sight some appear so trivial that no one looking just at language would bother to note them[, they] become worthy of mention only when it is realized that certain animal systems – and certain human systems other than language – lack them' (Hockett in Wang 1982, pp. 5–6). The design-features are: vocal-auditory channel; broadcast transmission and directional reception; rapid fading (transitoriness); interchangeability; total feedback; specialisation; semanticity; arbitrariness; discreteness; displacement; productivity; traditional transmission; duality of patterning (ibid., p. 7).

505   Fitch and in Arbib 2013, p. 500.
506   Fitch and Jarvis in Arbib 2013, p. 511. On the similarities in the vocal learning process in songbirds and human infants, see Lipkind et al. 2013, pp. 104–8.

complex propositions allows it to represent an infinite variety of meanings and frees it, in principle, from the exigencies of affect. However, the discrete tones and pitch sets that supply grist for the musical mill in most cultures are rather unique to music. Also, for humans the speaking voice is a highly significant biological sound whose emotional colouring draws on our repertoire of innate nonverbal emotional expressiveness. We routinely express emotion through the modality of speech rather than music; nothing compels music to convey emotion.[507]

And 'overall', they conclude, 'no single criterial attribute, save perhaps that of propositionality, distinguishes between language and music clearly and comprehensively'.[508] And while this 'single criterial attribute' of 'propositionality' produces an immense gap between language and music and an even larger one between the communicative capacities of humans vs. other animals, that discussion can be postponed; for of interest here is the matter of vocal learning and meaningful sound production.

'Singing', insists Alfred Tomatis, an ear, nose, and throat doctor who studies and treats singers with vocal problems, 'is a basic human function', 'a response to the need for self-expression and self-exploration'; '[i]t creates body awareness and allows the singer to explore the environment through the impact on the body of returning sound. Even more important, it feeds and stimulates the nervous system'.[509] Whether or not human beings sing, as Tomatis insists, 'by instinct' or whether singing should be considered, as some have argued, a direct ancestor of language, it is not so far-fetched to note with Tomatis that '[l]anguage has rhythms, nuances, inflections, and timber, exactly like music', nor to conclude that 'the ability to intone must have come before spoken language'.[510] This view seems substantiated by Cross et al. who approach music and language 'as constituting different manifestations of the human capacity to communicate' (which 'may take very different forms in different cultural contexts'), and search for 'proximate motivators' that 'are likely to apply to a broader range of communicative systems than language alone'. Among these proximate motivators, they find that '[f]or vocal-learning species, there seems

---

507 Ian Cross et al. in Arbib 2013, p. 544.
508 Cross et al., in Arbib 2013, p. 550. Differentiating the levels of vocal capacity, the authors explain: 'All vocal animals produce innate calls expressive of emotional states. ... In addition, a subset of these callers acquires and produces learned song. ... Finally, a single species (humans) add a third something, dependent on the crux of the second (i.e. vocal production learning); namely spoken language and vocal music' (ibid., p. 555).
509 Tomatis 2005, pp. 7–8.
510 Tomatis 2005, p. 5.

to be an intrinsic pleasure in vocalizing (e.g., in forms such as babbling, subsong, or imitation)' – as is evidenced by infants who 'vocalize well before their vocalizations are intentionally communicative, perhaps because vocalizing is intrinsically pleasurable'.[511] Etymologically speaking, 'aesthetics', as Herbert Marcuse reminds, pertains primordially to the senses and derivatively to beauty.[512] And these musings on the vocal-learning based affinities between music and language and on the 'intrinsic pleasure' in vocalising seem to point toward what might be called the aesthetics of linguistic sound(s) – to which I return in concluding the following ruminations on the (corporeally-grounded) production of phonetically meaningful sounds.

6.6.6.6 'The Sound Shape of Language'[513]

Because the Saussurean *Course* defines the linguistic sign as a 'sound image' (*image acoustique*), Derrida was not incorrect in levying a phonocentric charge against it.[514] But the phonocentrism of the *Course* is rather muted. For, having defined language/*langue* as the sole object of a linguistic science which 'is possible only if the other elements [of speech] are excluded', the *Course* could happily 'dispense with' speaking.[515] For the purposes of the *Course*, a phonetic alphabet that *graphically* represents signifying sound images suffices for the silent rendering of sound. The *Course* tellingly emphasises that while 'it would

---

511   Cross et al. in Arbib 2013, p. 547, p. 548. Elaborating other such proximate motivators for human communication, Cross et al. write: 'For humans (and perhaps some other primate species), vocal and gestural communication serves to co-regulate affective states between the caregiver and infant, and to enhance a sense of mutual affiliation. Communication can have prosocial effects, not just for dyads but also for larger groups: we may gain pleasure from collective and synchronized performance which, in turn, reduces social uncertainty and helps bond the group, enhancing the effectiveness of group action and identity, particularly when directed against potential external threats …. Of course, once we can behave linguistically or musically, we can be motivated to co-opt these communicative resources for other ends: "inner speech" may be deployed to reduce uncertainty in attention-based coordination or to manage communication, whereas self-directed music may be produced as a means of affect regulation …' (ibid., p. 548).

512   Marcuse 1969, p. 24. See also Marcuse 1978, p. 62, p. 66, p. 69. *Oxford English Dictionary* (online): 'aesthetic: Ultimately from the ancient Greek αἰσθητικός of or relating to sense perception, sensitive, perceptive; αἰσθητός sensible, perceptible; the stem of αἰσθάνεσθαι to perceive'. The *Wikipedia Online Dictionary* notes that the usage of aesthetics in the sense of being '*concerned with beauty*' was a German coinage of the mid-nineteenth century; though adopted into English in the early nineteenth century, this usage was controversial until late in the century.

513   This section heading is borrowed from Jakobson and Waugh 1979.

514   Saussure 1959, p. 66.

515   Saussure 1959, p. 15.

be impossible to provide detailed photographs of acts of speaking [*parole*]', 'linguistic signs are tangible', making it 'possible to reduce them to conventional written symbols'.[516]

Such *de facto* ostracism of sound from language leads linguistics into what Vološhinov called an 'abstract objectivism' that leaves language as silent as the words inscribed on a headstone.[517] The point here is not to erase the immeasurable human value of writing, but to give voice to the human significance of speaking. A silent language is without intonation; and the lack of intonation, as mentioned more than once above, collapses the various meanings that can be phonetically conveyed through vocalisation into the same abstractly objective signifier which maintains its 'concreteness' only in opposition to the other graphically represented signifiers that it is not. Silenced too is the sound of interlocution and therewith 'the life of language – that is to say, language as a human practice', the accounting for which is, the historical-materialist Lecercle insists, 'the essential task of the study of language'.[518] An abstract objectivism that banishes speaking/*parole* from language, that treats sounds silently, and leaves only mute graphic representations of sound is, so argue Roman Jakobson and Linda Waugh, already listing toward 'overexaggerating the role of arbitrariness in language and minimizing the role of onomatopoeias and of sound symbolism'.[519] It is therefore not surprising that the 'Saussurean' *Course* (and the traditions deriving from it), after having acknowledged the existence of relatively non-arbitrary auditory signs in the form of onomatopoeia, quickly dismisses them as not only 'limited in number, but also ... chosen somewhat arbitrarily, for they are only approximate and more or less conventional imitations of certain sounds'.[520] Nor is it surprising that those swimming in a Saussurean current might conclude that such once motivated, non-arbitrary signs are irrelevant to the understanding of language, that 'the true nature of language' as a

---

516   Ibid.
517   Vološhinov 1973, p. 48, pp. 52–61 *et passim*. Vološhinov was referring specifically to the Saussurean *Course in General Linguistics*, but the term is applicable to any such hypostatising of *langue*.
518   Lecercle 2009, p. 108. (All three instances of 'language' in this citation are *langage* in the French original, see Lecercle 2004, p. 103). Lecercle, inspired in this regard by Deleuze and Guattari, insists that a Marxist philosophy of language/*langage* 'does not consider the distinction between *langue* and *langage* to be essential' (Lecercle 2009, p. 210; Lecercle 2004, p. 193). I do not consider that distinction essential but, as I shall explain in detail in Chapter 8, I do consider it a temporary methodological necessity in order to elaborate, as the Saussurean *Course* does, the internal structure and logic of sign systems (and this seems, to me at least, in keeping with Lecercle's position).
519   Jakobson and Waugh 1979, p. 182.
520   Saussure 1959, p. 69. Following citation, ibid., p. 17.

semiotic system is to be sought in the allegedly wholly 'arbitrary' linguistic sign. Here too a definitional fiat creates a foregone conclusion. However, casting a glance at language through the two lenses of Lecercle's depiction of 'the life of language/*langage*' as a human interlocuting (and aesthetic/sensual) practice and of C.S. Peirce's tripartite delineation of signs provides a much different view.

Others, before and outside the Saussurean tradition, were/are neither so hasty nor so dogmatic. Alfred Wallace, Darwin's contemporary, had long since suggested that 'mouth-gesture' is 'a factor in the origin of language' and 'the expressiveness of speech': 'In our own language, and probably in all others, a considerable number of the most familiar words are so constructed as to proclaim their meaning more or less distinctly, sometimes by means of imitative sounds, but also, in a large number of cases, by the shape or the movements of the various parts of the mouth used in pronouncing them, and by peculiarities in breathing or in vocalisation, which may express a meaning quite independent of mere sound-imitation'.[521] In order to revitalise language/*langue*, to reanimate its users, and to hear the linguistic logic of sound, it is worth listening to what we might call the 'sounds of meaning'.

These can be heard by listening to what is nicely expressed in the title of a work by Jakobson and Waugh: *The Sound Shape of Language*. Following an alternative, though now less prominent tradition in language study that views speech as an audial affair, Jakobson and Waugh take onomatopoeia and sound symbolism more seriously.[522] And I would like to view their reflections on the 'sound shape of language' through the unusual lens of C.S. Peirce's tripartite differentiation among 'iconic', 'indexical', and 'arbitrary' signs.[523] This lens reveals

---

[521] Alfred Russel Wallace, 'The Expressiveness of Speech, Or, Mouth-Gesture as a Factor in the Origin of Language', in *The Alfred Russel Wallace Page*, http://people.wku.edu/charles.smith/wallace/S518.htm, p. 1.

[522] Jakobson and Waugh (1979, p. 182) name Georg von der Gabelentz, Alber Wellek, Maurice Grammont, Otto Jesperson and Edward Sapir as contributors to the understanding of the 'sound shape of language'. See ibid, pp. 177–88.

[523] C.S. Peirce, 'What is a Sign?' (http://www.marxists.org/reference/subject/philosophy/works/us/peirce1.htm), 1894. There is a degree of conceptual awkwardness in this discussion resulting from Jakobson's and Peirce's different usages of 'symbols'. Whereas Peirce uses 'symbols' to refer to linguistic signs whose meanings are arbitrary and determined by convention, Jakobson understands 'symbols' as being linked (even if established by convention) in some motivated way (e.g. visual or audio resemblance, contiguity) to that which they symbolise – criteria that Peirce uses to define indexical signs characterised by likeness. Because of the similarity between Peirce's indexical signs and Jakobson's symbols, both motivated by likeness, I am here treating Jakobson's symbols in terms of Peirce's indexical signs. And I will substitute for Peirce's 'symbols' the term 'linguistic signs'. Peirce

a more textured view of language and the signs of which it consists. A consideration of the 'sound shape' of language through this Peircean lens suggests that it consists not only of arbitrary signs (to be addressed in Part 3), but also of two kinds signifying sound images that may be thought of as iconic and indexical – and that matter profoundly to a consideration of language as a human practice.

Jakobson's and Waugh's linking of shape (generally considered a visually or tactically apprehended attribute) to the auditory realm of sound is perhaps as unusual as the suggestion to connect the auditory with 'iconic' signs that are generally exemplified visually. The iconic representation of 'watch for deer', for example, takes the form of a road-sign containing a visual re-presentation, a pictorial mimicry, of a deer. But sounds can be iconic too. This is graphically rendered in Albert Wellek's phrase 'die *Tonmalerei der Sprache*', literally 'the tone-painting of language' or, less awkwardly, 'linguistic tone-painting'. Similarly, 'onomatopoeia' – from the Greek onoma = name, poiein = making – is the making (or painting) of words that mimic the sounds of that which the words are intended to signify: 'cock-a-doodle-doo' is intended and heard as a mimicry, a representation of (that no one would mistake as) the sound of the rooster.[524] And even if onomatopoeia is not (or perhaps: no longer) the most noble form of signs in mature languages, Jakobson and Waugh join that tradition arguing that it still belongs essentially to languages and plays an essential role in them.

To gain some perspective on the significance of onomatopoeia in the linguistic life of the human species we might cast a glance at the work of anthropological linguist Mary LeCron Foster who has speculated (in ways complementary to Jakobson's and Waugh's) on the logic of meaningful sound production in 'primordial' language(s). Whether human polyglotism had a single or multiple lineage, whether there was originally, as linguist Vitaly Shevoroshkin suggests, a 'proto-world language', a 'mother tongue' that is the ancestor of all living languages,[525] is certainly an intriguing question; but like so many evolutionary

---

himself was never quite content with the term 'symbol' which, he noted, 'has so many meanings' and had in an earlier essay used 'tokens' instead (Peirce 1992, pp. 225–8; p. 226).

524 The audial counterpart to the argument that pictorial representations are conventional takes the form of the claim that even onomatopoeic forms are 'arbitrary'. But this argument is based on a specious cross-linguistic contrast. The well-known fact that roosters too speak different languages (e.g. an English-speaking rooster crows cock-a-doodle-doo, while a German rooster crows 'ke-ke-keree') does not prevent fluent speakers (regardless of whether or not native) of a language from recognising its 'sound shape' as a mimicry, a representation (in the sense of 'standing for', not of a 're-presentation') of the rooster's crowing; and they would not mistake the sound as that of, says a dog or lion.

525 See Shevoroshkin 1990.

questions that have surfaced in this cartographic sketch, it will here be sidestepped. Although LeCron Foster's analysis is embedded in the evolutionary question of language origins, our particular interest is her reflection on the relation between sound and meaning in onomatopoeic words produced through sound mimicry.

LeCron Foster proceeds in effect, if not explicit intent, from Wallace's reminder that 'though to us words are for the most part mere conventions, they were not so to primitive man. He had, as it were, to struggle hard to make himself understood, and would, therefore, make use of every possible indication of meaning afforded by the positions and motions of mouth, lips, or breath in pronouncing each word'.[526] Beginning similarly with the assumption that 'all meaning interchange, whether linguistic or not, depends on bodily movements or the result of those movements',[527] LeCron Foster assumes further that gestural meaning interchange preceded linguistic, and asks how the transformation from gestural to linguistic might have occurred. She hypothesises that earliest language, like gesture, was a form of mimicry. And she concludes that it is 'this human faculty for oral mimicry that makes human language possible and must be the clue to its phylogenetic emergence. Language, at its inception, must have been based not on the production and learning of arbitrary sounds, but on the reproductions of sounds as mimicry'.[528]

Far from being arbitrary, word-making in its earliest forms, LeCron Foster argues, was quite literally 'onomatopoeic': words were made of sounds intended to mimic, to resemble (or: as icons of) the sounds associated with that to which they referred, their referent. Combining its etymologically literal meaning with its current meaning, *onomatopoeia* means the *making* of a word that sounds like that which it names – and I emphasise *making* to recall that languages are artefacts, made-objects, and that the purpose, even if not consciously intentional, behind their making is not irrelevant to their significance (see Chapter 2). In contrast to mature language that 'is composed of linked sounds' (also *made*), this protolanguage, Foster hypothesises, must have consisted of 'sounds produced individually'. She calls these sounds *phememes*. Like (but preceding) *phonemes*, *phememes* were the smallest units of linguistic sound; but unlike phonemes, phenemes were also bearers of meaning 'at the earliest stages of language [when] sound and meaning were undifferentiated', 'minimal units uniting distinctive features of sound and meaning'.[529] As sound

---

526 Wallace, http://people.wku.edu/charles.smith/wallace/S518.htm, p. 3.
527 LeCron Foster in Sheets-Johnstone 1992, p. 211.
528 LeCron Foster in Sheets-Johnstone 1992, p. 218.
529 LeCron Foster in Sheets-Johnstone 1992, p. 221; LeCron Foster in Washburn and McCown 1978, p. 78. See also LeCron Foster in Foster and Brandes 1980.

units invested with meaning by sound mimicry, phememes are onomatopoeic icons; their meanings 'were a function of their mimetic articulatory characteristics'.[530] The transformation of phememes into phonemes meant on the one hand that these basic sound elements lost their meaning; but on the other hand it made possible the development of proto-language into language[531] – the latter characterised by 'duality of patterning' (i.e. consisting of 'phonemes', basic sound elements that bear no meaning, that can be combined to form meaning-bearing sequences of phonemes, i.e. morphemes and words) which is the foundation for the immense lexical wealth of mature language whose predominant feature is the (as I argue in Part 3: relative) arbitrariness of linguistic signs.[532]

Between the iconic onomatopoeic and the (relatively) arbitrary linguistic signs, however, there is a rather large class of phonic signs that may be thought of as analogous to indexical signs. These can be articulated through Jakobson's and Waugh's discussion of 'sound symbolism' which includes onomatopoeia, but is much broader; for it includes not only words that mimic their meaning, but also those whose phonic signifiers 'have a direct, immediate relation to meaning', whose 'features have sound-symbolic properties and synesthetic values, associated with their binary nature'[533] – a relation that is not onomatopoeic *re-presentation*, but sound-symbolic *representation* (i.e. a standing-in-for based on likeness).

Jakobson and Waugh launch their inquiry in the wake of Otto Jespersen's 'vehement attack against the narrow antiquarianism' that 'disregard[s] the ety-

---

530 LeCron Foster in Sheets-Johnstone 1992, p. 224.
531 LeCron Foster explains this development in 'gradualist' terms. 'Over time the meaning of the sounds themselves became obscured because as the system developed the sounds came to be pronounced in rapid succession, often causing fusion between what had originally been separate sounds. Concatenations of sounds then became conventionalized with particular rather than generalized meanings, a change which also contributed to the loss of original analogical meanings. As these meanings were obscured, the sounds gradually became phonemes, meaningless but conventionalized units of sound, which achieved meaning only through their combination with other sounds as they evolved into words, roots, or affixes'. 'Shifts in both sound and meaning over time as concatenation with other sounds or sound sequences occurred obscured the original meanings of the sounds'. 'Slight but progressive changes in meaning over time, coupled with similarly progressive joining together of separate units into words, brought about the loss of phememic meaning and instead invested meaning in words formed of sequences of phonemes in roots and affixes'. All citations from LeCron Foster in Sheets-Johnstone 1992, p. 219; p. 221, pp. 221–2.
532 LeCron Foster in Sheets-Johnstone 1992, p. 221.
533 This quote is the Editor's Note to an abridged version of *The Spell of the Speech Sound* that Jakobson co-authored with Linda Waugh. Waugh is one of the two editors (the other is

mological creativity of the living speech community, and assign[s] the creation and use of echoic and symbolic words solely, if at all, to former ages'. They insist that 'the natural correspondence between sound and sense is a constantly renewable and vital process', whereby, as Jespersen believed, 'languages in the course of time grow richer and richer in symbolic words' and develop progressively 'towards a greater number of easy and adequate expressions – expression in which sound and sense are united in a marriage-union closer than was ever know to our remote ancestors'. Jespersen's 'remarkable chapter discusses the direct imitation of the audible phenomena by sound production and the use of speech sounds, their groups, reduplications, lengthenings, and omissions, to designate, metonymically or metaphorically, sound producers, movements, things and appearances, states of mind, sizes and distances'.[534]

In a fascinating discussion too lengthy to review here, Jakobson and Waugh summarise studies delineating the contours of the sound shape of language. Topics addressed in these studies include: the symbolic value of vowel sounds; sound synaesthesia and the colours of sounds (as manifested in oppositions such as lighter and darker, smaller and bigger, quicker and slower, more and less pretty, more and less friendly, bitterer and sweeter sounds carrying corresponding meanings; and they relate the story of a blind man who, after hearing definitions of the colour scarlet finally felt he had understood its meaning: 'like the sound of a trumpet'); word affinities, reduplication (flip-flop), and phonetic symbolism; and 'sound-symbolic ablaut' ('the morphological utilization of the substitution of features in certain consonants or vowels within the root of a word and sometimes also within its affixes [which] is a particular example of the use of single sound differences in the direct service of grammatical meanings'; e.g. in Yoruba *birì* and *bírí* meaning large and small respectively).[535] And in a concluding passage worthy of lengthy citation, Jakobson and Waugh argue that

---

Monique Monville-Burston) of the volume in which this version appears: *Roman Jakobson: On Language* (Cambridge, MA: Harvard University Press, 1990, pp. 422–437), p. 422. It seems likely, if not certain, that Waugh wrote this note; regardless, it is an excellent concise summary of the argument.

534 Both citations Jakobson and Waugh 1979, pp. 182–3.
535 This synopsis of Jakobson's and Waugh's summary of work on the links between sound and meaning is gleaned from Jakobson and Waugh 1979, pp. 183–204. The rest of the essay (pp. 204–20) summarises work on the sound-sense relation in mythopoeic usage, verbal taboo, 'glossolalia' (the connection of 'the human and divine worlds on the one hand as prayers from the former to the latter and on the other hand as messages transmitted from the divine power to the assembled human body in order to inspire, unity, and emotionally exalt it'; ibid., p. 211), and also verse, children's verbal art, and poetry.

> any distinctive feature [of language] is built on an opposition which ... carries a latent synesthetic association and thus an immediate, semantic nuance. This *immediacy* in signification of the distinctive features acquires an autonomous role in the more or less onomatopoeic strata of ordinary language. The habitual relation of *contiguity* between sound and meaning yields to a bond of *similarity*. This phenomenon goes beyond the limits of onomatopoeias proper and succeeds in creating submorphemic links between words of diverse origin. It is this similarity in sound and meaning which even assumes an active role in reviving or condemning lexical archaisms and in furthering viable neologisms.
>
> ...
>
> The tension between two structural principles – contiguity and similarity – permeates the whole of language. If, as mediate building blocks of meaningful entities, the distinctive features serve to connect sound and meaning by virtue solely of contiguity, the inner sound symbolism peculiar to these features strives to burst forth and to sustain an immediate similarity relation, a kind of equivalence between the *signans*, and the *signatum*.[536]

Notwithstanding the Saussurean claim that 'the true nature of language' can only be deciphered through the 'arbitrary' (and silent) linguistic sign, the analysis of the 'sound shape' of language indicates that human languages exist by virtue of voice, and that the truly human nature of language(s) cannot be fully grasped by dispensing with the voice and the meaning-bearing sounds it speaks. Though the 'arbitrary sign' may be the key to deciphering the semiotic logic of language, iconic linguistic signs in the form of onomatopoeia and indexical signs in the form of sound symbolism give body and texture to natural languages.

Fitting here as a conclusion to these reflections is Jakobson's and Waugh's caution that the 'significance of the play on words (*jeu de mots*) in the life of language [that] should not be underestimated'.[537] For 'it is precisely "play" and the mythopoeic transforms [sic] of language which help to dynamize the autonomous semantic potential of the distinctive features and of their complexes'. Fitting, because this invocation of play recalls the discussion of singing, speaking, and aesthetics with which I began this inquiry into phonation. Play, certainly a sensual activity, returns us to the realm of aesthetics. And phonic

---

536   Jakobson and Waugh 1979, pp. 235–6.
537   Jakobson and Waugh 1979, p. 236. Following citations in this paragraph, ibid.

play, the 'intrinsic pleasure in vocalizing' that plays on the 'play' (here in the sense of leeway, flexibility) of sounds is not only essential to intonation, poetry, and song lyrics, but it is also ubiquitous in the prosody of everyday speaking and integral to the transformations that are the history of a given language. However necessary an 'abstract objectivist' approach may be to the understanding of the anatomy of silent signs, it is inadequate 'to account for the life of language' as 'a human practice' – which requires an understanding of the physiology of speech and the phonetics of language, both inseparable from the corporeal organisation of the 'apes who speak', and grasping their meaningful and playful aesthetic significance as a human practice.[538]

Although the human vocal apparatus can emit an impressive range of sounds, not all of those sounds are phonic or linguistically useful; in Susanne Langer's terms, not all of its 'mouthy little noises' can be called words. Once delineated within the sonic repertoire as essential to speech, the phonic can be studied in (at least) two ways: *phonetics*, 'the study of sounds, their properties and formation, and the perceptual cues that allow listeners to recover them'; and *phonology*, 'the study of their organization within the systems of particular languages in the formation of higher-level linguistics units'.[539] While it would seem reasonable to expect harmony among the acoustically attuned who reject the Saussurean ostracism of sound from linguistics, encounters with the cacophonic debates over all things pertaining to language should prepare us for discordant tones. And, as Stephen Anderson reports, '[p]ractitioners of each field have long tended to be somewhat dismissive of those in the other field': 'The early phonologist Prince Nikolas Trubetzkoy famously suggested that phonetics is to phonology as numismatics is to economics'; and Trubetzkoy's colleague, Roman Jakobson, dismissed the vocal apparatus as 'merely a

---

538   On the role of play in the human practice of languaging, see Robin Kelley 1997. Though Kelley does not use these terms, the first chapter of this book that takes social scientists to task for how they 'construct the ghetto' is a critique of the kind of approaches that Vološinov called 'abstract objectivism': analyses based on the assumption that the meaning of a game, whether the language game 'the dozens' or jump rope, can be derived simply from an understanding of the structure of the game, perhaps also in conjunction with a social situating of the game, but that completely miss the human significance of the game because they completely exclude the actual people who play the game, that is: they completely miss the significance of play as human practice. I address his critique of 'abstract objectivist' social science in Chapter 9.

539   'Phonic' refers not to sounds in general (that would be sonic) nor even to all vocally produced sounds. It is reserved for sounds of, or relating to, speech; from the Greek *phōnē* meaning voice.

physiological prerequisite'. Meanwhile, 'otherwise sensible phoneticians regard phonological arguments as mere artful conjuring with no empirical basis'.[540] Agreeing with Anderson's judgement that 'both are wrong about the triviality of the other's pursuits', I am here interested in the fundamental point of agreement between the two subdisciplines and in the more phonetic question of the relation between linguistic sounds and the vocal apparatus, not as a mere physiological prerequisite, but as a means of speech production.

Given their dispute, it does not seem trivial to say that both phonetics and phonology are concerned with the same sounds, but with different attributes: the former with the acoustic properties of meaning-bearing sounds and the latter with those sounds as bearers and expressions of meaning. Nevertheless, both are agreed that that there is a structural logic to meaning-bearing sounds. Phonologists would agree with acoustic phoneticist Kenneth Stevens who (acknowledging his debt to Jakobson among others) reiterated the fundamental phonic fact that 'though there are a large number of possible speech sounds in the languages of the world, it is well known that a small inventory of sounds appears over and over in language'.[541] And although only phoneticists treat it as a crucial object of analysis, neither side would deny (not even Jakobson despite his reduction of the vocal apparatus to a mere physiological prerequisite) that the logic underlying the range of sounds that become the sounds of speech is a corporeal one: the corporeal logic of the human vocal apparatus. I therefore conclude this discussion of the corporeal foundations of speech with a brief look at phonic matter in relation to the means of its production.

As one of the main figures in the phonologically pioneering Prague School of Linguistics, Jakobson chose 'to leave the territory of phonetics, the discipline which studies sounds solely in their motor and acoustic aspects, and [...] enter a new territory, that of phonology, which studies the sounds of language in their linguistic aspect'.[542] Jakobson and his colleague Trubetzkoy sought to settle this unexplored phonological territory by identifying what they considered the rather limited number of fundamental acoustical 'quanta' of which all natural languages are composed.[543] Trubetzkoy, in Jakobson's estimation, made 'the first attempt at a phonological classification of the vowels and consequently a typology of the vocalic systems of the whole world'; and Jakobson found it

---

540 All citations except Jakobson's comment from S. Anderson 2004, pp. 121–2. Jakobson's comment in 1978, pp. 5–6.
541 Stevens and Keyser 1989, p. 81.
542 Jacobson 1978, p. 20.
543 Jakobson 1978, p. 3; p. 24.

'quite appropriate' that Trubetzkoy's accomplishment was viewed as a kind of phonological counterpart of 'the famous periodic table of chemical elements established by Mendeléeff'.[544] The comparison is apt, for Jakobson and like-minded sought to identify the elemental components underlying the entire range of spoken languages, to take an 'over-all inventory of distinctive features' in the production of speech sounds which would 'foreground the problem of the universal rules underlying the phonemic patterning of languages'. The development of this inventory, Jakobson predicted, would 'permit us to reduce the list of distinctive features used in the languages of the world' and show that the 'supposed multiplicity of features proves to be largely illusory'.[545]

The phonetic counterpart of the phonological search for an 'over-all inventory' would be the International Phonetic Alphabet, the first such published by the International Phonetic Association. The Association was founded by a group of French and British linguists and language teachers in 1886, and published the first International Phonetic Alphabet two years later. Over the last century-and-a-quarter of its existence the Phonetic Alphabet has undergone several revisions according to the Association's scholarly guidelines. In its most recent iteration (2005), the Alphabet contains, on a single page, the inventory of the 107 letters, 52 diacritics, and four prosodic marks from which the world's multiplicity of alphabets and languages is constructed.[546]

The mode of scholarly production being what it is, such inventories will always be disputed and revised. In phonological circles there is much disagreement over how exactly to determine the 'quantum' level, how exactly to delineate the basic meaning-bearing unit of sound; arguments have been advanced in favour of phonemes, sub-phonemic 'distinctive features', morphemes, and larger 'exemplar-based' units such as words, phrases, or even entire sentences.[547] And the International Phonetic Alphabet will no doubt be expan-

---

544 Jakobson 1978, p. 50. For a discussion of language elements (though in grammatical rather than phonological terms) treated as analogous to chemical elements, see Baker 2001, Chapter 5, pp. 123–56.
545 Jakobson and Halle 1956; all citations, p. 27.
546 International Phonetic Alphabet, Wikipedia, http://en.wikipedia.org/wiki/International_Phonetic_Alphabet. Recalling the discussion of singing and languaging above, it is worth noting here that Fitch and Jarvis find a further affinity in the 'existence of the International Phonetic Alphabet and musical notation capable of transcribing much of the world's music [which] demonstrates that there are finite limits on the sounds used in speech and song' (Fitch and Jarvis 2013, in Arbib 2013, p. 511). Worth noting too is that they refer in this context to Jakobson's work on the limited distinctive features of language (Jakobson et al. 1957).
547 This information from conversation with Spike Gildea, Professor of Linguistics, University of Oregon, 16 June 2014.

ded somewhat with further analysis of already examined languages, and new analysis of as yet unstudied ones. But regional disputes over phonological quanta and the inevitable problem of incompleteness are matters that can, for present purposes, be circumvented. For unsettled issues and necessarily incomplete undertakings notwithstanding, the results thus far are significant for the matter at hand, namely: whether the sound shapes of languages are arbitrary or in-formed by a corporeal logic.

If the signifying sound images of natural languages were truly arbitrary, then there would be no limits (other than the corporeally-determined outer limits of the human vocal apparatus) on the perhaps infinite number of vocal noises that would serve as signifying sound-images; without phonic limits, word noises would show such variation that no generality could be as 'overwhelmingly valid' as Stephen Anderson judges Jakobson's undertaking; nor could something like the International Phonetic Alphabet be developed.[548] That such a small set of phonetic features suffices to inventory the world's languages may seem incredulous at first glance; but it makes sense to a corporeal second glance. For, the reason why the sets of easily-combined, meaning-bearing sounds that produce speech both fluid and fluent is almost infinitesimally small compared to the total number of sounds in the human vocal repertoire can be traced directly to the corporeally-established capacities and limits, of the human vocal apparatus that produces linguistic sounds and the hearing apparatus that 'consumes' them.

As Michael Kenstowicz summarises, the 'study of sound systems of the many different languages described over the past two centuries strongly suggests that the sounds of speech are drawn from a tightly constrained, *universal phonetic alphabet* with a surprisingly rich internal structure' – a structure Kenstowicz concludes, that 'in large part reflects categorizations imposed by the vocal apparatus'.[549] In elaborating the 'most basic properties' or 'design features' of a 'language articulation system' that both satisfy the conditions established by the vocal apparatus and 'may subserve vocabulary acquisition', Kenstowicz points to three: 'Surely one requirement is that the system be able to assign different lexical items distinct articulations that are detectable by the human ear. Second, the faster the item can be articulated and the more quickly the information contained in the acoustic signal can be recovered, the better. Third, the system itself must be easy to learn and to operate'.[550]

---

548   S. Anderson 1985, p. 125.
549   Kenstowicz 1994, p. 13.
550   Kenstowicz 1994, p. 12.

The relatively brief International Phonetic Alphabetic may be viewed as the result of filtering the entire range of sounds of which the human vocal apparatus is capable of producing through these three phonic design features characteristic of the diverse multiplicity of languages that has been constructed on so small a foundation. If there is a universal attribute of all human languages, it is that they consist of vowels and consonants. *Phonetically* speaking, 'vowels are distinguished from consonants in terms of how they are articulated in the vocal tract, and the associated patterns of acoustic energy. In this approach, consonants are defined as sounds made by a closure in the vocal tract, or by a narrowing which is so marked that air cannot escape without producing audible friction. Vowels are sounds that have no such stricture: air escapes in a relatively unimpeded way through the mouth and nose'.[551] The phonetics of vowel and consonant production are described in terms of the instruments and the manner of articulation. Vowels are defined by four criteria: the part of the tongue that is raised; the extent to which the tongue rises in the direction of the palate; the position of the soft palate; the kind of opening made at the lips. Consonants are defined by six criteria: the source of the air stream, its direction; the state of vibration of the vocal folds; the position of the soft palate; the place of articulation in the vocal tract; the manner of articulation. The places of consonantal articulation number eleven and are defined in terms of two referent points: 'the part of the vocal tract that moves (the "active articulator") and the part with which it makes contact (the "passive articulator")'.[552] And the manner of articulation of consonants number four: total closure, intermittent closure, partial closure, and narrowing.[553] The possible permutations of

---

551   Crystal 1987, p. 152. All information in this paragraph and its notes is cited or paraphrased from this entry.

552   Those eleven places are: bilabial, both lips are involved in the articulation; labio-dental, the lower lip articulates with the upper teeth; dental, the tongue tip and rims articulate with the upper teeth; alveolar, the blade (and sometimes the tip) of the tongue articulates with the alveolar ridge; retroflex, the tip of the tongue is curled back to articulate with the area between the rear of the alveolar ridge and the front of the hard palate; palato-alveolar, the blade (and sometimes the tip) of the tongue articulates with the alveolar ridge with a simultaneous raising of the front of the tongue towards the hard palate; palatal, the front of the tongue articulates with the hard palate; velar, the back of the tongue articulates with the soft palate; uvular, the back of the tongue articulates with the uvula; pharyngeal, the front wall of the pharynx articulates with the back wall; glottal the vocal folds come together to cause a closure or friction. See Crystal 1987, p. 155.

553   There are three modes of *total closure*: *plosive*, a complete closure is made at some point in the vocal tract, the soft palate is raise, and air pressure thus builds up behind the closure, which is then released explosively, as in [p] and [b]; *nasal*, a complete closure is made at some point in the mouth, the soft palate is lowered, so that air escapes through the nose,

the languages built from this handful of speech sounds produced with these vocal instruments are perhaps legion; but the fact all languages are built upon a fraction of that handful indicates that they are not in the least arbitrary. For the same corporeal mode of vocal production that makes those permutations possible is also subject to design features that limits the phonic range of human speech.

As Kenstowicz's list of design features clearly states, the audial range of human ears for the reception of speech sounds also plays a crucial role in language construction. And Kenneth Steven's work elucidates the phonic attributes that satisfy the audial *desideratum*. Seeking to explain the cross-linguistic recurrence of a rather small number of sounds, Stephens analysed the qualities of the speech sounds that are rapidly produced by the vocal apparatus and whose acoustic properties make them easily distinguishable by the listening interlocutor. Speech sounds, he discovered, are neither linear, nor continuous, nor only quantitatively differentiated, but are instead discontinuous and discrete. Each distinctive speech sound can be maintained on a kind of 'plateau' despite small quantitative adjustments in the articulatory organs (tongue, lips, etc.); yet eventually a point will be reached that marks an abrupt break and produces a qualitative change in acoustical output. As summarised by Kenstowicz, Stevens's research exposes 'a nonlinear (*quantal*) relation between the articulatory and the acoustic/auditory dimensions'. Discrete speech sounds can be likened to a series of 'plateaus' of 'stable acoustic output[s] across a range of articulatory targets', each of which is surrounded by 'boundary region[s] where small changes in articulation coincide with abrupt changes in the acoustic correlate'. Each 'acoustic steady state generated by the articulatory plateau identifies the corresponding feature's acoustic correlate'. The 'major functional advantage for such quantal relations between articulation and acoustics [is that] the articulator does not have to hit a precise target, but has a considerable

---

as in [m] and [n]; *affricate*, a complete closure is made at some point in the mouth, the soft palate is raised, air pressure builds up behind the closure, and is then released relatively slowly, e.g. the *ch* or *dg* sound in the English words *church* and *judge*. *Intermittent closure* is of two kinds: *roll* or *trill*, one articulator raps rapidly against another – typically the tongue tip against the alveolar ridge or the tongue back against the uvula, in the different kinds of trilled *r*, heard for example in many English, French and German accents. *Partial Closure* is *lateral*, a partial closure is made at some point in the mouth, in such a way that the air stream is allowed to escape around the sides of the closure, as in various kinds of *l* sound. *Narrowing* is *fricative*, two vocal organs come so close together that the movement of air between them causes audible friction, as in [f], [z], [h]. All of the above, with some changes in punctuation and with some phrases deleted, cited directly from Crystal 1987, p. 157.

margin of error in which to produce the desired acoustic effect [and] presumably allows for faster articulation'.[554] It also helps explain how languages are constructed such that, despite the diverse individual voices each as unique as fingerprints, the speakers of a given language can variously produce a given sound that nonetheless remains within a recognisable range.

Elaborating this functional advantage Lieberman explains that quantal sounds facilitate vocal communication by providing both 'acoustic salience' and 'acoustic stability'. Acoustic salience 'derives from the ability to produce an abrupt change in the cross-sectional area of the supralaryngeal vocal tract'. This allows (in addition to the labial consonants such as [b], [p], and [m] and the dental consonants [d], [s], and [t] that all primates can produce) the vocalisation of the vowels [a], [i], [u] and the velar consonants [g] and [k]. Easier to perceive, quantal sounds provide 'acoustic salience' and are 'better suited for vocal communication', and it is therefore unsurprising that quantal sounds 'occur more often in different human languages'. This salience is complemented by 'acoustic stability' which is the ability to produce identifiably distinct sounds 'without being extraordinarily precise when we position our tongue'. This facilitates identification of the same phoneme even if it is produced differently because of differences in individuals' vocal cords or dialects.[555] The complexity, sophistication, and fine-tuning of the human instruments of speech production provide, in short, 'optimal acoustic signals' for speech; they provide the sharpness and clarity of sound manipulation needed for both an extensive vocabulary consisting of fine phonemic distinctions and for easy and quick identification by the listener, in short for the rapid transmission of information through vocal communication.[556] As Lieberman concludes in what is both tautology and understatement, 'a human surpralaryngeal vocal tract is a *necessary* condition for human phonetic ability' which 'does not seem a trivial part of human linguistic ability' – nor, he might well have added, a trivial part of the formation of human languages themselves.

As long as this cartographic narrative has been, it obviously offers only a rather incomplete sketch. A detailed portrait would include all socio-economically

---

554   All citations from Kenstowicz 1994, p. 188.
555   Citations on acoustic salience and stability from Lieberman 1975, p. 58. It is telling that when anthropologist Robert McCarthy used Neanderthal vocal tracts (reconstructed from fossils) to simulate a Neanderthal voice, and concluded that Neanderthals had fully articulated speech, he qualified this claim by noting that 'they wouldn't have been able to produce these quantal vowels that form the basis of spoken language'. See Highfield 2008.
556   Lieberman 1975, p. 160. Next citation ibid., p. 120, p. 121.

A HISTORICAL-MATERIALIST CARTOGRAPHY   501

and culturally relevant aspects of human corporeal organisation: the heart, blood, and circulatory system; the lungs and respiratory system; the liver and its bile; the spleen about which Baudelaire vented, etc. But here I have only been able to address some of the more fundamental attributes of the uniquely human corporeal organisation that shape patterns of human experience that in turn in-form the making of human worlds of material, social, and semiotic artefacts. And in the following summary and concluding chapter to Part 2, I address the relation between these corporeally framed patterns of human experience and forms of cognition.

CHAPTER 7

On the Corporeal Constitution of Cognition and Subjecthood

> [T]here is no evidence that our current form of language is much more than 50,000 years old. We were becoming human long before that, and our humanness is founded in our distant past, not uniquely created by our most recent forms of behavior.
> ROLAND FLETCHER[1]

∴

> With the term 'presence of mind' [*Geistesgegenwart*], language reveals that the secret of success is not housed in the mind. It is thus not the *that* or the *how* of the mind, but only the *where* of the mind that decides. Mind can only be present in the moment and in place – it accomplishes that by committing to a tone of voice, to a smile, a silence, a glance, a gesture. For only the body creates presence of mind.
> WALTER BENJAMIN[2]

∴

> 'I', you say and are proud of this word. But that which is greater is that which you do not want to believe – your body and its great reason: it does not say 'I', rather it does 'I'.

---

1 Fletcher 1993, p. 18. Since Fletcher wrote his book on the evolution of human behaviour in *The First Humans: Human Origins and History to 10,000 BC*, the origin of human language has been pushed back to approximately 200,000 years (see Pinker 1994). Nevertheless, as argued at length in the previous chapter mapping human corporeal organisation, Fletcher is right in arguing that we were becoming human long before we developed the 'language instinct'.
2 Benjamin 1972, p. 352; my translation. The original is: *Dass das Geheimnis des Erfolges nicht im Geist wohnt, verrät die Sprache mit dem Wort 'Geistesgegenwart'. Also nicht das Daß und Wie – allein das Wo des Geistes entscheidet. Daß er nur im Augenblicke und im Raum zugegen sei, das schafft er nur, indem er in den Stimmfall, das Lächeln, das Verstummen, den Blick, die Geste eingeht. Denn Gegenwart des Geistes schafft allein der Leib.*

> There is more reason in your body than in your best wisdom. And who knows for what purpose your body requires precisely your best wisdom?
>
> FRIEDRICH NIETZSCHE[3]

∴

> We do not have bodies, we *are* bodies.
>
> WILHELM REICH[4]

∴

7.1 Introductory Overview

When in *The German Ideology* Marx simply but profoundly defines consciousness (*das Bewußtsein*) as nothing other than conscious being (*das bewußte Sein*), which is itself 'the life-process of real individuals', it is obvious from the context that he was thinking of the social determinations of that life-process and thus of consciousness. It is, however, worth remembering that the section in which he establishes this relation between life-process and consciousness begins by announcing what Eagleton called his 'breathtaking wager' on corporeal organisation as the 'first fact' in the consideration of human history. This of course does not preclude the socio-cultural determinations of historically specific forms of consciousness, but invites us to consider first the corporeal organisation that is an even more fundamental form-determinant (*Formbestimmung*) of human life-processes and hence of particular forms of consciousness. And the purpose of the previous chapter's cartographic undertaking was to delineate in outline form the corporeal organisation that is the form-determinant, that establishes the range and limits, of human life-processes and therefore of the human forms of consciousness that always consist of specific socio-culturally mediated, but still all too human contents. The matter of socio-cultural mediations will be addressed in the following chapters.

---

3 Nietzsche 1976b, p. 300; my translation. For a slightly different translation, see Nietzsche, 'Of the Despisers of the Body' in *Thus Spoke Zarathustra* (Nietzsche 1969, p. 62).

4 This statement is attributed, without citation, to Wilhelm Reich by Mannfred Faßler (1996), pp. 222–31, p. 226, my italics). I have inverted the order of the two sentences in this passage whose original form is: *Wir sind Körper, wir haben keinen Körper.*

Here the focus is on the relation between corporeality and forms of consciousness, between corporeality and cognition.

At least since Descartes, and almost obsessively so since the launching of the poststructuralist project aimed primarily at 'decentring' post-Cartesian 'Western' philosophy, matters of cognition and forms of consciousness have invariably become imbricated with the question of the knowing subject and determinations of its subjecthood and subjectivity. Although widespread throughout the humanities and some social sciences, the concern with subjecthood is rarely posed on the natural science side of the disciplinary divide – although this may well be not so much because of lack of interest, but rather a consequence of the abyss of mutual unintelligibility between the 'natural' and 'human' sciences that C.P. Snow long ago noted. But as suggested by the previous chapter's sketch of the relation between human corporeal organisation and the range, limits, and patterns of human experience, students of human evolution, paleoanthropology, human anatomy and physiology would have a good deal to contribute to the understanding of the corporeal roots of human cognition and to the constitution of subjecthood. And one valuable exception to the at least *de facto* isolationism among 'natural' and 'human' scientists is the abyss-bridging 'dialectical biology' of Richard Levins and Richard Lewontin that views every organism as the subject as well as the object of its own evolution or history.[5] To claim that an organism is both subject and object of its history extends to all organisms Marx's aphorism that people make their own history, but not as they please; and it is also another way of signifying what in the poststructuralist lexicon is called a 'decentred subject'. The previous chapter provided in barest outline a sketch of the corporeally-grounded capacities of human subjects who make their own history and of the corporeally-grounded limits that 'decentre' them or make them into also objects of their own history. Here, in the form of summarising theoretical reflection on the results of my cartographic undertaking, I approach the problematic of human subjecthood through reflection on the relation between corporeality and cognition. To avoid confusion: my concern here is not with the socio-culturally specific contents of concrete subjectivities, one manifestation of which will be addressed in Part 4. Here the concern is rather with the general form and contours of human cognition and subjecthood in a form that is both abstract and essential, both necessary and necessarily insufficient.

Because the discussion in the 'human sciences' of cognition, subjecthood, and subjectivity has for almost a century been dominated by semiotic ap-

---

5 Levins and Lewontin 1985.

proaches that treat cognition and subjecthood as an effect of language, I begin, for orientation purposes, with a brief presentation of such 'linguistiocentric' approaches followed by an equally brief discussion of alternative approaches that take the role of corporeality in these matters much more seriously. Following this introductory discussion, I proceed to articulate my take on the relation between corporeality and cognition. With the help of various authors offering alternatives to the linguistocentric approach to cognition and subjectivity, I first explain how I understand cognition and its relation to corporeality. This includes explaining how I approach, and what terminology I use, in addressing, the mind-body question. Then in a discussion of the 'wisdom of the body', I elaborate three forms of corporeally grounded 'tacit knowledge' that are both forms of knowledge themselves and that in-form our conscious 'acts of understanding and knowing'.[6] These are: the body as itself a body of knowledge; the tacit knowledge involved in all human action; and the patterns of bodily experience that in-form human patterns of thought and action. In short: proceeding from the 'first fact' of human corporeal organisation, from Benjamin's insistence that 'only the body creates presence of mind', I undertake both an anthropo-centring and a corporeal decentring of human subjects – that is to say: I seek to explain both the corporeally-delineated range, and the corporeally-delineated limits, of the species-specific field of human cognition that is our anthropocentric fate – the range and limits that establish the contours of always already corporeally-decentred human subjecthood.

7.2 A Glance at 'Linguistocentric' Conceits Concerning the Constitution of Cognition and Subjecthood

The pet poststructuralist/postmodernist-inspired project for a good half-century now, and closely tied to the project of exposing the 'embodiedness' of minds, has been that of decentring the 'subject' or 'subjects'. Despite all claims to the contrary, that is not exactly a novel undertaking. I noted in the Introduction Freud's enumeration of Copernicus, Darwin, and himself as practitioners of the decentring project; and I explained why I think (as did Foucault) that Marx should be added to the group. But what is new in the latest round of deconstructing and decentring the subject is that the discussion of subjects, subjecthood, and subjectivity, like that of bodies and embodiedness, has in the wake of the 'linguistic turn' been 'hegemonised' by ultra-constructionist dis-

---

6   M. Johnson in Hampe 2005, p. 16.

course insisting on the thoroughgoing linguistic and/or cultural construction of subjects and their subjectivity – the result of which is a treatment of really living individual subjects as no more than linguistic and/or cultural constructions. Gustav Bergmann who coined the term 'linguistic turn' thought of it as a kind of intellectual 'style' initiated by Wittgenstein's notion of language as a 'game'[7] And in explicitly comparing a science of linguistics to study the rules of chess, the Saussurean *Course in General Linguistics* established the methodological foundations and outlined a research programme that has lain at the heart of both structuralist and (despite their scepticism about the structuralist optimism in attaining truths) poststructuralist projects throughout the twentieth and into the current century. This will be addressed at great length in Chapter 8. Here I will just note to preface the following discussion that the single-minded focus on the rules of the game and neglect of the game itself privileges an abstract formalism and treats the living history of human subjects as merely contingent and therefore beneath the level of the scientific gaze.

On the basis of such assumptions, many rather bold claims have been rather emphatically made about the relation between language structure and subjectivity. The *Course* itself pronounces that 'our thought – apart from its expression in words – is only a shapeless and indistinct mass. [...] Without language [*la langue*], thought is a vague, uncharted nebula. There are no pre-existing ideas, and nothing is distinct before the appearance of language'.[8] Taken out of context, C.S. Peirce's claim that 'My language is the sum total of myself; for the man is the thought' has been wielded apodictically and axiomatically.[9] Heidegger insisted that 'language speaks' and that 'language is the house of being';[10] Lacan that 'the world of words creates the world of things'; Derrida, 'il n'ya pas de hors-texte'. Umberto Eco offers a taxonomic rendering with his classification of human beings as 'semiotic animals'. The problem is not necessarily with the term 'semiotic animals', but rather with the way in which Eco's apodictic claims that 'languages are what constitutes human beings as such', and that 'signification encompasses the whole of cultural life', let the adjective 'semiotic'

---

7   Bergmann 1954, pp. 30–1. It should be noted that Wittgenstein, in contrast to many of those who took up the notion of language as game, rooted language in the communicative and social act of speaking.

8   Saussure 1959, pp. 155–6.

9   See Peirce 1868. By treating this statement as self-evident and indubitable, Kaja Silverman ignores Peirce's elaboration of the relation of language to speaking and listening subjects and to the objects of the world about which they speak (Silverman 1983, p. 18). Peirce's views on speech, language and the world will be central to, and addressed in, Chapters 8 and 9.

10 The phrase is Martin Heidegger's 1985, p. 10 *et passim*.

overwhelm, to the point of disembodiment, the animate form signified by the noun 'animals'.[11] Judith Butler insisted that 'There is no subject prior to its constructions' – those constructions being a 'crossroads of cultural and political discursive forces'.[12] Emile Benveniste insisted that language is 'the possibility of subjectivity' and is 'constitutive of *all the coordinates that define the subject*'.[13] Approvingly citing Benveniste's claims, and with the same aura of tautological self-evidence, Kaja Silverman adds one of her own, namely that 'without language there would be no subjectivity'; with a circular logic she retrieves subjects as discursive interlocutors only to disappear them; as she announces rather pre-emptively in her Preface that 'signification occurs only through discourse, that discourse requires a subject, and that *the subject itself is an effect of discourse*'.[14] Though their coiners often wielded these ideas with more nuance than is implied by these apodictic formulations, such phrases privilege language as *the* constitutive factor of human consciousness; and their axiomatic formulations have been repeated interminably, too often uncritically, in countless works ranging across such diverse fields as literature, philosophy, cultural and intellectual history, including the history of science, and in several social science disciplines.[15]

Those who have taken the linguistic turn are correct (tautologically so) in insisting on the obvious fact that human thought, as it has evolved, would be impossible without language. And because the uniquely human faculty of speech is so obviously the key to the imperial dominion of the functionally naked and speaking ape that became capable of supplementing, often overwhelming, nature with culture, it seems almost impossible to overestimate the role of language not only in human history, but in making the histories of *Homo sapiens* possible at all. Perhaps, however, that *seeming* impossibility of overestimation has led to the exaggerations that make the 'linguistic turn' often seem like a tumble through a pan-linguistic looking glass. Despite the valuable insights of the 'linguistic turn' into the expression of meaning through lin-

---

11   Eco 1986, p. 12; Eco 1979, p. 46. For further comment on non-language centred approaches to cognition, see Appendix 7.1.
12   Saussure 1959, pp. 111–12; Lacan 1984, p. 39; Butler 1993, p. 124.
13   Benvensite 1971, p. 227.
14   Silverman 1983, p. 45; p. vii, my italics.
15   Because my purpose in this chapter is to develop a historical-materialist approach to corporeality, cognition, and subjecthood, I only mention these linguistic-turn positions, and also the alternative positions in the following section, in order to establish the dimensions of the debate. But see Chapters 8 and 9 for a critique of the synchronic, structuralist approach to language emanating from the Saussurean *Course in General Linguistics* that propelled the linguistic turn and set its trajectory.

guistic signs and its contributions to a much-needed decentring of the centred 'Western' subject, the methodological barriers erected along the path leading into that turn produce a tunnel vision that excludes all but language from the much broader field of linguistics. It is thus not surprising that language is then (mis)taken as the single constitutive factor and the definitive (indeed the only) attribute of (human) subjecthood. From this viewpoint, speaking individuals appear only as simple prerequisites through whose mouths language not only speaks but also, through being spoken, transforms the merely corporeal bearers of speech capacity, the performers of speech, into subjects who can say and, only then, think 'I'. But once thought is reduced to language, and once language is granted the power of speaking and, therewith, the power to impose, by and through a given vernacular, a particular linguistic order on natural things and social relations, there remains nothing, at least nothing of significance, outside of language.[16]

---

16   Lacan's claim that 'the world of words creates the world of things' carries a secular echo of the Christian notions, advanced in the gospel of John, that 'in the beginning was the Word' and that 'the Word became flesh'. But, we should ask: what creates the 'world of words'? How is it created? What are its contents? In the cosmogony of the Hebrew Bible, that comes closer to answering those questions than does its Christian offspring, the world of words pales when compared with the world of creation. (All citations in the following, Alter 2004, pp. 17–22.) Despite the anthropocentric right that the Lord God gifted in *Genesis* to His human creation, the right to 'hold sway' over all of His other creations, a reader sceptical of exaggerated claims about the power of language might also read it as a parable warning against 'linguistocentric' hubris. When God turned His attention to creating the first human in His own (albeit naked and mortal) 'image' and 'likeness', He had already put in a rather busy week of work, during which He created heaven and earth, sun and moon, sea and land, in which He fashioned animate forms, flora and fauna, creating a garden of grass, plants, trees, fruits and flowers in which a 'swarm of living creatures' could live. And to top off this busy week, he finally fashioned 'humus from the soil' into human being. In taxonomical terms this being might be called *Homo loquens*; for, the Lord gave His human creation not only the right but, with the gift of the corporeal capacity for speech, also the power to name His other creations. His curiosity apparently piqued in musing about how His human creation would name his (linguistically) mute cohabitants, what signs he would affix to the referents of his speech acts, the Lord brought each of His other creations before the human 'to see what he would call it, and whatever the human called a living creature, that was its name'. But given the vast difference between God's supreme power of creation and the not insignificant but, in comparison, relatively paltry human power of giving names to, creating linguistic signs for, God's already-existing creations, it is easy to imagine the Lord's attitude when observing His human creation making up names as tinged with sympathetic paternalist amusement at His child's linguistic play – perhaps not unlike the delight of the zoologists, whose understandable pleasure at their accomplishment of teaching the chimpanzee Washoe some 350 words in American sign-language I would imagine as also tinged with a bit of parental amusement. Be that as it may, the point

When speech and language are seen, not as crucial dimensions of human thought, but rather as alone the possibility and practice of thought, then it is all too easy to get caught up in a self-validating circular logic leading to the conclusion that the inverse is also true, that there is no human thought outside of language. The reduction of cognition to language is a rather impoverished notion of cognition. As Mark Johnson notes, although the restriction of 'the term "meaning" only to that which can be structurally articulated' might be 'useful ... as a strategy for formalizing aspects of our thought and language, it is far too restrictive to capture the fully embodied expanse of human meaning'.[17] And the dubious axiom that language is the possibility of thought, that thought without language is merely a 'shapeless and indistinct mass', 'a vague uncharted nebula', unjustly sentences thought to life in a 'prisonhouse of language'.[18]

The reduction of cognition to thought, and of thought to language, enables in turn exaggerated proclamations about subjecthood: that human subjects are wholly constituted by language, that language is 'constitutive of *all the coordinates that define the subject*'. It is, however, a very inflated notion of language that would posit it as the sole prerequisite and content of cognition and subjecthood. And it is a very impoverished notion of human cognition and subjecthood that would limit it to language. The refusal to approach speech and language as products of social interaction among human subjects, to consider the *madness* of speech and language, results in a fetishised elevation of language onto, as the pretender to, the throne of the 'unmoved mover', as the metasubject that constitutes individual subjects and their subjectivity by speaking through them; and the flip-side of this elevation is a reified reduction of human subjecthood to a disembodied effect of but one form of its own meaning-producing objectifications.

7.3   A Glance at Alternative Approaches to Cognition and Subjecthood

The first step in coming to terms with cognition is to establish terminological clarity. Proponents of the primacy of language tend to equate language not only with linguistically articulated 'thought', but with cognition in general.

---

  is that in *Genesis* it is not the world of words that creates the world of things, but rather the world of things that provides content for the world of words, and that in-forms thought. (The matter of words and things, signs and referents, is addressed in detail in Chapters 8 and 9.)

17 M. Johnson in Hampe 2005, p. 29.
18 The term is of course borrowed from Jameson 1972.

I will proceed, however, from a broader and etymologically justified understanding of cognition. According to the *Oxford English Dictionary*, the English signifier 'cognition' derives from the Latin *cognitiōn-em*, meaning 'a getting to know, acquaintance, notion, knowledge, etc'. And it is worth noting that even the *OED*'s 'philosophical' definition of cognition goes well beyond the realm of language and refers to 'the action or faculty of knowing taken in its widest sense, including sensation, perception, conception, etc.' – what Johnson called 'the fully embodied expanse of human meaning'.[19] It is not surprising that the 'philosophical' definition of cognition does not include in that 'etc.' feeling and volition – which from a corporeal perspective can certainly play a formative role in cognition. But what is important here is that, in contrast to one-dimensionally linguistocentric definitions, this 'philosophical' definition, even without considering feeling and volition, presents a broader, multidimensional understanding of cognition that requires us to do what should be obvious: to go beyond language and linguistics to various other disciplines – cognitive, biological, anatomical, paleoanthropological, etc. – in order to grasp the corporeal foundations and the dimensions of cognition that bear directly on the matter of determining the coordinates of subjecthood. Accordingly, I will first glance at a brief sample of what I take to be more insightful approaches to cognition and then make an argument in favour of establishing human corporeal organisation as the site of the human subject and as the foundations of inescapably 'decentred' forms of subjectivity.

In his 'classic'[20] study of the *Biological Foundations of Language* Eric Lenneberg, a student of both cognitive psychology and linguistics, ignored the various injunctions against consideration of extra-linguistic determinants of language.[21] He explicitly rejected the strong version of the so-called, but somewhat

---

19   *Oxford English Dictionary*, on-line edition. Improperly excluded from cognition in this definition are 'feeling and volition' which also play essential roles in how we perceive certain things (Impressionist painters, of course, made a living from this insight). But here, to indicate the direction of my discussion, a definition of cognition not limited to linguistically articulated thought will suffice.

20   Haspelmath et al. 2001, p. 95.

21   These included: the long-lasting effects of the ban which in 1866 the Linguistic Society of Paris imposed on its members, forbidding them to read, at any of its meetings, any papers on the topic of language evolution (see Kendon 1991, p. 200.); and also the spell cast by the misnamed 'Sapir-Whorf theory of language'. Though Lenneberg was convinced that language must have evolved, he did not think it possible or necessary to explain how it evolved in order to elaborate what he saw as the inescapably biological foundations of language – a question also outside the orthodox linguistic pale. And although working at Harvard in the 1960s when and where the so-called Sapir-Whorf theory held sway, Lenneberg was fully unpersuaded.

misnamed 'theory of linguistic relativity' espoused by Edward Sapir and Benjamin Lee Whorf who, like Benveniste, held language responsible for human cognition. Lenneberg doubted that 'natural language is a biasing factor in the formation of concepts in general' and was also 'doubtful about any strong claim upon the 'constraint' of words upon its speaker's cognitive capacities': the 'concepts tagged by the vocabulary of natural languages are not completely arbitrary as may be seen from the large degree of semantic correspondences between languages'. And although 'translation always brings out some absence of correspondence between two languages', *'the experience of the physical environment finds expression in all languages*. It is mostly the aspect of mode of reference and the metaphorical extensions that vary'.[22] In an explicit challenge to the Sapir-Whorf theory, yet based on Whorf's own research, Lenneberg insists 'that the cognitive processes ... are largely independent from peculiarities of any natural language and, in fact, that cognition can develop to a certain extent even in the absence of knowledge of any language'; and he adds that 'reverse does not hold true; the growth and development of language does appear to require a certain minimum state of maturity and specificity of cognition'.[23] Based on the understandable assumption that 'cognitive function is species-specific', Lenneberg logically concludes that human 'language is the manifestation of species-specific propensities. It is the consequence of the biological peculiarities that make a human type of cognition possible'. Inverting the linguistic theory of cognition, he insists that 'cognitive function is a more basic and primary process than language, and that the dependence-relationship of language upon cognition is incomparably stronger than vice versa'.

Lenneberg has many fellow travellers in a variety of disciplines. Also rejecting the notion that language is foundational for cognition, philosopher J.N. Findlay insists: 'It is not language that delimits kinds and descriptive features in our phenomenological neighbourhood, but the kinds and descriptive features that distinguish themselves in that neighbourhood that reflect themselves in our language. And it is the extreme uniformity of our psychophysical structure which determines the extreme uniformity, certain if anything is certain, of the world as it appears to us human subjects'.[24] Adam Kendon, biologist

---

22   Lenneberg 1967, p. 356, my italics. See in this regard my discussion of signs and referents in Chapters 8 and 9. Most pertinent here is the discussion (see Chapter 9) of Predag Matvejević's book, *Mediterranean: A Cultural Landscape* that chronicles the similar vocabularies referring to things pertaining to the sea in the different languages of the many and culturally rather diverse peoples living on the shores of the Mediterranean Sea.

23   Lenneberg 1967, p. 364. Following citations in this paragraph, ibid., p. 371; pp. 374–5.

24   Findlay 1982, p. 550. A reminder that 'to reflect' does not have to be taken, as do the 'lin-

and experimental psychologist studying cognition and the possibility of a gestural origin of language, points out that 'before a child uses language he or she already appears to possess concepts which language then represents'. The 'crucial point' is that in order 'to be able to acquire linguistic expressions, [a child] must first have a system of concepts in place. Language does not create the conceptual system, at least it does not in the very first place. It serves to represent it'.[25] Comparative studies of cognition in human and ape infants document, as David Premack reports, the 'thoroughgoing superiority of the pre-language child on every measure used'; this indicates, Premack concludes, that 'the cognitive advantage to the human is not one introduced by language. ... The addition of language to the proto-human did not create a difference but amplified one that already existed. For proto-human intelligence already greatly exceeded that of the ape'.[26] And Elizabeth Spelke's studies of infant cognition lead to similar conclusions: '[T]he organization of the world into objects precedes the development of language and thus does not depend on it'.[27]

Non-linguistic cognition is not limited to dividing the world into things that become referents of linguistic signs. What Heidegger insightfully called (before myopically overlooking it – see Chapter 4) a hidden 'bodily problematic' opens onto wide vistas of non-linguistic, corporeally-grounded cognition. Spelke suspects 'that language plays no important role in the spontaneous elaboration of physical knowledge. To learn that objects tend to move at smooth speeds, for example, one need only observe objects and their motions; one need not articulate the principles of one's theory or communicate with others about it'.[28] As J.J. Gibson exemplifies with an outfielder chasing a flying baseball or a cat after a rolling ball of yarn, a theoretical knowledge of physics is not required for a tacit and practically efficacious perceptual understanding of the laws of physics. Also drawing on studies of the conceptualising abilities of pre-linguistic chil-

---

guistically turned', as 'to replicate': anyone who has cast a stone into a body of still water would know that reflections can be distorted or, more neutrally, can alter the form of what is being reflected. Findlay's comment about the 'features in our phenomenological neighborhood', like Lenneberg's that 'the experience of the physical environment finds expression in all languages' (see note 22), are relevant to the question of the rehabilitation of the referent addressed in Part 3.

25   Kendon 1991, p. 207. By 'represent', Kendon does not mean 're-present' or replicate, but 'represent' in the sense of 'standing for', 'signifying'.
26   Premack in Weiskrantz 1988, p. 64. Premack adds that 'the difference between ape and human intelligence lies not in the ability to profit by school; it lies rather in the ability to have invented school'.
27   Spelke in Weiskrantz 1988, p. 181.
28   Spelke 1988, pp. 181–2.

dren as well as of the prevalence of non-linguistic transmission of (culturally specific) practical knowledge, anthropologist Maurice Bloch similarly argues: that 'language is not essential for conceptual thought'; 'that much of knowledge is fundamentally non-linguistic'; 'that concepts involve implicit networks of meanings which are formed through the experience of, and practice in, the external world'; and, in recognition of the refractive (but not tyrannical) power of language, 'that, under certain circumstances, this non-linguistic knowledge can be rendered into language and thus take the form of explicit discourse, but changing its character in the process' – in short, that human cognition, subjectivity, is the ground of language, not vice versa.[29] Practical knowledge, Bloch explains, 'seems to be passed on in ways unknown to us'; the operations connected with practical domains 'not only *are* non-linguistic but also *must* be non-linguistic if they are to be efficient' – from which 'it follows that much of the [cultural] knowledge which anthropologists study necessarily exists in people's heads in a non-linguistic form'. And he concludes furthermore that 'we should see linguistic phenomena as a *part* of culture, most of which is non-linguistic'.

Similarly, neural psychologist Don M. Tucker who also sees language as the (very important) tip of the cognitive iceberg. He suggests that only 'people with no training in psychology' would see language as 'the defining property of the human mind' and argues instead that 'only the surface of meaning is conscious' whereas the 'mechanisms of experience are largely unconscious'. Although 'language, captured in the words of a culture, became an effective, disembodied vehicle of mind [,] ... it remains a product of bodily structures in each generative act. By recognizing the visceral and somatic frames of corticolimbic network organization, we may approach the bodily context of the mind's language in a fresh way'.[30] Although what follows will probably not be the 'fresh way' that Tucker had in mind, its approach to the problems of body and mind, subjecthood and subjectivity, 'up from the body' is radically different from that of the language-centred – and one that, while different in content, does, I think, run in the same direction as that pointed out by the various thinkers mentioned in this and the preceding few paragraphs.

While acknowledging and admiring the astonishing power of language to express in words not only the worlds we perceive, but also unseen worlds that we imagine, we must also acknowledge that there is much more to cognition and thought than is dreamt of in language-centred approaches to cognition and subjectivity. As Michael Polanyi put it so succinctly, even within the range

---

29   Maurice Bloch 1991, p. 186. Following citations from Bloch, ibid., p. 186; p. 189; p. 189; p. 192.
30   Tucker 2007, p. 43, p. 139, p. 141, p. 242.

of our corporeally defined experience, we 'know more than we can tell'. How often do we sputter in utter frustration some form of the statement, 'I don't have the words to say what I mean'; 'I can't put this into words'? Metaphor in general, and poetry in particular might both be linguistic attempts to counter the inability of language to say what we mean. There must, then, be more to cognition than language. And the pursuit of that 'more' points in the direction of a historical-materialist theory of subjecthood.

7.4   Of Bodies and Minds, Corporeality and Cognition

The problematic of the subject is inseparable from the mind-body question. As often noted in the preceding, the Western philosophical mainstream was grounded in a mind-body dualism that designated the mind as the site of reason. Although it first appeared explicitly with Descartes and modern philosophy, the notion of subjecthood is grounded in the same mind-body dualism that has been running through the Western philosophical mainstream since Plato and Aristotle. And although poststructuralist/postmodernist critics of that philosophical tradition have succeeded in decentring the 'logocentric' subject, they have not, their claims to the contrary notwithstanding, succeeded in overcoming mind/body dualism; for they did not at all shift the site of subjecthood away from the mind whose thoughts are allegedly made, and made known, through language alone. Because of its intimate connection to the question of subjecthood, my first step will be to clarify what I take to be a historical-materialist stance on the mind-body relation.

While struggling in the *1844 Manuscripts* to develop a materialist notion of the mind/body relation, Marx wrote that 'Thinking and being are indeed *different*, but are nonetheless in *unity* with each other'.[31] This straightforward and not inaccurate, but still very abstract comment is a decent place to start. Still unanswered, of course, is the question of how exactly to understand this 'unity' of body and mind. To answer this question adequately, it is necessary to avoid reductionism, whether in the form of the idealist tyranny of the mind ('centred' or 'decentred') over the body or the materialist tyranny of the body over the mind. The challenge is to delineate the relation between body and mind in such a way that avoids conflating them, subsuming one to the other, or leaving them as integral but mutually indifferent parts of a whole; more specifically, how to elaborate a 'differential unity' of mind and body.

---

31   Marx 1844 in Tucker 1978, p. 86.

The notion of a 'differential unity' is a dialectical designation that goes beyond both an impossible dualism and an easy monism.[32] 'Differential unity' signifies the inseparable relation of mind and body as components of human corporeal organisation; it preserves their differences, acknowledges the proper locus and logos of each, and also recognises their necessary interdependence. This approach does not at all deny the cognitive, reflective and imaginative capacities of the mind. But it does insist that corporeality is essential to cognition as itself a 'cognitive apparatus' and also as a reservoir of absolutely indispensable, unconscious (by which I do *not* mean 'instinctual' – see below) 'tacit knowledge' that fundamentally in-forms cognition. Thus, as I shall elaborate in the following, corporeality itself establishes the coordinates of the subject.

The first step, however, is to discover or invent an adequate term to signify this differential unity of body and mind. As I have explained often in the preceding (esp. Chapter 4), the term 'embodied minds', regularly forwarded in poststructuralist-oriented analyses as beyond mind-body dualism, seems, to borrow Maxine Sheets-Johnstone's unforgettably apt formulations, no more than 'a lexical band-aid put on a three-century old metaphysical wound' inflicted by Cartesian dualism; and the programme of 'embodied knowledges' that follows from this formulation 'actually takes the body itself for granted in its entire epistemological enterprise; functioning as an indexical, the body is simply the place one puts one's epistemology', an 'epistemological receptacle'.[33]

There are, however, three other terminological possibilities, proposed by Mark Johnson, Michael Steinberg, and Sheets-Johnstone herself, that are worth considering. These three advocates seem to be designating the same content, and in ways compatible with my notion of a 'differential unity of mind and body'. And because they attach different terms to the same essential content, a debate about the strengths and weaknesses of each might seem a mere terminological quibble. But in quibbling over, and explaining my preference among, the three signifiers, I can give more texture to that signified content.

Mark Johnson suggests John Dewey's notion of 'body-mind'. In Dewey's words: 'body-mind simply designates what actually takes place when a living body is implicated in situations of discourse, communication, and participa-

---

32 I cobbled together 'differential unity' from Marx's statement in the *1844 Manuscripts* that 'Thinking and being are indeed *different*, but are nonetheless in *unity* with each other' (Marx 1844 in Tucker 1978, p. 86).

33 See Sheets-Johnstone 1994, p. 66. Sheets-Johnstone refers specifically to 'embodiment' as the 3-century old metaphysical wound, but her words are equally applicable to 'embodied mind'. See also Sheets-Johnstone 2011.

tion. In the hyphenated phrase body-mind, "body" designates the continued and conserved, the registered and cumulative operation of factors continuous with the rest of nature, inanimate as well as animate; while "mind" designates the characters and consequences which are differential, indicative of features which emerge when "body" is engaged in a wider, more complex and interdependent situation'.[34] Although Dewey certainly treats the body as far more than a simple prerequisite, a vessel bearing the mind, and although he attributes to the body its own essential role in cognition, I find the term 'body-mind' not quite appropriate. For there is, it seems to me, a hint of dualism in its hyphenation – a sense that the two parts, though both indispensable and mutually interdependent, are related as parallels rather than in a differential unity.

Although he defines the relation between body and mind in a manner similar to Dewey, Michael Steinberg suggests a different name. Situating the mind firmly in the body, he insists that 'We are not thinking beings at all but bodies that think and without the body thinking wanders into irrelevance'.[35] Elaborating, he explains:

> We incarnate knowledge of our environment as we bring forth and refine our responses to it. Our acts literally incorporate social, personal, and genetic history; all are present in the body that in hearing, seeing, and responding is continually transformed. These transformations and the knowledge they embody do not require any level of awareness. Reflection serves to turn some of the implicit comprehension of the flesh into explicit discourse, but the knowledge exists and is manifested in behavior whether it's explicit of purely embodied. Just because an organism cannot tell us what it knows doesn't mean that it knows nothing.

Steinberg concludes therefore that '[l]ike all other animals, we are *thinking bodies*'. Although I do find the term 'thinking body' more appropriate than Dewey's body-mind precisely because it implies a more immediate and intimate relation between corporeality and cognition, my one reservation is its at least implicit equation of cognition with thinking. It seems clear that Steinberg, as well as Dewey and Johnson, would agree that thinking is not the only dimension of cognition.

---

34   John Dewey cited in Johnson in Hampe 2005, p. 22.
35   Steinberg 2005, p. 23. Following two citations, ibid., p. 41, my italics. I have also altered the order of Steinberg's sentences: the last sentence cited ('Like all other ...') precedes the previously cited sentences ('We incarnate knowledge ...').

For this reason, I prefer Maxine Sheets-Johnstone's notion of the 'mindful body'.[36] Not only does it avoid the hyphenated hint of dualism, but it firmly situates the mind in a species-specific body; and it also suggests a broader and deeper notion of cognition. The 'mindful body' encompasses not just the conscious cognitive processes of thinking and reflection, but also the tacit cognitive processes that in-form our 'acts of understanding and knowing'.[37] First of all, the term 'mindful body' forces us to consider the different ways in which different species are mindful, the variations caused of course by differences in the cognitive apparatuses (sense organs, brain, kinaesthetics) and their capacities. And because it better encompasses the greater breadth of the relation between corporeality and cognition than either 'body-mind' or 'thinking body', approaching the body as mindful allows us to address not only the corporeal roots of thinking, the corporeal structuring of our 'acts of understanding and knowing', but also the epistemological efficacy of corporeal organisation as itself a body of knowledge and as a reservoir of 'tacit knowledge'. These are the issues that delineate the *corporeal* coordinates of subjecthood and that, following further elaboration of the notion of 'mindful body', will be addressed in the remainder of this chapter.

7.5   The Corporeal Coordinates of Subjecthood

7.5.1   *Animate Form as Subjecthood*

One of the curious things about both linguistically or culturally ultra-constructionist approaches to subjecthood, and also Marxist approaches deriving from Althusser's notion of the 'interpellation' of the subject, is that they completely avoid a very simple and very basic question, namely: what were subjects before they became linguistically (or culturally) constituted or interpellated subjects? The lack of an answer to this question seems to imply that the 'subjectivation process' is practiced on mere matter lacking in any and all art. And although Deleuze and Guattari (see Chapter 4) take an earthy step toward corporeality in describing human bodies as 'desiring machines' that perform all kinds

---

36   See Sheets-Johnstone 2011. As the following elaboration makes clear, this use of the 'mindful body' refers to the cognitive capacities of the human brain that frames the ways in which we can be aware of the world or, in Mark Johnson terms, the ways in which we mentally 'have' the world. It is not to be confused with 'mindfulness' in its Buddhist or New Age version – each of which, in its own way, seeks to still the body to prevent it from encroaching on the mind.

37   M. Johnson in Hampe 2005, p. 16.

of bodily functions ('eating, shitting, fucking, urinating, etc.'), it is not insignificant that all other sexually-reproducing species do so as well.[38] While it is crucial to determine the particular ways in which a given species eats, shits, etc., this notion of corporeality is rather limited. What must be added are the particular ways in which a species perceives (what kind of sensory organs with what range), moves (in locomotion, in interacting with objects and with conspecifics), and works, (satisfies its needs and makes its world). Far from being a *tabula rasa* awaiting inscription, prescription, discipline, and/or interpellation, corporeality (and not just that of humans) is itself, I shall argue, both a site and a source of the objectifying capacities that allow human beings (among other species) to make their worlds consisting of material, social, and semiotic artefacts – the site and source, in short, of subjecthood. If agency is the key attribute of subjecthood, and if by agency we mean the purposeful navigation of the world (whether in the form of doing, knowing, speaking, or, as I call it: objectifying; and regardless of whether that navigation is 'right' or 'wrong', 'centred' or 'decentred'), then subjecthood may more appropriately be understood, not as the 'end of the chain'[39] by which a nebulous, non-descript entity is interpellated, inscribed, linguistically constituted, or performed into subjecthood, but as the starting point, that is: subjecthood is the always already existing condition that is grounded in the corporeal organisation of an organism's animate form.

This is the position articulated by Maxine Sheets-Johnstone in *The Roots of Thinking*. As we might surmise from that title, Sheets-Johnstone insists that only if we begin with 'the living [human] body' will we be able to grasp the roots of [human] cognition: 'The key to an understanding of the dynamics of the reciprocal relationship between hominid thinking and hominid evolution lies in deepened understandings of the body, specifically, in corporeal analyses of a hominid animate form and tactile-kinesthetic body'. By 'animate form', she means 'a species-specific body with all its various spatial conformations, and attendant everyday postures, modes of locomotion, movements, and gestures. In broad terms, animate form is equivalent to the spatiality of the body in all its dimensions'. And the *tactile-kinesthetic body*, she explains, 'is the sentiently felt body, the body that knows the world through touch and movement. It is not the body that simply *behaves* in certain observed or observable ways, but the body that resonates in the first-person, lived-through sense of any behaviour. It is the experienced and experiencing body. The thesis that thinking is modelled

---

38   Deleuze and Guattari 1986, p. 1.
39   Lecercle 2009, p. 208.

on the body thus links thinking to spatial and sentient-kinetic life'.[40] Because 'sentient' life must include not only the tactile sense, but all of the internal and external sensory apparatuses inherent in an animate form, I would amend by expanding Sheets-Johnstone's concept of the 'tactile-kinesthetic body' to the 'sensory-kinesthetic body'; but with that amendment, I follow the general path of her argument.[41]

To understand the 'natural history' of consciousness, Sheets-Johnstone begins with the relation between the sensory-kinesthetic body and what we might have to call 'self-consciousness': 'A creature's corporeal consciousness is first and foremost a consciousness attuned to the movement and rest of its own body. When a creature moves, it breaks forth from whatever resting position it was in; it *initiates* movement, and in ways appropriate to the situation in which it finds itself'. This 'corporeal consciousness' consists structurally of 'four kinetic dimensions of spontaneity':

> A creature's initiation of movement is coincident with its kinesthetic motivations, its dispositions to do this or that – turn, pause, crouch, freeze, run, or constrict; its kinesthetic motivations fall within the range of its species-specific movement possibilities. ... [T]hese possibilities are the basis of its particular repertoire of 'I cans', a repertoire that may not only change over the lifetime of the animal as it ages, but that may be selectively distinguished insofar as the animal can run faster, for example, or conceal itself more effectively than other members of its group; as enacted, any item within its repertoire of 'I cans' is undergirded proprioceptively (kinesthetically) by a sense of agency.[42]

Adopting the notion of 'I-cans' from Edmund Husserl, Sheets-Johnstone gives it concrete corporeal content. By taking the species-specific corporeality (which *is* the organism as animate form) as her starting point, she re-coins Husserl's concept of 'I-cans' into a notion of 'bodily I-cans', the range of which is established by the capacities and limits embedded in that corporeality:

---

40 All quotations in this paragraph from Sheets-Johnstone 1990, pp. 4–5.
41 This amendment is not inconsistent with Sheets-Johnstone's perspective, for in a later work (1998, p. 134) she essentially makes the same amendment. Elaborating further the Husserlian term 'animate organism', she explains that it 'refers in more and more refined ways to living beings whose animateness is the foundation of their perceptual world, including the perceptual world of their own bodies'.
42 Sheets-Johnstone 1998, pp. 70–1.

> The term 'animate form' adumbrates corporeal matters of fact and possibilities. [...] [A]nimate forms are intending and knowing subjects. They are creatures caught up in making their way in an ever-changing world. They are creatures whose bodily logos endows them with a capacity for survival [which includes the capacities for what I am calling the objectifying practices involved in world-making], but a capacity that is always at the mercy of *circonstances*, as Lamarck modestly termed what we now know to be the fragility of ecological balances and relationships.[43]

In this way, Sheets-Johnstone redefines the coordinates of subjecthood: the capacities embedded in the corporeality of animate forms, the corporeal 'I-cans', constitute the *I* who *can* – and also the *I* who has a sense of self: 'creatures know themselves ... in ways that are fundamentally and quintessentially consistent with the bodies they are. They know themselves in these ways not by *looking* ... but proprioceptively, or more finely, kinesthetically, i.e. in ways specific to movement alone, sensing their bodies as animate forms in movement and at rest'.[44]

> This primal animateness, this original kinetic spontaneity that infuses our being and defines our aliveness, is our point of departure for living in the world and making sense of it. It is the epistemological foundation of our learning to move ourselves with respect to objects, and thus the foundation of a developing repertoire of 'I cans' with respect to both the natural and artefactual array of objects that happen to surround us as individuals in our particular worlds. It is in effect the foundation of our sense of ourselves as agents with a surrounding world. But it is even more basically the epistemological foundation of our sense of who and what we are. *We literally discover ourselves in movement.* We grow kinetically into our bodies.

---

43 Sheets-Johnstone 1998, p. 368.
44 Sheets-Johnstone 1998, pp. 70–1. Following two indented citations, ibid., p. 136; p. 138. See also. Rejecting the 'primacy of language', Margaret S. Archer insists on the 'primacy of [corporeal] practice'. She notes the tacit recognition of the corporeal roots of cognition in subjectivity even in the thought of the social constructionist Emile Durkheim, who 'wanted to conceive of the "self" as "indeterminate material", awaiting the social impress, conceded that all animals, ourselves included have the capacity to make "rudimentary distinctions in the flux of experience", otherwise they could not navigate the natural environment' (Archer 2000, p. 121).

> In effect, *movement forms the I that moves before the I that moves forms movement*. Spontaneous movement is the constitutive source of agency, of subjecthood, of selfhood, the dynamic core of our sense of ourselves as agents, subjects, selves. [...] Our very emergence as cognizing subjects is grounded in our original kinetic spontaneity.

Although these passages focus on *human* animate form and subjecthood, the ability to navigate the world and its objects depends on a certain amount of proprioception. That proprioception includes knowing which corporeal instruments are fit for the various kinds of cognitive processes, '[t]hat we in some way perceive our eyes, our ears, and the other parts of our body', was, Giorgio Agamben notes, already understood by Hierocles of Alexandra in the fifth century BCE, who explained: 'if we want to look at something, we direct our eyes and not our ears at it, and when we want to listen, we incline our ears and not our eyes, and if we want to walk, we do not use our hands for this but our feet and legs'.[45] And as Gibson made clear with the example of a cat's knowledge of the angle and corresponding speed it needs to take in order to intercept a ball of yarn, this awareness of the self's abilities and limits, this sense of 'being-in and moving-about the world', is an embodied sense of self and agency that is not limited to *Homo sapiens*. The corporeally rooted species-specific coordinates of animate (that is to say: mindful) bodies are what make animal organisms of all kinds both always already subjects endowed with agency, cognition, and a reservoir of tacit knowledge, that is: centred subjects; and also, because inescapably subject to their own corporeal limits, always already, decentred subjects. My redirection of Nagel's question, 'What is it like to be a bat?' to 'What is it like to be human?' is nothing more than positing the question that follows from the Delphic injunction to 'know thyself'. The remainder of this chapter will be devoted to giving more specific content to these notions.

7.5.2 What Is It Like To Be a Human? The Wisdom of the Body and (Human) Subjecthood[46]

In his reflections on the question of whether human beings could grasp 'what it is like to be a bat', Thomas Nagel concludes that we can at best 'ascribe general *types* of [bat] experience on the basis of [the bat's] structure and behaviour'.[47] Nagel certainly recognises the value of establishing those general types

---

45 Hierocles, cited in Agamben 2015, p. 50.
46 The first part of this title is an adaptation of the title Thomas Nagel's 1974 essay 'What Is It Like to Be a Bat?', and the second part from Walter B. Cannon (1932).
47 Nagel 1974, pp. 435–50; p. 439. Following citation ibid. Nagel recognises the difficulty of mutual understanding among humans with different experiences, and mentions specific-

through studying an organism's cognitive apparatus and behavioural habits. But he makes what should be the obvious point that it is simply 'beyond our ability to conceive' what it is like to be a bat; and he acknowledges that we can do no more than form 'a schematic conception' of bat-hood. Rephrasing this conclusion in terms used here: we can never know what it is like to be a bat because we do not have the corporeal organisation to experience, navigate, apprehend, and comprehend the world as does a bat – and without which we have no access to the subjective experience of a bat (or any other species, for that matter).

One would think that would-be responders to a reposing of Nagel's question about the *Dasein* of *Chiroptera* as a query into what it is like to be a human primate would have an advantage: not only able to consider the objective conditions of human experience, i.e. human corporeal organisation, but also having an insider's perspective on human subjective experience(s). But as noted often in the preceding chapters, neither the mainstream of the Western philosophical tradition nor the currently prevailing ultra-constructionist tendencies in the humanities and social sciences have shown much interest in the essential corporeal contributions to human subjectivity. The philosophical mainstream has treated the body at best as a simple prerequisite of subjectivity; and ultra-constructionists proclaim that subjective experience is wholly constituted through linguistic or cultural semiotics and that the body itself is a linguistic or cultural construction. Neither of these not so distantly related approaches to the mind-body relation would be anything but appalled by the suggestion that corporeal organisation could even affect, let alone be a definitive constitutive factor in, human subjective experience and in the constitution of human subjects. And if we cannot know what it is like to be a bat because we can only delineate the conditions and general types of the subjective experience of bats based on analysis of their structure and behaviour, neither can we know what it is like to be human if we focus only on subjective experience and leave the corporeal conditions and constitution of subjective experience to the insidious bias of neglect.

---

ally the impossibility of a sighted person to know how the world is perceived by a blind person (ibid., p. 449). But as is clear from the telling anecdote related by Jakobson and Waugh about the blind person, who after hearing definitions of the colour scarlet, finally felt he had understood its meaning, that the colour scarlet is 'like the sound of a trumpet', it is the general sameness of their corporeal organisation that provides the basis for a mutual understanding (Jakobson and Waugh 1979; see Chapter 6, note 526). To a bat, such a comparison would truly be incomprehensible because of the vastly different visual and audial apparatuses. The reference to 'having a world' is from M. Johnson's *The Body in the Mind* (1987), and will be addressed shortly.

The necessary (if necessarily insufficient) first step of a historical-materialist response to Nagel's question posed to our own species would be to investigate the human corporeal organisation that is the 'first fact' of human life, experience, and history, in order to understand 'the general types of human experience on the basis of the animal's structure and behaviour' – to understand human corporeal organisation not only as the form-determinant that establishes the conditions and the range of contents of human subjectivity and as an essential participant in the process of knowledge production, but also as itself a body of knowledge. That first step is of course a rather big one – so big that the lengthy attempt in the preceding chapter to map the corporeal organisation that frames human experience, and the attempt to articulate the relation between corporeality and cognition in this one, is far from complete. But although that cartographical sketch of human corporeal organisation is still too incomplete to allow the drawing of definitive conclusions, it is, I think, sufficiently suggestive of some of the ways in which human corporeality structures, frames, and organises human subjective experience(s) and also of some of the guiding threads of a historical-materialist research programme of thinking history 'up from the body'. And by way of providing a historical-materialist response to Nagel's question redirected to our own species, I offer in the following a concluding summary of the 'wisdom of the body' as portrayed in the preceding and present chapters, and organised around the work of three distinct but very compatible perspectives on the relation between corporeality and cognition: Konrad Lorenz's view of the body of an organism as a *Wissenschaft*, a body of objectified knowledge; the notion of the 'cognitive unconscious' developed by Mark Johnson and George Lakoff; and Michael Polanyi's elucidation of 'tacit knowledge'. Together these perspectives help in excavating and articulating the profoundly corporeal roots of cognition.

7.5.2.1   Corporeal Organisation as *Wissenschaft*, an 'Open Book' of an Organism's 'Body of Knowledge'

Ernst Mayr, as Philip Lieberman noted, has pointed out time and again that the structure and physiology of any living organism necessarily reflect its evolutionary history.[48] Similarly Konrad Lorenz in his 'Search for a Natural History of Human Knowledge', the subtitle of his book *Behind the Mirror*,[49] depicts an organism's evolution as a process of absorbing information about the world it inhabits; and he roots the epistemological process in a cognitive apparatus not

---

48   Lieberman 1991, p. 11.
49   Lorenz 1973. On the problems with using Lorenz, see Müller-Hill 1988 and Deichmann 1992. Further comment on Lorenz and National Socialism, note 62 below.

limited to just the 'mind' or even the brain, but consisting rather of the entire body. He views 'evolution, that eons-long process of genesis in the course of which all organisms have confronted the givens of reality and, as we say, "adapted" to it', as 'one of knowledge' that 'produces in the organic system actual images of the outside world'.[50]

Lorenz exemplifies this by noting that '[t]he fish's motion and the shape of its fins reflect the hydrodynamic properties of water, which possess [sic] these properties irrespective of whether there are fins moving through it or not'.[51] And with a nod to Goethe's perspicacity, he adds that 'the eye is an image of the sun and of the physical properties of light, which are present irrespective of whether the eye is there to see the light or not'.[52] More generally, as he noted elsewhere: 'Every species of animal and plant has adapted itself to its environment in a process of adjustment lasting eons; in a sense each species is the image of its environment. The form of the horse's hoof is just as much an image of the steppe it treads as the impression it leaves is an image of the hoof'.[53] Not just morphology, however, but also an organism's information acquisition devices are, and provide, images of its environment: 'The sense organs and central nervous system enable living organisms to acquire relevant information about the world and to use this information for their survival. ... Everything we know about the material world in which we live derives from our phylogenetic-

---

50 *Behind the Mirror* 6. Translation altered: Taylor translates *äonenlang* as 'age-long' when it is more accurately rendered 'eons-long'. This is a trifle, but more serious is the translation of *in dessen Verlauf sich alle Organismen mit den Gegebenheiten der Wirklichkeit auseinandergesetzt und – wie wir zu sagen pflegen – angepaßt haben* as 'in the course of which all organisms have come to terms with external reality' (Lorenz 1982, p. 17). The use of 'come to terms with external reality' renders the organism more passive than does '*auseinandergesetzt*' which refers to the confrontations between the organism and the 'givens of reality' – a process in which the organism, as Levins and Lewontin put it, is not only an object, but also a subject of its own evolution.

51 In terms of Walter Benjamin's historical-materialist monadology (addressed in Chapter 10 below), the corporeal organisation of a given organism reflects the entire universe from its particular perspective.

52 Lorenz 1973, p. 6. Marx may have been thinking of Goethe's comment when in the *1844 Manuscripts* he wrote: 'The sun is the *object* of the plant – an indispensable object to it, confirming its life – just as the plant is an object of the sun, being an *expression* of the life-awakening power of the sun, of the sun's *objective* essential power'. Generalising, he concludes: 'A being which does not have its nature outside itself is not a *natural* being, and plays no part in the system of nature. A being which has no object outside itself is not an objective being. A being which is not itself an object for some third being has no being for its *object*; i.e., it is not objectively related. Its being is not objective', and: 'An unobjective being is a nullity – an un-being'. Marx 1844 in Tucker 1978, p. 116.

53 Lorenz 1972, pp. 1–2.

ally evolved mechanisms for acquiring information'.[54] With the reminder that the term 'information' itself 'primarily means "giving form"', Lorenz concludes that 'what an organism learns of external reality is 'impressed' or 'imprinted' on it', quite literally in-corporated into, embodied in the organism.[55]

Lorenz's general insight that an organism's morphology is 'in-formed' by and about its environment is, as stated, in need of qualification. This is supplied by Donald Campbell who agrees that an organism's morphology (e.g. the shape of a horse's hoof) certainly expresses 'knowledge' of the environment (the steppe). He adds, however, the caveat that this knowledge is expressed 'in a very odd and partial language, and in an end product mixed with "knowledge" of other contingencies'. Campbell exemplifies that 'odd and partial language' with the immense biodiversity of aquatic organisms all 'in-formed' by the same hydrodynamic law: 'The hydrodynamics of sea water, plus the ecological value of locomotion, have independently shaped fish, whale, and walrus in a quite similar fashion. Their shapes represent independent discoveries of this same "knowledge" expressed in this case in similar "languages". But the jet-propelled squid reflects the same hydrodynamic principles in a quite different, but perhaps equally "accurate" and "objective" shape'. He thus concludes that the *'Ding an sich* is always known indirectly, always in the language of the knower's posits, be these mutations governing bodily form, visual percepts, or scientific theories'.[56] Neither arbitrary nor determined, the quite diverse morphologies and ethologies (in the etymological sense of behavioural logic) of aquatic species are different, relatively motivated ways of knowing the same environment. An organism's corporeal organisation may thus be appropriately viewed as the oddly expressed, particular rationality of a species – what we might call a 'decentred' knowledge of the world objectified in a corporeal form that is functionally commensurate with the organism's needs and capacities.

---

54   Lorenz 1972, p. 6. In addition to morphology and the sensory apparatuses, Lorenz insists here also that ethology, '[t]he behaviour of men and animals, in so far as it is adapted to their environment, is an image of that environment'. This important point is, however, formulated too generally and needs the qualification that Donald Campbell gave it. See next paragraph in text and next note here.

55   Lorenz 1972, pp. 22–3. Arguing similarly, psychologist Richard Gregory writes that '[e]ven the simplest living organisms are supreme examples of potential intelligence [which Gregory defines as "the power of knowledge to solve problems"], as they are solutions to incredibly difficult problems, which were solved over millions of years by the brainless blind steps of natural selection. So although plants are hardly intelligent in the kinetic intelligence sense of psychologists [the capacity for "knowledge production"], they embody immense potential intelligence as created through evolution, though its processes are blind' (Gregory in Gregory and Marstrand 1987, p. 6; pp. 7–8).

56   Campbell 1987, p. 85.

The information absorbed into an organism's morphology is, to give an evolutionary twist to Judith Butler's terminology, a performative process of interaction with its environment, a 'process of materialization that stabilizes over time'. What it produces, however, is not what she calls the 'effect' of 'boundary, fixity, and surface we call matter', but the *actual* boundary, fixity, and surface, the outer form, and also the entire internal anatomy and physiology making up the corporeal organisation of a species. And here the 'materialization' is not just a consequence of a process of performative repetition that moulds a supposedly infinitely malleable, culturally constructed body that could relatively easily be performatively altered. It is rather the far less malleable corporeal organisation of an organism's natural body – a natural body that itself evolved through the organism's interaction with the world outside itself and within the possibilities and limits imposed by both its own corporeal organisation or *Bauplan* and the environment it inhabits. The corporeal organisation of a given organism quite literally *is* objectified knowledge of its environment, a body of knowledge, a corporeal *Wissenschaft*. And the succession of changes in the corporeal organisation of an organism, its morphogenesis, might be seen as the history of that organism's science.[57] What Marx said of technology, namely that it can be read as an 'open book of human essential powers', we might similarly say of an organism's corporeal organisation namely: an organism's corporeal organisation is the organism's evolutionary history objectified – and can be read as 'an open book', a graphic memoire, of that organism's heritage and life process, its interaction with and knowledge of its environment.

In addition to signifying a 'body of knowledge', the term *Wissenschaft* also refers to the systematic pursuit of knowledge. And Lorenz extends this sense of the term to the 'cognitive apparatus' embedded in an organism's corporeal organisation. From Egon Brunswick, he borrows the term 'ratiomorphus' (of rational form) to describe the 'sensory and nervous processes [that] take place in areas of our nervous system which are completely inaccessible to our consciousness and our self-observation'. 'Ratiomorphus' are those processes that, 'although ... closely analogous to rational behaviour in both formal and functional respects, ... have nothing to do with conscious reason'.[58] From this standpoint there is nothing oxymoronic about the notion of 'unconscious reason'; for an organism's ratiomorphus processes are essential to its cognitive appar-

---

57   If one were interested in translating this into Thomas Kuhn's terms, one could argue that each species-specific corporeal organisation is its 'paradigm' and its phenotypic changes are its normal science until they accumulate so much that speciation, the development of a new 'paradigm', occurs. See Kuhn 1962.
58   Lorenz 1972, p. 119. All citations in this and following paragraph, ibid., pp. 6–7.

atus, and therewith to its ability to acquire not just information, but meaningful information. Invoking a 'realist' epistemological perspective and appealing to that 'common sense' so often derided by the philosophical tradition, Lorenz insists that the 'cognitive apparatus' of a given species 'is itself an objective reality which has acquired its present form through contact with and adaptation to equally real things in the outer world'. As such, it produces referentially accurate information about actual things and events occurring in the world: 'everything we know about the material world in which we live derives from our phylogenetically evolved mechanisms for acquiring information'. He therefore concludes that 'whatever our cognitive faculty communicates to us corresponds to something real'; for '[t]he "spectacles" of our modes of thought and perception ... are functions of a neurosensory organization that has evolved in the service of survival'.

These 'spectacles' include the (Kantian) categories of 'causality, substance, quality, time and place' (which can, of course, be given diverse, culturally-specific contents). Anticipating scepticism from 'transcendental idealists' who argue that our cognitive 'spectacles' produce 'some unpredictable distortion of reality which does not correspond in the least with things as they really are, and therefore cannot be regarded as an image of the outer world', he counters (with what also serves as an anticipatory response to poststructuralist sceptics): 'What we experience is indeed a real image of reality – albeit an extremely simple one, only just sufficing for our own practical purposes; we have developed "organs" only for those aspects of reality of which, in the interest of survival, it was imperative for our species to take account, so that selection pressure produced this particular cognitive apparatus'. The reality that we humans can know is thus (and the immense variation in culturally specific determinations of that reality notwithstanding) an inescapably 'anthropocentric' one – and for that reason, an inescapably limited one.

Lorenz is fully aware that 'no scientific understanding of man's physiological functions can in any way detract from the value of the higher activities based on these functions'.[59] His point is simply to show that there is more to knowledge production than conceptualisation, that it does not debase the 'higher' mental forms of cognition to recognize that they are based in and substantively informed by the 'lower' corporeally rooted and produced forms of tacit cognition. Lorenz elaborates this by situating his view in relation to Kant's explanation of the 'higher' forms of knowledge, perception, and conception in the *Critique of Pure Reason*. He argues that the facts of evolution discovered since Kant's

---

59   Lorenz 1972, p. 4. Following citation in this paragraph, ibid., p. 9.

time make possible the reconciliation, not of the mind with the '*Ding an sich*', but of the 'transcendental structure of the mind' with aspects of reality. Lorenz agrees that a cognitive apparatus pre-structuring experience exists '*a priori* to the extent that it is present before the individual experiences anything, and must be present if experience is to be possible'. But he differs in two important ways from the idealist philosopher.

First, whereas for the pre-Darwinian Kant the mind's transcendental structure, that which brings conceptual order to the contents of perception, is simply there, *a priori*, Lorenz offers an evolutionary perspective in place of Kant's essentialist explanation of an organism's cognitive apparatus: 'the system of sense organs and nerves that enables living things to survive and orient themselves in the outer world has evolved phylogenetically through confrontation with, and in adaptation to, that form of reality which we experience as phenomenal space'.[60] Secondly, (and echoing Darwin's refutation of Plato's claim that our 'imaginary ideas' arise from 'the preexistence of the soul' and not from 'experience' with the simple response, 'read monkeys for preexistence'[61]), Lorenz argues that this 'transcendental structure of the mind' is not pure *Geist*, but is rather firmly and polymorphously rooted in human corporeal organisation; this includes not only the organs of sense perception that pre-structure what aspects of the world we can perceive and thereby determine the range and limits of possible experience and knowledge, but also corporeality itself as a body of incorporated knowledge.

The 'realism' and the 'universality' of this line of reasoning about the peculiarly human cognitive apparatus does not at all entail a simple reductive explanation of the (culturally variable) *contents* of human consciousness as products of natural selection. The claim is not that there is one truth, and that that is Western, but rather that there is one set of species-specific *mechanisms* of knowledge acquisition (brain organisation, sense organs, corporeal form itself).[62] Because the range and limits of the cognitive apparatus vary

---

60 Lorenz 1972, p. 9. Translation altered. There is a probably typographical error in the translation of the phrase in the German original '*in Auseinandersetzung mit und in Anpassung an*'. This is translated as 'through confrontation with *an* adaptation to' (my italics). However, the 'und' should clearly be translated as *and*, not *an* – which I have done in the text. See Lorenz, *Die Rückseite des Spiegels*, p. 21.
61 Darwin, 'M Notebook', in Darwin 1980, p. 64.
62 Having defended this general point about knowledge mechanisms, it must also be noted that certain aspects of these claims are more than a little problematic. Although he recognises that one must see all the similarities between humans and animals before one can realise the vastness of their differences (Lorenz 1972, p. 168), he overestimates the similarities in believing that the human ethology can be approached in the same way as that

from one species to the next (not excluding humans), the 'reality' that each species can apprehend is unique to that species. Although we humans can create artificial means (e.g. telescopes and microscopes, infrared and ultraviolet goggles, hearing aids) to experience things beyond the range of our own sensory apparatuses and can thereby glimpse aspects of realities constructed by other species, we still cannot experience the world as do creatures with a different set of corporeal instruments with a different range of sensory powers. Although we can create and use radar, we cannot perceive the world as does a bat, nor therefore can we know what it is like to be a bat; although we can create ultra-violet detecting devices, we can neither perceive the world as does a bee, nor know what it is like to be a bee. One need not at all deny the historical importance of differences among human culturally-specific constructions of reality to acknowledge that those differences are minute compared to the vast incommensurable and therefore truly incomprehensible differences among corporeally-rooted species-specific framings of cognisable realities.

The 'real' knowledge of which Lorenz speaks, moreover, is meaningful because efficacious knowledge of the world – knowledge that can, however, be formulated in countless culturally-variable ways. The malevolent properties of a poisonous (to humans) fungus, to take a simple example, can be explained through botany or magic; but whether the proffered explanation is botany or animism, it is real, efficacious knowledge if it keeps people from eating it and dying. Lorenz's reflections, in short, delineate the outer limits of our cognitive apparatus (thereby suggesting grounds for intellectual humility, to which he himself should have paid more attention): 'What little our sense organs and nervous system have permitted us to learn has proved its value over endless years of experience'; and we may, he insists, 'trust' that knowledge 'as far as it goes'.[63] But he hastens to add that that is not very far: 'For we must assume that reality also has many other aspects which are not vital for us ... and for which we have no "organ", because we have not been compelled in the course of our evolution to develop means of adapting to them. We cannot hear what is transmitted on wavelengths inaccessible to our receiving apparatus, nor can

---

of other species. In short, he feels he can apply the same approach and general behavioural 'laws' to humans as to animals, which effectively negates the way in which culture mediates behaviour patterns; he does not acknowledge the degree to which human social organisation is relatively 'voluntary' in contrast to the relatively 'programmed' social behaviours of animal species. The dangerous political implications of such instinctually determinist notions when applied to humans are fairly obvious.

63   This and following citations in this paragraph, Lorenz 1972, p. 7. Lorenz's concluding comment on our literal and metaphorical limitations is not included in the English edition; see Lorenz, *Die Rückseite des Spiegels*, p. 19.

we know how many such wavelengths there are'; we are, in short, '"limited" in the literal and also in the metaphorical sense of this word'. Translated into the terms of contemporary discourse, Lorenz's argument is that on the basis of its corporeal organisation, an organism is always already a knowing subject – and always already a decentred one.

7.5.2.2 Corporeal Organisation as Paradigm/Episteme/Form-Determinant: The Cognitive Unconscious and Tacit Knowledge

One could agree with all of the above and acknowledge that an organism's knowledge of its world, its reality, is inscribed in its corporeal organisation that in turn lets itself be read as an 'open book' of its evolutionary history, yet argue, as is *de rigueur* after the linguistic/cultural turn, that that is all ancient prehistory, that the advent of language and the 'properly human' knowledge of *Homo sapiens qua loquens* has superseded corporeal knowledge and rendered the body's 'open book' a 'quaint and curious volume of forgotten lore' – a nice narrative of times long gone by, but of only antiquarian interest and irrelevant to human worlds of language and culture.[64] But if, as argued above, the morphology of, and the ratiomorphus information acquisition devices embedded in, an organism's corporeal organisation are themselves objectified images of its environment, we might say, borrowing from Thomas Kuhn, Michel Foucault, and/or Karl Marx that that corporeal organisation is itself, respectively, paradigmatic, epistemic and/or form-determining, that is: corporeal organisation establishes the conditions or an organism's knowledge production and informs its knowledge of the world. And the activation and use of those information acquisition devices produce a vision of the world in the species-specific image of its own corporeal organisation, a world that reflects the extent and limits of the organism's ability to apprehend what lies outside it. To elaborate further these (human) ratiomorphus processes that 'have nothing to do with conscious reason', we turn first to Johnson's and Lakoff's notion of the cognitive unconscious and then to Polanyi's elaboration of tacit knowledge.

In proposing a 'cognitive unconscious', Johnson and Lakoff diverge sharply from the Western philosophical mainstream for which '*cognitive* means *only* conceptual or propositional structure' and which would therefore consider the term 'cognitive unconscious' oxymoronic.[65] Undeterred, Lakoff and Johnson proceed to investigate dimensions of the cognitive process that for 'many philosophers [are] not considered cognitive at all', namely those 'mental operations

---

64   The phrase is from Edgar Allen Poe, *The Raven*.
65   This and following citations in this paragraph, Lakoff and Johnson 1999, p. 12.

and structures that are involved in language, meaning, perception, conceptual systems, and reason'. Recognising that 'our conceptual systems and our reason arise from our bodies', they use 'the term cognitive for aspects of our sensorimotor system that contribute to our abilities to conceptualize and reason'. And '[s]ince cognitive operations are largely unconscious, the term *cognitive unconscious* accurately describes all unconscious mental operations concerned with conceptual systems, meaning, inference, and language'.

Emphasising what we might call the corporeal depth of cognition, Johnson elsewhere insists on the 'crucial point' that 'understanding is not only a matter of reflection, using finitary propositions, on some preexistent, already determinate experience'.[66] Instead,

> *understanding is the way we 'have a world', the way we experience our world as a comprehensible reality*. Such understanding, therefore, involves *our whole being* – our bodily capacities and skills, our values, our modes and attitudes, our entire cultural tradition, the way in which we are bound up with a linguistic community, our aesthetic sensibilities, and so forth. In short, our understanding *is* our mode of 'being in the world'. It is the way we are meaningfully situated in our world through our bodily interactions, our cultural institutions, our linguistic tradition, and our historical context. Our more reflective acts of understanding (which may involve grasping of finitary propositions) are simply an extension of our understanding in this more basic sense of 'having a world'.

The all too human world(s) that human beings have are, in short, the all too human world(s) that human beings make.[67] And before proceeding with the discussion of the cognitive unconscious, it is necessary to comment on the making of the worlds we have.

If we were to ignore for the moment the artificiality of isolating knowing from doing and making, and instead situate Johnson's and Lakoff's undertaking in Kantian terms, their concern is with the corporeal roots of what Kant took to be 'pure' reason, that is: with the unconscious corporeal means of knowledge production and the corporeal framing or patterning of the conscious knowledge produced. And these means of knowledge production include not

---

66 M. Johnson 1987, p. 102. Following citation, ibid.
67 Of the two meanings of the verb 'to have' that could fit here, the intended meaning is clearly 'to experience', and not 'to possess' – at least not in the sense of exclusive private ownership. The reference is to those aspects of the universe outside of us of which we can, because of the range and limits of our cognitive capacities, have experience.

only the perceptual instruments and capacities but also the kinaesthetic instruments and capacities, all of which are embedded in our corporeal organisation and frame how we experience, how we perceive and negotiate the world – how we 'have' the world. I fully agree, but as might be expected given my focus on objectification as a multi-dimensional process of making human worlds, I would add that we also need to consider the other essential dimension of how we 'have our world(s)' – the corporeal foundations of what might in Kantian terminology be categorised as 'practical reason', that is: our kinaesthetic abilities that are not only essential to our perceptual and conceptual ways of having and navigating our world(s), but also constitutive of the actual *making* of the worlds we have – worlds consisting (as argued above, Chapter 2) of material artefacts and social relations as well as the semiotic systems and ideas made in knowledge production.

Helpful again in terms of the question of worldmaking is Levins's and Lewontin's notion of the organism as subject and object of its own evolution introduced above. They reject the notion that organisms just find and occupy prefabricated niches, and insist rather that organisms are acting subjects that actively make themselves at home in the world, that make their own niches, not as they please, but in accordance with their own bodily needs and capacities interacting with environmental affordances; and in so doing they remake their sector of the world in the image of their own corporeal organisation. It is, in short, an organism's kinaesthetic capacities, not only for locomotion, for moving about in, navigating, the world, but also for moving and manipulating the objects of the world (whether trees for beavers, dirt for burrowing creatures, or just about everything for human beings including damming rivers, deforesting woodlands and decapitating mountaintops) that give shape to the world(s) it makes. Because of the unique capacities and dexterities of the human bodily toolkit, not least among which is the capacity for speech, *Homo sapiens* has succeeded in making worlds in its own image immeasurably far beyond the capacities of any other species. Nevertheless, even if in radically varying degrees, humans and other organisms are all acting subjects that make the worlds that they 'have' – albeit, because subject to corporeal limits and constraints, not as they please. In the following, therefore, I consider the corporeal foundations of both the 'pure reason' involved in knowing and the 'practical reason' involved in doing and making as inextricably intertwined moments of the cognitive unconscious that together are the 'universal' (always socio-culturally mediated) constituents of the world(s) human beings make and have.

Although Johnson and Lakoff do not use the term, it does not seem too much of a stretch to classify the contents of their cognitive unconscious with Michael

Polanyi's category of 'tacit knowledge'. And although Polanyi does not use the term, it seems not much of a stretch to see in Johnson's and Lakoff's cognitive unconscious the site of tacit knowledge production and the repository of tacit knowledge. That is, in any case, how I shall use those terms in the following.

In a statement that fits rather well with Johnson's and Lakoff's elaboration of the cognitive unconscious, Michael Polanyi introduces his standpoint and the starting point of his investigation of 'tacit knowledge' by announcing his intention to 'reconsider human knowledge by starting from the fact that *we can know more than we can tell*'.[68] From this standpoint, all echoes of the Saussurean linguistocentric claim that 'our thought – apart from its expression in words – is only a shapeless and indistinct mass', that '[w]ithout language, thought is a vague, uncharted nebula', are not only hyperbolic, but also backward.[69] Rather than reduce cognition and knowledge simply to language, Polanyi undertakes the more challenging task of attempting to explain how we can know more than we can tell – a 'fact [that] seems obvious' even if 'it is not easy to say exactly what it means'.[70] Nevertheless, he is certain that the tacit dimension of all knowledge must be traced (to put it in Eagleton's terms) 'up from the body'. 'Our body', Polanyi avers, 'is the ultimate instrument of all our external knowledge, whether intellectual or practical. In all our waking moments we are *relying* on our awareness of contacts of our body with things outside for *attending* to those things'; '[b]ecause our body is involved in the perception of objects, it participates thereby in our knowledge of all other things outside. Moreover, we keep expanding our body into the world, by assimilating to it sets of particulars which we integrate into reasonable entities. Thus do we form, intellectually and practically, an interpreted universe populated by entities, the particulars of which we have interiorized for the sake of comprehending their meaning in the shape of coherent entities'.

In contrast to the semiotic turn toward the body taken by cultural ultra-constructionists, Polanyi, beginning with the 'fact', obvious but difficult to explain exactly, that 'we can know more than we can tell', takes a corporeal turn; like Lorenz, Lakoff and Johnson, Polanyi understands the body as itself an essential and constitutive means of knowledge production. In thus alluding to what may be called a 'corporeal logos' (and what may be the key to the hid-

---

68 M. Polanyi 1967, p. 4. Citations in the following paragraph, ibid., p. 4; pp. 15–16; p. 29.
69 Saussure 1959, p. 111, p. 112. The limits of what might I call the 'linguistocentrism' inherent in synchronic semiotic approaches to knowledge production and subjecthood derived from the 'Saussurean' text (and the question of whether Saussure or the editors should be held responsible for the text that emerged) are addressed in detail in Chapter 8.
70 This and following citations, M. Polanyi 1967, p. 4; pp. 15–16; p. 29.

den bodily problematic that Heidegger recognised but left unexplored), Polanyi suggests that the body is fundamental to cognition, an epistemologically essential, even if 'mute' contributor to knowledge production. 'Explicit knowledge', the conscious knowledge whereof we can speak, is, Polanyi explains, rooted in 'tacit knowledge' that is acquired through 'subception' ('learning without awareness').[71] Tacit knowledge is that knowledge of which we are not conscious, that we do not know we have, that we cannot articulate, but which we nevertheless use essentially in all our cognitive acts. 'All knowledge', Polanyi insists (in a comment that resonates with Lorenz's on ratiomorphous processes and Johnson's and Lakoff's on the cognitive unconscious), 'is *either tacit or rooted in tacit knowledge. A wholly* explicit knowledge is unthinkable'.[72] Polanyi recognises two dimensions of tacit knowledge: tacit knowledge itself that he calls 'actual' tacit knowledge (see below) and the tacit roots of 'explicit knowledge'. I begin with the latter and elaborate the tacit constitution of explicit knowledge with the help of Johnson's and Lakoff's elaboration of image schemata that in-form conscious thought and reasoning.

To explain the relation between corporeality and cognition, 'the body in the mind', Johnson investigates 'the bodily basis of meaning, imagination, and reason'.[73] Reacting against 'linguistocentric' excesses, he seeks 'to understand *linguistic* meaning as a special case within the broader notion of *meaningfulness in general*'; his 'investigation is thus oriented toward figuring out how it is that a large range of structures arise out of our bodily experience and provide patterns that are meaningful to us and that influence our reasoning'.[74] To mediate between general corporeally-rooted experiential patterns and particular meaningful experiences, Johnson and George Lakoff adopt Kant's formal definition of 'schemata' as 'nonpropositional structures of the imagination',[75] but give it corporeal content by planting these structures of the imagination firmly in the body. Johnson and Lakoff coined the term 'image schemata' whose use 'focuses on embodied patterns of meaningfully organized experience (such as

---

[71] 'Subception' defined by R.S. Lazarus and R.A. McCleary as 'learning without awareness'. Cited in M. Polanyi 1969, p. 143.
[72] M. Polanyi 1969, p. 144.
[73] These are the title and subtitle of M. Johnson 1987.
[74] M. Johnson 1987, p. 18. I should note that in some of the texts cited in this section the authors use the Greek plural 'schemata' and in others the Anglicisation 'schemas'. I cite them as they are found in the cited texts.
[75] M. Johnson 1987, p. 29. As Johnson notes, Kant viewed the imagination not simply in terms of artistic creativity, fantasy, and fiction, but as 'the very means by which we have *any* comprehensible structure in our experience' (ibid.).

structures of bodily movements and perceptual interactions)'.[76] As such, these corporeally derived image schemata embedded in the mind are foundational in giving order and meaning to experience:

> Image schemata exist at a level of generality and abstraction that allows them to serve repeatedly as identifying patterns in an indefinitely large number of experiences, perceptions, and image formations for objects or events that are similarly structured in relevant ways. Their most important feature is that they have a few basic elements or components that are related by definite structures, and yet they have a certain flexibility. As a result of this simple structure, they are a chief means for achieving order in our experience so that we can comprehend and reason about it.[77]

> In order for us to have meaningful, connected experiences that we can comprehend and reason about, there must be pattern and order to our actions, perceptions, and conceptions. *A schema is a recurrent pattern, shape, and regularity in, or of, these ongoing ordering activities.* These patterns emerge as meaningful structures for us chiefly at the level of our bodily movements through space, our manipulation of objects, and our perceptual interactions.

Whereas Kant depicted schemata as rather rigid 'procedures for generating images that can fit concepts', Johnson and Lakoff grant them greater elasticity, defining them instead as 'a *continuous structure of an organizing activity*' and insisting that 'even though schemata are definite structures, they are dynamic patterns rather than fixed and static images ...'; and they are 'dynamic in two important respects':

> (1) Schemata are structures *of an activity* by which we organize our experience in ways that we can comprehend. They are a primary means by which we *construct* or *constitute* order and are not mere passive recept-

---

[76] As will be clear in the following discussion, Johnson's notion of image schemata is expansive; and in this respect, it differs significantly 'from what has come to be the standard meaning of the terms in recent cognitive science' that generally 'regards schemata as abstract conceptual and propositional event structures'; or, in the results of a survey of schema theory, as 'a cluster of knowledge representing a particular generic procedure, object, percept, even, sequence of events of social situation [that] provides a skeleton structure for a concept that can be "instantiated", or filled out, with the detailed properties of the particular instance being represented' (M. Johnson 1987, p. 19).

[77] M. Johnson 1987, p. 28. Following citations in this paragraph, ibid., p. 29; p. 29; pp. 29–30.

acles into which experience is poured. (2) Unlike templates, schemata are flexible in that they can take on any number of specific instantiations in varying contexts. It is somewhat misleading to say that an image schema gets 'filled in' by concrete perceptual details; rather it must be relatively malleable, so that it can be modified to fit many similar, but different, situations that manifest a recurring underlying structure.

Based on a 'cross-reading' of Johnson's and Lakoff's 'pathbreaking 1987 publications' that introduced their notion of image schemata, Beate Hampe produced a 'condensed characterization of their original conception' that provides an excellent summary of the part image schemata play in the 'cognitive unconscious':

- Image schemas are *directly meaningful* ('experiential'/'embodied'), *preconceptual* structures, which arise from, or are grounded in, human recurrent bodily movements through space, perceptual interactions, and ways of manipulating objects.
- Image schemas are highly *schematic* gestalts which capture the structural *contours* of sensory-motor experience, integrating information from multiple modalities.
- Image schemas exist as *continuous* and *analogue* patterns *beneath* conscious awareness, prior to and independently of other concepts.
- As gestalts, image schemas are both *internally structured*, i.e., made up of very few related parts, and highly *flexible*. This flexibility becomes manifest in the numerous transformations they undergo in various experiential contexts, all of which are closely related to perceptual (gestalt) principles.[78]

Crucial here is that the source of these image-schemata that in-form our conscious thought and reasoning processes is the body as animate form dwelling in and interacting with the world. Image-schemata are thus the mode in which the body is 'in the mind'; for they are

> recurring patterns of organism-environment interactions that exist *in* the felt qualities of our experience, understanding, and thought. Image schemas are the sort of structures that demarcate the basic contours of our experience as embodied creatures. They depend on how our brains work, what our physiology is like, and the kinds of environments we inhabit. They are one of the most basic means we have for discrimination, differentiation, and determination within our experience.[79]

---

78 Hampe in Hampe 2005, pp. 1–2.
79 M. Johnson in Hampe 2005, p. 31. Following citation, ibid.

The 'philosophical significance' of image schemata, Johnson concludes, 'lies in the way they bind together body and mind, inner and outer, and thought and feeling. They are an essential part of embodied meaning and provide the basis for much of our abstract inference'.

The range of meaning constituted by image schemata is expanded and enhanced by means of 'metaphorical projection from an image schema generated in [bodily] experience onto the nonphysical, or less clearly structured domain'.[80] That is to say: a given corporeally structured pattern of experience, the 'source domain', serves as an ordering principle for a less corporeally immediate, or more 'abstract' domain of experience. Our sense of balance, for example, established by our vestibular sensibility is metaphorically projected onto, as a criterion of evaluation, works of art or notions of justice. The path of directed locomotion is projected metaphorically as the structure of any kind of purposeful activity, as the physical path toward a concrete goal, but also as a notion of time as motion; 'Walking and traveling', Rebecca Solnit notes, 'have become central metaphors in thought and speech, so central we hardly notice them'.[81] Cyclic structure (of heartbeat, breathing, digestion, waking/sleeping, seasons, the course of life) 'constitutes one of our most basic patterns for experiencing and understanding temporality. It provides us a way of understanding an enormous range of event sequences and, metaphorically interpreted, even nontemporal sequences such as numbers'. Our bipedal verticality not only gives us a particular spatial orientation of up and down, but a schema of scale, of more and less, rising and falling, and 'is figuratively extended to cover abstract entities of every sort (numbers, properties, relations, geometric structures, entities in economic models, etc.)'. Because of our bilateral symmetry, 'we project RIGHT and LEFT, FRONT and BACK, NEAR and FAR, through the horizon of our perceptual interactions'. Moreover, 'the very concept HORIZON is image-schematic. Our perceptual fields have focal areas that fade off into a vague horizon of possible experiences that are not currently at the center of our conscious awareness'; it is thus 'no surprise that we have a CENTER-PERIPHERY image schema'. And '[b]ecause of our ongoing bodily encounter with physical

---

80   M. Johnson 1987, p. 99. The following examples of cyclic structure and verticality from ibid, p. 121; pp. 123–4; p. 124. The examples beginning with right-left and through the end of the paragraph, from Johnson in Hampe 2005, p. 20. Johnson (1987, p. 126) provides a 'partial list of schemata', derived from corporeally-framed patterns of human experience, that includes: container, blockage, enablement, path, cycle, part-whole, full-empty, iteration, surface, balance, counterforce, attraction, link, near-far, merging, matching, contact, object, compulsion, restraint removal, mass-count, centre-periphery, scale, splitting, superimposition, process, collection.
81   Solnit 2001, p. 73.

forces that push and pull us, we experience the image-schematic structures of COMPULSION, ATTRACTION, and BLOCKAGE OF MOVEMENT .... The bodily logic of such force schemas will involve inferences about speed of movement, the rhythmic flow of movement, whether a moving object stops and starts, and so on'.

Johnson and Lakoff continue the exploration of image schemata into their neurological grounding and seek to explain how corporeally constituted patterns of experience are 'hardwired' into the human brain and shape and form human 'meaning, understanding, and rationality'.[82] This neuropsychological dimension of image schemata is beyond the scope of this study – fortunately so, because it is also beyond my ability to do justice to it. But it is obviously an immense and rich new field in the investigation of human experience and cognition that has already drawn a number of interested researchers from a variety of fields.[83] Pointing even more deeply into corporeal organisation as the foundation of human cognition, it is further evidence of both the immense horizon opened up when corporeal organisation is taken as the first fact of history – and also of the immensity of Marx's wager on writing history 'up from the body'.[84] But for present purposes, the point is that our explicit conscious

---

82 'How Schemata Constrain Meaning, Understanding, and Rationality' is the title of Chapter 5 of M. Johnson 1987, pp. 101–38.
83 See the contributors to Hampe 2005.
84 As Johnson noted during a presentation to my seminar on 'Mapping Human Corporeal Organization' (15 January 2009), he has been criticised over an issue that is of utmost importance here, namely: that he allegedly presumes the universality of image schemata and therewith, too, a universality of bodily form and experience, and thus fails to recognize racial, ethnic, and/or gender differences in bodily form and/or experience. But the appropriate response to this criticism is already contained in his insistence on the elasticity and flexibility of each schema. Image-schemata are *not*, he insists, 'mere passive receptacles into which experience is poured', but 'a primary means by which we *construct* or *constitute* order'; an image schema 'can take on any number of specific instantiations in varying contexts' and 'must be relatively malleable, so that it can be modified to fit many similar, but different, situations that manifest a recurring underlying structure'. He explicitly states that '[i]nsofar as meanings involve schematic structures, they are relatively fluid patterns that get altered in various contexts' and 'are never wholly context-free' (M. Johnson 1987, p. 30). And elsewhere, arguing against the pretence 'that one's understanding consists only of one's beliefs', and insisting instead that 'these beliefs are merely the surface of our embodied understanding which we peel off as abstract structures', he concludes with an even more explicit statement on the levels of mediation involved in the formation of our conscious beliefs: 'It might be more satisfactory to say that our understanding is our bodily, cultural, linguistic, historical situatedness in, and toward, our world'; accordingly, 'image schemata, their abstract extensions, and their metaphorical elaborations constitute a great part of the constraining structure of this understanding' (ibid., p. 138).

knowledge is pre-formed and in-formed by the corporeal constitution of our cognitive apparatus that is itself a species-specific mode of knowledge production – a corporeal *Wissenschaft*.

Turning now to the 'actual' tacit knowledge situated in human corporeal organisation, Polanyi notes that it is 'indeterminate' in the sense that its content *cannot be explicitly stated*.[85] This actual but indeterminate knowledge pertains to doing and manifests itself 'in the way we possess a skill'. We are all familiar with this inarticulate form of knowledge. We have all marvelled at some form of corporeal grace of dancers and divers, ice skaters and skiers, gymnasts and basketball players, etc. whose seemingly incredible corporeal feats almost invariably provoke the common response: 'How did she/he do that?' And when that question is posed to the performers themselves, they are almost invariably forced into the realm of metaphor to explain a kind of knowledge that cannot be expressed conceptually. Thus, we find countless examples of metaphorical attempts to express an otherwise inexpressible kind of corporeal knowledge: athletes of various kinds claiming to be 'in the zone'; baseball players on a hitting streak for whom 'the baseball looked like a grapefruit'; a basketball player (Allen Iverson) after scoring 55 points in a game explaining (in appropriately mixed musical and maritime metaphors): 'I just caught the rhythm. The basket looked like an ocean'.

To pose the questions aimed at the epistemological underpinnings of such metaphors: how does a basketball player *know* at what angle and with what arc

---

While I fully agree with Johnson's point here, I would make a slight amendment to the phrase 'constituted a great part of the *constraining* structure of this understanding' and reformulate it as 'constituted the *framing* structure of this understanding'; *framing* in my view more accurately establishes the range of understanding, and entails not only constraints and limits but also the capacities and possibilities, that is to say: human corporeal organisation is the general form-determinant of human cognition that will vary in its socio-cultural specifics. That having been said, Johnson's insistence on the flexibility and fluidity of image schemata, and their culturally specific metaphorical elaborations is an anticipatory response to, and refutation of, critics who accuse him of a misplaced universalism. He is simply pointing out what should be obvious, namely that we humans are a species characterised by certain biological universals, by a species-specific sensory-kinesthetic body whose particular corporeal organisation gives rise to specific specific patterns of behaviour, experience, and cognition. And the image schemata constituted by that experience are flexible enough to undergo a great variety of socio-cultural mediations and to manifest themselves in a great variety of socio-culturally specific refractions.

85 M. Polanyi 1969, p. 141. Polanyi notes that the form of tacit knowledge in which explicit knowledge is rooted is also 'indeterminate', but in a different, open-ended sense of opening an 'indeterminate range of *anticipations* in any knowledge bearing on reality' – which seems rather similar to what Johnson and Lakoff have to say about the flexibility of image schema.

and force to release the ball? how does a figure skater *know* how to coordinate the many leg and arm movements with speed and timing in order to leap in the air, perform three rotations of her body, and come back down, landing on the ice on two almost razor-thin blades without collapsing into a corporeal heap? How does a moderately advanced string player so consistently unerringly *know* not only a sequence of notes on a cello, viola or violin, but also exactly where to place the fingers to get exactly the right sound while producing up to sixteen notes per second.[86] And such questions are not limited to the glamorous performances of athletes and musicians, but can also be asked of what are considered more mundane kinds of activity. One need only take the time to observe any person experienced at any kind of task – whether involving the fineness and delicacy of say watchmaking, the brute labour in a coal mine or steel foundry, the routinised speed of a typist, or my mother moving about the kitchen, or knitting for hours while carrying on (often multiple) conversations, watching television, and only very occasionally glancing at the work she performed without interruption and without missing a stitch – in order to witness the harmony of a corporeal logos and a corporeal aesthetic at work: a body of knowledge engaged in what Marx called 'sensual activity' (*sinnliche Tätigkeit*).[87]

Although the appellation is of more recent coinage, the matter of 'muscle memory', the seemingly unconscious motor prowess that is the foundation of proficiency in any form of corporeal activity, had already intrigued Plato and Aristotle. The association of memory, generally considered an attribute of mind, with a corporeal attribute such as muscle might mislead one to think that the term is merely metaphorical, that the muscles behave as if they had a memory, but they really do not. But if 'muscle memory' is taken, not metaphorically, but literally, then it is most apt. And in Polanyi's view, it must be taken literally, for it refers to an inexpressible, but nevertheless 'actual' knowledge:

> If I know how to ride a bicycle or how to swim, this does not mean that I can tell how I manage to keep my balance on a bicycle or keep afloat when swimming. I may not have the slightest idea of how I do this or even an entirely wrong or grossly imperfect idea of it, and yet go on cycling or swimming merrily. Nor can it be said that I know how to bicycle or swim and yet do *not* know how to coordinate the complex pattern of muscular acts by which I do my cycling or swimming. I both know how to carry out

---

86 This information provided by Emma Tepfer, violist and former student in my 'Bodies and Artifacts' (2004) seminar based on this project.
87 See esp. 1st and 5th theses on Feuerbach, in Marx and Engels 1973, p. 5.

these performances as a whole and also know how to carry out the elementary acts which constitute them, though I cannot tell what these acts are.[88]

Although it cannot be expressed other than metaphorically in the linguistic act of speaking, 'actual knowledge' is literally expressed in the corporeal act of doing. Thus, '[i]t is characteristic of our body that it submits to operations, the particulars of which are virtually unknown to us, and that these largely unspecifiable operations cannot be replaced effectively by any focally controlled operations. This offers us evidence of our capacity *to integrate and endow with meaning things of which we possess only a subsidiary awareness*'.

Not only is this 'actual knowledge' linguistically inexpressible, but its seemingly 'unconscious' and 'automatic' aspects often confounds language itself. We frequently hear said of the seeming unthinking and automatic character, the pure grace, of a well-cultivated corporeal action that 'no one can teach that', 'he's a natural', 'she's a born talent', etc. – in short: that the action is 'instinctual'. It cannot be denied that certain 'in-born' or 'natural' factors play a role in skill; bodily proportions, sensual acuities, etc. certainly establish the range of probabilities that a given person will excel in a given corporeal activity. But it is too hasty to view such skills as just 'natural' or 'instinctual', for the 'learning' that produces 'actual knowledge' is in the doing.

Reflecting on such loose and reductionist use of the 'instinctual', P.B. and J.S. Medawar note that '[a]s a figure of speech, performances are sometimes described as instinctive when all that is intended is reference to the functional aptitude of a performance combined with its prompt and effective execution'. And they adduce the tendency of 'accomplished drivers' to describe their skill as 'instinctive' to illustrate Alfred North Whitehead's wisdom on this matter. As Whitehead heretically insisted: 'It is a profoundly erroneous truism, repeated by all copy books, and by eminent people when they are making speeches, that we should cultivate the habit of thinking what we are doing. The precise opposite is the case. Civilization advances by extending the number of important operations which we can perform without thinking about them'. To which the Medawars add:

> We regard this as a profound observation which most people will be able to bear out from their own experience. Learning a new repertoire of neuromuscular performances such as driving a car or skiing is precisely learn-

---

88   M. Polanyi 1969, pp. 141–2. Following citation in this paragraph, ibid., p. 184.

ing *not* to be obliged to think about them. It is learning to react promptly and appropriately to each stimulus as it presents itself. Our behaviour must be quasi-instinctual, for these are performances in which ratiocination has no part, though judgment – it is to be hoped – will have been exercised by insuring against the breakage of one's limbs that so often accompanies skiing and other people's misjudgements when driving a car or, as English people absurdly say, 'motoring'.[89]

The irony here is that in some tongues (e.g. English, Italian) this idealist binary that relegates corporeal doing to the realm of the 'instinctual' is undermined by language itself, which acknowledges the body's 'actual knowledge' when we ask: 'do you *know* how to swim, do you *know* how to ride a bicycle, drive a car etc.?'[90] This of course, as Polanyi noted, questions not whether we can put into words the 'complex pattern of muscular acts' required, but whether we have the tacit embodied knowledge to know how to perform the act, whether we can *do* it.

Rudolf zur Lippe uses the term *Körpergedächtnis* to differentiate such seemingly automatic, but very much learned behaviour from more properly 'instinctual' motor-reflex reactions. To render zur Lippe's usage appropriately, *Körpergedächtnis* must be translated and understood literally (not metaphorically) as the 'body-memory' – the body's memory in both senses: as the faculty that memorises and as the storehouse of the memorised.[91] Almost synonymous with 'cognitive unconscious', *Körpergedächtnis* carries a more active connotation than 'unconscious': *Gedächtnis*, memory, is etymologically linked to the verb *denken*, to think, and thus to a bodily logos that is as fundamental as it is ubiquitous. And whether we call it the cognitive unconscious or *Körpergedächtnis*, it is impossible to imagine any activity, from walking and

---

89 Medawar and Medawar 1983, p. 161.
90 In Italian *sai guidare* is literally 'do you know how to drive?'; *sai inglese* literally 'do you know [how to speak] English?' German by contrast does not use the verb 'to know' in such situations, but the verb 'can': *kannst Du fahren? Kannst Du englisch?*
91 I am grateful to Professor Doktor Monika Unzeitig (Institut für Deutsche Philologie, Universität Greifswald) for this etymological clarification. It should be noted, as the above examples clearly indicate, that zur Lippe's use of *Körpergedächtnis* corresponds to what Polanyi calls 'actual' tacit knowledge – knowledge that is indeterminate in the sense that 'it cannot be explicitly stated'. Because of its intimations of unconscious thinking and memory, zur Lippe's term more graphically suggests the contours and texture of this corporeal logos than does Polanyi's reference to 'actual' tacit knowledge. But in the terms that I am using, *Körpergedächtnis*, like Polanyi's notion of 'actual' tacit knowledge, belongs to that dimension of the cognitive unconscious concerned with 'practical' reason, kinaesthesis.

talking to working and playing that does not depend essentially on the tacit knowledge stored in the body's memory.

The cognitive unconscious should thus be viewed both as the body's memory, its storehouse of tacit knowledge and also as the site of what might be called the body's 'mental operations'. Although this too must sound self-contradictory to philosophical idealists and cultural ultra-constructionists, it is rendered plausible by Polanyi's discussion of the process of 'tacit integration' whose 'speed and complexity', he argues, 'far exceeds in its own domain the operations of explicit inference' and explains 'how intuitive insight may arrive at unaccountable conclusions in a flash'.[92] This 'tacit integration' is essential to all corporeal activities, whether motoring, knitting, in Gibson's examples of the 'perceptual knowledge of the laws of physics' evident in an outfielder chasing after a flying baseball or a cat a ball of yarn – or in that which the linguistocentric claim as the exclusive dimension of human cognition, the linguistic capacity of speaking primate. Acknowledging the obvious point that 'language expands human intelligence immensely beyond the purely tacit domain', Polanyi insists that 'the logic of language itself – the way language is used – remains tacit' and that therefore 'it is easy to see that the structure of tacit knowing contains a general theory of meaning which applies also to language'.

Elaborating the '*semantic function* of tacit knowing', Polanyi writes:

> A *set of sounds* is converted into the *name* of an object by an act of tacit knowing which integrates the sounds to the object to which we are attending. This is accompanied by a characteristic change in our impression of the sounds. When converted into a word they no longer sound as before; they have become, as it were, transparent: we attend from them (or through them) to the object to which they are integrated.[93]

By means of its capacity for speedy and complex tacit integration, the attending body plays an essential role in the production of linguistic meaning: it makes sense of, by linking, disembodied sounds to their embodied referents.[94]

---

92   M. Polanyi 1969, p. 144. Following citation, ibid., p. 145.
93   M. Polanyi 1969, p. 145. Polanyi's reflections here indicate that the meanings of linguistic signs cannot be grasp without their referents. This is in contrast to synchronic semiotic approaches to language the deny the relevance of both speaking/*parole* and the referent to the meaning of signs. This matter is addressed in detail in Chapter 8.
94   This corresponds to Lieberman's explanation of the 'automatization process' essential to speech that 'converts a series of *learned* motor instructions into a 'subroutine' that is stored in the motor cortex and executed as a complete whole', that allows us rapidly and unthinkingly to execute the 'complex voluntary articulatory manoeuvres involving the tongue,

Without the tacit knowledge of meaningful sound production stored in the *Körpergedächtnis*, language use in speaking, and therewith language (certainly as we know it), would be impossible. If linguistic content is fundamentally (if not exclusively) rooted in the body's perceptual capacities and if the practice of language is made possible by a body that, among many other things, also tacitly knows how to speak, then it seems fair to conclude that the 'coordinates that define the subject' are broader and deeper than language and are embedded and embodied in corporeal organisation. Polanyi, at least, seems to agree: 'The way the body participates in the act of perception can be generalized further to include the bodily roots of all knowledge and thought. ... Every time we make sense of the world, we rely on our tacit knowledge of impacts made by the world on our body and the complex responses of our body to these impacts'. And 'such', he concludes, 'is the exceptional position of our body in the universe'.[95]

What must not be forgotten, however, as Johnson, Lakoff, and Polanyi explicitly recognise, is that that 'exceptional position of our body in the universe' is not a static one, but the ever-changing position of a body in motion. Maxine Sheets-Johnstone conceptualises this 'primacy of movement' with her reference to human animate form as (in my slightly amended version; see above) a 'sensory-kinaesthetic body'. To capture the corporeal aesthetics, the

---

lips, velum, larynx, and lungs' that allow us to produce in rapid succession differentiated and meaningful sounds. Lieberman 1991, pp. 48–51.

95   M. Polanyi 1969, pp. 147–8. Polanyi's position has affinities with that similarly phenomenological position of Merleau-Ponty who writes: 'Our bodily experience of movement is not a particular case of knowledge; it provides us with a way of access to the world and the object, with a "praktognosia", which has to be recognized as original and perhaps primary. My body has its world, or understands its world, without having to make use of my "symbolic" or "objectifying function"' (Merleau-Ponty 1966, pp. 140–1). Citing approvingly an article by A.A. Grünbaum on '*Aphasie und Motorik*', he concludes that 'motility is the primary sphere in which initially the sense of all significations is engendered in the domain of represented space' (ibid., 142). Merleau-Ponty cites Grünbaum's German phrase, *der Sinn aller Signifikationen* which the English translation renders as 'the meaning of all significances'; but I have translated it more literally and, I think, more accurately as 'the sense of all significations'. Motility is for Merleau-Ponty so primary that it leads to 'a new meaning of the word "meaning"', that is the opposite of how 'intellectualist psychology and idealist philosophy' conceive of meaning. For these traditions, 'all meaning was *ipso facto* conceived as an act of thought, as the work of a pure "I"'; and they were accordingly 'unable to account for the variety of experience, for the element of senselessness in it, for the contingency of contents'. Merleau-Ponty, on the other hand, insists that 'bodily experience forces us to acknowledge an imposition of meaning which is not the work of a universal constituting consciousness, a meaning which clings to certain contents' (preceding three two citations, ibid., pp. 146–7).

ON THE CORPOREAL CONSTITUTION OF COGNITION AND SUBJECTHOOD   545

patterns of movement involved in all human action from working to playing to thinking, she borrows and elaborates the term 'kinetic melodies' coined by Russian neurologist Aleksandr Romanovich Luria:

> Kinetic melodies that are inscribed in our bodies are dynamic patterns of movement. They constitute that basic, vast, and potentially ever-expandable repertoire of [what Edmund Husserl called] 'I cans', permeating human life: walking, speaking, reaching, hugging, throwing, carrying, opening, brushing, running, wiping, leaping, pulling, pushing. The basic kinetic repertoire is indeed virtually limitless, being constrained only by age, inclination – and pathology. Its sequential complexity and intricacy are similarly virtually limitless, not only with respect to everyday 'I cans' such as writing, tying knots, for example, but with respect to dancing, diving, skiing, performing surgical procedures, administering medical courses of action, learning artistic modes of applying and of sculpting a piece of wood, and so on. In each instance, knowledgeability is not simply a know-*how*, a lesser form of knowledge that is 'merely physical'. Kinetic melodies are saturated in cognitive and affective acuities that both anchor invariants and colour and individualize the manner in which any particular melody runs off.[96]

Summarising their omnipresence, Sheets-Johnstone notes that 'Luria's concept of kinetic melodies is an experientially-based concept rooted in the kinetic dynamics of life as normally lived. "Kinetic melody" thus describes *an experienced kinetic event*: writing one's name fluently, reciting the months of the year, solving an arithmetical problem'. Here too a historical-materialist perspective would insist on two steps that would render explicit what is implicit in Sheets-Johnstone's examples: first by noting that all the examples of doing that she lists are also forms of making: whether of dances, dives, knots, sculptures, sentences, or social relations; and then by establishing the categorial complement of the 'I can do' in the form of 'I can make' – which opens onto the whole question of the worldmaking capacities and made worlds that will be addressed in detail when developing a historical-materialist corporeal semiotics in Chapter 10.[97]

---

96   Sheets-Johnstone 2009, pp. 255–6. Following citation of Luria on 'kinetic melodies', see Luria 1966, p. 226.
97   In discussing these issues with Maxine Sheets-Johnstone at least a decade ago, I mentioned (I cannot recall the exact words) that work and making are perhaps the most decisive and certainly the most world-altering of human bodily I-cans. She replied that

Here it is worth noting in passing the suggestiveness of the term 'kinetic *melodies*' to describe the motions of making and doing. If we were to pursue the aesthetic intimations of Luria's metaphorical likening of patterns of movement to melodies, we might speak of kinaesthesia not only as a proprioceptive sensing of the body in motion, but also as a corporeal kin-aesthetics, as the purposeful and graceful motion permeating all aspects of the lives of animate human forms ranging from locomotive navigation of the world to the various forms of material, social, and semiotic worldmaking. The notion (resembling Herbert Marcuse's view on aesthetics and emancipation) that an emancipated corporeal kinaesthetics is a necessary dimension of human freedom will reappear in the conclusion to this undertaking. For now, however, the task is to conclude this chapter by reviewing the preceding reflections on the wisdom of the body.

The dimensions of the wisdom of the body discussed in the preceding – corporeality as a body of knowledge or *Wissenschaft*, a corporeally constituted cognitive unconscious as the site of tacit knowledge both theoretical and practical, and corporeal kinetic and kinaesthetic melodies – pertain in varying degrees to the 'structure and behaviour' of all animal organisms and are in varying degrees constitutive elements in the subjective experience of any animal organism, be it a bat, a human, or any other motile heterotroph. Like that of any other creature, the corporeal organisation of *Homo sapiens* may itself be considered a particular, evolutionarily-adapted paradigm (Kuhn), a particular episteme (Foucault), a particular form-determinant (Marx). Whether we call it a paradigm, episteme, or form-determinant, the key factor is that an organism's species-specific corporeal organisation establishes what I would call (borrowing Benveniste's term) the 'coordinates' of its corporeally constituted and corporeally decentred subjecthood: corporeal organisation establishes patterns of human experience; it in-forms the cognitive unconscious; it establishes the range and limits of the possible patterns of meaningfully subjective experience; it frames what it is like to be a human being by framing the range and kinds of the socio-culturally specific worlds that human beings can know and make – the worlds that human beings can have.

---

she had never considered that point before, but that, once called to her attention, it seems self-evident.

Conclusion to Part 2: What It Is Like To Be a Human: Corporeally Constituted Patterns of Human Experience and Subjecthood

In addressing the question of corporeality and cognition in Chapter 7, I presented a case for the corporeally-constituted decentred subjecthood of animal organisms; and I argued that the coordinates of an organism's subjecthood are established by its particular corporeal organisation, by its morphology, anatomy, physiology – as Nagel put it, by its 'general structure and behavior'. Taking up Nagel's recognition that the understanding of the 'general structure and behavior' of an animal is insufficient to understand what it is like to be such, I solicited, in querying what it is like to be a human, the help of Lorenz, Johnson and Lakoff, Polanyi, Sheets-Johnstone and zur Lippe, all of whom address the corporeal coordinates and constituents of human subjective experience. Taken together, their work facilitated a more mediated articulation of the 'mind-body' problem, of the link between an organism's corporeality and its subjective experience or cognition; and they did so by explaining corporeal organisation as itself an embodiment of knowledge or corporeal *Wissenschaft*, as the realm of the cognitive unconscious or *Körpergedächtnis*, and as the site of the wisdom of the body, of the tacit knowledge that in-forms both its 'pure' and 'practical' reason, and as the site of kinaesthetic melodies.

In this respect Chapter 7 may be considered a set of theoretical reflections prompted by the (still incomplete) mapping of human corporeal organisation presented in Chapter 6. And now, after having made those theoretical reflections, it may, as a means of summarising and concluding Part 2, be worth presenting in schematic outline the results of that cartographic undertaking to delineate the corporeal coordinates and contours constitutive of human subjective experience and subjecthood. Though of course incomplete, the chart outlines some of the more obvious patterns of human experience: the way(s) in which human beings make the world(s) they have, the world(s) they know, and the world(s) in which they make themselves at home. It outlines in short some of the key elements that frame what it is like to be a human.

What It Is Like To Be a Human: A Chart of Corporeally Constituted Patterns of Human Experience

Biorhythms

Cosmic/Astrophysical
- Circadian, circalunar, circannual rhythms
  - established by the astrophysical place of the earth in the solar system, earth's rotations and revolutions of moon around earth and earth around sun.
  - Climatological Conditions and Seasonal cycle (largely established by place of earth in solar system and the tilt of its axis, yet varying according to North/South coordinates)

Geophysical
- Terrestriality
- Terranean (a rarely used term meaning 'of earth' that I use to signify a creature living on, not under, the ground)

Physiological
- Rhythms of Life: Heartbeat; Breathing rhythm: inhalation/exhalation
- Diurnal rhythm of waking/sleeping
- Life-cycle phases:
  - birth, prolonged infant helplessness, childhood, puberty, adult, aged or 'senior', death
  - for human females:
    - menarche, menstrual cycle to menopause
    - possibly the cycle from pregnancy to birth and cycles of breastfeeding
- Warm-bloodedness and normal body temperature, 98.6° give or take a few degrees
- Hetereotrophism: cycle of ingestion, digestion, excretion

Morphological

Stature
- Upright
  - Vertical body axis
    - upright posture that directs perceptual organs
    - and structures apprehension of external space
  - Bipedal locomotion
  - Bipedal locomotion plus heterotrophism = purposeful locomotion

CONCLUSION TO PART 2: WHAT IT IS LIKE TO BE A HUMAN

- Bilateral Symmetry
  - Anterior polarity of mouth and organs of prehension
  - Expansion of cognitive possibilities
  - notions of 'right' and 'left'
- Body Size
  - physical capacities to manipulate heavier objects (crucial to human worldmaking)
  - brain size
  - life span

Limbic Structure: Arms and Legs, Hands and Feet (rather than fore- and hindlegs and paws)
- Two Legs, pendactyly-toed feet.
  - Bipedality
  - Energy-efficient walking
- Two arms and pentadactyly-fingered hands
  - used for carrying (thus freeing mouth for other uses, most notably speaking)
  - Very flexible arms and shoulders
  - Very flexible prehensile hands and opposable thumbs
    - Gripping and grasping
    - Highly-skilled manipulation of objects in making, throwing, etc.
    - Touch-sensitive Fingertips

Vocal Apparatus
- Supralaryngeal tract
  - pharynx and oral and nasal cavities, flexible tongue and lips capable of controlling sound emission and producing enough controlled sounds and combinations of sounds to make an extensive, well-defined vocabulary

Sexual Apparatus
- Sexual Dimorphism and the intersexual permutations thereof
  - Poles establishing the range of gender constructions

Structure of Brain and Perceptual Systems (see below: Cognitive Apparatus)

Cognitive Apparatus
Perceptual Systems and the Constellation of the Senses
- Binocular, Stereoscopic Vision; the dominant primate sense
  - Clear and distinct delineation of objects at rest and in motion

- Accurate situating of objects, stationary and moving, in three-dimensional space
- A world of colours (also helpful in delineating and situating objects) on the electromagnetic spectrum between ultraviolet and infrared
- The 'nearing' of distant objects (e.g. stargazing, for perceptual pleasure or astrophysics, brings stars that are millions of light years away the range of our visual experience)
- the 'distancing' of near objects with the glaring gaze
- Hearing
  - Duration
  - Pitch
  - Loudness
  - Quality
- Touch
  - Geometric variables like shape, dimensions and proportions, slopes and edges, curves and protuberances
  - Surface variables like texture and roughness/smoothness
  - Material variables a like heaviness or mass, density and rigidity/plasticity
  - Temperature
  - Pleasure/pain
- Smell
  - Foul and fragrant
  - Smell and memory
  - Smell as source of attraction and repulsion
  - Weakness of human olfactory capacities gives smells a certain ineffable power
  - Smells are language-resistant, inarticulate
  - The immediacy of smells gives them a power beyond what we would expect given human olfactory weakness
- Taste
  - Salt, bitter, sweet, sour, umami
  - Linked physiologically (and socially) to smell
- Vestibular
  - Balance
  - Sacred and profane uses of temporary disruption of balance
- Proprioceptive
  - Sense of self

Brain (among its many functions, I note only the following as the most pertinent here)
- Separation of Sensory from Motor Apparatus allows time for reflection between stimulus and response – which is the
  - prerequisite for expanded realm of consciousness:
    - memory
    - consideration of context
    - anticipation and expectancy
    - language use

Social Behaviour

Reproduction
- Sexual
- Viviparous
- Prolonged period of child-rearing (given weakness and vulnerability of human infants)

Sex Decoupled from Reproduction
- Sexuality
- Love

Social Touch
- Erotic (in the Freudian sense of pertaining to the life-instinct): loving touch and psychic well-being
  - The functionally naked ape and the body's polymorphous sensitivity to touch
- Aggressive

If, as Marx put it, consciousness (*das Bewußtsein*) is nothing other than conscious existence (*das bewußte Sein*), and if conscious existence is the real life-process (*wirklicher Lebensprozeß*) of really living individuals, then that real life-process that frames cognition and consciousness is itself framed not only by particular socio-cultural mediations, but more generally and fundamentally by the first fact of human history, namely the corporeal organisation that establishes the patterns of possible human experience and allows human beings to make their own history – but not as they please.

Postscript: The 'Principle of Hope' as a Corporeally-Constituted Pattern of Human Experience

Ernst Bloch finds in human awareness what he calls an 'anticipatory consciousness' that is characterised by a 'principle of hope'. Although he does not explicitly use the term, Bloch does situate the roots of this hopeful, anticipatory consciousness in what I call a corporeally-grounded pattern of human experience. 'Hope', writes Bloch, 'with its positive correlate: the still unclosed determinateness of existence', is 'superior to any *res finita*'.[1] And leaving no doubt about its species-wide range, he insists that '[e]xpectation, hope, intention toward possibility that has still not become', is 'a basic feature of human consciousness'. This hopeful orientation of human consciousness toward the future is not, however, a pure figment of the imagination, but has instead corporeal roots, has its origins in the body, more specifically (and echoing Marx's notion that the first 'moment' in human existence is the satisfaction of material needs): in the stomach and hunger. To summarise a long and complex argument all too briefly, but I hope not too unfairly: although hunger is the primary moment of existence, the primary drive throughout the animal kingdom, what differentiates *Homo sapiens* from all other species is the way in which humans are conscious of hunger. The expanse of the temporal horizons of human consciousness, in terms of both memory of past experience and an anticipatory orientation toward the future and its openness, extends with the human capacity for making which requires both memory of how things are made, with what materials, how to find them, etc. and an anticipation of their future use.

This expansion of consciousness toward the future, however, is not without an unsettling, but ultimately all too human aspect: 'Conscious [human beings are] the most difficult of all animals to satisfy; [they are] – in gratification of [their] wishes – the animal which makes detours. If [they lack] what is necessary for life, [they feel] the lack like no other creature: hunger-visions surface. If [they have] what is necessary, then with its enjoyment new desires surface which torment [them] differently, but no less intense than the previous naked privation'.[2] Although this formulation perhaps smacks a bit too much of a cross-fertilisation of two Western literary icons, Prometheus and Faust, it is not hard to imagine members of a hunting and gathering society with a sense of time radically different from the linear notions of the capitalist West feasting on a

---

1 E. Bloch 1986, p. 6. Following citation, ibid., p. 7.
2 E. Bloch 1986, p. 49. The first bracketed term is my translation of Bloch's *'der bewußte Mensch'* as 'human beings' (see Bloch 1976, p. 54); and, in the following brackets, the verbs and pronouns are adjusted accordingly.

bountiful hunt and harvest and imagining the future as an eternal recurrence of that moment of satisfaction – and in that sense perhaps saying to the moment (as did Faust in expressing what might well be called his utopian vision) 'verweile doch, Du bist so schön' ('Abide awhile, you are so fair'). For Bloch, the combination of corporeal needs (ever changing in their specific socio-cultural expressions) and the consciousness of a future horizon is what makes human consciousness an anticipatory one imbued with a principle of hope.[3] And that principle is much more deep-seated and widespread than one would think from looking only at utopian literature that treats utopia not only as no place but as not possible. Bloch insists rather that the principle of hope, the anticipation of a realisable utopia, is ubiquitous and manifested in the countless everyday daydreams that, because of the nature of human drives and human consciousness, are part of everyone's life.

Having begun work on *The Principle of Hope* as a Jewish Marxist in Hitler's Germany, Bloch was all too acutely aware of how utopian dreams could be turned into nightmares – and that is exactly the kind of historically-specific question concerning socio-cultural mediations that a historical-materialist *Wissenschaft* must investigate. But his elaboration of the corporeally-rooted pattern of experience that gives rise to the principle of hope provides a very material starting point for that investigation. And given the US presidential election campaigns in 2016 and 2020, it seems fairly obvious to me at least that we come much closer to understanding the enthusiastic rank and file support for a neo-fascist like Donald Trump (or for fascist prototypes Hitler and Mussolini) by approaching those supporters in terms of their hopes and utopian impulses, rather than, as is so common, by simply dismissing them as 'uneducated', 'gullible', 'crude', 'deplorable', and/or 'racist'; for even if we were, for the sake of argument, to assume that all of those accusations were true, they would only describe, but not explain, why their modest dream of a 'comfortable happiness' should lead them to think that Donald Trump could realise it. Such an understanding of those who really are economically vulnerable and whose lives teeter on precarity is a crucial prerequisite not only of alleviating their situation, but also, and as a first step, of a politics aimed at gaining the support of those otherwise susceptible to simplistic scapegoating solutions.

---

3 Related issues addressed in Appendix 10.3: 'On Pain, Pleasure, and Playfulness in Human World(s)making'.

Bibliography

Abella, Alex 2009, *Soldiers of Reason: The RAND Corporation and the Rise of American Empire*, Boston: Houghton Mifflin.

Ackerman, Diane 1991, *Natural History of the Senses*, New York: Vintage Books.

Ackerman, Diane 2004, *An Alchemy of the Mind: The Marvel and Mystery of the Brain*, New York: Scribner.

Adler, Jerry 2013, 'Why Fire Makes Us Human', *Smithsonian Magazine*, https://www.smithsonianmag.com/science-nature/why-fire-makes-us-human-72989884/.

Adorno, Theodor 1973, *Minima Moralia*, Frankfurt: Suhrkamp.

Adorno, Theodor 1974, *Eingriffe: Neuen kritische Modelle*, 8. Auflage, Frankfurt am Main: Suhrkamp.

Adorno, Theodor and Max Horkheimer 1969 [1944], *Dialektik der Aufklärung: philosophische Fragmente*, Frankfurt: S. Fischer Verlag.

Adorno, Theodor and Max Horkheimer 2002, *Dialectic of Enlightenment: Philosophical Fragments*, translated by Edmund Jephcott, Stanford: Stanford University Press.

Agamben, Giorgio 1998, *Homo Sacer: Sovereign Power and Bare Life*, translated by Daniel Heller-Roazen, Stanford: Stanford University Press.

Agamben, Giorgio 2014. 'What is Destitutent Power?' translated by Stephanie Wakefield, *Environment and Planning D: Society and Space*, 32: 65–74.

Agamben, Giorgio 2015, *The Use of Bodies*, translated by Adam Kotsko, Palo Alto: Stanford University Press.

Alberti, Leon Battista 1971, *Della Famiglia*, translated by Guido Guarino, Lewisburg: Bucknell University Press.

Alder, Ken 2002, *The Measure of All Things: The Seven-Year Odyssey and Hidden Error That Transformed the World*, New York: Free Press.

Alexander, Jeffrey C. 1988, 'The New Theoretical Movement', in *Handbook of Sociology*, edited by Neil Smelser, Newbury Park, CA: Sage Publications.

Alexander, R. McNeill 1991, 'Characteristics and Advantages of Human Bipedalism' in *Biomechanics in Evolution*, edited by J.M.V. Rayner and R.J. Wootton, Cambridge: Cambridge University Press.

Alexander, R. McNeill 1992, *The Human Machine*, New York: Columbia University Press.

Alpern, Mathew 1982, 'Eye Movements and Strabismus' in *The Senses*, edited by H.B. Barlow and J.D. Mollon, Cambridge: Cambridge University Press.

Alter, Robert 2004, translator and editor of *The Five Books of Moses: A Translation with Commentary*, New York: Norton.

Althusser, Louis 1971, *Lenin and Philosophy and Other Essays*, translated by Ben Brewster, New York: Monthly Review Press.

Althusser, Louis 1976, *Essays in Self-Criticism*, London: New Left Books.

Althusser, Louis 1986, *For Marx*, translated by Ben Brewster, London: Verso.

Althusser Louis and Étienne Balibar 1987, *Reading Capital*, translated by Ben Brewster, London: Verso.

Alvarez, Maximillian 2019, 'Against the Pundits' Class', *The Nation*, 4 October, https://www.thenation.com/article/class-media-labor/.

Amadea, S.M. 2003, *Rationalizing Capitalist Democracy: The Cold War Origins of Rational Choice Liberalism*, Chicago: University of Chicago Press.

Amin, Samir 2010 [1978], *The Law of Worldwide Value*, New York: Monthly Review Press.

Amin, Samir 2013, *Three Essays on Marx's Theory of Value*, New York: Monthly Review Press.

Amin, Samir 2014, 'Contra Hardt and Negri: Multitude or Generalized Proletarianization', *Monthly Review*, 66, no. 6, November.

Anderson, Perry 1976, *Considerations on Western Marxism*, London: New Left Books.

Anderson, Perry 1983, *In the Tracks of Historical Materialism*, London: Verso.

Anderson, Perry 1988, 'Modernity and Revolution' in *Marxism and the Interpretation of Culture*, edited by Cary Nelson and Lawrence Grossberg, Urbana: University of Illinois Press.

Anderson, Stephen R. 1985, *Phonology in the Twentieth Century: Theories of Rules and Theories of Representations*, Chicago: University of Chicago Press.

Anderson, Stephen R. 2004, *Doctor Dolittle's Delusion: Animals and the Uniqueness of Human Language*, New Haven: Yale University Press.

Andrews, Kenneth R. 1984, *Trade, Plunder and Settlement: Maritime Enterprise and the Genesis of the British Empire, 1480–1630*, Cambridge: Cambridge University Press.

Appadurai, Arjun 2003, 'Commodities and the Politics of Value' in *The Social Life of Things: Commodities in Cultural Perspective*, edited by Arjun Appadurai, Cambridge: Cambridge University Press.

Archer, Margaret S. 2000, *Being Human: The Problem of Agency*, Cambridge: Cambridge University Press.

Arbib, Michael A. (ed.) 2013, *Language, Music, and the Brain: A Mysterious Relationship*, Cambridge, MA: MIT Press.

Archibald, W. Peter 1989, *Marx and the Missing Link: Human Nature*, Atlantic Highlands: Humanities Press.

Arendt, Hannah 1958, *The Human Condition*, Chicago: University of Chicago Press.

Arendt, Hannah 1977 [1963], *Eichmann in Jerusalem: A Report on the Banality of Evil*, New York: Penguin.

Aristotle 1941, *The Basic Works of Aristotle*, edited by Richard McKeon, New York: Random House.

Arrighi, Giovanni 2009, 'The Winding Paths of Capital', Arrighi interviewed by David Harvey, *New Left Review*, 56, March/April: 61–94.

Asimov, Isaac 1988, 'Standing Tall', in *Fantasy and Science Fiction*, 74, no. 1: 123–33.

Aston, T.H. and C.H.E. Philpin (eds) 1985, *The Brenner Debate: Agrarian Class Structure and Economic Development in Pre-Industrial Europe*, Cambridge: Cambridge University Press.

Bachelard, Gaston 1969, *The Poetics of Reverie*, translated by Daniel Russell, New York: Orion Press.

Bakhtin, Mikhail M. 1981, *The Dialogic Imagination: Four Essays*, edited by Michael Holquist, translated by Caryl Emerson and Michael Holquist, Austin: University of Texas Press.

Balibar, Étienne 1992, 'Foucault and Marx', in *Michel Foucault, Philosopher*, edited by Timothy J. Armstrong, New York: Routledge.

Balibar, Étienne 2017, *The Philosophy of Karl Marx*, London: Verso.

Bannerji, Himani 2005, 'Building from Marx: Reflections on Class and Race', *Social Justice*, 32, no. 4: 144–60.

Barrell, John 2004, *The Darkside of the Landscape: The Rural Poor in English Painting, 1730–1840*, Cambridge: Cambridge University Press.

Barth, F. 1975, *Ritual and Knowledge among the Baktaman*, New Haven: Yale University Press.

Barthes, Roland 1967, *Elements of Semiology*, New York: Hill and Wang.

Barthes, Roland 1972, *Mythologies*, New York: Hill and Wang.

Barthes, Roland 1984, *The Fashion System*, translated by Matthew Ward and Richard Howard, New York: Hill and Wang.

Baudelaire, Charles 1970, *The Painter of Modern Life and Other Essays*, translated and edited by Jonathan Mayne, London: Phaidon.

Baudelaire, Charles 1989, *Flowers of Evil*, edited by Marthiel and Jackson Mathews, New York: New Directions Publishing Co.

Baudrillard, Jean 1981, *For a Critique of the Political Economy of the Sign*, Candor, NY: Telos Press.

Baynes, Thomas Spencer 1888, 'Labour Laws', in *The Encyclopedia Britannica*, 9th edition, Vol. 14.

Beattie, J.M. 1986, *Crime and the Courts in England 1660–1800*, Princeton: Princeton University Press.

de Beauvoir, Simone 1992, *The Prime of Life*, translated by Peter Green, New York: Paragon House.

Bejjani, Fadi J. and Johan M.F. Landsmeer 1989, 'Biomechanics of the Hand', in *Basic Biomechanics of the Musculoskeletal System*, edited by Margareta Nordin and Victor H. Frankel, Philadelphia: Lea and Febiger.

Bell, Graham A. and Annesley J. Watson (eds) 1999, *Aromas: The Chemical Senses in Science and Industry*, Sydney: University of New South Wales Press.

Benjamin, Walter 1968, *Illuminations*, translated by Harry Zohn, New York: Shocken Books.

Benjamin, Walter 1972, 'Der Weg zum Erfolg in Dreizehn Thesen', in *Gesammelte Schriften*, Bd. IV.1, Frankfurt: Suhrkamp Verlag.

Benjamin, Walter 1974, *Gesammelte Schriften*, Bd. I.2, Frankfurt: Suhrkamp Verlag.

Benjamin, Walter 1989, *Das Passagen-Werk*, in *Gesammelte Schriften*, Bd.V.1, edited by Rolf Tiedemann, Frankfurt: Suhrkamp Verlag

Benjamin, Walter 1992, *Aussichten: Illustrierte Aufsätze mit zahlreichen Abbildungen*, Frankfurt: Insel Verlag.

Benjamin, Walter 2002, *The Arcades Project*, translated by Howard Eiland and Kevin McLaughlin, Cambridge, MA: Harvard University Press.

Benjamin, Walter 2003, *Selected Writings, Volume 4: 1938–1940*, edited by Howard Eiland and Michael W. Jennings, Cambridge, MA: Harvard University Press.

Bentham, Jeremy 1965, *An Introduction to the Principles of Morals and Legislation*, New York: Hafner Publishing.

Benthien, Claudia 2002, *Skin: On the Cultural Border between Self and the World*, New York: Columbia University Press.

Benton, Michael J. 2005, *Vertebrate Paleontology*, 3rd edition, Malden, MA: Blackwell.

Benton, Ted 1979, 'Natural Science and Cultural Struggle', in *Issues in Marxist Philosophy*, Vol. II, edited by John Mepham and D-H. Ruben, New Jersey: Humanities Press, pp. 101–42.

Benveniste, Emile 1971, *Problems in General Linguistics*, translated by Mary Elizabeth Meek, Coral Gables: University of Miami Press.

van den Berg, J.H. 1974, *Divided Existence and Complex Society: An Historical Approach*, Pittsburgh: Duquense University Press.

Berger, John 1991, 'Why Look at Animals?', in Berger 1991, *About Looking*, New York: Vintage International.

Berger, John 2016, *Landscapes*, London: Verso.

Bergmann, Gustav 1954, 'Logical Positivism, Language, and the Reconstruction of Metaphysics', in *The Metaphysics of Logical Positivism*, New York: Longmans, Green and Co.

Berlant, Lauren 2011, *Cruel Optimism*, Durham, NC: Duke University Press.

Berlin, Adele and Marc Zvi Brettler (eds) 2004, *The Jewish Study Bible*, Oxford: Oxford University Press.

Berman, Marshall 2017, *Modernism in the Streets: A Life and Times in Essays*, London: Verso.

Bhattacharya, Tithi (ed.) 2017, *Social Reproduction Theory: Remapping Class, Recentering Oppression*, London: Pluto Press.

Bickerton, Derek 1990, *Language and Species*, Chicago: University of Chicago Press.

Bickerton, Derek 1995, *Language and Human Behavior*, Seattle: University of Washington Press.

Biernacki, Richard 1999, 'Method and Metaphor after the New Cultural History', in *Bey-*

ond the Cultural Turn, edited by V.E. Bonnell and L. Hunt, Berkeley: University of California Press.

Bindoff, S.T. 1976, *Tudor England*, London: Penguin.

Bloch, Ernst 1973, *Erbschaft dieser Zeit*, Frankfurt: Suhrkamp.

Bloch, Ernst 1975, *Über Methode und System bei Hegel*, Frankfurt: Suhrkamp.

Bloch, Ernst 1976, *Das Prinzip Hoffnung, Erster Band*, Frankfurt: Suhrkamp.

Bloch, Ernst 1985 [1923], 'Aktualität und Utopie: Zu Lukács' *Geschichte und Klassenbewusstsein*', in *Philosophische Aufsätze zur objektiven Phantasie*, in *Ernst Bloch: Gesamtausgabe*, Bd. 10, Frankfurt am Main: Suhrkamp Verlag, pp. 598–621.

Bloch, Ernst 1986, *The Principle of Hope*, Vol. 1, translated by Neville Plaice, Stephen Plaice, and Paul Knight, Cambridge, MA: MIT Press.

Bloch, Maurice 1991, 'Language, Anthropology and Cognitive Science', *Man*, 26, no. 2: 183–98.

Blondel, Eric 1991, *Nietzsche: The Body and Culture*, Palo Alto: Stanford University Press.

Bohrer, Ashley J. 2019, *Marxism and Intersectionality: Race, Gender, Class and Sexuality under Contemporary Capitalism*, Bielefeld: Transcript Verlag.

Bonefeld, Werner and Kosmas Psychopedis (eds) 2000, *The Politics of Change*, Basingstoke: Palgrave.

Bonefeld, Werner and Kosmas Psychopedis (eds) 2005, *Human Dignity: Social Autonomy and the Critique of Capitalism*, Farnham: Ashgate.

Bonner, John 1980, *The Evolution of Culture in Animals*, Princeton: Princeton University Press.

Bourdieu, Pierre 1991, *Language and Symbolic Power*, translated by Gino Raymond and Matthew Adamson, Cambridge, MA: Harvard University Press.

Bowsky, William M. 1981, *A Medieval Italian Commune: Siena under the Nine, 1287–1355*, Berkeley: University of California Press.

Braddick, O.J. 1982, 'Binocular Vision', in *The Senses*, edited by H.B. Barlow and J.D. Mollon, Cambridge: Cambridge University Press, pp. 192–200.

Braga, Ruy 2019, *The Poltiics of the Precariat: From Populism to Lulista Hegemony*, Chicago: Haymarket Books.

Braudel, Fernand 1966, *The Mediterranean and the Mediterranean World in the Age of Philip II*, translated by Siân Reynolds, New York: Harper & Row.

Braverman, Harry 1975, 'Work and Unemployment', *Monthly Review*, 27, no. 2: 18–31.

Braverman, Harry 1998, *Labor and Monopoly Capital*, New York: Monthly Review Press.

Brenner, Johanna 2000, *Women and the Politics of Class*, New York: Monthly Review Press.

Broberg, Gunnar 1983, *Linnaeus, the Man and His Work*, Berkeley: University of California Press.

Brown, Heather A. 2012, *Marx on Gender and the Family: A Critical Study*, Chicago: Haymarket Books.

Brucker, Gene A. 1967, 'Introduction', in *Florentine Diaries and Diarists*, edited by Gene A. Brucker, Long Grove, IL: Waveland Press.

Brüggemann, Heinz 1973, *Literarische Technik und soziale Revolution*, Hamburg: Rowohlt.

Bruner, Jerome Seymour, Alison Jolly, and Kathy Sylva (eds) 1976, *Play: Its Role in Development and Evolution*, London: Penguin Books.

Bryceson, Deborah Fahy 1983, 'Use Values, the Law of Value and the Analysis of Non-Capitalist Production', *Capital and Class*, 20, Summer.

Buchli, Victor (ed.) 2002, *The Material Culture Reader*, Oxford: Berg.

Buisseret, David 2003, *The Mapmakers' Quest: Depicting New Worlds in Renaissance Europe*, Oxford: Oxford University Press.

Burkett, Paul 2014, *Marx and Nature: A Red and Green Perspective*, 2nd edition, Chicago: Haymarket.

Burkett, Paul 2018, 'Some Notes on Kohei Saito's *Karl Marx's Ecosocialism*', *Climate and Capitalism*, 8 January, https://climateandcapitalism.com/2018/01/08/on-kohei-saitos-karl-marxs-ecosocialism/.

Butler, Judith 1993, *Bodies that Matter: On the Discursive Limits of 'Sex'*, New York: Routledge.

Butler, Judith 1995, 'Conscience Doth Make Subjects of Us All', *Yale French Studies*, 88: 6–26.

Butler, Judith 2004, *Precarious Life: The Powers of Mourning and Violence*, London: Verso.

Butler, Judith 2016 [2009], *Frames of War: When is Life Grievable?* London: Verso.

Butler, Judith 2019, 'The Inorgranic Body in the Early Marx: A Limit-Concept of Anthropocentrism', *Radical Philosophy*, 2, no. 6, https://www.radicalphilosophy.com/wp-content/uploads/2019/12/rp206_butler.pdf.

Cagan, Robert H. (ed.) 1989, *Neural Mechanisms in Taste*, Boca Raton, FL: CRC Press.

Callinicos, Alex 1982, *Is There a Future for Marxism?* Atlantic Highlands: Humanities Press.

Calvin, William H. 1983, *The Throwing Madonna: Essays on the Brain*, New York: McGraw-Hill.

Campbell, Donald T., 1987, 'Evolutionary Epistemology', in *Evolutionary Epistemology, Theory of Rationality, and the Sociology of Knowledge*, edited by Gerard Radnityzky and W.W. Bartley, III, La Salle, IL: Open Court, pp. 47–89.

Camus, Albert 1955, *The Myth of Sisyphus and Other Essays*, New York: Vintage.

Carello, Claudia and Michael Turvey 2000, 'Rotational Invariants in Dynamic Touch', in *Touch, Representation, and Blindness*, edited by Morton A. Heller, Oxford: Oxford University Press, pp. 27–66.

Carrier, D.R. 1984, 'The Energetic Paradox of Human Running and Hominid Evolution', *Current Anthropology*, 25: 483–95.

Carruthers, Bruce G. and Wendy Nelson Espeland 1991, 'Accounting for Rationality', *American Journal of Sociology*, 97, no. 1.

Cartmill, Matt 1974, 'Rethinking Primate Origins', *Science*, 184, no. 4135: 436–43.

Carver, Terrell 2013, 'The German Ideology Never Took Place', *Marxismo Critico*, https://marxismocritico.com/2013/05/06/the-german-ideology-never-took-place/.

Case, Anne and Angus Deaton 2020, *Deaths of Despair and the Future of Capitalism*, Princeton: Princeton University Press.

Casey, Edward S. 1993, *Getting Back into Place: Toward a Renewed Understanding of the Place-World*, Bloomington: Indiana University Press.

Cassady, Joslyn 2007, 'A Tundra of Sickness: The Uneasy Relationship between Toxic Waste, TEK ["Traditional Ecological Knowledge"], and Cultural Survival', *Arctic Anthropology*, 44, no. 1: 87–97.

Cassady, Joslyn 2010, 'State Calculations of Cultrual Survival in Environmental Risk Assessement: Consquences for Alaska Natives', *Medical Anthropology Quarterly*, 24, no. 4: 451–71.

Cassirer, Ernst 1970 [1944], *An Essay on Man*, New Haven: Yale University Press.

de Certeau, Michel 1997, *Culture in the Plural*, Minneapolis: University of Minnesota Press.

Chakrabarty, Dipesh 2000, *Provincializing Europe: Postcolonial Thought and Historical Difference*, Princeton: Princeton University Press.

Chakrabarty, Dipesh 2004, 'History and Historicality, Review of Ranajit Guha, *History at the Limit of World History*', *Postcolonial Studies*, 7, no. 1: 125–30.

Chambers, J.D. 1953, 'Enclosure and Labour Supply in the Industrial Revolution', *The Economic History Review*, 5, no. 3: 319–43.

Chari, Anita 2015, *A Political Economy of the Senses: Neoliberalism, Reification, Critique*, New York: Columbia University Press.

Chatfield, Michael 1977, *A History of Accounting Thought*, Huntington, NY: Robert E. Krieger.

Chen, Michelle 2016a, 'Until Last Year, No One Was Tracking Workplace Injuries', *The Nation*, 22 March, https://www.thenation.com/article/until-last-year-no-one-was-tracking-workplace-injuries/.

Chen, Michelle 2016b, 'In the Time it Takes to Read this Article, a Person Will Die at Work in the US', *The Nation*, 27 April, https://www.thenation.com/article/in-the-time-it-takes-to-read-this-article-a-person-will-die-at-work-in-the-us/.

Chomsky, Noam 2006a [1967], 'Biolinguistics and the Human Capacity', in *Language and Mind*, Cambridge: Cambridge University Press.

Chomsky, Noam 2006b [1967], 'Linguistic Contributions', in *Language and Mind*, Cambridge: Cambridge University Press.

Clark, Brett, Daniel Auerbach, and Karen Xuan Zhang 2018, 'The Du Bois Nexus: Intersectionality, Political Economy, and Environmental Injustice in the Peruvian Guano Trade in the 1800s', *Environmntal Sociology*, 4, no. 1: 54–66.

Classen, Constance 1993, *Worlds of Sense: Exploring the Senses in History and Across Cultures*, London: Routledge.

Clastres, Pierre 1989, *Society Against the State*, translated by Robert Hurley and Abe Stein, Cambridge, MA: MIT Press, Zone Books.

Cocks, Joan 1998, 'Complementarity or Contradiction', Response to Fracchia, 'Foucault, Marx, and the Historical-Materialist Horizon', *Intellectual History Newsletter*, 20: 16–18.

Cohen, J.M. 1969, *Christopher Columbus: The Four Voyages*, London: Penguin.

Collins, Patricia Hill and Sirma Bilge 2019, *Intersectionality*, Cambridge: Polity Press.

Conrad, Joseph 1997, *Heart of Darkness*, in *Heart of Darkness and The Secret Sharer*, New York: Penguin/Signet.

Cook, Michael 2003, *A Brief History of the Human Race*, New York: Norton.

Cooke, Roger 1997, *The History of Mathematics: A Brief Course*, New York: John Wiley & Sons.

Corballis, Michael C. 1991, *The Lopsided Ape: Evolution of the Generative Mind*, Oxford: Oxford University Press.

Corballis, Michael C. 2003, 'From Hand to Mouth: The Gestural Origins of Language', in *Language Evolution*, edited by Morten H. Christiansen and Simon Kirby, Oxford: Oxford University Press, pp. 201–18.

Corbin, Alain 1986, *The Foul and the Fragrant: Odor and the French Social Imagination*, Cambridge, MA: Harvard University Press.

Corrado Pope, Barbara 1977, 'Angels in thee Devil's Workshop: Leisured and Charitable Women in Nineteenth-Century England and France', in *Becoming Visible: Women in European History*, edited by Renate Bridenthal and Claudia Koonz, Boston: Houghton Mifflin Company, pp. 296–324.

Covert, Bryce and Mike Konczal 2017, 'Accidental Advocates', *The Nation*, 9 October, 9.

Craig, Neville (ed.) 1848, *The Olden Time*, Vol. 2, Pittsburgh: Wright and Charlton.

Crary, Jonathan 2014, *24/7: Late Capitalism and the Ends of Sleep*, London: Verso.

Crenshaw, Kimberlé 1991, 'Mapping the Margins: Intersectionality, Identity Politics, and Violence Against Women of Color', *Standford Law Review*, 43, no. 6: 1251–99.

de Crèvecoeur, Hector St. John 1963, *Letters from an American Farmer and Sketches of Eighteenth-Century America*, New York: Signet Classic.

Crosby, Alfred W. 2009, *The Measure of Reality: Quantification and Western Society, 1250–1600*, Cambridge: Cambridge University Press.

Cross, Ian et al. 2013, 'Culture and Evolution', in *Language, Music, and the Brain: A Mysterious Relationship*, edited by Michael A. Arbib, Cambridge, MA: MIT Press, pp. 541–62.

Crystal, David 1987, 'The Sounds of Speech', in *The Cambridge Encyclopedia of Language*, Cambridge: Cambridge University Press, pp. 152–59.

Csikzenthmihalyi, Mihaly and Eugene Rochberg-Halton 1981, *The Meaning of Things: Domestic Symbols of the Self*, Cambridge: Cambridge University Press.

Culler, Jonathan 1976, *Ferdinand de Saussure*, London: Penguin.
Darby, H.C. 1933, 'The Agrarian Contribution to Surveying in England', *The Geographical Journal*, 82, no. 6: 529–35.
Darlington, William M. 1893, *Christopher Gist's Journals with Historical, Geographical and Ethnological Notes and Biographies of his Contemporaries*, Pittsburgh: J.R. Weldin & Co.
Darwin, Charles 1980, 'M Notebook', in *Metaphysics, Materialism, and the Evolution of Mind: Early Writings of Charles Darwin*, Chicago: University of Chicago Press.
Darwin, Charles 2006, *The Expression of the Emotions in Man and Animals*, in *From So Simple a Beginning: The Four Great Books of Charles Darwin*, edited by Edward O. Wilson, New York: Norton.
Dati, Gregorio 1967, *The Diary of Gregorio Dati*, in *Two Memoirs of Renaissance Florence*, edited by Gene A. Brucker, Long Grove, IL: Waveland Press.
Dauvé, Gilles 2017, 'Federici vs. Marx', on website *Communists in Situ*, https://cominsitu.wordpress.com/2015/12/03/federici-vs-marx-gilles-dauve/, accessed 14 April 2017.
Davidson, Iain and William Noble 1993, 'When did Language Begin?' in *The First Humans: Human Origins and History to 10,000 BC*, edited by Göran Burenhult, McMahons Point NSW, Australia: Weldon, Owen Pry Limited.
Davidson, Neil 2012, *How Revolutionary were the Bourgeois Revolutions?* Chicago: Haymarket Books.
Davis, Angela 1983, *Women, Race & Class*, New York: Vintage Books.
Davis, Mike 2018, *Old Gods, New Enigmas: Marx's Lost Theory*, New York: Verso.
Dawkins, Richard 1989, *The Selfish Gene*, Oxford: Oxford University Press.
Deleuze, Gilles and Félix Guattari 1986, *Anti-Oedipus: Capitalism and Schizophrenia*, translated by Robert Hurley, Mark Seem, and Helen R. Lane, Minneapolis: University of Minnesota Press.
Delvecchio Good, Mary-Jo, Paul E. Brodwin, Byron J. Good, and Arthur Kleinman (eds) 1992, *Pain as Human Experience: An Anthropological Perspective*, Berkeley: University of California Press.
Derrida, Jacques 1976, *Of Grammatology*, translated by Gayatri Chakravorty Spivak, Baltimore: Johns Hopkins Press.
Derrida, Jacques 1981, *Positions*, translated by Alan Bass, Chicago: University of Chicago Press.
Dery, Luis Camara 2002, *A History of the Inarticulate: Local History, Prostitution, and Other Views from the Bottom*, Manila: New Day Publishers.
Descartes, René 1999, *The Philosophical Writings of Descartes*, Vol. I, edited by John Cottingham et al., Cambridge: Cambridge University Press.
Devlin, Keith 2011, *The Man of Numbers: Leonardo's Arithmetic Revolution*, New York: Walker and Company.
Diamond, Jared 1997, *Guns, Germs, and Steel: The Fates of Human Societies*, New York: Norton.

Dill, D.B. et al. 1964, *Adaptation to the Environment*, Washington, D.C.: American Physiological Society.

Dodson, Edward O. and Peter Dodson 1985, *Evolution: Process and Product*, 3rd edition, Boston: Prindle, Weber and Schmidt.

Dodwell, Peter C. 1995, 'Fundamental Processes in Vision', in *Sensation and Perception*, edited by Richard L. Gregory and Andrew M. Coleman, London: Longman.

Dominy, Nathaniel J. and Peter W. Lucas, 2001 'Ecological Importance of Trichromatic Vision to Primates', *Nature*, 410: 363–6.

Dominy, Nathaniel J. 2004, 'Fruits, Fingers, and Fermentation: The Sensory Cues Available to Foraging Primates', *Integrative and Comparative Biology*, 44, no. 4: 295–303.

Douglas, Mary and Baron Isherwood 1996, *The World of Goods: Towards an Anthropology of Consumption*, New York: Routledge.

Duden, Barbara 1987, *Geschichte unter der Haut. Ein Eisenacher Arzt und seine Patientinnen um 1730*, Stuttgart: Klett-Cotta Verlag.

du Gay, Paul 1997, *Production of Culture/Culture of Production*, London: Sage.

Dundes, Lauren (ed.) 2003, *The Manner Born: Birth Rites in Cross-Cultural Perspective*, Walnut Creek, CA: AltaMira Press.

Dunn, John 1967, 'Consent in the Political Theory of John Locke', *The Historical Journal*, 10, no. 2: 153–82.

Dunn, John 1968, 'Justice and the Interpretation of Locke's Political Theory', *Political Studies*, 16, no. 1: 68–87.

Dunn, John 1969, *The Political Thought of John Locke: An Historical Account of the 'Two Treatises of Government'*, Cambridge: Cambridge University Press.

Dupre, John 1991, 'Comments on Biology and Culture', in *The Boundaries of Humanity: Humans, Animals, Machines*, edited by James J. Sheehan and Morton Sosna, Berkeley: University of California Press.

Durrell, Gerald 2004, *Birds, Beasts, and Relatives*, London: Penguin.

Eagleton, Terry 1990, *The Ideology of the Aesthetic*, Oxford: Blackwell.

Eagleton, Terry 2011, *Why Marx was Right*, New Haven: Yale University Press.

Ebrey, Patricia Buckley (ed.) 1981, *Chinese Civilization and Society: A Sourcebook*, New York: The Free Press.

Eco, Umberto 1978, 'Semiotics: A Discipline or an Interdisciplinary Method?' in *Sight, Sound, and Sense*, edited by Thomas A. Sebeok, Bloomington: Indiana University Press.

Eco, Umberto 1979, *A Theory of Semotics*, Bloomington: Indiana University Press.

Eco, Umberto 1986, *Semiotics and the Philosophy of Language*, Bloomington: Indiana University Press.

Eldredge, Niles 1995, *Reinventing Darwin: The Great Debate at the High Table of Evolutionary Theory*, New York: John Wiley & Sons.

Eldredge, Niles 2004, *Why We Do It: Rethinking Sex and the Selfish Gene*, New York: Norton.

Eldredge, Niles and Stephen Jay Gould 1972, 'Punctuated Equilibria: An Alternative to Phyletic Gradualism', in *Models in Paleobiology*, edited by T.J.M. Schopf, San Francisco: Freeman Cooper, pp. 82–115.

Eldredge, Niles and Ian Tattersall 1982, *Myths of Human Evolution*, New York: Columbia University Press.

Elias, Norbert 1992, *Time: An Essay*, translated by Edmund Jephcott, Oxford: Blackwell.

Elias, Norbert 2000, *The Civilizing Process: Sociogenetic and Psychogenetic Investigations*, Revised Edition, translated by Edmund Jephcott, Oxford: Blackwell.

Elson, Diane 1979, 'The Value Theory of Labour', in *Value: The Representation of Labour in Capitalism*, edited by Diane Elson, London: CSE Books.

Engels, Friedrich 1883, *Dialektik der Natur*, in *Marx-Engels Werke*, Vol. 20, 1973, Berlin: Dietz Verlag.

Engels, Friedrich 1886, *Ludwig Feuerbach und der Ausgang der klassischen deutschen Philosophie*, in *Marx-Engels Werke*, Vol. 21, 1975, Berlin: Dietz Verlag, pp. 259–307.

Engels, Friedrich 1859, 'Karl Marx, "Zur Kritik der politischen Ökonomie"', in *Marx-Engels Werke*, Vol. 13, 1975, Berlin: Dietz Verlag.

Engels, Friedrich 1999, *The Condition of the Working Class in England*, edited by David McLellan, Oxford: Oxford University Press.

Eribon, Didier 1991, *Michel Foucault*, Cambridge, MA: Harvard University Press.

Erikson, Paul et al. 2013, *How Reason Almost Lost its Mind: The Strange Career of Cold War Rationality*, Chicago: University of Chicago Press.

Evans, E.P. 1982, 'Basic Physics and Psychophysics of Sound', in *The Senses*, edited by H.B. Barlow and J.D. Mollon, Cambridge: Cambridge University Press.

Eyre, Eric 2020, *Death in Mud Lick: A Coal Country Fight against the Drug Companies that Delivered the Opioid Epidemic*, New York: Scribner.

Falk, Dean 1992, *Braindance: New Discoveries about Human Origins and Brain Evolution*, New York: Henry Holt & Co.

Farago, Jason 2018, 'Was Australopithecus an Artist?', *New York Times*, 1 February, https://www.nytimes.com/2018/02/01/arts/design/nasher-sculpture-center-dallas-first-sculpture-review.html.

Faulkner, Neil 2013, *A Marxist History of the World: From Neanderthals to Neoliberals*, London: Pluto Press.

Fausto-Sterling, Anne 1993, 'The Five Sexes: Why Male and Female are not Enough', *The Sciences*, 33, no. 2: 20–4.

Fausto-Sterling, Anne 2000, 'The Five Sexes Revisited', *The Sciences*, 40, no. 4: 19–23.

Federici, Silvia 2014, *Caliban and the Witch: Women, the Body and Primitive Accumulation*, Brooklyn: Autonomedia.

Federici, Silvia 2018, *Witches, Witch-Hunting, and Women*, Oakland, CA: PM Press.

Federici, Silvia 2019, *Re-enchanting the World: Feminism and the Politics of the Commons*, Oakland, CA: PM Press.

Feenberg, Andrew 1991, *Critical Theory of Technology*, Oxford: Oxford University Press.
Feuerbach, Ludwig 1841a, 'Einige Bemerkungen über den "Anfang der Philosophie" von Dr. J.F. Reiff', in *Sämtliche Werke*, Vol. III, 1975, Frankfurt: Suhrkamp Verlag.
Feuerbach, Ludwig 1841b, *Das Wesen des Christentums*, in *Sämtliche Werke*, Vol. V, 1976, Frankfurt: Suhrkamp Verlag.
Feuerbach, Ludwig 1843, 'Grundsätze einer Philosophie der Zukunft', in *Sämtliche Werke*, Vol. III, 1975, Frankfurt: Suhrkamp Verlag.
Findlay, J.N. 1982, 'An Ontology of Senses', *The Journal of Philosophy*, 70, no. 10: 545–51.
Fine, Robert 1997, 'Civil Society Theory, Enlightenment and Critique', *Democratization*, 4, no. 1: 7–28.
Fink, Eugen 1981, 'Operative Concepts in Husserl's Phenomenology', in *Apriori and World: European Contributions to Husserlian Phenomenology*, edited by W. McKenna, R.M. Harlan, and L.E. Winters, The Hague: Nijhoff, pp. 56–70.
Finley, M.I. 1973, *The Ancient Economy*, Berkeley: University of California Press.
Fitch, W. Tecumseh and Erich D. Jarvis 2013, 'Birdsong and Other Animal Models for Human Speech, Song, and Vocal Learning', in *Language, Music, and the Brain: A Mysterious Relationship*, edited by Michael A. Arbib, Cambridge, MA: MIT Press.
Fletcher, Roland 1993, 'The Evolution of Human Behavior', in *The First Humans: Human Origins and History to 10,000 BC*, New York: HarperCollins.
Flynn, Andrea and Susan R. Holmberg, 'America Needs Economic Rights: Now Is the Time to Push for Them', *The Nation*, 11 January, https://www.thenation.com/article/franklin-roosevelt-economic-bill-rights/.
Foley, R. 1987, *Another Unique Species*, New York: Longman.
Foley, R. 1992, 'Evolutionary Ecology of Fossil Hominids', in *Evolutionary Ecology and Human Behavior*, edited by Eric Alden Smith and Bruce Winterhalder, New York: Aldine de Gruyter.
Foriani, Francesca 2005, *The Marvel of Maps: Art, Cartography and Politics in Renaissance Italy*, New Haven: Yale University Press.
Foster, John Bellamy 2000, *Marx's Ecology*, New York: Monthly Review Press.
Foster, John Bellamy 2011, 'The Ecology of Marxian Political Economy', *Monthly Review*, 63, no. 4.
Foster, John Bellamy 2017, 'The Meaning of Work in a Sustainable Society', *Monthly Review*, 69, no. 4: 1–14.
Foster, John Bellamy 2018, 'Marx, Value & Nature', *Monthly Review*, 70, no. 3: 122–36.
Foster, John Bellamy 2020, *The Return of Nature: Socialism and Ecology*, New York: Monthly Review Press.
Foster, John Bellamy and Paul Burkett 2000, 'Marx and the Dialectic of Organic/inorganic Relations', *Organization and Environment*, 14, no. 4: 403–25.
Foster, John Bellamy and Paul Burkett 2018, 'Value Isn't Everything', *Monthly Review*, 70, no. 6: 1–17.

Foster, John Bellamy and Brett Clarke 2018, 'Marx and Alienated Speciesism', *Monthly Review*, 70, no. 7.

Foster, John Bellamy, Hannah Holleman and Brett Clark 2020a, 'Marx and the Indigenous', *Monthly Review*, 71, no. 9: 1–19.

Foster, John Bellamy, Hannah Holleman and Brett Clark 2020b, 'Marx and Slavery', *Monthly Review*, 71, no. 3: 101–22.

Foster, Mary LeCron 1978, 'The Symbolic Structure of Primordial Language', in *Human Evolution: Biosocial Perspectives*, edited by S.L. Washburn and Elizabeth R. McCown, Menlo Park, CA: Benjamin/Cummings Publishing, pp. 77–122.

Foster, Mary LeCron 1980, 'The Growth of Symbolism in Culture', in *Symbol as Sense: New Approaches to the Analysis of Meaning*, edited by Mary LeCron Foster and Stanley H. Brandes, New York: Academic Press, pp. 371–97.

Foster, Mary LeCron 1992, 'Body Process in the Evolution of Language', in *Giving the Body its Due*, edited by Maxine Sheets-Johnstone, Albany: SUNY Press.

Foster, Russell G. and Leon Kreitzman 2004, *Rhythms of Life: The Biological Clocks that Control the Daily Lives of Every Living Thing*, New Haven: Yale University Press.

Foucault, Michel 1964, 'Nietzsche, Freud, Marx', in *Transforming the Hermeneutic Context: From Nietzsche to Nancy*, edited by Gayle L. Ormiston and Alan D. Schrift, Albany: SUNY Press, pp. 59–67.

Foucault, Michel 1972, The *Archaeology of Knowledge and the Discourse on Language*, translated by A.M. Sheridan Smith, New York: Pantheon Books.

Foucault, Michel 1973, *The Birth of the Clinic*, New York: Pantheon Books.

Foucault, Michel 1975, *Surveiller et punir: Naissance de la prison*, Paris: Gallimard.

Foucault, Michel 1976, 'La grande colere des faits', in Michel Foucault, *Dits et ecrits*, Vol. III, 1994, Paris: Gallimard.

Foucault, Michel 1979, *Discipline and Punish: The Birth of the Prison*, New York: Vintage.

Foucault, Michel 1980, *Power/Knowledge: Selected Interviews and Other Writings 1972–1977*, edited by Colin Gordon, translated by Colin Gordon et al., New York: Pantehon Books.

Foucault, Michel 1983, 'The Subject and Power', in *Michel Foucault: Beyond Structuralism and Hermeneutics*, edited by Hubert Dreyfus and Paul Rabinow, Chicago: University of Chicago Press, pp. 208–28.

Foucault, Michel 1988, *Technologies of the Self: A Seminar with Michel Foucault*, Amherst: University of Massachusetts Press.

Foucault, Michel 1990a, *Michel Foucault: Politics, Philosophy, Culture*, edited by Lawrence Kritzman, New York: Routledge.

Foucault, Michel 1990b, *The History of Sexuality: Volume 1: An Introduction*, translated by Robert Hurley, NY: Vintage.

Foucault, Michel 1990c, 'Nietzsche, Freud, Marx', in *Transforming the Hermeneutic Context*, edited by Gayle L. Ormiston and Alan D. Schrift, Albany: SUNY Press.

Foucault, Michel 1991, *Remarks on Marx: Conversations with Duccio Trombadori*, translated by R. James Goldstein and James Cascaito, New York: Semiotext(e).

Foucault, Michel 1997, *Michel Foucault: Ethics, Subjectivity and Truth* in *Essential Works*, Volume I, edited by Paul Rabinow, New York: New Press.

Foucault, Michel 2000, *Power: Essential Works of Foucault 1954–1984*, Vol. 3, New York: The New Press.

Foucault, Michel 2008, *The Birth of Biopolitics: Lectures at the Collège de France, 1978–1979*, translated by Graham Burchell, New York: Picador Palgrave Macmillan.

Fox, John 2015, *Marx, the Body and Human Nature*, London: Palgrave Macmillan.

Fracchia, Joseph 1991, 'Marx's *Aufhebung* of Philosophy and the Foundations of Historical-Materialistic Science', *History and Theory*, 30, no. 2: 153–79.

Fracchia, Joseph 1998, 'Foucault, Marx, and the Historical-Materialist Horizon', *Intellectual History Newsletter*, 20.

Fracchia, Joseph 1999, 'Dialectical Itineraries', *History and Theory*, 38, no. 2: 169–97.

Fracchia, Joseph 2003, 'Whose Burden? Review Essay of Allan Megill, *Karl Marx: The Burden of Reason*', *History and Theory*, November: 378–98.

Fracchia, Joseph 2004, 'On Transhistorical Abstractions and the Intersection of Historical Theory and Social Critique', *Historical Materialism*, 12, no. 3: 125–46.

Fracchia, Joseph 2005a, 'Beyond the Human Nature Debate: Human Corporeal Organization as the "First Fact" of Historical Theory', *Historical Materialism*, 13, no. 1: 33–61.

Fracchia, Joseph 2005b, 'The Untimely Timeliness of Rosa Luxemburg', in *Social Autonomy and the Critique of Capitalism*, edited by Werner Bonefeld and Kosmas Psychopedis, Farnham: Ashgate, pp. 105–30.

Fracchia, Joseph 2008, 'The Capitalist Labor Process and the Body in Pain: The Corporeal Depths of Marx's Concept of Immiseration', *Historical Materialism*, 16, no. 4: 35–66.

Fracchia, Joseph 2011, *Verwertung der Sachenwelt – Entwertung der Menschenwelt: Zur Rolle des menschlichen Körpers in Marx' Kritik der politischen Ökonomie*, in *Kapital & Kritik: Nach der "neuen" Marx-Lektüre*, Werner Bonefeld and Michael Heinrich (Hrsg.), VSA Verlag: Hamburg, pp. 65–92.

Fracchia, Joseph 2012, *kulturelle Wende* in *Historisch-Kritisches Wörterbuch des Marxismus*, Bd. VIII.1, Hamburg: Argument-Verlag, pp. 362–78.

Fracchia, Joseph 2013, 'The Philosophical Leninism and Eastern "Western Marxism" of Georg Lukács', *Historical Materialism*, 21, no. 1: 69–93.

Fracchia, Joseph and Richard Lewontin 1999, 'Does Culture Evolve?' *History and Theory*, 30, no. 2: 52–78.

Frede, Wolfgang 1976, *Zur Entwicklung der gesellschaftlichen Kräfte im Marxschen Frühwerk*, Göttingen: Göttinger Beiträge zur Gesellschaftstheorie.

Frege, Gottlob 1980 [1884], *The Foundations of Arithmetic: A Logico-mathematical Enquiry into the Concept of Number*, translated by J.L. Austin, Evanston, IL: Northwestern University Press.

Frege, Gottlob 1892, 'Über Sinn und Bedeutung', *Zeitschrift für Philosophie und philosophische Kritik*, NF 100, S. 25–50. English translation by Max Black, May 1948, *The Philosophical Review*, 57, no. 3: 209–30.

Freud, Sigmund 1929, *A General Introduction to Psychoanalysis*, translated by G. Stanley Hall, New York: Boni and Liveright.

Freud, Sigmund 1962, *Civilization and its Discontents*, translated by James Strachey, New York: W.W. Norton.

Friedland, Roger and John Mohr 2004, *Matters of Culture: Cultural Practice in Sociology*, Cambridge: Cambridge University Press.

Funnell, Warwick 2001, 'Distortions of History, Accounting and the Paradox of Werner Sombart', *Abacus*, 37, no. 1: 55–78.

Fusfeld, Daniel B. 1957, 'Economic Theory Misplaced: Livelihood in Primitive Society', in *Trade and Market in the Early Empires: Economies in History and Theory*, edited by Karl Polanyi et al., New York: Free Press.

Gabrielle, Vincent 2018, 'Gamified Life', *Aeon*, https://aeon.co/essays/how-employers-have-gamified-work-for-maximum-profit.

Garland, Robert 2009, *Daily Life of the Ancient Greeks*, Westport, CT: Greenwood Press.

Garson, Barbara 1988, *The Electronic Sweatshop*, New York: Simon and Schuster.

Gatrell, V.A.C. 1994, *The Hanging Tree: Execution and the English People, 1770–1868*, Oxford: Oxford University Press.

Geertz, Clifford 1973, *The Interpretation of Cultures*, New York: Basic Books.

Gehlen, Arnold, 1997, *Der Mensch. Seine Natur und seine Stellung in der Welt*, 13. Auflage, Wiesbaden: Quelle & Meyer Verlag.

Geldard, Frank 1972, *The Human Senses*, 2nd edition, New York: John Wiley & Sons.

Geras, Norman 1971, 'Althusser's Marxism: An Account and Assessment', *New Left Review*, 171: 57–86.

Geras, Norman 1983, *Marx and Human Nature: Refutation of a Legend*, London: Verso.

Gerth, H.H. and C. Wright Mills (translators and editors) 1970, *From Max Weber: Essays in Sociology*, Oxford: Oxford University Press.

Gibbs, Jr., Raymond W. 1994, *The Poetics of Mind: Figurative Thought, Language, and Understanding*, Cambridge: Cambridge University Press.

Gibson, James J. 1966, *The Senses Considered as Perceptual Systems*, Westport, CT: Greenwood Press.

Gibson, James J. 1979, *The Ecological Approach to Visual Perception*, Boston: Houghton Mifflin.

Giménez, Marthe E. 2018, *Marx, Women and Capitalist Social Reproduction*, Chicago: Haymarket Books.

Godelier, Maurice 1988, *The Mental and the Material: Thought, Economy and Society*, translated by Martin Thom, London: Verso.

Godzich, Wlad 1986, 'Introduction' to Paul de Man, *Resistance to Theory*, Minneapolis: University of Minnesota Press, pp. i–xviii.

von Goethe, Johann Wolfgang 1963, *Faust*, translated by Walter Kaufmann, Garden City, NY: Anchor Books.

Goldstein, R.J. 1991, 'Introduction' to Michel Foucault, *Remarks on Marx: Conversations with Duccio Trombadori*, translated by R. James Goldstein and James Cascaito, New York: Semiotext(e).

Goldthwaite, Richard A. 1990, *The Building of Renaissance Florence: An Economic and Social History*, Baltimore: Johns Hopkins University Press.

Goodman, Nelson 1978, *Ways of Worldmaking*, Indianapolis: Hackett.

Gorz, André (ed.) 1976, *The Division of Labour: The Labour Process and Class-Struggle in Modern Capitalism*, Atlantic Highlands: Humanities Press.

Gorz, André 1982, *Farewell to the Working Class*, Boston: South End Press.

Gorz, André 1985, *Paths to Paradise*, London: Pluto Press.

Gould, Stephen Jay 1977, *Ever Since Darwin*, New York: Norton.

Gould, Stephen Jay 1977, *Ontogeny and Phylogeny*, Cambridge, MA: Harvard University Press.

Gould, Stephen Jay 1980, *The Panda's Thumb*, New York: Norton.

Gould, Stephen Jay 1995, 'Evolution by Walking', *Natural History*, 104, no. 3: 10–15.

Gould, Stephen Jay and Richard C. Lewontin 1979. 'The Spandrels of San Marco and the Panglossian Paradigm: A critique of the Adaptationist Programme', *Proceedings of the Royal Society B*, 205: 581–98.

Graeber, David 2018, *Bullshit Jobs: A Theory*, New York: Simon & Schuster.

Gramsci, Antonio 1973, *Letters from Prison*, edited by Lynne Lawner, New York: Harper and Row.

Gramsci, Antonio 1977, *Selections from the Prison Notebooks*, edited and translated by Quintin Hoare and Geoffrey Nowell Smith, New York: International Publishers

Gramsci, Antonio 1987, *The Modern Prince and Other Writings*, New York: International Publishers.

Gramsci, Antonio 2000, *The Gramsci Reader: Selected Writings 1916–1935*, edited by David Forgacs, New York: New York University Press.

Greenough, William T. 1990, 'Brain Storage of Information from Cutaneous and Other Modalities in Development and Adulthood', in *Touch: The Foundation of Experience*, edited by Kathryn E. Barnard and T. Berry Brazelton, Madison, CT: International Universities Press.

Gregory, Richard 1970, *The Intelligent Eye*, London: Weidenfeld and Nicolson.

Gregory, Richard 1987, 'Intelligence based on Knowledge – Knowledge based on Intelligence', in *Creative Intelligences*, edited by Richard L. Gregory and Pauline K. Marstand, Norwood, NJ: Ablex, pp. 1–8.

Gregory, Richard 1990, *Eye and Brain: The Psychology of Seeing*, 4th edition, Princeton: Princeton University Press.

Gregory, Richard et al. (eds) 1995, *The Artful Eye*, Oxford: Oxford University Press.

Gregory, Richard L. and Andrew M. Coleman (eds) 1995a, *Sensation and Perception*, London: Longman.

Greimas, Algirdas Julien 1987, 'Toward a Semiotics of the Natural World', in *On Meaning: Selected Writings in Semiotic Theory*, Minneapolis: University of Minnesota Press.

Greshko, Michael 2018, 'World's Oldest Cave Art Found – And Neanderthals Made It', *National Geographic*, 22 February, https://news.nationalgeographic.com/2018/02/neanderthals-cave-art-humans-evolution-science/.

Griffin D.R. (ed.) 1982, *Animal Mind – Human Mind*, Report of the Dahlem Workshop, Berlin 1981, Berlin: Springer Verlag.

Griffith, Richard 1970, 'Anthropodology', in *The Philosophy of the Body*, edited by Stuart F. Spickler, Chicago: Quadrangle Books.

Grimm, Richard E. 1973, 'The Autobiography of Leonardo Pisano', *Leonardo Quarterly*, 11: 99–104.

Grosz, Elizabeth 1994, *Volatile Bodies: Toward a Corporeal Feminism*, Bloomington: Indiana University Press.

Grünberg, Emil 1932, *Der Mittelstand in der kapitalistischen Gesellschaft*, Leipzig: Hirschfeld Verlag.

Guha, Ranajit 2002, *History at the Limit of World History*, New York: Columbia University Press.

Gutting, Gary and Johanna Oksala 2019, 'Michel Foucault', in *The Stanford Encyclopedia of Philosophy*, edited by Edward N. Zalta, Spring Edition, https://plato.stanford.edu/archives/spr2019/entries/foucault/.

Hacking, Ian 1983, *Representing and Intervening: Introductory Topics in the Philosophy of Natural Science*, Cambridge: Cambridge University Press.

Hagen, William W. 2002, *Ordinary Prussians: Bandenburg Junkers and Villagers, 1500–1840*, Cambridge: Cambridge University Press.

Hagen, William W. 2011, 'European Yeomanries: A Non-immiseration Model of Agrarian Social History. 1350–1800', *The Agricultural History Review*, 59, Part II.

Haila, Yrjö and Richard Levins 1992, *Humanity and Nature: Ecology, Science, and Society*, London: Pluto Press.

Haldane, J.B.S. 1985, 'On Being the Right Size', in *On Being the Right Size and Other Essays*, edited by John Maynard Smith, Oxford: Oxford University Press.

Hallpike, C.R. 2008, *How We Got Here: From Bows and Arrows to the Space Age*, Milton Keynes: AuthorHouse.

Halpern, Richard 1991, *The Poetics of Primitive Accumulation: English Renaissance Culture and the Genealogy of Capital*, Ithaca: Cornell University Press.

Hampe, Beate (ed.) 2005, *From Perception to Meaning: Image Schemas in Cognitive Linguistics*, Berlin: Mouton de Gruyter.

Hampe, Beate 2005 'Image Schemas in Cognitive Linguistics: Introduction', in *From Perception to Meaning: Image Schemas in Cognitive Linguistics*, edited by Beate Hampe, The Hague: Mouton de Gruyter.

Hartmann, Heidi 1997, 'The Unhappy Marriage of Marxism and Feminism', in *The Second Wave: A Reader in Feminist Theory*, edited by Linda Nicholson, New York: Routledge, pp. 97–122.

Hartman, Saidiya 2019, *Wayward Lives, Beautiful Experiments: Intimate Histories of Riotous Black Girls, Troublesome Women, and Queer Radicals*, New York: W.W. Norton & Co.

Haspelmath, Martin et al. (eds) 2001, 'Biological Foundations of Language', in *Language Typology and Language Universals: An International Handbook*, Vol. 1, Berlin: de Gruyter.

von Haselberg, Peter 1977, 'Wiesengrund-Adorno', in *Text + Kritik*, Sonderband zu Theodor W. Adorno, edited by Heinz Ludwig Arnold, München: Text + Kritik.

Hayakawa, S.I. 1941, *Language in Action*, New York: Harcourt Brace.

Hayman, Ronald 1981, *Kafka: A Biography*, Oxford: Oxford University Press.

Hegel, G.W.F. 1970, *Enzyklopädie der philosophischen Wissenschaften*, in *G.W.F. Hegel: Werke in zwanzig Bänden*, Vols. 8, 9, 10, Frankfurt: Suhrkamp Verlag.

Hegel, G.W.F. 1973, *Vorlesungen über die Philosophie der Geschichte*, in *G.W.F. Hegel: Werke in zwanzig Bänden*, Vol. 12, Frankfurt: Suhrkamp Verlag.

Hegel, G.W.F. 1974, *Phänomenologie des Geistes*, in *G.W.F. Hegel: Werke in zwanzig Bänden*, Vol. 3, Frankfurt: Suhrkamp Verlag.

Hegel, G.W.F. 1975, *Grundlinien der Philosophie des Rechts* in *Hegel*, in *G.W.F. Hegel: Werke in zwanzig Bänden*, Vol. 7, Frankfurt: Suhrkamp Verlag.

Heidegger, Martin 1962, *Being and Time*, translated by John Macquarrie and Edward Robinson, New York: Harper & Row.

Heidegger, Martin 1985, *Unterwegs zur Sprache*, Frankfurt/Main: Vittorio Kostermann.

Heller, Agnes 1976, *The Theory of Need in Marx*, New York: St. Martin's Press.

Heller, Agnes 1981, 'Paradigm of Work/Paradigm of Production', *Dialectical Anthropology*, 6, no. 1: 71–9.

Heller, Joseph 1999, *Catch-22*, New York: Simon and Schuster.

Hertz, Noreena 2021a, *The Lonely Century: Coming Together in a World that's Pulling Apart*, New York: Random House.

Hertz, Noreena 2021b, Interviewed by Doug Henwood, *Behind the News: Doug Henwood's radio archives*, https://shout.lbo-talk.org/lbo/RadioArchive/2021/21_02_11.mp3.

Herz, Rachel 2007, *The Scent of Desire: Discovering Our Enigmatic Sense of Smell*, New York: HarperCollins.

Hewes, G.W. 1973, 'Primate Communication and the Gestural Origin of Language', *Current Anthropology*, 14: 5–24.

Hibbert, Christopher 1975, *The House of Medici: Its Rise and Fall*, New York: William Morrow & Co.

Highfield, Roger 2008, 'Neanderthals Speak for First Time in 50,000 Years', *The Telegraph*, 16 April.

Hill, Christopher 1996, *Liberty against the Law: Some Seventeenth-Century Controversies*, London: Allen Press.

Hirschman, Charles, Samuel Preston, and Vu Manh Loi 1995, 'Vietnamese Casualities During the American War: A New Estimate', *Population and Development Review*, 21, no. 4: 783–812.

Hobbes, Thomas 1970, *Leviathan: of the Matter, Forme and Power of a Commonwealth Ecclesiastical and Civil*, London: Collier-MacMillan.

Hobsbawm, Eric 1962, *The Age of Revolution 1789–1848*, New York: Signet.

Hobsbawm, Eric 1975, 'Class Consciousness in History', in *Aspects of History and Class Consciousness*, edited by István Mészáros, New York: Herder and Herder, pp. 5–21.

Hockett, Charles F. 1982, 'The Origin of Speech', in *Human Communication: Language and Its Psychobiological Bases*, Readings from *Scientific American*, edited by William S.-Y. Wang, San Francisco: W.H. Freeman, pp. 4–12.

Hodge, Robert and Gunther Kress 1988, *Social Semiotics*, Ithaca: Cornell University Press.

Hodgson, Derek 2017, 'Costly Signaling, the Arts, Archaeology and Human Behaviour', *World Archaeology*, 49, no. 4: 446–65.

Hodos, W. 1982, 'Some Perspectives on the Evolution of Intelligence and the Brain', in *Animal Mind – Human Mind*, edited by D.R. Griffin, Berlin: Springer Verlag.

Holdcroft, David 1991, *Saussure: Signs, System, and Arbitrariness*, Cambridge: Cambridge University Press.

Holloway, John n.d., 'Read *Capital*: The First Sentence, Or *Capital* Starts with Wealth, not with the Commodity', in *Grundrisse: zeitschrift für linke theorie & debate*, https://www.grundrisse.net/english-articles/Read_Capital_The_First_Sentence.htm.

Honneth, Axel and Hans Joas 1988, *Social Action and Human Nature*, Cambridge: Cambridge University Press.

Hoppit, Julian 2000, *A Land of Liberty? England 1689–1727*, Oxford: Oxford University Press.

Horkheimer, Max 1935, *Bemerkungen zur philosophischen Anthropologie*, in Horkheimer 1977, *Kritische Theorie*, Frankfurt: S. Fischer Verlag, pp. 200–27.

Horkheimer, Max 1947, *The Eclipse of Reason*, Oxford: Oxford University Press.

Horkheimer, Max 1967, *Zur Kritik der instrumentellen Vernunft*, Frankfurt: Fischer Verlag.

Horkheimer, Max 1977, *Kritische Theorie*, Frankfurt: S. Fischer Verlag.

Houlgate, Stephen (ed.) 1998, *The Hegel Reader*, Oxford: Blackwell.

Howard, Robert 1985, *Brave New Workplace*, New York: Penguin.

Hughes, H. Stuart 1958, *Consciousness and Society: The Reorientation of European Social Thought, 1890–1930*, New York: Vintage Books.

Huizinga, Johan 1954, *The Waning of the Middle Ages: A Study of the Forms of Life, Thought and Art in France and the Netherlands in the XIVth and XVth Centuries*, New York: Doubleday.

Huizinga, Johan 1966, *Homo Ludens: A Study of the Play Element in Culture*, Boston: Beacon Press.

Huxley, Julian 1960, *Evolution after Darwin*, Vol. III, edited by Sol Tax and Charles Callender, Chicago: University of Chicago Press.

Hyppolite, Jean 1969, *Studies on Marx and Hegel*, translated by John O'Neill, New York: Harper & Row.

Ingold, Tim and Jo Lee Vergunst (eds) 2008, *Ways of Walking: Ethnography and Practice on Foot*, Farnham: Ashgate.

Innes, Joanna and John Styles 1986, 'The Crime Wave: Writing on Crime and Criminal Justice in Eighteenth-Century England', *Journal of British Studies*, 25: 380–435.

Isaacson, Walter 2008, *Einstein: His Life and Universe*, London: Simon and Schuster.

Jablonski, Nina 2012, *Living Color: The Biological and Social Meaning of Skin*, Berkeley: University of California Press.

Jablonski, Nina 2013, *Skin: A Natural History*, Berkeley: University of California Press.

Jacoby, Russell 1971, 'Towards a Critique of Automatic Marxism: The Politics of Philosophy from Lukács to the Frankfurt School', *Telos*, 10: 119–46.

Jacoby, Russell 1981, *Dialectic of Defeat, Contours of Western Marxism*, Cambridge: Cambridge University Press.

Jakobson, Roman 1978, *Six Lectures on Sound and Meaning*, translated by John Mepham, Cambridge, MA: MIT Press.

Jakobson, Roman 1980, *The Framework of Language*, Ann Arbor: Michigan Studies in the Humanities.

Jakobson, Roman 1990, 'Langue and Parole: Code and Message', in *On Language*, Cambridge, MA: Harvard University Press, pp. 81–109.

Jakobson, Roman and Linda Waugh 1979, *The Sound Shape of Language*, Bloomington: Indiana University Press.

Jakobson, Roman and Morris Halle 1956, *Fundamentals of Language*, The Hague: Mouton & Co.

Jameson, Fredric 1972, *The Prisonhouse of Language: A Critical Account of Structuralism and Russian Formalism*, Princeton: Princeton University Press.

Jameson, Fredric 1981, *The Political Unconscious*, Ithaca: Cornell University Press.

Jameson, Fredric 1991, *Postmodernism or, The Cultural Logic of Late Capitalism*, Durham, NC: Duke University Press.

Jameson, Fredric 2014, *Representing Capital: A Commentary on Volume One*, London: Verso.

Jarman, Neil 1998, 'Material of Culture, Fabric of Identity', in *Material Cultures: Why Some Things Matter*, edited by Daniel Miller, Chicago: University of Chicago Press, pp. 121–45.

Jay, Martin 1973, *The Dialectical Imagination: A History of the Frankfurt School and the Instiutte of Social Research 1923–1950*, Berkeley: University of California Press.

Jay, Martin 1993, *Downcast Eyes: The Denigration of Vision in 20th Century French Thought*, Berkeley: University of California Press.

Jay, Martin 2020, *Splinters in Your Eye: Frankfurt School Provocations*, London: Verso.

Jefferson, Thomas 1815, Letter to Francis C. Gray, 4 March, https://founders.archives .gov/documents/Jefferson/03-08-02-0245#print_view.

Jeffries, Stuart 2017, *Grand Hotel Abyss: The Lives of the Frankfurt School*, London: Verso.

Jephcott, E.F.N. 1974, translation of Theodor Adorno, *Minima Moralia*, London: Verso.

Jevons, William Stanley 1876, *Money and the Mechanism of Exchange*, New York: D. Appleton and Co.

Johnson, Anthony 2008, *Solving Stonehenge: The New Key to an Ancient Enigma*, London: Thames & Hudson.

Johnson, Mark 1987, *The Body in the Mind: The Bodily Basis of Meaning, Imagination, and Reason*, Chicago: University of Chicago Press.

Johnson, Mark 2005, 'The Philosophical Significance of Image Schemas', in *From Perception to Meaning: Image Schemas in Cognitive Linguistics*, edited by Beate Hampe, Berlin: Mouton de Gruyter.

Johnson, Walter 1999, *Life Inside the Ante-bellum Slave Market*, Cambridge, MA: Harvard University Press.

Johnson, Walter 2000, 'The Slave Trader, the White Slave, and the Politics of Racial Determination in the 1850s', *The Journal of American History*, 87, no. 1: 13–38.

Jonas, Hans 1970, 'The Nobility of Sight: A Study in the Phenomenology of the Senses', in *The Philosophy of the Body: Rejections of Cartesian Dualism*, edited by Stuart F. Spicker, Chicago: Quadrangle Books.

Jones, Gareth Stedman 1973, 'Engels and the End of Classical German Philosophy', *New Left Review*, 79: 17–36.

Jones, Jonathan 2018, 'So Neanderthals Made Abstract Art? This Astounding Discovery Humbles Every Human', *The Guardian*, 23 February, https://www.theguardian.com/ artanddesign/2018/feb/23/neanderthals-cave-art-spain-astounding-discovery-humbles-every-human.

Jonna, R. Jamil and John Bellamy Foster 2014, 'Beyond the Degradation of Labor: Harry Braverman and the Structure of the US Working Class', *Monthly Review*, 66. no. 5: 1–23.

Jonna, R. Jamil and John Bellamy Foster 2016, 'Working-Class Precariousness', *Monthly Review*, 67, no. 11: 1–19.

Jütte, Robert 1981, 'Poor Relief and Social Discipline in Sixteenth-Century Europe', *European Studies Review*, 11: 25–52.

Jütte, Robert 2005, *A History of the Senses from Antiquity to Cyberspace*, Cambridge: Polity Press.

Kafka, Franz 1970, *The Trial*, New York: Schocken Books.

Kafka, Franz 1979, 'In der Strafkolonie', in *Erzählungen*, Leipzig: Reklam.

Karasek, Robert and Töres Theorell 1990, *Healthy Work: Stress, Productivity, and the Reconstruction of Working Life*, New York: Basic Books.

Karma, Roge 2019, 'The Gross Inequality of Death in America', *The New Republic*, 10 May, https://newrepublic.com/article/153870/inequality-death-america-life-expectancy-gap?fbclid=IwARıqfkE-2lTXWnuUQFRNTlWP4TnPjk8Qt53lIMHUURlClp5io_ZNI3 fZ1YA.

Karpf, Anne 2006, *The Human Voice: How This Extraordinary Instrument Reveals Essential Clues about Who We Are*, New York: Bloomsbury.

Karpinski, Louis C. 1921, 'Hermann Von Helmholtz', *The Scientific Monthly*, 13, no. 1: 24–32.

Katz, David 1935, *The World of Colour*, London: Kegan Paul.

Katz, David 1989, *The World of Touch*, translated by Lester E. Krueger, Hillsdale, NJ: Lawrence Erlbaum.

Kelley, Robin D.G. 1997, *Yo Mama's DisFunktional! Fighting the Culture Wars in Urban America*, Boston: Beacon Press.

Kelly-Gadol, Joan 1987, 'Did Women Have a Renaissance', in *Becoming Visible: Women in European History*, 2nd edition, edited by Renate Bridenthal, Claudia Koonz, and Susan Stuard, Boston: Houghton Mifflin.

Kelso, J.A. Scott and David A. Engstrom 2006, *The Complementary Nature*, Cambridge, MA: The MIT Press.

Kemple, Thomas 1995, *Reading Marx Writing*, Stanford: Stanford University Press.

Kendon, Adam 1991, 'Some Considerations for a Theory of Language Origins', *Man*, 26: 199–221.

Kenstowicz, Michael 1994, *Phonology in Generative Grammar*, Cambridge, MA: Blackwell.

Keverne, E.B. 1982, 'Chemical Senses: Smell' and 'Chemical Senses: Taste', in *The Senses*, edited by H.B. Barlow and J.D. Mollon, Cambridge: Cambridge University Press.

Kiaer, Christina 2005, *Imagine No Possessions: The Socialist Objects of Russian Constructivism*, Cambridge, MA: MIT Press.

Kidron, Michael 1974, *Capitalism and Theory*, London: Pluto Press.

King, Peter 2006, *Crime and Law in England, 1750–1840: Remaking Justice from the Margins*, Cambridge: Cambridge University Press.

Kisch, Bruno 1965, *Scales and Weights: A Historical Outline*, New Haven: Yale University Press.

Klein, Herbert Arthur 1974, *The Science of Measurement: A Historical Survey*, New York: Dover.

Klein, Richard 1989, *The Human Career: Human Biological and Cultural Origins*, Chicago: University of Chicago Press.

Kocka, Jürgen 2013, *Geschichte des Kapitalismus*, München: C.H. Beck.

Konner, Melvin 1991, 'Human Nature and Culture: Biology and the Residue of Uniqueness', in *The Boundaries of Humanity: Humans, Animals, Machines*, edited by James J. Sheehan and Morton Sosna, Berkeley: University of California Press.

Kopytoff, Igor 2003, 'The Cultural Biography of Things: Commoditization as Process', in *The Social Life of Things: Commodities in Cultural Perspective*, edited by Arjun Appadurai, Cambridge: Cambridge University Press, pp. 64–90.

Kosík, Karel 1986, *Die Dialektik des Konkreten*, Frankfurt: Suhrkamp.

Kovacs, Maureen Gallery trans. 1989, *The Epic of Gilgamesh*, Stanford: Stanford University Press.

Krell, David (ed.) 1977, *Martin Heidegger: Basic Writings*, edited by David Farrell Krell, New York: Harper & Row.

Kroeber, A.L. and Clyde Kluckhohn 1952, *Culture: A Critical Review of Concepts and Definitions*, Cambridge, MA: Peabody Museum, Harvard.

Kuhn, Thomas 1962, *The Structure of Scientific Revolutions*, Chicago: University of Chicago Press.

Kula, Witold 1986, *Measures and Men*, translated by R. Szreter, Princeton: Princeton University Press.

Kummer, H. 1982, 'Social Knowledge in Free-Ranging Primates', in *Animal Mind – Human Mind*, edited by D.R. Griffin, Berlin: Springer Verlag.

Lacan, Jacques 1977, *Ecrits: A Selection*, New York: Norton.

Lacan, Jacques 1984, *Speech and Language in Psycholanalysis*, Baltimore: Johns Hopkins University Press.

Laclau, Ernesto and Chantel Mouffe 1992, *Hegemony and Socialist Strategy: Towards a Radical Democratic Politics*, London: Verso.

Laitman, Jeffrey T. 1987, 'Tracing the Origins of Human Speech', in *Anthropology: Contemporary Perspectives*, edited by Phillip Whitten and David E.K. Hunter, Boston: Little, Brown & Co.

Lakoff, George and Mark Johnson 1999, *Philosophy in the Flesh: The Embodied Mind and its Challenge to Western Thought*, New York: Basic Books.

Lamberg-Karlovsky, C.C. 1993, 'The Biography of an Object: The Intercultural Style Vessels of the Third Millennium B.C.' in *History from Things*, edited by Steven Lubar and W. David Kingery, Washington, D.C.: Smithsonian Institution Press, pp. 270–89.

Lanbein, J.H. 1983, 'Albion's Fatal Flaws', *Past and Present*, 98: 96–120.

Landes, David 1972, *The Unbound Prometheus: Technological Change and Industrial Development in Western Europe from 1750 to the Present*, Cambridge: Cambridge University Press.

Landes, David 2000, *Revolution in Time*, Cambridge, MA: Harvard University Press.

Langer, Susanne K. 1974, *Philosophy in a New Key: A Study in the Symbolism of Reason, Rite, and Art*, Cambridge, MA: Harvard University Press.

Laqueur, Thomas 1990, *Making Sex*, Cambridge, MA: Harvard University Press.

van Latwick-Goodall, Jane 1971, *In the Shadow of Man*, New York: Dell.

Leakey, Mary 1084, *Disclosing the Past*, Garden City, New York: Doubleday.
Leakey, Richard E. and Roger Lewin 1977, *Origins*, New York: E.P. Dutton.
Lebovics, Herman 1969, *Social Conservatism and the Middle Class in Germany, 1914–1933*, Princeton: Princeton University Press.
Lecercle, Jean-Jacques 2004, *Une philosophie Marxiste du langage*, Paris: Presses Universitaires de France.
Lecercle, Jean-Jacques 2009, *A Marxist Philosophy of Language*, Chicago: Haymarket Press.
Lefebvre, Henri 2004, *Rhythmanalysis: Space, Time and Everyday Life*, London: Verso.
Lefebvre, Henri 2008, *Critique of Everyday Life*, Vol. I, translated by John Moore, London: Verso.
Le Gros Clark, W.E. 1960, *The Antecedents of Man*, Chicago: Quadrangle Books.
LeGuérer, Annick 1992, *Scent: The Essential and Mysterious Powers of Smell*, translated by Richard Miller, New York: Kodansha International.
Lemke, Thomas 2001, 'The Birth of Bio-Politics – Michel Foucault's Lecture at the Collège de France on Neo-Liberal Governmentality', *Economy & Society*, 30, no. 2: 190–207.
Lemke, Thomas 2002, 'Foucault, Governmentality, and Critique', Archived copy (PDF) of paper delivered at *Rethinking Marxism Conference*, Amherst, 21–24 September.
Lemke, Thomas 2005, 'A Zone of Indistinction – A Critique of Giorgio Agamben's Concept of Biopolitics', *Outlines. Critical Social Studies*, 7, no. 1: 3–13.
Lemke, Thomas 2011, *Bio-Politics: An Advanced Introduction*, New York: New York University Press.
Leibniz, G.W. 1989, *The Principles of Philosophy or, the Monadology*, in *Philosophical Essays*, edited and translated by Roger Ariew and Daniel Garber, Indianapolis: Hackett Publishing, pp. 213–25.
Lenin, V.I. 1969, *What is to be Done?* New York, International Publishers.
Lenneberg, Eric H. 1967, *Biological Foundations of Language*, New York: John Wiley and Sons.
Leroi-Gourhan, André 1993, *Gesture and Speech*, translated by Anna Bostock Berger, Cambridge, MA: MIT Press.
Lester, Toby 2012, *Da Vinci's Ghost: Genius, Obsession, and How Leonardo Created the World in His Own Image*, New York: Free Press.
Leutenegger, W. 1972, 'Newborn and Pelvic Dimensions in *Australopithecus*', *Nature*, 240: 548–69.
Lévi-Strauss, Claude 1963, *Structural Anthropology*, Vol. 1, translated by Clair Jacobson and Brooke Grundfest Schoepf, New York: Basic Books.
Lévi-Strauss, Claude 1970a, *The Savage Mind*, Chicago: University of Chicago Press.
Lévi-Strauss, Claude 1970b, *Tristes tropiques: An Anthropological Study of Primitive Societies in Brazil*, translated by John Russell, New York: Atheneum.

Levin, David Michael (ed.) 1993, *Modernity and the Hegemony of Vision*, Berkeley: University of California Press.

Levins, Richard and Richard Lewontin 1985, 'The Political Economy of Agricultural Research', in *The Dialectical Biologist*, Cambridge, MA: Harvard University Press, pp. 208–24.

Levy, J. 1982, 'Mental Processes in the Nonverbal Hemisphere', in *Animal Mind – Human Mind*, edited by D.R. Griffin, Berlin: Springer Verlag.

Lewen, David 1993, *Modernity and the Hegemony of Vision*, Berkeley: University of California Press.

Lewin, Robert and Robert A. Foley 2004, *Principles of Human Evolution*, Malden, MA: Blackwell.

Lewins, Tim 2004, *Organisms and Artifacts: Design in Nature and Elsewhere*, Cambridge, MA: The MIT Press.

Lewontin, Richard 1991, *Biology as Ideology*, New York: HarperCollins.

Lewontin, Richard and Richard Levins 2007, *Biology Under the Influence: Dialectical Essays on Ecology, Agriculture, and Health*, New York: Monthly Review Press.

Lichtman, Richard 1990, 'The Production of Human Nature by Means of Human Nature', *Capitalism, Nature, Socialism*, 4.

Lieberman, Philip 1975, *The Origins of Language: An Introduction to the Evolution of Human Speech*, New York: Macmillan.

Lieberman, Philip 1991, *Uniquely Human: Speech, Thought, and Selfless Behavior*, Cambridge, MA: Harvard University Press.

Lieberman, Philip 1994, 'Human Speech and Language', in *The Cambridge Encyclopedia of Human Evolution*, Cambridge: Cambridge University Press.

Lieberman, Philip 2006, *Toward an Evolutionary Biology of Language*, Cambridge, MA: Harvard University Press.

Liebrucks, Bruno 1964, *Sprache und Bewusstsein, Bd. I, Spannweite des Problems*, Frankfurt am Main: Akademische Verlagsgesellschaft.

Lienhardt, Godfrey 1961, *Divinity and Experience: The Religion of the Dinka*, Oxford: Clarendon Press.

Linebaugh, Peter 2006, *The London Hanged: Crime and Civil Society in the Eighteenth Century*, London: Verso.

Livingstone, Margaret and David Hubel 1995, 'Through the Eyes of Monkeys and Men', in *The Artful Eye*, edited by Richard Gregory et al., Oxford: Oxford University Press.

Livni, Ephrat 2018, 'A New Theory Claims Homo Sapiens Beat Out Neanderthals because of Art', *Quartz*, 13 February, https://qz.com/1205270/art-made-homo-sapiens-smarter-than-neanderthals-and-better-equipped-to-survive/.

Locke, John 1997, *An Essay Concerning the True Original, Extent, and End of Civil Government* in *Two Treatises of Government*, Cambridge: Cambridge University Press.

Lollini, Massimo 2011, 'Vico's Wilderness and the Places of Humanity', *Romance Studies*, 29, no. 2: 119–31.

Lonitz, Henri (ed.) 2001, *Theodor W. Adorno and Walter Benjamin: The Complete Correspondence, 1928–1940*, Cambridge, MA: Harvard University Press.

Lorenz, Konrad 1972, 'Introduction' to Wolfgang Wickler, *The Sexual Code: The Social Behavior of Animals and Men*, New York: Doubleday.

Lorenz, Konrad 1973, *Behind the Mirror: A Search for a Natural History of Human Knowledge*, translated by Ronald Taylor, New York: Harcourt Brace Jovanovich.

Lorenz, Konrad 1997, *The Natural Science of the Human Species*, translated by Robert D. Martin, Cambridge, MA: MIT Press.

Lorey, Isabell 2015, *State of Insecurity: Government of the Precarious*, London: Verso.

Löwith, Karl 1984, *From Nietzsche to Hegel*, New York: Garland Publishing.

Lubar, Steven and W. David Kingery 1993, *History from Things*, Washington, D.C.: Smithsonian Institution Press.

Lukács, Georg 1970, *Geschichte und Klassenbewußtsein*, Neuweid: Luchterhand.

Lukács, Georg 1971, *History and Class Consciousness: Studies in Marxist Dialectics*, translated by Rodney Livingstone, Cambridge, MA: The MIT Press.

Lukács, Georg 2000, *A Defence of History and Class Consciousness: Tailism and the Dialectic*, translated by Esther Leslie, London: Verso.

Luria, A.R. 1978, *Cognitive Development: Its Cultural and Social Foundations*, translated by Martin Lopez-Morillas and Lynn Solotaroff, Cambridge, MA: Harvard University Press.

Lutz, Tom 1999, *Crying: The Natural and Cultural History of Tears*, New York: Norton.

Luxemburg, Rosa 1899, *Sozialreform oder Revolution*, in Luxemburg 1974, *Gesammelte Werke* Bd. 1/1, Berlin: Dietz Verlag.

Machiavelli, Niccoló 1995, *The Prince*, translated by George Bull, London: Penguin.

Machiavelli, Niccoló 2001, *The Art of War*, Cambridge, MA: Da Capo Press.

MacKenzie, Donald 1984, 'Marx and the Machine', *Technology and Culture*, 25, no. 3.

Macpherson, C.B. 1962, *The Political Theory of Possessive Individualism: Hobbes to Locke*, Oxford: Oxford University Press.

Manetti, Giannozzo 1966, *On the Dignity of Man*, in *Two Views of Man*, translated and edited by Bernard Murchland, New York: Frederick Ungar Publishing.

Manta, Irina D. 2011, 'The Puzzle of Criminal Sanctions for Intellectual Property Infringement', *Harvard Journal of Law and Technology*, 24, no. 2: 469–518.

Maquet, Jacques 1993, 'Objects as Instruments, Objects as Signs', in *History from Things*, edited by Steven Lubar and W. David Kingery, Washington, D.C.: Smithsonian Institution Press, pp. 30–40.

Marcuse, Herbert 1960, *Reason and Revolution: Hegel and the Rise of Social Theory*, Boston: Beacon Press.

Marcuse, Herbert 1969, *Essay on Liberation*, Boston: Beacon Press.

Marcuse, Herbert 1978, *The Aesthetic Dimension*, Boston: Beacon Press.

Marcuse, Herbert 2005, *Heideggerian Marxism*, edited by Richard Wolin and John Abromeit, Lincoln: University of Nebraska Press.

Margolin, Stephen 1976, 'What Do Bosses Do? The Origins and Functions of Hierarchy in Capitalist Production', in *The Division of Labour: The Labour Process and Class-Struggle in Modern Capitalism*, edited by André Gorz, Atlantic Highlands: Humanities Press.

Markus, Gyorgy 1978, *Marxism and Anthropology*, Assen: Van Gorcum.

Markus, Gyorgy 2001, 'Walter Benjamin or The Commodity as Phantasmagoria', *New German Critique*, 83: 3–42.

Martin, Emily 1991, *The Woman in the Body*, Boston: Beacon Press.

Marx, Karl 1962 [1867], *Das Kapital*, Vol. I, in *Marx-Engels Werke*, Vol. 23, Berlin: Dietz Verlag.

Marx, Karl 1964, 'Provisorische Statuten der Internationalen Arbeiterassoziation', in *Die Gründung der 1. Internationale: Dokumente und Materialien*, edited by Richard Sperl and Günter Wisotzki, Berlin (East): Dietz Verlag.

Marx, Karl n.d. [1857–58], *Grundrisse der Kritik der politischen Ökonomie*, Frankfurt: Europäische Verlagsanstalt.

Marx, Karl 1857–58, *Fragmente des Urtextes von 'Zur Kritik der Politischen Ökonomie'*, in Marx, *Grundrisse der Kritik der politischen Ökonomie*, Frankfurt: Europäische Verlagsanstalt.

Marx, Karl 1971, *Theories of Surplus Value*, Moscow: Progress Publishers.

Marx, Karl 1973 [1857–58], *Grundrisse: Foundations of the Critique of Political Economy*, edited and translated by Martin Nicolaus, Frankfurt: Europäischen Verlagsanstalt.

Marx, Karl 1973a [1844], *Auszüge aus James Mills Buch "Éleméns d'économie politique"*, in *Marx-Engels Werke Ergänzungsband I*, Berlin: Dietz Verlag.

Marx, Karl 1973b [1844], *Ökonomisch-philosophische Manuskripte aus dem Jahre 1844*, in *Marx-Engels Werke Ergänzungsband I*, Berlin: Dietz Verlag.

Marx, Karl 1973c, *Das Kapital*, Bd. III, in *Marx-Engels Werke*, Bd. 25, Berlin: Dietz Verlag.

Marx, Karl 1975 [1859], *Kritik der politischen Ökonomie*, in *Marx-Engels Werke*, Vol. 13, Berlin: Dietz Verlag.

Marx, Karl 1976 [1843], *Zur Kritik der Hegelschen Rechtsphilosophie* and *Einleitung zur Kritik der Hegelschen Rechtsphilosophie*, in *Marx-Engels Werke*, Vol. 1, Berlin: Dietz Verlag.

Marx, Karl 1976 [1843a], 'Luther als Schiedrichter zwischen Strauß und Feuerbach', in *Marx-Engels Werke*, Vol. 1, Berlin: Dietz Verlag.

Marx, Karl 1976 [1879–80], *Randglossen zu Adolph Wagners 'Lehrbuch der politischen Ökonomie'*, in *Marx-Engels Werke*, Vol. 19, Berlin: Dietz Verlag.

Marx, Karl 1977 [1846–47], 'Das Elend der Philosophie', in *Marx-Engels Werke*, Vol. 4, Berlin: Dietz Verlag.

Marx, Karl 1978 [1859], 'Preface' to *The Critique of Political Economy*, in *Marx-Engels Reader*, edited by Robert Tucker, New York: Norton.

Marx, Karl 1981 [1894], *Capital*, Vol. III, translated by David Fernbach, London: Penguin Books.

Marx, Karl 1990 [1867], *Capital*, Vol. 1, edited by Ernest Mandel, translated by Ben Fowkes, London: Penguin Books.

Marx, Karl and Friedrich Engels 1973 [1845], *Die deutsche Ideologie*, in *Marx-Engels Werke*, Vol. 3, Berlin (East): Dietz Verlag.

Marx, Karl and Friedrich Engels 1978 [1848], *The Manifesto of the Communist Party*, in *The Marx-Engels Reader*, edited by Robert Tucker, New York: Norton.

Marx, Karl and Friedrich Engels 1975, *Marx-Engels: Selected Correspondence*, Moscow: Progress Publishers.

Mascia-Lees, Frances E. and Patricia Sharpe (eds) 1999, *Tattoo, Torture, Mutilation, and Adornment: The Denaturalization of the Body in Culture and Text*, Albany: SUNY Press.

Matvejević, Predag 1999, *Mediterranean: A Cultural Landscape*, translated by Michael Henry Heim, Berkeley: University of California Press.

Mayr, Ernst 1982, *The Growth of Biological Thought: Diversity, Evolution, and Inheritance*, Cambridge, MA: Belknap/Harvard University Press.

Mbembe, Achille 2001, *On the Postcolony*, Berkeley: University of California Press.

McBrearty, Sally and Alison S. Brooks 2000, 'The Revolution that Wasn't: A New Interpretation of the Origin of Modern Human Behavior', *Journal of Human Evolution*, 39: 453–563.

McCrone, John 1991, *The Ape that Spoke: Language and the Evolution of the Human Mind*, New York: Avon Books.

McLellan, David 1973, *Karl Marx: His Life and Thought*, New York: Harper.

McGowen, Randall 1987, 'The Body and Punishment in Eighteenth-Century England', *The Journal of Modern History*, 59, no. 4: 651–79.

McGowen, Randall 1994, 'Civilizing Punishment: The End of the Public Execution in England', *Journal of British Studies*, 33, no. 3: 257–82.

McGowen, Randall 1995, 'The Well-Ordered Prison: England, 1780–1865', in *The Oxford History of the Prison*, edited by Norval Morris and David J. Rothman, Oxford: Oxford University Press, pp. 79–109.

McGowen, Randall 2003, 'History, Culture and the Death Penalty: The British Debates, 1840–70', *Historical Reflections/Réflexions Historiques*, 29, no. 2, *Interpreting the Death Penalty: Spectacles and Debates*, Summer 2003: 229–49.

McGowen, Randall 2004, 'The Problem of Punishment in Eighteenth-Century England', in *Penal Practice and Culture, 1500–1900: Punishing the English*, edited by Simon Deveraux and Paul Griffiths, Basingstoke: Palgrave Macmillan, pp. 210–31.

McGowen, Randall 2007, 'Managing the Gallows: The Bank of England and the Death Penalty, 1797–1821', *Law and History Review*, 25, no. 2: 241–82.

McKenon, Richard (ed.) 1941, *The Basic Works of Aristotle*, New York: Random House.

McMahon, Thomas A. and John Tyler Bonner 1983, *On Size and Life*, New York: Scientific American Library.

McMurtry, John 1978, *The Structure of Marx's World-View*, Princeton: Princeton University Press.

McNally, David 2001, *Bodies of Meaning: Studies on Language, Labour, and Liberation*, Albany: SUNY.
McNally, David 2017, 'Intersections and Dialectics', in *Social Reproduction Theory: Remapping Class, Recentering Oppression*, edited by Tithi Bhattacharya, London: Pluto Press, pp. 94–111.
McNally, David and Sue Ferguson 2015, 'Social Reproduction Beyond Intersectionality: An Interview', *Viewpoint Magazine*, https://www.viewpointmag.com/2015/10/31/social-reproduction-beyond-intersectionality-an-interview-with-sue-ferguson-and-david-mcnally/.
Medawar, P.B. and J.S. Medawar 1983, *Aristotle to Zoos: A Philosophical Dictionary of Biology*, Cambridge, MA: Harvard University Press.
Meehan, Therese Connell 1990, 'A Role for Therapeutic Touch', in *Touch: The Foundation of Experience*, edited by Kathryn E. Barnard and T. Berry Brazelton, Madison, CT: International Universities Press.
Megill, Allan 2002, *The Burden of Reason*, Lanham, MD: Rowman & Littlefield.
Merleau-Ponty, Maurice 1964, *The Primacy of Perception*, Evanston, IL: Northwestern University Press.
Merleau-Ponty, Maurice 1966, *Phenomenology of Perception*, translated by Colin Smith, London: Routledge & Kegan Paul.
Merleau-Ponty, Maurice 1973, *Adventures of the Dialectic*, Evanston, IL: Northwestern University Press.
Meyer, Raymond 1988, 'Translator's Comments', in Axel Honneth and Hans Joas, *Social Action and Human Nature*, Cambridge: Cambridge University Press.
Mezzadra, Sandro 2011a, 'The Topicality of Prehistory: A New Reading of Marx's Analysis of "So-Called Primitive Accumulation"', *Rethinking Marxism*, 23, no. 3: 302–21.
Mezzadra, Sandro 2011b, 'Bringing Capital Back In: A Materialist Turn in Postcolonial Studies', *Inter-Asia Cultural Studies*, 12, no. 1: 154–64.
Mezzadra, Sandro 2011c, 'How Many Histories of Labour? Toward a Theory of Postcolonial Capitalism', *Postcolonial Studies*, 14, no. 2: 1–20.
Michels, Robert 1925, *Zur Soziologie des modernen Parteiwesens in der modernen Demokratie* 2. Auflage, Leipzig: Alfred Kröner Verlag.
Miller, Daniel 1998, *Material Cultures: Why Some Things Matter*, Chicago: University of Chicago Press.
Miller, Peter 1994, 'Accounting and Objectivity: The Invention of Calculating Selves and Calculable Spaces', in *Rethinking Objectivity*, edited by Allan Megill, Durham, NC: Duke University Press.
Miller, Peter and Christopher Napier 1993, 'Genealogies of Calculation', *Accounting, Organizations and Society*, 18, no. 7/8: 632–47.
Miller, Peter and Michael Power 2013, 'Accounting, Organizing, and Economizing: Connecting Accounting Research and Organization Theory', *The Academy of Management Annals*, 7, no. 1: 555–603.

Moir, Cat 2020, 'The Archimedean Point: Consciousness, Praxis and the Present in Lukács and Bloch', *Thesis Eleven*, 157, no. 1: 3–23.

Montag, Warren 2013, *Althusser and His Contemporaries: Philosophy's Perpetual War*, Durham, NC: Duke University Press.

Moore, Henrietta 1990, 'Paul Ricoeur: Action, Meaning and Text', in *Reading Material Culture*, edited by Christopher Tilley, Oxford: Basil Blackwell, pp. 85–120.

Moore, Jerry D. 1997, *Visions of Culture: An Introduction to Anthropological Theories and Theorists*, Walnut Creek: Altamira Press.

Moore, Pamela 1998, Annotation on *The Body in Pain*, in LITMED: *Literature, Arts, Medicine Data Base*, http://litmed.med.nyu.edu/Annotation?action=view&annid=309.

Montagu, F. Ashley 1978, *Touching: The Human Significance of Skin*, New York: Harper and Row.

de Montaigne, Michel 1958, *Essays*, translated by J.M. Cohen, London: Penguin.

More, Thomas 1965, *Utopia*, Harmondsworth: Penguin.

Moretti, Franco 2005, *Graphs Maps Trees*, London: Verso.

Morris, David B. 1991, *The Culture of Pain*, Berkeley: University of California Press.

Morris, Rosalind 2016, '*Ursprüngliche Akkumlation*: The Secret of an Originary Mistranslation', *boundary 2*, 43, no. 2.

Most, Kenneth S. 1979, 'Sombart on Accounting History', Working Paper No. 35, *Academy of Accounting Historians, Working Paper Series*, March.

Mumford, Lewis 1961, *The City in History: Its Origins, Its Transformations, and Its Prospects*, New York: Harcourt, Brace & World.

Nadeau, R. 1991, *Minds, Machines and Human Consciousness*, Chicago: Contemporary Books.

Nagel, Thomas 1974, 'What is it Like to be a Bat?' *The Philosophical Review*, 83, no. 4.

Napier, J.R. 1993, *Hands*, revised by Russell H. Tuttle, Princeton: Princeton University Press.

Neale, Walter C. 1957, 'The Market in Theory and History', in *Trade and Market in the Early Empires: Economies in History and Theory*, edited by Karl Polanyi et al., New York: Free Press.

Negt, Oskar 1982, '*Naturrechtlicher Restposten oder Legitimationsfassade?*', *Frankfurter Rundschau*, 127, 4 June: 10–11.

Negt, Oskar 1988, 'What is a Revival of Marxism and Why Do We Need One Today', *Marxism and the Interpretation of Culture*, edited by Cary Nelson and Lawrence Grossberg, Urbana: University of Illinois Press.

Negri, Antonio 1978, '*Manifattura ed ideologia*', in *Manifattura, società, borghese ideologia*, edited by P. Schiera, Rome: Savelli.

Netzloff, Mark (ed.) 2010, *John Norden's The Surveyor's Dialogue, 1618: A Critical Edition*, Burlington, VT: Ashgate.

Netzloff, Mark 2010, 'Surveying and Social Dialogue', Introductory essay to *John Norden's the Surveyor's Dialogue*, Burlington, VT: Ashgate, pp. xiv–xl.

Ng, Karen 2009, 'Hegel's Logic of Actuality', *The Review of Metaphysics*, 63, no. 1: 139–72.
Ngugi wa Thiong'o 1965, *The River Between*, Oxford: Heinemann.
Nietzsche, Friedrich 1968, *The Will to Power*, translated by Walter Kaufmann and R.J. Hollingdale, New York: Vintage Books/Random House. German: *Der Wille zur Macht: Eine Auslegung alles Geschehens* § 436, Project Gutenberg EBook: https://www.gutenberg.org/files/60360/60360-h/60360-h.htm#Page_239.
Nietzsche, Friedrich 1976a, *Die fröhliche Wissenschaft*, in *Friedrich Nietzsche: Werke* II, Frankfurt: Verlag Ullstein.
Nietzsche, Friedrich 1976b, 'Von den Verächtern des Leibes', in *Also Sprach Zarathustra*, *Friedrich Nietzsche: Werke* II, Frankfurt: Verlag Ullstein.
Nietzsche, Friedrich 1976c, *Zur Genealogie der Moral*, in *Friedrich Nietzsche, Werke* III, Frankfurt: Ullstein.
Nicolaus, Martin 1973, Foreword to Karl Marx, *Grundrisse*, New York: Vintage.
Nightingale, Florence 1979, *Cassandra*, Old Westbury, NY: The Feminist Press.
Noble, David 1984, *Forces of Production: A Social History of Industrial Automation*, New York: Knopf.
Noble, William and Iain Davidson, *Human Evolution, Language and Mind*, Cambridge: Cambridge University Press.
Nöth, Winfried 1990, *Handbook of Semiotics*, Bloomington: Indiana University Press.
Novick, Peter 1988, *That Noble Dream*, Cambridge: Cambridge University Press.
Ollman, Bertell 1971, *Alienation: Marx's Conception of Man in Capitalist Society*, Cambridge: Cambridge University Press.
Orwell, George 1937, *The Road to Wigan Pier*, London: Victor Gollancz LTD.
Ostler, Jeffrey 2019, *Surviving Genocide: Native Nations and the United States from the American Revolution to Bleeding Kansas*, New Haven: Yale University Press.
Patterson, H. Orlando 1979, 'Slavery in Human History', *New Left Review*, 1/117: 51–67, https://newleftreview-org.libproxy.uoregon.edu/issues/I117/articles/h-orlando-patterson-slavery-in-human-history.pdf.
Patterson, H. Orlando 1982, *Slavery and Social Death: A Comparative Study*, Cambridge, MA: Harvard University Press.
Pawel, Ernst 1985, *The Nightmare of Reason: A Life of Franz Kafka*, New York: Vintage.
Pecora, Vincent 1989, 'The Limits of Local Knowledge', in *The New Historicism*, edited by H. Aram Veeser, New York: Routledge, pp. 243–7.
Peirce, Charles Sanders 1868, 'Some Consequences of Four Incapabilities', *Journal of Speculative Philosophy*, 2: 140–51.
Peirce, Charles Sanders 1894, 'What is a Sign?' https://www.marxists.org/reference/subject/philosophy/works/us/peirce1.htm
Peirce, Charles Sanders 1932, 'Divisions of Signs', in *Collected Papers of Charles Sanders Peirce*, Vol. II, *Elements of Logic*, edited by Charles Hartshorne and Paul Weiss, Cambridge, MA: Harvard University Press.

Peirce, Charles Sanders 1992, 'On the Algebra of Logic: A Contribution to the Philosophy of Notation', in *The Essential Peirce: Selected Philosophical Writings*, Vol. I, 1867–1893, Bloomington: Indiana University Press.

Perelman, Michael 2000, *The Invention of Capitalism: Classical Political Economy and the Secret History of Primitive Accumulation*, Durham, NC: Duke University Press.

Petty, William 1888, 'Of the People of England', in *Essays on Mankind and Political Arithmetic*, Elibron Classics Replica Edition of the edition published in London, Cassell and Co.

Philip, J.A. 1966, *Pythagoras and Early Pythagoreanism*, Toronto: University of Toronto Press.

Pico della Mirandola, Giovanni 1948, 'Oration on the Dignity of Man', in *The Renaissance Philosophy of Man*, edited by Ernst Cassirer, Paul Oskar Kristeller, John Herman Randall, Jr., Chicago: University of Chicago Press.

Pilbeam, David 1989, 'TITLE???', in *Human Biology: An Introduction to Human Evolution, Variation, Growth, and Adaptability*, edited by G.A. Harrison et al., Oxford: Oxford University Press.

Pinker, Steven 1994, *The Language Instinct: How the Mind Creates Language*, New York: William Morrow.

Plato 1961, *Collected Dialogues*, edited by Edith Hamilton and Huntington Cairns, Princeton: Princeton University Press.

Plessner, Helmut 1980, *Die Stufen des Organischen und der Mensch*, in *Gesammelte Werke*, Bd. IV, edited by Guenther Dux et al., Frankfurt: Suhrkamp.

Plucknett, Thomas F.T. 1956, *A Concise History of Common Law*, 5th edition, London: Buterwort and Co.

Plumb, J.H. (ed.) 1961, *The Italian Renaissance*, New York: American Heritage Publishing.

Polanyi, Karl 1957, *The Great Transformation*, Boston: Beacon Press.

Polanyi, Karl 1957a, 'Aristotle Discovers the Economy', in *Trade and Market in the Early Empires: Economies in History and Theory*, edited by Karl Polanyi, Conrad M. Arensberg, and Harry W. Pearson, Glencoe, IL: Free Press.

Polanyi, Karl, Conrad M. Arensberg, and Harry W. Pearson 1957, *Trade and Market in the Early Empires: Economies in History and Theory*, New York: Free Press.

Polanyi, Michael 1967, *The Tacit Dimension*, Garden City, NY: Anchor Books.

Polanyi, Michael 1969, 'The Logic of Tacit Inference', in *Knowing and Being: Essays by Michael Polanyi*, edited by Marjorie Grene, Chicago: University of Chicago Press.

Pomeranz, Kenneth 2001, *The Great Divergence: China, Europe, and the Making of the Modern World Economy*, Princeton: Princeton University Press.

Poovey, Mary 1998, *A History of the Modern Fact: Problems of Knowledge in the Sciences of Wealth and Society*, Chicago: University of Chicago Press.

Porter, Theodore M. 1994, 'Objectivity as Standardization: The Rhetoric of Impersonality in Measurement, Statistics, and Cost-Benefit Analysis', in *Rethinking Objectivity*, edited by Allan Megill, Durham, NC: Duke University Press, pp. 197–237.

Porter, Theodore M. 1995, *Trust in Numbers: The Pursuit of Objectivity in Science and Public Live*, Princeton: Princeton University Press.

Porter, Theodore M. 2001, 'Modern Facts and Postmodern Interpretations', a review of Mary Poovey, *A History of the Modern Fact*, *Annals of Science*, 58: 417–22.

Pradella, Lucia 2010, 'Beijing between Smith and Marx', *Historical Materialism*, 18: 88–109.

Pradella, Lucia and Thomas Marois 2015, *Polarising Development: Alternatives to Neoliberalism and the Crisis*, London: Pluto Press.

Premack, David 1988, 'Minds with and without Language', in *Thought Without Language*, edited by L. Weiskrantz, Oxford: Clarendon Press, pp. 46–65.

Prinz, Arthur 1969, 'Background and Ulterior Motive of Marx's "Preface of 1859"', *Journal of the History of Ideas*, 30, no. 3: 437–50.

Proust, Marcel 1981, *Remembrance of Things Past*, Vol. I, translated by C.K. Scott Moncrieff and Terence Kilmartin, New York: Random House.

Psychopedis, Kosmas 1981, *Gesellschaftswisenschaftliche Begründung und Historische Reflexion*, Göttingen: Habilitationsschrift, Georg August Universität.

Psychopedis, Kosmas 1995, 'Emancipating Explanation', in *Open Marxism* 3, edited by Werner Bonefeld et al., London: Pluto Press.

Psychopedis, Kosmas 2000, 'New Social Thought: Questions of Theory and Critique', in *The Politics of Change*, edited by Werner Bonefeld and Kosmas Psychopedis, Basingstoke: Palgrave.

Psychopedis, Kosmas 2005, 'Social Critique and the Logic of Revolution', in *Human Dignity: Social Autonomy and the Critique of Captialism*, edited by Werner Bonefeld and Kosmas Psychopedis, Farnham: Ashgate.

Pullam, Geoffrey 1989, 'Comment on "The Great Eskimo Vocabulary Hoax"', *Natural Language and Linguistic Theory*, 7: 275–81.

Rabb, Theodor 1967, *Enterprise and Empire: Merchant and Gentry Investment in the Expansion of England, 1575–1630*, Cambridge, MA: Harvard University Press.

Rabb, Theodor 1974, 'The Expansion of Europe and the Spirit of Capitalism', *The Historical Journal*, 17, no. 4: 675–89.

Rabinbach, Anson 1990, *The Human Motor: Energy, Fatigue, and the Origins of Modernity*, Berkeley: University of California Press.

Radick, Gregory 2007, *The Simian Tongue: The Long Debate about Animal Language*, Chicago: University of Chicago Press.

Radin, Max 1925, 'Fundamental Concepts of the Roman Law', *California Law Review*, 13, no. 3: 207–28.

Randles, W.G.L. 2000, 'Classical Models of World Geography and their Transformation Following the Discovery of America', in *Geography, Cartography and Nautical Science in the Renaissance*, Aldershot: Ashgate.

Ransom, John S. 1997, *Foucault's Discipline: The Politics of Subjectivity*, Durham, NC: Duke University Press.

Rees, John 2000, Introduction to Georg Lukács, *A Defence of History and Class Consciousness: Tailism and the Dialectic*, translated by Esther Leslie, London: Verso.

Reichelt, Helmut 1973, *Zur logischen Struktur des Kapitalbegriffs bei Karl Marx*, Frankfurt: Europäische Verlagsanstalt.

Reichelt, Helmut 1983, 'Zur Dialektik von Produktivkräften und Productionsverhältnissen', in *Producktivkräfte und Produktionsverhältnisse*, edited by Helmut Reichelt and Reinhold Zech, Frankfurt: Ullstein.

Reiss, Timothy J. 1996, 'Denying the Body? Memory and the Dilemmas of History in Descartes', *Journal of the History of Ideas*, 57, no. 4: 587–607.

Reiss, Timothy J. 2004, 'Calculating Humans: Mathematics, War, and the Colonial Calculus', in *Arts of Calculation*, edited by David Glimp and Michelle Warren, New York: Palgrave Macmillan.

Relethford, John H. 1994, *The Human Species: An Introduction to Biological Anthropology*, 2nd edition, Mountain View, CA: Mayfield Publishing.

Richards, Graham 1986, 'Freed Hands or Enslaved Feet? A Note on the Behavioural Implications of Ground-dwelling Bipedalism', *Journal of Human Evolution*, 15: 143–50.

Richeson, A.W. 1966, *English Land Measuring to 1800: Instruments and Practices*, Cambridge, MA: MIT Press.

Riggs, Lorrin A. 1965, 'Visual Acuity', in *Vision and Visual Perception*, edited by Clarence H. Graham et al., New York: John Wiley and Sons.

Roberts, Derek F. 1981, 'Selection and Body Size', in *Food, Nutrition, and Evolution: Food as an Environmental Factor in the Genesis of Human Variability*, edited by D. Walcher and N. Kretchmer, New York: Masson Publishing.

Robinson, Cedric J. 1984, *Black Marxism: The Making of the Black Radical Tradition*, London: Zed Press.

Robinson, Cedric J. 2000, Preface to 2000 edition of *Black Marxism: The Making of the Black Radical Tradition*, Chapel Hill, NC: University of North Carolina Press.

Robinson, Cedric J. 2019, *Cedric J. Robinson: On Racial Capitalism, Black Internationalism, and Cultures of Resistance*, edited by H.L.T. Quan, London: Pluto Press.

Rosdolsky, Roman 1973, *Zur Entstehungsgeschichte des Marxschen 'Kapital'* Vols. 1–2, Frankfurt: Europäische Verlagsanstalt.

Rosenberg, Daniel 2015, 'Whence Data?' *The Berlin Journal*, 28: 18–22.

Rosenberg, Karen R. and Wenda R. Trevathan 2003, 'The Evolution of Human Birth', *Scientific American*, 13, no. 2: 80–5.

Rossi-Landi, Ferruccio 1983, *Language as Work and Trade*, translated by Martha Adams et al., Massachusetts: Bergin & Garvey.

Rousseau, Jean-Jacques 1921, *Emile, or Education*, translated by Barbara Foxley, London: J.M. Dent and Sons, http://oll.libertyfund.org/titles/2256.

Rubin, Gayle 1997, 'The Traffic in Women: Notes on the Political Economy of Sex', in *The Second Wave: A Reader in Feminist Theory*, edited by Linda Nicholson, New York: Routledge, pp. 27–62.

Rubin, I.I. 1982, *Essays on Marx's Theory of Value*, translated by Miloš Samardźija and Fredy Perlman, Montréal: Black Rose Books.

Ryan, Alan 1965, 'Locke and the Dictatorship of the Bourgeoisie', *Political Studies*, 13: 219–30.

Ryan, Alan 1984, *Property and Political Theory*, Oxford: Basil Blackwell.

Sahlins, Marshall 1972, *Stone-Age Economics*, Chicago: Aldine-Atherton.

Sahlins, Marshall 1976, *Culture and Practical Reason*, Chicago: University of Chicago Press.

Saito, Kohei 2017, *Karl Marx's Ecosocialism: Capital, Nature, and the Unfinished Critique of Political Economy*, New York: Monthly Review Press.

Sandars, N.K. trans. 1972, *The Epic of Gilgamesh*, London: Penguin.

Sartre, Jean-Paul 1968, *Search for a Method*, translated by Hazel E. Barnes, New York: Vintage Books.

Sartre, Jean-Paul 1975, 'Portrait of an Anti-Semite', in *Existentialism from Dostoyevsky to Sartre*, edited by Walter Kaufmann, New York: Penguin/Meridian, pp. 329–45.

de Saussure, Ferdinand 1959, *Course in General Linguistics*, edited by Charles Bally and Albert Sechehaye, New York: Philosophical Library.

de Saussure, Ferdinand 1983, *Cours de Linguistique générale*, Paris: Payot.

Savage-Rumbaugh, Sue et al. 1998, *Apes, Language and the Human Mind*, Oxford: Oxford University Press.

Sayers, Sean 1998, *Marxism and Human Nature*, London: Routledge.

Scheler, Max 1976, *Die Stellung des Menschen im Kosmos* in Scheler, *Gesammelte Werke*, Bd. 9, edited by Manfred S. Frings, Bern: Franke Verlag.

Schevill, Ferdinand 1909, *Siena: The Story of a Medieval Commune*, New York: Charles Scribner's Sons.

Schiebinger, Londa 1993, *Nature's Body: Gender in the Making of Modern Science*, Boston: Beacon Press.

Schierup, Carl-Ulrik and Martin Bak Jørgensen 2018, *Politics of Precarity: Migrant Conditions, Struggles and Experiences*, Chicago: Haymarket Books.

Schiller, Friedrich 1993 [1795], *Über die Ästhetische Erziehung des Menschen in Einer Reihe von Briefen*, Stuttgart: Philipp Reclam.

Schmidt, Alfred 1973, *Emanzipatorische Sinnlichkeit: Ludwig Feuerbachs anthropologischer Materialismus*, München: Carl Hanser Verlag.

Schmidt, Alfred 1974 [1962], *Der Begriff der Natur in der Lehre von Marx*, Frankfurt: Europäische Verlagsanstalt.

Schor, Juliet 1992, *The Overworked American: The Unexpected Decline of Leisure*, New York: Basic Books.

Schumpeter, Joseph A. 2008 [1942], *Capitalism, Socialism and Democracy*, New York: Harper.
Sebeok, Thomas (ed.) 1977, *The Perfusion of Signs*, Bloomington: Indiana University Press.
Sebeok, Thomas 1978, *Sight, Sound, and Sense*, Bloomington: Indiana University Press.
Sebeok, Thomas 1991, *A Sign is Just a Sign*, Bloomington: Indiana University Press.
Sebeok, Thomas A. and Jean Umiker-Sebeok (eds) 1991a, *Biosemiotics: The Semiotic Web*, Berlin: Mouton de Gruyter.
Semple, Janet 1993, *Bentham's Prison: A Study of the Panopitcal Penitentiary*, Oxford: Clarendon Press.
Sennett, Richard and Jonathan Cobb 1972, *The Hidden Injuries of Class*, New York: Vintage.
Sewell, William H. 1999, *The Concept(s) of Culture* in *Beyond the Cultural Turn*, edited by Victoria E. Bonnell and Lynn Hunt, Berkeley: University of California Press.
Sheehan, James, J. and Morton Sosna 1991, *The Boundaries of Humanity: Humans, Animals, Machines*, Berkeley: University of California Press.
Sheets-Johnstone, Maxine 1990, *The Roots of Thinking*, Philadelphia: Temple University Press.
Sheets-Johnstone, Maxine (ed.) 1992, *Giving the Body its Due*, Albany: SUNY Press.
Sheets-Johnstone, Maxine 1994, *The Roots of Power: Animate Form and Gendered Bodies*, Chicago: Open Court.
Sheets-Johnstone, Maxine 1999, *The Primacy of Movement*, Amsterdam: John Benjamins Publishing.
Sheets-Johnstone, Maxine 2009, *The Corporeal Turn: An Interdisciplinary Reader*, Exeter: Imprint Academic.
Sheets-Johnstone, Maxine 2011, 'Embodied Minds or Mindful Bodies: A Core Twenty-First Century Challenge', in *The Primacy of Movement*, 2nd edition, Amsterdam/Philadelphia: John Benjamins Publishing.
Sheets-Johnstone, Maxine 2011a, 'Embodied Minds or Mindful Bodies? A Question of Fundamental, Inherently Inter-related Aspects of Animation', *Subjectivity*, 4, no. 4: 451–66.
Shepard, Paul 1978, *Thinking Animals: Animals and the Development of Human Intelligence*, New York: Viking Press.
Shevoroshkin, Vitaly 1990, 'The Mother Tongue: How Linguists Have Reconstructed the Ancestor of All Living Languages', *The Sciences*, May/June: 20–7.
Shryock, Andrew and Daniel Lord Smail 2011, *Deep History: The Architecture of Past and Present*, Berkeley: University of California Press.
Shumway, David 1989, *Michel Foucault*, Boston: Twayne Publishers.
Silko, Leslie Marmon 1992, *Almanac of the Dead: A Novel*, New York: Penguin Books.
Silverman, Kaja 1983, *The Subject of Semiotics*, Oxford: Oxford University Press.

Simmel, Georg 2007, *Philosophy of Money*, London: Routledge.
Smail, Daniel Lord 2008, *On Deep History and the Brain*, Berkeley: University of California Press.
Smarsh, Sarah 2018, *Heartland: A Memoir of Working Hard and Being Broke in the Richest Country on Earth*, New York: Scribner.
Smith, Adam 1976, *An Inquiry into the Nature and Causes of The Wealth of Nations*, Chicago: University of Chicago Press.
Smith, Anthony 1968, *The Body*, New York: Walker and Company.
Smith, David Eugene 1926, 'The First Great Commercial Arithmetic', *Isis*, 8.
Smith, Jillyn 1989, *Senses and Sensibilities*, New York: John Wiley & Sons.
Smith, Mark 2007, *Sensing the Past: Seeing, Hearing, Smelling, Tasting, and Touching in History*, Berkeley: University of California Press.
Smith, Paul 1988, *Discerning the Subject*, Minneapolis: University of Minnesota Press.
Sohn-Rethel, Alfred 1973, *Geistige und körperliche Arbeit*, Frankfurt: Suhrkamp Verlag.
Sohn-Rethel, Alfred 1978, *Warenform und Denkform*, Frankfurt: Suhrkamp Verlag.
Sokolowski, Robert 2000, *Introduction to Phenomenology*, Cambridge: Cambridge University Press.
Solnit, Rebecca 2001, *Wanderlust: A History of Walking*, New York: Penguin Books.
Solnit, Rebecca 2018, *Call Them by Their True Names*, Chicago: Haymarket Books.
Sombart, Werner 1902, *Der Moderne Kapitalismus*, 1. Band, München: Verlag Von Duncker & Humblot.
Sombart, Werner 1924, *Der moderne Kapitalismus*, 2. Band, erste Hälfte, München: Duncker und Humboldt.
Sombart, Werner 1967, *The Quintessence of Capitalism: A Study of the History and Psychology of the Modern Business Man*, translated and edited by M. Epstein, New York: Howard Fertig.
Soper, Kate 1981, *On Human Needs*, Atlantic Highlands: Humanities.
Spelke, Elizabeth S. 1988, 'Origins of Physical Knowledge', in *Thought Without Language*, edited by L. Weiskrantz, Oxford: Clarendon Press, pp. 168–84.
Spivak, Gayatri Chakravorty 1988, 'Scattered Speculations on the Question of Value', in *In Other Worlds: Essays in Cultural Politics*, New York: Routledge.
Stavrianos L.S. 1981, *Global Rift: The Third World Comes of Age*, New York: William Morrow & Co.
de Ste. Croix, G.E.M. 1981, *The Class Struggle in the Ancient Greek World*, Ithaca: Cornell University Press.
Stearns, Peter N. et al. 2003, *Documents in World History*, Vol. 1, London: Longman.
Steinberg, Michael 2005, *The Fiction of a Thinkable World: Body, Meaning, and the Culture of Capitalism*, New York: Monthly Review Press.
Stevens, Kenneth N. 1998, *Acoustic Phonetics*, Cambridge, MA: MIT Press.
Stevens, Kenneth N. and Samuel Jay Keyser, 1989, 'Primary Features and their Enhancement in Consonants', *Language*, 65, no. 1: 81–106.

Stone, Lawrence 1966, 'Social Mobility in England, 1500–1700', *Past and Present*, 33: 16–55.

Straus, Erwin W. 1958, 'Aesthesiology and Hallucinations', in *Existence: A New Dimension in Psychiatry and Psychology*, edited by Rollo May et al., New York: Basic Books.

Straus, Erwin W. 1970, 'Born to See, Bound to Behold: Reflections on the Function of Upright Posture in the Esthetic Attitude', in *The Philosophy of the Body: Rejections of Cartesian Dualism*, edited by Stuart F. Spicker, Chicago: Quadrangle Books.

Stuchin, Steven 1989, 'Biomechanics of the Wrist', in *Basic Biomechanics of the Musculoskeletal System*, edited by Margareta Nordin and Victor H. Frankel, Philadelphia: Lea and Febiger.

Suomi, Stephen J. 1990, 'The Role of Tactile Contact in Rhesus Monkey Social Development', in *Touch: The Foundation of Experience*, edited by Kathryn E. Barnard and T. Berry Brazelton, Madison, CT: International Universities Press.

Susman, R.L. 1994, 'Fossil Evidence for Early Hominid Tool Use', *Science*, 265: 1570–3.

Swetz, Frank 1987, *Capitalism and Arithmetic: The New Math of the 15th Century*, La Salle, IL: Open Court.

Synnott, Anthony 1993, *The Body Social: Symbolism, Self and Society*, London: Routledge.

Tallis, Raymond 1995, *Not Saussure: A Critique of Post-Saussurean Literary Theory*, New York: St. Martin's Press.

Tanner, Nancy Makepiece 1987, *On Becoming Human*, Cambridge: Cambridge University Press.

Tawney, R.H. 1962, *Religion and the Rise of Capitalism*, Gloucester, MA: Peter Smith.

Taylor, A.J.P. 1976, *The Hapsburg Empire: 1809–1918*, Chicago: University of Chicago Press.

Thirsk, Joan 1967, 'Enclosing and Engrossing', in *The Agrarian History of England and Wales*, Vol. 4, edited by Joan Thirsk, Cambridge: Cambridge University Press.

Thompson, E.P. 1963, *The Making of the English Working Class*, New York: Vintage Books.

Thompson, E.P. 1967, 'Time, Work-Discipline and Industrial Capitalism', *Past and Present*, 38: 56–97.

Thompson, E.P. 1975, *Whigs and Hunters: The Origin of the Black Act*, New York: Pantheon.

Thompson, E.P. 1978, *The Poverty of Theory*, New York: Monthly Review Press.

Thompson, E.P. 1991, 'The Moral Economy of the English Crowd in the Eighteenth Century', in *Customs in Common*, NY: The New Press, pp. 185–258.

Tigar, Michael E. 2000, *Law & the Rise of Capitalism*, New York: Monthly Review Press.

Tilley, Christopher 1999, *Metaphor and Material Culture*, Oxford: Blackwell.

Tilley, Christopher 2002, 'Metaphor, Materiality and Interpretation', in *The Material Culture Reader*, edited by Victor Buchli, Oxford: Berg, pp. 23–7.

Timpanaro, Sebastiano 1980, *On Materialism*, London: Verso.

Tomatis, Alfred A. 2005, *The Ear and the Voice*, translated by Roberta Prada and Pierre Sollier, Lanham, MD: Scarecrow Press.

Trevathan, Wenda R. 1987, *Human Birth: An Evolutionary Perspective*, New York: de Gruyter.
Trevathan, Wenda R. 1988, 'Fetal Emergence Patterns in Evolutionary Perspective', *American Anthropologist*, 90, no. 3: 674–81.
Trevathan, Wenda R. 1996, 'The Evolution of Bipedalism and Assisted Birth', *Medical Anthropology Quarterly*, 10, no. 2: 287–90.
Trubetzkoy, Nikolai 1969, *Principles of Phonology*, translated by Christiane A.M. Baltaxe, Berkeley: University of California Press.
Tuchscheerer, Walter 1968, *Bevor 'Das Kapital' entstand. Die Herausbildung und Entwicklung der ökonomischen Theorie von Karl Marx in der Zeit von 1843–1858*, Berlin.
Tuck, Richard 1979, *Natural Rights Theories: Their Origin and Development*, Cambridge: Cambridge University Press.
Tucker, Don M. 2007, *Mind from Body: Experience from Neural Structure*, Oxford: Oxford University Press.
Tucker, Robert 1978, *The Marx-Engels Reader*, New York: Norton.
Tully, James 1980, *A Discourse on Property: John Locke and his Adversaries*, Cambridge: Cambridge University Press.
Turnbull, Colin 1962, *The Forest People: A Study of the Pygmies of the Congo*, New York: Simon & Schuster.
Vilar, Pierre 1976, *A History of Gold and Money, 1450–1920*, London: New Left Books.
da Vinci, Leonardo, 1970, *The Notebooks of Leonardo da Vinci, Compiled and Edited from the Original Manuscripts*, 2 Vols., 3rd edition, edited and translated by Jean Paul Richter, New York: Phaidon.
Vogel, Lise 2013, *Marxism and the Oppression of Women: Toward a Unitary Theory*, Chicago: Haymarket Books.
Vološhinov, V.N. 1973, *Marxism and the Philosophy of Language*, translated by Ladislav Matejka and I.R. Titunik, Cambridge, MA: Harvard University Press.
Vonnegut, Kurt 2011, *Breakfast of Champions*, New York: Dial Press.
de Vries, Jan 1976, *The Economy of Europe in an Age of Crisis, 1660–1750*, Cambridge: Cambridge University Press.
de Vries, Jan 2007, *European Urbanisation 1500–1800*, London: Routledge.
Vygotsky, Lev 1986, *Thought and Language*, Cambridge, MA: MIT Press.
Wade, Nicolas 2007, *Before the Dawn: Recovering the Lost History of Our Ancestors*, London: Penguin.
Wall, Patrick 2000, *Pain: The Science of Suffering*, New York: Columbia University Press.
Warneken, Bernd Jürgen 2010, *Populare Kultur*, Köln: Böhlau Verlag.
Weatherford, Jack 1997, *The History of Money: From Sandstone to Cyberspace*, New York: Three Rivers Press.
Weber, Max 1958, *The Protestant Ethic and the Spirit of Capitalism*, translated by Talcott Parsons, New York: Charles Scribner.

Weber, Max 1972, *Wirtschaft und Gesellschaft: Grundriss der verstehenden Soziologie*, 5th revidierte Auflage, Tübingen: J.C.B. Mohr.

Weber, Max 1973, 'Die "Objektivität" sozialwissenschaftlicher u. sozialpolitischer Erkenntnis', in *Gesammelte Aufsätze zur Wissenschaftslehre*, 4. Auflage Tübingen: J.C.B. Mohr.

Weber, Renee 1990, 'A Philosophical Perspective on Touch', in *Touch: The Foundation of Experience*, edited by Kathryn E. Barnard and T. Berry Brazelton, Madison, CT: International Universities Press.

Werrett, Simon 1999, 'Potemkin and the Panopticon: Samuel Bentham and the Architecture of Absolutism in Eighteenth Century Russia', *Journal of Bentham Studies*, 2, http://discovery.ucl.ac.uk/648/2/002__1999__S.Werret_1999.pdf.

Wheen, Francis 2006, *Marx's Das Kapital: A Biography*, New York: Grove Press.

White, Hayden 1975, *Metahistory: The Historical Imagination in Ninenteenth-Century Europe*, Baltimore: Johns Hopkins University Press.

Whitehead, Alfred North 1967, *Science and the Modern World*, New York: Free Press.

Whitehead, Alfred North 1979, *Process and Reality*, New York: Free Press.

Whitfield, Philip 1982, *The Rhythms of Life*, edited by Edward S. Ayensu and Philip Whitfield, New York: Crown Publishers.

Whitman, Walt 1885, 'Slang in America', *The North American Review*, 141, no. 348: 431–5.

Whitman, Walt 1958, *Leaves of Grass*, New York: Signet.

Whitman, Walt 1969, *The Portable Walt Whitman*, New York: Penguin.

Williams, Raymond 1977, *Marxism and Literature*, Oxford: Oxford University Press.

Williams, Raymond 1983, *Key Words: A Vocabulary of Culture and Society*, New York: Oxford University Press.

Wilson, Edward O. 1975, *Sociobiology: The New Synthesis*, Cambridge, MA: Harvard University Press.

Wilson, Edward O. 1978, *On Human Nature*, Cambridge, MA: Harvard University Press.

Wilson, Edward O. (ed.) 2006, *From So Simple a Beginning: The Four Great Books of Charles Darwin*, New York: Norton.

Wilson, Frank R. 1999, *The Hand: How its Use Shapes the Brain, Language, and Culture*, New York: Vintage Books.

Witt, Ronald G. 2012, *The Two Cultures and the Foundation of Renaissance Humanism in Medieval Italy*, Cambridge: Cambridge University Press.

Wittgenstein, Ludwig 1999 [1921], *Tractatus Logico-Philosophicus*, translated by C.K. Ogden, Mineola, NY: Dover Publications.

Wolin, Richard and John Abromeit (eds) 2005, *Heideggerian Marxism: Herbert Marcuse*, Lincoln: University of Nebraska Press.

Wood, Ellen Meiksins 1999, *The Origin of Capitalism*, New York: Monthly Review Press.

Wrangham, Richard 2010, *Catching Fire: How Cooking Made Us Human*, London: Profile Books.

Wrightson Keith 2003, *English Society 1580–1680*, London: Routledge.
Wyschograd, Edith 1981, 'Empathy and Sympathy as Tactile Encounter', *Journal of Philosophy*, 6: 25–43.
Zilhão, João 2007, 'The Emergence of Ornaments and Art: An Archaeological Perpsective on the Origins of "Behavioral Modernity"', *Journal of Archaeological Research*, 15: 1–54.
Zimmer, Carl 2018, 'Neanderthals, the World's First Misunderstood Artists', *New York Times*, 22 February, https://www.nytimes.com/2018/02/22/science/neanderthals-cave-paintings-europe.html.
Zuckerman, Joseph D. and Frederick A. Matsen III 1989, 'Biomechanics of the Shoulder', in *Basic Biomechanics of the Musculoskeletal System*, edited by Margareta Nordin and Victor H. Frankel, Philadelphia: Lea and Febiger.
Zupko, Ronald Edward 1975, *British Weights & Measures: A History from Antiquity to the Seventeenth Century*, Madison: University of Wisconsin Press.

Index

abstractions 97, 99, 156–57, 162, 179–80, 182, 186, 203, 206, 249, 282–83, 285–86, 586–87, 1068, 1354
accumulation 164, 166, 196–97, 807, 872, 875, 956–57, 961, 963, 992, 995, 1222, 1224, 1228, 1231–32
Ackerman, Diane 335, 347, 353–55, 358–60, 363–66, 369, 373–75, 377–78, 380, 433–34, 436, 1283
Adorno, Theodor W. 60, 245, 771, 773, 782, 818, 823, 1175–76, 1295, 1297–99, 1301, 1305–6
advertising 122, 415, 477, 759, 817, 1039, 1046, 1085–86, 1165, 1171, 1208
aesthetics 138, 183, 333, 370, 486, 493, 546, 631–32, 634, 654, 716–17, 729–30, 1283, 1286, 1288–90
Africa 296, 382, 401, 406, 917, 958, 1097, 1222, 1237, 1264–66
Agamben, Giorgio 521, 1206, 1337, 1339–54
agency 206, 232, 518–19, 521, 766, 783, 936, 1039, 1087, 1151, 1163, 1175, 1285, 1298–99, 1333
agriculture 70, 293, 837–38, 952, 960, 984, 1036, 1190, 1403
Alberti, Leon Battista 843, 861–62, 864, 909, 914, 981
alienated labour 58–59, 61, 64, 75–77, 79, 137, 1113, 1189
alienation 3, 55–56, 60, 62, 64–65, 76, 78–79, 84, 86–88, 773, 971–72, 1212, 1215, 1375, 1378
Althusser, Louis 15, 91, 159, 170–71, 208, 217, 245, 788, 790–92, 795, 801, 1209–10, 1212–17, 1293–96
anatomy 161, 199, 273, 313, 322, 325, 327, 384, 386, 394, 462–64, 585–86, 1002–3, 1247, 1250
Anderson, Perry 87, 274
animals 65–66, 259–60, 299–303, 317, 347–48, 354–56, 391–93, 397, 428–30, 476–77, 683–84, 1201–3, 1218, 1220–21, 1258–59
apes 67, 312, 319, 382–83, 386, 409, 456, 463, 480, 482, 512, 1202–5, 1247, 1251, 1258

Appadurai, Arjun 139, 662–68, 1268–69
architects 72, 720, 722, 835, 853, 1048, 1108, 1218
Arendt, Hannah 9, 66, 218, 252–53, 257–62, 265, 722, 1032, 1220
Aristotle 7–9, 150, 276, 317, 356, 364, 436, 829, 832, 857, 866, 869, 879
arithmetic 861, 891–92, 894–96, 907, 917, 1315, 1392, 1416
artefacts 31–33, 105–9, 137–42, 262–65, 654–56, 658–60, 674–79, 685–89, 697–735, 737–49, 751–52, 754–59, 761, 1268–70, 1277–78
artefactual mendacity 724, 727, 734, 746, 753, 757, 760
artefactual monads 701–2, 705, 722, 737, 743
Australopithecines 27, 382–84, 388, 397–99, 404, 421, 423, 427, 456, 684, 1247

bacteria 70, 297, 299, 453, 472, 1024, 1204, 1254–55
Bank of England 1010–11
Barthes, Roland 434, 563, 654–57, 664, 668, 738, 788, 1267–68
behaviour 222–23, 313, 401, 406, 412–13, 421, 423, 462, 521–23, 629, 631–32, 797–98, 864, 1095–96, 1297–98
being-in-the-world 65, 255, 299, 396, 558, 567, 682, 702, 823, 836, 863, 886, 1243
Benjamin, Walter 37, 198, 204, 560, 695, 699–702, 720, 724, 736–37, 741, 743, 748–49, 765, 772–73, 1381–82
Bentham, Jeremy 995, 1021, 1024–27, 1037–38, 1156, 1357–58, 1360–61, 1382
Berkeley, George 1318
biology 26, 222, 231–32, 400, 406, 1203, 1237–38
biopolitics 1020, 1205, 1337–40, 1346, 1350
bipedalism 358, 382–86, 389–90, 397, 403, 410, 412, 417, 421
birth 6–7, 307, 408–10, 412–14, 416, 548, 562–63, 671–72, 715, 717, 879, 883–84, 888, 1342, 1391
Bloch, Ernst 1, 20, 183, 215, 377, 552, 624, 1174, 1183, 1196, 1284, 1354

INDEX 597

bodily instruments 61, 65, 69–70, 72, 74–75, 267, 271, 275–77, 280–81, 402, 404, 1074, 1108, 1282–83, 1286
body size 214, 343, 397–400, 405, 429, 549
bookkeeping 820, 900, 906–7, 910, 913–14, 1309
brain 30–31, 301–4, 310–11, 313, 332–33, 339–40, 342–46, 358–60, 362–67, 383–85, 405–7, 456–58, 1245, 1247–48, 1252–53
Braverman, Harry 978, 1100, 1133, 1136–37, 1149
bureaucracy 1028–32, 1034, 1036, 1052–53, 1364–65
Butler, Judith 68, 233–39, 242–43, 310, 507, 602–3, 608, 610, 1158, 1177, 1289, 1296

capital 163–66, 175–84, 186–91, 193–96, 198–200, 204–5, 806–17, 951–54, 1063–71, 1080–92, 1099–1108, 1112–22, 1125–29, 1131–38, 1140–51
capital accumulation 807, 812, 838, 898, 954, 961, 986–87, 992, 995, 1119, 1360
capitalism 190–92, 195–99, 815–17, 827–28, 897, 900, 955–58, 1089–90, 1227–29, 1231–32, 1311–13, 1317–20, 1325–26, 1351–53
capitalist labour-process 1106–7, 1109, 1111, 1113, 1115–19, 1121–23, 1125, 1127, 1133–35, 1139–41, 1147–49, 1151, 1153, 1157, 1179–80
capitalist societies 169–71, 183, 193–94, 767–68, 775–76, 784–85, 814, 826–27, 972, 1159–60, 1170–72, 1177, 1227–29, 1231–35, 1305–7
Cartesian subject 845, 856–58, 860, 862, 971–72
cartography 213, 288, 290, 322, 887, 917–22, 943, 950
causality 148, 188, 342, 347, 527, 827, 1343–44
Chakrabarty, Dipesh 189–92, 196, 198–99, 202, 205, 568, 807, 839, 1237, 1239, 1317
childhood 306–7, 337, 361, 371, 414–15, 548, 617, 926
citizens 11, 116, 149, 723, 836, 863, 870–71, 938, 950, 1094, 1166, 1267, 1328
city-states 835–36, 872–74, 1310
class 182–83, 195–97, 381, 766–67, 781–83, 812–14, 952–53, 988–89, 1101–4, 1132–34, 1157–59, 1291–92, 1323, 1334–35, 1383–84
class consciousness 15, 698, 770, 778, 781–83, 809, 1057, 1204, 1292, 1334, 1404
class genocide 982, 988–89, 1100–1101
classical liberalism 101, 949, 1356, 1358, 1363
class struggle 85, 767, 772, 781–85, 812–13, 967, 970, 1158–59, 1163, 1176, 1214–15, 1294
commodity exchange 169, 173, 661–62, 664, 666–67, 874, 876, 902–3, 1062, 1065–66, 1068–69, 1073, 1076, 1080–81, 1086
commodity fetishism 87, 165, 625, 654, 667, 773–76, 809, 1075, 1077–78, 1080, 1119, 1121, 1127, 1288–89, 1298
commons 958–60, 967, 976, 995–96, 1005–6
communication 126–27, 133–34, 469–74, 476–79, 482, 486, 584–87, 589–91, 594–96, 599, 604, 612, 1249–52, 1254, 1256–57
consumption 259, 650, 654, 656–57, 661–64, 666–67, 687, 689, 726–27, 1066, 1068, 1070–71, 1151, 1266–67, 1271
contemplation 7, 55, 60, 228, 260, 262–63, 357, 697
corporeal capacities 32, 73–75, 109, 271, 281, 732–33, 735, 742, 1108, 1112, 1116, 1135, 1140, 1187, 1192
corporeality 31–32, 44, 46, 213, 218, 221, 262–65, 295, 355, 504–5, 515, 517–20, 708, 1068–71, 1086
 and cognition 13, 36, 213–14, 504–5, 514, 516–17, 523, 534, 547, 1261
corporeal semiotics 31, 33, 36–37, 557–60, 685, 701, 703–5, 711, 715, 733–35, 739, 741–45, 747–49, 751–61, 765–66
countryside 836, 838, 869, 871, 883, 951, 983, 996, 1324
Crosby, Alfred 38, 818–21, 850–54, 858, 865, 874–75, 887, 891–92, 913–14, 918, 928–30, 970, 1037, 1386
cultural anthropology 625, 645, 1054, 1205
cultural relativism 48, 243, 589, 1264, 1266

Darwin, Charles 4–6, 21–24, 26–30, 94–95, 347, 349, 459, 483, 528, 849, 1203–5, 1352
Dasein 252, 254–57, 594, 708, 1267, 1320

death 9–11, 256–57, 264, 279–80, 414–15, 421–22, 425–26, 562–63, 1005–6, 1013–14, 1049–50, 1336–37, 1351–52, 1376, 1400
death camps 1339–44, 1347–48, 1352–53
death penalty 1005–7, 1011, 1013, 1333, 1336
democracy 723, 1328, 1342–46, 1348, 1367
Derrida, Jacques 138, 153, 221, 454–55, 479, 486, 506, 606, 619, 1251, 1349–50
Descartes, René xvii, 10, 252, 321, 324–25, 337–38, 365, 504, 855–58, 860, 969–70, 1179–80
dexterities 31–32, 253, 275–77, 279, 281, 283, 319–20, 391–92, 396, 708, 712, 1072, 1074, 1115–16, 1118
  corporeal 45, 277, 280–81, 402, 1117
Discipline and Punish 789, 793–94, 799, 992, 994, 1020, 1337, 1391
double-entry bookkeeping 819–20, 861, 864–65, 896–99, 901–6, 910, 912, 914–15, 950, 1038, 1092–93
dualism 244, 515–17, 657, 686, 688–90, 717, 734–35, 1262–63

Eagleton, Terry 16, 18, 45, 73, 91, 107, 248, 453, 503, 713, 962, 1192, 1205
Economic-Philosophical Manuscripts 2, 44, 52, 58–59, 80, 707, 1109, 1209
emancipation 123, 149–51, 362, 380, 390, 420, 546, 729, 805, 848, 1151, 1317
embodied knowledges 244, 515
emotions 117, 268, 326, 347–48, 361, 365–67, 377–78, 381, 430, 445, 482–83, 485, 614, 967, 971
enclosures 197, 838, 943–44, 954–56, 958–60, 967, 976, 981, 988, 996, 1016, 1174, 1324–25, 1371
energy 219, 279, 295, 300, 307, 437, 440, 448, 1114–15, 1117–18, 1134, 1141, 1150, 1160, 1373
Engels Friedrich, 2–3, 5, 26–28, 43, 52–53, 83–85, 275, 1060–61, 1110, 1179, 1203–7, 1219, 1224–25, 1375–78
Enlightenment 11, 818, 823, 855, 930, 1037, 1299, 1301, 1304–6, 1314, 1379
entrepreneurs 828, 832, 887, 900, 912, 914, 922, 1031, 1056, 1090, 1092–93, 1359

environment 69–70, 74, 252–53, 271, 273, 305, 362–63, 484–85, 524–26, 530, 532, 681–83, 685, 1220–21, 1362
epistemological break 15, 36, 77, 91–92, 148, 177, 203, 774–75, 1209–10, 1212–15, 1217
evolutionary history 5, 94, 269, 319, 325, 523, 526, 530
  human 94–95
evolutionary process 5, 27, 95, 243, 311, 325, 360, 421, 1112
exchange-value 90, 661–62, 903, 1059–63, 1066–73, 1080, 1084, 1086, 1173, 1192, 1207–8, 1303, 1367–68
exploitation 87–88, 782–83, 813–14, 961, 963, 966, 1125–26, 1147–49, 1158–59, 1227–29, 1231, 1234, 1236, 1238, 1291–94
  and oppression xx, 196–97, 750, 962, 1180, 1185, 1195, 1225, 1227–31, 1236–38, 1316, 1319
expropriation 164, 949, 951, 953, 955, 957, 960, 962, 966, 1034, 1184, 1187, 1322, 1326, 1328
extended body 67–68, 71, 707, 712, 766, 769, 838, 1071, 1074, 1110–11, 1151, 1153, 1164–66, 1187, 1190
eyes 124, 301–3, 323–26, 328–35, 337–40, 342–49, 351–52, 395–96, 422, 433–34, 521, 524, 821–22, 854–55, 1124
  primate 332, 342–43, 345, 855

factories 806–7, 810, 972, 978–79, 1009, 1016, 1019–20, 1041, 1090, 1095–96, 1133, 1137, 1143, 1147, 1153–55
false consciousness 151, 806, 1297–99
Federici, Silvia 197, 955, 959, 961, 966–67, 969–76, 988, 994, 1389
Feuerbach, Ludwig 44, 53, 55–62, 64–65, 75–80, 83, 86, 117, 121, 144, 1199, 1207, 1210, 1212
fingers 316, 318–20, 380, 436, 450, 540, 587, 846–48, 1051, 1246
food 107, 279–81, 299–301, 305, 326, 358–59, 377–79, 383, 452, 639, 644, 657–58, 667, 694, 1246
form-determination 170, 185–86, 1063, 1208, 1238
Foucault, Michel 38, 46, 54, 153, 242–43, 768, 771–72, 785–808, 991–95, 1014–21,

INDEX

1174–75, 1240, 1297–99, 1337–40, 1355–59, 1361–64
Freud, Sigmund   4, 16, 27, 46, 113, 419, 421, 444, 711, 735, 753, 849, 861

gallows   1006–7, 1010–12, 1014, 1334, 1336
Geist   9–10, 54–56, 63, 102, 112, 175, 256, 407, 528, 643, 819, 827, 900, 903
Geldard, Frank   328, 334–35, 352–53, 355, 360, 379–80, 437
German Ideology   1–5, 12, 17–18, 52–53, 59–61, 77–78, 82–86, 88, 90–91, 95–98, 104–5, 156–62, 1206–7, 1209–16, 1224
Gibson, James J.   123, 143, 274, 395, 437–40, 512, 521, 613–14, 643, 1074, 1220–21, 1252
Gilgamesh   423–26, 716, 867
Gould, Stephen Jay   19, 22, 26, 28, 30, 214, 287, 346, 384, 386, 401–2, 413, 1180, 1205
Gramsci, Antonio   31, 137, 152, 209, 276, 767, 881
Grundrisse   154–55, 158–61, 166, 168–69, 175, 177, 187, 274, 733, 1062–66, 1080, 1115, 1182–83, 1186–89

Halpern, Richard   21, 90, 798, 808, 837–38, 966
Harrison   313, 318, 327, 383, 387–88, 398–99, 401, 406–7, 456, 1410
Hegel, G.W.F.   6–7, 10–11, 13–15, 53–55, 59–63, 75–81, 91, 112, 117–18, 159–60, 175–81, 268, 355–56, 1199
Heidegger, Martin   36, 216, 218, 252–57, 263–64, 506, 512, 696, 708–9, 716, 740, 868, 1282, 1284
Heller, Agnes   44, 49, 105, 277, 279, 805, 1062, 1107, 1114–18, 1151, 1186, 1218, 1371
hierarchies   115, 196–97, 322, 348, 432, 1013, 1237
historical development   156, 177, 282, 402, 881, 953, 1222, 1224
historical materialism   xxi, 1, 3, 5, 29, 34, 59, 61, 251–52, 557, 559, 643, 1227, 1315–17
historical theory   xxi, 1–2, 13–14, 16, 18, 93, 97, 155, 157, 186, 188–89, 741–42, 1061, 1236, 1238
History and Class Consciousness   15, 778, 1204
Hobbes, Thomas   111, 116, 609, 819, 855, 883–86, 905, 936, 969–70, 990, 1021, 1331

Hobsbawm, Eric   780–83, 785, 886, 896, 1291
hominids   382–85, 390–91, 396, 398, 404–6, 410, 412–13, 416, 419–20, 427, 429, 432, 456, 474–75, 482–84
Homo economicus   245, 451, 969
Homo erectus   102, 129, 385, 399, 405–6, 457–58, 1247–48, 1251
Homo habilis   129, 397–98, 456–58
Homo oeconomicus   170, 827, 1024, 1303, 1358–64
Homo sacer   1339–42, 1347–49, 1366
Homo sapiens   4–5, 27–29, 69–72, 222–23, 242–43, 267–68, 274–75, 277–78, 288–89, 349–50, 384, 452–53, 1110, 1252, 1285–86
Horkheimer, Max   771–72, 778, 782, 784, 1029, 1095, 1298, 1300–1301, 1303–7, 1397
human beings   53–55, 61–69, 93–96, 100–102, 110–11, 117–18, 139–46, 222–23, 257–58, 268–69, 713–15, 960–64, 1107–10, 1284–88, 1349
  nature of   55–56, 79, 1199, 1359
  brain of   30, 151, 200, 275–76, 283, 288, 307, 325, 338, 343, 428, 469, 517, 538, 1143
  consciousness   102, 132, 214, 268, 325, 341, 507, 528, 552–53, 855, 1219, 1408
  corporeality   4, 61, 63, 66, 214, 222, 232, 286–87, 1058, 1067, 1074, 1154, 1162, 1184, 1192
  senses   123–25, 325, 380, 402, 428, 1289, 1393
  species-being   57, 64–65, 76, 81, 88, 1360

imagination   72, 136, 370–71, 373, 534, 705–6, 708, 716–17, 728–29, 731, 734–35, 988, 1108–9, 1284–85, 1287–88
immanent logic   132, 160, 205, 1089–90, 1092–93, 1300, 1329
immiseration   xxi, 961, 1056, 1122, 1125–26, 1133–34, 1146, 1148–51, 1159, 1183, 1213
inequalities   197, 760, 987, 1004, 1170–71, 1246, 1328, 1331
infants   306, 399, 410, 412–14, 416, 442, 444–47, 486, 1002, 1245, 1284
instrumental reason   717, 818, 823, 1029, 1299–1303, 1305–6

intersectionality 197, 1185, 1225–27, 1229, 1383, 1385–86, 1407
intimacy 336, 348, 366, 375, 378, 380, 448, 693, 1284
Isherwood, Baron 656–57, 659, 661–62, 664, 668, 686, 689, 694

Jablonski, Nina 320, 386, 427–32, 441, 446, 449, 1246
Jakobson, Roman 355, 460, 480, 488–89, 491–93, 495–96, 1256
Jameson, Fredric 95, 137, 181, 509, 651, 1068, 1071

knowledge production 14–15, 18, 20, 46–47, 151, 153–54, 182, 184, 188–89, 525, 527, 532–34, 1209–10, 1214–15, 1319–20

labour-power 953, 970–72, 1042, 1071, 1073, 1106, 1113–21, 1128–29, 1132–34, 1136, 1138, 1163, 1168, 1170
Lakoff, George 530, 532–34, 536, 538–39, 544, 547
land 830–31, 833–34, 836–37, 867–68, 876, 878–80, 921–23, 939–43, 945–50, 958–60, 981, 983, 1003–4, 1324–25, 1327–28
landlords 193, 809, 941–42, 959, 990, 1035
larynx 463–66, 468, 481, 544, 1247–48
laws 166–68, 564–66, 568–69, 814, 871, 875–79, 984–85, 987, 995–96, 998, 1003, 1006–8, 1012, 1031, 1330–31
Lecercle, Jean-Jacques 460, 477–79, 481, 487, 518, 605, 611–14, 616, 618, 700, 1255
  historical-materialist 487
lectures xiv, 791, 1201, 1253, 1338, 1363–64, 1392
legal status 878, 964
legislation 810–11, 813, 916, 967, 991–92, 994–96, 998, 1024, 1090, 1336, 1382
legs 109, 229, 304, 314, 383, 386–90, 392, 394, 396, 398, 400, 402, 436, 540, 549
Lenneberg, Eric 461–63, 465, 467–69, 510–12, 638–39, 1261
Leroi-Gourhan, André 280, 299–300, 302–3, 305, 311, 361, 368, 370, 373, 380, 383, 405, 452, 454, 457
Lieberman, Philip 269, 458, 463–66,
Lienhardt, Godfrey 671–74, 679, 686, 690–91

life-cycle 299, 306, 414–15, 425, 441, 664, 671, 679, 706, 719, 724, 726, 737, 748, 1269
life-process 103, 200, 503, 682, 774, 778, 780, 803, 812–13, 991, 1075, 1209, 1297
life-worlds 141, 190, 296, 630, 1235, 1332–33
linguistics 133, 135, 487, 494–96, 506, 508, 510, 564–71, 577, 579, 605–6, 619–20, 738, 1260, 1268
Linnaeus, Carl 288, 304, 364, 420, 451, 456, 1201–2, 1243–44
Locke, John 195, 259, 813, 884–86, 949, 978–79, 981, 984–85, 990, 1003–6, 1119, 1128, 1326–34
logic 167–68, 175, 179–82, 189–92, 194–95, 280, 282, 767–68, 805–7, 811–12, 1027–28, 1091–92, 1230–36, 1238–39
Lorenz, Konrad 292, 333, 341, 391, 523–29, 533–34, 547
love xix–xx, 64, 105, 112–13, 115–19, 124, 145, 414, 421–22, 424, 426, 445, 447, 1196, 1200
Lukács, Georg 768, 771–78, 782, 784, 809, 814, 1057, 1059, 1075–77, 1119–21, 1157, 1295, 129

Machiavelli, Niccolò 881–86, 922–23, 936, 1021, 1310
machinery 1017, 1066, 1125, 1135, 1137, 1140–43, 1146, 1148–49, 1374
Macpherson, C.B. 879, 881, 949, 1004, 1325–32
mammals 303–6, 308–13, 318, 320, 327, 332, 334–35, 352–53, 388, 392, 419–20, 426–27, 442, 445, 1243–44
manual labour 8, 47, 137, 150, 153, 965, 1146, 1155
manufacture 404, 804, 837, 1137–40, 1221, 1267–68
Marx, Karl 1–7, 11–22, 25–32, 43–54, 57–69, 71–88, 93–112, 151–73, 175–82, 951–62, 1057–89, 1106–18, 1131–51, 1209–19, 1314–20
  late 87, 1061, 1114, 1117, 1371
  mature 49, 181, 810, 1115, 1145, 1186, 1191–92
Marxism 246, 248, 624–25, 633, 635, 773, 775, 785–87, 1206, 1209, 1214, 1315–16, 1319, 1383–84

INDEX 601

masses 267, 439–40, 450, 550, 617, 838–39, 953–54, 958, 979, 983, 991–92, 994, 1127–28, 1131, 1315–17
material culture 401–2, 652, 654, 658, 668, 671, 674, 676, 680, 683, 685, 690, 692, 1260, 1272–73
materialism 21, 41, 51, 58, 64, 83, 621, 625, 755, 1289, 1387, 1416
  scientific 1372–73
materiality 54, 63, 104, 107, 112, 217, 219, 233–38, 602, 669, 676, 684–85, 1071, 1260–61, 1264
material metaphors 372, 675–76, 678, 680, 690, 1261, 1272, 1274
mathematicians 850, 861, 887–89, 891–92, 1141, 1230, 1314
McMurtry, John 72, 74–75, 96, 110, 246, 275, 1108, 1220, 1241
Megill, Allan 30, 83, 85, 87, 90–91, 881
Merleau-Ponty, Maurice 232–33, 346, 544, 602, 771, 1278
metaphor 293–96, 346–47, 370–73, 474–76, 539, 572–73, 674–75, 732–33, 735, 930, 1053, 1117, 1260–62, 1272
middle classes 951, 1100–1101, 1103–4, 1271
mind-body dualism 10, 151, 252, 514–15, 860
  gendered 1034
Mollon, J.D. 331, 333–35, 344, 351, 353, 359–60
monads 37, 560, 695, 698–701, 713
money 118, 832–33, 848, 865–66, 873–77, 900–902, 910–11, 928–29, 941–42, 948–49, 952–53, 1028, 1069–70, 1080–82
  invention of 885, 981, 1004, 1327–28, 1331
Montagu, Ashley 301, 413, 433–38, 440–49, 1246
Montaigne, Michel de 323, 356–57, 362
mortality 9, 259, 263, 280–81, 412, 415, 423, 425, 747, 1039, 1047, 1052, 1284, 1303
music 31, 275, 351, 353, 356, 373–74, 466, 483–86, 631, 850

Napier, Christopher 317–20, 450, 820, 900–901, 915–16
natural history 5, 27, 64, 94, 181, 265, 355, 519, 953, 964, 1201, 1204
natural resources 712, 716, 868, 1060, 1165, 1172, 1306

natural sciences 3, 23, 27, 57, 97, 166, 470, 1144, 1204, 1206, 1212, 1237
natural world 68, 70, 95, 103, 109, 141–42, 868, 1021, 1058, 1061, 1151, 1153, 1164–65, 1190, 1199
nature 61–63, 65–68, 74, 80–83, 127–30, 140–44, 248–50, 259–61, 867–69, 884–85, 1071–72, 1109–12, 1211–12, 1300–1301, 1305–6
nervous system 343–44, 485, 526, 529, 1145
niches 68, 70, 74, 82, 110–11, 271, 273, 277, 310, 453, 532, 951, 989, 1369
Nietzsche, Friedrich 16, 18, 43, 46, 144–45, 357, 503, 613–14, 619, 788, 821, 1284, 1288

objectification 13, 31–33, 44–45, 49–53, 58–61, 64–66, 71–76, 78–80, 104–8, 111–13, 116–21, 141–44, 273, 705, 814–15
olfaction 327, 360–61, 363, 368, 375, 379–80
organs 123, 219, 268, 275, 300–301, 303, 317, 350–52, 408, 433, 436–38, 481–82, 527–29, 1138, 1143

pain 226–30, 435, 437, 439, 447–48, 450, 711–14, 753–55, 1013–14, 1024–27, 1049–50, 1166, 1171, 1279–85, 1287–88
Peirce, Charles Sanders 488–89, 506, 574, 588, 592, 607–10, 709, 738, 1261
philosophy 2–4, 9–12, 14–16, 43–44, 46–47, 54–56, 77, 83–84, 148–51, 175–76, 698–701, 1212, 1214, 1390–92, 1401–2
Pilbeam, David 313, 318, 327, 383, 387–88, 398–99, 401, 406–7, 456, 1410
Plato 7–8, 10, 148, 150, 252, 258, 268, 321, 324, 356, 364, 454, 854, 857, 1200–1201
poetry xv, 356, 370–71, 373, 492, 494, 514, 610, 616–17, 650, 657, 717, 861, 1287
Polanyi, Karl 169, 170–71, 533–34, 539–44, 547, 725, 824–27, 829–34, 838, 951–52, 958, 1078, 1162, 1164–65, 1223, 1302, 1410
political economy 114, 808–9, 954–55, 980–81, 1062, 1064, 1069–71, 1077–78, 1298–99, 1354, 1356, 1360, 1364, 1385
poor laws 995–99, 1001–2
Poovey, Mary 819–21, 883, 891, 905–13, 950, 1022–23, 1307–9, 1354, 1410
Porter, Theodor M. 766, 822, 841, 881, 905, 909, 1021, 1038, 1052, 1163, 1175, 1308, 1366

poverty   630–31, 750, 955, 979, 981, 985–86, 996–97, 999, 1001, 1003, 1007–8, 1156–58, 1169, 1171, 1193
practical activity   155, 157, 208, 253–54, 256, 263, 635, 654, 683, 1285
practical reason   532, 542, 547, 635–36, 643–45, 1272, 1413
prehistory   27, 172, 834, 1242–43, 1325
productivity   484, 860, 940, 990, 1009, 1045, 1185, 1187, 1193, 1333
Psychopedis, Kosmas   xxi, 11, 178–79, 190, 282, 1176, 1181–83, 1186, 1191, 1196

Rabinbach, Anson   1114–18, 1151, 1186
race   22, 24, 196–97, 231, 233, 244, 283–84, 963–64, 1225, 1227–29, 1231–32, 1234, 1337–38, 1345
rationality   538, 767–69, 797, 800, 811, 814, 824–25, 1031–32, 1093–94, 1201, 1300, 1355, 1358, 1360–62, 1364–65
raw materials   109, 122, 127, 205, 254, 781, 859, 1060, 1071, 1078, 1109–10, 1150–51, 1162–63
Reading Capital   183, 191, 795, 1181
reality   71–72, 154–55, 176–77, 282–83, 285–86, 434, 440–41, 527–30, 602, 612, 629–30, 637–38, 1108, 1356, 1362–63
reification   112, 118, 122, 619, 625, 627, 771, 773–78, 1050, 1059, 1073, 1075, 1077–78, 1119–20, 1122
relative surplus-value   1018, 1126, 1134, 1137, 1141, 1147–49, 1162–63, 1306
Relethford, John H.   70, 301–3, 306, 308, 313–15, 343, 382, 389, 391, 397, 404, 420
Renaissance   828, 835–36, 841, 844–45, 849, 852–53, 855, 866, 888, 904, 907, 1036–37
reproduction   259–60, 297, 299, 310, 313, 342–43, 414–16, 418–21, 424, 432–33, 551, 831, 973, 975–76, 1294
revolution   4, 7, 88, 208, 548, 629, 839, 1178–79, 1183, 1214
Robinson, Cedric J.   196, 1237, 1304–5, 1315–17, 1319–20
Rossi-Landi, Ferruccio   106–7, 113, 127, 130–32, 563, 1255
ruling class   197, 767, 770, 976, 987, 1194, 1334, 1336

Sahlins, Marshall   614, 635–39, 642–46, 648–49, 657, 1264–65
Sapir-Whorf theory of language   510
Sartre, Jean-Paul   357, 594, 687, 697–98, 786, 1313, 1349
Saussure, Ferdinand   36, 125–26, 131–32, 134, 454, 459, 479–80, 486–87, 557, 561–73, 579–81, 603–4, 619–21, 1259–60
Sayers, Sean   246–51, 1241
Scarry, Elaine   31–32, 37, 702–3, 705–17, 719–20, 722–28, 730–34, 736, 739–41, 747, 752–53, 755–57, 760, 1279–82, 1284
Schumpeter, Joseph   813, 820, 866, 904, 910, 914, 940, 1088–92, 1095, 1175
science   561, 566, 568–70, 619–21, 818–19, 849, 851–52, 881, 1143, 1145–47, 1214–17
self-preservation   1132, 1300–1301, 1304–6
semiology   561, 570–71, 619, 621, 738, 1264, 1268, 1381
semiotic artefacts   32–33, 46, 104, 106–7, 120–21, 203, 269, 280–81, 290, 670, 752
semiotic systems   24, 50, 126, 134, 136, 199, 481, 488, 557, 581, 586, 630, 634, 637, 647
sense organs   61, 81, 117, 275, 310, 331, 339, 341, 435–36, 517, 524, 528–29, 1146, 1278
sexuality   235, 239, 242, 374, 414–15, 421–22, 424, 789, 796, 802, 1227–29, 1231–32, 1234, 1240
slavery   196, 879, 983–84, 998, 1236–37, 1315–19, 1409
Smith, Adam   170, 173, 952, 954, 978–80, 983, 985–86, 990–91, 1023, 1060–61, 1139, 1170, 1354, 1356, 1358
Smith, Anthony   313, 353, 355, 360, 437, 439
Smith, Paul   181, 810
social body   196–97, 731, 742, 746, 800, 1008, 1012–13, 1135, 1140, 1217
socialism   198, 204, 773, 1091, 1187, 1241, 1288–89, 1332
social relations   86–88, 101, 111–16, 168–71, 673, 676–77, 680, 689–90, 730–31, 733, 824, 956–57, 1069, 1079, 1140–41
    rural   838, 953, 993, 1035, 1323–24
social topography   181–82, 188, 192, 194, 202, 733–34, 742, 780, 784, 812, 814, 1075, 1077, 1081, 1292

INDEX 603

Socrates 6–7, 10–11, 13, 15, 54, 117, 119, 151, 1202, 1241
Sombart, Werner 819–20, 829, 864, 897, 899–904, 906–7, 913, 915, 950, 1088–89, 1091–93, 1095, 1098, 1311–12
soul 7–8, 43, 341, 351, 366, 581, 633, 639, 700, 747, 932, 1142, 1148–49, 1191, 1201
sovereignty 478, 874, 932, 1005, 1019, 1029, 1339–41, 1343, 1347–48, 1353
space 20, 194–95, 315–16, 331–33, 336, 339–41, 354, 535–36, 804, 839–40, 915–21, 940–41, 962, 1014–16, 1226
species-being 65, 71, 80, 86–87, 94, 105, 247, 283, 406, 443, 703, 761, 1211, 1358, 1361
speech production 127–28, 131, 458, 463, 468–69, 477, 480–81, 500, 618, 1248–49
state 101, 112, 114–15, 439, 784, 883–85, 933–34, 975–76, 985–87, 1003–4, 1048–50, 1327–28, 1330–33, 1345–46, 1356–57
state of nature 884, 1004, 1332
Straus, Erwin 351, 356, 392–93, 395–97, 448–49
structuralist 33, 125, 128, 131, 138, 140, 179, 200, 202, 506, 562, 589, 624
structure-in-dominance 170, 733
subjecthood 214–15, 502–5, 507–9, 511, 513–15, 517–19, 521, 523, 525, 527, 529, 531, 533, 535, 547
  corporeal coordinates of 517
subjection 28, 728, 807, 870–71, 969, 992, 1019, 1024, 1156, 1182, 1294, 1300, 1348
surplus-value 1113, 1118–20, 1122, 1127, 1129, 1133, 1140, 1148, 1150–51, 1154–55, 1159, 1186, 1189, 1192, 1306

Tallis, Raymond 459, 570, 578, 594, 601–3, 608, 647, 649
Thompson, E.P. 624, 780–83, 785, 924–26, 928, 930, 937–38, 979, 982–87, 1005, 1102, 1131, 1224, 1291
Tilley, Christopher 372, 589, 671, 674–83, 686, 690–93, 1261, 1272, 1274–75
time xiv–xv, 306–7, 339–41, 345, 366–70, 453–54, 748–50, 916–18, 920–22, 924–29, 944–46, 1017–20, 1039–42, 1128–29, 1131
  abstract 924, 928

historical 20, 97, 146, 233, 238, 251, 612, 614, 743, 820, 907, 919–20, 1208, 1305, 1309
tools 68–69, 127–29, 154, 252–57, 260–61, 263, 310–11, 403–5, 457, 462, 643, 848, 851–52, 1141–42, 1149
  prehistoric 405, 457
torture 224, 752–53, 992, 1149, 1151, 1156, 1279
totality 57, 103, 114, 137, 142, 144, 159, 179, 188, 193, 196–97, 255, 788, 800, 963
transhistorical abstractions xxi, 156, 162, 702–3, 730, 746, 761, 1061
transportation 684, 870, 922, 943, 1007–9, 1275, 1343

ultra-constructionism 24, 219, 221, 241–42, 322, 1054, 1240, 1246, 1266
universality 57–58, 70–71, 156, 173, 249, 290, 528, 538, 788, 1183, 1218–19, 1265, 1355, 1371
use-value 19, 642–45, 661–63, 712–13, 1060–76, 1080, 1082–86, 1102, 1109, 1112–13, 1115–17, 1121, 1207–8, 1300–1301, 1367–68

valorisation process 183, 186, 189, 662, 784, 839, 1075–76, 1083–84, 1104, 1106, 1113–14, 1135–36, 1232–34, 1318, 1325
  capital's 1142, 1146
violence 7, 85, 260, 629–30, 1156, 1158, 1194–95, 1228, 1231–32, 1307, 1313, 1336, 1376, 1384
Vološinov, Valentin 565, 568, 581, 604, 612, 614, 700, 1255

wage-labour 951–52, 980–81, 984, 990, 1000, 1059, 1128–29, 1142, 1148, 1227, 1229, 1315, 1318, 1325, 1369
Wala
  people of 679–81, 683, 691, 1275
  Wala canoes 674, 676–79, 681, 684, 690, 1054, 1272, 1274
Weber, Max 448, 622–23, 824–25, 827–30, 863–64, 900–901, 951–52, 1028–31, 1053, 1088–92, 1094–95, 1097–98, 1310–11, 1364–65
Whitman, Walt 136, 610–11, 614, 617–18, 697, 912, 1418

Wilson, Stephen   974
Wordsworth, William   xx, 700
workhouses   245, 806, 985, 992, 1001–2, 1019
world history   64, 827, 1385, 1415

worldmaking   44, 46, 61, 93, 141, 288, 532, 549, 559, 701, 706, 708, 721, 730, 1394
   human   15, 256, 286, 559, 711
   semiotic   546